Anthony Wayne

Trouble Shooter of the American Revolution

Anthony Wayne

Trouble Shooter of the

American Revolution

by

HARRY EMERSON WILDES

GREENWOOD PRESS, PUBLISHERS
WESTPORT, CONNECTICUT

E
207
·W₃₅ W₅
1970

Reprinted by arrangement with
Harcourt Brace Jovanovich, Inc., New York

First Greenwood Reprinting 1970

Library of Congress Catalogue Card Number 70-106701

SBN 8371-3383-1

Printed in the United States of America

TO KIKI

Preface

A BIOGRAPHY of any hero should speak for itself; if it cannot by its content explain its point of view, its author has failed dismally in his purpose. In presenting this life of Wayne, the first to put the warrior-statesman in his proper social, economic, political, and military setting, I shall not attempt to prejudice the reader in advance. That the "trouble-shooter of the Revolution" has never before been presented in all his many facets is remarkable enough; what is even more remarkable is the fact that, in spite of our ignorance of many phases of his career, Wayne has won the love and admiration of his countrymen. It is a striking testimony to his warmth of personality and to his force of character.

Any biography of this scope is inevitably the work of many minds. No one man can independently glean all the information that he needs for such an extensive study, or rely entirely on his own interpretation. This is especially true of a life of Wayne, whose career took him to more different parts of the North American continent than did the career of any other important military figure in the Revolution. In preparing this book, I have visited every place that Wayne touched; and everywhere I have had the help of many generous men and women. I am deeply grateful to them for having made this book possible.

My heaviest debt of gratitude is to the Historical Society of Pennsylvania for permission to use its enormous wealth of Wayne material. To Julian P. Boyd, former librarian at that institution and now librarian at Princeton, who suggested this biography, to President Edward Robins, and to the officers and councilors of the Historical Society of Pennsylvania, who unlocked their long-sealed manuscripts for my use, I express my most sincere thanks. In carrying out the task of collating material, the staff of the Historical Society was of inestimable assistance.

A similarly heavy debt is also owed to William Wayne of Waynesborough, who made available the magnificent store of private papers still in possession of the Wayne family. These documents, many of which had been so long secluded that they were believed forever lost, clarify the General's personality and explain incidents long unknown or misunderstood. To Mr. Wayne, for allowing unrestricted access to these vitally important papers, I offer my deep appreciation.

For special aspects of Wayne's life, I have been privileged to enjoy advice, criticism, and assistance from experts in their special fields. The late Edward Warlock Mumford, secretary of the University of Pennsylvania, searched diligently among the university's records for documentary evidence of Wayne's matriculation, as did Horace Mather Lippincott, editor of the university publications, and Ralph Morgan, president of the Alumni Association. Thomas Ridgway, Esq., checked material concerning Wayne's theatrical activities.

Stephen H. P. Pell, director of the Fort Ticonderoga Museum, together with Milo H. King, general manager, and Eleanor M. Murray, librarian, opened the resources of that excellent institution for my use. Ola M. Wyeth, librarian of the Savannah Public Library, and Mrs. Dolores B. Floyd of the Georgia Historical Society, graciously cleared up troublesome problems about Wayne's life in the South, as did Randolph G. Adams, director, and Howard Peckham, curator of manuscripts, of the William L. Clements Library at the University of Michigan. To those who guided me about long-forgotten haunts of Wayne, Marmaduke Floyd at Richmond and Kew and Miss Marguerite Quarles at Green Springs, I acknowledge my gratitude.

Major James R. Jacobs, biographer of the *Tarnished Warrior*, generously advised me on affairs relating to Wilkinson, as did Mrs. John Trotwood Moore, librarian of the Tennessee Historical Society, and Nina M. Visscher, librarian of the Kentucky State Historical Society.

For the Ohio-Michigan incidents, I am indebted to the Honorable Roy G. Fitzgerald, president of the Dayton Historical Society; Harlow Lindley, director, and P. Freeman Mooney, curator of manuscripts, at the Ohio Archeological and Historical Society; Leland D. Baldwin, librarian of the University of Pittsburgh; Eleanor S. Wilby, librarian of the Historical and Philosophical Society of Ohio; Bertha K. Kraus, curator of manuscripts at the State Library of Ohio; F. Clever Bald of the Detroit Institute of Technology; and, for Indian material, to John M. Oskison of Estrella, Oklahoma, and John Walton Caughey of the University of California. Professor Milo M. Quaife of the Burton Historical Collection, Detroit, has been extraordinarily helpful in his searching, though sometimes caustic, suggestions.

Mary Vining's relations with Wayne are based upon data received from Thomas Robins—whose family traditions trace through his great-great-grandfather, Thomas Rodney, cousin and contemporary of Mary Vining—and from Mrs. Henry Ridgely of Dover, president of the Public Archives Commission of Delaware and a direct descendant of the Vining family. The late Mrs. Francis de H. Janvier of New Castle, vice-president of the Public Archives Commission, Leon de Valinger, assistant state archivist, and Mrs. William D. Denny of Dover worked assiduously in clearing up imaginative misconceptions concerning the Wayne-Vining relationships, and to them I am deeply indebted.

Miss Katherine B. Blake, director of the Erie Public Museum, studied the printed records and the traditional accounts to discover the facts about Wayne's death, burial, and subsequent exhumation, while Catherine Cate Coblentz, literary editor of the *National Historical Magazine* of the Daughters of the American Revolution, has been extremely helpful in solving numerous knotty problems. To them also I express my gratitude.

Upon the completion of the manuscript, I have had greater or smaller portions of it read for comment and criticism by many of those whom I have already mentioned. I am under the deepest obligations to Frederic R. Kirkland, Thomas Ridgway, Roy G. Fitzgerald, Albert Idell of Primos, Pennsylvania,

Milo M. Quaife, and Kay Dealy of Philadelphia for their often severe but always friendly and extremely helpful suggestions. Mr. Kirkland was particularly keen in spotting errors of interpretation about Colonial and Revolutionary Pennsylvania and in suggesting improvements in style, and Mr. Ridgway was invaluable for his knowledge of both history and law. Stephen H. P. Pell read and approved the chapters on Ticonderoga. Christian Sanderson of Chadd's Ford checked the story of Brandywine, upon which he is an acknowledged authority, while Edward W. Hocker, librarian of the Germantown Historical Society, and the best expert upon that region, commented kindly upon the account of the battle of Germantown. Miss Quarles, of the Association for the Preservation of Virginia Antiquities, read and passed favorably upon the chapters relating to her state. If, despite their efforts, errors either of omission or of commission have crept in, the responsibility is not theirs but mine alone, for they have done their utmost. No one but myself will ever know how great their help has been.

I confess my gratitude to an able, though slave-driving editor, Lambert Davis, and to a conscientious and imaginative copy-editor, Isabel Ely Lord, who have brought a huge manuscript into order.

Lastly, but only to indicate that the debt is greatest, I thank Helen Jaquette Wildes for constant and always inspiring aid during the whole course of gathering, collating, writing, and editing the work. Without her, it could never have been completed.

HARRY EMERSON WILDES

Valley Forge, Pennsylvania

CONTENTS

ILLUSTRATIONS

Anthony Wayne   *Frontispiece*

MAPS

Anthony Wayne

Trouble Shooter of the American Revolution

CHAPTER I

Dragoon's Blood

WAYNESBOROUGH's three hundred and eighty acres are a farmer's paradise. From the long plateau that tops the South Valley Hills, rich-soiled fields of Chester County slope slowly southward for a mile or more until they touch the slender stream, Crum Creek, that flows to meet the Delaware. Beyond the Crum rise oak and hickory forests, blazing bright in autumn with their scarlet, gold, and bronze, broken by ravines through which swift waters rush. Eastward, twenty miles away, lies Philadelphia, metropolis of colonial days; westward stretch the townships that are called the Land of Goshen, fat farming country where for two full generations peace and plenty have reigned uninterruptedly. Behind the long plateau, protecting it from drifting snow and piercing wintry gales, stand the South Valley Hills, gently sloping on the side toward Waynesborough, but falling rapidly upon the northern side. Here, even yet, are tangled woods, overgrown with grape and cat brier, cluttered by rotting fallen timbers.

Certainly old Captain Anthony Wayne, veteran of Marlborough's continental wars, leader of King William's dragoons at the Battle of the Boyne, thought the scene delightful when he came to settle there in 1724. The sixty-year-old Britisher, worn out by warfare, tired of wandering in Holland, Germany, and Ireland, sought quiet and security on a fertile Pennsylvania farm. Among the Welsh and Quaker planters of the Land of Goshen and the Great Valley that lay behind the hills, Captain Anthony established a homestead that has been occupied by his descendants for eight succeeding generations.

The brown three-story, field-stone house, white-pointed with broad bands of mortar, that was begun by Captain Anthony remains a gem of Georgian architecture. The seasoned soldier, mindful even in a Quaker neighborhood of wars and riots, built it partly as a fort. Its broad door, strongly built; with sheet-iron set between its double planking, hand-wrought bars, and a mighty iron lock, was a safeguard against sudden attack. Within the house, convenient alcoves were provided as a storage place for muskets so that defenders might be well prepared, and at the head of the great staircase leading to the master's bedroom on the second floor more barriers were built behind which the cavalry commander might fight such Frenchmen, Indians, or Stuart partisans as might invade the peaceful farm. More typical of Waynesborough hospitality is the friendly lantern hanging from an iron ring above the doorway to cast generous light upon the entrance and upon the wide brick terrace that spreads before the house. Within, large square rooms, white-painted and comfortable, warmed by eleven huge fireplaces, afford ample space for gracious living. In winter, when solid shutters close the windows against drafts and when great logs burn in all the downstairs rooms and in many of the upper chambers, candlelight glows gaily against the glass and crystal of the drawing-room.

For fifteen years old Captain Anthony Wayne enjoyed his Chester County farm, aided in the later years by his blunt, brawny son Isaac, militia leader, politician, and Assemblyman. Then in 1739 the dragoon commander died, leaving Waynesborough to Isaac and Isaac's small but wiry wife, Elizabeth Iddings, daughter of an English Quaker who was a neighbor of the Waynes. Filial though he was, Isaac could not deny a feeling of relief when the testy cavalryman lay at last in the churchyard of St. David's in Radnor. In his later years, Captain Anthony had been a trial to his son and to the little Quaker bride. He was forever reminding them that the Waynes had always been noted for their military prowess. From the time the family first appears in English records, in Derbyshire in the early fifteenth century, there had been soldiers in the clan. For Isaac to be married to a nonresistant Quaker had been a severe shock to the warrior's family pride.

Captain Anthony had been indignant, too, because Isaac seemed remiss in marital duties. All the Waynes had been prolific parents. The dragoon's great-grandfather had raised nine children to maturity; his grandfather had been sire of eleven; Anthony's father and Anthony himself had each reared ten. But although Isaac's brothers and sisters had fulfilled their family duties, Isaac himself seemed destined to be childless. Constantly, as he passed seventy, the ancient warrior reminded Isaac of his obligation to produce a family; he exhorted the embarrassed Elizabeth to greater efforts.

The old man died before a child was born to Isaac. Perhaps it was just as well, since that child was a daughter. Not for six years after the dragoon's death was Captain Anthony's ambition gratified. (A second daughter would later complete the family.) On New Year's morning, 1745, the Anthony Wayne who was to be the Revolutionary general was born at Waynesborough. The boy would have delighted the old dragoon, for young Anthony, stocky, sturdy, and muscular, was pure Wayne in his physique, from his faintly reddish hair and hazel eyes and ruddy skin down to the huge feet that always marked the Waynes. He had the quick, flashing temper of his grandfather, and the sharply jutting jaw of all his military ancestors. None of the Quaker Iddings characteristics showed themselves, nor did he possess the cunning, managerial skill of his politician father. Anthony Wayne was precisely the type of grandson that the dragoon would have desired.

Possibly Isaac would not have been so well pleased had he been able to foresee the future. After a brief term of militia service against Indians on the Pennsylvania frontier, he had come back to Chester County to lead the Whig group of independent voters against the Tory faction of Judge William Moore. In political meetings throughout the county, in the vestry at Anglican St. David's, in the halls of the provincial Assembly, Isaac and Judge Moore clashed constantly, though socially they remained warm friends. Isaac hoped that when the boy grew up young Anthony would become a lawyer, capable of running for the Assembly and perhaps of taking Judge Moore's place upon the bench. Robert Shannon, a well-recommended British overseer versed in farming, tanning, and the care of livestock, would then manage the estate, setting Anthony free for statesmanship and the arts of gracious living.

But as the boy grew older he showed no signs of scholarship. Isaac's brother Gilbert, master of the school attended by children of the Waynesborough neighborhood, was frankly disappointed at young Anthony's lack of interest in books. Again and again, Gilbert Wayne protested that the boy was wasting his time. "Your affection blinds you, Brother Isaac," the school-teacher declared. "You mistake your son's capacity. I cannot tell what occupation suits him best, but I am certain that he will never make a scholar. I must be candid with you. Unless Anthony pays more attention to his books, I shall be under the painful necessity of dismissing him from school."

At Isaac's strong insistence, Gilbert relented, although increasingly the boy's attention wandered. Latin held no charms for him, except for the one term when he read of Caesar's victories in Gaul; he hated the long, prosy oratory of men who merely mouthed big words; he could not see the sense of taking time to puzzle out his sums. But, as Gilbert saw, when lesson time was up, the stocky stripling became at once alert. The first one out of the classroom, he bustled about impatiently outside, shouting to his playmates to hurry. He was, it seems, commanding general of a schoolboy army. His playmates, armed with sticks and stones, drilled daily under Tony's watchful eye. He marshaled them with careful strategy; he led them in maneuvers, drilling them unmercifully; he raced them across the fields to charge imaginary Indians; he re-enacted famous battles of the recent wars against the French.

On one occasion, when he was fourteen and when the news of battles at Ticonderoga was fresh in people's minds, he had his "soldiers" throw up earthworks in the schoolyard so that he and they could act out the whole campaign. Gilbert Wayne came out of the schoolhouse just in time to see his pupils in the heat of bitter battle. Anthony was running straight up to the fort, his nose bleeding from a hit by a stone; three other boys, heads down, each with one hand extended to ward off stones, the other tightly clutching a sharp stick as a bayonet, dashed after him, yelling wildly. Francis Johnston, one of Tony's best friends, cowered with a pair of badly frightened "Frenchies" behind the earthworks of Ticonderoga.

The schoolmaster cast aside his dignity and shouted, but the determined "general" did not hear. His soldiers, less obsessed by battle, stopped suddenly. Anthony, all alone, climbed the breastworks, grabbed the handkerchief that fluttered from a crooked stick, and demanded that the fort surrender. Then he saw his uncle. His jubilation ended quickly, but before he walked back to Gilbert to take his punishment for fighting, he demanded that Francis Johnston give over the lath sword that the French general wore. Proudly clutching the trophy, young Anthony took the caning that his uncle administered. "I think," said Gilbert that night to Isaac over the rum punches, "that Anthony may perhaps make a soldier."

Fatherlike, Isaac clung to a hope that Tony would improve in his studies. Thinking that a change of scene might cure the boy's dislike for books, and that in new environment and under a more skilled tutor than Uncle Gilbert Tony would find new interests, Isaac arranged to enter him at the Philadelphia Academy, then entering its eighteenth year. Gilbert would have scoffed at the idea, so the father kept his reasons to himself. To Anthony, concealing indulgence under a mask of harshness, Isaac said that the boy must not dare to fail: "It is, my son, the last chance I shall give you. If you do not persevere, I shall take you out of school and send you to do the hardest labor on the farm."

Certainly Isaac was not literal in his threats; he hoped to waken the boy's determination. No matter how low the lad might sink in scholarship, he never would be reduced to grubbing with a hoe nor to the tedious tasks of laboring in the tanning vats. The Waynes were folk of substance who understood the gulf that lay between the life of a gentleman and the work of bound boys. Isaac, with his six horses, ten cows, and ten sheep, and with the ownership of four servants—more than all the other residents of Easttown township combined—would never have reduced his son to humiliating manual labor. His threat to take the boy from school meant merely that he would put him under Shannon's careful tutelage.

Tony's own preference was for war. Historic Blue Ball Tavern on the Lancaster Road, not a mile from Waynesborough, was a military rendezvous. Officers on their way to fight the French at Fort Duquesne mustered there, talking of their plans. Tony, too young to join the army but old enough to slip into the Blue Ball taproom, drank in soldier talk. To his surprise, he learned that military life was not all fighting. Grown men at the Blue Ball talked more of cutting military highways through the wilderness than about the storming of redoubts; they spoke of building forts and making bridges, of scouting and of safeguarding supplies, of maneuvering and sentry go, of drill and discipline. Young Anthony discovered that mathematics and engineering were requisites for waging successful war, and that skilled surveyors were essential if victory was sought. Such taproom talk underscored Isaac's advice. Tony agreed to go to the academy, provided there should be less Latin and more science in his study program. Isaac promised that a commission might be purchased for the boy in one of the crack Guards regiments. The father was not wholly candid in the matter; Isaac firmly believed that the French war was drawing to its close, and that when once the French were driven from America, a long unbroken period of peace would put an end to Tony's military prospects.

2

Chester County farmers, even those as urbanely sophisticated as Assemblyman Isaac Wayne, held a low opinion of the city. Since the death of William Penn in 1718 a new generation had come to power in Philadelphia, a more aggressive, less spiritual folk than the old Quaker stock. Staidness, sobriety, and honesty were no longer as fashionable as in the Founder's day; that toleration of all religious beliefs which Penn had stressed had so far enlarged itself as to become neglect of and indifference to all religion. Isaac hesitated to send his son to town, yet the alternative was to keep Tony at home, where the boy would increasingly devote himself to hunting and riding to the detriment of a broader education. Philadelphia, too, for all its metropolitanism, remained devoted to the pacifism of its Quaker settlers. The British garrison, though growing in prestige and in importance, had not yet modified the peaceable and quiet nature of the town. In such a capital, Isaac thought, the restless boy might lose something of his love of war games; in any case, a study of mathematics, science, and surveying would prepare him for a civil as well as for a military career.

In the autumn of 1759, when Anthony was not quite fifteen, he rode along the narrow, rutted trail that led from Lancaster to Philadelphia. The road was crowded. Scores of hopeful migrants were on their way to take up free land on the frontier. Stolid Germans trudged patiently westward, seeking peace in Pennsylvania, bearing on their backs their scanty stock of tools, seed, and stores. Young Anthony Wayne could not understand their attitude of docile resignation; he felt closer kin to the forceful, brisk Scotch-Irishmen, those sandy-haired, freckled folk who seemed always spoiling for a fight. These reckless, swaggering fellows shouldering their way toward Lancaster captured his imagination; they must be, he thought, grandsons of old Captain Anthony's dragoons. Though Wayne possessed no single drop of Celtic blood, he looked upon himself as Irish because his grandfather had once lived in Ireland. Invariably he set aside the seventeenth of March as a holiday; in later years, he prized his membership in that social club of convivial Irishmen who called themselves the Friendly Sons of St. Patrick. Foreigners were not the only pioneers whom he met moving westward toward the frontier. English immigrants were on the road, spare lanky men with grim determined faces who spoke seldom but always with authority; a few Yankees, thin-lipped and flinty, pushed creaking barrows loaded with trade goods. Tony did not like these men; they were too cold, and they had disciplined their thoughts. He preferred men who were forceful and who gave full rein to their impulsiveness.

Philadelphia proved exciting. The broad, placid Delaware,

filled with as many as two hundred ships from England and the West Indies, beckoned Anthony to overseas adventures that he was never fortunate enough to undertake. The handsome homes of rich importers gleamed with silver and with crystal and the deep richness of their furniture and paneling seemed, through their endless oilings and polishings, to be satin-soft. The grounds of country homes equaled the best in all America in their artistic landscape gardening. Wayne, who liked the open, took but little pleasure in shaded walks bordered by evergreens carefully clipped into pyramids and cones, but beyond Eighth Street the open fields began, and from here to the Schuylkill, nearly two miles distant, were woods and farmlands. Forest giants as tall as anything that he had known at Waynesborough were not far beyond the little city's limits. Here Wayne wandered, as long as the weather stayed mild enough for outdoor exercise.

His fellow students did not share his interest in roaming in the wilderness. Most of them were younger than the Chester County boy, interested in more puerile sports. Tony had not long outgrown schoolboy skirmishes, but he had grown accustomed to man-talk at the Blue Ball; these youngsters at the Academy, the progenitor of the later University of Pennsylvania, were childish. Anthony was growing more mature; he preferred adult society.

By moving for the summer to Waynesborough, Anthony escaped the dreadful yellow-fever epidemic of 1760, which carried off several of his classmates; by the time of his return in the autumn, the danger of infection had passed. In this second year, the stocky, handsome youth knew Philadelphia better; he became more social than he had been during his first days in the city. He sought gayer company, particularly at stables where race horses were kept. There are no account books available to show whether he won or lost, or even if he placed bets on his favorites, but hot-blooded Tony was not one to take his pleasures calmly. A country boy who knew horseflesh thoroughly, the high-strung youngster could not keep himself aloof from the stables. It is a safe conjecture that he backed his choice in races and, in the absence of warning letters from his father, it is an equally safe assumption that his losses could not have been extensive. Isaac would never have missed an opportunity to write a stinging letter to a wastrel son.

More dangerous than his patronage of racing was his discovery of wine. Liquor, to be sure, was nothing strange to boys of Anthony's upbringing; Waynesborough, like other large plantations, had its cider press, and on occasion tried its hand at brewing. Rum was a specific, and Isaac Wayne, who fancied himself a connoisseur of food and drink, bought Madeira by the barrel. Tony, in common with all other boys of his class, regarded liquor as a customary adjunct to a proper meal. In Philadelphia, however, drinking had become a social art. Close to the academy, in a smart Race Street inn, college boys and adolescent townsmen met to talk and drink. For two-and-six a boy might buy a quart of wine, enough to last two friends an evening. Billiards were available, too, and though Chester County rustics still regarded the game as an invention of Satan, Tony held no such narrow prejudices. He soon became an excellent player. With wine and whist, loo and billiards, the Race Street tavern attracted gay youths. No doubt it wrecked many a promising college career for boys who took their dissipations too intensely, but the diversions did not hinder Tony's advancement. He moved forward rapidly in surveying and astronomy.

By 1763, in his nineteenth year, Anthony Wayne was proficient in his chosen work, though one need not go the lengths of his son, his first biographer, who asserts that "his attachment to mathematical science was so ardent and his zeal to reach its summit so great that . . . his manuscripts excited the attention and elicited the applause of distinguished professors." None of those masterpieces are extant, and hence the opinion of the enthusiastic only son cannot be checked, but the comment is certainly exaggerated.

Anthony did not return at once to Waynesborough; Philadelphia offered too many charms. He thought again of war as an engineering officer, and he believed that if he stayed in the metropolis he would have a stronger chance of winning a commission. He entertained at times disturbing thoughts about military life. The brilliant officers whom Wayne had met at the

Blue Ball unanimously advised against his entering the service, particularly now that peace with France was but a few weeks off. They pointed to old Captain Benjamin Loxley, the dingy artillery commander who had long been thrust off in a corner because he lacked strong connections at the War Office; they warned that Pennsylvanians, no matter how well qualified for promotion, had little chance to progress. The best post that the unhappy Ben Loxley could secure was that of permanent Philadelphia commandant; Wayne, they said, would fare no better. But always at that point, it seemed, Otway's regiment paraded through the streets, brave in gold and scarlet, its fifes squealing the "Grenadiers' March," its drums valiantly beating time. The thrill of Otway's music drowned out the warning.

Two other reckless officers, drunken, gay, and uninhibited, lent added glamour to military life. Driving full tilt through the streets in their racing carriage, one of the thirty wheeled "chairs" in the capital, Ogle and Friend—names as closely linked as those of Castor and Pollux—treated Philadelphians as a conquered people. Strangely enough, the populace registered no protest; instead, the two swaggering captains won the hearts of Philadelphia youth. Wayne watched them race along the road. Once he saw them come to a fenced-off section and dash their horse and chair against the barrier. He looked with frightened fascination as they were thrown, parabola-fashion, from their seats. But when he leaped forward to their assistance, he was relieved to see them jump up and, with not a glance at the wreckage of their chair, stroll off laughing heartily.

Captain Charles Lee, too, a stoop-shouldered cadaverous Englishman who loved his spaniels more than he did human beings, glided through Philadelphia streets to leave behind him, before his departure for Britain, a trail of myth and romance. Survivor of the Ticonderoga expedition and of Braddock's disaster, Lee had just come from the Indian country, where he had been adopted as a member of the Mohawk tribe. Whisperers in drawing-rooms gossiped that he was married to a Mohawk "princess," that he had horsewhipped a man, and that he was the author of a series of scurrilous pamphlets. Wayne paid no heed to gossip; certainly there was no charm to Anthony Wayne, who had heard too much about Indians from his father, in the idea of marrying a squaw, but Lee's shrewd personality attracted him. Lee's adventures with the famous 44th were fascinating. For only £900, thought Wayne, he too might buy a captaincy in that crack regiment. Then he could look down with cold disdain upon the "mohairs," the civilians in mufti.

Peace, however, was at hand; Isaac, looking calmly into the future, thought that the purchase of a commission was unjustifiable. The boy would do much better at surveying. Chester County needed competent men. Perhaps, too, rumors had reached Waynesborough that young Anthony was spending too much time at race tracks and in taverns and that he was consorting too freely with officers like Ogle, Friend, and Lee. Whatever may have been the reason, Isaac summoned Anthony to come home at once, to start surveying in Easttown township.

CHAPTER II

To Make a Fortune

A NY INDUSTRIOUS man may make a fortune in a few years."
Anthony Wayne's optimism seldom flagged; wherever he
might be, he followed rainbow trails to wealth. Now in May,
1765, he was in Nova Scotia as colonizing agent for a land-
speculation syndicate. His letters home glowed with the promise
of riches soon to come. "I have been this three weeks back
a-surveying the coast between Halifax and Cape Sable," he
wrote John Hughes, close friend and intimate business associate
of Benjamin Franklin. "I have found some very fine land . . .
equal to any I have ever seen. I am confident that this will be
a place of Great Importance in a very short time. . . . I need
say no more of the land than this . . . it is sufficient to produce
any kind of grain whatsoever." From a Chester County farmer,
accustomed to rich, generous soil, this compliment to Nova
Scotia land was praise indeed—but possibly the twenty-year-
old's excitement had been too much for him. To this day that
land is not famous for its grain, though apples and hay grow
in profusion and butter and cheese produced there match those
of any other land. Wayne, however, was not consciously exag-
gerating Nova Scotia possibilities; he always viewed his prospects through rosy lenses.

Anthony's hazel eyes were bright with delight; he lived in a
seventh heaven. From routine work in mapping farms and
woodlots in well-established Chester County he had been trans-
ported suddenly to membership in a speculating company. All
his phrases show his deep excitement; he was ebullient with joy.

Perhaps his schoolboy races won him his opportunity. Vi-
sionary Alexander McNutt, the Londonderry enthusiast who

planned Nova Scotia settlements, was a friend of Andrew Lewis, father of a lad against whom Tony had run races in Philadelphia. Young Anthony's intensity, his burning ambition, appealed to the promoter. McNutt needed a manager to care for his interests in the North; as soon as he was ready to send settlers to Nova Scotia, he invited Tony Wayne to lead the expedition. Inwardly, Anthony was enthusiastic over the opportunity, but with that deep-seated caution which always underlay his seeming impulsiveness, he made inquiries before he gave his answer. He asked about his pay, and was told that he would get no cash other than enough for his expenses, but that he would be given 5,000 acres of land. Ordinary settlers, he was reminded, must pay a royalty on all crops grown, but his grant would not be subject to that tax. All that he grew would be his, and since the land would cost him nothing, his profit would be high. When he protested that he was investing time and skill and energy in return for merely a free farm, McNutt replied by painting Nova Scotia prospects in glowing colors. Successful colonization, he said, would push the price of Nova Scotia acres to high levels; by managing the colony successfully, Anthony would enhance the value of his farm. In a few short months he could sell out at a tremendous profit.

Because the invitation still seemed to him peculiar, Anthony investigated further. He went to Mayor Matthew Clarkson, a veteran land speculator, to ask his advice; he found that Clarkson thought so highly of the scheme that he had formed a syndicate to take a one-fifth interest in the McNutt development. Judge William Moore also urged him to accept the offer, pointing out that Tony could pick up 5,000 acres of good land for a few months' work as manager. The Franklin clique, headed by the great philosopher, reinforced the Clarkson and Moore recommendations, since it too held a one-fifth interest in the venture. Dr. William Smith, head of the university in Philadelphia, was another enthusiastic investor. With shrewd businessmen supporting it, the project seemed certain to succeed. These men were investing money to pay the expenses of colonists who would go to Nova Scotia. If they, who knew finance, were confident that through royalties on crops and by enhancement of land values the scheme would prosper, surely, thought Anthony, the risk could not be great. If it succeeded, he would be independently wealthy; if by any remote possibility the venture failed, he would not be too old to come home again to Waynesborough.

Anthony's willingness to accept McNutt's invitation was increased by an offer from the Franklin clique. That canny group, always alert to seize an opportunity, invited him to throw in his lot with them, taking his 5,000 acres in the same area with their 25,000-acre allotment. Thus the resident manager would be their special agent, since by caring for his own land he would also protect their interests. In return for this service the clique would help Anthony in Philadelphia. They had a finger in every Pennsylvania pie. Anthony could not lose. With nothing to risk but a few months of labor, he was entering the inner circle of a great land-speculation venture. After less than a year at Waynesborough, he accepted both McNutt's offer and the pay of 4 shillings per day offered by Franklin's friends, and took ship for Nova Scotia early in the spring of 1765.

Arriving with McNutt at Halifax on March 29, after a two-week passage marred by a three-day nor'easter, Wayne discovered that McNutt had grossly magnified the chances for success. There were, to be sure, thirty-four families of settlers, enrolled in New York by the high-pressure salesmanship of one Reuben Haines, to whom McNutt paid so much a head for recruiting colonists, but none of them were farmers; worse still, few were of the pioneering breed. McNutt turned them over to Wayne for protection, and they clung to him helplessly, unable to strike out for themselves. Unlike the swaggering rawboned Scotch-Irishmen whom Wayne had seen shouldering their way west along the road to Lancaster, these men were timorous, devoid of self-reliance.

Moreover, McNutt in Nova Scotia was far less friendly than he had been in Philadelphia. Learning that Wayne considered himself an agent of the Franklin clique rather than of his own, McNutt turned cool. Beyond a formal introduction to Montague Wilmot, Governor-General and Commander-in-Chief of Nova Scotia, McNutt assumed no responsibility for Wayne's success, but left the boy to his own devices. Wayne succeeded well enough to be invited to dine with Wilmot at the rude log house which was the colony's palace; he made friends with the Halifax gentry, and went off on a six weeks' surveying trip with Parson Lyon, but in none of these was Alexander McNutt of any real assistance.

To his amazement, Wayne soon discovered that no actual colony existed; worse yet, that although the syndicate was to control 200,000 acres (at a yearly rental of 1 farthing an acre), the land had not yet been allotted or even surveyed. Governor Montague Wilmot seemed loath, indeed, to come to any decision as to when the colony might start. With the rashness of youth, Wayne assumed that the delay was due to inactivity; he wasted no time in hiring chain-carriers to help him chart the coast. Then, when he knew something of the island, he pushed himself into the Governor's office and demanded to be given the best unoccupied land in Nova Scotia. Wilmot hesitated. By evasion and delay, the Governor postponed his answer. Wayne insisted that since everyone was ready to begin a settlement, Wilmot must sign the grants that would put the colony into operation. Unless, Anthony explained, immediate steps were taken, no settlers could be brought to Nova Scotia until another year had passed, for any immigration must be made in summer in order to get men established before winter should set in. Such postponement, as it happened, was precisely what the Governor preferred. McNutt, he had heard, planned to transport Irishmen to Nova Scotia, and Wilmot feared that Irish Catholics, by combining with French Canadians, might stage a plot to upset British rule. He had sent word of his fears to London; he was delaying action until he should receive a reply, together with instructions concerning his future actions.

Wayne, baffled by the smooth diplomacies of Governor Montague Wilmot, lost his head; he threatened that unless the grant was made at once, he would advise his friends to cancel the project entirely. Wilmot laughed and said that he did not think that this drastic action would be taken. He went further, and declared that since Wayne felt so strongly on the matter, it would be well to cancel the entire arrangement. He would withdraw his permission for the colony. Wayne protested angrily, as the clever Governor had anticipated. Wilmot had no intention of putting an end to the matter; he sought only to gain time until his orders should arrive. He knew that Wayne had no authority to speak for McNutt or for the other members of the syndicate, but was their agent only, with limited powers. He pretended to be mollified when Anthony apologized for losing his temper; but he said the syndicate must now agree to plant four hundred families on the island within a four-year period.

Wayne believed that McNutt secretly connived at the delay, hoping, so Wayne suspected, to obtain special favors by betraying the Clarkson-Franklin interests. In writing to Hughes, Wayne expressed his indignation at what he termed "this despicable and unjust proceeding." He was angry, too, because the members of Wilmot's council, while bland and friendly in private conversation, invariably voted in Wilmot's favor when put to public test. Wayne was sure that McNutt was at the bottom of this duplicity; he assured Hughes that if it should prove at all possible, every effort would be made to freeze out McNutt from any share in such grants as should eventually be made.

In the privacy of Wayne's log hut at Halifax, the surveyor fumed and swore at Montague Wilmot's tyranny. However, he dared not let his public protests be too vehement, lest Wilmot add more onerous provisions. Curbing his resentment, he drew up a most respectful letter, begging leave to show that the new terms could not be carried into execution. In a very different vein from that in which he had written Hughes, he suggested that the soil was too thin to support so large a population. "In almost every township, there is scarce one-third part of the lands fit for culture without manuring—which will require time to raise stock for that purpose." He proposed that Wilmot mend his requirements and that the syndicate be permitted to send two hundred families, half the number that Wilmot asked. The letter was an error. Wilmot, pretending to be angry at the slur on Nova Scotia soil, forced an apology, and compelled Wayne to cool his heels for weeks until the Governor was ready to receive him. When the long-awaited instructions arrived, Wilmot at length relented.

On October 31, the Nova Scotia government granted to McNutt's associates a tract of 100,000 acres on the north bank of St. John's River, on condition that within four years the company settle one Protestant person for each 200 acres. Since colonial families were never very small, this population clause was really a Wayne victory; certainly, five hundred people, the minimum number called for in the 100,000-acre tract, would be far easier to recruit than the two hundred families Wayne had offered to secure. Other provisions were not so favorable. Wilmot slipped in new requirements: that a third of the entire area was not only to be planted but must be fenced within ten years; that all gold, silver, and coal found within concession boundaries were reserved for the Crown; and, by a curious demand, that 30,000 square yards, or 6 acres, were to be sown to hemp. Just how that plant was to be grown in Nova Scotia, Wilmot failed to explain, and evidently Anthony forgot to ask. Thinking only of the victory as to the number of colonists required, the young manager accepted the conditions; moreover, he contracted to take another 100,000 acres, on precisely the same terms—including the hemp fields—on the Petitcoodia River. He was thus obligated to produce within four years a colony of at least a thousand people.

But the Governor had one more trump card up his sleeve. The land, to Wayne's amazement, was not the highly desirable territory he had surveyed. He had requested the southern coast, close to the fishing-banks along the ocean, but when Wilmot handed over the deed, the grant faced Northumberland Strait, on the northern shore. Anthony had not visited the neighborhood; he knew neither the quality of the soil nor the physical features of the grant. The work that he had done in mapping watercourses, in scouting the best locations for roads and ferries, in locating marshes, meadows, roads, and mountain passes, and in finding springs and ores must be done again. His colonists would be comparatively isolated, too, since they would have access to the sea only by a long sail northward around Cape Breton.

Little, however, could be done in Nova Scotia at that season of the year. Cold weather was approaching, and Wayne, rather than spend a winter in the field alone, resolved to go home to Philadelphia to explain the circumstances as best he could. By the time he reached Pennsylvania at the end of November, he had recovered his self-confidence. Nova Scotia, he insisted again, as in his letter to John Hughes, was well worth developing. All through the winter of 1765-66 Anthony Wayne kept busy in Philadelphia, explaining to his fellow directors of the syndicate about the possibilities of Nova Scotia settlement. He did not mention that he had been reduced to a steady diet of pork, rum, and bread and butter, with a lump off "a loaf of white shuggar" for dessert. Nor did he add that he had been dependent for his bread upon the willingness of fishing-schooner captains to sell him portions of their stores.

Though he was absent from Nova Scotia, Wayne did not cease his efforts for his colony. As each vessel came to Philadelphia with immigrants, he interviewed the new arrivals, seeking to persuade them that the crowded middle colonies needed no more men, and that good land was occupied as far as the Indian country beyond the Susquehanna. From his own observation, he told them of the swarms of settlers moving westward on the road to Lancaster; he warned newcomers that frontier life was harsh and dangerous. Nova Scotia, on the other hand, was virgin soil, where an enterprising colonist, working with the McNutt associates, could prosper. If they would take passage with sufficient food and stores to last them until crops were gathered, Wayne, Franklin, and McNutt would ask no payment for the land other than a small share of the harvest. Even if they could not pay the costs of getting themselves established, the syndicate would gladly advance credit without demanding interest. Franklin's group alone laid out more than £200 for passage money, cattle, and provisions. Thirteen families accepted Wayne's inducements. They sailed north, with Wayne's persuasive words still ringing in their ears:

"Any industrious man may make a fortune there in a few years."

2

Social doors swung wide open to the returned adventurer. That Wayne had as yet few settlers was overlooked; the fact that he controlled a colony established the Nova Scotia manager as a person of distinction. Always a man's man, ready to drink or ride or tell a story, twenty-one-year-old Anthony Wayne mixed well. He went on pigeon shoots and bagged more than his share of game; at cider frolics he talked knowingly about horses. At taverns, in late afternoons and evenings, he matched glass for glass with hardened drinkers, yet kept a head clear enough to play respectable backgammon, and nerves sufficiently controlled to make a run at billiards.

Physical activities attracted him, but intellectual matters left him cold. When the conversation turned on Franklin's theorizing or upon the new books of the French philosophers, young Wayne sat silent, drumming with his square finger-ends upon the table, shifting restlessly in his chair. Sometimes, when he had been rash in making forthright statements, tavern companions badgered him to desperation with their arguments; then in a sharp burst of anger he blistered them with oaths; he branded them as "caitiffs," the omnibus word which served him as description for everything he did not like.

There was never a doubt about his political stand. Men at the City Tavern, his accustomed place of resort now that he had outgrown the collegiate atmosphere of Race Street, counted on him to oppose the Stamp Act, even if his patron John Hughes was the collector; they knew that he would blast the caitiff Lord Townshend who wished to tax America. They were certain, too, that if the Massachusetts idea of a Congress of the Colonies should be accepted, Wayne would agitate for Pennsylvania to join it; they suspected that he was a Son of Liberty. On matters such as these, Wayne's voice was always loud and gruff, in the manner of one who would batter down all opposition. He was not a thinking man; he was a man of action. He did not oppose the King, nor condemn the monarch as not wholly sane; he blamed the King's friends for misleading George. Like all true Whigs, he believed firmly that an independent Parliament, with Americans included, should be supreme.

John Cox, one of the syndicate, made Anthony a member of a small fox-hunting set which started off at dawn on crisp mornings to look for sport in the open fields and woods that lay beyond the city. Anthony enjoyed the sport; it was vigorous, blood-stirring, and exciting, and it brought him into contact with important people who were kindred spirits.

Two days before Christmas, 1765, he took part in a gala chase. Rising long before dawn, he snatched a few bites of breakfast and trotted out to Darby, southwest of the city across the Schuylkill, to join thirty sportsmen in an all-day hunt. By eleven o'clock they had run three foxes to ground. After an elaborate noonday dinner, rich in meats and game and wine, they set out for a late-afternoon run. The fox proved vigorous, but the riders and their thirty dogs prevailed. According to accounts from supposedly veracious men, the fox eventually climbed a tree. Levi Hollingsworth, one of the most dignified merchants of the town, clambered after him, driving the bewildered fox to the far end of a limb, from which, as Hollingsworth pursued with shouts and shakings of the bough, the fox fell among the waiting dogs. After a double fox hunt netting four brushes, sportsmen should be tired, but Wayne had not finished riding. As the hunters turned back toward Philadelphia, he trotted northward, cutting across fields and fording creeks to reach Waynesborough to spend Christmas with the family.

The holiday was joyful. Parson William Currie preached a special sermon at St. David's, where ever since old Captain Anthony's time the Waynes had been pewholders and vestrymen. After service, neighbors from Easttown and Tredyffrin, across the South Valley Hills, crowded Waynesborough to hear the furloughed colonist talk about his venture. Over and over again Anthony told of Wilmot's tortuous evasions, but he ended always on a happy note of triumph. He did not mention the fence clause, nor talk about hemp-planting; he stressed, instead, his victory in the matter of population. With his usual enthusiasm, he exaggerated Nova Scotia's riches. Even to these prosperous planters, comfortably established on fertile farms, he promised wealth if they would emigrate. His parents listened eagerly to all the repetitions; to them, as well as to the neighbors, Anthony's adventures were new. During his absence they had heard little from their son. Mails were few, depending on the favor of ship captains and casual travelers; even had Tony written, letters would have been delayed in Philadelphia until a neighbor chanced to stop in at the city's tiny post office. Anthony, moreover, was not then a ready penman; during his Nova Scotia stay he had sent but seven letters back to Pennsylvania, and these were to his business partners.

Abraham Robinson, near neighbor of Waynesborough, listened eagerly, as did his brother Tom, both youngsters of Anthony's own age. Their interest, however, was but curiosity; neither had any intention of moving to the North. Clever Dr. Sharp Delany, the Philadelphia doctor and apothecary, was interested too; he had known Anthony in town, but only as a casual acquaintance. At Waynesborough, where his wife's relatives the Robinsons had brought him, Delany developed a deep fondness for the enthusiastic colonial promoter. If ever the Franklin clique ceased to look after Anthony's Philadelphia interests, he said, he would be happy to be of service.

Hannah Van Leer, Anthony's elder sister, also listened as she sat primly by her husband's side. Never close to her brother —whom, indeed, she still considered childish—she felt pride but not elation at his success. She could not keep from thinking about other matters. Anthony, she mused, had not explained his lingering so long in Philadelphia; he should have hurried home at once instead of trying to recruit more colonists. She suspected that he had been loitering in taverns with good-for-nothing fellows instead of thinking of Waynesborough and his relatives, his neighbors, and his parents. No such concern worried gay fifteen-year-old Ann Wayne, third and youngest of the children. She could not keep her admiration in control. Squirming with delight at her big brother's popularity, squeal-

ing with high-pitched laughter at his stories, no matter how
often Anthony repeated them, she prodded him to tell about
the man who chased the fox up a tree and about his trips in
Nova Scotia when he lived on ham and rum. Regardless of her
sister's sharp but low-voiced rebukes, and of the gentle hand
laid by her mother on her arm, Ann giggled incessantly. She
was insistent that her friend Mary Penrose admire her brother
too.

Mary, bright, nervous daughter of one of Philadelphia's
prominent shipbuilding families, was visiting Chester County
to see her sister, the bride of Abraham Robinson. She had, she
shyly insisted, little use for men. Her brothers, Tom and
Joseph, stocky, brawny, and quick-witted, had been too huge
and strong for their delicate little sister. She could not play
their games or understand their wit; often her trustfulness
and inexperience made her the butt of their jokes. If all men
were like her brothers, Polly Penrose vowed, she would be
happy as a spinster. Fatherless since she was three, she had
always been her mother's little girl, coddled and protected
except by her rough brothers. But Anthony Wayne seemed
different. His bravery, his confidence, his tone of authority, and
his charm fascinated the impressionable girl. At sixteen, she
was a hero-worshiper; this ruddy, hazel-eyed man with the
jutting jaw looked, she imagined, as if he wished to guard her
against trouble. When Anthony glanced in her direction, her
broad, well-featured face glowed delightedly. Even without
Ann's constant song of praise for Tony, Mary Penrose would
have been impressed.

Anthony, as yet, knew nothing about girls. His life had been
too full of masculine adventure. Away from home since adoles-
cence, he had swaggered with soldiers and with students; he
had caroused with schoolmates at the Race Street inn and with
men older than himself at the City Tavern; he had chased
foxes and he had explored the Nova Scotia wilderness. Women
were still an unknown quantity. His sisters, one so severe and
prim, the other so silly and shrill, were the only girls he
knew; by manhood, he had even forgotten Mary Wayne, his
cousin, who had lived with the family for a few years in his

early youth. Mary Penrose, therefore, brought a new thrill to
Anthony. She attracted him as irresistibly as she was herself
drawn to him. When she smiled and dropped her eyes con-
fusedly, he felt strange, and for the first time uncertain of
himself; when she giggled and then, unexpectedly, grew very
serious, Anthony was baffled; he gave her credit for an un-
plumbed depth of mind. Conscious of her presence, anxious to
be noticed, he raised his voice, so that without his seeming to
be speaking to her she would hear every word he said; but
when he had blurted out some vigorous remark that seemed
too rough for dainty minds, he blushed with self-consciousness.
He squared his shoulders, and tried to look severe. Then, worried lest he frighten the shrinking little lady, he toned his
sternness with a smile. Mary Penrose, glancing sidewise from
her downcast eyes, thought that no one had ever been so handsome as this man who had done such gallant deeds.

The courtship was brief. When Anthony Wayne laid siege
to a fortress, he carried it by storm; besides, he had to sail for
Nova Scotia soon. He dared not leave so wonderful a girl to
be snapped up by someone else while he was gone. In a whirlwind of love-making, Anthony Wayne won the promise of shy
Polly Penrose, if, she said, he could secure her mother's consent. Wayne had no difficulty with Mrs. Penrose; he did not
know his gifts as yet, but he always had a devastating way with
women. When he asked Mrs. Bartholomew Penrose for her
daughter, he did it, all unwittingly, in a fashion that made the
mother think that it was she he loved.

On March 25, 1766, in Christ Church, Philadelphia, the
Rev. Richard Peters, president of the board of trustees of the
Philadelphia Academy, married Anthony Wayne and Mary
Penrose. Two weeks later, the bride and groom sailed off for
Nova Scotia.

3

Polly Penrose Wayne, gently nurtured in the refinements
of America's metropolis, felt penned and helpless. Smells of

tar and bilge upset her badly; the stuffy little schooner, plunging heavily in choppy seas, was unbearable. During the greater portion of the journey she was sick. Boston was a relief, for Anthony took her ashore to stay a day or so while the schooner unloaded its scanty cargo and stowed more goods, but as soon as the ship cleared the bay the respite was followed by more seasickness. When she was able to come up on deck, she found the weather, though spring was well advanced, cold and raw and clammy. The ship held close to land, but all that she could see was barren rock, or straggly birch and pine, green in color but twisted into strange shapes by constant winds. The sight was cheerless, and when fog closed in, the dead, gray world was worse. Noise of countless gulls, like hollow-voiced ghosts, drove her to distraction. Once she heard a loon, which sounded to her frightened mind like a lost soul calling from the sea. What, she wondered, could induce a man to forsake society to live in such a barren, haunted land?

Anthony reassured her. The voyage, he said, was unusually dismal. On his last trip North, he lied, a hot sun had shone; he had sat on the deck all the way to Halifax, browning himself; the sea had been as smooth as glass. His voyage home, though in winter, had been pleasant too; he had enjoyed good company. This caitiff weather, he said brightly, could not last. At Halifax she would be happy again. That harbor, big enough to hold half a hundred ships of the line, was pleasant, for when Sir Edward Cornwallis founded the naval station in 1749 as a rival to French Louisbourg, he picked a place where smooth, hill-bordered waters offered safe retreat; but the town was disappointing. There were no quays; wharves were rudimentary, and though streets were wide, houses were of shabby wood, crudely shingled with rough, uneven slabs. Polly Wayne, homesick for neat, brick-built Philadelphia, where Quaker housewives scrubbed their steps and washed their pavements daily, cried despairingly. The shy bride, who had not yet passed seventeen, was lonely. Anthony could go into the wilderness to make surveys, or dash up and down the coast to look after his colonists or to consult the Governor, but in her clapboarded, unpainted shack in Halifax Polly had little to occupy her mind.

She sewed and, in good Philadelphia fashion, she kept her house immaculate; she drank tea with the other ladies of the town. Much of the time, however, she spent waiting for Anthony to complete his work and take her home to Pennsylvania.

Even Indians were disillusioning. In Pennsylvania, redskin visitors were common; braves smelling of rancid butter walked with their strange rolling gait about the streets. No one expected Indians to be clean or dainty, but these tiny, stupid-looking Micmacs, with their deep-yellow color and their black pig-eyes, stank of rotten fish. Their young girls were bearable, clad in red-flowered yellow flannel over a short blue petticoat, their sugar-loaf caps, woven with rushes, above their five-foot pigtails. Polly bargained with them for their porcupine-quill workbaskets, patterned in red, yellow, white, brown, and black, and thought that she bought trophies cheaply. When, however, she told Anthony of her bargains, he laughed scornfully and said that she had paid a double price.

Her husband had his troubles, too. Under the pretext of new instructions from London, Wilmot issued more stringent rules. No man, he decreed, could take up more than 1,000 acres—a bitter blow to the syndicate members, each of whom planned to patent for himself at least 10,000 acres—nor could even 1,000 be taken unless the owner paid a fee of £5 sterling. By dint of continued pleading and by sweetening the surveyor with "a wine present" worth £7 6s., which he charged to Hughes, Wayne acquired 6,000 acres in his own name on a four-mile river front, but in the absence of men to work the ground this was a hollow victory.

He worked energetically to make the colony prosper, riding so assiduously about the island that he killed a horse; but his men were far too few. Instead of the thousand people whom he had promised to import, his colony had less than fifty. The soil, which Wayne had so confidently asserted to be as good as any in the world, would not grow grain enough to feed the settlers. Even after wheat was harvested in 1766, his men went on short rations; before winter came, he had to buy flour for their food; the bill came to more than £50. When he went to pay this unexpected charge, he learned to his chagrin that merchants declined his offer of a draft on Philadelphia; they demanded to be paid "in best Burlington pork," a commodity selling at a premium. Wayne protested, calling the demand an extortion, but Wilmot upheld the merchants. Under such conditions, Anthony decided, there was nothing he could do to help the colony progress. He resigned his managership and, to Polly's intense delight, went home to Philadelphia. He still claimed his Nova Scotia lands, though Wilmot insisted that if he abandoned the acres, title would be lost. By strict interpretation of the grant, Wilmot was correct.

When Wayne left, the colonists were in deep distress. Pressed by the syndicate for repayment of money advanced for food and passage, disillusioned at the sterile soil, the settlers faced starvation. They had discovered coal at Monckton, but by express provision of Wilmot's grant the mineral belonged to the Crown. Their only recourse was fishery, but for this they owned neither equipment nor experience, and in any case the voyage to the Banks was roundabout. Samuel Weathered, Wayne's successor, wrote six piteous letters begging for assistance. He secured thirty barrels of flour, four oxen, and a small flock of sheep, but by some unforgivable oversight the bulk of this relief was left behind at Halifax when the last schooner of the season sailed for Northumberland Strait; the syndicate was put to extraordinary expense in chartering a special ship.

Anthony Wayne was glad to be free from the responsibility of colonial management. Happily he returned to Easttown to work the farm and the tannery in partnership with Isaac. He did, however, test his Nova Scotia popularity once again when, a year after his resignation, he forwarded a shipment of Waynesborough leather to Joseph Scott, a Halifax acquaintance. He hoped that Scott would sell it at a price at least as high as it would bring in Philadelphia; he asked for payment either in cash, in fish oil, or in rawhides from the cattle which the syndicate had sent. The quondam colonial proprietor plunged, with his characteristic energy, into the tanning business. He and Isaac entered partnership. Their land now spread into the three townships of Easttown, Willistown, and Charlestown. The business prospered. Isaac's flock of ten sheep grew to fifty, and there were six servants instead of four. Waynes-borough was not only the richest farm in Easttown, but it be-came one of the largest of the county. Under Shannon's watch-ful eye, Wayne supervised a leather factory that did business as far off as the British West Indian islands.

Polly Wayne, who had always hated Halifax, was pleased to be at home. She vowed that never again would she leave Chester County.

"In Time of Peace . . ."

INCREASINGLY the leather business took Wayne to the city—or such was his excuse for riding into town. More and more, the social Anthony who liked good company preferred town delights to country living. Philadelphia taverns, filled nightly with as gay a crowd as that of London, appealed to his love of fellowship. He liked the formal dinners that newly elected officials gave to celebrate their inauguration, though he despised the growing practice of offering only cold collations in place of the time-honored banquets; he felt happy at meeting new arrivals, such as that strange William Alexander from somewhere in New Jersey, who called himself Lord Stirling and who insisted that he was a rightful peer; he enjoyed conversing with all types of people, even though he was intolerant of those who disagreed with him. When George Emlen, for example, said that human bodies were composed of sulphur, mercury, and salt, Wayne laughed so loudly and pounded the tavern table with such vigor that everybody else stopped short in their conversations to stare open-mouthed at Wayne's derision. When chipper Dr. Benjamin Rush, whose Edinburgh diploma was not yet dry, talked earnestly about freeing all the slaves, Wayne laughed again at the idea that "curly-heads" were capable of culture, but when Rush switched to his other favorite crusade, asking for prohibition of hard liquor, Wayne thought the young doctor's ideas absurd. Rush was a good fellow and Wayne enjoyed his company—if only Ben would talk sense.

Anthony made a particular point of coming into town in the autumn after crops were in, for then the Jockey Club held races at its rope-marked course in Center Square. It was one of the few diversions of which Polly thoroughly approved, since the Penrose family were noted horsemen, and the sport was patronized by leaders of society. Timothy Matlack, convivial Quaker who had been read out of meeting for his eccentricities, Will Allen, whose father was chief justice and whose mother was the daughter of the provincial attorney general, and Joseph Galloway, vice-president of the Philosophical Society, led the racing set.

Wayne's best enjoyment, next to sitting round the dinner table with a group of good companions, was the theater. It was a relatively new diversion, for although Philadelphia had seen plays when Anthony was still at Gilbert's school, few dramas had been given while he was at the academy. Actors opened a strange, new world to him, a realm in which passion and play of personality were displayed. Anthony, who liked to dramatize situations in which he appeared, looked upon the theater as the highest art; it was the only art he would ever appreciate. Playgoing offered constant entertainment. David Douglass's American Company, fresh from six years in New York, Rhode Island, and the South, opened a big red theater on South Street where, three nights a week, they gave a repertoire of forty dramas that ranged from Shakespeare's plays, Dryden's *All for Love*, and Farquhar's *Beaux' Stratagem* to the flimsiest of farces. Anthony genuinely enjoyed all of them. His first trip to the theater, made on the opening night when, purely to be fashionable, he sat in a box behind a big square pillar, had been disappointing, but later, when he learned that experienced playgoers chose seats on the front gallery bench, he relished the drama. When the Americans played Shakespeare, he missed few performances. Falstaff he thought a perfectly drawn character.

During four winter months, Douglass produced good plays at his Southwark Theater to constantly increasing audiences. Quaker opposition, roused because of the unusual length of the season and the evident popularity of the company, cast about for some good means of ending what the Friends believed a menace to good morals. In February, 1767, they circulated a petition asking the Assembly to close down the Southwark on the ground that it was "too expensive, hurtful of business and destructive of frugality."

Wayne indignantly spluttered when the Quaker action became known. He roundly applauded Governor John Penn for pigeonholing the remonstrance. When, twenty years later, he was himself a member of the Assembly, he took an active part in defending the theater against other Puritans who attempted to bar drama from the commonwealth.

Even in 1767, Wayne violently opposed censorship of any kind. He was one of the small number who protested when Douglass shelved a performance of Thomas Forrest's comic opera, *The Disappointment,* because the manager feared that the play contained "personal reflections . . . unfit for the stage." Nor did the substitution of Thomas Godfrey's *The Prince of Parthia* mollify him, for though this play is famous in theatrical annals as the first American drama ever to be produced, Wayne found it tedious. The Godfrey play was never repeated.

Polly saw no virtue in acting; socially, players were beyond the pale. She had, moreover, like almost every other Pennsylvania lady, a distinct objection to the cast, since, according to teatable gossip, two late-comers, the tall, handsome comedian John Henry, and an actress named Nancy Storer, the toast of the town, had arrived on the same ship from Jamaica. Polly hinted broadly that the two were not above reproach, and though the Governor himself had recently come to Philadelphia accompanied by a woman who was not his wife, she hated to see such freedom become the fashion. She was glad that her delicate condition gave her good excuse for not taking tea with the Governor's lady; she would not, under any circumstances, be put in a position to recognize that actorfolk existed. Boys in the balcony who threw orange skins upon the gentlemen below she thought truly represented the social tone of theaters. When Anthony reproached her for talking nonsense and said that ladies were "dragons for politics and scandal," Polly tightened her lips and refused to speak of the matter further.

She would have been far more disturbed had she known how her husband's thoughts were again dwelling upon the idea of settling colonies in distant sections of America. Increasingly, in coffeehouse and tavern, men were talking of Ohio River regions where rich grass grew waist-high and game was plentiful. Anthony became as excited as he had been over Nova Scotia. Travelers spun incredible yarns of sixty-pound wild turkeys, of clouds of pigeons that darkened the sun at noon, and of rivers filled with catfish that weighed a hundred pounds. Now that the French were cleared away, this vast inland empire, Anthony predicted, would be the seat of a rich nation. Matthew Clarkson, one of Wayne's Nova Scotia partners, had come home enthusiastic for the West, and although he admitted that Indians were troublesome, he was sure that settlement was feasible. Forgetting his Nova Scotia disappointment, or believing that he could avoid repeating the mistakes made in the North, Clarkson planned colonies in the vast prairie beyond the Alleghenies. Often he repeated, as Wayne nodded agreement: "Every great fortune made within the past fifty years has been in land."

There were difficulties in the path of settlement, not least of which were stringent prohibitions, based upon solemn treaties, against white men's taking up land in areas reserved for Indians. This barrier, Wayne predicted, would be removed shortly, for if the colonial movement toward freedom should go further, all former treaties with Indians would be null and void. Wayne insisted that Western development would progress with great rapidity as soon as London's restraining hand was loosened.

Signs showed that America was restless. Wayne and his intimates were reading eagerly a series of anonymous communications to the *Pennsylvania Chronicle* in which a clever correspondent who called himself a farmer, but who was obviously well skilled in law, argued that the British Parliament had no right to legislate for the colonies without their consent. The tone of these *Farmer's Letters*, as they were later to be called when their authorship was acknowledged by John Dickinson of Pennsylvania, was quiet, conciliatory, and optimistic, but they contained an ominous note of threat of force unless the British changed their tactics. Wayne, deeply stirred, swung himself excitedly into the movement for colonial rights; in coffeehouse discussions he insisted that the "British Rebels" (as he always called them) should be curbed before they wrecked the framework of the British Constitution. The Stamp Act, to be sure, had gone, ushered out on a gala night when every Philadelphia house was brightly lighted in token of the city's joy, but popular resentment still ran high. American patriots loudly cheered the small group of British liberals led by John Wilkes—who was considered martyred by the Crown for criticizing the King's speech in the famous No. 45 issue of the *North Briton* newspaper. Wayne, like every other fervid Colonial, considered forty-five a sacred number. They gathered, whenever possible, in groups of forty-five; at formal dinners they stretched the number of toasts to that magic symbol; in every possible way they stressed the number.

Wayne's Irish-born comrades of the Friendly Sons of St. Patrick set up another popular figure when, at their annual banquet in 1769, they toasted Pasquale Paoli, a Corsican revolutionist who was fighting French royal tyranny in his little island. Few knew much about the man, for no American had either seen or corresponded with him, but the *Pennsylvania Journal*, in a column-long notice of James Boswell's *An Account of Corsica*, lauded Paoli as a vigorous warrior against oppression. Paoli's popularity grew as Wayne's Irish friends publicized his heroism. Three weeks after the St. Patrick's Day dinner, the Sons of Liberty celebrated Paoli's forty-fifth birthday, thus linking the Corsican even more closely to the radical cause. As soon as the usual perfunctory toasts had been drunk to the King and to the royal family, Paoli became the dominating theme. The third toast was to the revolutionist; Wayne drank it amid tumultuous applause.

As the banquet progressed, other friends of America were honored, but none, not even Wilkes, Isaac Barré, or William Pitt, received as frequent mention as Paoli. Excitement mounted. At the twelfth toast, "The Spirit of Paoli to every American!" the assembly roared approval; the thirteenth, "May Paoli meet with equal renown but a happier fate than the younger Brutus!" evoked a shout of wild acclaim. The forty-fifth and final toast brought Wayne and his fellow diners to their feet: "To liberty and loyalty; liberty anyhow, loyalty if not incompatible with liberty!" Less than a month thereafter, Pasquale Paoli was badly beaten by the French and was compelled to flee from Corsica. His rebellion collapsed, but his example continued to inspire American patriots. Out in Wayne's own neighborhood, Joshua Evans christened a new tavern in honor of the rebel; Anthony's address thereafter, for those who wrote him letters, was "At the sign of the Paoli Tavern."

Spirits continued to mount against British rule. Philadelphians cursed and kicked a man who bought a Cheshire cheese in violation of nonimportation agreements; they pulled the nose of another "traitor" who purchased a butt of wine from a British ship. The radicals did not lose their sense of humor; they turned their ire into caricature by ordering that the cheese and wine be given to the prisoners in the city jail and that, to make the feast complete, the two offenders must buy bread for all the inmates. However, loyalty toward England still existed during the sweltering summer of 1769; it stopped suddenly in the following spring. Report of the Boston Massacre, where five people were killed, ran flamelike through Philadelphia. When, a month later, loyal Britons planned their annual St. George's Day festival, only twenty men could be collected.

Wayne sat glowering as celebrants filed into the City Tavern for their jubilation. In other years, he would have joined them at their banquet of roast beef and plum pudding; like them, he would have drunk deeply in honor both of St. George and of George the King. He would have worn the cross that every loyal Briton sported on the anniversary, and he would have gone with them to finish out the evening at the playhouse, singing loudly "God Save the King," "Rule Britannia," and "Britons, Strike Home" at every intermission. In 1770, however, Wayne sat silent in his seat.

Philadelphia had turned unusually cool toward its mother country. When in June the King's birthday came, citizens conveniently forgot that it was customary to picnic on the banks of the Schuylkill, firing cannon in honor of the monarch and drinking his health in many bowls of punch. The capital was grimly sullen. British officers, pets of society in happier times, felt the sting of disapproval. Ogle and Friend were no longer tolerated; their commander ordered them to tone down their pranks. When Lieutenant Ramsey of the 42nd, the Black Watch Highlanders, got drunk and rode his horse up the steps of Mrs. Graydon's boardinghouse, through the parlor and into his bedroom, Philadelphians did not smile. Muscular Major George Etherington, combing the city for a civilian to play rackets with him, saw the people turn their backs; as recruiting officer for the Royal Americans, enlisting Tories for the British Army, Etherington was the most unpopular of all the officers. Cynically he told his cronies that unless men changed their attitude toward him, he would punish them by refusing to guide them further into the city's low-life resorts. Colonel Frank Richardson, a former Pennsylvania Quaker who now wore the king's scarlet uniform, was hooted as he walked the streets; small boys shouted shrilly that only Creoles, Carolinians, and dancing masters wore red coats.

With anti-British feeling growing more intense, young men hesitated to embark on Western enterprises; Ohio, though appealing to both adventurous and wealth-desiring people, attracted few migrants. Wayne and his associates stayed East, drilling and studying tactics. They dared not openly admit the imminence of strife with England, but they urged their fellows to provide themselves with arms "in consequence of prevailing apprehensions of a war with France"; they spent their evenings discussing Marshal Maurice de Saxe's newly published *Mes rêveries*, in which the art of war was clarified. They envied Maryland militiamen who had Charles Lee to train them; they regretted now that nowhere in the colonies was there a military school.

Fashionable young men, Wayne among them, flocked to Francis Mentges' salle d'armes to study swordsmanship, though some preferred to go to their old dancing master Pike, who had forsworn his ballroom to teach fencing. Pike was not particularly skillful, but he was a better pedagogue than Mentges; the latter could defeat Pike at will, but Pike's students were more adept than Mentges'. Wayne, who studied under Mentges, was particularly proud of his master's skill; in later years, when Francis Mentges was an officer in his command, Anthony pushed his tutor forward at every opportunity.

Wayne, however, did not remain in Philadelphia during the time when anti-British feeling was mounting. The farm and the tannery called him home; besides, he could not stay away while Polly was pregnant. During the summer of 1770 he became the father of a daughter, a blonde, blue-eyed baby. With unexpected departure from the names ordinarily given to Wayne daughters or to Penrose girls, he called her Margaretta. He had hoped for a son, but Margaretta cooed so prettily that he forgave her sex. Even after her brother Isaac was born two years later, Margaretta—Peggy, he called her—remained his favorite child.

After the thrills of Philadelphia, Waynesborough was dull. The big brown mansion, filled with women, offered few masculine distractions for restless Anthony. When work was done, he fell into the habit of riding over to the Blue Ball, to Paoli, or to the Leopard Tavern. Sometimes, for wider acquaintanceship, he went downhill to David Howell's inn at Tredyffrin, or out in the Great Valley to the Warren Tavern where Peter Mather was the host. Mather, however, was too Tory for his taste; though the landlord was always most obsequious when entertaining the half-owner of Chester County's richest farm, Anthony preferred the less elaborate Howell inn, where everyone was strongly Whig.

He loitered once too often at his little table underneath the big buttonwood at Howell's tavern. One blistering September evening in 1771, when farmers, tired out from their harvesting, stopped by for refreshment, Wayne was the unlucky victim of a serious predicament. He himself was innocent, but, like many others who attempt to stop a barroom brawl, he was the victim of his good intentions. Mrs. Jacob Malin, wife of the master of Malin Hall, a big estate at the next crossroads to the west, had missed her husband. Suspecting that he was at Howell's tavern, she rode there to bring him home. She found him sitting quietly with Wayne and Caleb Jones, but when she tried to take him back to Malin Hall, she was suddenly attacked.

A drunken tavern girl, Phoebe Stewart, seeing a woman bend-
ing over one of the men she had already marked for her own,
leaped on Mrs. Malin's back, dragged her to the ground, and
in a rough-and-tumble match tried to scratch the wife's eyes
out. Malin jumped to protect his wife and was in turn assaulted. Others joined the fracas; Wayne and Jones grabbed
Phoebe's arms to pull her off. Mather, who was passing by en
route to his own tavern, leaped from his horse to stop the scrim-
mage, but a strong Whig partisan coming from the taproom
saw the Tory and assaulted him. Howell, dodging irresolutely
about the milling crowd, called weakly for the fight to stop.

The brawl ended when Wayne pulled Phoebe away from
Mrs. Malin, but the affair was not complete. Malin took his
wife home, then rode to enter a complaint with Judge William
Moore, Isaac's political enemy but Anthony's partner in the
Nova Scotia venture. Moore issued a warrant for Phoebe's arrest, binding her under bail of £100 to keep the peace. Phoebe,
sobered but still angry, countered by swearing out a warrant
against Jones and Wayne, alleging that they had assaulted her.
Moore bound Jones under a £50 bond and Wayne under a bond
of half as much, but because he thought Phoebe at fault, he
added an additional £50 bond for her, to assure that she would
prosecute the charges. Evidently the affair was settled amicably,
for exhaustive search of Chester County court records yields no
further mention of the case. Phoebe dropped her charges
against Anthony Wayne and Caleb Jones, but her £50 bond
to prosecute was not collected. Moore's dockets show that he
received 51 shillings in fees for issuing warrants and taking
depositions, but fail to indicate how the matter ended. Perhaps
Phoebe lived thereafter under bond to keep the peace, for her
name appears no more as a disturber. Nor is there the slightest
evidence to show how Polly felt about her husband's innocent
participation in the brawl, though it is significant that after that
her attitude toward Anthony was cooler and more distant.

2

Late May brings pleasant weather to southeastern Pennsylvania. By that time, the reluctant spring which comes half-heartedly to Chester County, alternating balminess with sharp reminders that winter has not vanished, is at last resolved to stay. The countryside glows green with growing grain; the trees, casting away their half-year's gray-brown barrenness, paint the hills in emerald. The air above this profusion of fertility is clear and sweet.

Anthony Wayne in late May, 1774, sensed no beauty in the scene. Sitting on his broad veranda beside the spicy box bush planted by the grandfather for whom he was named, Anthony was reading his copy of the *Pennsylvania Packet*. The news was ominous. After June 1, Parliament had decreed, Boston was to be barred from trade; Lord North had threatened in debate that should the colonists resist, troops would fire upon the citizens. Lieutenant-General Thomas Gage, His Majesty's commander-in-chief, whom Wayne had once helped to welcome at the City Tavern, was ordered to be ruthless in suppression of sedition. Wayne's anger flared. He flung the paper to the floor and overturned his chair as he pushed himself to his feet. His old dog Castle, mouthing toothlessly a heel of bread as he lay helpless in the sun, lifted his head painfully an inch or two, pathetically ready to protect his master against sudden danger. White-haired Darby, Waynesborough's ancient butler, moved as quickly as his age and dignity permitted toward the veranda door. Shannon, in the stable yard, froze in his steps, racking his brain to remember if there were orders he had not obeyed. Old Isaac, feeble now like Castle, querulously complained about his son's noise. "This news, Father! It's war! We must not let those caitiffs treat us so. If Boston is condemned, Philadelphia's turn will come. Lord North is making slaves of us. We must resist."

Old Isaac also was a Whig, but as an old man and a politician he was not impulsive; his Wayne blood had long since cooled to caution. He told his son to pick up the four-page paper and read the fine-print paragraph aloud. Anthony blurted it out and Isaac had to ask him to read it more slowly and distinctly. The impetuous Anthony read the item dutifully, and without a pause, as though his remarks were a portion of the news itself, he added: "You see, sir, I am right. That means war. Now, I think my friend John Cadwalader has a good idea. He suggests recruiting a militia to protect Philadelphia. I think that I should do the same in Chester County."

Isaac closed his eyes and thought a moment. As a soldier and the son of a soldier, he thought of warfare as a normal way to settle difficulties, but he knew that Tory sentiment was strong, and that if Whigs began to arm, loyalists of Judge William Moore's stamp would do the same. Frankly, he did not think that Chester County was as yet ripe for drastic action. He told his son this, and though Anthony was certain that the younger men were strong in opposition to Parliamentary tyranny, his father's advice seemed reasonable. Tony turned, instead, to organizing a Chester County committee of safety to collaborate with similar groups in other sections. He collected also a subscription for food and clothing for the relief of Boston. Canvassing for funds to help the Massachusetts sufferers, his father pointed out, would not only provide useful aid but would give an admirable opportunity for sounding out the sentiment of the neighborhood.

Anthony, it soon developed, was closer to public opinion than his aging father. The community, aroused by Dickinson's *Farmer's Letters,* eagerly united against aggression; even Judge Moore, the Tory, protested against Parliament's action in closing Boston Harbor and against General Gage's high-handed dissolution of the Massachusetts legislature. Chester County freemen chose a thirteen-man delegation to a Provincial Council of Delegates to meet in Philadelphia. Anthony Wayne was the Easttown member. Though the Chester Countians were able men, when Wayne surveyed his colleagues from other counties, he feared that voters did not take sufficient care in choosing representatives. When, therefore, the time grew near for electing men to the Assembly which, since Penn's time, had made laws for the province, Wayne called a caucus of all the voters to meet at the Turk's Head Tavern. His summons indicates that he not only recognized the seriousness of the times but also that he was acquainted, perhaps through his father, with the tricks of politicians.

"It becomes all and every of your Duties to attend as the time is drawing to a Crisis that calls for men of the first abilities both for lerning, prudence and unshaken fortitude in order to withstand and ward off the impending blows big with the fate of British America. . . . The perplexity now and hurry at the Day of Election Renders it a very Inept time for a Deliberate conversation . . . and the Dificulty for each Elector to alter or to procure pen and ink to alter their respective Tickets often is the cause of their turning them in as they come to hand which would not be the case had they time and opertunity to correct names at their leisure which at this previous meeting they may have."

Wayne signed his call simply "A Freeman of Chester County," but the neighbors did not long remain in doubt about its authorship. When the caucus met, Anthony Wayne rose to his feet and made a speech which cut straight to the heart of the situation. Beginning by apologizing, as he did three different times, for his youth and inexperience, he insisted that the main purpose of the British was to assert their right to tax America and to destroy colonial charters.

"England does not dare fall on all America at once," he pointed out, "but on one colony only, hoping that it will not be protected by its sister colonies. 'Divide and conquer' is the sum of politics. One of the chief members of the British Senate has said that this is meant to enslave America.

"Shall we then be deemed the abject slaves he mentions? Shall we remain idle and tame spectators whilst a despotic Parliament are making a footstool of a sister colony to mount and trample on the high reared head of American liberty?

"Forbid it, Virtue, and forbid it, Shame. Let us modestly, yet manfully, show our decent protest, and by every moderate, constitutional means within our reach, let us endeavor to obtain our redress and that equitable independency which as part of the British Empire we are indubitably entitled to." He closed by urging the appointment of a committee of correspondence. "Let all party and personal pique be removed far aside. Appoint men of understanding and integrity, without regard to religion or to occupation."

Evidently his mention of "equitable independency" caused worries among loyalist neighbors, for a few weeks later he and his caucus friends issued a public statement disclaiming any intention of "overthrowing the Constitution." Wayne as chairman of the caucus committee announced: "This Committee have thought proper to declare . . . their abhorrence even of an idea so pernicious in its nature; as they ardently wish for nothing more than a reconciliation, on constitutional principles, with that state from whom they derive their origin." The disclaimer was convincing, for at the election the caucus ticket triumphed overwhelmingly. Anthony Wayne became one of the Chester County delegates to the Pennsylvania Assembly.

As a legislator, Wayne was more valuable at sampling public opinion than he was as an originator of laws; he was more adept at cloakroom conversation than in public oratory. His name is attached to no bills introduced, but that he was much more than a shrinking first-termer and that his special talents were recognized and used is shown by his election to head the all-important committee to "carry into execution the association of the late Continental Congress." He was, in other words, the one man chosen as liaison officer to present Pennsylvania's suggestions to her sister provinces.

More than any other rural representative, moreover, Anthony Wayne moved on terms of absolute equality with the social sets of Philadelphia. He and his neighbor Francis Johnston, Dr. Sharp Delany, and a new acquaintance, Thomas Hartley of York, together with Thomas Penrose, his brother-in-law, circulated among the gay gatherings of the city, endlessly talking the necessity for stubborn opposition to the British despots; with young Dick Peters, nephew of the rector who had married him, Wayne helped promote war spirit in the taverns.

Such service was of great value in a town founded and dominated by pacifistic Quakers.

Wayne's services were not confined to tavern life. His friend Benjamin Rush, the doctor with such remarkable ideas, took him into drawing-rooms where Anthony, poised and graceful now in feminine society, fluttered the dovecotes. Susceptible Hetty Griffits, the "sweet Miss Biddles," one of whom later married James Wilkinson, Sally Robinson, the clever, witty, scintillating sister of Wayne's friend Thomas Robinson, quipped and danced and dined with the handsome young Assemblyman. Wayne, in turn, was deeply smitten with them all and though he did not, being married to Polly, flirt too outrageously, he adopted them one and all as his protégées. Sally Robinson, indeed, was hailed throughout the city as "Wayne's daughter."

Anthony frequently interpreted for his colleagues the importance of minor items in the news. Always a connoisseur of irony, he chuckled heavily when the *Pennsylvania Packet* reprinted Franklin's clever article "Rules by Which a Great Empire May Be Reduced to a Small One"; he saw that every legislator received a copy. The next week, his eye lit upon an obscure paragraph reporting that an Indian chief in Georgia, Emisti-Siguo of the Creeks, was warring on the Choctaws. His agile mind evolved a scheme for enlisting that chief in Whig interests. If the plan succeeded, Wayne suggested, the colonists could find Indian allies against the "British Rebels"; by setting one tribe against another all over America, the Indians might even kill each other off. Nothing came of his scheme; his fellow legislators lacked the vision to put it into practice. Ten years later, Anthony would recall the advice when his troops would be warring against Emisti-Siguo, later to be named Guristersijo, in a campaign to clear the Creeks from Georgia. Anthony would narrowly escape death at that chief's hand; he would himself slay the Indian leader.

He proposed other policies to the Assembly and to civilians in Philadelphia's drawing-rooms. He urged Hetty Griffits and Sally Robinson to follow the example of certain Carolina belles who had resolved not to drink tea until the tax trouble ended. He firmly pressed the nonimportation policy; he asked farmers not to kill their sheep until Pennsylvania was self-sufficient in her wool supply; he warmly advocated that every freeman oil a gun and be prepared for military duty. When in April, 1775, news came of Lexington and Concord, Wayne knew that war must be waged until either the "British Rebels" or the Americans were victorious.

New influences beat in upon his mind. Believing with Thomas Paine that "We live not in a world of angels," he combined his legislative duties with activity in raising regiments. With Francis Johnston's aid, he enlisted his Chester County neighbors; he bought muskets and bayonets; he studied Saxe and brushed up on his once-hated Caesar to improve his knowledge of strategy; he hunted up materials for uniforms. Paine filled his ears with the arguments which later saw the light in *Common Sense;* it was from Paine that Anthony learned to call the King the Royal Brute.

Unhappily, domestic troubles put a temporary halt to Wayne's patriotic service. Old Isaac fell critically ill; the son was obliged to hurry back to Waynesborough. He arrived just in time to promise the dying Isaac that he would take care of his mother. Old Isaac died in December, 1775; he had lived to be seventy-six, three years longer than his father, the dragoon commander. Young Anthony, now head of the clan, stayed in Chester County long enough to see his father buried in the family plot at St. Dayid's, and to transact the necessary legal business. Then, hurrying back to the city, he ended his legislative service. When in that same month Congress authorized a Continental Army, to include four Pennsylvania battalions, Wayne was ready for the call. On January 3, 1776, he was commissioned colonel. The date is important. American officers, taking over the military customs of the British, assumed from the beginning that officers longest in service should have preferment. Men whose commissions bore an early date felt that their honor had been wounded if late-comers attained higher rank. Except in the case of foreign officers, brought into American service from French, Polish, or German armies, neither efficiency nor special claim gave privilege to new arrivals. Even in such cases, American officers complained bitterly; on several occasions, they resigned their commissions rather than serve under "strangers."

Wayne was in the third rank of Pennsylvania officers. Brigadier-General Thomas Mifflin, merchant and Washington's aide-de-camp, who had been so vigorous a partisan of freedom that John Adams called him "the animating soul of the Revolution," stood alone. Next to him came two colonels commissioned before January, 1776; these were William Thompson of Carlisle, veteran of the French and Indian War, and John Bull, a peppery neighbor of Wayne's from close to Valley Forge. By virtue of their longer service, both these colonels held claims superior to those of Wayne. Bull, however, less than three weeks after Wayne's appointment threw up his commission. Four colonels were appointed simultaneously on January 3, 1776. Arthur St. Clair, ensign with Amherst and large landowner in western Pennsylvania, because of his British Army service enjoyed preferred position, though his commission was dated on the same day as that of Anthony. Anthony contested St. Clair's higher status from the start. Seven months before, in June, 1775, the Assembly, in appointing Wayne to a recruiting committee, referred to him in an official document by the honorary title "Colonel." This, Anthony contended, was tantamount to an appointment, and as such gave him precedence over both St. Clair and Bull. Washington, however, would not accept Wayne's interpretation, but recognized only the actual commission. During the remainder of the war a long conflict for precedence continued, Wayne sulking because his claim was disregarded.

Wayne's command, officially named the Fourth Pennsylvania Battalion, met difficulties in its underofficers. Johnston, who worked mightily to raise the regiment, was entitled to be lieutenant-colonel, but both Joseph Penrose, Polly's brother, and Caleb Parry, tavern-owner at the Leopard, applied for the position. Both had strong claims, the former because of his powerful Philadelphia connections and because of his relationship to Wayne, the latter because his wife was sister of the Speaker of the Assembly. Wayne recommended Johnston; the two rival applicants received lieutenant-colonelcies in other regiments.

Wayne desired that Tom Robinson, Sally's brother, should be named a major, but Persifor Frazer, a neighbor from the Brandywine, also applied for the post. Neither was successful, for the Pennsylvania Assembly, in the hope that Pennsylvania Germans might be encouraged to enlist, named Nicholas Hausseger to the position. Both Frazer and Robinson served as captains.

Captaincies offered less tribulation, since any man who raised a group of sixty-eight privates was entitled to command his company if no higher office was available. In addition to Frazer and Robinson, Wayne's captains included John Lacey, a young thin-skinned former Quaker, Caleb North, an ironfounder of northern Chester County, Frederick Vernon, and James Moore, whom rivals regarded as Anthony Wayne's special pet. Just at the last moment, another volunteer appeared with an application that Wayne would have been delighted to grant. His boon companion, Thomas Hartley, hoped for a commission as lieutenant-colonel, but as the post was filled by Francis Johnston, Wayne could not honor the request. Fortunately it was possible, even at that late moment, to add him to Colonel William Irvine's Sixth Battalion, commissioned just a week after Wayne's Fourth was mustered into service.

New regiments were sorely needed. Fired by the desire to add Canada to the list of rebellious colonies, Brigadier-General Richard Montgomery and Colonel Benedict Arnold had led converging expeditions against the chief cities of the North. Montgomery, racing up the Hudson and over Lake Champlain, had unexpectedly fallen upon Montreal in November, 1775, and had taken it, together with great stores of food and munitions; Arnold, after enduring terrible hardships in a march through the wilderness of Maine, had appeared on the same day before Quebec. These initial successes unfortunately were followed by reverses. On New Year's Eve, just four days before Wayne received his commission, the Colonials had launched a desperate midnight attack upon Quebec, and though they had gained the lower town and had fought in hand-to-hand conflict for the remainder of the city, they had been beaten off. Montgomery had been killed; Arnold had been badly wounded; a third of the Continental Army, including Virginia's intrepid

Colonel Daniel Morgan, chief of the frontier riflemen, were prisoners.

Despite the setback, Arnold clung to his position before Quebec. Plodding old Brigadier-General David Wooster still held Montreal, and if fresh troops hurried up from the south, there was bright hope that Canada might yet be captured for the Continentals. Haste was essential, since Britain was preparing an expeditionary force under General John Burgoyne to reinforce Sir Guy Carleton's army, but the British could not reach the St. Lawrence until June. If additional American troops could be hurried to Canada before Burgoyne arrived, Quebec would fall and the Continentals would win control of Canada. More than actual possession of Canada was involved. Military strategists were well aware that Quebec, Montreal, and the St. Lawrence controlled the key to success. If Carleton and Burgoyne held the river, they could send troops south via Lake Champlain and the Hudson, thus cutting off New England from the Southern colonies and so weakening the patriot defenses. But if the Americans controlled the St. Lawrence, no such back-door approach would be feasible; Britain must advance from the seacoast only.

Wayne and his fellow colonels pressed their preparations so as to hurry fresh troops to the North. The Fourth Pennsylvania, camped at Marcus Hook on the west bank of the Delaware, drilled feverishly to put itself in readiness to march.

3

"I without hesitation inroled myself under the banner of my Country, being young and full of fire; Patriotism beat high in my breast . . . My Patriotism was pure and irristable, including all the principles of social and Public virtue, imbracing an Enerjective devotion to support the liberty, the Independence, and political safety of my native Country against the strong arm of British oppression, invasion and Tyroney, offering up on the Altar of Public weal, the sacrifice of my private interest and social Felicity." The words were John Lacey's, but the sentiments could have been those of any of Wayne's officers, those novices in military matters who had everything to learn and no one to instruct them who knew any more than they. All had patriotism and devotion; few had patience, tact, or tolerance; each was thoroughly convinced that anyone who was not one hundred per cent Whig was the blackest of reactionary Tories. Lukewarm civilians were suspect; enlisted men who asked for pay or uniforms or who complained about their rations or their discipline seemed mutinous.

Wayne's men, drilling in the snow at Marcus Hook, were patriotic too, but they grumbled incessantly. Free farmer boys, unused to discipline, did not understand why they must mount guard on winter nights when no enemy was near; they saw no sense in endless drills with broomsticks. They groused about the food, and they raised a mighty roar when Wayne informed them that they must come upon parade shaved and with freshly powdered hair; they hated orders which compelled them to keep silent while on drill. After their long day's work, they certainly had no desire to ramble in the evenings, but they protested vigorously at Wayne's order that they stay indoors after nine o'clock at night. They had, they said, volunteered to free their province from tyranny; this discipline was servitude.

The soldiers ran their leaders ragged. Noncommissioned officers met gales of raucous laughter when they tried to carry out their orders; the captains rushed helplessly to Hausseger, but he shifted his problems to Lieutenant-Colonel Francis Johnston, who as senior officer in camp wrestled with the matter. Pathetically, he passed the difficulty on to Wayne: "In Heaven's sake, give your attendance at this place as soon as possible. The men are almost naked, and have little or nothing to shelter them from cold at night. Their rations are not dealt out to them agreeable to ye resolves of Congress. I am afraid that they will mutiny. The trouble will be too great for me to bear."

Wayne was already doing two men's work in Philadelphia. Busily running from office to office, cadging guns from Dick Peters, now secretary of the Board of War, hurrying tailors into finishing the blue uniforms faced with white which his Fourth

Battalion was to wear, and cajoling authorities into giving him some cash to pay the troops kept him fully occupied, but in addition the Pennsylvania Committee of Safety thought he ought to be their agent. Knowing that he was an engineer and that he had studied fortification, the committee bade him build defenses for the Delaware. Wayne, after reading Saxe, adopted a European device used to halt cavalry charges. He suggested that great wooden beams be chained together at Marcus Hook, and that long iron spikes be driven into the framework so that ships attempting to ascend the river would be impaled and sunk. Upon his recommendation, several rows of the spiked traps were sunk below the surface of the stream. Thus enemy vessels evading the sharp spikes were forced to come within range of shore batteries. The chevaux-de-frise worked admirably. Not until the passageway through the maze was betrayed to British skippers in 1777 were enemy vessels able to ascend the river.

Anthony had less good fortune with other recommendations made to the Committee of Public Safety. Commissioned to find arms for Pennsylvania troops, he discovered a store of muskets suitable for his Fourth Battalion. But when he asked the committee to buy the guns, the statesmen took no action. The postponement was unfortunate, because Washington, then gathering all available men to hold Canada against Carleton and Burgoyne, was asking that troops be rushed at once. Wayne, impatient to get into action, cursed the committee because his men were armed with nothing better than "damned tomahawks."

It was at this juncture that he received the urgent appeal from Johnston. Wayne hurried down to Marcus Hook. The situation was indeed appalling. Neither Congress nor the state had sent money or supplies, and the men were living on food illegally confiscated. In mid-February one company slept tentless in the open air; none had more than one blanket for every three soldiers; no detachment was completely clad. Men huddled about fence-rail fires to keep from freezing. The Colonel knew his men were justified in protesting, but he was a stickler for discipline. No matter how correct the men might be, nor how negligent were Congress and the Pennsylvania authorities, privates must not murmur against their superiors. Wayne did not hesitate. He ordered six men whipped thirty-nine lashes on their naked backs from a cat-o'-nine-tails. The next man who disobeyed, he threatened, would get a hundred strokes and have his torn skin washed with salt. If they deserted and were caught, he would have them shot.

Civilian complaints could not be thus summarily treated. A Chester County delegation came to camp complaining that Captain Vernon had kidnapped their servants. One Sunday morning, they declared, just as church service was beginning, he broke into meeting and carried off half a dozen indentured laborers. When masters protested, Vernon told them to be still and mind their business. He had, they said, "tossed civil people out of doors"; he had even gone so far as to throw one protesting landowner into the fire. Wayne knew that Captain Vernon had been wrong, but, like other Continental officers, he put recruiting above justice. He called Vernon to his quarters, repeated the complaints in the presence of the civilians, and then sent Vernon out to bring back a report. He must have accompanied the order by a wink, for nothing was done to set the bound men free. Some days thereafter, when the matter was still officially under investigation, Vernon's company hurried off to the North, taking the redemptioners along. The matter, Wayne remarked "regretfully," was then entirely out of his control.

Serious complaint came, too, from householders in Marcus Hook and Darby. By congressional resolution, allowances were made to private citizens on whom troops were billeted, but these sums were small and, more serious still, even this money was not paid. Johnston lightheartedly solved the difficulty to his own satisfaction by battering down doors while shouting merrily the Scripture verse "Knock and it shall be opened unto you," but the people were not amused. At Darby, Captain Lacey promised that Colonel Wayne would personally pay a bonus to owners on whom troops were billeted. He told Wayne of the arrangement, and the latter, absorbed with some other problem, absent-mindedly agreed. Both Lacey and his colonel promptly forgot all about the matter.

The house-owners did not forget; they hounded Lacey for their money. He, all innocence, responded blithely by referring them to Wayne and he too, like Vernon, marched away to New York en route for Canada. For a fledgling captain to accuse a colonel of deception, lying, fraud, and negligence, as Lacey confesses that he accused Wayne, would in any professional army subject the rash youth to court-martial, but, in its early days at least, the Continental Army had delightful informality. With Lacey absent, Wayne could do nothing, but when the Colonel arrived later in New York, his first act was to hurry Lacey back to Philadelphia to beg the Pennsylvania Committee of Public Safety for the funds. Meanwhile, Wayne gave Lacey's company to James Moore. The transfer broke John Lacey's heart. He had been boastful that his company was the best clad in the Fourth Battalion, for he had persuaded Darby women to sew uniforms while other captains waited for the Philadelphia tailors to complete their work; he had, moreover, twenty rifles, one for each three men, whereas other companies, if they had any weapons at all, had only muskets. Outside John Lacey's company, there was scarcely another rifle in the battalion.

A restless regiment, doomed to daily routine drills and led by jealous captains, could not possibly be happy. Officers and men alike rejoiced when orders came for them to go to Canada. Reports that came to Wayne indicated that the situation there was far from satisfactory. Bumbling old Wooster, inefficient and incompetent, had hopelessly confused his preparations. Arnold, recognized as the brains of the expedition, had been shelved to the boring duty of guarding Montreal, and although made a brigadier, was sulking in disgust. Major-General Philip John Schuyler, the Albany nabob whom Washington had assigned to the Northern Army "to sweeten and keep up the spirits" of the expeditionary force, had quarreled violently not only with Wooster but with most of the New Englanders in the command. At the moment when Wayne's men were ordered North, Schuyler was stationed at Ticonderoga, at the foot of Lake Champlain, where he was superintending the transport of supplies. But, through no fault of Schuyler, mud, slush, and snow so blocked communications that food, munitions, and troop reinforcements intended for Canada piled up at Ticonderoga in inextricable disorder.

Congress, worried over Canadian affairs, probed deeply into the military and political situation. Deposing Wooster, that body named Major-General John Thomas, a physician, to command the expedition. To find out the truth about what had been happening in the North, it sent Benjamin Franklin, Samuel Chase, "a born leader of insurrection," and Charles Carroll of Carrollton as a commission to investigate Canadian affairs. These men, struggling through the snow, met a retreating army that had already fled a hundred miles from Quebec to Sorel, and which was ravaged by smallpox.

Such was the situation when Wayne and his Fourth Battalion were ordered North. The Pennsylvanians, confident of success, welcomed the assignment, believing that when reinforced by them Thomas would be able to recapture Canadian territory that Wooster had abandoned and, indeed, to take Quebec itself. Wayne in particular was optimistic. Anxious for conference with Washington, he planned to hurry to New York to consult the Commander-in-Chief before the main body of his troops should arrive. Though he was suffering with a cold caught at Marcus Hook, he left for Philadelphia on April 17, 1776. Leaving his troops to follow him, he took a shallop up the Delaware as far as Trenton, and pushed on that same day to Princeton. It was a long, tiring journey, but he forgot his weariness when he found good company at the inn. He laughed heartily and long at a recital of the way a volunteer German, General de Woedtke, had collapsed a few days earlier. The man, he heard, grew saddle-sore at Princeton and called upon his orderly to find a feather and anoint him frequently with goose grease. The soldier almost mutinied at the assignment, yet he did his duty; but goose grease gave the General no relief. Thereafter the General lay in stately dignity upon his rotund stomach. Next day a cart, heavily straw-cushioned, was pressed into service to take the supine General on his way.

At record-breaking speed, Wayne followed the General's trail on horseback to Amboy. There he took a sloop across the bay into New York. He arrived late in the evening of Thursday, April 18, the day after leaving camp. He was supremely happy, believing that he was on the verge of action. Always in times of strong emotion he turned melodramatic. In a letter written to Tom Robinson, he showed his eagerness: "Since the sword must determine whether we shall be freemen or Slaves, I most fervently pray that all intermission may be cut short and that those wretches who brand us with vile epithets, vain boasters and cowards, may meet us front to front, when, if we turn aside, may God shut the door of mercy on us." On the eve of momentous happenings throughout all his campaigns Wayne almost invariably sent letters couched in language such as this. On the same day that he sent his flamboyant hope of battle, he dispatched to Polly an eighteen-line scrawl saying merely that he had arrived and that his cold was much improved.

Anthony was not to enter instantly into a battle. Washington, hearing that the Colonel had been trained in engineering, gave him assignments in that field. Three companies of the Wayne battalion were hurried North, but their commanding officer, with the rest of his men, was held for three weeks on Long Island. Soldiers waited, fingering the "damned tomahawks" that were their only weapons, while Wayne planned forts and laid out trenches. Frequently, in their idleness, they drew down Wayne's amused rebuke for their mischief-making, the least of which was riding Tories out of town on rails. But at least they ceased to grumble. They were at last getting food enough to keep them healthy. A pound of beef or salt fish daily, with a pound of bread, half a pint of beans or peas, a pint of milk, and a quart of spruce beer, and now and then a special issue of half a pint of rice—this is scarcely luxurious, but compared to the scanty fare of Marcus Hook it seemed Lucullan.

Despite his itch for action, Wayne enjoyed himself. Residents gave parties to the officers; regiments vied in entertainments. New York was filled with pretty girls who liked the uniforms that colonels wore, and Anthony was always spick-and-span, his hair perfectly powdered, his boots shining. In the first days of his stay he proudly wrote his Philadelphia "daughters" of the gaiety, but then he reflected that they might think him fickle. Thereafter his letters were confined to tales of how hard he was working and of his hopes of following his advance companies to Canada.

On May 10, he was at last allowed to leave. He made no secret of his happiness; he gloated over Francis Johnston and other officers who were condemned to stay behind until those "damned tomahawks" could be exchanged for first-class guns. Lacey, back from Darby, made an extravagant gesture of good-will to show that he did not hold a grudge against his colonel— he dipped into his scant captain's pay of $20 a month to buy Wayne a ten-gallon keg of cherry wine. He hoped that Wayne would drink it as the sloop *Half-Moon* took him up to Albany.

Wayne could never resist the chance to hold a party. That afternoon, after dinner, as the sloop moved before a brisk south wind past the Palisades, he gathered his brother officers together. They broached the keg of cherry wine. The officers drank heartily, though it puckered their mouths, but Wayne spat his first mouthful out on the deck. He swore roundly that the stuff was poisoned. "I'd rather drink rot-gut," he raged. "Lacey shall pay for this." Other liquor was brought, and toasts continued. Wayne, recovering from his violent anger, had the skipper take the Lacey keg below, under instructions to send it back. It would teach John Lacey, Wayne said, grinning, to be more careful in the future about his choice of wine.

The episode was just another instance of the ill luck that pursued the well-meaning Lacey. No drinking man himself, he had taken a wine merchant's word for quality, and thinking that 9 shillings a gallon was a fair price to pay, he had bought the keg for Anthony Wayne's pleasure. When it came back to him, plus a bill for haulage, Lacey was brokenhearted. He was sure that Wayne was so angry at the Captain's presumption that he had refused even to sample the fine, expensive wine. From that time on, John Lacey was certain that Wayne was plotting to disgrace him.

Wind and tide turned against the *Half-Moon,* so a night was spent at anchor, but in the morning the voyage continued. Wayne sailed past Stony Point, on the post road between New England and the middle colonies; he entered the Highlands, where the current flows swiftly and where the channel winds. His engineer's eye saw that strong fortifications here on each side of the Hudson could command the stream, and when the sloop stopped to take on water and buy fresh meat, he made a quick inspection of the ground. A few years later, he would camp in this vicinity, and he would then study the terrain almost inch by inch.

On the evening of May 13 the sloop arrived at Albany, a mile-long thread of settlement nestled in a hollow. The town itself was disappointing, Wayne declared; in fact, he thought it not much more advanced than Halifax, for its gabled dwellings, opening upon dirty, crooked, unpaved streets, housed only "Hollanders who could speak no English." He found them "shy of strangers, impolite and mulish." He felt happier when he was greeted by Tom Robinson and Jim Moore, his favorite captains. He had a hurried glance at his battalion before darkness closed down, and he was annoyed to find the men dirty and bewhiskered. According to Tom Robinson, the uniforms, though splendid on parade, were difficult to clean; the white facings picked up dirt. Wayne felt the explanation unconvincing, and he ordered all his men to spruce up their appearance.

Philip Schuyler also met Wayne at Albany, and invited him to take up quarters at the Schuyler mansion, the largest in the colony. Wayne was delighted, for Schuyler hospitality was famous; Britishers whom Wayne had met before the war had told how Schuyler and his wife, who was a Van Rensselaer, entertained all military officers and how travelers of note were expected to stop there as a matter of course. He had heard, too, of the pretty Schuyler girls, and though he was true to Polly and to his Philadelphia "daughters," he was no man to run away from beauty. "The General's daughters," he confessed, "are accomplished, fine, sweet girls, and very handsome. Had I been single, perhaps I might have made some impression, but, as that was not the case, it would have been cruel to endeavor to win the affections of an innocent, good girl. I therefore studiously endeavored to keep out of the way of temptation, but was, notwithstanding, necessitated to pass four or five evenings out of six (being the time I was in Albany) in their company." The confession, it should perhaps be noted, was written to one of the Robinson boys, and was no doubt composed with an idea that Sally might see it. Not even Anthony Wayne's ingenious wit explained precisely what compulsion "necessitated" that frequent presence. He neglected to mention that the fine, sweet girls were making him a red cockade for his tricorn hat.

On Sunday, May 19, Wayne held a final review. His men, well shaved and powdered, their uniforms spotless and their newly acquired guns glittering brightly in the sun, made an impressive appearance. Everyone in the city turned out to see the sight; Wayne, standing by the side of General Schuyler, felt that everyone was tremendously impressed. The three Schuyler girls assured him that "it was the finest battalion they had ever seen," a real compliment from girls who had seen crack British Guardsmen drill in their honor.

Next day the Pennsylvanians took up the march from Albany along the Hudson northward to the wilderness that lay between the falls of that stream and the waters of Lake George. They were on the great strategic communication line which they were set to guard, the road down which all successful invasions from Canada must come, the path by which the British must move to cut off New England from the South. It was the road, too, by which the Continentals must advance to capture Canada, the same route which had been followed in the French and Indian War.

North of the Hudson's waterfalls, the troops plunged into the forest. The distance to Lake George was only eight miles, but the pine woods were densely thick. Soldiers who had gone before had suffered miseries when snow still lay upon the ground and when this portion of the way had been a trackless wilderness. But now, in May, ice and snow had melted, and though the ground was soft, marching was not difficult. Once arrived at the lake shore, flat-bottomed bateaux took the troops onward to Ticonderoga. A hundred vessels, with blankets for sails, moved steadily along Lake George, giving to the imaginative John Lacey the appearance of "the Gretian fleet going to the seage of Troy." Even Wayne, never a man to show much enthusiasm over scenery, was deeply impressed by the size of the squadron and by the beauty of the views. "A hundred miles," he wrote, "would be a short ride to see the glorious sight. The prospect far exceeds any idea I had ever formed."

CHAPTER IV

On to Canada

BEFORE a fine, fair wind, the crude single-masted flatboats brought Wayne's Fourth Battalion to Ticonderoga, citadel of Continental defense. At this gateway on "the war-path of the nations," the men debarked to refit themselves for the last stage of their journey to reinforce the Northern expedition. They had been drilled for half a year in intensive discipline.

Under the shadow of high, green-forested Rattlesnake Hill, which Americans called Mt. Defiance, a powerful stronghold had been built. For a musket shot's distance from the broad plateau on the point of the peninsula, a tangled abatis of heavy tree trunks, overlapped and interlacing with sharp points bristling outward, made land approach extremely difficult. So thick was this barricade that soldiers could stand behind it as a breastworks, protected against enemy fire but able to level their guns at an attacking force through notches cut in the upper· tier of logs. From the central portion of the abatis, the ground sloped upward to the fort, thus compelling assailants to scramble uphill through a wilderness of fallen timbers under withering musket fire without being able to draw a bead upon a single defender of the fort.

This was but the approach to the defenses. Half a mile distant from the fort, battery emplacements formed an outer guard, backed by a long redoubt and by a broad, deep moat. When these were passed, the fort itself loomed high, with its wedge-shaped demilunes, stone curtain walls, and a star-shaped trench with counterscarps. Wayne approved the formidable protection of this perfectly designed stronghold. Ticonderoga—which he, like every other soldier, called "Ty"—seemed impregnable against assault, particularly as the Canadian expeditionary force stood between it and the British.

News from the North, moreover, was more cheerful. Burgoyne had not arrived from England, and Carleton's army was in danger of being trapped between Arnold at Montreal and Thomas's men farther down the St. Lawrence. Brave, energetic John Sullivan, a brigadier whose personal characteristics were akin to Wayne's, had just arrived in Canada with reinforcements for the Colonials, and he was pressing insistently for aggressive action against the British.

Wayne hastened forward eagerly. Again embarking his men upon bateaux, he sailed eighty miles northward on Lake Champlain, passing Isle aux Noix, the low, marshy, wooded island which marks the head of the lake, and entering the swift-flowing Sorel River, which empties into the St. Lawrence. Sixteen miles downstream was the little town of St. John's, with its outpost Chambly, only a dozen miles east of Montreal. The Pennsylvanians were well within the frontier of Canada.

Colonel Wayne had not intended to delay, not even to examine the huge French *radeaux*, wooden scows built to float heavy guns across the lake, but rain fell heavily. Rather than drench his troops, the Colonel insisted that his men stay all day in their tents. It proved an unfortunate command, for the ground was low and level, and the rainfall flooded the encampment. The coming of the sun on Sunday morning, June 2, was a welcome sight to soldiers who stood wringing water from their clothes and blankets. Sensitive Captain Lacey suffered further shock at this wet camp. Hoping to recover leadership of his men, he asked the Colonel for reinstatement. Wayne, cursing the wetness, impatiently waiting for his men to dry, refused to listen. He stormed at Lacey, calling him a mutineer. A colonel's orders, Wayne shouted, must not be questioned by a captain. Lacey, mumbling that he had meant no harm—"My motives," he said, "were pure and laudable"—backed out before Wayne's blast.

When the sun returned, Wayne felt happier; he felt sorry for the Captain and sought to redress the hurt that had been inflicted. He invited Lacey to dinner, hoping to restore good

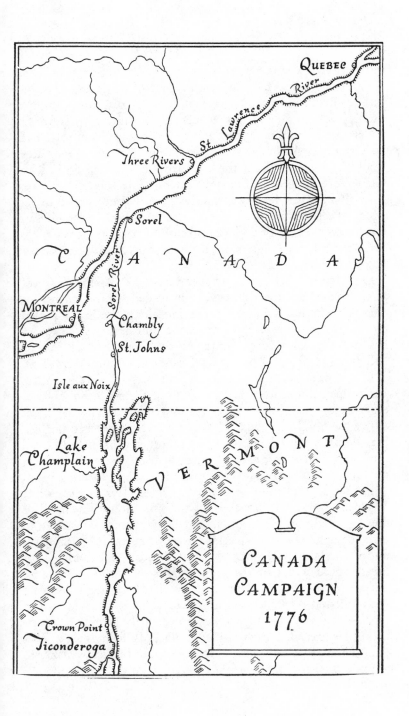

relations. The Captain accepted, out of policy rather than from desire, since, he said, "I felt such a load of degradation, of injured innocence, of the purest motives of patriotism, such a deadly blow to all my future hopes of comfort or preferment under such an absolute tyrant and partial commander that I had no appetite." Anthony Wayne was more tactful than Lacey would have believed. At the pig barbecue to which he had invited the Captain, the Colonel won back the subordinate's regard. Before the feast was finished Lacey had agreed to let Moore keep command of the company, while Lacey himself was to become special courier between Wayne's battalion, Arnold at Montreal, and the main body of the expedition farther down the Sorel.

On Monday, June 3, Wayne resumed his march. The river at this point was too dangerous for loaded bateaux to be entrusted to it, but soldiers floundering along the banks pulled empty flatboats downstream while the remainder of the troops tramped the sandy roads, portaging the supplies which Wayne had brought from Albany. At Chambly, six miles from St. John's, the Sorel calmed again and the bateaux were reloaded. From this point onward to the mouth of the river the way was easy. Before entering the American rendezvous at the point where the Sorel met the St. Lawrence, Wayne beached his flatboat flotilla upon a level sandy shore, ordered his men to clean their guns and uniforms, and gave them a good night's sleep; on June 5 he sailed them triumphantly to their meeting-place.

He found the camp despondent. Three days before, while Wayne's troops lay drenched in the rain, John Thomas had died of smallpox. Sullivan, second in command, was eager to take the aggressive, but his men were starving. The camp required twelve hundred pounds of pork and an equal amount of bread each day, but so low were supplies that the soldiers were on one-sixth rations. Wayne's stores saved the day. Sullivan, with well-fed men and healthy reinforcements, ordered an immediate advance. Burgoyne was momentarily expected; anticipating his arrival, Sullivan sent Wayne, William Irvine, William Thompson, and Arthur St. Clair, all Pennsylvanians, to attack a British outpost on the St. Lawrence.

The enemy held Trois Rivières, forty-five miles below the mouth of the Sorel, about halfway between Quebec and Montreal. The town was ringed by swamp, and Thompson, commanding the party, planned to fall upon it simultaneously from four directions. If the scheme succeeded, the garrison would be forced to surrender. Then, with Trois Rivières safely in American control, shore forts capable of preventing Burgoyne's ships from going up the river might be erected.

At midnight on June 9 Thompson led his troops along the south bank of the St. Lawrence close to Trois Rivières. After dark the men embarked upon bateaux, and at two in the morning they gained the north shore, where Trois Rivières was located. They found themselves amid thick woods and dense swamp undergrowth. Doggedly they stumbled forward, splashing into pools in the pitch-black night. Thompson, St. Clair, and Wayne had each stressed the need for silence, but no column of 1,400 men could move noiselessly under such conditions. Their guns rang loud when they hit against trees; the breaking of tree limbs and the sound of men falling into hidden creeks could be heard for a long way. The British garrison could hear the army coming.

Day breaks early in June in Canada. By four o'clock, while Wayne and his comrades floundered in the swamp, dusk turned into dawn. By this time they had expected to be close to the town, advancing in four converging columns; instead they were some distance from it, and hopelessly confused and out of line. The bogged troops could not even see the river. Each man was sopping wet; those who had slipped carried useless belts of sodden cartridges. Many men had lost their boots, some even their stockings, in the mire; all were bedraggled and in despair. At six o'clock the vanguard, if such a military term can be applied to the disordered mob, came out again upon the riverbank. They saw themselves directly opposite a fleet of British frigates! Burgoyne's ships had come up in the night, unknown to the Americans. The warships fired heavy broadsides on the frightened Continentals. The troops turned and ran, dodging back of trees, turning Indian-fashion to pop away at frigates with their soggy ammunition.

Wayne had not expected to lead the army, for his superior, General Thompson, was in command, but Thompson was missing. He and Irvine were completely lost, floundering somewhere in the swamp. They tried to extricate themselves by following the sounds of gunfire, but were so confused that they could not make their way to safety. In their absence, Anthony Wayne was the commanding officer. It was his first time under fire, but, as usual in an emergency, he kept his head with admirable self-possession. Gathering his men within the woods, he planned a dash against the town. The enemy anticipated him. While he waited, a force of British regulars marched out to meet him. Luckily, he had near by Captain Sam Hay's riflemen, who belonged to Irvine's battalion, and these skilled marksmen, together with Wayne's own infantry, kept up such a steady fire that the regulars retreated.

Wayne's spirited resistance deceived the British leaders. General Simon Fraser, commandant of the outpost, was certain that no small body of Americans could fight so bitterly. He rushed down to the water front, cupped his hands, and shouted to the warships to send reinforcements. "For God's sake, wake up out there!" he yelled. "Send us all the guns you have. The rebels are here, three thousand of them. They're only a mile away." Wayne had, as a matter of fact, less than 800 men to fight Fraser's 2,000 veterans.

With ships bombarding from the river and a powerful garrison entrenched behind high breastworks, Wayne realized that direct assault would not be feasible. Withdrawing to the safety of the woods, he ordered company after company to slip away to the rear, while the constantly diminishing force kept up sufficient fire to cover their retreat. For an hour this withdrawal movement was continued until, when only twenty riflemen and six officers remained "to amuse the British," Wayne ceased his pretense of attack.

Getting back to Sorel was not easy, however. The small guard left at the flatboats had either run away or left the bateaux to join the battle, and now British sailors were in possession, with their squadron ready to blow any bateau out of water if it tried to cross. Wayne and Lieutenant-Colonel Will

Allen, the racing man, of St. Clair's battalion, were reduced to plunging through the marsh again, unfed and without a chance for rest. At dusk on June 11, after sixty hours of constant struggle, they got back safely to a point opposite the Sorel. Bateaux were sent across to ferry them to camp. The Americans had lost 25 killed and 200 prisoners, including Thompson and Irvine; the British loss was 8 dead and 9 wounded. Not until after every survivor was safe did Wayne reveal the fact that during the engagement he had been slightly wounded in the leg.

His report of the event is characteristic. In a long, detailed account to Benjamin Franklin, Wayne told all the happenings at Trois Rivières. "I believe it will be universally allowed that Col. Allen and myself have saved the army in Canada." Writing to Polly, he sent an eight-line message announcing that he had lost a quarter of his men, and that "If I live, you'll hear from me soon. Adieu, my dear Girl, God bless you and my children." The next letter that he wrote to her was exactly two months later.

2

Sand breastworks on a swampy shore were of little value against six of the biggest warships in the world; a shattered, beaten army, sick with smallpox, could not defeat Carleton and Burgoyne's 13,000 stalwart veterans. It is no wonder, then, that John Sullivan, hearing greatly exaggerated reports of overwhelming British strength, looked for safety in the south. His scouts told him that the triumphant Britons had pushed ahead with lightning speed. According to the frightened scouts, Burgoyne had moved upstream almost as fast as they could run away from him. Even now, they said, he was close to the mouth of the Sorel; in a few hours more, he would surround Sullivan's main camp. They advised General Sullivan to push at once for Ticonderoga.

Sullivan felt hopelessly alone. In such circumstances, it was customary for American generals to hold war councils, so that before acting the leaders could weigh a number of proposals and cull the best features from several suggestions. Sullivan had no such opportunity; he was obliged to act largely upon his own initiative, without aid from experienced assistants. Trois Rivières had cost the Americans serious losses in officer personnel. Thompson and Irvine were prisoners; St. Clair, the only colonel with war experience, was hors de combat in his tent with a sharp snag through his foot; Wayne was wounded in the leg. Brigadier-General Benedict Arnold could have given wise advice, but Arnold was at Montreal, vainly battering at that town's defenses. Sullivan ordered immediate retreat to Chambly and St. John's.

Arnold, as it happened, was worrying about Sullivan. Couriers had reported to him that Burgoyne had reached the Sorel and that Sullivan was in danger, but Arnold did not wish to come away from Montreal unless the situation was critical. He sent his teen-age aide-de-camp Captain James Wilkinson to scout the situation. Wilkinson, trotting through the woods, short-cutting to Sullivan's headquarters, suddenly spied Burgoyne's British army. Luckily, the enemy did not see the aide. The young officer pulled his horse about and rode rapidly back to Arnold, to tell that General that the enemy was within fourteen miles of Montreal, and that unless Arnold left at once, he would be captured. Arnold immediately put his army on the march for safety, heading for St. John's; Wilkinson, facing about again, resumed his ride toward Sullivan.

In later years, James Wilkinson was guilty of deceits and treacheries, and there are ugly rumors that he tried to sell his nation to the British and the Spaniards, but on this stormy day in June, 1776, he saved an American army from annihilation. His information enabled Arnold to escape a British trap; his ride to warn John Sullivan prevented that officer from being captured. Wilkinson rode his horse until the animal gave out, then, commandeering another from a parish priest, he rode to Chambly. He found Sullivan's men amazingly remiss. No sentinels were placed; no watch was kept; at nine o'clock, when Wilkinson came into camp, he found the exhausted troops asleep.

"I rode through the encampment, entered the fort by the drawbridge, dismounted and presented myself to General Sullivan without being halted or even hailed. The general and his companions, Colonels St. Clair, Maxwell and Hazen, all appeared astonished at my information." "Scotch Willie" Maxwell, in broad dialect, exclaimed: "Be the Lard, it cannot be possible!" "Be the Lard, sir," Wilkinson impudently answered, "you don't know what you're talking about."

A hurried council agreed that the best thing to do was to call up reserves from farther down the Sorel and to withdraw while escape was possible. Wilkinson, tired as he was, volunteered to go still farther, since Sullivan was underofficered, to find Brigadier-General Baron Frederick de Woedtke, the goose-grease man, who was with the reserves somewhere in the rear. Moses Hazen lived at St. John's, but his directions were misleading; Wilkinson got lost in a torrential midnight rain and fell into the river. He groped about in the inky-black woods, stumbled upon a bridge, crossed it, and burst into a filthy cabin. He was so exhausted that, forgetful of his mission, he threw himself upon the floor and slept till dawn. Then, waking to continue his search for the Prussian general, he met Will Allen, Wayne's companion on the retreat from Trois Rivières. "Where's De Woedtke?" Wilkinson asked. "Drunk, no doubt," said Allen. "We're retreating, so you'll find him in our van."

Wilkinson told Allen that Sullivan and Arnold needed help, lest the whole Canadian expedition be defeated, but Allen was not hopeful. "This army's conquered by its fears," he said. "You'll get no aid. Try Colonel Wayne; if anyone can help, he is your man." Wilkinson looked further, and found Wayne, "as much at his ease as if he was marching to a parade of exercise." Wayne heard the story, and agreed with Allen that De Woedtke was drunk or with a squaw. "His engagements are in the field of Bacchus or Venus," he said. "In the former he's famous, and he often attempts the latter." Taking immediate command himself, Wayne halted at the bridge and posted a guard with instructions to stop every man who tried to pass. Within a few moments he had a detachment of miscellaneous troops, drawn from all the regiments, to lead against the enemy. Wayne, wounded and limping, with characteristic courage set off to challenge the whole British Army. "The very men," said Wilkinson admiringly, "who only yesterday were retreating in confusion, before a portion of the enemy, now marched with alacrity against their main body."

When Wayne and Wilkinson had gone two miles, Lacey came breathlessly from Arnold to announce that the latter had escaped and that he would meet them at St. John's. The need for Wayne's detachment, therefore, faded; the Colonel faced about to rejoin Sullivan. That commander was suffering from a bad case of nerves. Outposts of the camp, seeing an advancing column, raised a shout that British troops were coming. Sullivan, anticipating the worst, prepared for battle. Drums beat the call to arms. "Colonel Wayne halted his column," said Wilkinson, "and pulled out his spyglass. He seemed to enjoy the panic that his appearance caused." Then, telling Wilkinson that the excitement might interrupt the progress of the men in getting out of danger, he bade the aide ride forward with a white flag to reassure the General.

Sullivan, Wayne, and Wilkinson, with some aid from the hobbling St. Clair, now put the army into full retreat. Knowing that Burgoyne was near, and that Arnold had left Montreal, they realized that the Canadian expedition was completely finished and that the only possible maneuver was to lead the army to a place of safety. By withdrawing from untenable positions they could form a junction with Arnold's veterans and so strengthen their defenses. The retreat ranks rightly with the great flights of history; certainly its hardships were severe and its perils dangerous. Sullivan's shattered 3,000, penniless and unsupplied, without food, clothing, or munitions, so ravaged by disease that seven New England regiments contained, all told, only 1,000 men, raced through the wilderness, while a splendidly equipped superior force of Hessians and British regulars, aided by hundreds of Indians, threatened on every side.

Yet the withdrawal was no disordered flight. On the very day when hope was blackest, Wayne's general order warned that any man who should be found "dirty, with a long beard, or his breeches-knees open" must do double duty and receive no rations. "For the colonel lays it down as a position, that every soldier who neglects to appear as decent as the nature of his situation will admit, is unfit for gentlemen's company, and is a coward." Men who had just emerged from sixty hours in a swamp must have thought the order unreasonable, but Wayne made no exceptions. Over and over again during the course of his campaigns he insisted on good grooming; each of his companies had a special barber whose task it was to shave the soldiers and dress their hair, at a cost of fourpence a man each week. In consequence, his men suffered much less from sickness than did soldiers in other commands.

Baggage, heavy guns, and tools were piled upon bateaux, together with scores of smallpox patients, while men fit for duty marched along the marshy shores of the Sorel, keeping sharp watch for the enemy. All went well for a few miles until the wind died down, becalming the flat-bottomed scows. Soldiers waded to the boats and tried to push them up the river, but the mud was deep and poles could get no proper hold. Once more the troops got soggy-wet, walking in the waist-high mud and water pushing the heavily loaded bateaux before them. When they approached rapids, deeper water and more uncertain footing made such methods dangerous. Men on the shore pulled the scows by ropes while others poled the flatboats from the rocks. At one place, which the men called Point Despair, bateaux had to be unloaded and portaged round a rift. Weary, hungry soldiers carried smallpox victims, and then came back to tug heavy guns and water-logged baggage. Two days and nights of constant toil were spent in bringing the army back.

Not knowing where the British were, Sullivan and Wayne worried constantly; time and time again they called their men to arms to guard against attacks that never came; over and over, nervous soldiers fired blindly into the dark woods at some sudden, or imagined, sound. The army had not lost its nerve, but it was jittery.

On Sunday, June 16, while rain fell in torrents, information came that the British were just outside Chambly, and so the Americans, without pausing for more than a hasty bite of cold pork and sodden johnnycake, again took to the march.

Leaving the town ablaze, two sawmills, four small schooners, and a number of flatboats burning, Sullivan and Wayne set out for St. John's, where Arnold waited. They had scarcely cleared Chambly when Burgoyne's advance hurried into the village.

At St. John's also the British were too close. Hurriedly, the Americans carried flaming torches through the town. The work was barely finished before the head of the enemy column came in sight. Arnold stripped saddle and bridle from his horse, shot the animal through the head, and pushed the last boat from shore. Leaving St. John's blazing high with burning barracks and warehouses, he rowed past the burning floating *radeaux;* but the fires were not set soon enough to cause complete destruction. Burgoyne's men quenched the flames, though the *radeaux* sank in midstream, blocking traffic. Fortunately for the safety of the Continentals, Burgoyne halted his pursuit after having cleared Sullivan out of Canada. The Americans continued as far as Isle aux Noix, where, on June 19, they made a temporary halt.

Wayne's fears that the island was unhealthful proved well grounded. The low, clover-covered island, which took its name from dense hazel bushes on its northern point, was marshy and malarious, but the army fell victim to other ailments. New England soldiers, camped on the eastern shore, were hard hit by smallpox and fever. John Lacey, who went to pay a visit to the sufferers, was overwhelmed: "My eyes never before beheld such a seen, nor do I ever desire to see such another—the Lice and Maggots seme to vie with each other, were creeping in Millions over the Victims; the Doctors themselves sick or out of Medicine. . . . I examined the Burying Ground of each Camp, found two large holes dug in the Earth, one for each Camp—while there I saw several Corps brought, carried by four Soldiers in a blanket, one holt of each corner. . . . On their arriving at the pit or Grave, those next to it let go of the blanket, the other two giving a Hoist rolled the dead body into the pit where lay several bodies already deposited in the same way, with no other covering than the Rags in which they dyed, heads and points as they happened to come to the place. In this manner, the burials continued all day, as soon as the breeth had left the unfortunate Victim, the body was thus laid on a dirty Blanket and toted off to the silent Toom, without a sie from a Friend or relative, or a single morner to follow it. In the evening the dirt in front of the General Grave, or deposit of the dead, was thrown over the Dead bodies, leaving a new space open for the next Day. This seene of human retchedness and missery ingrossed my daily visits. The New England and New York Camp was the most infected with the smallpox scarcely a single one of them survived."

Jerseymen and Pennsylvanians, camped on the west side of Isle aux Noix, were victims of an uncomfortable but less dangerous malady. Their constant diet of salt pork, flour, and spruce beer—the drink was warranted to keep off scurvy—kept them running to the improvised latrines. Regiments standing on parade were steadily decimated as the soldiers dropped their guns and ran; from twenty to sixty men out of companies of sixty-eight fell victim to the flux. Even some of the dignified officers could not contain themselves, but raced hurriedly to relief.

Sullivan, who had led his men successfully from military danger, could not cope with smallpox and loose digestive systems. He had his sick carried into open flatboats, unprotected from the hot sun and without soft pallets for the sufferers, to be sent to Crown Point and Ticonderoga for better medical attention. In leaky boats, with water slopping all about the sick, Pennsylvania soldiers rowed the victims down Lake Champlain. The journey required five days, during which oarsmen and patients had nothing to eat but the inevitable rancid salt pork and unbaked flour.

Disease was not their only enemy. Though Burgoyne had given up the chase and was camping peacefully at what was left of St. John's, his Indian allies roamed widely searching for stragglers. On June 24 they found soldiers fishing on the west bank of the lake. Helpless on the island, Wayne watched the massacre that followed. Falling suddenly upon the careless fishermen, the Indians tomahawked four men and took six others prisoner. One captain, Wayne saw, escaped by climbing to safety when the Indians were not looking; another officer, a young ensign, suffering from sudden spasms that had called him into the woods for a moment, had not been noticed by the savages. These alone survived. As soon as the Indians burst into sight, Wayne called for men to man the boats, and a party hurried to rescue the fishermen, but before his men could cross the lake the Indians had vanished, taking their captives with them. Only the four scalped bodies remained; the prisoners were never recovered.

Two days later, after Sullivan had sent a note to Schuyler declaring that the camp at Isle aux Noix was "the most dismal spectacle ever furnished from one army in this quarter of the globe," the unhappy expeditionary force withdrew by slow stages down the lake. When the men arrived at Crown Point on July 2, their condition was pitiable. An army that had originally numbered 5,000 men was now reduced by sickness, death, and desertion to less than half that number. Colonel Jonathan Trumbull, the adjutant-general who inspected them on their arrival, wrote: "I can truly say that I did not look into tent or hut in which I did not find a dead or dying man."

CHAPTER V

Winter at Golgotha

Ticonderoga, which seemed so formidable to Americans en route to Canada, looked less impressive when they hurried back. Nervous because Burgoyne was on their heels, fearful that thousands of British, Indians, and Hessians infested the thick forests of birch and pine, worried lest the enemy somehow slip between Ty and the Hudson and so cut off their retreat, certain of the Continental leaders were unnecessarily alarmed.

Even in this atmosphere of jitters a forceful and determined man like Wayne could have instilled confidence into the troops, but unfortunately the army had no clear-cut leadership. Congress, playing politics, had recalled Sullivan from his command before news of either Trois Rivières or the retreat had been received in Philadelphia; in his stead that body named Major-General Horatio Gates, a retired officer of the Royal Americans and special pet of Massachusetts, to lead the Canada contingent. But in making the appointment Congress also specifically declared that Philip Schuyler should command the Northern Army. The dispute between the two generals, while friendly, was insistent. Each, jealous lest the other gain undue credit, countermanded such orders as his rival issued, thus throwing the army into hopeless uncertainty. Subordinates took sides; the army at Ty pulled wires and played politics at a time when unified leadership was desperately needed.

Luckily, the British did not come, though they were momentarily expected. Again and again sentries, hearing strange sounds in the woods at night, ran to rouse the garrison. Over and over again men grabbed their guns and took their places on Ty's wide stone platforms waiting for the word to fire. The troops lived in a constant state of tension; the fort was constantly on the alert. Carleton and Burgoyne, commanding overwhelming forces of admirably equipped soldiers, could bring down their invaders at will, yet, cautiously, they hesitated. Their ill-timed prudence may have cost their country the war; had they pushed ahead, Ticonderoga would have fallen, the whole Hudson Valley would have been at Britain's mercy, and the rebel colonies would have been split apart.

Wayne was certain that the enemy was frightened. Convinced that Ticonderoga was impregnable, he boasted that the very sight of its gray walls would give the enemy "cannon-fever." The 3,500 men garrisoning the fortress rendered it, he reiterated, proof against attack, especially when so many of those men were well-drilled Pennsylvanians. "I have the finest and best regiment in the Continental service," he asserted. "We are viewed with admiration and pleasure by all the officers in the army."

He was particularly proud of his Fourth Battalion when, on the occasion of one alarm, a hundred men, many of them with bandages about their foreheads or with their arms in slings, poured out from the hospital when they heard the warning gun. Someone asked if any more were on the way. A sergeant snapped reply: "Yes, blast your eyes! Every sick man who can stand!" Wayne, ever a good publicist, turned the incident into excellent copy for the Pennsylvania journals. He wrote out in detail the story of the invalid volunteers and sent it to Dick Peters with instructions to publish the account in all the papers.

Anthony was overjoyed when in November, after it was certain that the British had retired to winter quarters, orders arrived recalling Sullivan, St. Clair, and Gates from Ticonderoga and appointing Anthony Wayne commandant of the fort. Nominally he was to be under Schuyler's control, but since that general was to winter in Albany, Anthony was left largely to his own devices.

Complete control at Ty proved not as sweet as he had anticipated. Ticonderoga was an isolated post, distant from civilization and without the resources of society. As commandant he ranked all other officers; he had no friends of equal rank as intimates. Such officers as remained were largely Yankees from Massachusetts and Connecticut, with strange notions of equality and democracy. Anthony did not like the fellows, and he could not share their interests. Increasingly he was thrown back upon himself for recreation; he was reduced to reading, a pastime which he relished only in small degree, or to drinking with his Pennsylvania subordinates. More often, Anthony Wayne was lonely. No doubt his isolation made him sharp and testy; certainly it led him to find fault more frequently with his subordinates. He lost his merry joviality and ceased to be a good companion; he grew gloomy and despairing. In the winter cold that set in by the middle of November, he began to lose his confidence.

Wayne was particularly aggrieved because his garrison was cut. When he became the commandant, he had 3,500 able-bodied men, but soon Washington, relying upon assurances that Ty was safe, withdrew many of the regulars to reinforce the army of the Middle States. The terms of militiamen expired and no men were sent to take their places. Wayne thus lost 1,000 soldiers, and although he bombarded Schuyler with appeals for reinforcements, no men came. Letters sent to influential friends at Philadelphia, bidding them intercede with Washington for more troops, remained unanswered. Schuyler seemed deaf; Washington, implicitly relying on that general's suave assurance that Ticonderoga was impregnable, thought the stronghold needed no additional defenders.

Wayne had, to be sure, a brief moment of delight when messengers ran in to announce that new men were coming into camp. He buckled on his sword belt and went out to welcome the arrivals; he waited impatiently as they approached in clouds of powdery, hard snow. But when they drew nearer, he was shocked to see that they were round-cheeked children. Angrily, he burst out to his aide: "Why, these are babies! They can't possibly be more than twelve years old! What good are they to us?" To Wayne it seemed as though these Albany Dutch newcomers had come to Ty upon a picnic. Numbering merely 724, the boys had only one month to serve before they must be sent back to their homes; they had no guns; their officers were enemies to discipline. "I would rather," Wayne said bitterly, "risk my life and reputation and the fate of America on two hundred good soldiers than on all these now on this ground."

When he was in good spirits, he could see humor in his situation; he spoke with levity upon his plight in having to hold with youngsters a post that required 5,000 veterans. He liked to go out to the parade grounds to watch his adjutant, Major Michael Ryan, drilling Albany Dutchmen who could speak no English. " 'Tis said there is some consolation in Hell itself," he chuckled. "Even here I meet with something to divert me, when it does not set me raving. When Major Ryan parades the Guards and orders them to be silent, they one and all begin to gabble Dutch; when he orders them to rest their firelocks, they lay them down upon the ground, butts and muzzles intermixed as being the most natural state of rest; when he orders them to march, they make off at full speed to their respective huts. Ryan pursues and flogs them; he gets a Dutch interpreter. In the course of three or four hours, perhaps, he mounts a guard. They answer one good purpose, however. After tattoo, they allow no one to pass or repass; the countersign is of no use to them." It was a tremendous comedown from the time when Wayne assumed command. Now that he was leading raw Dutch boys, many of whom preferred iron-tipped spears to heavy muskets, his pride was chastened.

Materially, the garrison prospered. Wayne, always prompt to protest when his men were not spick-and-span, shouting vigorously that his troops were destitute and naked if they had no spare equipment, registered no protests against lack of proper clothing. He did, in late spring, ask for stockings, shoes, and blankets, a reasonable request after a hard winter in the North, but otherwise he was content.

Food was plentiful at Ticonderoga. Wayne's very first days saw him reveling in good victuals. Dinners of venison, mutton, beef, potatoes, peas and beans, washed down with copious drafts of porter, wine, and punch, put flesh on his bones. He delighted in the red-fleshed lake trout and the sweet white perch with which Champlain abounded; he enjoyed bear meat and other game shot in the woods. Some men protested that at times their flour was so coarsely ground that it was little better than chopped forage, but even this bad meal was edible when it was made into a batter with meat juice, lard, and water and fried. On such occasions, the addition of chocolate or tea sweetened with maple sugar made a filling, if not particularly appetizing, dinner. Once or twice, barrels of salt pork had to be thrown away because they had been so badly pickled that the meat was "rusty," and there was one distressing day when Wayne had to destroy thirty-four quarters of beef, totaling a ton and a half, because it was so tainted as to be unfit for use.

But these unfortunate occasions were rare; for the most part, food was wholesome, sweet and edible. Fresh vegetables, to be sure, were scarce in winter, as in every rural community of the time, but the men were well accustomed to such hardships. An unexpected gift of two hundred bushels of turnips made a pleasing break to men who expected nothing but salt meat and bread, but even in the winter Wayne had milk, molasses, and dried peas, to say nothing of eight gallons of Madeira. Anthony did not, however, try the delicacy recommended by New Englanders. When fresh meat failed, they went out on the rocky hills to hunt for rattlesnakes. Four-foot rattlers, they declared, with bodies thick as a man's calf, might smell like goat, but if boiled long enough, the snakes provided good, rich soup. Yankees cut the meat in slices, boiled it thoroughly, then, throwing the meat away, they drank the soup with relish. It made them strong, they said; it built up their resistance.

Wayne suffered more from cold than from any other hardship. Chester County winters are seldom mild, and the Colonel had not anticipated much discomfort, but when Ty's mountain frosts began to bite, he realized that Northern cold was much more sharp and keen than that of Pennsylvania. He bundled up in heavy clothes, and kept a roaring fire, but the arctic weather chilled him to the bone. Dr. James Thacher, a Massachusetts surgeon, tried in vain to reassure his leader. According to that Yankee, the winter was extremely temperate; little snow fell; though the ground was frosted hard, storms were rare. It was, however, too cold for Wayne; looking out over the ice of Lake Champlain, he was certain that this spot was the most frigid in America. He shivered as he wrote to Sharp Delany: "I was so congealed that after turning before the fire for three hours by *Shrewsbury Clock* I was not half thawed until I had put one bottle of wine under my sword-belt at dinner. I have been toasting you all, but can't *toast myself,* for by the time that one side is warm the other is froze; however, I'll still keep to the internal application." His fire kept high as soldier orderlies piled wood into the open fireplace, and Wayne congratulated himself on his foresight in having huge stocks of logs laid in for just such emergencies. His winter orders included a regular detail of troops to cut wood on the mountains. By storing logs, the garrison would have a big reserve in the event of a British siege.

By Christmas Wayne was heartily sick of the whole place. He saw the fort only as an isolated frontier garrison that might be the most important stronghold in the North but which was nonetheless a lonely backwoods post. He longed to be released from his icebound prison. He poured out his bitterness against Ticonderoga in all his letters home: "It appears to be the last place of the world that God made, and I have some ground to believe it was finished in the dark. That it was never intended that man should live in it is clear. . . . I believe it to be the Ancient Golgotha or place of Skulls—they are so plenty here that our people for want of Other Vessels drink out of them."

That bitter criticism of the place was no mere passing whim on Anthony Wayne's part. He thought the stricture so apt that in letters written months apart he used the same phrases. Wayne did not like Ticonderoga; he did not hesitate to make his distaste clear. There was no reason why he should enjoy his stay. No man who craves brisk action could be satisfied cooped up on an icebound spit of land; no soldier who delighted in campaigns could be happy cutting firewood and setting an abatis. Wayne longed to be with Washington, fighting the British in New Jersey; instead he was assigned to engineering tasks, building blockhouses, and trying to throw up a stone redoubt.

Even in this defensive work he suffered handicaps. Congress commanded that great timber caissons should be sunk across the narrow channel between Fort Ticonderoga and the eastern shore and that when these were chained and riveted together, a floating bridge should be constructed. The barrier would serve a double purpose, giving access to Mt. Defiance, and guarding the channel. With ice a foot deep on the lake, however, no such work could be completed.

2

Wayne was sure that Schuyler stole his mail. Impatiently waiting at Ticonderoga for the ice to melt, he found that time dragged heavily. One great relief would have been a steady rain of correspondence, but few letters trickled into camp. There was, he said, an insurmountable barrier set up at Albany. Some caitiff, whom he suspected but could not prove was Philip Schuyler, either tore the letters up or turned them over to the British. Wayne's friends were certain of Schuyler's guilt. Dr. Samuel Kennedy, senior surgeon at the hospital, which Anthony invariably called the house of carnage, accused that "infamous villain, G. S—r" of not only stopping the mail but also of disrupting military service. Disdaining both Wayne's indirection and Kennedy's cautious elisions, Colonel Hartley categorically charged that Schuyler personally robbed a courier of all letters intended for the North.

Probably Wayne was not averse to using the "envious devil of Albany" as a scapegoat for personal deficiencies. There is no doubt that postal service was faulty, but Anthony was far from perfect as a correspondent. Always quick to chide a friend who might be negligent in writing, he himself was thoughtless. Dr. Sharp Delany, his best friend in Philadelphia, wrote four newsy letters which somehow slipped past the "insurmountable barrier," but Anthony replied with only one; Abraham Robinson, Sally's brother, sent eight or nine notes during Wayne's Ticonderoga stay, but received only two letters in reply.

Philadelphians, to be sure, had much to say. Living closer to the scene of military operations, they told Wayne about the progress of the war, how the British, surprised at Trenton and beaten at Princeton, had been pushed back into northern Jersey, and how Pennsylvanians who had fled panic-stricken into the interior of the state at the approach of Howe's army had returned shamefaced to the capital. They told of Congress and of its futile debates, of intrigues among politicians, and of the tribulations of Pennsylvania. That state, unlike its neighbors, was torn by violent internal dissension, not only between patriots who wanted freedom and Tories who stood by the King, but between radicals who sought social as well as political revolution and cautious liberals who merely wished a change of sovereignty.

Anthony, on his part, had little to reply. Nothing happened at Ticonderoga outside the narrow routine of camp life. When he sat down to write about such matters, he wrote interestingly and well, but though he talked freely and with originality and vibrance, he could not master the art of gossiping on paper. His pen was not a facile instrument; never was he known to set down casual occurrences. After he had damned Golgotha and the house of carnage, he had nothing more to say.

His friends, immersed in exciting happenings, could not properly interpret Anthony's long silences. Some thought him selfish and secretive; others, particularly young ladies, assumed that he had ceased to care for them. They wrote appealing little letters, begging him to think of them more often; they chided him for his neglect. Then, when he failed to send immediate replies, they dropped him from their lists of correspondents. Sometimes the favored few who received his letters were annoyed at Anthony's carefulness when writing about controversial affairs. In private conversation, he was outspoken—no one ever doubted where he stood—but on paper he was cautious. His conservative friends at Philadelphia, pleading with him to help them overthrow the Pennsylvania constitution, "this damnatic conventie," resented his wariness; they felt that he was too discreet.

Publicly, he conducted himself with equal wariness when Schuyler was abused. Wayne did not trust the Albany nabob, although he did not go so far as to assert, as so many of his friends asserted, that Schuyler was a traitor. Eagerly Anthony listened to reports that fashionables were criticizing Schuyler, especially at that Albany tavern which was called Liberty Hall, and that they were reporting Schuyler as being sick of the war. Gossip declared that Schuyler had remarked that political control had "devolved to the lowest and most desperate of the people" and that he "considered American liberty and American slavery as synonymous terms." Wayne heard the charges, but did not spread them further. It is significant also that he did not write or say a word in defense of his superior officer.

Thoroughly convinced that Philip Schuyler did not understand the art of war and that he was incompetent, Wayne acted as an independent leader, going through the motions of obedience by inquiring Schuyler's wishes, but exploding with indignation when the General sent orders to be carried out. One order, in particular, made Wayne lose his temper. Schuyler approved a rule whereby recruiting officers from any state could sign up for the duration of the war any man in any regiment who had enlisted for a shorter term. If this permission should stand, recruiting parties from New England states which offered small cash bounties to volunteers could raid the Pennsylvania ranks to steal away Wayne's admirably trained soldiers. The Fourth Battalion, few members of which were enlisted for the duration, might become a Massachusetts regiment.

Bad blood broke out between the Pennsylvania officers and the Yankee leaders. In their anxiety to enroll every man, Massachusetts agents drenched the troops with rum so that the men would sign up when too drunk to know what they were doing. They went so far as to visit hospitals to enlist the sick. Pennsylvania regiments were left with few save "scourings and sweepings, food for worms, sharp-looking caitiffs, hungry, lean faced villains" whom no one else desired. Pennsylvania officers resented Massachusetts' raiding. Had the Yankees been men of honor and of gentlemanly breeding, they insisted loudly, such practices could never have occurred. Openly they insulted Easterners, calling them caitiffs without honor. New England troops, they said, except for the Pennsylvanians bought into service, were trashy mixtures of Negroes, boys, and Indians.

When the Yankees persisted, the gentlemanly Pennsylvania officers lost their self-control. On Christmas night, after a particularly long session with the bottle, Lieutenant Colonel Thomas Craig and Captain Thomas Moore broke open Colonel Asa Whitcomb's door. Whitcomb, with true Massachusetts thrift, was making shoes. His son, a private in the regiment, sat peacefully at a bench, sewing leather; another son, the Colonel's orderly, was cleaning up the room. To Craig's delicate sensibilities, the idea of a colonel's using his quarters for manufacture and demeaning his high rank by letting his sons do common labor was disgraceful. Craig upset the shoemaker's bench, kicked tools and leather about the room, and when Whitcomb protested, Moore punched him in the eye. The Whitcombs yelled for help, and the Massachusetts men rushed to their arms, but before the Yankees could be organized, Moore brought up his battalion. Several shots were fired in the excitement, miraculously without killing anyone, although several Massachusetts men were wounded.

Wayne protected his Pennsylvanians. As commandant, he went through the motions of arrest, but he had no notion of punishing them. He knew that Whitcomb's regiment had but a week to stay in camp and that they had declared that nothing on earth could induce them to stay a moment longer. If, he reasoned, court-martial proceedings should be delayed, no witnesses would remain to testify against Craig and Moore. He "forgot" to call the court-martial.

Craig played upon Colonel Whitcomb's good nature. He called to his soldiers from his hut, where he was placed in theoretical imprisonment, to go out and shoot a big fat bear and to bring it into camp. Then, when the bear was shot, Craig invited Whitcomb and the Massachusetts officers—but not the private or the orderly—to dine with him at a reconciliation feast. Whitcomb accepted, whereupon Wayne temporarily released his friends from their detention so that they might entertain the man whose eye they had blacked. After much bear and rum, Whitcomb, in mellow mood, signed a paper releasing Craig and Moore from liability. His signature was shaky, and Whitcomb later had no memory of having signed the document, but Wayne, convinced that Whitcomb had relented, released both Craig and Moore.

Schuyler learned of the affair when Major Daniel Whiting, also a victim of Craig's fists, complained directly to the general commanding the Northern Army. Schuyler demanded that Wayne explain. Wayne grew angry. Whiting, he thundered, should have protested at Ticonderoga, not to Albany. He complained to Schuyler that Whiting had overstepped military procedure. Moreover, Wayne pointed out to his superior, the action was useless, because no witnesses remained at Ticonderoga. They had all, he said, "run away in the clouds of the night, some before and all as soon as their times expired." Easterners, Wayne remarked, were always running off for home. "I hope," he added naïvely, "that my conduct on this occasion will meet your approbation."

Of course it did not. Schuyler became apoplectic. Since he could not bring Massachusetts men back to camp to testify, Schuyler had the accused officer on his hands, with no means for escaping gracefully from the situation. Wayne, chuckling at the hole into which the General had been plunged, made life as pleasant as he could for Craig by sending one of that officer's best friends, Sally Amos, a camp laundress, to keep him company. Craig and Sally enjoyed themselves for sixty days until, in blank despair, Schuyler released the man for lack of evidence. In Craig's triumphant phrase, he was "acquitted with honor."

Nothing that Wayne did after that pleased the General. Almost immediately after Wayne issued pointed orders forbidding inoculation against smallpox, Schuyler required Dr. Jonathan Potts to perform that operation on the whole Ticonderoga garrison. Then, when Wayne called for Potts to come to camp, Schuyler flatly refused to let him go. Wayne commanded Potts to report at once, "notwithstanding the orders of General Schuyler." Poor Potts was worried, but Gates, a better friend to Wayne than Schuyler had ever been, sent five surgeons up to Fort Ticonderoga. They arrived "with sleeves rooled up."

3

Wayne craved a brigadier's commission, but the hurdles were numerous and high. Before he could obtain a higher post, he must win endorsement from his immediate superior, that caitiff Schuyler, and from Washington, the Commander-in-Chief; he must also be approved by a state Assembly that was packed with hostile politicians. The endorsement was a matter that, by military custom, depended almost solely upon length of service; now that Wayne was senior colonel of the Pennsylvania Line neither Schuyler nor Washington could recommend another candidate without disrupting army tradition. The approval of the Assembly was, however, almost unobtainable.

Wayne's friends, unhappily for Anthony, were members of the wrong faction. Though Rush, Franklin, and Peters, his chief supporters in the national administration, swung much weight in Congress and the Board of War, they had slight influence with the state Assembly. Congress, swaying to the winds of politics, frankly turned over to the states the right to name their army officers. Pennsylvania's quota of generals in Continental service was therefore picked by state officials, those radical Whigs who disliked Wayne's conservative ideas; Congress would ratify only those names which came with state endorsement. Rush, who for all his unusual notions possessed sound political sagacity, suggested that Wayne come down to Philadelphia to lobby; he warned that he must butter the Assembly with flattery and attention.

Wayne refused to lobby, holding that the action would be undignified. He threatened to resign, hoping that when Pennsylvania realized the danger of losing her only dynamic and aggressive military leader, the commonwealth would give him his reward. In his note to Rush he coined another of that long list of pet phrases which was to stud his correspondence. There were many of these standardized expressions, such as that which he had used in his caucus speech to Chester County voters—

"Forbid it, Virtue, and forbid it, Shame"—or like that which, on an unfortunate occasion, he used the same day both to Polly and to his "daughter" Sally Robinson—"Fortune is a fickle goddess and like some other females, changed for the first new face she saw." In later years he would add other clichés; it would be possible to compose an entire letter out of Wayne's repetitive expressions. A new one came to be a favorite; within a month he sent it to Rush, Gates, and Francis Johnston:

"I cannot submit to be commanded by an officer whom yesterday I commanded. This, Sir, is a pride common to Gentlemen and Soldiers. . . . Whenever the Honorable Congress thinks they can be better served by a Gentleman *younger in Rank* than myself, I shall with the utmost chearfulness Return to my *Sabine field*."

Evidently, Anthony had added Horace to his list of favored authors, though how, with his small knowledge of Latin, he could read the poet is food for wonderment. Perhaps it was a mere allusion, for certainly Wayne's taste could never run parallel to the peaceful slothfulness that Horace enjoyed among the Sabine hills. Wayne was much more akin to the colorful, dramatic swashbucklers of his beloved *Henry IV*, whose passages he was continually quoting.

He had fewer compunctions against lobbying in the interests of his subordinates. When Will Allen, the racing man, resigned his lieutenant-colonelcy rather than subscribe to the Declaration of Independence, Wayne pushed the claims of his good friend and neighbor Persifor Frazer, though he was not in the least unhappy when the more convivial Joseph Wood won the promotion; when there were vacancies among the majors, Wayne pressed Peters to consider personal friends for the positions.

The sad example of John Shee probably restrained Anthony from giving up his commission. Shee, colonel of the Third Battalion, resigned when he was next in line for promotion to a brigadiership. No one seemed to know why he left, the common explanation being that his wife was unhappy at his being in the service, but Philadelphia boiled with rumors. Dick Peters, receiving one of Wayne's threats to quit, dashed off a hurried and rather hysterical appeal to Wayne to reconsider: "For God's sake, don't think of resigning. We want good officers. Shee has resigned and thereby rendered himself despised by the best friends he ever had. I have not seen him and I wish I never may. He keeps out of town and has fallen, never to rise again." Peters was not gifted as a prophet; Shee became a prominent merchant and was for twelve years treasurer of Philadelphia. Neither Peters nor Wayne could foretell that Shee would thus come back to public favor; all that they could see was that no officer dared resign, "notwithstanding he should receive fifty publick affronts," without suffering obloquy.

Wayne ceased now to mention resignation, though he would recur to it at a later time; he turned his attention to drill and discipline. A circular letter, sent to his captains, expresses his philosophy of leadership in more detailed fashion than he would ever again declare it:

"I wish for nothing more than to see discipline introduced . . . it lays much in your power to establish it without the appearance of the least Hate or Resentment to Individuals by enforcing your Authority with Judgment and Setting a proper example by obedience to all orders of your Superiors.

"Necessary severity must be accompanied with great tenderness and moderation and so displayed on every occasion as to appear void of all Manner of Design and totally the Effect of a Natural Disposition—by this means you will Render yourselves at once beloved and feared.

"I must, therefore, not only for the Good of the Service in General, but for your own Sakes, Request that you'd pay more attention to your duty—make a point of Reading Military Authors and be particularly Attentive to the manoeuvring of the men. . . . For my own part, I would much rather lead Gentlemen to their duty by a silken thread than be necessitated to make use of coercive rules."

Perhaps Anthony's off-the-record advice on methods of recruiting was even more shrewd than his analyses of what makes a warrior: "The best and surest way to get men is to win the Effections of all the handsome Country girls." Undoubtedly, more pretty country girls would have enlivened lonely Ticonderoga; certainly Wayne's men missed the joys of feminine

companionship. Hard labor, grim discipline, and wintry blasts
disheartened the warriors; they wished for gaiety. The few
laundresses in camp were not enough to go around.

Three months of isolation proved enough for one company
of riflemen. In February, when the ice was thick and snow was
deep, they packed up their belongings and announced that they
were going home. When Wayne refused to let them off, they
told him that their terms of service had expired a month before, and that no power under Heaven could restrain them
from departing. Wayne looked about him, but saw no trustworthy troops who might stand by him in a battle with the re-
calcitrants; he feared that other troops would follow their example. He could not hold them back by law, so he tried force.
Shrugging his shoulders, throwing out his arms as if the whole
affair were quite beyond control, he asked if they would name
one of their number as their spokesman.

A sergeant stepped out from the company, saluted smartly,
and told Wayne that he would represent the men. Wayne then
whipped out a pistol, pointed it directly at the sergeant, and
forced that soldier to his knees. Standing over the cowering
fellow, with pistol aimed at the sergeant's head, Wayne snapped
out to the riflemen to get back to their tents. "You'll stay," said
he, "ten days longer. If, by that time, we have reinforcements,
I will let you go; if no one comes to take your place you will
stay here until the war is over." Their spirits broke at once;
unanimously, they agreed to stay with Wayne; the cowering
sergeant was almost abject in his thanks that Wayne had not
been more severe. Wayne did not forget the incident; a few
months later, he was instrumental in having their leader cashiered from the army for another, and much milder, derelic-
tion.

New York's militiamen, those Albany boys who could not
understand the English language, had more pride. They were
building abatis; at least, such were their orders, but they rebelled. Those doughty lads had volunteered to rid their state of
redcoats; this logging enterprise was bringing them no glory. On
a freezing February morning, therefore, they went on strike;
Major Henry Hay found them sitting snugly by a roaring

campfire, gabbling Dutch stories with their idle Captain Fitch. Hay shouted angrily, but the Dutch boys did not move. Fitch, condescending to turn from the blaze a moment, languidly inquired if Hay had something on his mind. The Major spluttered, and the Dutch troops smiled. When Fitch translated to them Hay's orders that they get to work, they burst out laughing. Captain Fitch patiently explained to Hay that the militiamen had not the faintest notion of doing more of such degrading work.

"We did not come here to cut abatis," he told his astonished Major. "We came to keep guard and to defend the garrison. We do not think an abatis is needed."

"You do what you're told to do," snapped Hay. "Who the hell are you to think what's needed? You've got your orders; go to work."

Fitch, newly appointed to his office, was amazed. Sincere in his belief that he was fighting for freedom against tyranny, he could not understand why Hay turned purple and choleric. "Why," said he, "I never thought that I would be in an army where I had no right to think for myself. We work when we get ready." Nor did Hay's apopleptic threats to throw him in the guardhouse have the least effect. He and his Albany friends lounged comfortably while Hay raged. Hay's report to Wayne indicates that poor Henry Hay had not made the least impression on the strikers, "After a great deal of argument," he told Wayne, "I left him."

Anthony was no man to accept defeat. Angrily, he roared to Hay that he would settle this himself. He threw open his door, and rushed bareheaded to the militia camp. Coming to the first man that he met, he demanded to know what caused the mutiny. The private, Josiah Holliday, was not one of the strikers, but as a fellow Yorker he told Wayne that the men believed they had a right to refuse improper duty. Wayne listened to part of his sentence, then, jumping to the conclusion that Holliday was justifying mutiny and probably inciting others to it, he laid the fellow cold with a smashing blow of his fist. When Holliday staggered to his feet again, saluting in a dazed fashion, Wayne sharply ordered him to the guardhouse. Onlookers

were horrified at the injustice; Captain Aaron Coe protested
that Holliday was guiltless, and that Wayne's attack was unprovoked. Wayne wheeled upon him and demanded if that
meant that Coe too was a mutineer. "No, sir," replied Coe,
"but you asked Holliday for his opinion. Every soldier has a
right to give his views on any occasion without being punished
for it."

Wayne answered by throwing Coe also into the guardhouse,
whereupon thirty-five majors, captains, and lieutenants of the
New York militia signed a formal protest. They demanded,
as their right, that when Coe and Holliday were tried the
proceedings should be before a court-martial of New York
officers. There was no doubt, either in their minds or in
Wayne's, that the result of such a trial would be triumphant
acquittal. Anthony refused to grant that demand, and in writing a report to Schuyler on the matter, he urged Philip Schuyler also to refuse. That general, despite his animosity toward
Wayne, stood by the Colonel and ordered Wayne to name a
court of his own choosing, which would have doomed the prisoners to death. Before the trial could be held, Schuyler took
another look at the Articles of War and found therein a flat
command that militia court-martials must be made up of officers from the same provincial corps as the accused. Wayne, realizing that he would be beaten, turned on all his charm and
made peace with Coe and Holliday without a trial. He closed
the case by telling Schuyler: "Captain Coe and his coadjutor
Holliday have been brought to proper sense of their error and
they are much humbled. All officers now do duty with alacrity,
and, like a child when in need of correction, promise never to
err again."

His troubles, however, were not over. On the very day that
he wrote finis to the Coe-Holliday case, another militia regiment, impatient at its long stay, "began to grow impertinent."
Wayne did not hesitate to take strong measures of persuasion.
"I have been necessitated," he reported, "to put some of the
officers in irons, kick and pull the noses of others, by which
means I have brought them to a sense of their duty. To say
anything severe to them has just as much effect as if you were

to cut up a Butcher's Choping block with a razor. By G—d, they feel nothing but the down Right blows which, with the dread of being whipt thro' the Small Guts keeps them in some awe."

4

Ticonderoga had become Golgotha to Wayne. Lacey swore that the man's true nature cropped out under stress. "The Colonel is a Tyrant," Lacey raved, "of an implacable temper, once offended always cruel and unforgiveing, waiting only like a Beast of Prey to make a sure and safe stroke on his prey. He sacrifices largely on the Alter of self pride and Ambitious Tyranny."

John Lacey was a prejudiced observer; a warm, sensitive youngster who craved friendship, he was hurt because Wayne did not admit him to his inner circle of bosom friends. His jealousy showed itself in catty comment. Captain Robinson, he said, invariably shirked duty and "never fails to faint at the sight of human blood." Moore was a bully with profligate and debauched morals, "mean, cringing and servile, a flatterer crouching at the Colonel's feet." These were Wayne's favorites. "None of the other Officers were suffered to approach them or invited to eat or drink a drop at the Colonel's festive board. The Colonel's partiality to them was such as to disgust all the other officers."

Unquestionably Lacey's strictures were exaggerated, but there was sufficient truth in them to make the camp a whirlpool of jealousy. The friends clung close together; the absence of one of them for even a brief time was enough to make them feel the separation keenly. When Colonel Joseph Wood was called away to Pennsylvania, only to be unlucky enough to break his ankle stepping from his carriage, Wayne wrote him that he was lonely: "By my soul, I did not know the value of your friendship until you left me—the benefit and pleasure of your Company until I lost it. I conceit I am talking to you—I often order my boy to call Colonel Wood to breakfast, dine or Sup, and frequently get to your House before I recollect that you are in a Christian Country." Wood's temporary escape from that damned Golgotha plunged Wayne into a fit of morbid despair; he thought that he would never again see civilization.

Polly wrote him pretty letters, whose sentiments were better than their spelling, and in them she overflowed with love, but they were infrequent and devoid of news. Had they been sent by post, they never could have come to him, for Polly thought that he was stationed at a place named "Tycontarogae," but since she entrusted them to military couriers for delivery, they could not go astray.

"O my Dear if a hundred miles jarney would find me but one day with you with what pleasant would I set out this moment to meat one that is forever dear to me," she wrote. But, then, abandoning that vein, she showed herself the motherly spouse. "It gives me a great deal of trouble to hear that you have bean so long with the tuth ack. Mr. Robinson told me just now that Tommy rote word that they cold not prevale on you to have it out let me beg on you my Dear to try to get rid of that most horid pane and try to take great care and not get cold in your jaw if you should get it out." The only other personal note in that letter was the brief remark that "Your Daughter has been purely but is now very harty and goes to school."

As guides to late eighteenth-century spelling and pronunciation, the messages of Polly Wayne, "your Loveing Wiffe," are of more interest to orthographers than they were to her husband. She seems to have been devoted, but careless; she was more wrapped up in her children than in Anthony, who was a glutton for attention. In one letter, telling of her son Isaac's solicitude, she gave more insight into what was happening to Waynesborough people than all her other letters put together:

"I returned last Friday from Philadelphia with a havey hart I may wenter to say as Ever any Boddy traveled twenty miles. My company was small only a sarvent and my dear little son, my comfort and a gayn to my Greaf for when i wold tolk to him he would seme to be quite delited and have many a deverting saying. And when he wold se me cry he would look at me and say don't cry wot dus Mammy cry for i ancer him becays your Daddy is gown to the wars then he wold ancer my Daddy com a gayn when he has run all the Sholders in and made them blead." But that was all the news she sent, except that she had been obliged to fire John Cassel for drinking too much, and that she was happy that Anthony had not died in Canada.

"I heard the Shocking a Count of your being in a Battle before i larnt wether you was a mong the liveing Or the Dead which made me so very unhappy that i culd nither Rest Day nor Night. Very Desires as i was to se the papers yet i dreded the Site for fear i Shold Discover the mans Death or imprisment who is as Dear to me as my one life. Sure my fear was removed when i heard my Col° was a live and harty and behaved like a hero o the joy i felt at that time would not a low me to think of the Poor men that is killed and takeing. But now my hart acks for them and thar near Coneckshon they have left to greave for them."

There was another letter saying that she had the colic, but after that the silences closed in; she did not write for almost a year thereafter. The neglect could not have been wholly Anthony's fault; he wrote several times to a wife who would not answer. Tony thought of her, and he dreamed of getting home to Waynesborough, though that return was constantly postponed. She may have been miffed because his notes were short, impersonal, and at times peremptory, or she may have been disturbed by gossip that her husband was more interested in Sally than in his wife.

If Polly stood aloof, Sally Robinson, his "daughter," remained a source of joy. He looked back on the pleasant rural dances he had enjoyed with her; he assured her that no vicissitude of fortune "can ever eradicate a fix't and tender friendship"; he warmed her heart by telling her, "If I could only be favored once a Month with a Single line from you—I should be more than Reconciled to remain in this more than bad country." Sally, however, was soon to be lost to him; having given up all hope of ever marrying him, she had been captured by the whirlwind courtship of Dick Peters. Wayne's plea for monthly letters was not granted, but Sally, with that de-

light which all brides take in matchmaking, even in this case
with a married man, flirted mildly with her absent Colonel.
"I can love my Husband and esteem my friend," she answered
him, but she continued by seeking to transfer his allegiance.
"Hetty Griffits was my Bride Maide. She thanks you for remembering her, says a thousand fine things of you, among the
rest that she feels a violent freindship for you, wishes to see
you."

Anthony rose promptly to his opportunities. Lest either of
them be made jealous by a note sent to the other, he wrote a
joint letter, addressed to "My Dear Girls"—incidentally, he misspelled Hetty's name by calling her "Miss Griffith"—in which
he expressed his solicitude for their worries while "The British
Rebels and their savage auxiliaries were ravaging the Jersies"
just before the American successes at Trenton and Princeton.
"How did you feel—did your fortitude fail you—or were you
so much the Heroines and Americans as to determine to foregoe
ease and affluence—and seek for Liberty in a little Country
Cottage far distant from the din of War—the pomp of State—
the Luxury of a Town?" He himself, he assured them, had
been torn by anguish at their danger. "I was racked with Different and Contending passions—pity—duty—Revenge—and one
of a more tender Nature took their turns to Reign." His soldiers burned with ambition to take vengeance on the British.
In a glowing, and imaginary, account of their interview with
him, he assured his girls of the army's devotion:

"Hearing of the Horrid crimes Committed by our Savage
Enemy—shocking to humanity and which Modesty forbids to
mention—my worthy soldiers stung to the Souls at the Recital—
grasping more fast their arms—cried with one Voice lead us—
instantly lead us to Death or Vengeance.—Indeed, sir, we will
sell our lives or Liberties at as high a price as you yourself will
Estimate and at too dear a rate for Britons to make many purchases.

"Could I have followed the dictates of my Heart, I certainly
should have taken them at their Word but duty held me fast—
it was my business to prevent a Junction of the Enemies Armies

and with a handful to keep at bay their whole Canadian force—
this task I have hitherto performed—"

He closed his letter by assuring them both that they would
"always retain a warm and tender seat in the Memory of yours,
most Sincerely" and reminded them that he had not been
favored by a single line from any friend on earth for many
tedious months. Hetty responded with a sweet, gushing, most
maidenly letter, skillfully composed so as to recall to Anthony
the pleasant times they had enjoyed talking of books and plays
and parties. Though she evidently hoped to draw replies from
Wayne, and though she succeeded in that design, she was a
shade too gentle, too ladylike, too coy, for Anthony's taste. Her
poetic touch in tracing the soft tear that stole down Sally's cheek
when that married lady thought of Wayne defeated its purpose; it made him think of Sally when, Hetty thought, he might
better have been thinking of his correspondent.

He grew so homesick that he turned toward poetry. In the
Ticonderoga fortress, surrounded by hard-boiled soldiers who
would have scoffed at verse, Anthony Wayne composed the only
stanzas that he ever wrote. His first writing was an ambitious
piece addressed "To a Young Lady on Her Expressing Some
Doubt of the Sincerity of a Lasting Fidelity in Her Admirer":

> Had I a Heart to falsehood fram'd
> I ne'er could Injure you;
> For tho' your tongue no promise claim'd
> Your Charms would make me true.
> To you no Soul shall bear Deceit,
> No Stranger offer wrong;
> But friends in all the aged you'll meet,
> And lovers in the Young.
> But when they find that you have blest
> Another with your Heart,
> They'd bid aspiring passion rest
> And act a Brother's part.
> Then, Lady, dread not here Deceit,
> Nor fear to Suffer wrong,
> For friends in all the ag'd you'll meet
> And Brothers in the Young.

As poetry the ode lacks that ineffable something that made Keats and Shelley great, but Wayne was no professional. He was a soldier, not a literary giant, but he knew how he felt toward Sally. He knew also how he felt toward Richard Peters, who must have had a twinge of worry over Anthony's continued correspondence with his charming bride. A second poem, the last the warrior ever wrote, is inscribed "To a Friend When Accused of Endeavoring to Supplant Him in the Affections of a Lady and Deemed by Him a Breach of Faith and Friendship."

> Friendship is the bond of Reason
> But if Beauty disapprove,
> Heaven absolves all other treason
> In the heart that's true to love.
> The faith which to my friend I swore,
> As a civil oath I view;
> But to the charms which I adore,
> 'Tis Religion to be true,
> Then if to one I false must be,
> Can I doubt which to prefer?
> A breach of Social faith with thee,
> Or Sacrilege to love and her?

Some jealous husbands might construe the verses as an open declaration of war, or of piracy, but Richard Peters did not seem to mind. Perhaps, with Wayne far off in Ticonderoga, he believed that he was safe; absence makes the heart grow fonder, but it cuts down propinquity, which is far more dangerous. Close observers of propriety might note, too, that though Sally married Dick in August, and though Francis Johnston speeded his congratulations, Anthony nursed his sorrows much longer. He did not get around to writing Dick a letter of congratulation until November 12: "Use my daughter well—you can't treat her better than she deserves—She tells me she is realy happy— I know it's in your Power to keep her so." Then, possibly feeling that his emotions were about to run away with him, he hurried to write about the army.

By that time, his worst pangs of jealousy were over. He was recalling a motto which he and Francis Johnston had created for their guidance, "A Bottle and a kind Landlady cures all again." Bottles were plentiful at Ticonderoga, and kind landladies were not absent. Wayne was living in a hastily built house, one of the grander structures of Ticonderoga because it owned a cellar, and in his case the "landlady" was poetic license, but the lady herself was very real and very kind. The charmer was Mrs. Udney Hay, wife of a Quebec timber merchant. Hay was not only a stanch Whig and a true devotee of independence, but he was a brevet lieutenant-colonel and assistant deputy quartermaster-general. Mrs. Hay had become, without a shadow of a doubt, the mascot of Ticonderoga.

Some suspected that Udney Hay was chiefly tolerated for his wife's good company, and though that is probably an unfounded accusation, commanding officers developed a habit of sending the assistant deputy on long boat voyages up Lake George to purchase "green sauce" (vegetables) for the mess while they consoled the pretty wife. Wayne was particularly devoted to the lady; she was his hostess when he gave dinners to his friends; she saw that soldier orderlies polished up his pewter dishes and laundered his two tablecloths until they were crisp and white.

Good fortune, however, could not last. The Hays were summoned down to Albany. Wayne was plunged into despair. "I was beginning to be a favorite," he lamented, "now I am as completely secluded from Society as Adam was before the formation of Eve. . . . I must try and converse with some femail friend or other."

He sublimated his desires by writing letters to Sally and Hetty, but that was unsatisfactory, and Joseph Wood, to whom he trusted the letters for delivery, came back with discouraging reports. Joe may have been sulking because all the time that he talked to Sally Dick Peters stood so close at hand that Wood could not "collect the postage." Wood vented his disappointment by declaring that although the girl was happy, "Dick can't child her," a singularly inept prediction for a couple who would in time produce six children. Perhaps, too, Philadelphia was too rich for Joe's blood, for in a burst of enthusiasm, Wood wrote Wayne: "My God, what swarms of fine girls in this town. I wish my friend and I had the setting of some of their tails." No doubt Anthony wished so himself, though it was gross libel to say of him, as Wood went on to say: "You and I like to be in love, so it's no matter who, so we have a sweetheart. It's a pretty amusement, and does very well for a leisure hour."

There were, to be sure, ladies like Sally Amos with the army, but many of them were soldiers' wives, and most of the rest were of that group which never is maid, wife, or widow. As commanding colonel, Wayne could not steal girls from private soldiers, and the few other damsels were either "black," which meant Indian, or closely guarded. Anthony was compelled to find his romance in his thoughts, in lyrical reports of his friends who wandered down to Albany to see the Schuyler girls, or in letters from his friends in Philadelphia. Those letters, it might be added, were sometimes extraordinarily frank. In passages that would make a Broadway columnist blush for his restraint, Wayne's friends informed him what swains were giving their ladies the "flankanade," and what was going on in more or less polite society. It was cold comfort for a love-hungry colonel, but he had to make the best of it.

Wayne was happy, then, when word came at last that he had been promoted to a brigadiership, that St. Clair was to take over Ty, and that he himself was to leave at once to join Washington and the main army. He dashed off a letter to Albany, hinting that his red cockade was tarnished and that it would be much appreciated if the Schuyler girls made him a new one; he gave a final dinner to his friends; and on April 28, 1777, he left Ticonderoga forever.

St. Clair, always Wayne's malignant rival, reported maliciously that Wayne had left both garrison and fortifications in poor condition. "Instead of having been improved during the winter which was expected they are much worse than when I left them, a very strong abatis on which the security of Mt. Independence chiefly consists having been almost entirely burned up for firewood and a great part of the Breast works."

CHAPTER VI

The Politicians Call

MONEY TROUBLES held Anthony interminably at Albany. Since he had assumed command at Golgotha not a single penny had been paid him for his food, although as a colonel he had been entitled to six rations daily and as a brigadier he was presumably drawing twelve. No money had arrived for such purposes; Wayne had paid the entire cost of food for his servants and his staff from his colonel's pay of $75 monthly or from the $125 which a brigadier received.

Arriving at Albany, he visited the office of the deputy commissary-general to present a food bill of £53 16s. 10d., accrued since he had taken over Ty. That officer demurred, questioning the thousand pounds of beef which Wayne and his half-dozen orderlies had eaten. The amount, Anthony insisted, was not exorbitant, amounting, as it did, to less than seven pounds of beef per day for all Wayne's staff of servants, but the auditor challenged the item; he criticized, too, the outrageous price of fivepence per pound that Wayne had paid for beef. Nor was the deputy convinced that half a dozen men could possibly consume a gallon of milk per day, although it averaged but a pint apiece. For a fortnight Anthony battled to obtain approval of the bill, but he was constantly put off by excuses and delays. Although he was in a hurry to join Washington at Morristown, New Jersey, he was held immobile until the fussy actuary would approve the bills.

Again, as on his journey north, Anthony spent much time with the pretty Schuyler girls, since his distaste for their father did not include the younger generation. He sat talking with them while they sewed upon a new bright-red cockade to replace the worn-out rusty decoration he had worn at Golgotha. Then, when the two weeks' auditing of bills was over and Wayne at last received a warrant for the money he had spent for rations, he resumed his journey. With Major Michael Ryan, a physician, and a small escort of troops guarding his two wagon-loads of baggage, he took the land route along the Hudson to West Point. From there he struck through the valley of the Ramapo to ride across the iron lands of northern New Jersey. The scenery was pleasant and the people most hospitable, but roads were poor. Not until May 20, almost a month after leaving Ty, did Wayne arrive at Morristown. He was somewhat thinner now than when he had last been with the main army, but his jutting jaw was still thrust forward in the same dynamic, confident way that his former associates so well remembered.

Anthony was shocked when he met Washington, for the commander, not yet wholly recovered from a severe attack of typhoid, was drawn and pale and physically unsteady, not at all like the vigorous, athletic figure whom Wayne had known before the war at Philadelphia's City Tavern. Washington's spirit, however, was unbroken; in talking with Wayne he showed himself a clear-thinking, coldly analytical strategist. His policy was to await British moves. Like Quintus Fabius Maximus, the Delayer, he wished to wear down his opponent by avoiding action and by harassing the enemy; he feared that large-scale operations in the open field would end in disaster.

Yet there was reason, he told Wayne, to think that Sir William Howe, now that spring had come to stay, would take advantage of good weather, probably by marching once again across New Jersey to the capital, or perhaps by trying a northern thrust straight up the Hudson to join Burgoyne's southward-moving army. Washington guarded against both dangers by remaining watchfully at Morristown. If Howe went north, then, by hastening over the same roads that Wayne had used in coming into Morristown, Washington could attack the British rear; if Howe struck south, he must first force the Continentals out of their mountain stronghold. Burgoyne could be watched by St. Clair's enlarged Ticonderoga garrison, and by Gates and Schuyler.

Wayne headed a division of eight Pennsylvania regiments. The work was, by rights, a major-general's job, for the division was composed of two brigades, each of which should have had a brigadier of its own. But since Pennsylvania's political disorders made it impossible for that harassed commonwealth to secure its proper quota of high officers, and since, with Mifflin doing quartermaster service and St. Clair commanding Ty, no Pennsylvania major-generals were available, Wayne, as senior brigadier, assumed responsibility. Shortage of ranking generals continued almost to the close of the Revolution, thanks to Pennsylvania's politicians; throughout the war Wayne would be carrying a major-general's load, but without the prestige or the perquisites of that rank. At Morristown, he commanded eight of Washington's forty-three Continental regiments, and they were, as everyone confessed, the flower of the army, but though he bore one-fifth the burden of the American force, he ranked lower than men (such as Arthur St. Clair) who had far less responsibility. The inequality irritated Wayne; he brooded over the injustice. More and more he came to feel that persecution was his lot, and that St. Clair was his evil genius.

His underofficers were congenial souls. The First Brigade included James Chambers's 1st Pennsylvania, with Tom Robinson and Richard Butler as lieutenant-colonels; Tom, of course, he knew well; Butler, cut from Wayne's own pattern, became a bosom friend. The 13th included red-faced, merry colonel Walter Stewart, the handsomest man in the army, and Wayne's intimate friend. If anyone could ever take the place of Joseph Wood, Walter, who was never happy unless he was in love, was the man. The 7th and the 10th were also members of the First Brigade, but neither possessed men who made a lasting impression on their brigadier.

Probably the Second Brigade was Wayne's special favorite. Under a new arrangement, Pennsylvania had shuffled her regiments so that Francis Johnston, leading the 5th, commanded many of Wayne's old comrades. The 4th Regiment, led by Dick Butler's brother William, marched in this brigade, and also Daniel Brodhead's 8th and Richard Humpton's 11th. For these last two men Wayne cared little. Brodhead, icy, jealous, and unduly covetous of promotion, watched Wayne too intently, seeking to discover flaws in leadership that would prove Anthony incompetent and Brodhead more deserving of command. Humpton, slow, stupid, and routineering, heavy in both thought and speech, was too suspicious. Wayne distrusted both; he far preferred their subordinates, his schoolboy playmate Caleb North and his fencing master, Major Francis Mentges.

2

Troubles piled upon Anthony. Once the immaculate dandy, he looked now, he thought, exactly like a scarecrow. At Ticonderoga, where he had been supreme, his clothes had not mattered greatly, for his associates were no better dressed than he; even at Albany, in the Schuyler salon, he could pass off his worn-out uniform as temporary traveling garb. As a brigadier, he told the pretty Schuyler girls, he would have clothes so brilliant as to dazzle all beholders. At headquarters, among Washington's smartly garbed officers, Tony felt disgraced. His bright new cockade illumined a cocked hat whose gold lace was badly tarnished; his fine blue-and-white coat had long since given way to one which had once been red but was now a dingy, seedy brown. Since Mrs. Hay was not at hand to watch his laundry, Anthony gave up perforce the use of white cravats; his stock was a rusty greenish-black. Curry, the fashionable Philadelphia tailor, was hurrying a new jacket and a pair of lambskin breeches, tanned as soft and fine as even Dandy Tony could desire, but Curry took a week to make the garments. In the meantime Wayne stayed shabby, hating to look at himself, hating even more to have dapper aides-de-camp see him in such a condition.

His men were clad worse. Chambers's troops had never been completely uniformed; they had gone forth to fight in loose brown, fringed-edged hunting-shirts such as frontiersmen wore, and these, from constant wear, were ragged. Other Pennsylvanians, more smartly garbed, laughed at the Chambers boys,

holding them up to ridicule; many of the soldiers, too thin-skinned to stand derision, deserted rather than remain the butts of their associates. Wayne tried to get them better clothing; knowing that Continental storehouses at Morristown were empty, he appealed to Pennsylvania pride to dress the troops. No answer came to his appeals; Pennsylvania politicians, too preoccupied with factional disputes to give proper care to their troops, marked time while the soldiers suffered. Wayne did not relax his efforts. Showering the officials with demands for help, calling upon every man of prominence to pull wires for the as-sistance of the army, he found himself buried in an avalanche of letter-writing. Night after night he quit his cronies to sit by candlelight alone in his quarters, writing moving accounts of the hardships of his Pennsylvanians. This, together with the paper work of straightening out details of accounts, muster rolls, and pay lists, bored him beyond belief. Like his friend Francis Johnston, he insisted that such activities destroyed the mind. "By Heaven my very Brain is," he insisted, "coddled into a kind of Pasty, composed of old *Musty Papers.*"

Polly worried him, too. After sixteen months of absence from Waynesborough, he was eager to be home, but army duties intervened. For the past nine months not a line had reached him from his wife, though he had sent a monthly letter home; he was impatient to know what was happening at the farm. Yet when at last she sent a note, it held no cheer, for Polly said that she was ill and that she was becoming more despondent. She suggested that he allow her to put Waynesborough under a sharecropping agreement and that she sell the livestock. There was no mention of her coming to the camp, though Anthony had hoped that since Martha Washington, Lucy Knox, and Catherine Greene were with their husbands at Morristown, Polly might come too. But Polly had resolved in Nova Scotia that she would never again stir from Chester County. All that Anthony could do was to encourage her to keep her courage high and to call upon the neighbors for aid in getting in the harvest. He sent her $260, more than two months' pay, to buy more cows. They would, he said, be of advantage in the fall.

On top of this, politicians, remiss about assisting him with uniforms, pestered him for his support. To fight George Bryan's and Timothy Matlack's ultrademocratic constitution, Rush and his conservative friends used the name of Anthony Wayne, hero of Trois Rivières and commander of the van at Morristown. They had tried before to drag him into the political arena, but he had side-stepped adroitly. Now, with an election coming on, they appealed once more. "Suppose," wrote Rush, "you write to some of your old friends in Chester County to concur with us in overthrowing the Constitution. Nothing but a new convention will restore union to us." Peters added his plea to Rush's appeal. "Our *fallen* Pennsylvania wants you," Dick declared. "Some change must be made or the power of this important state will never be exerted for the salvation of American liberty." Peters proposed that Wayne secure a furlough and come down to electioneer in person; he went so far as to suggest that the visit would make Sally very happy. Canny Dick was not above using pretty Sally as a bait to lure her old admirer.

But on the eve of British summer movements Wayne could not be spared from army duty. Again he evaded, writing Rush a noncommittal note which talked at length about pushing Britons out of Jersey but which said not a word about the Pennsylvania constitution of 1776; he answered Peters only by demanding that his Board of War send clothing to the troops. Pennsylvania's neglect was, he said, astonishing. He used another of his literary tags:

"I would rather risque my life, my reputation and the fate of America on 5000 men neatly uniformed than on a third more, equally armed and disciplined, covered with Raggs and Crawling with Verman." This original version was not as effective as a later, and more frequent, repetition:

"I have an insuperable bias in favor of an elegant Uniform and a Soldierly Appearance, so much so that I would rather risque my life and Reputation at the head of the same men in an attack, clothed and appointed as I could wish, merely with bayonets and a single charge of ammunition, than to take them as they appear in common with sixty rounds of ammunition."

Anthony Wayne was not cut out to be a politician; he could not be noncommittal indefinitely. Repeated hammerings broke him down; he did not go to Chester County to make speeches, but he did write Rush an unequivocal endorsement of the conservative position. Borrowing phrases from Francis Johnston's blasts of half a year before, Wayne went on record as declaring: "General St. Clair and many other Gentlemen of the Army can witness that at the very first view of your sickly Constitution I pronounced it not worth Defending"—precisely what Frank had written Wayne. "In my opinion the only way to open the eyes of the people would have been to try to put it into execution; the Defects would not only be seen but felt."

Rush exaggerated Wayne's importance as a vote-getter. Conservative Philadelphia County supported enemies of the ultra-democratic government, but upstate Pennsylvania sent down a solid radical delegation. Rush sadly accepted the inevitable, but he predicted dire misfortune: "I need not point out to you the Danger and folly of the Constitution. It has substituted a mob government to one of the happiest governments in the world. Nothing more was necessary than to abolish the royal and proprietary power of the State. A single legislature is big with tyranny. I had rather live under the government of one man than of seventy-two. They will soon become like the Thirty Tyrants of Athens. Absolute authority should belong only to God."

A second John Lacey turned up, to make Wayne's cup of discontent full to overflowing. Major Michael Ryan, his adjutant at Golgotha and his companion on the trip from Albany, suffered wounded feelings when Wayne preferred other friends. He wrote a tearful letter of complaint: "Your manner of treating me this while past fully convinces me that you are determined to part with me. . . . I defy anybody to censure my conduct yet I am treated as a person unworthy of being taken notice of. At Morristown I was never in your company but once and that was accidentally, when every other brigade major not only lived with his brigadier but was always with him wherever he was invited. . . . I am generally as clean dressed as my situation will admit of."

Wayne acted tactlessly; he turned stiff and formal, and wrote sarcastically: "I am very sorry that I have not conducted myself

in a manner pleasing to Major Ryan. It was not my fault if the
Major was not invited with myself the few times I dined out
of my own quarters. I *had* no intention of parting with Major
Ryan but as he wishes to quit his present and get into another
department, I can only assure him of best wishes." It was a
brutal blow, and Ryan felt it deeply, but there was nothing
that could be done to mollify the overformal General. Poor
Michael Ryan temporarily lost a soft and pleasant association
with a brigadier whom he admired.

Billeted at Deacon Ephraim Sayre's on Bottle Hill, at what
is now Madison, Anthony enjoyed a happy social life. He gave
gossipy and social parties; his quarters resembled a fashionable officers' club. He was invariably bubbling with good
stories; his mulatto servant, whom he had given a wooden
sword to wear, mixed the best rum punches in the camp. At
dinner parties, where sound port and good Madeira flowed,
boon companions laughed and sang, to the horror of his host.
The Deacon would have much preferred another billeting, but
when he gently asked if Wayne could not be transferred to a
less strait-laced house, he was reminded that during the larger
portion of the winter the Sayre house had not been requisitioned for the army, and that in any case he would not be bur-
dened long.

The reassurance rested on sound authority. Rumors came into
camp that Howe and Cornwallis had increased their forces at
New Brunswick, both by enlisting loyalists and by troopships
from overseas, and that the British were building a sort of portable bridge, as well as a large number of flatboats. Washington
was sure that the bridge was intended to be laid upon pontoons
when Howe arrived at the banks of the Delaware, and that he
intended to carry the flatboats on wagons down to Trenton or
some other crossing of the river. Evidence pointed to an early
British advance on Philadelphia. Washington, thinking that
Morristown was too far north for a good base against such
moves, planned to transfer his camp to a more southerly position. By marching to the Raritan River, he would be in good
position to intercept the enemy if they should start advancing
upon Philadelphia. His 5,738 effective men would not match

the more than 10,000 trained troops which Howe concentrated
at New Brunswick, but the very fact that they were ready to
engage in action might dissuade the British from undertaking
an attack.

3

Jocund Colonel Phil Van Horne sat on his porch at Convivial Hill admiring the late June scenery. Before him stretched
a wide tree-shaded lawn, running downhill to the highway that
connected Somerville and Bound Brook; to the east ran the
placid Middle Brook; great fields of ripening wheat, meadows
from whose acres came the sweetness of the first hay harvest,
groves of cherries, red-dotted with their sour fruit, lay almost
endlessly upon his right. Phil Van Horne, master of Convivial
Hill, was thoroughly content.

Convivial Hill well deserved its name. Though Colonel Phil
Van Horne lacked the luxuries of his aristocratic neighbor Lord
Stirling, his hospitality never flagged. On summer evenings his
lawns were gay with girls in pink and white, coming to call upon
the Van Horne daughters; slim officers in their gala best, be-
decked with ruffled shirts, gold epaulets, and all the varied
reds and blues, browns, greens, and white of Continental soldiers, bowed low in formal greeting. The huge white-paneled
entrance hall, running Colonial fashion through the house, led
into spacious rooms on either side, where older, more sedate
gentry and their ladies grouped to talk of politics, of neighborhood occurrences, and of the endless social and domestic crises
of the times. Not even Lord Stirling's near-by English manor
house contained such merriment as Van Horne's daughters
caused upon the lawn, nor as much deep-seated happiness.
Convivial Hill, famous in North Jersey for its hospitality, was
the capital of charm and laughter. Van Horne, standing now
upon his porch, one hand spread-eagled against the glistening
white pillar, spied Old Man Martin coming with the mail.
Something was afoot, for Martin was not letting his bony horse
amble while he himself knitted stockings, as had been his cus-

tomary practice, but the reins were drawn taut and the whip was rising like a flail. The postman was bringing news that Wayne planned to camp along the Middle Brook. Old Man Martin's bright eyes, snapping happily beneath his red wig and his rusty cocked hat, danced merrily as he spread the report. Grinning to show his broken teeth, he stepped down from his battered sulky, to run, in all the glory of his bright-blue, yellow-buttoned coat, scarlet waistcoat, leather smallclothes, and blue yarn stockings, to the master of Convivial Hill. Then, fearful lest some other traveler anticipate him in his self-appointed heraldry, he ran back breathlessly to whip up his horse and pass the word along.

Phil Van Horne called his servants into action. His big Dutch ovens at Convivial Hill began a constant baking, to turn out at the very least three or four batches of fine white bread before sunrise. The task involved the servants' staying awake all night; it meant that much wood must be cut, and that fresh barrels of flour must be rolled in from the storehouses, but there were slaves for this, and Phil Van Horne was not accustomed to consider what extra labor his commands involved. He looked to his Madeira, finding to his satisfaction that there were at least two pipes of it on hand; this meant two hundred gallons, which would assuredly supply the officers, and he saw that there was beer enough to care for all emergencies. He warned the girls to get into their best, which drove them into ecstasies of giggling. He saw that fires were laid—though not too high, just enough to take off chill and to dry up the damp—in his four big bedrooms on the second floor. When his preparations were complete, he settled down to wait the coming of his guests.

Unfortunately Old Man Martin spread his news too widely. Stopping at every farmhouse on the way from Morristown to Princeton, bawling his report at every crossroads hamlet, bursting in at every tavern on the route, he broadcast the word that Washington and Wayne were marching. From half a score scattered places Tories hurried to inform Sir William Howe and Lord Cornwallis. Soon New Brunswick, only ten miles from Convivial Hill, was flooded with British agents bearing Martin's tidings.

The British leaders held rapid conference. Too cautious to begin a march on Philadelphia while an American army of unknown strength threatened their rear, Howe and Cornwallis wondered whether they dared storm the new positions. The Continental Army, they were well aware, was but half the British force; even the rumored addition of large detachments of New Jersey and North Carolina militiamen, eager fighters but unseasoned, would not bring the Americans up to British strength. Wayne controlled the passes through the hills and Washington was strongly posted in the south end of the basin, behind three sets of strong earthwork defenses. Cannon planted on the summits commanded the valley of the Raritan; a well-built fort at Chimney Rock controlled the narrow paths that wound along Middle Brook. In the absence of authentic information about the numbers and especially about the artillery of the Americans, Howe hesitated to attack.

Howe turned himself into an actor. With elaborate nonchalance, he ignored the Americans. Splitting his strength, in open violation of sound military tactics, he sent divisions off upon divergent routes. Surreptitiously, Cornwallis slipped away from camp, marching at midnight on the road toward Millstone, a maneuver intended to convince the Americans that the British were really serious about attacking Philadelphia, and with careful cunning Howe saw to it that the Continentals had quick news of the movement. Thus, thought Howe, Wayne, completely fooled, would rush out from his stronghold to attack the British rear and cut off Howe's communications. Meanwhile, a second expedition set off toward Princeton. Each hour that the two divisions marched, it appeared, the British forces would be more distant from each other; an American attack upon either force, so Howe wanted Wayne to think, would inevitably prosper.

The Americans were both cagy and observant. The "deserter" who came to the Middle Brook to reveal the British military "secrets" found Wayne and Washington remarkably cool. Spies had reported that both British columns were without their heavy baggage, and that the field guns and munition stores remained close to New Brunswick. If Wayne had rushed out to attack, Cornwallis would have turned at once; the second British column would have caught the Continentals on an unprotected flank; the main force at New Brunswick would have opened up with all its power on the American rear. It was a well-planned trap, and had it worked, the Continental Army must have been destroyed. But Wayne and Washington remained in their positions. Howe's playacting failed to draw them forth. The British columns sheepishly returned to their old base.

Anthony settled down for a brief spell of relaxation at Convivial Hill, but his repose was not long-lived. Fat, red-faced Major General James Grant, smarting under the ignominious retreat of the British, confident that one regiment of British grenadiers could throw Wayne's two brigades into confusion, struck suddenly at Wayne's advanced position. But Anthony, alert and well served by skilled scouts, heard of Grant's approach before the British reached the Continental lines. In a sharp skirmish on June 16, 1777, Wayne's men not only smashed the British advance but chased Grant for some miles. "This Hero," Wayne jubilantly reported, "had his Coat much dirtied, his Horse's Head taken off and himself badly bruised for having the presumption at the head of seven hundred British troops to face five hundred Pennsylvanians."

A month later, his Convivial Hill merriment was again disturbed when news arrived that Burgoyne, with 9,000 men, had outwitted St. Clair and had taken Ty without a battle. St. Clair, thinking the fort impregnable, had left Mt. Defiance unguarded. Burgoyne, dragging cannon up steep, winding paths, had posted guns commanding Ticonderoga, and St. Clair, facing annihilation or capture, had slipped away along the eastern shore of Lake George. Wayne, incoherent with rage, thundered that St. Clair deserved court-martial.

Hetty Griffits made him feel happier by a gentle note assuring him that she thought of him continually and asking when she might again enjoy the pleasure of his company. That delight was not to be postponed long. Washington, fearing a renewed attack on Philadelphia, ordered Wayne to hasten down to Chester to train recruits. Wayne disliked militiamen, but he

enjoyed whipping young soldiers into shape; Chester was, moreover, but a few short miles from Naaman's Creek, where Sally
often spent her time, nor was it far from Philadelphia, where
both Hetty Griffits and the City Tavern awaited him. On July
24 he took the road from Morristown to his new assignment.

4

The City Tavern seethed with criticism. Angry talk raged about
the cost of living. Loaf sugar had skyrocketed to 15 shillings a
pound; salt, so necessary in curing meat and in preserving
food, especially now that torrid weather was at hand, was equally
expensive. Rum had shot up to 40 shillings a gallon for the
poorest domestic quality, and tea was almost unobtainable. The
City Tavern circle blamed the extraordinary prices on the fact
that Pennsylvania was controlled by dangerous democratic
demagogues. Some of them, indeed, thought that it would be
salutary if British soldiers overran the city. "I had rather they
came to Philadelphia than not," said John Adams, slowly.
"Either the furnace of affliction would refine it of its impurities,
or it would be purged as by fire. This town has been a dead
weight upon us; it would be a dead weight upon the enemy."
Wayne writhed at such talk, yet he thought it wiser not to be
involved in civilian argument. He was sorry now that he had
stopped at the City Tavern on his way to Chester; for the first
time in his life he disliked tavern company. He left the inn
and walked up the street to pay a fleeting call on Hetty Griffits.
The conversation there was more enjoyable. For all her demure-
ness and her shy retirement, Hetty was a girl to whom a man
could talk. Most Philadelphia ladies aired an artificial modesty;
if Anthony talked to them about his favorite novel, *Tom Jones,*
they blushed and said such topics were unbecoming; they pretended, though everyone knew better, that they never read
novels. Hetty, on the other hand, held vigorous opinions; her
literary criticisms were often over Anthony's head, but they
were always interesting. He sat with her and chatted; when

Tom Jones palled, he told her that his thoughts would never leave her, a sentiment which she cherished far more warmly than his literary views. The call on Hetty Griffits took the bad taste of the City Tavern from his mouth, but the evening grew late; ten o'clock approached. Reluctantly, Anthony took his leave to go to Chester to drill recruits.

Wayne liked Pennsylvanians better than he did Yorkers or Yankees. Wherever you found them, militiamen were clumsy enough; gawky farmer boys and gangling apprentices could not be turned at once into smart soldiers. They tripped over their own feet when they were told to wheel; they dropped their guns in practicing the manual of arms; drill was punctuated by the ringing sounds of long squirrel-rifle barrels clanging against each other. They were good-humored about it, to be sure, for when they made mistakes they laughed out loud; they spat out curses at their own stupidity. As youngsters, they were happy, pleasant cubs; when he thought of them as soldiers, Wayne, the disciplinarian, tore his hair.

You could, however, talk to them in English. Those Albany fellows had just stood with mouths agape, not understanding anything that you were saying, but the Pennsylvanians, even those German boys from Berks and Lancaster counties, knew something of the English language. You might have difficulty understanding them when they talked back, for upstate Dutchmen spoke with thick, guttural tones, and frontier Irishmen had a broad and mellow brogue, but soldiers did not often dare to speak to officers. It made little difference if you failed to understand what troops were saying; the important thing was that the soldiers should grasp your meaning, and obey it.

Wayne drilled them until they nearly dropped. He could not teach them much about the bayonet, the weapon which he had come to think was indispensable, for squirrel guns were not adapted for it; if you stuck a bayonet into the muzzle of a six-foot rifle, you had a lance too long to be of any use. Wayne did not like the squirrel gun, though it was his own state's special contribution to the art of war and though it could shoot with exceptional precision; he wanted bayonets. Dan Morgan, his frontier friend who, now that he was exchanged out of his

Canadian prison, was organizing a corps of Rangers, was welcome to the six-foot rifle. Wayne did the best he could; he
made his boys maneuver, drill, and perform the manual of arms
at every opportunity. He had them take the precious flints from
their guns and put in wooden stoppers, so that they could practice the motions of firing and loading without using up their
flints.

It was fortunate that he had those fellows down at Chester,
away from the distractions of the capital. Country boys, unused
to city life, would have gone mad over Philadelphia's rum and
dissipation; discipline would have disappeared. At Chester,
Wayne had the militiamen to himself; the energetic brigadier
in his bright-blue coat and lambskin breeches had his hunting-
shirted recruits entirely to himself. For two crowded weeks,
until the ninth of August, those youngsters were his to mold
as he saw fit.

Anthony liked the ladies, and he delighted in good fellowship, but his soldiers looked upon him as a merciless slave-
driver. They did not have much time to rest when Wayne
cracked orders, but when he turned them over to old John
Armstrong, hero of Kittanning in the French and Indian War,
they were excellent soldiers; unseasoned, certainly, to the whine
of warlike bullets, but thoroughly drilled. They marched with
heads up and with springy step; their files stretched straight;
their actions were precise. Wayne knew that Major-General
Armstrong could make good use of them.

He had a day or two now to spend at Waynesborough before
going back to duty. It was his first furlough in the war, unless
that two weeks' stay at Albany be so considered; he had not seen
Polly for almost a year and a half. Wives of other generals,
even of colonels, had come to Morristown to call upon their
husbands, but Polly had begged off. Anthony suspected that she
did not care to come. One gathers that he did not have too good
a time on his return. Polly was sinking deep into despondency;
she complained that she was sickly and that her burdens were
too heavy. Shannon was a first-rate overseer, but he was no
businessman; he did not take advantage of his opportunities.
Polly had to run the farm and tannery herself, with such help

as William Hayman, husband of pert young Ann, could spare from his own duties. Nor was she grateful to Hayman for his help; instead she found fault that he came alone to Waynesborough, leaving Ann, whom Polly loved devotedly, at the distant Hayman home. Polly grumbled, too, because Anthony would not let the farm be sharecropped; she protested that his sudden coming had upset her plans; she found fault with him because he sent a worn-out war horse to be put to pasture and to be fed, in addition, with oats twice or three times a day; she objected strenuously to his demanding her best horse in exchange for the broken-down animal.

These, however, were unimportant matters when contrasted with her burning indignation at Wayne's neglect. His letters, she said, were brief, formal scrawls, telling nothing but bare outlines of military movements, sending his love to his children and his mother, but almost never a word to her. When he grew personal, it always was about Margaretta or Isaac, never about his wife. Anthony retorted hotly that at least he wrote, but that she had kept tight-lipped. All that he had heard of Waynesborough, he reminded her, had come from other sources, from Abraham, from Sharp Delany, or from Sally Robinson.

That mention loosed the floodgates; Polly broke down in tears. She had heard too much of Sally; Abraham Robinson, for all his loyalty to Anthony and to his sister Sally, had told about the correspondence. Polly was intensely jealous. Anthony, stupid, like most men, in the ways of handling injured wives, certain in his own soul that he had meant no harm, irritated her beyond endurance. "Well," he said, "she wrote to me, when you did not. She went out of her way to buy me tea, two pounds of it. It cost her £10. She searched out the material for this jacket that I wear; she sent me a jar of pickled oysters. Certainly, I wrote to her because she was so considerate." Perhaps the pickled oysters were too much; Polly fled back into her silences. Thenceforward, her letters, which, though rare, had overflowed with love, were as coldly impersonal as those which Anthony sent her.

There was difficulty, too, between Anthony and his mother. The old lady, wrapped up in memories of her husband Isaac,

consoled only by religion, stood aloof from her son. She thought
of him as still a little boy, though he was married and the father
of children, but her emotions were not warm enough to demonstrate whatever affection she still felt. She was, moreover, completely occupied in caring for a stricken sister, Priscilla, who had
gone completely out of her head and who gave Mrs. Wayne
no rest by day or night. Financial misunderstandings drove
mother and son apart. Before Anthony had gone to Canada,
there had been a formal settlement of old Isaac's estate, and
since Waynesborough was solely under Anthony's control, a
bond had been drawn up whereby he agreed to pay his mother
£50 a year annuity. Mrs. Wayne had then moved most of her
personal belongings to Priscilla's house, in adjacent Newtown;
she had grown out of touch with affairs at her old home. Amidst
all Anthony's troubles, he had overlooked his duty, or else the
yawning Schuyler gulf at Albany had swallowed his letters to
his mother. She complained that since his departure for the
North she had received but one brief note, and that more than
a year ago, soon after the annuity had been arranged. He had
failed to pay a single cent of the debt.

But if the grown-ups were cool in their reception, seven-year-
old Margaretta and her brother Isaac were shrill-voiced with
excitement. Margaretta, already the little lady because she had
been a year or more at school in Philadelphia, buzzed happily
about her father, displaying her accomplishments. Anthony was
particularly pleased to see how well she read and how adept she
was at writing; he admired the polish she was acquiring under
Mrs. Powel's care. Isaac, Polly thought, was still too young for
this; much to Anthony's disgust, she wanted him to stay a baby.
Anthony believed a boy of five should start to school, to learn
to be a man. "Don't neglect the charge about my little Girl and
Boy," he solemnly warned Polly. "Let no *mistaken fondness*
be a means of keeping them from school, for that is the Rock
that parents frequently split upon."

He was especially worried lest in that feminine household,
where only Shannon and old Darby represented manhood and
virility, Isaac grow up to be too soft and gentle. Pleased by the
boy's boasting that Daddy would "run the sholders in and make

them blead," he vowed to find his son a proper sword and uniform to wear. Even should he not return from this campaign, he hoped that Isaac would become a warrior: "I hope that my Boy will not turn aside from Glory, tho' the path should be marked with his father's blood."

Except for his delight in seeing the children, Anthony's visit to Waynesborough had not been happy; he was glad to start out again on Monday, August 11, to rejoin the Continental Army. Washington, in the meanwhile, had moved south into Pennsylvania. Howe, embarking all his army aboard ship, had sailed off for some unknown destination, which might be Charleston or Halifax, the West Indies or even England, but which was far more likely to be Philadelphia. The Americans, completely in the dark concerning Howe's intentions, thought it wiser to be close to the capital. They were now encamped twenty miles north of Philadelphia, along the banks of Neshaminy Creek.

Wayne rode to the camp. He found the army jubilant. News had just arrived that Nicholas Herkimer's 800 New York militiamen, those despised Albany Dutchmen, had beaten off an enemy attack at Fort Stanwix (now Oriskany) after a bloody battle of six hours; he learned, too, that Washington had at last decided to fight Indians in redskin fashion by sending up Dan Morgan's frontiersmen Rangers to sharpshoot from behind the shelter of trees and rocks. That meant, as Wayne well knew, that Pennsylvanians would exchange those six-foot squirrel rifles for good muskets, the kind that could be fitted with a bayonet; it meant, too, that the Commander-in-Chief was evidently determined to take the aggressive against the enemy.

As usual, Wayne was in the van; Washington sent him down the Philadelphia road to take post closest to the city. An express rider had brought word that British ships were sailing up the Chesapeake; revised opinions now agreed that Philadelphia would somehow be the enemy's objective. Wayne, accordingly, went with his Pennsylvania troops as spearhead for the American advance. He was flattered by the responsibility. He bubbled with enthusiasm, his conversation sparkled.

No doubt his quarters contributed to Wayne's joy, for Anthony lived at the great manor house of Graeme Park, near Gwynedd, north of Philadelphia, where Elizabeth Graeme Ferguson, petite and witty social arbiter of the capital, kept a summer home. She was a poet and a scholar, and read French as readily as most women of her times read English; her conversation dripped with puns and epigrams. Anthony knew her well, for everyone in Philadelphia life had been her friend; she was a protégée of the Rev. Richard Peters, who had married him to Polly, and though she was six years older than the Brigadier, she was as young in spirits as any girl he knew. Wayne camped his troops in Mrs. Ferguson's great woods, that 500-acre tract of parkland which she stocked with deer and game; he himself found quarters in the finely built great house, where Mrs. Ferguson and her young companion, Miss Stedman, made him extremely welcome. He hated to leave; he hoped that he would come again with frequency. "You're very welcome," Mrs. Ferguson replied. "Do come again to Graeme Park as a convincing proof that you enjoyed your stay. But when you do return, I own that I should prefer to see you with a smaller retinue."

Wayne raged when he discovered that sutlers accompanying his division took off with them, in breaking camp, one of his hostess's best slaves, together with a yoke of excellent oxen. The sutlers then fled from camp, and in hurrying away during the broiling summer heat drove one of the animals until it dropped dead from exhaustion. Wayne tried to recover the stolen property and to punish the thieves; he promised Mrs. Ferguson that he would do everything within his power to see that justice was accorded her, but his efforts were vain.

CHAPTER VII

The Fight for Philadelphia

SEVEN O'CLOCK on a summer Sunday morning is not a time to see a city at its best, but Wayne had not come to view the sights of Philadelphia. The army was upon the march; authentic information had arrived that Howe's armada was well up the Chesapeake, and that the British planned to drive through southern Chester County to the back door of the capital. By hurrying from the Neshaminy to Philadelphia and beyond, the Continentals were on their way to intercept the British movement. It was late August, but the atmosphere was clear and not too hot. During the night a sharp thunderstorm drenched the town, leaving in its aftermath some smoldering ruins fired by lightning, but the rain laid the dust and cooled the air; a brisk, refreshing breeze, faintly acrid with the smoke of wet, charred timbers, made travel pleasant. The subaltern and twelve horsemen who led the American advance enjoyed their early morning ride.

Behind them, strung out in a long column, twelve men wide, came Washington's Grand Army, stepping briskly down the well-paved middle of Front Street, wheeling smartly to the right to swing out Chestnut Street to Center Woods. They marched to quicksteps played by fifes and drums; they wore small sprigs of green as hat cockades; some carried flowers in the barrels of their muskets. The soldiers marched with unaccustomed lightness, for Washington, to make them look more spruce, freed them for this day from carrying camp kettles and other bulky baggage. These, with the women of the camp, were carted round the outskirts of the city, to rejoin the army when the parade was over. Wayne's report on City Tavern talk inspired the dress parade; Washington staged it to reawaken local patriotism. The demonstration would have been more forceful had he waited until a later hour, when churchgoers were in the streets or when Philadelphia gentry took their Sunday strolls, but Howe's near advance prevented a delay. It was unfortunate that the Continental Army, groomed so admirably, arrived in town when breakfast was upon the table.

Many of the ladies, to the extreme regret of dapper officers, were, as it happened, out of town. Responding to their state's appeal, they were at the seashore, sixty miles away, boiling great panfuls of ocean water to make a coarse, gray salt, of curious look and villainous taste, for preventing fresh meat from spoiling in summer heat. Many of Philadelphia's officers could not see their girls as the army marched through the city. Wayne had better luck; his orders led him, after leaving Philadelphia, back to Naaman's Creek, where he was to wait fresh news of Howe. It seemed likely that he would spend at least two days, and probably more, at this pleasant retreat, and Wayne took the opportunity to patch up his troubles with Polly. He sent her a note inviting her to meet him there, and to bring the children, but as usual his wording was curt; to Polly's mind, it seemed a military order. She resented, too, her husband's freedom in acting as if he were the host at Sally's home; her jealousy flared. She ignored the invitation.

Sally, too, grew cool. She knew, of course, that Howe was near and that all Continental officers were absorbed in military matters, but Tony had never before been too busy to notice her; she wondered if he had been smitten by Hetty Griffits, the substitute she had herself picked out, or worse, by some unknown charmer. When, womanlike, she protested his neglect, he said that he was busy "doing the work of three general officers"; he turned back to his papers and resumed his writing. Sally, piqued, flounced away, resolving not to show him any signs of interest until he should mend his ways and be properly remorseful.

Wayne was, as it happened, drawing up a plan of war to send to Washington. He had been rereading Caesar; those Latin lessons at Uncle Gilbert's school, much as he had de-

PENNSYLVANIA CAMPAIGN
1777 ~ 1778

spised them at the time, were paying dividends. Caesar, he read, had beaten back the Gauls, bravest of ancient warriors, by striking suddenly at their unprotected flanks; he suggested now that 2,500 picked men fall upon the British. Caesar had acted thus successfully at Amiens and at Alesia; the maneuver ought to work for Americans, bravest of modern soldiers.

However, Howe too had studied Caesar; British armies were less careless than unlettered Gauls. By strengthening outposts and by bringing up artillery he had made his flanks powerful. Nor did Washington follow Wayne's suggestion as to strength. Instead of selecting 2,500 men, he let William Maxwell, with but 600 soldiers, lead an attack. On September 3, at Cooch's Bridge in northern Delaware, Maxwell's small detachment, fighting for the first time under their newly adopted Stars and Stripes, was overpowered. Howe swept onward toward Philadelphia.

Hastily, Washington moved his army to the steep banks of Brandywine Creek, twenty miles southwest of the capital. As a defensive position the location was superb. Where the main road crossed the creek, at Chadd's Ford, the stream was narrow, but its banks were high and forested. Continental cannon, posted on the heights, commanded Howe's approach. To ford the creek British soldiers must wade waist-high in water, cross a marsh, and then climb a steep and well-defended hill under constant fire of artillery and musketry. To take Chadd's Ford by a direct assault was absolutely impossible. Wayne held the key position, standing with the artillery on high ground east of the creek. To his left were Armstrong's militiamen, whom he had drilled at Chester; on his right stood Sullivan, Adam Stephen of Virginia, and Lord Stirling. Behind Wayne, Nathanael Greene waited with a full division in reserve.

To meet these 11,000 Americans, Howe had 16,000 British and Hessian veterans, with heavier guns. Two skilled strategists, Cornwallis and Wilhelm, Baron Knyphausen, a sixty-year-old German, aided the British leader. Classic warfare called for a direct assault, but Howe commanded sufficient men to dare an unprofessional attack. Americans regarded him as hidebound, cautious, and unimaginative, but again, as at the

Battle of Long Island in 1776, Howe threw conventions to the winds. By splitting his army into two columns he tricked the rebels.

The morning of September 11, 1777, was peculiarly fitted for his purpose. Thick fog prevented scouting; even had the day been clear, the Americans had no cavalry. So long as no spies or deserters escaped from his ranks, Howe could act in perfect secrecy. Knyphausen opened fire on Wayne's position as though determined to force a passage at Chadd's Ford, while Howe and Cornwallis stumbled through the fog on a seventeen-mile cross-country march, to ford the Brandywine far beyond the rebel right. The movement was risky, for if Washington learned of the march in time, he could fall upon the distant flanking troops while they were far away from Knyphausen, and thus smash the divided British forces. Howe gambled that the fog would last long enough for him to get across the creek before Washington learned what was afoot. While Knyphausen's artillery pounded Wayne and Armstrong, the main force of the British, guided by loyalists who knew the country even in the fog, would roll up the American right flank.

Washington should never have been caught in such a situation. Precisely the same maneuver had been tried before, at the disastrous Battle of Long Island; he should have been alert to danger. A slight shift in assignments would have won the day. Had Wayne been stationed on the right instead of in the center, Howe's scheme would have failed, for Anthony was well acquainted with the narrow roads that wound among the hills of Brandywine; he was familiar with the fords. Wayne would have watched these points of weakness; Washington, unable in the fog to scout efficiently, took precautions which at any other time would have been more than adequate, but which at Brandywine were not enough.

Knyphausen played his role with extraordinary skill. Steadily he hammered Wayne, as though laying down an artillery barrage; when Wayne answered, Knyphausen faltered as if he had been overwhelmed. Maxwell, who had a small advance detachment on the west side of the stream, was deceived by Knyphausen's clever acting; he drew up his few men to chase the fleeing Hessians. Wayne jubilated; his Pennsylvanians, both regulars and militiamen, had beaten back the British! Washington, completely misled, prepared to cross the Brandywine; he called up Greene's reserves and sent orders for Sullivan and Armstrong to advance.

Rumors cluster thick about Brandywine, most of them manufactured long after the engagement by nonmilitary people who were not present at the battle. One, completely unfounded, tells a sparkling tale of how proud Hugh, Earl Percy, riding on the long circuitous detour, reined in his horse, and suddenly exclaimed: "I know this landscape; I have seen it in a dream. This is where I shall be killed." He called his servant Clifford, gave him his watch and purse, entrusted to him a few last messages to be delivered to his friends, then, spurring his horse, dashed forward into battle and was shot. It is a most engaging story when narrated by some credulous sentimentalist, but it has no solid basis. No Earl Percy and no legitimate member of that famous line died at Brandywine, for none was present at that battle.

Another glowing story tells that "old Squire Cheyney" spurred from Thornbury, five miles from the battlefield, to warn Washington that Howe was on the march. He rode up, breathless and disheveled, to a scoffing group who would not credit his report; he called on Wayne and Frazer to testify that he was a true patriot; he jumped down from his sweating horse to draw a sketch map in the dirt so that the officers might realize that he knew whereof he spoke; he offered to remain a hostage to be executed if he were lying. There is, no doubt, a shred of truth in this Thomas Cheyney legend, though in the course of years the tale has been embroidered lavishly. The officer, a county lieutenant of forty-six who would not be named a squire until another year had passed, told Sullivan that he had seen the British marching, but Sullivan had word from his own officers that they had ridden out beyond the lines without seeing any sign of an approaching army. Sullivan, quite naturally, preferred to take the word of his professional observers, particularly when there was no confirmation of the Cheyney report by any civilian. The Quaker residents of the Brandywine

Valley, following their pacifist practice, sent no such word. In fact, they ignored the presence of both armies save for a notation entered in the Birmingham Meeting minute book which reads: "Today there was much confusion outside."

Not until two o'clock in the afternoon, when the fog lifted and when Howe and Cornwallis completed their long detour, did the Americans actually know that Howe had outmaneuvered them again. Washington was in a dangerous position; Knyphausen, no longer acting out a role, pressed a violent attack against Wayne's central position at Chadd's Ford; Howe and Cornwallis, safely over the Brandywine, fell on the unsuspecting Sullivan's right flank. Instead of one battle at the Brandywine the struggle developed into four different fights at places difficult for the Americans to reinforce.

Incredible confusion wrecked any hope that the Americans might yet hold for victory. Sullivan's position was desperate enough, with the British on his flank and in his rear, and with a steep hill between his division and a marsh-bordered creek; maneuvering his men in such a situation was a delicate affair involving cool calculation and precise timing. To make matters worse, destroying all hope of smooth operations, the generals thought of prestige first and danger second. Military etiquette required that troop detachments be deployed with regard to the seniority of commanding officers. Sullivan, as head of the division, was entitled to hold the post of danger on the right. He issued orders that would put his men upon that flank, facing the enemy, but when his soldiers marched to that position, they found it occupied by Chevalier Prud'homme de Borré, who, though only a brigadier, considered himself, as a foreign expert, superior to Major-Generals Sullivan and Stirling.

Stirling, also aiming at the right, found De Borré usurping the position, but Stirling, rather than argue the matter, avoided trouble with the Frenchman by continuing his march still farther to the right. Sullivan, arriving at the place where the right flank should have been, followed Stirling's example; he too swung around the Frenchman's troops, and continued past the post that Stirling took. The troops were at last in what Sullivan considered proper order. The silly, childish jockeying for position left an open gap of half a mile between Wayne's center and the Sullivan flank. Howe's agile cavalry discovered the wide opening. British soldiers poured between the two American detachments. De Borré solved the problem in a manner satisfactory to himself by rushing off in haste; he did not stop until he had reached Philadelphia, where, resigning his commission, he took ship for France and safety. Lafayette and Count Pulaski (newly come from Poland) rallied De Borré's bewildered troops.

Washington and Greene rushed to close the gap on the American right; Wayne also moved to help his fellows. Anthony knew now that Knyphausen commanded but a portion of the British Army, but underestimating the numbers as sadly as he had previously overestimated them, he left only a few men to defend the ford. Just as he was moving, Knyphausen launched a more determined drive; Hessian artillery opened up; hundreds of Knyphausen's men plunged into the Brandywine in mass attack upon the hill. Wayne could not leave his post. Holding the all-important center, he fought back Knyphausen's violent assault.

Sullivan was in distress. Washington and Greene were still racing to his aid when Howe swooped down. An American advance detachment was literally cut to pieces, an achievement of which the British 46th is so proud that to this day it wears a red badge on its caps in memory of the exploit. The Black Watch, with its somber tartan, pressed hard on Sullivan; the 40th singled out Lafayette's command and wounded that heroic Frenchman; the 15th Foot, an East Yorkshire regiment, drove Stirling's men into a wood.

Both sides fought desperately. Battle Hill, a strategic height just south of Birmingham Meeting House, changed hands eleven times within an hour. This was the conflict which the conservative Quakers described as causing "much confusion." Brigadier-General Thomas Conway, who had seen much service, said that he had never seen fire so intense. So bitter was the engagement that the 15th Foot used up all its ball; it moved ahead, snapping its empty guns, making so impressive a display by powder flashes that Stirling was wholly deceived. The regiment even yet bears the nickname of the Snappers.

Washington came up to Greene just in time to prevent disastrous rout. Sullivan's exhausted division fell back, Greene's regiments opening their ranks to let the tired men through. Then, doggedly fighting against superior odds, Washington engineered a masterly retreat. Greene's men held the British back while, one by one, the Continental regiments slipped away upon the road to Chester. When all the rest were gone, Wayne's men, still holding Chadd's Ford against the Hessians, were free to join their fellow soldiers.

Howe retained control of the Brandywine, at a cost of 579 casualties; the Americans lost approximately 1,000, including their wounded and those taken prisoner. Eleven cannon, two of which were trophies of Princeton, had to be abandoned when Washington retreated. Philadelphia now lay open to capture; all that Howe had to do was to advance along the great road to the city. Though he might face minor difficulties in crossing the Schuylkill, no serious obstruction blocked his path. The capital, however, was not now his main objective; that town was at his mercy, to be picked up whenever he desired, and he delayed in taking it. Far more important, both to Howe and Washington, was possession of the gun factories and powder mills at Warwick, Coventry, and Reading, directly north of the Brandywine, in the foothills of the mountains. If these could be kept from Washington, the Revolution would collapse.

Wayne, with characteristic courage, proposed a daring move. Three highways ran from Brandywine across the fertile Great Valley into the munition regions. The British held two of them; the third, a broad road that struck straight to Turk's Head, where Wayne had made his caucus speech, was unguarded. Why Sir William Howe should be so careless was none of Anthony's concern; it was enough for him that passage lay open. He urged Washington to dash along that road before Howe should realize his blunder; by hurrying into the Great Valley, the Continental Army could rearm and fill its ammunition pouches. Then, refitted and refreshed, the army could attack with confidence. It was admirable advice; had Washington followed it, he could have smashed an unsuspecting enemy. But Washington, always cautious, distrusted the bold move. He feared that Wayne was misinformed; dreading another battle, he ordered a retreat.

On September 12, the day after Brandywine, Washington led his battered army to the outskirts of Philadelphia. Wayne, meanwhile, skirted the capital to encamp at Merion, five miles west of Philadelphia on the road to Lancaster. Belatedly Washington was accepting Wayne's advice to rush westward on the Lancaster Road to a point near Waynesborough, from which they could cross the Great Valley to the iron centers. The route was roundabout and long, but it would place the Americans between the British and Warwick.

2

"There never was, nor never will be a finer opportunity of giving the enemy a fatal blow than the present—for God's sake, push on as fast as possible." No ordinary brigadier would dare to use such a tone to his superior; this urgent and imperative demand must have made a fearful dent in Washington's accustomed calm. Anthony Wayne, however, was no respecter of rank; when he thought Washington timorous and overcautious, he prodded his commander into action. Had one of Wayne's own captains dared send a note of such a character, Anthony would have blistered the presumptuous fellow with a searing blast, but Washington, understanding and forgiving, measured Anthony's enthusiastic optimism accurately. Far from taking offense at Wayne's peremptory demand, Washington approved of it. "Give me," he replied, "the earliest information of your moves, that I may know how to govern mine by them."

Confident that Brandywine had been only a check to Continental aspirations rather than a blow, Wayne, as usual, demanded action. Now that the Americans had refilled their ammunition pouches and replenished their artillery, Wayne wanted a counterstroke. He could not bear to think of Howe's resting unchallenged in the fertile farmlands, raiding Wayne's own neighborhood, burning barns filled to bursting with good harvests, sending scouts even into Waynesborough to worry Polly and the children. It was, he thought, the proper time to strike; he remembered Marshal Saxe's good advice: "Terror proceeds from that consternation which is the unavoidable effect of sudden, unexpected happenings."

Eight days after Brandywine, Howe was camped on the steep slopes of South Valley Hill. His rear was covered by the woods that mounted upward to the crest just by the Blue Ball, but his flanks were made vulnerable by main highways; on his front was a gently rolling open valley. Guns planted on the hilltops in his rear and on the summit of North Valley Hill, less than a mile from Howe's encampment, could pen the British in a narrow trap from which they could escape only by marching in the open valley under fire of Continental cannon. If Washington's main army, screened by the mountains, swung north and east to place themselves between Swedes' Ford and the British while Wayne blocked the highway to the west, the trap would be complete. Brigadier-General William Smallwood's Marylanders, coming north to join the Continental forces, could take the crest of the South Valley Hill and thus prevent Howe's escape. "It is," said Wayne, "the strongest ground I ever saw. We risked but little, the enemy their all." He demanded insistently that Washington attack at once.

Washington approved the plan. He ordered Wayne to lead an infantry division and a four-gun battery to the British left, while he himself hurried on the thirty-six-mile circuitous detour which would put his men between the British and the Schuylkill. At best, if the maneuver prospered Howe's army would be smashed to bits; at worst, Wayne could at least cut off the British baggage. For once, however, Washington's timing was at fault. Whether he underestimated the time that he would need for marching through the mountain region, whether he failed to consider the speed with which impetuous Wayne would make the short ten-mile trip to Howe's flank, or whether his plans went wrong by interception of dispatches, is difficult to ascertain; the fact remains that Wayne arrived at his ambush long before either Washington or Smallwood was in position. For two days Wayne waited, hidden in the woods. He vented his impatience by writing Washington, demanding that the Commander-in-Chief hurry faster.

His hiding-place was admirably chosen. Knowing every inch of the territory well, Wayne picked a forest meadow close to Paoli Tavern and near Waynesborough, less than four miles from Howe's headquarters. Well off the highroad, accessible from the valley only by a narrow woods path, though with a wide road west for escape in case of danger, he was certain that his lurking-spot would not be found by British scouts. Lest foragers be caught by Howe, Anthony, much to Polly's dismay, requisitioned ten of Waynesborough's fat cows. Properly butchered and skillfully carved, these animals yielded his 1,500 men perhaps five pounds of beef per soldier, enough to keep them well fed until the slower-moving Washington and Smallwood were ready to fight Sir William Howe.

Waiting patiently was never congenial to Anthony Wayne. Hearing nothing from either Washington or Smallwood, he decided to launch a single-handed attack with his small force against the British thousands, but when he came within half a mile of Howe's encampment, close to Howell's tavern, he changed his mind and hurried back to his hiding-place. The move, of course, was a mistake. No force of 1,500 men crashing through the woods within so short a distance of an alert enemy could escape notice. British sentries sounded an alarm; Howe's men rushed to arms; they waited Wayne's arrival.

Of this Wayne was unaware; he thought that he was undiscovered. He did not know that Howe had heard of his presence. Smoke columns rising from the fires that cooked the ten fat cows had given Howe a clue that men were camped in the vicinity; a few Continental soldiers, violating strict orders by firing their muskets to clear their guns of jammed cartridges, made it certain that troops were near. Howe had been expecting an attack, though from the intercepted messages that he had captured he thought that it would not be launched so soon. Far from being surprised by Wayne's proximity, Howe had ample information.

It was now Howe's turn to surprise the Continentals. Knowing that Great Valley farmers were strongly Whig and that gossip in the camp would soon seep through to Wayne, Howe let information slip that he was moving on to Philadelphia. At two o'clock in the morning of September 20, he announced, he would leave for Swedes' Ford to cross the yellow Schuylkill. His men, he was confident, would talk about the plans; any rebel spies in camp would soon hear of the arrangements. Only a few important commanders knew of Howe's real plans. A few regiments were to march off slowly to the east, carrying through the elaborate bluff, but more were to fall on Wayne's unsuspecting ambushers. Lieutenant-Colonel Thomas Musgrave of the 40th ("The Excellers," as they were called from their Latin numerals XL) was to climb the hill from Howell's tavern to the Lancaster Road, for the double purpose of opposing Smallwood if that laggard should arrive unexpectedly and cutting off Wayne's escape toward Philadelphia. Major-General Sir Charles Grey, with the Black Watch, was to conduct the main attack. By Howe's strategy, Grey was to move silently westward along the Swedes' Ford road. When he arrived in Wayne's vicinity, he was to race up the woods path. Either Howe knew nothing of the good road that led west from the rear of Wayne's encampment, or he thought it unimportant, for he left that way unguarded.

To make surprise more certain, Grey instructed all his men to use only the bayonet. Eighteenth-century armies, even crack Guards regiments, were never wholly trustworthy; marching soldiers, seeing shadows, fired recklessly; nervous privates, fingering their triggers, shot off muskets by mistake. Such noise, Grey knew, would advertise the arrival of his columns; in the darkness of a rainy night powder flashes would betray the exact location of the British. If Grey's men used cold steel, Wayne could not see exactly where the enemy was, while Britishers could thrust their bayonets toward anyone who fired a gun. Grey's orders ran counter to certain cherished traditions. Some regiments boasted proudly that their guns were always loaded; if their charges were withdrawn, their pride would be broken. For these, a special ruling was permitted; they could keep cartridges in their muskets, provided their flints were removed; thus Grey won the nickname "No-Flint." Other groups, with less ironclad customs, carried empty guns with bayonets plugged in the barrels.

As early as seven o'clock in the evening, Howe started his preparations. His soldiers, keyed up for an early morning departure, soon realized that important changes had taken place, and though some believed that these premature movements could be explained by fear of rainy weather later, others suspected an attack. Those who knew that Wayne was near were certain that Grey and Howe planned a surprise.

Of these altered preparations Wayne knew nothing. Happy in the belief that he understood Howe's plans, Wayne reacted precisely as the canny Britisher had hoped. As a careful general, he set guards about his camp; to keep his powder dry against the coming rain, he had guns and cartridge boxes wrapped; in order to be ready on the instant, he saddled and holstered his horse and threw a thick cloak over the animal to shield it from the wet. These were the precautions of a vigilant commander; they testified to his alertness and to his watchfulness. Then, certain that all was ready for an emergency, he told his men to rest. He did not let them know what action he was planning, lest news of his intentions leak to the enemy, but his tenseness, his nervous watchfulness, his more-than-customary inspections, caused them to suspect some sudden enterprise. Wayne's soldiers, hardened campaigners now, snatched a little sleep, but he himself was too excited to relax. Humpton, Hartley, Brodhead, and Ben Temple, a Virginian dragoon commander, killed time impatiently by checking up their final plans for the surprise. It was unnecessary, for Wayne and his colonels had long since perfected every arrangement, but they were too nervous to rest. None of them was at ease. Temple, restless as a boy, fidgeted impatiently; twice he mumbled some excuse to his companions and went out to look again at his pickets; again and again he congratulated himself that his mounted sentinels, his vedettes, were alert. Sloping-shouldered Brodhead, with thin lips pressed tightly together, drew innumerable little diagrams only to crumple up the papers and toss them to the floor. Slow-witted Humpton went over his orders again and again, mumbling in thick Yorkshire dialect, to memorize his part in the adventure. Methodical and plodding, Humpton always had to drive such things deep into his mind; he hated, more than anything else he knew, to change his plans and to make decisions quickly. He distrusted men who thought at lightning speed. Hartley tried to chat with Wayne, but each man's attention wandered; as tense as if they were adolescents starting on their first important enterprise, they pulled out their heavy watches a hundred times, to make sure that they would not miss the all-important moment to begin attack. Wayne thought that the night was almost gone; he looked at his watch and found that it was not yet ten o'clock.

Temple hurried in, clutching the sleeve of a frail old farmer. Wayne and Hartley leaped up from the table, where they had been about to start a game of cards; Humpton stared in heavy, open-mouthed astonishment; Brodhead, resting both elbows on the table, looked hard at the dragoon and his captive.

"I caught a spy—" said Temple.

"Spy!" roared Wayne. "You've got the chaplain's father! That's old Morgan Jones, our Davy's pappy. Look at him! He has the same long horse-face that our parson has. I've known this fellow all my life. If he's a spy, why, so am I."

The old man grinned toothless thanks. "I tried to tell him that," he said. "He thought I was a lobster-back without a uniform." But then he ceased his grin. He turned serious and earnest. "Tony, the British are coming. They'll be here almost any minute."

Wayne scoffed. He told the old man that he must be mistaken. "We hear," he said, "that Howe is marching just the other way; he's crossing Swedes' Ford at two o'clock."

"That's what he wants you to think," retorted Jones. "He's really coming this way. Josh Clayton's boy was in their camp. He says the soldiers there are talking of a change in plan. He got away from there at nine o'clock—dodged his way past the sentries, he said, when one of the fellows tripped over a root; he says that Howe had his men all in line and that they were ready to start."

Wayne knew the Clayton boy, and he was by no means certain that the lad was clever enough to interpret what he saw, but he took no chances. He ordered Temple to send out more vedettes; he doubled his pickets; he went out himself to see if all was well. Yet something went wrong with his arrangements. His new vedettes went but a scant mile before they met men upon the road. Josiah Stoddard, one of Ethan Allen's men at Ticonderoga, challenged sharply, but was answered by a friendly hail. Stoddard called for the countersign and was answered promptly by the proper words. Somehow, it seems, the American watchwords for that night—"Here we come—there they go"—had leaked to the British. Stoddard in spite of the responses was suspicious; he fired his pistol, dug his spurs into his horse's flanks, and galloped to the ambush. There was no answering fire from the advancing British; Grey's no-flint order remained in force.

Grey knew now that he could not catch Wayne by surprise, but since he was not far from the hiding-place, he double-quicked in the dark. At the crossroads forge he roused the blacksmith and forced him, still in his nightgown and slippers, to show him the woods path that led uphill to the camp. Another vedette challenged; he too fired and wheeled about.

Wayne, warned by his fleeing vedettes, bawled orders for his men to get in line. His foresight in having them sleep upon their arms, with their cartouche boxes covered by their coats, proved its wisdom now, for rain was falling heavily; had he been less careful, all the American powder would have been too drenched to use. Brightly burning campfires gave sufficient light for his men to scramble hastily into place. Wayne kept his head. He shouted to Temple to get the artillery started westward on the road away from camp; he yelled to Hartley to hold back the British advance until the troops were organized. He seized Humpton, goggling in the corner, and pushed him toward the flank, shrieking to him to get his men in motion. Humpton, dazed by the sudden happenings, wanted to argue, but Wayne cursed with such explosive force that Humpton was almost blown away.

Now, less than ten minutes after the vedettes had given

warning, the Black Watch van approached. Hartley fired, dropping some of the attackers, but the rest plunged forward. The British were difficult to see as they came out of the dark forest into the clearing; the Americans were silhouetted against their campfires. Temple did his job well; above the shrieks of wounded men Wayne heard the rumble of artillery wheels. Hartley's men stood firm, loading and firing with precision; on one side of the forest meadow, Brodhead coolly collected his men to take them off to safety. On the far side of the field, where Humpton was in charge, confusion reigned. Wayne swung about and yelled to Major Ryan. "Get over there to Humpton! Tell that fool to wheel about and take those men down White Horse Road. Do it quickly, too!" Ryan set out on the run. Racing along the edges of the camp, behind the lines of Hartley's dogged troops, he reached the bumbling Humpton. In breathless haste he blurted out Wayne's orders, but the bewildered Colonel, stupid and pig-headed, only half listened to the words. He grunted heavily and told Ryan to go back and say that everything would be all right.

There was difficulty finding Wayne. That enterprising, quick-thinking general was all over the ground at once. Pausing only to shout to his orderly Paddy to take the horse away, for it would be senseless to ride in such a constricted forest glade, he ran from post to post. He yelled praise to Hartley and told him to hold out a little longer; he ran over to Brodhead to start him after the artillery; he formed the 1st Pennsylvania as a guard to hold back the ever advancing Black Watch; he hurried over to Humpton to see what was delaying that officer. He saw, even in the firelight, that clumsy Humpton had made a mess of everything. Instead of taking the proper road, as he had been ordered to do by both Wayne and Ryan, Humpton had faced about and was sending his men into danger; they were brightly lighted by the campfires. The Black Watch, lunging forward with their swords and bayonets, had perfect targets.

Scores of Americans were cut down. Wounded men, run through by bayonets or slashed by swords, shrieked for quarter; the Black Watch, shouting triumphantly, pressed forward.

Someone snatched a brand to set fire to the few rude huts that the Americans had set up; the camp began to burn. Yells from wounded men were unheeded in the general excitement. Humpton's confused troops, firing raggedly against an almost invisible enemy, ran helter-skelter. The Colonel, now at his wit's end, barked orders that were contradictory when they were intelligible; Wayne, rushing into the danger zone, snapped out commands to get the men safely out by the one road that lay open. Meanwhile, Hartley and the 1st Pennsylvania stood stalwartly as the bulwarks of the camp.

Legends clustered in after years about this battle at Paoli. Remembering Wayne's energetic work of bringing order back after the Humpton chaos, some survivors swore that he had made a quick change in his uniform. The lining of his coat, they said, was red; Wayne, they declared, ripped off his coat and turned it inside out. Then, clad in what seemed in the firelight to be a British scarlet tunic, he took command of the Black Watch and ordered them to cease attack. Another story told how Wayne galloped on the saddled horse to take refuge in the middle of the big green box bush by the rear veranda of Waynesborough. Then, as the British swung about to chase the fleeing general, Wayne's troops filed off to safety. These stories were completely false, just as were the charges that the British deliberately massacred sick and helpless soldiers, and that Hessians—none of whom were actually present at the battle— butchered helpless men until the blood ran out the touchholes of their muskets. Paoli was a fertile field for propaganda; to stir Whig sympathies, clever minds imagined horrors to brand the invaders as heartless brutes.

The facts of the engagement were sad enough. More than 200 Americans died of bayonet thrusts, almost 100 more were seriously wounded. Grey, on the other hand, escaped with remarkably few casualties, only a dozen men in all. Yet the defeat was not a shameful rout. With half the numbers of the British, Wayne and Hartley blocked Grey's advance. When Humpton was at last set upon the proper road and when the artillery was hauled away, Wayne retreated slowly. For two miles, he fought a dogged rear-guard action. He escaped by the back road that

led northwest into the iron regions; almost immediately thereafter, he crossed the Schuylkill to rejoin Washington. While
on the march, he fell in at last with Smallwood's Marylanders,
who had heard the noise of battle, but who had hesitated, not
knowing what was happening, to rush into the engagement.

The unhappy Paoli affair had most unfortunate repercus-
sions. Humpton, the Colonel who had misconstrued commands,
filed formal charges that Wayne had been remiss. A court of
inquiry held to investigate the charges reported, strangely, that
the accusations, while not proved, possessed a certain residuum
of truth. Wayne, angered at this reflection on his military skill,
called for a court-martial. The trial, held under the presidency
of Lord Stirling, lasted four days, listening to a farrago of
"evidence" by Humpton, Brodhead, and Morgan Connor,
colonels who stood to win promotion if Wayne should be convicted. Ten other officers testified that Wayne had not been
alert. On Wayne's behalf, Hartley, Michael Ryan, Mentges,
and Butler gave detailed explanations of Wayne's carefulness;
on cross-examination, moreover, much of the prosecution's testimony turned out to be mere hearsay. Unanimously the court-
martial exonerated Wayne, declaring that he had done "everything that could be expected from an *active, brave* and *vigilant*
officer." Anthony was acquitted "with the highest honor."

In after years, Wayne's neighbors of Paoli commemorated
the disaster by a monument which voiced their detestation of
No-Flint Grey. Terming the affair an "atrocious massacre,"
they set up a stone announcing that the soldiers buried there
were "victims of cold-blooded cruelty" and of "British barbar-
ity." The inscription praises Wayne as an officer "whose military conduct, bravery and humanity were equally conspicuous
throughout the Revolutionary War."

3

Romantic fiction misleads readers. After a battle, a warrior's
first thoughts should be of patriotic service; his soul should

reek of glory. Mundane matters should, at such a time, be unimportant; spiritual concerns should be supreme. Wayne was cast in no such mold. Much as he would have enjoyed playing a conventionally romantic role, he was, in every instance, honest and sincere. After Paoli, his first worries were far removed from those which idealists expected. He wanted a clean shirt.

Polly, worried sick at the yells and shrieks from the woods to the west, torn by apprehensions, had no authentic news of what had happened. Wild rumors ran unchecked that every American had been bayoneted, that the British had driven all the Continentals into a raging fire where every rebel had been burned, that blood was rolling down the hill into the Great Valley in a crimson flood. No one knew the truth.

Then finally came news of Anthony, in the form of a letter from the iron country telling her, in his usual economy of words, "The Enemy made a hard push to camp on the night before last," but omitting all details. They had, he said, "some loss and thought prudent to halt." As a reporter of the battle Wayne was less than adequate, but he was not concerned with giving military data: "I am in great want of a Shirt or two— my boy Paddy carried all, with my other baggage to Reading." He closed his brief note with a request that made poor Polly uneasy, for in sending his best and kindest love to "our mothers, sisters and little children," he omitted any mention of herself, except to say in closing, "Adieu, my dear Polly." He signed it, as he did all his letters, most formally, "Ant^y. Wayne."

Wayne was not the only Continental officer to be concerned about his clothing in those hot, muggy September days. Major John Harper, taken at Brandywine, wrote, with British permission, on behalf of himself, Francis Johnston, and Persifor Frazer, his fellow prisoners, to ask for linen. Wayne, who had no spare shirts of his own and who on his precipitous retreat had no time to look for Harper's baggage, ignored the letter. A month later, Frazer repeated the request; it was a pathetic appeal, since the captured officers had enjoyed no change of linen since the battle. Anthony himself was more fortunate; Abraham Robinson rode to his aid with saddlebags of shirts after Polly gathered up every scrap of linen clothing she could find about the house; she borrowed from her neighbors to fit out Anthony. Dandy Wayne was well supplied.

With the shirts Abraham brought news of what had taken place at Waynesborough. On the night of the battle, he reported, polite British officers, one of whom may have been John André, knocked at the front door, saying that they had come to search the house. Though Polly assured them that she had not seen her husband for a month, and that no soldiers were concealed there, the party ransacked house and grounds. They were so thorough that they poked their bayonets deep into the big, spicy box bush that stood beside the rear veranda. Failing to find the General, the British then took Robert Shannon and Darby, the old butler, into custody as hostages for Waynesborough's good behavior. Abraham said, too, that Polly was despondent, that after Brandywine and Paoli she gave up hope of American success. Fearing another enemy raid, she purposed to sell the time of her indentured people at any price that she could get, lest they too be carried off.

Anthony lost his temper. Never one to show despondency about military setbacks, though he entertained blue devils on lonely evenings, he could not understand why Polly should despair. He wrote her a long letter, his most extensive since his leaving Marcus Hook, assuring her that the Americans were growing stronger all the time, that Howe could not possibly succeed, and that by spring the war must certainly be over. He added a note which, though it seemed to him merely an act of prudence, made Polly feel that his reassurance was pretense. "Remove," he said, "my books and Valuable Writings some Distance from my House." To Polly his request meant only that he expected British raiders to return at once. Her despondency blackened, nor was she happy in noticing that Anthony, sending his "kindest love and wishes to both our Mothers and Sisters" and asking her to "kiss our little people for me," again omitted any token of love for her. He closed with the proud boast: "My sword will shortly point out the way to Victory, peace and happiness."

His prediction was no idle boast. In their camp twenty miles above Philadelphia, American generals were drawing plans to smash at Howe's defenses around Philadelphia. Spies brought in word that the British Army was widely flung, that some regiments had been sent south of the city to invest Continental forts upon the Delaware, that certain regiments were beyond the Schuylkill westward of the capital, that others patrolled the water front, while some camped at Germantown, five miles above the city. Washington, Wayne, and other strategists believed that surprise attacks upon the Germantown positions might win great success. As has been noted, before a battle Anthony invariably anticipated death; he liked to dramatize himself as standing on the threshold of eternity, holding glory in his grasp. He therefore had a premonition that this Germantown engagement, scheduled for daybreak of October 4, would either end in triumphant American victory with himself riding at the head of cheering troops entering the capital, or that it would cause his death. The night before the battle he sat down to write another letter to his wife:

"I have often wrote to you on the eve of some expected and uncertain event but never on any equal to the present—before this reaches you, the Heads of many Worthy fellows will be laid low—dawn is big with the fate of thousands. . . . We cannot fear—My Heart sets lightly in its mansion—every Artery beats in unison and I feel unusual Ardour. . . . It is not in Mortal to Command Success nor length of days, if it shall be my fate to fall tomorrow I will not fall singly nor unavenged— a Bloody track shall mark my Setting Sun."

Polly could not help being impressed by Anthony's unwonted eloquence. In closing his letter, he made his usual request that she tell his "poor old Mother," his sisters, and other relatives that he was thinking of them all and, to her delight, he added: "May God protect and shield you. Adieu, my dear Polly, and believe me ever yours." He sealed the letter, addressed it, and dispatched it by a special rider; then he hurried to council to discuss final plans for the attack on Germantown.

Washington's carefully complex plan appealed to a surveyor's imagination. Mathematically exact, timed almost to a split second, the scheme was as modern as this morning's newspaper. Four separate columns were to fall simultaneously upon Germantown. Starting at seven in the evening from a point well out of range of British scouts, the troops were to march all night, quietly and without allowing a single spectator to escape, until, by two o'clock in the morning of October 4, they would each be within two miles of the enemy. They were then to rest, to eat a bite of breakfast and drink a swig of rum; at four, they would resume the march, taking care not to make a sound that would alarm enemy pickets; as soon as the first rays of the sun shot above the horizon, all four columns were to charge at once upon the enemy outposts. Not with guns, for that would make a noise, but with bayonets, as No-Flint Grey had taught the lesson at Paoli.

John Armstrong led the right wing of this well-ordered plan. Leading those Pennsylvania militiamen whom Wayne had trained at Chester, he was to strike Knyphausen's Hessians on the steep hills by Wissahickon Creek. By hammering them hard, Armstrong could keep those mercenaries out of Germantown and so make the task of other leaders easier. Armstrong said he understood; he filed off along the road that paralleled the Schuylkill, promising that at sunrise anyone who listened would hear his two guns bark. His 2,000 militia boys, nervous with excitement, boasted that by six o'clock no Hessians would be left alive.

Smallwood, dilatory at Paoli, swore that he and his Maryland militiamen would win the war by driving in the British right. He and Devil David Forman's Jerseymen together would clear their territory of invaders. He warned Nathanael Greene to look out for the British fugitives whom he and Forman would send flying. Greene, somewhat to the left, went with Major-General Adam Stephen's Virginians and Brigadier-General Alexander McDougall's New Yorkers to attack one section of the British center; Washington, Sullivan, and Wayne, in the center, flung themselves ahead to hit the keystone of Howe's line. If all worked well, the four columns, striking with deadly accuracy at exactly sunrise, would crumple the British guard. No section of the enemy could help another; Sir William Howe, facing simultaneous assault from every quarter, would be too flustered to send efficient help to any of the victims. A defeat of such magnitude, coming so soon after Saratoga, might drive Howe out of America.

Unhappily, everything went wrong. The fog, which except at Long Island always worked in Britain's interest, blanketed the roads with dense, clammy clouds; troops, unable to see the men ahead of them, floundered helplessly. They lost precious time; they strayed into wrong roads and took improper turnings; the schedule went to pot. Cautious old Armstrong was at least two hours late; Smallwood and Forman wandered everywhere except upon their proper roads. Couriers who tried to hold the several divisions in liaison with each other could not even keep their bearings with a compass. A Maryland colonel, Josias Carvel Hall, was knocked senseless when his horse carried him "under a cider-press" that Hall did not see in the fog.

Stephen, swigging whisky to keep the cold fog from his bones, got roaring drunk and led his men into strange places; then, seeing troops approaching, he violated instructions by ordering a vigorous fire. His Virginians shot valiantly and with deadly accuracy until horrified yells from the "enemy" disclosed, even to Stephen's rum-soaked brain, that they were shooting down fellow Americans, Colonel George Matthews's "Tall Virginians." Matthews wheeled about, and raced back to what he thought was Greene's protection, but, losing himself in the fog, he ran into a regiment of British soldiers. Poor Matthews was obliged to yield his sword. One of his soldiers escaped capture. Anna Maria Lane, wife of a private soldier, fought all day, receiving a severe wound that made her limp for the rest of her life. For years she boasted that she, a woman, had outfought all the Tall Virginians.

Before this time, Howe was well apprised of Washington's intention. The marching rebels, blundering through the fog, could not keep quiet; they tripped and fell, clanging their arms with betraying noise; they bumped their cannon into trees and made the bedlam worse by swearing irritably; they crashed and banged and thumped. Residents along the roads heard the passing army; in the fog and darkness Tories raced to warn the British that rebels were arriving. Howe heard of their approach

by three o'clock in the morning, two full hours before the attack
was scheduled to begin.

Under such circumstances, it was a miracle that the expedition made any sort of progress, yet Washington, Sullivan, and
Wayne strode forward almost on schedule time. At Mt. Airy,
or Beggar's Town—the name is a corruption of Mathias van
Bebber's pretty country town—they bayoneted British pickets
and captured a field piece; they pressed irresistibly into Germantown's one lane. Sullivan and Wayne, trusting that Armstrong and Greene, at least, if not Smallwood and Forman,
would close in on the flanks, dashed into the heart of the village.
Meanwhile Washington moved cautiously to clear up any British troops who might be lurking behind barns, stone walls, and
orchard trees. The American victory seemed complete. Happily
the Continental Army shouted its war cry—"Remember Paoli!"

Wayne, pushing irresistibly into the town, swept down the
east side of the Germantown road as far as the present site of
the high school, half a mile ahead of Washington. He won more
ground than any other leader, for Sullivan, on the west side of
the road, stopped halfway between Wayne and the Commander-
in-Chief, and Greene, far to the east of the village, was in un-
contested territory.

Yet, with triumph in his grasp, Wayne saw success snatched
away. The old Excellers, that famous 40th which had been so
troublesome at Brandywine and Paoli, proved again a stum-
bling-block. Lieutenant-Colonel Musgrave, rushing up to support his pickets, used Chief Justice Chew's stone house as a
fortress. Slamming tight the heavy ground-floor shutters and
barricading the oak front door, he stationed troops to bayonet
any rebel who might gain an entrance; he himself, with the
great majority of his 120 men, fired at the Americans through
windows on the second floor. The fog had lifted now; the troops
no longer groped in mist.

Against Wayne's excellent advice to keep Musgrave shut up
in his prison, book-trained American generals, chief among
them Massachusetts Henry Knox, played the classic game of
war. From time immemorial, textbook writers had stressed the
maxim that no fortified position should be left untaken in the

rear. This Chew house, a hasty council decided, was such a stronghold; it must, then, be reduced before the Americans continued their advance. Wayne fumed when he heard the decision; he protested that this would lose the battle. He and Sullivan, both now ahead of Washington, waited restlessly while Knox hauled up four six-pound guns to batter down the fort. An hour and a half was thus frittered away, giving Howe ample time to consolidate his forces. Armstrong's delay made it possible to transfer reinforcements from the Wissahickon; Greene's confusion allowed Howe to bring in soldiers from that distant flank. Even in the center Howe made gains, for Sullivan, alarmed when he discovered that he was alone, turned back to find what had become of Greene and Washington. The British thus recovered confidence; instead of retreating hurriedly to Philadelphia, as Howe had thought of doing, they came back to the battle. Sullivan and Wayne had to abandon the guns and men which they had taken.

The battle did not last long thereafter. With Howe uniting all his strength, with Cornwallis racing up from Philadelphia with more reinforcements, with half the American strength lost somewhere in the country, Washington's chance faded. He called off his men and ordered a retreat. For seven miles the British soldiers pursued them, Wayne fighting a persistent rear-guard action to keep them at a distance.

Germantown was a setback. The Americans lost 1,000 men, half of whom were prisoners; the British suffered casualties of only 500. North Carolina's brigadier, Francis Nash, was so badly hurt when he was toppled from his horse by a spent cannon ball that he died within a few days. Wayne had his roan horse shot from under him and his left hand was seared by the same ball; his left foot was badly bruised, though not enough to prevent his hobbling over to mount another horse. On the British side, Brigadier-General James Agnew of the 44th died at the very end of the battle, when a civilian sniper shot him through the star of his uniform coat. A medal granted to Musgrave's Excellers in commemoration of the victory was for many years thereafter awarded, as a sign of merit, to deserving officers and soldiers of the 40th. The medal, suspended on a

blue cord round the neck of the fortunate recipient, was regarded as equivalent to a decoration.

Yet, though Germantown was lost, the results were not disastrous. European military men, marveling at Washington's
strategic skill, looked upon Washington as an able general and
on his men as particularly well-trained soldiers. This realization
that the former colonists had forged an army capable of standing on terms of equality with crack British regiments did much
to win European sympathy for the patriotic cause. Germantown
and Saratoga convinced the French of the desirability of an
alliance with the Thirteen Colonies.

Two days after the battle, while Wayne was recuperating at
Pawling's Mill, twenty miles north of Germantown, he sent
another note to Polly, his third within a week. Anxious to mend
the steadily widening rift in their relations, he asked her to
come, under Abraham Robinson's escort, to visit him at camp.
But with his customary clumsiness where Polly was concerned
he hid his eagerness by a postscript rebuking her for thinking
of selling the remaining time of a favorite servant, Rachel. "I
would not have it done," he wrote severely, "for one thousand
Guineas." Polly, wounded by the reproof, worried by her responsibilities at Waynesborough now that Shannon was in British hands, would not take the time to go to see her wounded
husband. It was an unfortunate decision, for Anthony was convinced that Polly no longer cared for him.

CHAPTER VIII

Enter the Hannibals

WAYNE WAS sick and tired of masterly retreats, of cleverly contrived escapes, of brilliant withdrawals, and of dogged rear-guard actions; he wanted no more moral victories where the enemy kept everything but glory. Brandywine, Paoli, and Germantown left searing marks upon his mind; as a forthright man of practicality, he wished for tangible results. Doubt sprouted in him as to Washington's ability; he questioned if the Commander-in-Chief could lead the Continentals through to victory. Washington, he came to think, was much too slow, too hesitant, and overtimorous; he had not sufficient suppleness of mind. Whenever fortune smiled, George Washington missed his chance. Three times within a month before—at Brandywine, in the Great Valley, and at Germantown—he had thrown away his opportunity; if this irresolution should continue, Continentals might as well give up the war.

Perhaps, thought Wayne in charity toward his commander, the fault was not all Washington's. The Old Man—Washington was forty-five—meant well, and most of the time he had good judgment, but he lacked decision. Before he took important steps, Washington liked to call upon his generals for advice. He was, in Wayne's opinion, too fond of holding interminable councils of war, those everlasting jabber-meetings at which lion talkers spouted brag to each other, though, as Wayne well knew, those fiery orators were only lamblike fighters. Councils decided nothing; they merely postponed action; they wasted precious time which could be better spent in fighting. "A council of war," said Wayne disgustedly, "is the surest way to do nothing."

142

Four times during the autumn of 1777 Wayne pleaded with his commander to take the aggressive. Sir William Howe, besieged in Philadelphia, could be Burgoyned if Washington would act aggressively. All that would be needed, Wayne declared, would be to send an army down past the old Blue Bell Tavern at Darby to the banks of the Delaware, and thus cut off the British both by water and by land. To his delight, Washington agreed, and Wayne actually started out upon the expedition. "I am this moment ordered to march at the head of a Body of Troops to feel his strength," Anthony wrote Polly jubilantly. "The pleasing dawn of Success and Liberty will shortly spread its rays and Influence through this Our happy land. Toryism and Tyranny will quickly fall, Never to rise again. Let all our friends and Neighbors know this happy news, for the truth of which I pledge my faith and honor." But then, to Wayne's intense disgust, Washington recalled the expedition. Old Fabius had thought the matter over and had decided that Wayne's party could be cut off by a rear attack. It would be better, Washington declared, to try again some other time.

That second time did not come. Howe's naval auxiliaries, aided by traitors, broke open Wayne's chevaux-de-frise, thus making it possible for the British to get supplies by sea. Wayne, raging inwardly at Washington's caution, suggested that in view of these circumstances the Continentals try direct assault upon the city, but he was again overruled. Nor would Washington think of an attack upon New York, nor upon vulnerable British outposts. These were not the type of actions that Fabius, the cautious Roman, would have essayed. "We've tried Fabius," roared Wayne. "Let's see what Hannibal can do!"

Hannibal, it developed, had as his eighteenth-century counterpart none other than Horatio Gates, whose star was high in its ascendancy because of his recent capture of Burgoyne. Charles Lee, sour and embittered Englishman who made war in company with his spaniels and his doxy, was even yet, despite his misfortunes, a second idol, for he had campaigned widely with professional European soldiers, and he was credited with more knowledge of warfare than any other person in America. Pennsylvania's senior major-general, Thomas Mifflin, the quartermaster who did his fighting in the countinghouse, was another upon whom Hannibal's mantle had descended. None of the favored trio seems today to bear much similarity to the brilliant Carthaginian with whom they were compared; perhaps of all the generals of the Continental Army Wayne himself came closest to that model, but the eighteenth century was never scientifically exact in matters such as this. "Lee, Gates and Mifflin," Wayne said flatly, "will point by their conduct the line which I shall follow."

He was treading none too gently upon excessively thin ice, for there were intrigues stealthily afoot in November, 1777, to demote Washington and substitute one of these Hannibals in his stead. Congress buzzed with secret plots; in their retreat safely distant from the British danger statesmen whispered that Washington had failed. Rush was their tireless spokesman. To everyone who listened, ofttimes to those who tried to turn away, Rush thundered that Washington, the overrated general, had lost his grip, and that he was a tool of timid Greene, of bookbound Henry Knox, and of that boy adventurer from the West Indies, Alexander Hamilton. Even if he were a more determined personage, sneered Rush, nothing worth while could be expected from such riffraff as his generals. Sullivan, Rush had the temerity to say, was weak, undignified, and vain, a madman and a scribbler; Stirling, proud but lazy, was an ignorant drunkard; Stephen, as everyone now knew, was nothing but a sordid, cowardly sot, brave only in his boasting.

Wayne stood well with the inveterate conservatives. His views paralleled their own. He too wished for action. The Hannibals admired him for his dash and vigor; had he been of major-general rank, Wayne would certainly have been included in the list of those considered as George Washington's successor.

Peters likewise scattered pessimism. Never an admirer of the common people, distrusting democratic ways, he moved portentously behind the scenes of intrigue. Rush could be disregarded by friends of Washington as unimportant, on the ground that the "good doctor is too great a devotee of conviviality," but Peters could not be thrust aside. His influence in Pennsylvania's government was certainly not strong, but in national affairs his

power was very deeply rooted. As secretary of the Board of War
he pulled army wires in every matter except winning Wayne a
higher rank; as intimate of statesmen, he ran an inside track.
And since the Board of War was flirting with the Hannibals,
Peters was in a position to know much about plots against
George Washington.

Peters proved an able guide through political confusion. In
the midst of Wayne's criticisms of George Washington, when
he was edging ever closer to the Hannibals, Peters warned that
dangers lay ahead. He advised Wayne to talk more cautiously,
giving him the wise advice to cultivate domestic virtues. Dick
said that he himself had set a good example; delightedly, he
told Wayne of great news in the Peters household. Sally, he
announced, had made Dick a father, which implied that Anthony was now, by courtesy, a grandfather: "My *filial duty* calls
upon me to inform you that your Daughter has made you a
Grandfather by bringing me a son. She is very well and the
Buntling promises fair."

The news was somewhat surprising. Anthony remembered
the letter that Joseph Wood had sent him at Golgotha in which
Joe had licked his lips by saying that Peters was incapable of
children. He felt again a twinge of jealousy, so strong that he
delayed in writing Dick a letter of congratulation, as he had
delayed felicitations on the marriage; he envied Peters the
future that gloating Dick was promising himself: "I look forward to the time when I shall be busy in planting potatoes.
I shall not suffer anything to break in upon my rural Employ-
ments except now and then some Avocations and particularly
the very agreeable one of *planting* a man."

Wayne's thoughts were with Sally, but not with any other
lady, as Polly saw with pain when she received a letter asking
pointedly about the welfare of his war horse but omitting any
query as to how his wife might feel. He was glad to hear that
Robert Shannon, his overseer, had been freed from his captivity,
but it was plain enough that Anthony was writing merely duty
letters while his attention wandered elsewhere.

He was, as it happened, worried about how to keep his men
from freezing. Winter set in early in the fall of 1777, while

the Continental Army pitched its camps upon the hills of eastern Pennsylvania; sleet, snow, and rain beat down unmercifully upon an ill-clad, half-starved army. Officers and men who had lost their baggage at Brandywine looked like scarecrows; men without uniforms or blankets patched their clothes as best they could and stripped the dead to fit the living; but with winter pressing close these makeshifts offered scant relief. Unless new clothing came at once, the Pennsylvania troops would all desert. No one could expect men who were so close to their warm homes to suffer in silence; if Washington wished to maintain an army, he must protect them from the sleet and snow that even now were sweeping down from the Pennsylvania hills.

Wayne pressed for drastic action. He went to Washington for aid, but found that the harassed commander had no stores to draw upon. He then pleaded with his state to send relief, but members of the Pennsylvania Council of Safety, absorbed in petty politics, professed that Dandy Wayne was worried without cause. He thought of commandeering clothing, but as a mere brigadier he had no authority to confiscate such goods from civilians.

Other states were in similar predicaments. Wayne, attending a conference on how to compel them to work together, suggested that each send sufficient clothing for its troops. The plan won immediate approval; but Wayne, intent on fitting out his men before they froze, could not wait. He searched for a means to slash red tape and short-cut obstacles. By hurrying his own commissioners into the best available markets, Wayne bought up all the breeches that Pennsylvania had on sale and then took options on sufficient cloth to make five hundred coats. There was not a yard of cloth or a skein of thread in upstate Pennsylvania that Wayne did not control.

He met difficulties from an unexpected quarter. The Council of Safety, which Wayne not unnaturally supposed would be delighted to have its troops well clad, balked at paying for the clothing. Someone started a false rumor that Dandy Wayne was wasting money on unnecessary frills; the Council sent a letter reminding him that Congress had commissioned one James Mease as Clothier-General and that it would be disloyal for anyone to interfere with what Congress or James Mease planned for the comfort of the troops. Anthony received the Council's critical dispatch on Christmas Day, when snow flew blizzardlike about a starving tent colony on the hills of Valley Forge. He rubbed his eyes in sheer amazement that even Pennsylvania politicians could be so heartless and unfeeling. With chilling fingers holding a pen dipped in freezing ink, he wrote an anguished answer:

"I never pass along the line but objects strike my eye which give a painful, melancholy sensation. They almost induce me to wish that I was past either seeing or hearing. Indeed, sirs, nothing but the doubtful state that we are in keeps me in a service that has become intolerable."

Mease and the Council remained unmoved. Wayne's agents succeeded in rounding up sufficient shoes and cloth to garb every man in Wayne's command, but the Clothier-General offered one objection after another. He could not find, he said, that anyone had ever authorized Wayne to search for clothing; he refused to let the Pennsylvanians hire anyone but army tailors to make the uniforms; when Wayne offered to have the cloth cut by his own men at Valley Forge, Mease replied that no license had been issued for Wayne to employ his men in such an enterprise. Finally, when Wayne and Peters, slashing red tape, won permission for the goods to be withdrawn from Mease's warehouse for Wayne's use, the Clothier-General demurred because no definite date had been set for the release. And when at last a date was set, James Mease had gone upon vacation. With men shivering at Valley Forge for want of uniforms and with his storehouse shelves packed full of warm woolen cloth, Mease slammed the doors and went away. He would, his deputies declared, be gone indefinitely. Soldiers must wait until the boss returned, for deputies had no right to take the clothing from the shelves.

Eventually, the Clothier-General returned, refreshed by his vacation but still adamant in his bureaucracy. Of course, he said, Anthony Wayne could have the cloth, but unhappily the material could not yet be released. No buttons were available to make the uniforms, none, that is, that were approved. The only buttons that he had in stock were yellow, whereas rules distinctly stated that for Wayne's troops all buttons must be white. He was sorry, but until enough white buttons could be found, the clothing must remain in stock! Again Peters came to the rescue, winning a ruling from the Board of War that Wayne's men might wear yellow buttons. Mease reluctantly gave way before superior authority. Wagonloads of heavy woolen clothing rumbled into Valley Forge, five hundred coats and four hundred pairs of breeches, all with yellow buttons.

By this time, new needs were apparent. Wayne's brigade lacked shirts; his men, like Falstaff's troops, said Wayne, had but one shirt to a company. Anthony sent a requisition for the linen; to make sure that he would have enough in the event that Mease again proved dilatory, he asked for nine thousand shirts and for an equal number of uniforms; he added that he wished each man to have two pairs of shoes, a pair of garters, a stock, a pair of gaiters, and a hair comb. Mease, reading the requisition with growing horror, called the amount absurd. "I have already sent huge piles of shirts to Valley Forge," he complained. "The soldiers must be throwing shirts away."

For himself, Dandy Wayne picked up, here and there, fourteen yards of the best white India dimity, nine dozen hornmounted, double-gilt buttons—yellow ones—twenty-one shirt collars, and all the sewing silk that was upon the market. It was a huge supply, but he could take no chances on another shortage.

2

During the first terrible fortnight at Valley Forge, when storm, sickness, cold, and hunger ravaged the ill-clad army, Wayne suffered with his men. Sick with a stubborn cold that settled in his lungs, in constant pain because his breastbone, splintered when he fell from his shot horse at Germantown, cut sharply into his flesh, he endured their hardships. Waynesborough, where there was warmth and food and medicine, was scarcely five miles distant, but Wayne, refusing comforts, stayed in the open, directing the building of huts, visiting his sick, supervising foraging, encouraging his desperate men to hold out longer. Snow beat down upon him; he was continually wet; officers and men alike warned that if he continued his exertions, his cold would change into pneumonia; but until his men were housed he sought no refuge. During the arctic blizzards that swept the camp he slept in a canvas tent; for more hours than he slept he lay awake, shivering with cold and aching with pain.

When, by New Year's, the Pennsylvanians' huts were finished and roaring fires of oak and chestnut conquered the cold, Wayne asked for leave of absence. Army doctors said his case was serious and that he should be allowed to see his family physician, Sharp Delany, and to consult with Rush. Washington suspected that Wayne, who had not complained of illness, was seeking a pleasure furlough rather than a cure. He refused the furlough. Wayne would not argue with his leader; his cough and cold, together with the obvious lines of pain upon his features, should, he thought, have been sufficient evidence of his need for a vacation, particularly as he had been in constant active service for two years. He saluted his superior, turned about, and stalked away, but on coming to his quarters, he sat down to write a sharp demand to Peters, asking the secretary of the Board of War to get him congressional approval. "Procure leave of absence for me, otherwise I shall be necessitated to take it." Fortunately, before either desertion or congressional meddling became necessary, Washington relented. On New Year's Day, 1778, Wayne received a furlough.

Waynesborough needed his attention, because Shannon had been so long absent in a British prison and Polly was unable to manage the estate alone, but Wayne did not linger at his farm; he stood in too great need of medical care. Rush, the leading physician of the time, was sure that Anthony was tubercular; he prescribed rest. Wayne laughed at the suggestion, scouting the idea that anyone with such responsibilities could knock off work for any length of time; if only Rush or Sharp Delany would stop his cold, he said, he would continue in his duties. The two physicians patched him up, but Rush was never satisfied that Anthony was cured.

York, the nation's capital now that Philadelphia was in British hands, and Lancaster, Pennsylvania's largest inland town, buzzed with plots and rumors. Radicals such as George Bryan, draftsman of the state's ultraliberal constitution, and conservatives like Rush, agreed that army changes were essential, though on other matters they had no common ground. Native Americans waxed hot with indignation against foreigners who entered the army with high rank. De Borré's craven conduct at Brandywine was cited constantly to show that Frenchmen were rogues and cowards. For reasons of their own, the Hannibals approved young Lafayette, Washington's likable aide; they wished to send him on an expedition to the North, if only to detach the Marquis from Washington's staff. Wayne could not bring himself to ratify that choice. His first important split with the Hannibals came when he wrote Gates a note of protest: "The outcome of an expedition to Canada will be successful, but does it not deserve a serious thought before you commit the command to a *Stranger?* Was I assured that Gates or Mifflin was destined to that business, I would be content. The Honor of America and Common prudence bids you be careful to whom you commit so great a trust."

It is not unlikely that in default of Gates or Mifflin as a leader, Wayne, who knew the country well and who thrived best under an independent command, would have been willing to be nominated in their stead. It would have been an excellent choice, for Wayne was well tried in active service, whereas Lafayette had been but briefly under fire at Brandywine. Long weeks in an army hospital recovering from his wound were insufficient preparation for an expedition to the Northern wilderness. The preference of the Hannibals for Lafayette estranged Wayne from their company. When arguments rose high concerning army matters, Wayne thereafter was wholly on the side of Washington. Colonel Daniel Morgan, Pennsylvania-born leader of Virginia riflemen, taxed him one day with being hostile to the Commander-in-Chief, but was reassured by Wayne's reply that he could not criticize a leader "whom I love."

Wayne's one month's leave expired on February 1; his cold

was cured and his breastbone knitted. He rode back to Valley Forge, passing by Waynesborough, but staying only a few hours. Polly told again about her difficulties managing the farm and the tannery.

Brodhead, the ambitious colonel who had stood with Humpton in the court-martial proceedings, had made a mess of the command. A cold, unbending martinet, he had tried to make his men obey by force, when what they needed was gentleness and understanding. His routine discipline had been severe and brutal; soldiers recruited from near-by counties ran away from camp to find more food and warmer clothing at their homes. Wayne understood his men. He himself had used strict discipline to keep them controlled; his punishments had been harsh and quick. At Valley Forge, such methods were not desirable; the men stood more in need of sympathy than of the lash. Wayne's ability to inspire confidence brought order out of chaos. Within ten days he was able to tell Peters: "I have so much the Esteem and Confidence of my Troops that Desertion will no longer take place."

3

Long before the shirts and gilt buttons arrived, Wayne's men were off on active duty. His crack Pennsylvanians, smartly drilled, equipped with bayonets and muskets in place of squirrel-hunter rifles, marched in mid-February to round up cows. To some, the assignment may have seemed unworthy. Now that Mifflin, the merchant-warrior, had resigned, angry that Fabius would not recognize the merits of the Hannibals, and that St. Clair, still waiting his court-martial for the Ticonderoga matter, was suspended from the army, Wayne was senior general of his state. As such he might, like other leaders, have secured a quiet post at camp, waiting for the British to attack. But the restless Wayne could not be idle; he had to be in motion, even if it were only in foraging.

He was delayed in his departure. Some scurvy caitiff, a Tory without the shadow of a doubt, stole his best mare; once more he had to send to Waynesborough to draft another from Polly's little herd. Purely as a matter of form, for he expected to march as soon as he received another horse, he asked her a rhetorical question: "Are you better? When will you come to see me, or must I come to see you first?" She read a few lines farther before she realized what underlay his interest. If she would come at once, escorting the horse, she could bring with her a quart of wine for Tony's new friend, Priscilla Stephens, who lived close by his quarters at Valley Forge. Priscilla was ill; the wine would be good medicine. Polly ignored his invitation; she sent the horse, but neither came nor sent the wine.

Wayne's interest, as it happened, was not so much in Priscilla Stephens as in her namesake, his distant cousin Prissy Walker, in whose house he was quartered. When Anthony set out upon his foraging assignment, Prissy felt a deep personal loss. A few days after his departure she wrote a letter which, though sadly lacking in grammar and in spelling, is full of longing for the General's return. She addressed it to "My Dear jonerl." "When we Parted our iey folloed Whilst you Were in Sight, then a Gloomy Melancholy Spread over our Spirits with Such Oppression I was obliged to Retire to my Chamber to weep. . . . We long to hear from you by way of a Leter. My Love to thy dear Person, Colonel johnston and all inquiring friends if iny in Which dady and mamy and all the family joyns from your ever affectionate and truly loving Cousin whose Mental Prayer is for your Prosperity."

Wayne expected success at foraging. South Jersey, Delaware, and Maryland, always garden regions and thus far unravaged by war, were full of grain and cattle. In Delaware alone no less than seventeen thousand bushels of wheat, five thousand barrels of flour, and twelve thousand kegs of salt fish, to say nothing of corn, beans, and pickled pork, lay stored in barns, but there was no means of bringing these supplies to camp. British and American foragers had long since stripped the country of wagons and draft horses; the only food that could be brought to Valley Forge was that which came afoot.

Thousands of fat cattle, so Washington was informed, grazed, even in this wintry season, in counties south and east of Philadelphia. Raiding parties from Valley Forge, avoiding Philadelphia by a wide, semicircular swing, could drive these cattle into Valley Forge and so relieve the hunger of the soldiers. Major Henry Lee, the famous Light Horse Harry and father of Robert Edward Lee, volunteered to go to Delaware and Maryland; Wayne offered to round up beef cattle in South Jersey. The first portion of his assignment presented no difficulty. Striking almost due south from Valley Forge, close to his Waynesborough home, he went to Wilmington, and then, seeing that no British warships were near, on February 19 he crossed to the Jersey shore. He marched at once to Salem, where he issued orders commandeering all horses, cattle, sheep, and provender over a wide strip of territory between Salem and Billingsport, a district of three hundred and thirty square miles. Wayne promised to pay for hay and livestock in Continental paper.

No one questioned Jersey patriotism, but neither did anyone ever doubt Jersey's business shrewdness. Continental paper had not yet fallen to the depths it was to reach, but canny farmers were not anxious to exchange fat livestock for vague promises to pay. Promptly and with unanimity, farmers drove their cattle into woods and swamps to keep them hidden. Anthony had estimated that he would find at least three thousand head in each New Jersey county; instead he had much difficulty in rounding up a hundred and thirty animals. Even a hundred and thirty cows, however, meant more than sixty-five thousand rations of dressed beef, or at least a week's supply for such troops as remained at Valley Forge. More cattle, too, would be added as the search continued.

To drive the stock to Valley Forge involved a tedious journey. The Delaware does not freeze so far south as Wilmington; farther north, British scouts kept vigilance. Wayne herded his cattle by roundabout back roads, through central New Jersey, far to the east of Philadelphia, until, reaching Coryell's Ferry, at the present site of New Hope, he could cross the river into Pennsylvania. Danger was always present that the British, warned of his adventure, would strike hard to take the cattle from him.

His fears were well grounded. While Wayne with his 500

smartly uniformed troops slowly drove the cattle northward over frozen woods paths, a Salem Tory rowed off to a British guardship to tell of Wayne's activities. The British captain hurried the news to Philadelphia; while Wayne was en route with his cows, two enemy detachments, each consisting of about 2,000 men, crossed to New Jersey to catch Wayne in a trap. If their plan worked well, Wayne would be unable to advance lest a force four times his number overwhelm him; he could not retreat, because enemy detachments blocked the way.

Aaron Chew, a Jersey militiaman, saw the enemy arriving. At two o'clock in the morning of February 26, he galloped through a snowstorm to Wayne's camp at Haddonfield. Sentries challenged sharply, but Chew snapped out the proper countersign and passed the lines. He drew up at Wayne's quarters, shouting at the top of his lungs:

"Wayne! Wayne! General Wayne!"

The guard overpowered the militiaman and whistled for aid. This crazy fool, he thought, was drunk; he should be taken to the guardhouse. Wayne had only just gone to bed, after a drinking party in his quarters. He was deeply sunk in his first sleep, but the commotion just outside the house would have wakened Morpheus himself. He flung a window open.

"What's this? Quiet! What kind of caitiff business is this? I'll have you lashed."

Chew, still screaming, though the guardsmen, with their arms about him, vainly tried to shut his mouth, shouted:

"British coming! . . ."

"Where?" asked Wayne, thoroughly awake.

"Over the river, General. I saw them coming."

"How many? How long ago?"

The guards, convinced now that the noisy stranger was a messenger and not a spy, relaxed their hold. Chew came closer to the window:

"I can't tell you that, sir. It was snowing and too dark to see. But an hour ago I saw a boatload land on our side of the river. There was another just behind it. I heard someone say, 'We'll wait here till the others come.' I came here at once. I thought you ought to know."

"Sound the drums!" roared Wayne. "Get under arms! I'll come out there at once."

Even at that early morning hour, when he had slept so briefly, Wayne's mind moved quickly. He sent a few scouts, mounted on the better horses, back with Chew to see what was happening along the river; a small detachment drove the cattle farther inland. Wayne would have liked to send them deeper into the woods, but in the darkness and the snow he feared that many of the cows would stray; he ordered his drovers to keep to the roads but to move as fast as they could hurry the stock. Wayne, with the remainder of his men, formed to meet the enemy.

At Trenton, Count Casimir Pulaski, Polish adventurer who held a brigadier's commission and who had fought at Brandywine, had a small body of dragoons. Wayne scratched a summons, peremptory in style, demanding that Pulaski come at once. A courier could get the note to him by sunrise. The sensitive Pole was never one to shirk a battle, but he resented Wayne's curt command. Yet though he had but 50 men, he galloped immediately to join the battle. By noon he was with Wayne, alternately asking where the fighting was and protesting that he was not under Wayne's command.

Chew and the scouts by this time reported that the British forces numbered at least 4,000 men, and that more were on their way. Wayne calculated that even in the storm his cattle must be making progress toward safety, and that if he and Pulaski could delay the enemy, the livestock would be safe by nightfall. The British, he supposed, could not learn of his exact position during the few hours of daylight that remained. By slow withdrawal, it would be possible to save the cows. Pulaski would have none of it. Though he and Wayne together had less than 600 men, he boasted that they could win a victory: "My intention is to attack the Enemy by night. As strong as they may be, we can lose nothing, but gain profit."

For the first time, and the last, in all his military career Wayne hesitated; the odds, he thought, were far too great. Pulaski did not wait for Wayne's decision. His 50 dragoons charged the British van. So vigorously did he attack that the enemy leader, fearing that Wayne must have far more troops than he himself commanded, hurriedly retreated, leaving behind him much of his baggage. Pulaski wished to continue his charge to cut the fleeing enemy to pieces, but Wayne managed to restrain the impetuous Pole.

In the morning Wayne rode with Pulaski to the river. They saw the British, crowded at the ferry, waiting for flatboats to push their way through floating ice. Again Pulaski proposed a charge, but Wayne pointed out that in the daylight the British could see how few in numbers the Americans really were. If Pulaski would restrain himself until Wayne's 500 Pennsylvanians arrived, he would agree, even with such small numbers, to fight again. Action was not long delayed. Wayne was forced to fall back slowly. Pulaski lost a horse and four dragoons, but, after six hours in a strong northwest snowstorm, the British, still overestimating the strength that Wayne and Pulaski had at their disposal, "took the horrors" and embarked for Philadelphia.

The livestock now were safe. Wayne marched slowly along the back roads, picking up a few stray cattle here and there until, when well above Philadelphia, he sent off an advance consignment. Eighty-five fat cattle pushed ahead for Valley Forge. When they reached Pennsylvania, Wayne and the major portion of his men were still east of the Delaware. The movement was unfortunate. British raiders dashed swiftly north from Philadelphia. John Lacey, Wayne's luckless captain on the Canadian expedition, in command of picketing the area, was taken by surprise. Before he realized that raiders were about, they seized the cows and drove them within the British lines at Philadelphia. In any matter wherein Wayne and Lacey were concerned, poor John Lacey always was ill-starred. The Americans were luckier with the remaining forty-five Salem County cows. By taking a longer detour, these cattle, not so fat as when they left their pastures, arrived at length at Valley Forge. They gave sufficient beef for three days' rations for the army.

Wayne remained a month in Jersey, searching vainly for more animals and, with more success, contracting with a leather dealer for shoes for his division. His foraging, though not as productive as he had wished, won him a warm friendship. By bringing home thirty good horses as remounts for Lee's dragoons, he earned Light Horse Harry's enthusiastic thanks. Lee wrote Wayne a letter from the village now called Elkton. In it he thanked Wayne for the horses, and warned him against ever coming down to Maryland, where virtue was forgotten: "This town is perfectly in the virago stile. It is emblematical of old Sodom." Evidently as a result of careful investigation into Elkton's morals, he added: "There is one virtuous family within its confines." Unhappily for history, he did not give its name.

Further to show his appreciation for Wayne's gift of horses, Lee forwarded a special gift, discovered during his foraging activities: "General, you never in your life omitted one single opportunity but you afforded indubitable testimony of your attachment to malt liquor. I now present you with one barrel, excellent in quality." Wayne arranged a party at his Valley Forge quarters to celebrate the arrival of the beer. His special favorites among his colonels and majors gathered with him, and as the barrel came on, borne on the shoulders of Wayne's orderly, they raised a shout of triumph. Their merriment was short-lived, for though Lee had sent a barrel full of beer, couriers along the way had sadly lessened the amount. Only a few quarts sloshed about in the bottom of the barrel.

CHAPTER IX

An Army against Itself

WASHINGTON, ever the Fabius, stayed cautiously at Valley Forge, drilling troops in Baron von Steuben's new maneuvers; the Hannibals did nothing. At Reading, twenty-five miles up the Schuylkill, Mifflin, no longer Quartermaster-General but still one of the triumvirate on the Board of War, sat quiet as a statue; Gates, who once crushed Burgoyne, occupied his time by writing philosophical essays. Sir William Howe was immobile at Philadelphia. Wayne hated idleness. Restless, enterprising, and dynamic, he itched for action. He went to Washington with involved suggestions for prying Howe loose from the capital. "Bait him to come out," he urged. "Tell everyone that we will build a huge magazine of stores at Sunbury on the Susquehanna where Hartley is, so that Howe will go to capture it. Better yet, set up a magazine much further west, perhaps at Pittsburgh, where Brodhead is on guard. When Howe marches, both Philadelphia and New York will lie open to our attack."

Washington wondered what would happen if Howe could not be lured. Suppose, he said, that Howe preferred to stay at Philadelphia, quietly enjoying the delights of that metropolis. "Then, sir, we march upon New York." Washington remained unmoved. So did yet another of his interminable war councils, those "assemblies of mid-wives," as Alexander Hamilton called them. The council once more proved that it was the most certain way of doing nothing. Wayne, disgusted, thought again of resignation. But that would be worse. The Sabine fields lay near at hand, but they were dull, drearier than the camp. At Valley Forge Wayne enjoyed good company; he could always

work off excess energy by drilling soldiers in the new maneuvers. Waynesborough, on the other hand, had only cows to
offer, and the endless farmer grind. It would be lonely too,
since Polly had gone away to Maryland to mend her health.
It was her first absence from Chester County since the Nova
Scotia voyage, and it would be her last.

Even flirtation palled on Anthony. An old friend of his City
Tavern days, taking advantage of the fact that one could write
to general officers without paying postage, sent a cordial letter
hoping that his five years' absence had not erased her from his
memory. Wayne felt no thrill. Ann Wister had no such Attic
salt as Sally scattered; she did not sparkle like Miss Stedman
and Elizabeth Ferguson; she was notoriously content with John,
her husband. Anthony copied a line from one of his Ticonderoga
letters to Sally Robinson. He assured Ann Wister that she had
"too fixed and tender a Seat in my Memory ever to be eradi-
cated." But even as he wrote to her he thought of matters far
removed from mere flirtation; he dwelt more on her home in
festive Lancaster than on the lady's charms: "I am pleased to
find that your Interior Situation is such as to shield you from
the Savages of America and the More than Savage Britains, for,
believe me that there is not one single Vestige of Humanity
Remaining in the Troops of that Nation. They make war against
the very Arts and Sciences which the barbarous Goths and Van-
dals even Sought to Venerate and they carry it still further—
they make war against helpless Innocence, Beauty and Virtue
and stand Smiling on whilst the less barbous Indians plunge
the knife deep into the fair bosom of the prostrate tender and
trembling."

There had been Iroquois raids against isolated frontier settlements, and camp gossip had spread reports that British officers
had spurred the Indians into atrocities, but Wayne was not so
much thinking of actual massacres as of killing time by writing
thrilling letters to a girl for whom he did not care a pin. Nor,
evidently, was Ann more deeply moved; even with free postage,
she did not write again.

Soon thereafter, in early June, definite word arrived that the
British were at last ready to leave winter quarters. Some units

were already gone; heavy baggage and artillery were moved across the Delaware into New Jersey. Washington, always a devotee of councils, called one more to consider what should be done when Sir Henry Clinton, Howe's successor in command, cleared out of Philadelphia. Wayne, as always, wanted to fight. If the Americans hurried, he said, they could catch Clinton at the ferries and cut the British into bits. Or if Washington raced to Coryell's Ferry and fell upon the British flanks, as Caesar would have done, the enemy retreat would turn into a rout. Charles Lee shook his head. The thought of Continental soldiers attacking grenadiers shocked him. Steuben, drillmaster of the army, looked at Wayne aghast; it would be suicidal, he declared, to fight the British now. Louis Lebèque Duportail, engineering expert, drew maps to show that Wayne's plan was absurd. That Washington overruled his foreign experts shows that Americans fought the Revolution independently. Again, as at Germantown, Continentals, unawed by British reputation, ventured to attack a stronger, more experienced army.

Late June brings torrid weather to the Middle States; a heat wave sears the land. For a week the sun beats down with temperatures in the high nineties. Most of Pennsylvania and New Jersey enjoys balmy summer weather, but late June sees the summer at its worst. In just such a burning week the Continentals marched away from Valley Forge. Lee, still muttering about the folly of attacking grenadiers, led the van on the afternoon of June 18, 1778; Wayne followed two hours later with his Pennsylvanians, and with the troops that Thomas Conway had commanded before that would-be Hannibal resigned. They took the main road leading toward New York, marching in the evening well beyond the Schuylkill. Next day, at dawn, while Washington and the main army set out from Valley Forge, Lee and Wayne took up again their long tramp to Coryell's Ferry on the Delaware.

Their route ran thirty miles through open country, where there was little shelter. An early morning fog was wet and steamy; its soggy heat weighed down their uniforms. Later, rain set in, pouring in sheets that made the roads heavy with mud. Soldiers pushed their way through the thin fringe of

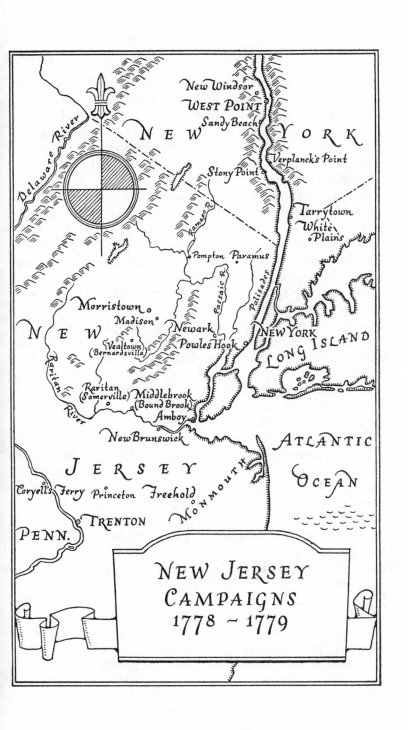

NEW JERSEY
CAMPAIGNS
1778 ~ 1779

ripening wheat along the roadway rather than slog through
sticky clay. Toward sunset the rainfall stopped and the sun
broke through the clouds, but this was small relief. Its heat
made heavy vapor rise from the drenched wool of the uniforms.
The troops pressed on, halting only to warm up rations by
smoky, wet-wood fires. They found it pleasanter to walk than
to relax in puddles of water; by splashing forward they hoped
to find shelter somewhere on the road. At midnight they
reached the Delaware, now a roaring, swollen torrent. Here
at last they rested under rude lean-tos of logs and plank.

In the morning of Saturday, June 20, Washington arrived,
his soldiers mud-splashed from head to foot. The army was
again united, close now to Clinton's line of march, but by no
means ready for an action. Guns were foul with mud and rust;
cartridge boxes dripped with wet; the officers' uniforms, once
gleaming and immaculate, with white facings glistening at neck
and cuff, hung like streaked and dirty bags. No one knew where
Clinton was. Wayne's advance detachment crossed the Delaware, halting on the far side to clean its guns and put equipment in good order, while scouts looked for the enemy. Washington, waiting on the Pennsylvania shore, mended the ravages
of the mud and storm. New cartridges were doled out and the
old ones were broken up to dry the powder.

Clinton, meanwhile, had moved slowly forward over roads
that led him through dense chestnut forests. His long baggage
train of heavy, clumsy wagons slowed his progress to a snail's
pace; he moved scarcely a mile an hour. He headed north,
although he did not even yet know whether he would cross
New Jersey by New Brunswick and so march all the way to the
Hudson, or whether he would go to Amboy, whence he could
take transports for New York. The British march was anything
but pleasant. Scotch Willie Maxwell dodged with his New
Jersey militiamen here and there about the British flanks, snip-
ping off stragglers, cutting off straying wagons. As Clinton's
unwieldy army lumbered forward, Maxwell hindered progress.
Whenever the British came to one of the innumerable creeks
or swamps along the road, they found bridges broken or huge
tree trunks felled across the way; Clinton had to halt to make

repairs. The two armies danced like boxers looking for an open-ing; both Washington and Clinton zigzagged in central Jersey for strategic advantage. In baking heat, the armies marched and countermarched until, early on the morning of Sunday, June 28, after a terrific thunderstorm, they met at Monmouth Court House near the present town of Freehold.

Lee, senior general under Washington, was nominal head of Wayne's advance corps, but Lee, as every general was aware, disliked the undertaking. He had no stomach for attacking grenadiers, but he was too proud to give up his right of leader-ship. Wayne wanted to follow the Paoli plan by falling upon the British rear and capturing Clinton's twelve-mile-long bag-gage train, while Washington and the main army hit the British center. Lee hesitated to co-operate. Only when Washington ex-pressly ordered him to fight did Lee consent, and then he agreed half-heartedly. He fumbled his assignment. Following his orders, he attacked the rear at dawn, expecting to be met by the second-rate troops usually put in charge of baggage. He found, instead, that Clinton had put crack Guardsmen in the rear. Lee, dazed at the thought of fighting well-trained grena-diers, turned to Wayne and asked advice.

"Push on," urged Wayne. "They're wavering."

"But, Mr. Wayne, the enemy outnumbers us. I hear that they have reinforcements coming up."

"Strike them before the reinforcements come. Our people can dislodge them."

"Mr. Wayne, you do not know the British grenadiers. We cannot beat them. I have fought among them and I know their spirit."

"By Heavens, General Lee, I know American spirit! My men are soldiers. Give them leadership and they will give you victory. Strike hard and strike quickly!"

Lee faltered. It would be wise, he said, to wait until more news arrived about the numbers of the British troops. He would not risk his men in fighting blindly. Better be cautious than foolhardy, better wait and see. Wayne grabbed Lee by the thin shoulders and spun him around. He pointed to Dick Butler, standing in a piece of thin woods, battering away with two field pieces at the grenadiers.

"Wait?" shouted Wayne. "Wait? Butler's up there now! We must not wait an instant. If we stay here, the enemy will cut him into pieces. He needs help. Rush him your support!"

"No, Mr. Wayne," Lee retorted slowly. "No advance. Mr. Butler must withdraw his men."

"My God, General Lee, you cannot be serious! Retreat? Advance, rather! Send him some men and we will push the enemy into that swamp at their rear. We must do so quickly before Butler uses up his ammunition."

Wayne swung his horse about and spurred to his regiments. He yelled to his men, waved his sword, and turned about to run to Butler's aid. To his amazement, Lee's men were already in retreat! Except for Wayne's division, men wavered all along the line. Spontaneously, for no orders had been given, troops moved back from the battlefield. Wayne was stunned. This must be treachery. Nothing else could possibly explain why Lee deserted Butler. Lee must be either a craven or in British pay. Wayne could not contradict the actions of the commanding general. He had no orders to withdraw, else he would have been guilty of disobeying commands. He was not forced to leave the field unless Lee sent him written orders. He took matters into his own hands. Avoiding any contact with the "traitor," lest Lee order him to retreat, Wayne took command. "Forward!" he yelled. "Strike and win!"

The Pennsylvanians cheered and charged. Running over the rising ground, they rushed gallantly to meet the grenadiers. Butler's hard-pressed regiment raised a shout; the British, panicky at the thought that this was Washington's main army, loosened ranks and stepped back toward their swamp. Monmouth's second half was far more glorious than its beginning. On the hottest day yet known to Jersey, Wayne's men, particularly Walter Stewart's Pennsylvanians and Nathaniel Rumsey's Marylanders, stood shoulder to shoulder with Dick Butler's regiment. Again and again the British formed to charge the woods; each time, Wayne's small force rallied to hurl back the flower of the veteran invader army. Soldiers, grimed and dirty, their tongues swollen by heat and thirst, too parched even to curse, fired and reloaded feverishly. In the brief intervals between rushes, they crawled to the edges of cedar swamps to gulp from stagnant pools and to drench themselves for coolness with hatfuls of the orange-colored water.

Both sides rushed reinforcements. Clinton's army, hoping to get forward toward New York, had split at dawn. Cornwallis, with half the British force, had left in morning dusk, that he might travel as far as possible before the raging sun burned down upon him. He double-quicked back now to help Sir Henry Clinton. Fresh Guardsmen flung themselves against Wayne's woods. Worn-out defenders, worrying lest Washington would never come, feared that they would run short of ammunition; they met the British with their bayonets. Some ran to the church at Freehold and grabbed up loads of prayer books and hymnals, then sped back to the woods, tearing out pages from the books for their comrades to use as wadding for their muskets.

Wayne hurried messenger after messenger to Washington, demanding haste and help. The Commander-in-Chief was already coming quickly. Starting from far behind the battlefield, according to his plans, he had not expected to enter action until Wayne and Lee had smashed the rear guard of the enemy. While he was moving leisurely, Lee's fugitives, streaming disorderly along the road, warned him that disaster lay ahead. A few moments later, he met Lee retreating from the battlefield. Washington lashed out at Lee in one of his few bursts of anger. Sending the craven to the rear in disgrace, he dashed forward. By this time the two armies were locked in battle, each side with all its strength, and each in advantageous situation. Clinton edged slowly away; the Americans, exhausted by their rapid march on a sweltering day, anxious about their ammunition, pressed a slight advantage, but could not push with too great vigor.

Even women took part in that daylong fight. Freehold residents who had fled to safety returned to carry water to the troops; wives of soldiers and camp followers braved British fire to bring jugfuls to the men. Mary Hays, wife of a private in the 7th Pennsylvania, won lasting fame for her service; gratefully soldiers, drinking the strong cedar-swamp water that she carried, called her "Molly Pitcher." But water-carrying proved too tame for energetic, mannish Molly Pitcher. When her husband fell, heat-struck, she took his place by his cannon, and served the piece until nightfall.

Even Wayne was glad when, after a burning day, both sides ended battle. Neither Americans nor British had won decided victory, but when darkness fell it was the British who withdrew. Clinton "took advantage of the moonlight" to move silently away; the Americans, sleeping heavily after their heroic labors, did not know that he had gone until sunrise the next morning. When dawn broke upon another torrid day, Clinton was far distant on the road to Amboy. Wayne counted up the costs of the engagement; the Americans had lost 75 dead and 270 wounded; the British casualties were 65 killed and 219 badly hurt.

Wayne gloated over the fate of British officers who only recently had staged extravagant mock tournaments at Wharton's house in Philadelphia. "Tell the Philadelphia ladies," he told Peters jubilantly, "that the heavenly, sweet, pretty red Coats, the accomplished gentlemen of the Guards and Grenadiers, have humbled themselves on the plains of Monmouth. The Knights of the Blended Rose and Burning Mountain have Resigned their Laurels to Rebel officers who will lay them at the feet of those Virtuous Daughters of America who cheerfully gave up ease and affluence in a City for Liberty and peace of mind in a Cottage."

He may have been thinking of his "daughter," though Sally had not written him since before the Battle of the Brandywine, but it is more probable that he had no particular young lady in mind; he was writing words that sounded well. Certainly, he laid no laurels before Polly. She was again melancholy; she alarmed him with reports that little Isaac was so sick that he would die. Wayne, fortunately, had better information; Dr. Delany told him that the illness was of minor consequence. In writing Polly, Wayne paid slight attention to Isaac's ailments, saying merely that he wished the boy to live to "fill and Discharge with Honor the Most Important Station in the gift of his Country." He added no word of personal regard for her.

2

Monmouth's aftermath was decidedly unpleasant. The whole army was torn by brawls and bitter hatreds. Accusations of knavery and treason flew recklessly about the mass; knots of officers, gathered in tiny, jealous cliques, whispered malicious gossip. Much of it centered about the stormy person of Charles Lee, who, according to both Lafayette and Charles Scott, had been called a poltroon by Washington himself. Lee, smarting under criticism, flared back that the confusion at Monmouth was wholly due to Wayne. Had Anthony followed orders, the hotheaded Englishman raved, the Continentals would have won that battle in the early morning. Lee gave no proof of his strange charge—indeed, no proof would be obtainable for such a ridiculous assertion—but he lost no chance to sneer at Wayne's alleged incompetence. St. Clair alone supported Lee, although only so far as Wayne was concerned. The Major-General, dining with his intimates, pointed out sourly that Wayne had been incompetent at Paoli and sneered that the court-martial members had not known their business. Conveniently, he neglected to comment on his own misfortune at Ticonderoga.

Anthony saw red. His quick tongue lashed out at both his detractors. At Monmouth, Wayne recklessly declared, St. Clair had jeopardized American success by failing to send help to the hard-pressed Pennsylvanians, though in his soberer moments Wayne must have known that St. Clair held no official position in the army at that battle and so could not have ordered troops about. As for Lee, that Hannibal whose caution cropped out only in the heat of battle, Wayne shouted, "His actions flowed from insanity—or a worse cause." Part of the dissension ceased at Paramus, a small Dutch town in northern New Jersey, ten miles from Newark, when the army halted for Lee's court-martial. Feuds, jealousies, and suspicions long current in the mess focused on the embittered prisoner, and when Charles Lee was suspended for a year, the social atmosphere was clearer. Then the army moved on to White Plains, just north of New York, where Washington hoped for greater harmony.

New Englanders, anxious to come closer to their homes, urged Washington to withdraw his army still farther east, oblivious, Wayne thought, of the evident fact that should the Continentals move far from the Hudson, Clinton could ascend that stream and thus cut off all access to the Middle States and to the South. Wayne warned against the danger; he pressed Washington to drive upon New York itself. Fabius wavered; he sought to satisfy both factions. First, he moved his men north to Fredericksburgh (now Patterson), close to the Connecticut boundary, in an attempt to please the Yankees. Then he pondered plans to split the army into several small divisions.

Wayne, holding pleasant parties at his quarters in Benjamin Haviland's stone house, thundered to his cronies that such schemes were suicidal. The day after the split was first proposed, at a gala dinner in commemoration of the anniversary of Burgoyne's surrender, as his tableful of intimates sat on Haviland's lawn under the shade of autumn trees he harangued them on the folly of splitting up the army. It would be better, he insisted, to keep the troops together, and if no drive were made upon New York, to build barracks for the army near White Plains or Morristown. He was so vehement that not even the roar of cannon—thirteen from each brigade—saluting the memory of Saratoga diverted him from his topic.

Wayne's plan prevailed, though it cost him a winter in the company of the Udney Hays, his old Ticonderoga friends. Colonel Hay had searched for a house for Wayne where the Colonel, his wife, and Anthony could spend a pleasant winter, but when Wayne was about ready to confess failure in his plan for making camp at White Plains or Morristown, Washington swung over to his point of view. The Hay family did not go along when the army left for New Jersey at the close of November.

Again boredom reigned. Wayne, brooding with a bottle, glowered as he thought of Charles Lee's accusations. They were old charges, but Lee was repeating them in Philadelphia; if the caitiff were unchecked, people might suspect that Wayne was cowardly. He moved to check the slander. "If it was your intention," he wrote, "to injure my military character in the eyes of the world, I know that you will have the candour to acknowledge it, as well as courage to accept my demand of *honourable redress.*"

Lee fought better battles with his pen than with his sword. This challenge to a duel gave him an opportunity to twist the truth and to re-establish himself with military folk. Lee assured Wayne that he had no thought of treating Anthony's military character with contempt, but that, on the contrary, he thought highly of him. "If ever I am restored to command," Lee promised, "I shall ask for you as my first brigadier." Had he paused here, the flattery might have soothed Wayne's pride, but Lee was seldom tactful. He went on to warn Wayne that a challenge would, in the long run, hurt Wayne more than himself: "However, if you persevere in your intention, as soon as I have taken final leave of Congress, published my case to the world at large, and am sufficiently recovered from my late accident to act with vigour, I will not decline your invitation."

His misfortune, as Wayne well understood, was a wound inflicted by Henry Laurens, Jr., Washington's aide-de-camp, in a duel caused by Lee's aspersions on the Commander-in-Chief. To promise Wayne a chance when Lee, inveterate intriguer, should "finish" with Congress, when he should complete a pamphlet explaining what had happened at Monmouth, and when his wound was wholly healed, was to postpone Wayne's duel to a very remote time. Wayne had to be content with slim satisfaction; in point of fact, his anger wore away and Lee, though never again his idol, became again a friend.

Yet Anthony's friendships were built on sand. A man of strong emotions, whose words crackled when he criticized, Wayne's snap judgments bit savagely into the feelings of associates. Some learned to discount his remarks; others, growing hardened, paid slight attention to his continual complaints. When Francis Johnston, his devoted friend, read Wayne's bitter sentence "No consideration will induce me to continue in a service where ten men die for want of necessaries for one that's killed in action," he was not alarmed, for he knew that Anthony understood no middle ground between a shining division fit for dress parade and a mob of ragamuffins. Dick Peters, unable to distinguish between Wayne's actual sufferings and his hyperbolic wrongs, fell into the habit of believing that everything Wayne said was much exaggerated. Almost everyone grew callous to Wayne's threat of going home to Sabine fields.

Anthony, angered at such indifference, cast off his old companions and formed new associations. Thus he was misunderstood, for disillusioned comrades who had been ruthlessly abandoned thought him cold and heartless. Nothing could be farther from the truth; Wayne was warm, impulsive, and affectionate, but to know him well, a man must be constantly in his presence, enveloped by his personality. There must be, in addition, a strong desire to stay his friend, for there were certain traits of Wayne's character which repelled as powerfully as other elements appealed. Many termed him boastful and bumptious, conceited and uninhibited; they disliked his heavy drinking and they resented his glaring favoritism. His trail was strewn with broken friendships that he never sought to mend. Living neither in the past nor in the future, he shed no tears for lost happiness, nor did he sigh for better days. He held fast to the present, enjoyed each moment as it came, and savored life completely. Once or twice, especially when writing to ladies, he voiced regrets for what might have been, but such expressions were more conventional than heartfelt.

He blossomed best when he was king; toward those whose rank was equal or superior to his own, Wayne held a curious mixture of suspicion and contempt. Invariably he picked out younger men as special protégés, only to cast them aside when they showed signs of jealousy. Not until after Monmouth was he convinced that Washington was as clever as the Hannibals, but once assured, Wayne never thereafter faltered in allegiance. Nathanael Greene alone among major-generals won his deep regard, but this was not wholly due to that officer's ability; Wayne was caught in vivacious Catherine Greene's social net, to begin a friendship that would be continued long after the war was over. Wayne distrusted Arnold and hated Schuyler;

he loathed foreigners in posts of high command. Lafayette was an exception, just as that warmhearted Frenchman was with everyone else.

His special hate went out to Arthur St. Clair, his fellow Pennsylvanian. Superficially, the men had much in common; each was cut from the same cloth, though St. Clair was colder and more shrewdly calculating than passionate Anthony Wayne. Knowing well that, despite St. Clair's longer military service, he was himself an abler general, Wayne sulked because St. Clair was a major-general while Wayne was but a brigadier. When St. Clair was not about, Anthony was an able officer; at Ticonderoga, Brandywine, Paoli, Germantown, and Monmouth he was incisive and aggressive. But whenever the two men served in the same division, they clashed openly.

After Monmouth, when the army was reorganized, Major-General St. Clair, exonerated for the surrender of Ticonderoga, replaced Wayne as commander of the Pennsylvanians, reducing him as brigadier to the rank of a subordinate in the division that he had led with such ability. Under military custom, this was unavoidable, but Wayne felt the blow to be unbearable. This "demotion," he blurted out angrily and injudiciously, was but another proof of St. Clair's malice. To serve under such a man would be humiliation not to be brooked by any man of spirit: "After two years' hard service, during all which time I have been honored with the command of the Pennsylvania Line, at the close of this Campaign I find myself superseded and put under a General Officer who has in the most ungenerous Envious Manner attempted to throw a *Stigma* on my Character . . . to be superseded at this late hour by a man in whose Conduct and Candor I can have no Confidence hurts me not a little. . . . I have, therefore, determined to return to domestic life, and leave the blustering field of Mars to the possession of Gentlemen of more worth."

Washington realized that the two Pennsylvania rivals were incompatible. Wayne, as everyone well knew, merited promotion, but unless a conservative Congress made terms with a radical Pennsylvania Assembly, neither Wayne nor any other Pennsylvanian could be advanced. The alternative was to de-

tach Wayne on some special assignment, but that involved taking him away from the regiments he had drilled and cared for
with such zeal.

Luckily, an alternative appeared. For weeks Wayne had been
clamoring for a furlough. Forgetting to mention that he spent
a month away from the army during the ordeal at Valley Forge,
Wayne insisted that he had not rested since the beginning of
the war; he asked for a vacation. To keep him at camp, under
St. Clair's direct authority, would invite a clash; to grant a furlough would allow time for a solution whereby the angry Brigadier could be removed from St. Clair's immediate control.
Beginning, therefore, with February 1, 1779, Wayne was
granted an indefinite leave of absence, which it was understood
he would spend chiefly at Philadelphia lobbying with Congress
and with the Pennsylvania Assembly for an improvement in
army matters.

3

"Like the bee, I move from flower to flower and sip the
honey from each rose." Anthony expected a seventh heaven of
delight. Walter Stewart told him that Philadelphia, once a
Quaker city that preached pacifism, had gone mad over the
army, and that any officer could count on endless entertainment.
"'Tis all gaiety," Stewart promised. "Every Lady and Gentleman endeavours to outdo the Other in Splendor and Show.
You will hardly dine at a Table but they present you with
three Courses and each of them in the most Elegant manner.
'Tis really flattering to the officers of the Army, the Attention
paid them by the people."

Wayne looked forward to savoring good things. Sequestered
four years, as he said, from the society of the fair—which was,
of course, an exaggeration—he thought himself entitled to indulgence. With Polly at Waynesborough, he let himself relax
in feminine society, particularly as Stewart chuckled that girls
had forgotten their inhibitions. "They have lost," said Stewart
with a reminiscent grin, "that native innocence in their manners

which formerly was their characteristick, and supplied its place
with what they call an Easy Behavior. They have really got
the art of throwing themselves into the most wanton and Amor-
ous Postures which their free manner of speech adds not a little
to. By Heaven, it is almost too much for a young Soldier to
bear."

Anthony Wayne, just past his thirty-third birthday, was both
youthful and vigorous; he enjoyed the honey of the Easy Behavior set. Warned in advance by Stewart, who had sampled
the flowers earlier, Wayne moved cautiously, having no wish
to suffer the fate of one of their mutual friends who, "on account of his getting the C—p last campaigne" had lost his
sweetheart. Not that the girl made much objection, for she had
"not quite so horrid an idea" of the ailment, but her mother
thought the disease a "crying and unpardonable sin." The difference in point of view between the generations, Wayne and
Stewart felt, indicated what a momentous change had come
about in Philadelphia's social views.

The General, fresh on furlough in the frigid February of
1779, was not disappointed. Glamorous because of his exploits
in four battles, he became a reigning favorite. From his lodgings at Sharp Delany's house on Second Street, he went out
nightly to dinners and dances. "I enjoy every moment and
participate in every Pleasure this place affords, for I must do
the Citizens this Justice to say that they have honored me with
every attention and treated me with every possible Politeness,
and what's very extraordinary, I have not turned more than
an hour or two with any one Lady."

No doubt Polly's gift of three stocks, a silk handkerchief,
and a pair of gloves enhanced his charms, just as Anthony's
new uniforms, decked out with silver buttons and lined with
closely woven white shalloon, helped make him irresistible.
(He owed his tailor at this moment a matter of £100 on an
account that now was more than three years old.) Neither these
thoughtful gifts nor her presentation of a warm jacket and
two pairs of knitted stockings impelled him to see Polly. He
much preferred to vision her at Waynesborough watching over
the fourteen new cows that she had purchased for the farm.

He did not tell her that he was coming to the city. He had, to be sure, sent word by Colonel Irvine in October that she might expect him at Christmas, but when he wrote in November, he failed to say anything about a furlough. That letter was instead filled with admonitions that she must send the children to good schools, that Peggy must learn dancing and improve her writing, and that Isaac must not be kept at home by any "mistaken notion of fondness," for he wanted him to make a figure in life. That November letter received close attention. To prove that Isaac was advancing nicely in his education, the boy scribbled childishly upon its margins. To this day, a hundred and sixty-three years after its receipt, it bears his infantile attempts at spelling, for Isaac laboriously scratched "Dan," "Katy," and his own proud title "Son" upon his "Pappy's" letter. That the capital "S" in "Son" is reversed adds just the proper homely, sentimental touch.

Polly was hardened to neglect; his sister Hannah Van Leer, who had sent five letters to her brother without receiving one reply, ceased to write, though in her last letter she said proudly that even the Tories admired Anthony's courage; his mother, who fervently reminded him over and over not to "forget your Makeer that saved you so many times," and who had offered to visit him if he could not spare the time to call on her, reluctantly admitted to herself that Anthony did not care to come. He did not completely forget his family. Early in March, he ordered a tierce of beer, forty-two gallons, to be sent to Polly, together with fish and oysters for Abraham Robinson, to show his gratitude for the latter's Christmas present of a pound of tea. Clumsy with his pen, he spoiled the effect of the gift by the cold curtness of his letters.

Wayne's stay in Philadelphia was supposedly a vacation, but he did have business to transact. Pennsylvania officers, distressed at the way politicians treated them, asked Wayne to represent them before the Assembly. Anthony was optimistic in the matter. With Hartley, Robert Morris, and numerous other powerful friends among its members, Wayne hoped to realize his ambition by being named a major-general, especially now that Thomas Mifflin had at last thrown up his commission and had left a vacancy for a Pennsylvania brigadier's promotion. To conservative dismay, the Assembly, on convening, continued radical, though by reduced majorities. Wayne's hope for promotion faded, but army relief was not a partisan matter. As legislative agent for the Pennsylvania Line, he pressed home the need for immediate help. He warned that the neglect in clothing troops, the policy of paying men in depreciated paper at a time of swiftly rising prices, and failure to pass pension laws were causing unrest.

Anthony's lobbying methods were strictly modern. To some Assemblymen, he threatened that unless they voted right, he would take the stump against them in their counties and use his prestige to cause voters to reject them. To others, he appealed on grounds of humanity and justice, knowing that if such Assemblymen understood aright, they would respond accordingly. "You are now," he told one wavering statesman, "sailing in the wide sea of politicks, forgetting that there are a few, poor, half-starved, naked fellows in the field who were once honored with your friendship. . . . Do you drink wine, eat veneson and get drunk, etc., as usual? If so, we may hope something from you, but if, on the contrary, you think much, eat little and sleep less and shut the door of friendship against honest fellows, agreeable to the present fashion, I'll none of you. I would much rather dine on frozen pork and Grog in camp than associate with such Caitiffs." Party feeling, he knew, ran high and, like many another lobbyist, he was plagued by men who promised much and gave assurance of good intentions and best wishes, but who when action was desired, broke their pledges. February passed with nothing done. The Assembly, Wayne saw, was more concerned with factional affairs than with helping army welfare.

Meanwhile, new complications arose in camp. Because enlistment times had expired, and since new recruiting was not sufficiently brisk to fill the gaps, Pennsylvania's three brigades were collapsed into two, with consequent lessening in the number of officers required. Congress and the Board of War, which should have handled such matters, passed over to the state the question of which officers should be dismissed and which retained. Many colonels, majors, captains, and lieutenants, now superfluous, found themselves slated for dismissal.

Because Wayne was at the seat of government, disgruntled army men believed that he personally decided who should stay and who should go. Ill will toward him increased, fanned mightily, Wayne believed, by Arthur St. Clair. Wayne argued vainly that he, a strong conservative, carried small weight with a radical Assembly; he suggested that Washington and St. Clair, his superiors, were far more influential; he urged that men dropped from the rolls consult with radical leaders. He could not escape appeals from personal friends who asked him to intercede on their behalf. There was the case of Major Francis Mentges, his one-time fencing master. Mentges had strong enemies in the service, owing partly to an aristocratic prejudice against associating with a former dancing master, but more to a belief that at the Battle of Long Island Mentges had skulked in a thicket while the fighting was in progress. By the new arrangement, Mentges was advanced to a lieutenant-colonelcy above men who had been his superiors. When news of his preferment came to camp, officers boiled in protest; a pleasant dance arranged at Millstone for the ladies of the neighborhood turned into an officers' mass meeting where men swore violently that they would quit the service.

Anger over appointments and dismissals, sweeping through the Pennsylvania regiments, brought other indignations to light. Wayne's men, incensed because the state treated them like stepchildren, approached the point of mutiny. Private soldiers enlisted for definite terms of service—usually for three years or for the duration of the war—could not quit the service, but officers had the privilege of resigning their commissions whenever they saw fit. At a stormy meeting Pennsylvania officers sent an ultimatum to the Assembly, declaring that unless effective aid was given, every Pennsylvania officer would throw up his commission on April 15, 1779.

Wayne was their Philadelphia mouthpiece. Busily, he moved among Assemblymen, explaining army grievances, pleading for some drastic change that would save Pennsylvania's brigades. To his dismay, while seeking relief for the brigades as a whole he found himself enmeshed in webs of personal intrigue; politicians made it evident that they would vote as he requested only if he took care of their personal friends. Wayne countered by distributing copies of laws passed by Massachusetts, New York, New Jersey, Connecticut, and Virginia, proving by their liberality that Pennsylvania had been niggardly in providing for her men. He threatened that unless the commonwealth showed itself as generous as other states, the shining Pennsylvania regiments would be leaderless and the state discredited.

These arguments were aimed at consolidating popular opinion, as was a formal memorial addressed to the Assembly; in private, Wayne pulled wires and dickered like a professional politician. Mentges retained his promotion, but the most violent of his critics was also moved up in rank. William McPherson, a Philadelphia-born British deserter who was one of Arthur St. Clair's protégés, gained a majority by brevet, but Wayne was skillful enough to mollify officers of lower rank by seeing that they were properly promoted. In return for these concessions from a radical Assembly, Wayne modified the army's stringent demands.

Three days after his memorial the commonwealth guaranteed that every Pennsylvania officer who served until the close of the war should, after he received seven years' half-pay from Congress, be granted half-pay by the state as an annuity for life; widows of men killed in service would also get half-pay. State lands granted to officers and men as bounty for war service would be tax-free so long as they remained in the possession of the men to whom they were allotted. Officers were to receive yearly a complete outfit of regimentals, to be paid for at prices current at the outbreak of the war. In addition, a state store system was set up whereby certain luxuries would be sold to Pennsylvania officers at standard prices. Rum, for instance, would be supplied at 5 shillings a gallon, no matter what the market price might be; sugar, coffee, and chocolate would be distributed at 3s. 9d. a pound, tea at 12s., soap at 1s. 3d., and tobacco at 9d. a pound.

So cleverly had Anthony Wayne handled legislators who were politically opposed to him that after compromises were complete and threats of resignation withdrawn, Pennsylvania's president, Joseph Reed, and the Supreme Executive Council appealed to Congress to promote him to a major-generalcy. They pointed out that Pennsylvania had but one such officer, Arthur St. Clair, since no one had been named to succeed Mifflin; they added that the commonwealth had but two brigadiers, Wayne and the captured Thompson, although in proportion to quotas assigned other states Pennsylvania deserved four. They recommended Wayne as a major-general, and suggested that Magaw and Irvine be appointed brigadiers. Had the latter clause not been included, Congress, which had at last taken over the right to name generals, would have favored Wayne. But by linking Magaw and Irvine with the Wayne suggestion, new questions of precedence came into play, for both men had been prisoners of war, and there were grave doubts whether captives should be rewarded by promotion; moreover, a Pennsylvanian, Edward Hand, one of St. Clair's partisans, had through political finagling already been made a North Carolina general. To increase Pennsylvania's brigadiers at such a time, Congress thought, would inevitably invite state jealousies. Wayne's nomination was accordingly pigeonholed.

Wayne gave no outward signs of disappointment, but his actions indicate that he was sadly downcast. Certainly he was bored, now that his lobbying had ceased; even the Philadelphia flowers palled upon him. He rode at last, after four months at Philadelphia, to see Polly at Waynesborough, and met a joyous welcome. Young Isaac, strutting about the lawn with a splendid sword and gold-laced hat that Anthony had sent when the boy entered school, was a fine figure of a youthful soldier. Polly herself, refreshed after her Maryland holiday, made him comfortable. But Waynesborough offered too tame a life for a restless officer. "I must try to get away from this place," he wrote Dick Butler. "The luxuriancy of the Soil, the domestic sweets and other pleasures and amusements which hourly present themselves have almost debauched me from the field."

He returned to Philadelphia, where he met one of the most agreeable and surprising experiences of his life. A messenger arrived from Wilmington with a handsome inlaid sword. The bearer, "Captain Brown"—there were six of them at that moment in the Continental Army, so that it is impossible to identify him more precisely—declared that it was a token of appreciation from a feminine admirer, but he gave no details, if indeed he had details to give. Anthony racked his memory, wondering who the lady might be. He thought of Sally, but she was at York with Richard Peters; he wondered if perchance Hetty Griffits, from whom he had not heard in months, had taken refuge in the mill town on the Delaware, but Hetty was not given to such gestures. He had few friends in Wilmington, though he knew the Reads, the Rodneys, and the Vinings.

The Vinings! It must be Mary Vining! Anthony did not know the lady well, though Lafayette had taken him to call upon Congressman John Vining while they were waiting for the British to appear at Brandywine. He remembered Vining's sister, a young girl alive with personality, a vibrant girl with snappy eyes who flirted with the Marquis in what Lafayette declared was perfect French spoken with a Versailles accent, and who, when Lafayette had been reduced to stammering adoration, turned her battery of charms on Anthony. He had responded in a clumsy, halting way, because the girl was so exciting that he could not keep his wits; he had told her that so long as he should live, his sword would be at her command. Then she had looked at his heavy service sword and made disparaging remarks about its quality. "For such a knight," she said, "a sword should be as graceful as his wit. You need, my general, a suaver sword."

So this was it! She had not forgotten him, though nine long months had passed. This must have been what Captain Brown had meant when he had given him the sword with the remark: "I was instructed to say, sir, 'I have been anxious to get it to you before, but the silversmith would not put it in my power.'" Anthony had something now to live for. The girl whose beauty and dynamic charm had captivated Lafayette, together with half the officers of the French contingent, had sent a sword to Wayne. She must have thought him more attractive than he had thought himself. His boredom disappeared; his chin went

forward and his shoulders shot back straight. With such a sword
as this, he would forever be her knight.

Press of business, which Anthony so often alleged to escape
unwelcome chores, prevented his going to Wilmington to thank
Mary Vining for the sword, if it were she who had presented
it. Washington put urgent duties upon him. As a solution of
the St. Clair-Wayne difficulties, the Commander-in-Chief had
promised that Wayne should have command of a new corps,
an elite brigade of Light Infantry, made up of crack companies
from several states. Time was drawing near when this brigade
would enter into action. At Washington's command, Wayne
began extensive correspondence with choice spirits whom he
wished as officers; he interviewed scores of applicants who
wished positions in this special corps. Reluctantly, Anthony put
aside the notion of a trip to Wilmington. In the late spring of
1779, he was immersed in army duties.

As finally perfected, the Light Infantry comprised four regiments, each of two battalions. Lieutenant Colonel Christian
Febiger, a Danish-born Virginian who had been Arnold's
brigade-major on the Canada expedition, headed the 1st Regiment, with Lieutenant-Colonel François Louis de Fleury, a
hero of Brandywine, and Major Thomas Posey of Virginia as
Febiger's aides. Dick Butler commanded the 2d, with Lieutenant-Colonel Samuel Hay of Pennsylvania and Major Jack
Stewart, an eccentric Marylander, as assistants. The 3d, under
Colonel Return Jonathan Meigs, who had been commended
by Congress for heroism at Long Island, Lieutenant-Colonel
Isaac Sherman, and Captain Henry Champion, all Connecticut
men, was largely a New England group. Colonel Rufus Putnam's 4th, with Majors William Hull of Connecticut and
Hardy Murfree of North Carolina, comprised both Eastern
men and Southerners.

In some respects, the line-up disappointed Wayne. He did
not have the close friends whom he wished for as associates;
neither Walter Stewart nor Josiah Harmar, each of whom had
asked for service under him, had been assigned to the Light
Infantry, though his friends Irvine and Johnston headed the
two brigades. Michael Ryan, whom Wayne refused to support

for promotion but whom nevertheless he wanted for his brigade-major, was out of the army, some said because his new bride disliked Wayne. There were too many Yankees and not enough Pennsylvanians in the corps to suit Wayne's taste. But on the other hand, the Light Infantry was, by all odds, the crack outfit of the army, and Wayne was very well pleased to have it in his charge.

The long-looked-for summons came at last when on June 24 Washington ordered Wayne to join the army. Anthony did not delay. Pausing only to buy for Polly twenty gallons of spirits, half a barrel of tongues, and two bushels of salt, which he left to be forwarded to her at Waynesborough, he wrote a hurried letter warning her not to neglect the education of his children, and speeded off for camp. Two days later he was at Washington's headquarters on the Hudson, ready for active service. On June 28 he took command of the Light Infantry.

CHAPTER X

"The Compleatest Surprise"

THIRTEEN hundred and fifty picked veterans, all of a size, stocky, sturdy fellows five feet eight inches tall, saluted Wayne. These soldiers, native-born Americans in their middle twenties who had seen at least two years of war, made up the crack Light Infantry. Drilled by Steuben for six months to within an inch of their lives, accustomed to minute inspections that eyed every last detail, they were a model corps. Wayne swelled with pride. Here at last was an elite brigade worthy of his leadership. With this praetorian guard he could accomplish wonders. Young as they were in organization, they showed esprit de corps. As Light Infantrymen, they were conscious of their worth.

Dandy Wayne would not have been himself had he been satisfied. His troops were well-nigh perfect; they drilled with marvelous precision; they were alert and energetic. But Wayne, inspecting them as they stood smartly at attention, saw flaws that made him wince. As he looked down the lines that stood ruler-straight before him, his eye caught a clash of color. These magnificent men, drawn from the lines of almost all the states, wore uniforms of different regiments. Next to a soldier in the white-faced coat of New England stood a man who wore New Jersey's buff; flanking a Pennsylvanian in red trimmings was a Carolinian whose buttonholes were edged with narrow tape. The general effect was blue, for such was now the common color of Continental clothing, but the coats differed in details. Wayne liked symmetry; he was distressed to see his perfect troops in a discordant garb. He asked the Commander-in-Chief for a distinctive elite uniform. Washington refused. Since the

Light Infantry was only a temporary corps, he would not permit so much as a distinctive red feather to set the men apart.

Even at his pleasant Light Infantry camp at Sandy Beach, five miles below West Point, Anthony could not escape St. Clair. That interfering general, restored to active service after his suspension, headed the Pennsylvania Line, which was stationed farther up the Hudson, near Washington's headquarters. St. Clair demanded that Wayne release Lieutenant Edward Butler, Dick's brother, in exchange for Lieutenant James Gibbon, a truculent sea lawyer whom St. Clair could not handle. Wayne's anger flared. Butler was his friend, a warmhearted, impulsive, hearty drinker of Wayne's inner circle; of Gibbon he knew nothing except that St. Clair was thrusting the man upon him. He resented St. Clair's assumption that Wayne, brigadier of an elite corps, was still under St. Clair's thumb, subject to whatever orders St. Clair chose to issue. Wayne believed that he was free of that caitiff's interference; if St. Clair were still master, Wayne might as well return at once to his Sabine fields.

Anthony appealed to Washington, and for once His Excellency supported Wayne. The transfer, Washington declared, need not be made unless Wayne desired the change. Anthony could have hugged his Commander-in-Chief; the words were equivalent to admission that Wayne and St. Clair were on a par, though their official ranks remained unchanged. He went back to his quarters with a broad grin on his face, and gleefully wrote out a message telling St. Clair that he would not surrender Butler. His happiness soon ended. To Wayne's intense resentment, Gibbon arrived in camp with a perfectly valid transfer into the Light Infantry. St. Clair, intent on ridding himself of a troublemaker, gave up an officer without receiving a replacement.

Other controversies also appeared. Noisy Colonel Samuel John Atlee of Lancaster, who had already stirred a row by running successfully for Congress while still on active army duty, caused confusion by demanding military promotion. William Irvine called on Wayne to take a stand against allowing Atlee's claim. If the boisterous Atlee were successful in being both a legislator and a military man, Irvine warned, dictatorship would not be distant. Wayne gladly endorsed Irvine's objections to Atlee's continuance in the army; he swallowed his distaste for St. Clair long enough to enroll the latter against the loud-laughing Congressman Atlee. Through the combined efforts of Wayne, Irvine, St. Clair, and Francis Johnston, virtually every Pennsylvania officer lined up in opposition to Atlee. Their objections proved forceful enough to bar the Congressman from further military service. In later years, Wayne's activity in this matter caused him embarrassment. Atlee's son, William Richardson Atlee, fell in love with Margaretta Wayne. The memory of his opposition to the father's promotion made it difficult for Wayne to welcome the lad as enthusiastically into the family as Margaretta wished, though Wayne overcame his prejudice against the boy, and the marriage took place.

The Light Infantry fretted for want of action. Sir Henry Clinton would not stir from his safe harbor in New York and Washington camped calmly up the river. The energetic Wayne as usual fidgeted with impatience. He begged for an attack upon the enemy, but Washington, whose men—except for the glittering Light Infantry—were poorly supplied, ill-equipped, and none too numerous, thought himself in no condition to risk a major battle.

Indeed, had Anthony's desire prevailed, the Continentals would have been unfortunate. The British wished to lure the rebels into a decisive general engagement in the open field, where superior British strength could crush the Revolution. As bait to draw Washington from safe mountain fastnesses, Clinton again made feints against strategic points. One column struck south into New Jersey, pretending to dash toward Easton, a great Continental storehouse; expeditions sailed up Long Island Sound to raid Connecticut; a third force, going suddenly up the Hudson, seized Stony Point, halfway up the river to Washington's camp.

Wayne's enthusiasm ran away with his caution. Had he translated his desires into aggressive action, the Continental Army would have been caught in Clinton's trap. Too confident of American strength, too sure that all the army was as prepared

and as powerful as his beloved Light Infantry, Wayne miscalculated the situation. Washington, fortunately, put brakes
on Anthony's impetuosity, so that no harm befell the Continentals. Patiently, he explained the relative positions of the
armies until Wayne too saw that reckless engagement would
destroy American chances. The lesson was not lost on Wayne.
Never again in his military career did he risk a battle unless
he was certain that every element of strategy was in his favor,
that all lines of communication were beyond attack, and that
all equipment was in order. Always careful, he learned from
Washington's example never to allow his hopes to dazzle his
reason. From this time onward, Wayne's respect for Fabius
mounted high.

Waiting never pleased Wayne, and time passed slowly on
the Hudson. With nothing active to occupy his mind, he grew
bored. Frank Johnston sent him a couple of dozen bottles of
porter, Lewis Farmer, a Philadelphia friend, gave him two
pounds of tea and twenty pounds of sugar, and there was liquor
in the camp; but Wayne fidgeted nervously. "I wish to god,"
he wrote to Light Horse Harry, "that we could form a junction in a Christian country. I am damned tired of this caitiff
place."

The fine edge dulled among his men. Trained to the minute,
anxious for action, the well-drilled Light Infantry slowly deteriorated. Wayne drove them hard; he marched them and
maneuvered them to keep them on their toes; but even Wayne
could not fill in all their time with empty drill. In leisure moments, Light Infantry energy broke loose. Dick Peters offered
a curious suggestion, which Wayne adopted eagerly. Peters had
heard an Irishman sing a ballad which pleased him so much
that he hit upon the notion that Wayne should teach his men
to sing. "I am a great Friend to Ballads," Peters said. "I believe that more can be achieved by a few occasional simple
Songs than by a hundred Recommendations of Congress, especially considering how few attend to read them. I wish often
to see Ballads dispensed among the Soldiery which, inspiring in
them a Thirst for Glory, Patience under their Hardship, a Love

for their General and Submission to their Officers would animate them to a Chearful Discharge of their Duty."

Peters was a century and a half before his time; in the first World War, and thereafter, his reasoning would be accepted. Wayne had slight confidence in the efficacy of ballads to sentimentalize his tough Light Infantry, but, agreeable to the wish of the secretary of the Board of War, he gathered his "musical colonels" about him and proceeded to give the boys a treat. He assured Peters that the innovation was a howling success and that the singing was done "with not a little eclait," but he failed to repeat the concert.

Instead of spending their spare time in caroling, the Light Infantry got into trouble. No chicken yard was safe; civilians watched their valuables; military storekeepers put double locks upon their doors and then sat up nights to see that Wayne's marauders kept their distance. Even officers lost their morale. Edward Butler, the man Wayne would not transfer, shouldered into Commissary Benjamin Rooney's office to demand some liquor; Rooney, nose-deep in paper work, misunderstood the call.

"I've flour and beef for you," he answered.

"To hell with that! I want some rum!" the officer shouted, pushing Rooney back against the shelves. Rooney apologized for his mistake; he told Butler that no rum had come, but that it would arrive within an hour. "You're a liar and a rascal," Butler fumed. "God damn you! You sit here doing nothing while we need rum. Go get it!"

Butler grabbed Rooney by the arm and spun the clerk about. He pushed Rooney toward the door, then, kicking with tremendous force, he sent him sprawling into the company street. Rooney lost his temper. He put his head down like a bull and butted Butler. The officer staggered back, caught himself against the door, and flailed the clerk with both fists. Rooney fell again. Butler kicked him while he lay upon the ground. When Wayne heard the story, he promptly took Butler's side. Ignoring the obvious fact that Butler began the row, Wayne held Rooney responsible. "No commissary can strike an officer," he said. "Put Rooney in the guardhouse for court-martial."

When the trial was held, Rooney told his story and was acquitted on the testimony of eyewitnesses who told of Butler's brutality. Rooney won release, but Wayne demanded another commissary. Rooney was transferred; Butler went unpunished.

Wayne was not immune to criticism. Too constant military service hardened him. His attitude toward civilians suffered change. On a former occasion when four officers had insulted peaceable inhabitants and slashed them severely with swords, Wayne had turned the culprits over to Governor George Clinton of New York to be tried as ordinary criminals. When the officers protested that their honor had been injured by their being arrested for their crime, he shot back angrily: "It has never yet been Deemed Honourable for Armed Men to Assault and Wound unarmed men." On the Hudson, Anthony Wayne's standards altered. Angered because Judge Abraham Van Ness was slow in ordering roads repaired, so that provision wagons could come up more easily, Wayne snarled at civilian officers.

The climax came early one morning while Wayne and his two aides, Major George Wright and Captain Benjamin Fishbourn, were still asleep. A dirty-looking fellow pushed into their quarters and wakened them. Wayne, seeing a stranger in his room, yelled for the sentry.

"Don't be alarmed, General," said the man. "I'm Constable Arrowsmith. I'm after Major Wright. I'm taking him to jail."

"You're crazy!" shouted Wayne. "Get the hell out of here."

"Not until the Major comes, too," retorted Arrowsmith.

"On what charge?" asked Wright.

"That makes no difference!" roared Wayne. "Charge or no charge, you can't break into my house. Where's your warrant, anyway?"

Arrowsmith ignored the questions, nor did he show a warrant. "Wright comes with me quietly, or I'll take him by force," he said. "I'm sent here by Judge Van Ness."

Fishbourn, sitting bolt upright in bed, laughed derisively. "You'll take him? By force? With the whole army here? Look at that doorway! It's full of soldiers! So you'll take Major Wright by force, will you?"

The blood ebbed away from Wayne's angry face; his color was less purple than when Arrowsmith had first come in. He had no desire to be made to look ridiculous. "You, fellow! What did you say your name is?"

"Constable Arrowsmith, sir."

"Arrowsmith! I thought so. We caught a spy named Arrowsmith in camp here several days ago. So, you're Arrowsmith, too? That's interesting!" Wayne motioned to his guards to put the constable under arrest. "He's a spy," said Wayne. "Take him to the guardhouse."

Word finally reached Van Ness that Wayne had jailed his constable. The Judge hurried to Wayne's quarters to demand Arrowsmith's release. Wayne kept the Judge cooling his heels until late in the evening, when in a stormy interview Van Ness swore upon his honor that Arrowsmith was not a spy. Wayne then set the constable free, but in the meanwhile Major Wright had left camp under Wayne's orders to go to Philadelphia. Van Ness brought new charges against Wright, but could not win his extradition from Pennsylvania.

Something had to be done to keep the crack Light Infantry from losing its morale, and to make good use of the high spirit of its officers. If they continued to stay idle in camp, Steuben's devoted work would be wasted. Wayne looked about for some objective that he might take without running the risk of bringing on a major battle. His eye fixed on Stony Point, the rugged promontory jutting half a mile into the Hudson, where the British, under Lieutenant-Colonel Henry Johnson, had a fort. So long as the enemy held Stony Point, they would menace the American defenses at West Point; if by a bold stroke Stony Point could be stripped from their possession, the moral effect would be incalculable. The British at New York would be thrown into confusion and dismay; American morale would shoot rapidly upward; most of all, the mighty Light Infantry would prove its worth. Wayne resolved on taking Stony Point.

2

Stony Point stuck out into the Hudson like a sore thumb. Rising abruptly from the water, it blocked navigation and commanded the channel. Without Colonel Johnson's permission, not even a skiff could pass the point. It was important, too, because the road from New England to the South passed within the shadow of the rock. King's Ferry, from Verplanck's Point on the east bank of the river to Stony Point at the base of the Palisades on the western side, usually carried the great bulk of Continental war materials that crossed the river, but with the British in control the road was blocked. There were other ferries, but they were several miles upstream and were by no means as convenient; they required longer haulage and were less desirable. Stony Point stood insolently like a little Gibraltar at the crossroads of traffic.

Wayne surveyed the stronghold. The rocky cliff was well defended. Even to approach the fort seemed impossible. One wet and swampy road led to it from the shore, but only at low water; at higher tides the Hudson swirled about the base of the promontory, drowning the road and making Stony Point practically an island. British warships swept the low ground with their guns; the soft morass left at the ebb was watched by pickets. He looked beyond the base. If attackers escaped ships and sentries, an uphill climb through a wilderness of fallen, tangled tree trunks led to three series of redoubts filled with brass twelve-pounders. When these were reduced, another, rougher abatis ran completely around the rock; beyond them came more trenches with heavier cannon and stronger garrisons.

Wayne scouted further. From neighboring farmers, living on the slopes of high, wooded Donderberg, a rough hill looming west of Stony Point, he learned that at very low tides when the moon was right, a sunken sandbar, normally under water, came close to the surface, giving a firm footway along the marsh edge from the riverbank to Stony Point. Captured foragers, together with deserters, under Wayne's persistent prodding divulged the fact that British pickets, knowing nothing of unusually low tides, did not guard that passageway.

Wayne pounded his fist upon his table. This forgotten sandbar was his key to victory. But, having learned caution from Fabius, he did not rush headlong to the capture; carefully he checked his facts. Without telling Febiger and Butler of his discovery, lest he color their reports, Wayne ordered them to make investigations in the neighborhood of Stony Point. He sent Captain Allan McLane, the best of his scouts, into Stony Point with a flag of truce, to see if the observant Delaware dragoon could spot a weakness in Colonel Johnson's defenses. McLane came back with an astonishing report. Johnson, certain that Little Gibraltar was impregnable, had not bothered about blindfolding the American. McLane had seen the double abatis and the several rows of redoubts; he had watched the grenadiers of the 17th lounging, waiting by their guns; he had seen the stone walls of the citadel that crowned the rock. But he had seen more. "General," he said, "the citadel is not complete. There's a wide gap at the west end. They've stopped building at a big rock; they've left an open space beyond it. When we get up there, we can walk right in."

Wayne rushed to Washington with his news, urging the Commander-in-Chief to approve a quick assault on Stony Point: "The Light Infantry can do it. I know these men. They're second to none in courage. They will follow me to victory and glory." Washington weighed the matter carefully. To capture Stony Point would regain control of the desirable King's Ferry; it would push the British outposts back and render West Point safer. Above all, the blow to British morale would be of inestimable importance. The Commander-in-Chief checked Wayne's report. He sent Colonel Rufus Putnam, an engineer, to map the terrain, and after Putnam submitted sketches, he himself reconnoitered the position, spying out the character and strength of Stony Point's defenses. He and Wayne rode over the Donderberg, with a few of McLane's dragoons as their escort, to make a final survey.

Finally, Washington was convinced that Wayne's scheme was

practicable. He drew up instructions calling for a Light Infantry assault at midnight on Thursday, July 15, 1779. The attack, it was understood, would be by bayonet alone. As he shook sand upon the paper to blot his signature, he asked Wayne, who stood near grinning with delight, if he were certain of success. "General," retorted Wayne, "if you give me permission, I'll storm Hell itself for you."

No one, not even Putnam, Febiger, Butler, or McLane, knew of the scheme that Washington and Wayne had contrived. Wayne's Light Infantry drew up in dress parade at eleven o'clock Thursday morning, expecting to be dismissed immediately to quarters. To their surprise, Wayne ordered them to march. They thought it was a practice maneuver, but when, leaving the Hudson, Wayne swung west along the base of Bear Mountain, the men began to wonder. By three o'clock, when Wayne led them by rough trails through the deep ravines of the Donderberg, they suspected something more than drill.

Wayne's actions betrayed his nervousness. He ordered two detachments, under Captains James Chrystie and Allan Mc-Lane, to round up stray civilians. The Donderberg was sparsely settled, but even one person could give warning to the British; he told them to bayonet every dog they saw, lest the animals bark and thus betray the presence of strangers. McLane and Chrystie captured two old women who were carrying chickens and vegetables to the fort; they confiscated twenty cows. On the south slope of the Donderberg, Wayne called his colonels into conference. For the first time he told them of his plan to surprise Stony Point; he sent them to the regiments to tell their men to keep strict silence, to keep in line, and to put pieces of white paper in their hats so that Americans could recognize each other in the dark. "I wish absolute obedience," Wayne concluded. "No man is to carry a loaded gun, except the few whom I particularly command to do so. Any other man who so much as moves his musket from his shoulder will be killed. Should there be any soldier so lost to every feeling of Honor as to attempt to retreat one single foot, or skulk in the face of danger, the Officer next to him is immediately to put him to Death."

The last sentence was superfluous; no man gave way in the

attack. One boy, however, frightened and confused, lost his head and stopped to load his musket. Without a word, his captain ran him through the body. As an incentive to victory, if any were needed, Wayne offered money prizes. The first man to set foot in the works was promised $500; the second man would receive $400; the third, fourth, and fifth were offered smaller sums.

While daylight held, Wayne arranged his columns. Six hundred men, under Febiger, Meigs, and Hull, with Wayne himself, marched upon the right; 500 others, led by Dick Butler, took the left. These were the bayonet troops, who were forbidden under pain of death to fire their guns. A small central column, headed by Hardy Murfree of North Carolina, was intended as a feint to distract the attention of Stony Point from the larger bodies on its flanks. Murfree's men were under orders to shoot quickly and often in order to give the impression of large numbers.

Advance volunteer detachments preceded Febiger and Butler. Each column had a Forlorn Hope of 20 pioneers, carrying axes and billhooks to clear away the abatis so that the fighting men would have a clear path to the fort. Sixty yards behind these suicide squads came groups of 150 picked shock troops, followed closely by the main columns. Command of the Forlorn Hope went to James Gibbon on the left and to Lieutenant George Knox of Pennsylvania on the right. Wayne would have preferred another man to Gibbon, but the cocky grumbler held a commission senior to that of any other volunteer, and by Revolutionary army custom he was entitled to the leadership. At eight o'clock, when darkness had closed down, Wayne halted on the farm of David Springsteel, two miles west of Stony Point. Here the men were to rest while waiting the word to start their final rush.

Wayne, as usual, expected to die in the battle. To clear his name of any accusations St. Clair might make, he wrote a final letter, dated "Eleven P.M., near the Hour and Scene of Carnage," to be delivered after his death to his best and dearest friend, Sharp Delany. With it he enclosed his correspondence concerning St. Clair. He took the opportunity to place himself squarely on the side of Fabius against the Hannibals:

"You have often heard me default the Supiness and unworthy torpidity into which Congress were lulled and that it was my opinion that this would be a Sanguinary Campaign in which many of the choicest Spirits and much of the best blood in America would be lost owing to the parsimony and neglect of Congress.

"If ever any prediction was true it is this, and if ever a great and good man was Surrounded with a choice of difficulties it is General Washington. I fear the Consequences, and See clearly that he will be impelled to make other attempts and Efforts to save his Country that his numbers will not be adequate to, and that he also may fall a Sacrifice to the folly and parsimony of our worthy rulers.

"I know that friendship will induce you to attend to the education of my little son and Daughter. I fear that their mother will not survive this Stroke. Do go to her and tell her her Children claim her kindest offices and protection.

"My best and Sincerest wishes to Mrs. Delany and family and all friends. I am called to Sup, but where to breakfast, either within the enemy's lines in triumph or in the other World." For Polly there was not a personal word of any sort, no letter and no further message.

Wayne snatched a short supper, picked up his spontoon, the sharp-pointed iron-tipped spear which all his officers carried in lieu of firearms, and went forth from Springsteel's to give his men the signal to advance. The three sections moved on schedule. At precisely midnight, in the bright moonlight both wings stepped out into the flat marsh that lay about the fort. Febiger and Wayne, taking the one good road, leading up the south slope of the point, came into the open at the exact moment that Butler's left wing sought the sunken sandbar on the north.

Both flanks met severe disappointment. Someone had miscalculated. The sandbar, which neighbors had predicted would be dry, was waist-deep under water; the road was still soft, with a foot of mire. Murfree's men, coming to the center, fired some minutes before the wings were ready to scale the cliffs. The premature fire worked well, for Colonel Johnson, utterly deceived, hurried half his force downhill to man the outer-line redoubts. He had no inkling that other rebels, wading silently on either side of Murfree, were flanking his defenses. The roar of cannon, pouring grape at Murfree's two companies, drowned out the noise of Forlorn Hope men smashing the abatis. The British could not understand why the Americans made such slow progress in attacking. "Come on, you rebels!" yelled the British 17th. "Come on and fight!" Murfree's men held their tongues, except for one irrepressible ensign who, knowing that the longer Johnson blazed away at this central feint, the better chance the wings would have, yelled back: "Take your time, my lads; we'll be there soon."

The Forlorn Hopes could not work fast enough; the advance guards caught up with them before more than a few logs were cleared. Without waiting for the abatis to be broken through, the men pressed forward. Logs, crisscrossed and piled irregularly, gave precarious footing in the midnight blackness; men slipped and fell, barking their shins, bruising their legs, and ripping their uniforms. Butler's left, wet to the neck after wading the sandbar, ran headlong into sharp-pointed tree trunks aiming outward at them. Wayne's column on the right, mud from head to foot, scrambled over the abatis.

Not until Wayne bayoneted his way past the first redoubt did Johnson realize that he had been tricked and flanked. He faced his men about to form a square, but in the darkness he could not finish the maneuver. Wayne swept past him into the midst of the second abatis; Butler pushed beyond the redoubts on the left. Fire intensified when the small garrison manning the citadel poured shot indiscriminately at both the British and the Continentals. Wayne fell when a musket ball grazed the side of his head; he lay senseless for a moment among the tangled logs. When he came back to consciousness, he saw his right wing pressing onward. He pointed with his spontoon to the citadel. "Carry me up to the fort, boys," he begged. "Let's go forward." Henry Archer and Fishbourn picked him up. Wayne dropped his spontoon, threw an arm about each man and, stumbling over logs, hurried as fast as he could after his advancing men.

"Old Denmark" Febiger, too, was wounded. A bullet plowed a furrow on the side of his big nose, but even with blood streaming down into his mouth, the Colonel pressed upward to the parapet. Major William Hull, who would command the army of the United States in the War of 1812, lost his hat when a bullet whizzed through it; a moment later his leg stung when a musket ball passed through his boot.

Wayne and Febiger, with the right wing, struck the parapet at the big rock near the west end; they pushed through the gap. At almost the same time, Butler, Gibbon, and the whole left column crowded up. There was no gap here, but Francis McDonald, a private soldier, climbed on the shoulders of a comrade and scaled the wall. He dropped down among the British and, by incredible luck, managed to unbolt the gate so that Butler's left column could push through. The garrison, overwhelmed now by both wings of the Light Infantry and outnumbered almost three to one, struggled desperately, but hopelessly. The Americans yelled loudly, "We've got the fort; it's ours!" and pulled down the British naval ensign. Ludwig Gutbreath, a Pennsylvania boy, handed it to Fleury, his commander.

The yells, of course, attracted attention. Johnson hurried uphill, only to find himself surrounded by rebel soldiers. In token of defeat, he handed his sword to Febiger. The private soldiers, dropping their guns, threw themselves upon the mercy of the Light Infantry. Half a mile across the river, at Verplanck's Point, a small British garrison of 70 men heard the American shouts, but, unable at that distance to make out the words, they thought it a British call of triumph. Brigade-Major Benson dragged a boat into the river and rowed across the Hudson to Stony Point. He found himself, to his dismay, surrounded by rebels, but he dodged from them in the dark and managed to escape. He rowed back with the bad news that the Americans had Stony Point. Only one other Englishman, Lieutenant Roberts of the artillery, escaped. He plunged into the river, swam a mile to the warship *Vulture*, and reported that

Wayne, using the same tactics that No-Flint Grey employed, had wiped out the stigma of Paoli.

The Light Infantry had killed 63 Britishers, all with the bayonet, at a loss to themselves of 15 dead and 84 wounded. They captured fifteen guns, three Negro boys, and 543 soldiers. Among the stores found at the fort were nine marquees, a hundred and thirty-one tents, two books on how to build a fort, and a speaking trumpet. Immediately after the capture of Stony Point, the cannon were turned upon Verplanck's Point and upon the *Vulture*. For more than an hour these objectives were bombarded with more than a hundred shells, but without effect. Neither Verplanck's Point nor the *Vulture* responded to the fire.

Wayne, still shaky from the two-inch scalp wound that clipped the hair above his forehead, sat down at once to write a brief report to Washington. His words, dated at Stony Point at two o'clock in the morning, rivaled Caesar's famous *"Veni, vidi, vici"*: "The fort and garrison with Col. Johnson are ours. Our officers and men behaved like men who are determined to be free."

In fuller dispatches later, written as he sat in Johnson's former quarters, a white bandage about his head, Wayne specially commended Fleury, Stewart, Butler, Meigs, Febiger, Hay, Lee, Fishbourn, and Archer. His alleged partiality in praising the last two, whose work had consisted in helping Wayne into the fort, was bitterly protested by those whom he neglected to mention. Gibbon was particularly indignant at having been omitted. Febiger wrote an anonymous letter to a Philadelphia newspaper, pointing out inaccuracies in Wayne's report and insisting that his own contributions had been minimized. Meigs protested that Wayne showed partiality, particularly by overpraising Southerners at New England's expense, a complaint echoed by Hull and by Colonel Isaac Sherman, who challenged Wayne to a duel; Major Thomas Posey went so far as to write a formal letter to Washington protesting against Wayne's injustice. In a series of conferences and letters, Wayne explained that he had no preferences and that he had not intended to cast discredit upon those whose names were omitted. When Congress awarded honors for the victory, Wayne received a gold medal, while silver medals were granted Stewart and Fleury; Knox, Gibbon, and Archer were promoted to be captains.

Though dissatisfaction was thus voiced at Wayne's distribution of honors, no one dissented from the belief that Stony Point was an overwhelming victory. Washington, arriving on the seventeenth from New Windsor with Greene and Steuben, enthusiastically praised the surprise attack; Steuben said that no European could have done better; Greene called the arrangements "the perfection of discipline. . . . It will," he said, "forever immortalize General Wayne." Other generals and statesmen were similarly congratulatory. Schuyler forwarded a letter warmly praising Wayne, to which Wayne replied at once that no other message "gave me half the pleasure I experienced from yours." Colonel Alexander Spottswood of Virginia termed it "the greatest stroke that has been struck this war," and Adam Stephen, in retirement since he was cashiered for drunkenness at Germantown, wrote that Wayne had "added dignity to the American arms and acquired immortal renown." John Armstrong was fulsome: "Once in an age, or in the course of some great Revolution, Heaven marks out some particular leader for an acquisition like yours at Stony Point."

Wayne was particularly happy to receive two letters from men who were not too friendly. St. Clair hurried a message of cordial congratulations: "It is the compleatest surprise I ever heard of." Charles Lee, living in a barrenly furnished house in Berkeley County, Virginia, with only his dogs for company— his doxy having deserted him—was particularly generous: "I do most sincerely declare that your action on the assault of Stony Point is not only the most brilliant, in my opinion, through the whole course of this War on either side, but that it is one of the most brilliant I am acquainted with in history." Rush wrote: "Our streets for several days ring with nothing but the name of General Wayne. You are remembered constantly next to our great and good General Washington. . . . You have established the national character of our country." It was a highly appreciated honor, too, for Wayne to receive from

Congress, through John Jay, its thanks for "this brilliant action that adds fresh lustre to our arms."

Anthony, always thin-skinned, noted that there were significant omissions in the list of those who sent congratulatory messages. Few of the major-generals sent a line of praise and not a single brigadier on active service wrote a word to him; the politicians, except his close friends Rush, Reed, and Delany, were strangely silent. No girl sent a note, though there was a brief scrawl from Polly, who was again convalescing from an illness; she was more concerned with her own troubles than with Anthony's triumph: "Through the hand of Our blessed god and the tender care my Mother and Sister has takeing of me i once more am raised so far of a bed of sleep as to be able to give you joy of your great Success."

He found great consolation in the despair of the British. Clinton was so disconsolate, both at losing Stony Point and at the failure of his Government to send reinforcements, that he pleaded to be relieved of service in favor of Cornwallis. Prior to the surprise, Clinton, by direct orders from London, had been sending raiding parties to the Chesapeake and to the Connecticut coast; through his subordinates he had been burning New Haven, Norwalk, and other towns close to the coast. Immediately after Stony Point the British, humiliated and disgraced by their defeat, called in their troops, thus sparing towns like New London, which was next upon the schedule for destruction, and saving New Jersey from similar depredations.

Stony Point enhanced American prestige. Continentals, proud that their bayonets were as keen as those of No-Flint Grey's men, certain that their Light Infantry could stand up to crack Guardsmen and grenadiers, assured that troops fighting in the open could dislodge British veterans from behind their barricades, swaggered proudly. A whole new folklore sprang up in the former colonies, a body of myth and legend glorifying the common soldier of America, and exalting their leaders into supermen.

Wayne had started on his march from Sandy Beach at eleven in the morning; he possessed Stony Point by one o'clock at night. There was mystic significance in the fact that this assault by troops of thirteen states had taken just precisely thirteen hours, especially as rumors ran that Wayne had thirteen teeth in each jaw. Reports spread that Wayne grew three extra toes after Stony Point.

American control of Stony Point did not endure long. On July 18, the day after Washington's inspection, the works were completely dismantled, and the Light Infantry withdrew. Clinton, sailing up the Hudson with a large troop detachment, occupied the promontory immediately and set up stronger, more nearly perfect, works. Washington, supported by the usual council of war, again remained immobile. He was certain that Clinton's objective was West Point, but until Clinton made a further move, he kept his army in position. Wayne, scarred with a cicatrice under the hair where the musket ball had grazed him, hoped that Washington would let him repeat the Stony Point assault, but Washington vetoed the suggestion.

The Light Infantry marked time in its camp, joyfully dividing the prize money of $158,640, for which the stores at Stony Point had been appraised. The sum was approximately $140 per man. In addition Fleury, to whom $500 was allotted for having been first to enter the works, added that sum to the men's share, and Knox, winner of the second award, turned over his $400 prize to the common pool. But when Sergeants Baker, Spencer, and Donlop, wounded soldiers who had followed Fleury and Knox, wished to give up their rewards, neither officers nor soldiers would permit them to sacrifice their prizes. The officers took for their particular use the three Negro boys captured at the fort. Wayne announced that it was the general wish to free the slaves "after a few years' service."

Wayne, smoking fine "segars" sent him as a present for taking Stony Point, took life easy. He dined out frequently, with brother officers, once or twice with Washington, and several times with the Udney Hays, before gracious Mrs. Hay rode off to the eastward.

CHAPTER XI

Part-Time General

WAYNE was not wanted at the camp. Although his stroke at Stony Point had been the most spectacular victory of the war, more inspiring than Saratoga, Anthony was a part-time general. When troops were active, he was indispensable; always the aggressor, he gave verve and spirit to the men; no other general showed such dash and enterprise. He was an asset in a brisk campaign; but in winter quarters Wayne was a heavy liability. Troubles always boiled about him. His feud with St. Clair was a source of much embarrassment to those who, by military courtesy, must show deference to the colorless and static Arthur St. Clair rather than to the more dynamic Anthony. When he obeyed the orders of his major-general, Wayne did so in a sullen fashion that set a bad example for his men; more often, he invoked those same sea-lawyer tactics that made Gibbon obnoxious. Officers of lower rank, seeing their brigadier contentious, followed his example. Whenever Wayne and St. Clair were in camp together, bad blood was evident. Their feud imperiled the welfare of the Pennsylvania Line.

Leisure weighed heavily upon Anthony. Essentially a lonely man, with few inner resources with which to entertain himself, he craved companionship. When company was convivial, he was delightful; he could be charming when, with a few choice spirits, he drank, feasted, and exchanged gay gossip. Among his intimates no other officer owned his gift of repartee; few others had his knack for turning scintillating phrases. He sparkled at the dinner table, but when he was alone he fell a prey to that morbidity which besets solitary souls. Reading offered only brief diversion. Always he read with Madeira or rum punch by his side; he gave more attention to the bottle and the bowl than to the book.

Gossip in the mess reported that in such a period of boredom Wayne made friends with the enemy. Captain Sir Thomas Wallace of the 17th British of the Stony Point garrison came to the American camp under a flag of truce to talk about exchanging prisoners. Wayne, finding him congenial, gave breakfast and dinner parties in honor of the Englishman. It was, as it happened, a time when American food supplies were low, and when, to quote Wayne's letter to a commissary, "The accumulated distresses occasioned by every possible extreme of cold, hunger and nakedness has rendered the troops desperate." But Wayne found ample food and drink to entertain the Britisher; he made warm friends with Wallace. Such hospitality, he thought, was proper toward a gentlemanly adversary; reversing his opinions of a year or two before, when he had told Ann Wister that all Englishmen were bloodthirsty savages, he said: "I wish to God that this Contest could be conducted with more liberality. For my part, I could eat, drink and fight with the Gentlemen alternately without affecting my principles, for I have no idea of being aware of Individuals."

There was no question of Wayne's patriotism, nor any thought that he had grown lukewarm toward the Continental cause. He had, as it happened, made his position clear to Wallace: "As the all-wise and benevolent author of Nature could never be so preposterously unjust as to despise this New World by making it tributary to a little Island, we must in justice conclude that He has pointed it out as the last asylum of liberty to mankind." Wallace did not agree with Wayne's politics, but he admired Wayne's broad-mindedness. Before the men parted, Wallace promised to send his host copies of all the latest British publications available at New York, and despite the unfortunate circumstance that some Continental soldier less chivalrous than Wayne stole Wallace's saddle and bridle while Wayne was entertaining the Englishman, Wallace fulfilled the promise. A big bundle of the *Annual Register,* the *Gentleman's Magazine,* and other London periodicals came into the American camp under a flag of truce. Wayne, in turn, caught the thief and sent him to the British, together with the saddle. The bridle, he regretted, could not be found.

Had the Wallace entertainments been mere conventional gestures, few could have criticized, but there is evidence of an aftermath that is more difficult to overlook. Wayne used his friendship to make arrangements for buying British goods and for smuggling them through the lines. He did so for no monetary gain; he strove to please a lady. American girls, cut off from purchasing new clothes from London shops, ignorant even of the latest fashions, thought themselves suffering severely from wartime hardships. Mary Vining, the dark-eyed Delaware beauty who had sent the sword, appealed to Anthony to help her.

Mary Vining was well accustomed to having officers chained to her chariot. Twenty-three and charming, daughter of a Chief Justice and sister of a Congressman, she had, through her dazzling beauty and her fascinating personality, bewitched the French and the British as well as the Continental Army. Her deep-set, big black eyes, snapping vivaciously under their long, heavy lashes, made men her slaves; her piquant wit disarmed them utterly. Wayne was her latest conquest. Since leaving Philadelphia for the campaign that culminated at Stony Point, he had thought of her frequently. Her tall, slim figure, her delicate rose-pink complexion, her graceful arms and hands, her full red lips, and her mass of blue-black hair haunted his dreams.

He wished to send her a gift that would show his gratitude for the sword and that would be worthy of her beauty. Wallace told him of New York shops filled with London importations, and Anthony, anxious to gain favor in the eyes of the loveliest girl in America, remembered her distaste for the clumsy homespun woolens of America. Wallace willingly agreed to help. He too had a sweetheart, Hester Kortright of New York, who he was certain would buy dress goods for Miss Vining. Wayne gave him 21 guineas and suggested that Miss Kortright use her judgment as to what was best. When the purchases were made, Wayne said, they could be wrapped into a neat parcel to be sent through the lines. Wallace promised that the British sentries would not interfere. The scheme worked perfectly; the clothes came quickly into Morristown and Wayne sent them down at once to Philadelphia. When Mary Vining opened her parcels at her brother's home, she clapped her hands and danced with glee at her lovely present. It would be pleasant to narrate that at the same time that Anthony refitted Mary Vining's wardrobe, he also bought a dress or two for Polly, but the thought did not occur to him. He commissioned Wallace to buy a few small gifts for Margaretta and for Mrs. Powel, mistress of her boardingschool, but he ordered nothing for his wife.

Meanwhile, camp atmosphere grew more electric. Charges of favoritism and of friendliness to the enemy sped through the cliques; rumor told how Wayne and his companions drank heavily each night. Again, as in the previous winter, Washington thought it wise to send Wayne off on a furlough. Wayne had enjoyed nearly half a year's absence from the army, and other generals fretted that they also deserved a vacation, but Washington feared that Wayne's continued presence might grow disturbing. Accordingly when the Light Infantry dissolved for the season on New Year's Day, Wayne received another leave of absence. It came as a present on his thirty-fifth birthday.

By spending the winter at the capital, Wayne escaped grueling hardship at Morristown. After four years of warfare, the national energies were exhausted; with little field activity to offer the inspiration of victory, enthusiasm for rebellion subsided; the French aid, so much relied upon, had thus far shown itself in little more than promises. Continental currency, unbacked by sufficient specie, slid steadily to ever lower values while prices skyrocketed. Shoes were $70 a pair and difficult to obtain even at that price; meat and grain were extremely scarce. To make matters worse, heavy snowstorms blocked Jersey roads, preventing provision wagons from approaching Morristown; on several occasions the men were wholly without food. Washington despaired of keeping his troops together.

"Our magazines are absolutely empty everywhere," he wrote to Reed, "and our commissaries entirely destitute of money or credit to replenish them. We have never experienced a like ex-

tremity at any period of the war. We have often felt temporary
want from accidental delays in forwarding supplies, but we had
always something in our magazines, and the means of procuring more. Neither one nor the other is, at present, the case.
. . . Unless, therefore, some extraordinary and immediate exertion can be made by the States from which we draw our supplies, there is every appearance that the army will infallibly
disband in a fortnight."

The chief state from which such help must be given was
Pennsylvania. New England, hard-hit by the winter, could offer little immediate relief; there were ugly rumors that some
states, such as Connecticut, flatly refused assistance. The South,
intent on aiding Charleston against Sir Henry Clinton's attacking fleet and army, had few goods to spare; the long overland
journey, moreover, would have required more wagons and draft
animals than could be brought together. Only the Middle States
were free to help the army, but these had been drained by previous campaigns; their resources were low. Washington relied
upon those states, refusing even to consider Pennsylvania's
agonized cries that her resources had been overestimated and
that too much was required of her. "Pennsylvania has it in her
power to contribute without comparison more to our success
than any other State in the two essential articles of flour and
transportation. . . . The matter is reduced to a point—either
Pennsylvania must give us all the aid we ask of her, or we undertake nothing."

It was then Wayne's peculiar task to serve again as liaison
officer between the army and the one state which could save
the Revolution. Throughout the severe winter of 1780, while
the army suffered at Morristown, Anthony Wayne worked to
swing statesmen to a realization of the emergency. His task
was difficult, for Pennsylvania was torn by factional disputes
wherein both radicals and conservatives preferred outright
Tories to each other, but Wayne, employing a new-found tact
which never had been expected of him, worked as intermediary. He was bitterly prejudiced against radical statesmen; he
thought them responsible for army sufferings, as well as for
his own inability to win higher rank. He warmly endorsed

Walter Stewart's indictment of politicians: "How much have those People . . . to answer for! What Uniform Ignorance and Stupidity have they made use of respecting the different departments of the Army. Should things come to a kind of conflagration, my Indignation, by Heaven, shall be levelled at a few of the White Wigs whose narrowness of Soul and shallowness of Head have reduced us to our present distresses."

Wayne also disliked the White Wigs, the politicians of both parties, but he knew that they held the key to military victory; he wooed their favor. It was his responsibility to bring them out of their "most wretched torpidity." Yet it was not so much the White Wigs who held up assistance, but rather the conservative bankers, merchants, and big businessmen who were reluctant to co-operate. They had never been keen for revolution, though they had been persuaded to take part in it; now that the legislators had resorted to the use of worthless paper money, they balked at further help. Wayne was particularly useful here, for these conservatives were largely his social intimates. Robert Morris was his friend; he had known the Willings and the Biddles from his boyhood. Since he too was a stanch conservative, he could approach them as a mediator; he could appeal to them as patriots to put the lives of Continental soldiers above money values. He found no pleasure in thus playing the game of the White Wigs, but he was above low partisanship.

Food was found in Pennsylvania, although only by draining the state dry. Following a January thaw, it was hurried into Morristown. Wayne then turned his attention to the clothing problem, in which he was greatly aided through the invention of a ladies' committee to collect by voluntary subscription supplies of money and linen for the army. By dividing Philadelphia and its suburban districts into areas for canvassing, sixteen hundred contributors, giving sums ranging from the 7s. 6d. of "colored Phillis" to the Marchioness de Lafayette's 100 guineas in specie, raised more than $7,500 in hard money. Much of the success of this drive was due to the splendid efforts of Esther Reed, wife of the president of Pennsylvania, and to Sarah

Bache, Franklin's daughter. Wayne regretted mightily that his relatives took so little part in raising money.

Absorption in military duty and his preference for gayer folk caused Wayne's close friends to drift away. Some, the flightier and more irresponsible, resented the time that he devoted to army problems; others, like Abraham Robinson and most members of his family, were angry because he failed to write. Robinson was point-blank in his frankness: "Your neglect of paying me and family the respect you formerly used to do and your not writing to me as you did the former campaigns has been the occation of my long silence." Polly, indignant, no doubt, because all that Anthony ever wrote to her nowadays was exhortations to educate the children and to see that Margaretta acquired social graces, ceased to write; there had been but two letters from her since his last furlough, and none whatever in the winter, though Anthony had sent eight notes to her. She was hurt because she had inadvertently found a note, forwarded from Sharp Delany's, and addressed to "Dear Molly," which on examination she had discovered was meant for Mary Vining, and not for herself. Undoubtedly she felt the sting of Anthony's sending new clothes to Mary Vining and to Margaretta while she remained forgotten and ignored; she also knew that in the first warm days of spring he hurried down to Delaware, ostensibly to inspect fortifications, but in reality to spend some time with Mary Vining. He had not once visited his home at Waynesborough.

Not that it had been necessary to delay that long to see the charming Delawarean. Mary, whom Wayne was now calling Molly, spent the winter at Philadelphia, savoring the gaieties of the capital. Even while Wayne was lobbying with Pennsylvania politicians, he kept his late afternoons free for teas at Molly's court, and he dined frequently in her company. He had considerable competition, since Congressmen and army officers flocked about, and in the middle of May Lafayette had come back from France with a coterie of brilliant friends to swell her suitors; but Wayne, though clumsier than the Versailles set, had a fresh, boyish enthusiasm which fascinated the lovely charmer. She liked to see him in his spick-and-span regimentals amid the shining silks and satins of her other suitors; she wore for his admiring eyes the splendid materials that Miss Kortright had sent over from New York. Wayne was captivated; he resented the time he had to spend at a victory dinner celebrating Spain's conquest of Pensacola from the British, and for the first time in his life he begrudged going to a banquet with his fellow Irishmen on St. Patrick's Day, even though there had been glorious news that Irish soldiers had crushed a British army of 3,000. He had gone to that dinner of .the Friendly Sons of St. Patrick under protest; when he discovered that the "news" of Ireland's victory had been false, he was inconsolable.

His time for play drew toward a close. Copies of the King's speech from the throne, brought to America, presaged an active season. Wayne wrote to Washington, again urging that, to counterbalance the recent fall of Charleston to the British, the Americans attack New York, but his suggestion was unheeded. So were his hints that he should head a revived, and much larger, Light Infantry Corps, an honor which, to Wayne's anger, was instead given to Lafayette, a major-general. In spite of Stony Point, Washington offered Wayne only his old post as brigadier in the Pennsylvania Line, subject to the hated Major-General St. Clair.

Anthony was brokenhearted; he meditated resigning from the service. To drown his grief, he got himself mixed up in a drunken altercation where he had to act as intermediary to save Light Horse Harry Lee from fighting a duel with a Congressman; he intrigued with the North Carolina delegation to have himself named a major-general from that state. Yet he could not forget that he had but two alternatives before him— either to serve beneath St. Clair or to retire to his Sabine fields. Often he had threatened the latter, but he chose the former.

He could not leave for camp until he straightened out accounts with both the state and the nation. Faced with a demand from the Pennsylvania state store that he pay for ninety gallons of spirits, forty gallons of rum, a hundred and twenty-three pounds of sugar, eighty pounds of coffee, twenty-eight pounds of chocolate, and nine pounds of tobacco bought by him during the six months ending January 1, and for a pipe of Madeira purchased during the spring, Wayne replied with a counterclaim for the ten fat cows commandeered at Waynesborough just before Paoli. The Continental financiers were glad to satisfy their debt, so they asserted, but when he saw the thirty-two thin cattle they offered in exchange, Anthony denounced them as scrawny, half-dead calves not worth the forage that they ate. He demanded that they be driven back into military stockyards, refusing to accept such poor animals, and he asked in exchange that he be paid the cash equivalent. He was awarded £15,000 in Continental paper, equal in hard cash to about $2,000, or at the rate of approximately 40 cents in specie for each pound of beef supplied. From this sum, he paid off the costs of his liquor and other luxuries.

With these transactions satisfied, he no longer had a valid excuse for lingering in Philadelphia. On June 9 he scratched a hasty note to Polly telling her that he was disappointed and distressed not to visit home, but that he must fly to camp. His only personal touch was the concluding line: "Adieu, a long adieu, but that we may again meet is the sincere wish of your affectionate, Ant^y. Wayne."

2

Wayne rejoined the army as it again moved northward to the Hudson. Following its second winter at Morristown, in the summer of 1780 the Continental force once more sought the highlands that controlled communications between New England and the South. As Wayne left Philadelphia, Washington slowly took his old road through Pompton and along the Ramapo to Fish Kill and West Point. Wayne overtook the army at Preakness Brook, close to the present city of Paterson. Sir Henry Clinton watched Washington's march, but made no move to halt its progress. Two recent efforts to attack New Jersey had collapsed; Clinton preferred to wait developments.

Comfortable and well fed, the British leader hoped by inaction to wear down American morale.

Wayne hated the thought of another idle summer. When Washington revealed that no aggressive act was planned, Wayne looked about for some objective that could keep his Pennsylvanians busy. He did not wish to see them rust; he wanted them sharp-edged and alert. Eastward, across the Passaic, stretched the English Neighborhood, where hundreds of Clinton's cattle, sheep, and horses grazed. Guarding them were "refugees," Tory sympathizers who had left their homes to seek protection under British guns. Some of these were peaceful victims of the war, others were in British military service as militiamen. These guerrillas had headquarters in a wooden blockhouse at Bull's Ferry in the very heart of what is now Jersey City. "Give me," Wayne said to Washington, "a few regiments, and I can clear the English Neighborhood. The refugees will run, and I can capture the cattle. A few pieces of artillery will batter down that blockhouse."

Wayne held, tucked away in the back of his mind, a more ambitious scheme. He could, he thought, by making sufficient demonstration, lure British troops across the river from New York. Landing-places on the Jersey shore were few; passages through the towering Palisades were easily defended. Any landing party must string through narrow defiles where it could easily be trapped. He would therefore let the British land without offering opposition, but when they entered the narrow passes, his Pennsylvanians, waiting in ambush, would fall upon them.

He said nothing of this plan to Washington, lest cautious Fabius veto the suggestion. Washington would doubt that Sir Henry would be reckless enough to rush men into a narrow gap; the Commander-in-Chief, unlike Wayne, would not gamble on the chance. So far as Washington knew, Wayne thought only of attacking the blockhouse and of raiding cattle. For this purpose, Washington allowed him four regiments, Colonel Stephen Moylan's dragoons, and four field pieces. Wayne posted Harmar with two regiments at the defiles; the rest, he estimated, could reduce the fort. Moylan flared up angrily when Wayne explained his share in the adventure.

"My men are fighters, sir, not ferrymen! We'll not agree."

"Oh, yes, you will," retorted Wayne, laughing. "It'll be disobedience of orders if you don't."

"But, damn it, General, we dragoons use sabers. We attack. We thrust with the lance. We've got no room for passengers on our horses."

"Carry them like women," Wayne explained. "Put them on pillions and have them put their arms around your men. All you have to do is to take those infantrymen to the field of battle. You won't fight."

"What do you mean, we won't fight? Dragoons fight better than foot soldiers any day."

"But not today," said Wayne. "Once you get them to the ground, you dragoons will chase cows. We're counting on you to collect the cattle."

"Chase cows! By God, General Wayne . . ."

Wayne tired of the comedy. He stiffened and his voice turned hard and cold: "Colonel Moylan, you have your orders. You will have each of your men mount a soldier behind him and proceed to the place I pointed out. After you make one trip, go back and pick up another load. Do this until you are ordered to stop. Then, you will drive off the cattle."

Moylan saluted silently, but as he left Wayne's quarters he thumbed his nose behind Wayne's back. Dutifully, his dragoons took up their soldier "wives" behind them, but they took a cavalryman's revenge by trotting their horses, jolting the "wives" every inch of the way to Three Pigeons Tavern at New Durham on the road to the Bergen blockhouse. There they unceremoniously pushed off the infantrymen, and clattered back to get another load. Once the infantrymen were ferried, Moylan's next task was not unpleasant. Wayne wanted guides; Moylan's men set out to round up civilians. The Irishman told his men with a wink that they were to let the guides "know the consequences of deception," and the bold dragoons embroidered with ready imaginations the warnings that they gave the people. He turned over to Wayne a score of cowed civilians ready to guide the regiments to the blockhouse.

Crashing through the blockhouse defense was not so easy as Wayne had anticipated. For more than an hour on July 21, his six-pounders banged away, from a distance of only sixty yards, while infantrymen waited impatiently. The guns were too light to batter down the walls; shot sank into the logs and stopped halfway. "The more we shoot," said a gunner ruefully, "the stronger that damned fort becomes. We're just plating it with iron."

Inside the blockhouse, seventy refugees, whom Harmar called "Negroes, Tories, and vagabonds," fired carefully through their loopholes, picking off officers while Wayne's infantrymen stood in line. Chambers's regiment lost patience. Men broke ranks and rushed pell-mell toward the blockhouse. Over the sharpened logs of the abatis they battered through the stockade into the enclosure about the fort. Men fell as the refugees fired and reloaded with frenzied speed, but the rush continued. No orders had been given for the dash. Jim Chambers, indeed, had been taken by surprise. He ran after his men, shouting for them to come back, but they paid no heed. Recklessly, with only bayonets as weapons, they charged the thick walls of the blockhouse. Firing ceased when the soldiers reached the fort. American artillery dared not fire, lest they kill more Pennsylvanians than British; refugees within the fort fell back from the loopholes lest bayonets thrust through from outside blind them.

Wayne rushed a second regiment into action, and its men swarmed about the blockhouse. They hammered against the ironbound doors; some few, who carried axes, chopped at the timbers. Angry soldiers poked the barrels of their guns through loopholes and fired blindly into the interior, killing five men and wounding eight in this undirected shooting. The action was a stalemate. The fort, sealed tight against attack, could not be taken, but neither could it fire against Wayne's men. The Pennsylvanians, yelling and cursing, found the bolted door planks too heavy to be broken through.

Wayne realized that the attack was hopeless. He could, by

long-continued siege, starve the blockhouse into submission, but he had neither time nor men to waste on such a move. By this time he knew that however Moylan might detest his job, he had driven off several hundred head of livestock from the English Neighborhood. Scouts brought news that the British in New York were doing just what Wayne anticipated. Transports loaded with troops were coming across the Hudson to land upon the Jersey shore. Wayne hurried his men away from the blockhouse in order to trap the British reinforcements. As the Pennsylvanians left, the refugees remanned the loopholes and fired upon the retreating rebels.

To Wayne's disgust, the British, who had seemed so anxious to fall into his trap, suddenly changed policy. Their transports stopped in midstream as though warned of danger. As Wayne watched, the ships swung about as if to come to Bergen Neck, above Wayne's present position. If they succeeded, the Americans would be pocketed between the blockhouse and the British reinforcements. Escape would be impossible, since Bergen Neck was a narrow peninsula with deep water on its flanks.

Standing in the open country, well out of gunshot from the fort, Anthony canvassed the situation. The British, it was certain, could not now be ambushed, and since the livestock had been rounded up, only danger would result from continuing the attack. He withdrew his regiments, first setting fire to British skiffs at the water's edge. He ordered the dry grass, parched by recent scorching weather, burned so that the British might not have forage; he could not know that the flames thus set would rage for two days, burning orchards and ruining other growing crops. His retreat was difficult. The refugees chased him four miles, firing indiscriminately into the mass of men and animals. The British recaptured many of the cattle and also took Wayne's body servant, his horse, and his personal belongings.

American losses were extremely heavy in comparison with the results achieved. At the cost of 90 men killed and wounded, the Continentals gained large meat rations for the army, and at the same time sharply reduced British stores of food and fodder. The loss of cattle rankled in the British mind. Sourly, they sought to gloss the affair by calling Wayne a drover who could conquer cows but who dared not face 3,000 British soldiers. Major John André, debonair aide-de-camp to the British leader, wrote a seventy-two stanza ballad, in the style of the famous fifteenth-century "Chevy Chace." André called his parody "Cow Chase," and published it in three installments of the *Royal Gazette*. Its style is not above reproach, for André's poetic talent has been overpraised, and its temper is worse. André, in telling of Wayne's expedition, accuses the General of cowardice.

> I, under cover of attack
> Whilst you are all at blows,
> From English Neighb'rood and Tinack
> Will drive away the cows

Wayne and Light Horse Harry, by the "Cow Chase" ballad, were cowboys with whom their supposed associate Lord Stirling failed to co-operate. It was Stirling's intention to participate, but, as André wrote,

> The self-made peer had sure been there
> But that the peer was drunk.

André scoffed, too, at the American insistence that the six-pounders could not penetrate the log walls of the blockhouse, for, as he wrote:

> Five refugees, 'tis true, were found
> Stiff on the block house floor,
> But then, 'tis thought, the shot went round
> And in at the back door.

But André's sharpest thrusts were aimed at Wayne, who, sitting in Yan Van Poop's tavern, Three Pigeons, meets "a lovely hamadryad," who weeps as she complains that her trees are being felled and who offers him her love in exchange for his protection:

> So Roman Anthony, they say,
> Disgrac'd th' imperial banner,
> And for a gypsy lost a day
> Like Anthony the Tanner.

He gibes at Wayne because in the pursuit by the refugees on his retreat, the American commander lost his personal supplies:

> His horse that carried all his prog,
> His military speeches,
> His corn-stalk whisky for his grog,
> Blue stockings and brown breeches.

And then, in the closing stanza of the ballad, he printed a quatrain that, in the light of contemporary happenings, was pathetically prophetic:

> And now I've closed my epic strain,
> I tremble as I shew it,
> Lest this same warrior-drover Wayne
> Should ever catch the poet.

Ironically, the last stanza of André's "Cow Chase" appeared in print on the very day that he was captured. His jailers pushed the New York newspaper containing the last stanzas through the bars of the cell where he was imprisoned, taunting him with being at the mercy of men whom he had maligned.

3

From major-generals down to privates, the army was decidedly unhappy. Unpaid, poorly clad Continentals, certain that fat civilians stole military funds, grumbled openly. Angry because they were held in service uselessly during the summer months of 1780 when they might be tending farms, they demanded their discharge. When officers refused them leave, pointing out that they had enlisted for the duration of the war, soldiers strung up effigies of their generals and lashed them publicly. Troopers threatened to desert; they were held in line only by repeated bribes of rum. Even when there was no thought of preferment, jealousies ran high. High-spirited youngsters snapped peevishly at each other over fancied slights. At mess tables and over gaming-boards, challenges flew recklessly; dueling was frequent.

Congress tangled the situation further. Decreeing that numerous small regiments should merge into larger units, it cut down the number of officers required. Many leaders, particularly of high rank, thus became supernumerary; they faced return to private life at a time when work for civilians was scarce and when men trained for military duty would have no scope for their special skill. It was, of course, one thing to grumble in the mess about camp hardships, but quite a different matter to be dismissed from service. Men who had ranted about their eagerness for freedom now abruptly changed their minds. They could not, they insisted, return to drab routines of countinghouse or farm. These too fished for favor; they plotted and connived to keep their places while men superior in service were released. For weeks, they backbit and knifed each other. Since readjustments would not take place until the end of the year, they had much time for intrigue.

The McPherson quarrel again cropped out. Once before, when Anthony lobbied and sampled flowers at the capital, he had made a temporary adjustment of this former Englishman's rank in the Continental Army, but the situation had grown worse. By St. Clair's political maneuvering, McPherson now held rank in the Pennsylvania Line over the heads of men of longer standing. Pennsylvanians protested. With Wayne's connivance, they went so far as to hand an ultimatum to George Washington, threatening that unless McPherson were removed, every Pennsylvania officer would resign. St. Clair took the ultimatum as a personal affront; he went to Washington, complaining of Wayne's insubordination. Wayne retorted that St. Clair violated army ethics and that the McPherson situation was intolerable. He angrily announced that he would quit the army rather than accept St. Clair's interference with the Pennsylvania Line.

Washington was much embarrassed. By strict interpretation of army rules, Wayne was guilty of disobedience of orders and of disrespect to an officer of higher rank. As major-general, St. Clair commanded both Wayne and the Pennsylvania Line; the McPherson appointment, having been made by Washington himself on St. Clair's recommendation, could not be withdrawn.

Yet Washington knew also that, by common custom and by codes of honor cherished in all professional armies, the Pennsylvanians had good ground for protest. He proved his wisdom by temporizing. Summoning McPherson to headquarters, Washington asked the Major to accept another post, in an independent command where questions of relative rank would not arise. Such an appointment was a remarkable compliment and though the Major did not accept it until after he consulted with St. Clair, he willingly took the transfer. Thus both McPherson and St. Clair were satisfied; the Pennsylvania officers, now rid of the interloper, also thought that they had won a victory.

Washington mollified Wayne cleverly. Calling the Brigadier into a conference, Washington assured him that as Commander-in-Chief he cherished the highest possible regard for Wayne's ability. The flattery was soothing; even more reassuring was Washington's insistence that at no time had St. Clair ever lodged an official complaint against him, and that the charge of insubordination was merely a personal matter that was not entered in the files. He closed with an apt quotation from one of Wayne's own speeches, delivered to officers of the Pennsylvania Line: "For God's sake, be yourselves—and as a band of Brothers—rise superior to every Injury—whether real or Imaginary." Outwardly, Wayne behaved politely; inwardly, he seethed. In writing to President Joseph Reed, Wayne took the opportunity to insinuate that St. Clair spread groundless gossip in the army. "Could I but once fix the Caitiff, this world would want a place to hold us both. I think I have drawn his picture and doubt not but that the same principles which induced him to throw out the Inuendo has produced others on other ocation and with other Gentlemen with more success altho' equally groundless."

More than anything else, Washington's actions at a moment of emergency proved his trust in Anthony Wayne and in the loyalty of the Pennsylvania Line. The Commander-in-Chief, riding back from Hartford where he had conferred with newly arrived French admirals and generals, came to West Point unexpectedly. Scarcely had the booming of the thirteen-gun welcoming salute died down over the fortress when Washington discovered Arnold's treachery. High-grade men of proved ability were needed immediately to hold West Point against the enemy; Washington sent at once for Wayne and his Pennsylvanians.

Word came to Wayne at eight o'clock in the evening of September 26. His men, worn out after a long day's practice march, were already sleeping, and Wayne had not the heart to rouse them. He questioned Washington's courier closely, learned that no enemy troops had marched for any distance up the Hudson, and that the 1,800 militia at West Point were under strict control. Under the circumstances, Wayne thought, he could afford to wait. But then he changed his mind, and at two o'clock he drummed his men awake and set them on the march. Tramping over the mountains in the dark, he drove his troops sixteen miles within four hours. The reception he received at West Point was worth the effort. "When our approach was announced," said Wayne, "General Washington thought it fabulous. He received us like a God and exclaimed, 'All is safe. I again am happy.' "

Arnold's treachery had been no surprise to Wayne. Ever since the Canadian expedition, he had held a low view of Arnold's ability. "I had," he said, "the most despicable Idea of him both as a Gentleman and a Soldier. He produced a conviction in me in 1776 that honor and Virtue were Strangers to his soul. He was naturally a Coward and never went in the way of Danger but when Stimulated by Liquor even to Intoxication." In separate letters to half a dozen friends at Philadelphia, including Robert Morris, Wayne related sordid incidents in Arnold's career.

"What think you of his employing Sutlers to retail the publick Liquors for his private Emolument, and furnishing his Quarters with beds and other furniture by paying for them with Pork, Salt, flower, etc., drawn from the Magazines?

"He has not stopped here. He has descended much lower and defrauded the old veteran Soldier, among others an old Sergeant of mine has felt his rapacity. By the Industry of this man's wife they had accumulated something handsome to support them in their advanced age, which, coming to the knowledge of this cruel Spoiler, he borrowed 4500 dollars from the poor Credulous Woman and left her in the lurch.

"The dirty, dirty act which he has been capable of committing beggars all description and is of such a Nature as would cause the *Infernals* [to] blush."

Wayne's stay in the "damned country" near West Point was short; his men, as soon as the first fear of British descent faded, went back to their northern-Jersey cantonment. Anthony found there a brand-new blue uniform awaiting him, complete with buff facings, yellow buttons, a pair of epaulets with the star of a brigadier gleaming from them, and a waving feather for his hat. The epaulets, he regretted, were not of the highest quality, for the most skilled craftsman had been absent from town at the time the uniform was ordered, nor was the feather as perfect as he wished, but Delany volunteered to get a better pair of shoulder ornaments, though warning that they cost at least $2,000, and Mary Vining promised him "a feather of taste." Wayne was sorry that regulations required that feather to be white; he would have much preferred one dyed scarlet or, failing that, a colored horsehair plume, falling from his hat like a red waterfall.

His men were less well equipped. Wayne drew up exhaustive lists of necessary goods, and sent copies to Congress, the Board of War, and Pennsylvania state officials; he prodded them for instant action. The two former groups, engrossed in what seemed to them more pressing matters, passed on his pleas to Pennsylvania. Reed replied with lavish promises. Each soldier, he declared, could have at once two hats, three shirts, and three pairs of good stout shoes, in addition to red-trimmed blue uniforms. Every last detail, said Reed, was ready, down to knives and forks and ivory combs for every man; the goods should soon be at camp. But the clothing did not come. Once more, red tape interfered. Just as Mease, during the Valley Forge winter, held up deliveries, so Reed, two years later, made excuses. Wayne waited five months, then, losing all patience, he sent Colonel Humpton down to Philadelphia to demand the clothing. Humpton found the city too delightful. Instead of searching for the goods, he embarked upon a spree. A second agent, sent to find out what had happened to Humpton, discovered him head down among his breakfast coffee cups, dead-drunk. After he sobered, the two men set out on their mission.

No one took the blame for the delay. Reed accused the Pennsylvania Council of delaying deliveries; the latter passed the buck to a purchasing agent, who in turn explained that French manufacturers, from whom the clothes had been ordered, were responsible. But the Frenchmen denied their guilt, declaring that Arthur Lee, one of the three American commissioners to France, had given no signal for delivery, while Lee pinned the blame on Franklin. The latter pointed out that no authority had been delegated to the commissioners by either Congress or the State of Pennsylvania. Meanwhile, the men were literally in rags, and winter was coming on. The Pennsylvanians, camped now on Jockey Hill near Morristown, worked hard, building a stockade, a citadel, and a triple redoubt, but they were hungry, naked, and unpaid. Wayne feared that unless immediate relief were given, his men would rebel.

"Our soldiers," he warned, "are not devoid of reasoning faculties, nor callous to the first feelings of nature. They have now served their country for near five years with fidelity. . . . They have not seen a single paper dollar in the way of pay for near twelve months. . . . However, I don't dispair at being able to restore harmony and content . . . if aided by a timely supply of stores and clothing. On the contrary, should we neglect rewarding their past services and doing justice to their more than Roman virtue, have we not ground to apprehend very disagreeable consequences from their defection?" In talking to his intimates, Wayne showed more pessimism; he predicted an uprising of the troops. Long before Christmas, 1780, he warned that trouble lay ahead. "I sincerely wish," said he, "that the Ides of January were come and past. I can't help cherishing disagreeable ideas about that period."

Nor was he reluctant to fix the blame. Not only were Reed's promises worthless, but, Wayne charged, the man worked secretly against the interest of the army. He suspected that the Pennsylvania president was two-faced, and he was right. Reed was not the only liar. High-pressure recruiting officers, roaming about the state enlisting likely youths, tricked volunteers. Since army agents received for each man enrolled a bonus whose amount depended on the length of time the rookie agreed to serve, recruiting officers deliberately misled candidates. Most frontiersmen could not read or write and hence had no idea what was printed on enlistment blanks; in the rare instances where a volunteer was literate, the fine-print legal technicalities were falsely explained. In Pennsylvania, enlistment forms read "for three years or during the war." Soldiers believed that three years was the maximum of service, even if the war were not then over; army chiefs construed the pledge as binding men until peace was signed, no matter how long fighting might continue.

Wayne's men, volunteering in 1776, by 1780 had more than served the time for which they thought they had agreed, yet discharge was not forthcoming. Moreover, they were angry because when they signed up, in the first flush of the independence fever, they received only a $20 bonus, whereas men who joined later were given six times that amount. Wayne hammered at the state to remedy these grievances, but nothing was done. Pennsylvania held out empty hands, insisting that she had already paid more than one-quarter of the entire expense of the Revolution, and that her resources were exhausted. Her Supreme Executive Council sent a long, complaining letter to Washington, protesting against her burdens. Primarily the letter dealt with quotas set by the army for supplies, but the words referred also to the demand that the state pay money to its soldiers: "The supplies demanded this year . . . are equal to eleven years' taxes and all other income of the State in its most prosperous days; besides which, all the expenses of the frontiers, satisfaction of the army, support of the government, and the vast variety of other charges. All these to be defrayed by money . . . which even the best Whigs will not take but for five or six times below its legal value."

Pennsylvania nevertheless scraped the bottom of her money barrel and managed to collect about $46,000. Reed sent off Lieutenant John Bigham with the money for distribution to the troops, but when six months elapsed without receiving a receipt, the state investigated. To Reed's amazement, he discovered that Bigham had spent all the cash "for necessities along the road." Bigham faced court-martial for embezzlement, but the extravagant lieutenant enjoyed exceptional political pull, for no decision was ever handed down, nor does Bigham appear to have been punished in any way whatever. Plaintively, the Supreme Executive Council remarked, "We cannot but expect mutinies, if injustice is thus done the soldiers with impunity."

Wayne blamed Reed and the civilian officers; he charged flatly that two-thirds of the food and clothing supposedly sent from Philadelphia also were stolen on the way. Washington, who did not feel that he was privileged to meddle in purely state affairs, expressed his sorrow for the men. "It would be well for the troops," he wrote, "if, like chameleons, they could live on air, or, like the bear, suck their paws for sustenance."

Not only were Pennsylvania officials corrupt and inefficient, but they were unbelievably stupid. Knowing that troops were clamoring for pay long overdue, and that veterans of longest service resented larger bonuses granted to later recruits, the state committed an unforgivable blunder. In December, it sent men with bags of gold to Morristown, but it allowed the troops to think that the money was for rookies. Rumors flew that every raw, untrained recruit was to have $25 in hard coin, but that veterans who had not received a dollar during the entire year were to be ignored.

The rumors, as it happened, were unfounded; the gold did go to all the troops, though each man's share was small; but soldiers who had faced privation, who had risked their lives in battle, and who had seen their comrades killed, who even now were naked and starved, supposed their rulers had deserted them. These sufferers, the flower of the Continental Army, had not lost devotion to the cause of freedom; they did not think of quitting the struggle for independence, but they did think that if only the Philadelphia lawmakers could see their misery, justice would at once be granted. They had before them the example of their leaders. Twice, at least, officers had threatened to resign unless their wrongs were righted; in the Mc-Pherson case, they had protested directly to Washington. News of these actions the officers supposed had been rigidly confined within their own restricted circle, but orderlies and servants, overhearing gossip, spread reports among the common soldiers. If officers could thus risk insubordination, and think it owing to their honor, privates could not see why they too should not appeal their case direct to Philadelphia. Food and clothing were certainly as important to them as prestige was to officers.

Wayne's extraordinary efforts, as he worked with his men in wind and cold and snow, building redoubts, directing the construction of huts, and taking part in other camp activities, convinced his men that he, and all his officers, shared their hardships. He managed to postpone their insurrection, particularly when at Christmas more rum arrived, "pretty good in quality but really pitiful in quantity." His men agreed to stick with him until New Year's.

At Christmas there was sufficient food to give the men an extra feast; rum flowed plentifully. The men rejoiced in their unexpected luck; officers, many of whom received parcels from home, pooled their gifts to make a holiday banquet. Wayne contributed a dozen bottles of port sent by Delany, three loaves of sugar, and two pounds of the green tea he liked so much; in addition, he shared with his officers a present of twenty bushels of oysters. For three successive nights officers held banquets at which, to quote a lieutenant's proud confession, "we got tolerable happy." The frolics kept up until late hours.

A growing fear shadowed the jubilations. The long-deferred matter of consolidating regiments, with the consequent dismissal of supernumerary officers, came again into the foreground. The impending shake-up loomed, for on New Year's Day the readjustments were to take effect. Indeed, at a dinner of field officers the affair burst into the open. Wayne was absent, dining with Washington, but other officers talked unrestrainedly. Wine flowed freely; voices rose high. Here and there, sharp-voiced interjections showed that tempers were fine-drawn. Walter Stewart, one of Wayne's closest intimates, rapped for silence. He stood facing the long table of flushed-faced comrades, then, raising his glass, he called a toast.

"I give you," he said, "Arthur St. Clair, most capable officer in the Pennsylvania Line, a man who holds our confidence!"

His hearers sat stunned. Not all were friends of Wayne, but everyone knew that Stewart was Wayne's boon companion. They sat silent, shocked by Stewart's outburst. Then a friend of St. Clair's clapped his hands; another cried, "Hear, hear!" From far down the table, one captain asked if Stewart was drunk or crazy.

"No," said Stewart slowly. "General Wayne is losing the confidence of his officers. He keeps officers who are incompetent because they are his favorites, while he forces good men out of service. I wish to God St. Clair had made the arrangements about who is to stay."

Major Tommy Moore, one of Wayne's Chester County neighbors, who had campaigned with Anthony since Ticonderoga, rose white-faced to his feet.

"You're much mistaken, Colonel Stewart," he protested. "What you say is false. By God, I know that General Wayne is a gentleman and a man of honor. His actions are those of a good officer. And, sir, I wear a sword to defend his honor. I am at your service, sir, whenever you think proper."

"You draw your sword," said Stewart slowly, "in defense of General Wayne's bad actions?"

"I know of no bad actions," Moore replied, "but on the contrary everything that is consistent with the honor of a gentleman. I take my leave, sir, and am at your service."

The meeting broke up in a buzz of excitement. Stewart, muddled by the wine, had blundered into a predicament. By every standard of military etiquette he was obliged to fight a duel with a friend upon a cause of which he really disapproved and in defense of words he really had not meant to say. Yet if he should back down, he might be branded as a coward. Stewart chose the braver course, for to confess himself wholly in the wrong was extremely difficult for a man of military honor. He called next day on Major Moore, apologized for his unfortunate remarks, explained that he had been drunk and that he wished to beg the pardon of both Wayne and Moore. Then, when Moore accepted his disclaimer of malicious intent, Stewart

sealed the renewed friendship by a hearty invitation to Major
Moore to dine with him.

The camp could not understand such actions, not knowing that
jealousies and back-biting were causing treacheries to long-
established friendships and breaches of old-time confidences.
Benjamin Fishbourn, once a hot-headed partisan of Anthony
Wayne's interests, was now secretly hand in glove with St.
Clair and was corresponding with that general to his own chief's
disparagement. Successfully pretending to be Wayne's best
friend, Fishbourn scathingly attacked Stewart as a man moved
by cunning artifice and by secret evil purpose. The policy not
only gratified Fishbourn's jealous envy but let St. Clair believe
that he was willing to be a spy on Wayne's private councils.
St. Clair's open friends cut Stewart dead as having shown
himself a coward.

Wayne, one of the few to keep his head in this time of stress,
ignored the whole affair, hoping, as he said, "to see perfect
harmony conspicuous in the Pennsylvania Line."

That harmony could not be assured. St. Clair still looked on
Wayne as a bitter personal enemy, capable of blowing up the
coals of discontent to kindle a fire of hostility; Fishbourn flitted
about undermining the confidence of brother officers in their
brigadier; Udney Hay hinted that jealousies at camp were being "hatched by some of the Devil's most intimate friends."

To make matters worse, not only officers were grumbling at
their treatment, but private soldiers, too, were restive. The
Christmas truce lasted little longer than the food and rum provided for their special holiday fare.

4

Colonel Richard Humpton rose unsteadily on New Year's
Eve, swaying slightly as he faced the Pennsylvania officers.
Loud talking ceased abruptly when he raised his glass. Waiting
for the ragged fringe of chattering to end, he cleared his throat,
then, when every officer down the long tables looked attentive,

Colonel Humpton, in his thick Yorkshire accent, proposed a toast: "Our friends who are departing: may they always be as happy as they have made their friends!" Every diner in the room, save only the supernumeraries, responded with a cheer; each man, even those who had been drinking heavily during the six-hour banquet, sprang to his feet and raised his wine glass.

Apparently, the troops outside the banquet hall responded to their colonel's toast, for as the officers stood, arms outstretched, cheering their departing comrades, the soldiers raised a shout. A musket coughed upon the right of the encampment; another answered on the left; a running fire of guns chittered in the Pennsylvania camp. Undoubtedly the excess officers who during most of the long banquet had sat slightly droop-shouldered by their disappointment warmed with pride at such a demonstration. Their solidarity with brother officers had long been demonstrated, but to have the common soldiers join was an unexpected tribute. While troops outside the hall cheered and shouted, the officers drank Humpton's toast. Solemnly, with every protestation of undying friendship, they filed up to their departing comrades and wished their friends farewell. Those who were to stay loaded down the unlucky ones with best wishes; they put a light touch to the situation by congratulating the supernumeraries on their luck in getting home; they hoped the excess officers would not steal away the pretty girls from those who had to stay in camp.

Noise outside continued; it grew louder and less regular. Colonel Humpton, flushed though he was with wine, felt uneasy; he sobered quickly. Unobtrusively, he weaved his way through groups of ensigns, lieutenants, captains, and majors toward the big plank door. As though to catch a breath of cold, refreshing air, he fumbled with the fastenings and edged the huge door open. Disorderly confusion met his eyes. Humpton investigated. Pennsylvanians were running about the camp's broad central avenue, where at this hour they had no right to be. Knots of soldiers who should have been in barracks yelled wildly to each other. Most of them, contrary to orders, had muskets in their hands, though the guns should have been

stacked long since and under careful guard. A skyrocket flew into
the air; the men rushed toward the parade grounds. Hastily,
Humpton got back into the banquet hall. His deep voice, rough-
ened by years of too much wine, boomed suddenly: "Attention!"

Officers, disciplined to instant obedience, stiffened; their hands
clapped to their sides. Many of them, holding half-filled
wineglasses, spattered themselves in their haste to follow orders.
Heavy silence blanketed the banquet room. Humpton, hesitat-
ing only a second, barked out rapid orders. "To post! The men
are out! Get them back into their huts! They've had too much
to drink. No man, except the guard, is to be loose!"

Officers poured out of the hall, running to their duty. Their
first thought, naturally, was that the British had attacked, but
Humpton's sharp commands made it certain that something else
was stirring. The men, they knew, had each been served a gill
of rum, and though rugged Pennsylvanians could stand much
more than that, some other supplies might have been tapped.
Perhaps the troops had managed to break into the rum stores.
Officers could take no chances; even the supernumeraries, now
technically out of service, took their accustomed places.

Strangely enough, the men were good-tempered. Laughingly
they said that they had heard alarms and had turned out to
fight. Willingly they went back into huts, and as long as their
superiors stood close by, the troops remained inside, though
cautiously they pushed their doors open now and then to scout
if the coast were clear. As soon as their superiors moved on,
privates streamed again into the streets. When officers turned
back, they dodged inside the huts again. For two hours the
game continued. Exasperated officers lost their tempers; soldiers,
laughing merrily, teased their leaders without doing anything
so obviously wrong that there could be a real excuse for punishment. At midnight, as the New Year came, the men abandoned
all restraint. Somewhere on the left a gun was fired. Every
Pennsylvanian, ignoring the officers, crowded into the open,
rushing again toward the parade ground. Some officers, frightened and hysterical, tried to stop the troops, but now the men
were not to be controlled. Leaders who opposed were mobbed
and captured; a few escaped by running.

Captain-Lieutenant Adam Bettin of the 10th was not so fortunate. Soldiers chasing an unpopular subaltern ran sharply about a corner at the intersection of two company streets. They saw an officer's uniform in the dim light and fired. Bettin died instantly. Lieutenant Nicholas White, also of the 10th, was shot through the thigh; Captain Samuel Tolbert of the 4th, who had risen from a sickbed to attend the farewell dinner, got a ball through the body. By this time the disorder was entirely out of hand. Officers had lost control completely. Men rushed to the artillery park to take possession of the cannon, but in their disorder they did not know when they had been successful. A trooper left as guard to keep the cannon safe in their hands was shot through the head.

Wayne, Stewart, and Dick Butler had been dining elsewhere. Now, summoned by the terrified underofficers, they galloped to the scene. Disregarding Humpton's warnings to be careful, Wayne rode up to the crowd.

"What's this about?" he demanded. "Why are you not in your quarters?"

Sergeant William Bowser, spokesman for the men, stepped forward. He was the ringleader; his men called him "major-general."

"We've been wronged, General, as you yourself well know. We are determined now to get our rights. We've no quarrel with you, sir; you've been very fair with us. If everyone had been as kind as you, this trouble never could have happened."

"Get your men back to the huts," Wayne answered. "Mutiny is no way to get your rights. Mutiny brings death. Put your men back in their quarters, and I'll get your rights for you, but I can do nothing while you act like this. You know me, and you all know that I keep my word, but you must do your part. I'll overlook this night's affair, as far as I can, but you must bring these men back."

"General," replied Bowser, "this has gone beyond your power. You have already done all that you could do. This business now is not with the officers here in Jockey Hollow; we must deal direct with President Reed and with his Supreme Executive Council. We may need to go to Congress to get justice. We thank you for your help, and we have no grievance against you, but we think that we must deal with the authorities in Philadelphia."

Wayne was about to argue, but firing broke out. Wayne thought that they were threatening his life. He rode closer to the men. Throwing open his military cloak, he cried:

"If you want to kill me, shoot me now! Here's my breast. Shoot!"

Bowser protested that no one wished to shoot the General. "We will not hurt any officer of this Line," he said. "No one will be in the least disturbed. We have nothing whatever against our officers. They have been our friends."

Drums began to beat; fifers started playing. As Wayne and Bowser talked, the men formed into regular platoons, with non-commissioned officers commanding. Front and rear guards were established in good military order. The troops, said Bowser, would march at once for Trenton. Thence they would go to Philadelphia.

"Don't," begged Wayne, "go over to the enemy!"

"We'll hang any man who tries to do that," Bowser assured him. "If the British come out while we are on the march, we'll turn back to fight them. We're still good patriots, but we want our rights."

"Well," said Wayne, "if that's the way you feel, I'll not leave you. Let me march with you. I'll lead you, if you insist on going. And, if you won't let me lead, I'll follow in your rear."

Anthony's position was peculiar. A stickler for military discipline, a martinet when in command of troops, he was torn between his love of orderliness and his passion for justice. These men, he knew, nursed justified grievances; he knew, too, that they had been cruelly wronged by careless politicians. He had seen them suffering with cold and hunger while Pennsylvania's leaders bickered over unimportant matters; he understood why these gallant soldiers had rebelled. But they were military men, sworn to obey their leaders, and in time of war disobedience brings death.

For once in his army career, Anthony Wayne blinked at mutiny. His sympathies responded to the men's wrongs, but underneath his quick acceptance of their arguments was still another motive. These Pennsylvanians were not officially his soldiers; they belonged to Major-General Arthur St. Clair, Wayne's enemy and rival. This mutiny was St. Clair's responsibility, but that wirepulling patriot was not in camp. Leaving his suffering men to celebrate a meager Christmas at Morristown, St. Clair had gone to Philadelphia, where parties were more pleasant. Wayne saw no reason why he should be asked to quell a mutiny largely caused by St. Clair's dodging his duty. Where, as at Ticonderoga, mutinies occurred in Wayne's command, he could be ruthless in suppression, but he was unwilling to pull St. Clair's chestnuts from the fire.

The troops, amazed but overjoyed at Wayne's decision, cheered him vigorously. They marched off in the cold, dark night, with Wayne, Stewart, and Butler tagging after. Before dawn, the mutineers reached Vealtown (now Bernardsville), where they rested; on the second day they reached their old camp ground at Middle Brook and on January 3 they halted at Princeton. Here they waited for an answer to appeals sent off ahead to Philadelphia. St. Clair, startled by the mutiny, sent back word that he would come to meet the troops, but they refused to treat with him; Wayne, they said to Anthony's delight, was the only general with whom they would talk. They drew up a list of grievances, dealing chiefly with complaints against recruiting methods and against harsh treatment by certain officers, which they asked Wayne to approve. This was equivalent to making him their spokesman and Anthony objected, but when Bowser pointed out that the men had no other avenue of approaching their superiors, Wayne consented to transmit their demands to the Pennsylvania officials. He sent the list to President Reed, adding a strong personal appeal for that official to come himself to Princeton. Meanwhile, Wayne softened the men's demands as best he could in private conferences with leaders of the mutineers.

Pennsylvania, faced by the virtually unanimous mutiny of her soldiers, surrendered. After a long series of conferences, at which proposals and counter-suggestions passed back and forth, Reed accepted the men's demands. Any soldier who had signed up

before January, 1777, for three years or the duration of the war
was released from service if he preferred freedom; those who
remained were offered better treatment. The mutiny was an
overwhelming victory for the troops. It was, however, deemed
impolitic to let men who had thus triumphed over their government return to camp, lest they contaminate regiments of other
states. The Pennsylvanians were withdrawn from Morristown;
most of the men who stayed in service were sent to distant units.
Wayne himself, the general who, in some sticklers' minds, had
compromised his position by co-operating with the common
soldiers, went back to Philadelphia on another furlough.

5

A hundred mellow candles winked in their tall, hand-wrought
silver holders, casting quivering flashes of soft light against
porcelain and crystal. The gentle yellow gleams shone gaily on
red and amber wines, on cream-white puddings and glossy
crimson jellies, on piles of golden oranges and on the quantities
of bright-hued artificial flowers strewn along the tablecloth.
Warm, hospitable color glowed from barons of roast beef,
golden-bronze roast turkeys, red-brown hams, and green and
golden vegetables.

Wayne and his companions sat comfortably at table in January, 1781, waiting for the president of Pennsylvania to begin
the feast in honor of Continental officers. Once again in Philadelphia, among civilized surroundings, far from the starvations
and mutinies of Morristown, Anthony's good humor expanded.
His soldier colleagues, whose bright new uniforms sparkled with
gilt and color, knew of his accomplishments; each of them, and
every Pennsylvania statesman who was present, was well aware
that it was he, and not Arthur St. Clair, his nominal superior,
who held the confidence of the troops. This dinner, tendered
by the commonwealth, though not arranged as any special tribute to Wayne's services in settling mutiny, was in reality an
ovation in his honor. It was the first of a long succession of

merry evenings in the capital. Once more relieved of active service, Wayne spent a third winter in Philadelphia, acting again as liaison officer between the army and the State of Pennsylvania, trying, as before, to spur the commonwealth into even greater effort, but in his moments of leisure savoring life completely.

Even within the year since his last furlough, Wayne learned, the city had been socially revolutionized. Worry had disappeared; long, grim-set faces had vanished. Citizens relaxed, certain now that Washington's men could keep the enemy from the gates; fear lessened; gaiety replaced solemnity. Some signs of the former spirit still remained, as in the wearing of homespun in place of finer English broadcloth, and in the boycotting of expensive imported "gewgaws" such as octagonal, balloon-shaped, frying-pan, and sugar-loaf metal buttons, but cynics suspected that the cutting off of trade with Britain explained such matters. Philadelphia swung far toward luxury.

Gentlemen, certainly, exhibited more interest in dress, as Anthony, the dandy, soon discovered. Only Quakers wore the round white hats of former years, and younger Friends who continued to affect the old style so tilted them that they rested diagonally over one eye instead of sitting uncompromisingly upon the head. Wayne saw fewer Quakers wearing conservative snuff-colored suits as he strolled the brick pavements of Philadelphia's streets; more and more men, especially among the younger generation, sported green, blue, and purple clothing, with scarlet or plum for evening wear. He noticed that despite the scandalized protests of old fogies, young bucks wore elaborately clocked white-silk hose to set off their well-turned legs. Conservatives wore boots, or if they made concessions to newfangled styles by using shoes, their stockings were dull-toned worsted, and their fastenings at ankle and knee were strings instead of silver buckles, but more and more these somber simplicities were looked upon as countrified and decidedly unfashionable.

Dandy Wayne belonged to a more modern set. Cocked hats and fantail coats, long embroidered silk waistcoats, foaming with lace at neck and wrists, tight velvet breeches, silver-buckled at the knees, white silk stockings and low red-heeled shoes, marked civilian gentlemen of his acquaintance. All carried little pocket combs to groom their curled, well-powdered hair. Without the slightest trace of affectation or self-consciousness, they paused before hall mirrors to set their locks in order.

At dances, teas, and dinners, Wayne found that manners had been changed, owing, he supposed, to the influence of French diplomats and officers with sophisticated European ways. Music was more prevalent; girls sang to the accompaniment of guitars and violins. Theodoric Bland, the gloomy Virginia Francophile whom Anthony had last seen at the head of barefoot dragoons, was holding a Parisian salon and was chattering away in what Wayne supposed was perfect French, though foreigners showed some difficulty in understanding the words. At the Assembly, Wayne resented the new custom of allotting all the handsome girls for the entertainment of foreigners.

He felt more at home in masculine society, even when he had to listen to Ben Rush talking interminably about abolishing liquor, giving girls as good an education as boys enjoyed, or freeing slaves. Taverns were full of gossip, such as that about the important French merchant who introduced his mistress as his partner in trade and so secured her entrance into Philadelphia society. He heard the strange tales of Armand, Marquis de La Rouerie, who left a Trappist monastery to join the American Army as colonel of cavalry, and of Major William Galvan, the Parisian who fell so deeply in love with a Philadelphia widow that he could not keep his mind on military matters. But when he heard that the Marquis de Chastellux, major-general of the French, called Philadelphia girls ridiculous because they used too much red, white, and blue paint and because "as staunch Whigs, they set no bounds to their liberty," he boiled with anger. Had the Marquis been in Philadelphia, Wayne would have challenged him to a duel. Had he known that De Chastellux referred particularly to "a certain Miss Viny," he would have murdered the man.

For Anthony was seeing much of Mary Vining. Daily they sleighed behind good horses through the narrow streets into the open country that lay a mile or so west of the Delaware. They took tea at famous rural inns along the Schuylkill, and visited the rich gardenlike estates of Wayne's friends Robert Morris and Richard Peters, who lived out at Belmont on a high bluff overlooking the Schuylkill and the city. They danced together at such times as Mary was not paired off with some important foreigner; they sat on tapestried sofas before the fire and gossiped. Even when he was not close by her side, Anthony liked to look at Mary as, dressed in the fashionable clothes that he smuggled through the sentry lines, she dominated intellectuals by her wit, scourged the stupid with her caustic tongue, and won the rest by beauty. Philadelphia, as might have been expected, talked scandalously about the pair. Dowagers whispered that with Polly Wayne so ill at Waynesborough, Anthony ought not to spend so much time with his new friend Mary; they drew young Margaretta, still at school, aside to give her sympathy, but Margaretta failed to understand their innuendoes. Men envied Wayne, but feared his quick temper too greatly to tease him; they knew, what their wives would not admit, that Mary's relations with the General were beyond rebuke.

Anthony liked to take the girl to see and hear new things. On one occasion he escorted her, with Margaretta, to call upon the venerable Stockbridge Indian, the Great Grasshopper, then in Philadelphia to seek "presents" from the Americans for help in war against the British. They found him clad in Bavarian court costume, a present from the French Ambassador, drinking spiced rum and telling of his warlike deeds. The Great Grasshopper, in his turn, stood with mouth wide open, marveling at Mary's high headdress, built up by wire and wool and artificial hair and fashioned into a tall steeple by pomade and oil. Each thought the other most exotic; they vowed a lasting friendship. Wayne drew the line, however, at Mary Vining's wish to visit incognito the newly opened gambling-house on Market Street where white men and freed Negroes staked 7s. 6d. a throw on dice, and where by house rules men might swear as lustily as they desired, but where they must not, on any provocation, strike a blow. Himself an ardent better, on horses, cards, or dice, he felt that this curiously named "E.O. Table" was no place for a lady.

Not all of Wayne's experiences were as pleasant as these jaunts with Mary Vining. His evenings at the City Tavern, where men sat about smoking cigars and drinking spiced rum punch, were filled with excited argument that at times degenerated into outright brawls. Anthony's good friend Thomas Craig, whom he had known well since Ticonderoga days, took part in such an angry colloquy ending, to everyone's horror, in a murder. Craig perhaps was innocent; certainly Wayne thought his friend incapable of taking life. To guard Craig against imprisonment, and quite possibly death, Wayne hid the man from constables and sheriff until the storm blew over. Craig warmly appreciated Wayne's service; Anthony's activity saved him from arrest. "It has been to me like oil to the wheels of a time piece," wrote Craig later, "though I once thought that I could readily submit to trial, I am now of a different opinion. This wild temper of mine is hard to conquer."

In his own relationships Wayne was less fortunate. The perennial St. Clair feud cropped out anew, as might have been anticipated, considering how freely Wayne's partisans spoke of St. Clair's inefficiency during the mutiny, and how frank St. Clair had been in criticizing Wayne for insubordination. Major Isaac Budd Dunn, aide-de-camp to St. Clair, babbled drunkenly to Fishbourn that Wayne plotted to displace St. Clair, and that the Major-General knew of Wayne's supposed disloyalty. Fishbourn, always ready to foment a quarrel, promptly tattled, and Wayne, violently angry, swore to make Dunn eat his words. The two men, however, failed to meet, though Wayne searched through the taverns to find Dunn, until one afternoon they met at a lady's tea party. Wayne, forgetting both himself and the courtesy owed his hostess, caught Dunn by the lapel and poured forth a stream of hot vituperation. Dunn, more calm and more considerate, took the abuse without flinching, but after he left the party he sent Captain Lawrence Keene to Wayne with a demand that the Brigadier apologize. Wayne's high position precluded him from dueling with a man like Dunn, who held a majority only by courtesy. He took no notice of Keene's message, but fired off instead an indignant protest to St. Clair, insisting that Dunn's comments could only have been based on slanders dropped by St. Clair himself.

St. Clair was embarrassed. He could not openly confess that he, a major-general, had been annoyed by Wayne's pretensions, for there was no evidence on which to base a charge of Wayne's impropriety, but neither could he deny that Wayne and a small clique of Pennsylvanians had, in every small way possible, exhibited contempt. He could not defend the drunken Major Dunn without producing witnesses, but if he produced such witnesses, he must perforce arrest his aide-de-camp for drunkenness; if he did not support the Major, then Dunn would feel, with justice, that St. Clair was weak, ungrateful, and caddish. In response to Wayne's message, brought by Dick Butler, St. Clair replied:

"You cannot suppose that I could entertain any Fears of being supplanted in the Command of the Pennsylvania Line, nor is it fair to imagine that if Major Dunn suspected you of intriguing for that Purpose, the sentiment is mine.

"You must be sensible that there was a Coldness for some time between You and me. . . . I may have mentioned in my Family, and most probably to Major Dunn, as he was more in my confidence, that I thought your Behavior not so candid as I could have wished, but it was a Subject on which I was very guarded and my Behavior to you must, I think, have convinced You that I had entirely forgot it, if it had been the Case—and, indeed, I am so well convinced of the Necessity of Harmony amongst Officers, especially those of high Rank that, I think, it should be matters of a much more serious Nature than Difference of Opinion that should disturb it."

Wayne accepted St. Clair's suave offer of an olive branch. Immediately upon receiving the reply, he sent Butler back with assurances of friendship: "The pain is now alleviated by your Reply. I, in turn, assure you that the Suspicions you harboured were as injurious to me as they were groundless; therefore, we have each been in error." The patched-up truce, based on flimsy half-apologies, prevented open outbreak, but neither general felt wholly convinced of the other's sincerity. Major Dunn, mildly rebuked by St. Clair for indiscretion, withdrew his challenge,

but in the privacy of his quarters he muttered that Wayne
had failed to meet the issue squarely.

This 1781 winter cost Wayne another friend, of very humble
station. One of his Chester County neighbors, an eccentric private soldier nicknamed by some the Commodore and by others
Jemmy the Rover, lost faith in Anthony. Jemmy, a chronic
deserter, whose roving temperament had never been curbed by
jails or lashings, misbehaved in some minor matter and by order
of the local constables was again taken into custody. He told his
guards that he was Wayne's good friend, and asked to be set
free; when they refused, he sent a messenger to the General
asking him to order a release. Wayne, not knowing anything
about the circumstances, did not intervene. When the messenger
returned with the news of Wayne's refusal, Jemmy could not
believe his ears. That Wayne, his protector and his friend, had
washed his hands of Jemmy was incredible.

"Anthony is mad," he mumbled to himself. "He must be mad,
or he would help me. Mad Anthony, that's what he is. Mad
Anthony Wayne."

The title stuck to Wayne. No officer employed it, but soldiers in the ranks, carried away by its rhythm and its euphony,
used it as a nickname. The disappointed mumblings of a half-
crazed common trooper became a nom de guerre. Years later,
Washington Irving, wholly misunderstanding the nickname,
jumped to the false conclusion that it was given Wayne because
of rashness, recklessness, and unbridled daring, and by so doing
not only smirched Wayne's military reputation as a cautious,
careful strategist who never took unnecessary chances, but in
addition gave him a stigma of mental unbalance which many of
Irving's uncritical readers accepted. The hasty sobriquet, be-
stowed carelessly by an eccentric private, detracted for many
years from a full recognition of Anthony Wayne's military
genius.

CHAPTER XII

Road to Yorktown

PENNSYLVANIA, chief granary and leading contributor to the army, in early 1781 was almost drained dry. Hard cash was missing; paper circulated at a ruinous discount. Merchants preferred to ship their goods to Cuba, who paid in Spanish dollars, rather than to an army which gave only depreciated promises to pay. Wayne learned that state laws requiring that one-third of the flour be delivered for army use were ridiculed and ignored. The Pennsylvania government hoped to aid the Continental cause, but with neighbor states conniving at the export of food, the commonwealth could not carry the load. It even asked Congress to embargo grain exports; it suggested that the nation confiscate outgoing vessels laden with foodstuffs. Congress, however, would not pass such drastic laws, since too many states profited by selling wheat to Cuba, and the gold thus gained would help to stabilize the currency.

Wayne's problem was twofold. He worked with Pennsylvania, striving to hold that state to high levels of co-operation at a time when other states lessened their loyalty; he buttonholed Congressmen to have them bring other states up to the Pennsylvania level. Unlike other years, New England was now cool to his appeals, for the war had long since moved away from that locality, but the South blazed with patriotic fever. Indeed, the South was now the center of hostilities. Still clinging to a plan of splitting asunder the rebellious colonies, in the fall of 1780 the British shifted active warfare to South Carolina, Charles, Earl Cornwallis, with 3,400 men, held Charleston, which had fallen into British hands in the preceding May; an American army of 1,500 Continentals and 600 militia was reeling from a disaster inflicted upon it at Camden. Although the rebels had a new commander, Nathanael Greene, in place of the beaten Gates, Cornwallis was making ready to march north into Virginia. Then, under the protection of a fleet in the Chesapeake, he could reduce Maryland and Pennsylvania; after this, complete conquest would be easy.

Cornwallis had good ground for optimism. A former Etonian and member of Parliament, he ranked among the best British generals. Cold, capable, and determined, vigorous, energetic, and resourceful, possessing the full confidence of War Minister George Germain and of Parliament, he was free from the handicaps that had shackled Howe, Clinton, and Burgoyne. No other British general inspired such respect for military skill, nor did any other enjoy his wealth of experience. With only a badly beaten army of less than half his numbers to check his northern drive, Cornwallis saw no reason to despair.

Yet Wayne kept confident. Two thousand mountaineers had caught 1,000 British loyalists on King's Mountain in the extreme northwestern part of South Carolina and had shot all who would not surrender. While Wayne had tried to stem mutiny in New Jersey, his friend Colonel Daniel Morgan won a brilliant victory at the Cowpens over Lieutenant-Colonel Banastre Tarleton, killing or capturing 800 crack British regulars. These two victories proved that Continentals could stand up against any attempt that Lord Cornwallis might make against Virginia. But Virginia, too, had troubles. Benedict Arnold, now a major-general in British service, celebrated the New Year by landing at Jamestown and plundering Richmond and the Tidewater area; only a few militiamen were on duty to prevent his ranging widely through the state. Washington sent Lafayette with 1,200 picked troops against Arnold, but it would take weeks for them to reach Virginia.

Wayne pleaded with Pennsylvania to re-establish its crack Line, and, despite its bankruptcy, somehow to raise money for supplies and pay. Even at the risk of issuing more paper and thus further depreciating the value of its currency, another effort was essential to keep the Union safe. To his delight, Congress voted to attach newly recruited Pennsylvanians to the

Southern army to fight Arnold and Cornwallis. To Wayne's bitter disappointment, less than half the old Pennsylvania Line stayed in service after the mutiny, and most of these, despite their mutinous reputation, were needed with Washington's main army in New Jersey as a check against Clinton's possible descent on Philadelphia. These were to remain under Arthur St. Clair; Wayne himself would lead the new men to the South. But at York and Lebanon, the rendezvous for recruits, only a few hundred men mustered. To get a larger number of first-class soldiers worthy of their task, Pennsylvania forgot bankruptcy and became more generous. The state promised new men larger cash bounties than rival states were giving. But the commonwealth could not grant more than £9 a man at a time when, by crossing the Delaware to enlist, soldiers could receive a £15 bonus. "The system of recruiting," said Wayne, "is the child of Council and altho' a monster of a *brat*, yet the parents wish to cherish it."

He appealed to two groups of possible recruits: to men on the far frontier who could not, by their isolation, know of the greater generosity of Pennsylvania's neighbors and who would gladly take the skimpy Pennsylvania bonus, and to old soldiers who might have a sentimental attachment to their old regiments. The former would undoubtedly discover in course of time that their bargain had been bad, and they too might mutiny; the loyalty of the latter was, to say the least, decidedly questionable; but Wayne had no other recourse. His pleas produced results, although recruiting progress was extremely slow. A few men at a time drifted into York to join the Pennsylvania ranks. While Lafayette and Greene wrote frantic letters begging Wayne to hurry, he could promise only an advance detachment by St. Patrick's Day and 1,200 additional troops by April 1. His men marked time, waiting for their numbers to increase, while Wayne bickered at Philadelphia with Congress and the state.

Wayne's inability to march immediately caused less worry to the American commanders than might have been anticipated. Greene pushed back the Cornwallis danger on March 15 by the Battle of Guilford Court House, near the Virginia-Carolina border. The Americans lost the engagement, but the British, battered in action, withdrew to Wilmington, far down on the North Carolina coast, to await reinforcements and supplies. An eighteen-day stay at that port delayed the British invasion of Virginia and so relieved the pressure on Greene.

For once, Wayne had sufficient guns, but clothing, as usual, caused concern. Experience, however, had taught him a few short cuts and when, by trickery, he diverted two thousand pairs of overalls, he kept his acquisition secret so that by asking for a full supply he could have an abundant stock. Estimating that he would have, at best, 1,500 men, Wayne requisitioned three thousand outfits of shirts, stocks, and coats, together with more overalls. He did not get all he asked—he did not think that he would be so fortunate—but he drew enough for the men enlisted under his command.

False rumors, for which Wayne was not responsible, unquestionably helped him win recruits and gain supplies. Philadelphia, always responsive to gusts of gossip, heard that Greene had crushed Cornwallis and had compelled the British to surrender. Amid the celebration that ensued, while bells rang, drums beat, fifes shrilled, and trumpets sounded, patriotic fervor mounted high. Wayne took full advantage of the excitement. He entertained statesmen at the tavern, filled their willing ears with predictions that Greene's victory was the precursor of final victory, and asked for just a trifle more cash to finish up the war. Politicians, swept away by enthusiasm, agreed to his requests. By the time the true accounts of Guilford reached the city, Wayne had spent the cash so freely granted. But then new hopes had been kindled, for Paul Jones came into port from successful sea raids, and there were rumors that the Comte d'Estaing's French fleet had smashed a British squadron, capturing ten men-of-war and taking forty-five transports out of a convoy of one hundred ships.

The story, as it happens, was completely false. Eight British vessels had intercepted a small French squadron bound from Newport to aid Lafayette, and after a sharp exchange of broadsides on March 16, had driven off the French. Thus the British kept control of the sea lanes to Virginia, preventing reinforcements from being sent to Lafayette; instead of being a great victory for the Americans, the action was a setback.

In spite of the fillip given to his plans by these untrue reports, Wayne was delayed for a much longer time at Philadelphia than he had expected. His hopes of sending off 1,200 men by April 1 faded when the authorities failed to vote funds to pay the men in good hard cash. Wayne spent the entire month of April arguing with statesmen that soldiers were entitled to be paid in currency that had an actual purchasing value. Such men as had enlisted deteriorated in barracks. Colonel Richard Butler, as restless a personality as Wayne himself, complained of prolonged idleness. The officers, he said, could drink, play cards, or even, as a last resort, try to lose themselves in the camp's dog-eared copy of Smollett's *Peregrine Pickle*, but the men grew "rusty" and undisciplined. "You may depend upon it, sir," he said, "the men are ruining by laying at these posts. Almost every house is a *tavern* and from the queen-less licentious life the men have led generally, I fear they will plague us with sickness. . . . There is nothing that will rouse them but British Guns and Drums or Jack Hatchway's pipe and, indeed, I wish he'd blow soon, or else their very souls will be petrified so that the Devil himself can't wake them."

The little army, without unity of determination, without definite policy, fell rapidly to pieces. As at Marcus Hook, in the first days of the Revolution, colonels, faced by growing unrest, appealed to him to take command.

Early in May, disorder came to a head. At Lebanon, where Dick Butler commanded, Sergeant John Maloney, a leader in the January mutiny and known from his habitual dapperness as Macaroni Jack, went to the guardhouse for a trivial offense. At court-martial, Macaroni Jack was convicted, and was sentenced to be lashed. Soldiers liked Maloney. His cleverness, his humor, and his watchfulness for their interests made him popular. His wife, one of the washerwomen accompanying the army, had been considerate and kind to men who needed nursing and other special care. Many felt that Macaroni Jack was facing an unduly harsh punishment for the small offense that he committed. Word of their objections reached the officers, who, always worrying about a renewal of the January mutiny, suspected a new outbreak. When Macaroni Jack, trussed up to the whipping-post, called out to the soldiers, "Help me, Brothers!" Butler thought the call an incitement to rebellion. The Colonel doubled his guard to beat back any attempt to rescue Macaroni Jack; then, after the prisoner had been whipped, he ordered Jack returned, handcuffed, to the guardhouse. Two days later, Maloney and a pair of deserters were sent to headquarters accused of sedition.

Wayne, meanwhile, arrived at York, on May 19. He found the camp disorderly, ill-kept, and badly officered. Rumors of rebellion met his ears. Only a few days before, three civilians had been charged with treason; at noon on the day of his arrival, a light horseman had charged the jail bent on freeing a comrade who was under arrest for assaulting a militiaman. The militia sentry on duty shot the horseman dead, but the incident was far from closed. The entire Light Horse vowed to attack the militia at night and wipe out every man in retaliation for their comrade's death. In such circumstances, Wayne readily accepted the idea that Macaroni Jack also was a villain, and that Jack Smith, who accidentally rolled a cannon ball close to a party of officers, had intended to murder his superiors. Wayne took little time for investigation. As soon as he calmed the Light Horse by promising to punish the sentry who had shot their friend, he ordered every prisoner brought to trial immediately before a court-martial whose members he knew would be severe. He was no longer lenient, as at Morristown, where the mutiny had been against St. Clair; the insubordination now was against his own authority.

His confidence in the court-martial was not misplaced. Macaroni Jack and Smith were both sentenced to death, together with the two deserters and Sergeant John Lillie, whose crime consisted in being out of his tent, drunk, at night. Both Smith and Lillie, the court-martial declared, had forfeited their lives for swearing at officers who arrested them. Not only were penalties extraordinarily severe, but punishment followed swiftly after conviction. Immediately after breakfast the next morning, all the men were ordered into line. Musicians led a march to the jail, followed by twenty picked marksmen; close behind them came the remainder of the army. At the guardhouse, troops were ringed about while the band played the "Dead March." When the last notes died, the troops stood in absolute silence as jailers brought out the prisoners. The men stood quietly as an officer read the death sentences aloud.

The procession formed again. Once more the band preceded, and twenty picked sharpshooters followed. On either flank, numbers of women sobbed and screamed for mercy for the men. The route led out of town to rising ground where rye fields were in blossom. Here the advance guard halted while the troops drew up in line. Maloney, Smith, and Lillie knelt, their backs to the blooming rye, their eyes bound by handkerchiefs. Each man's arms were tightly bound above the elbows, their forearms being free. Maloney's wife ran screaming to her husband, but an officer felled her; other women were held back by guards. Ten marksmen then advanced to within ten feet of their victims. An officer waved a handkerchief and the sharpshooters fired at Macaroni Jack. The shots could not miss. So close were the gun muzzles that the handkerchief binding his eyes blazed; his head was blasted from his body; his hands, clasped over his heart, flew into the air; blood and brains spattered the rye blossoms. The ten executioners stepped back to reload, while a second detachment came forward. Jack Smith was next to go; his head was blown to fragments. Lillie's turn followed, while, in the words of an awed spectator, "Even devils shrank back and stood appalled."

When the executions were complete, the entire army marched in double file past the death spot. Sharply barked orders commanded each man to look at the corpses as they lay in pools of blood. Lest any man miss the view, the troops then countermarched so that the file which had been farther from the victims passed by on the inside. "The sight," said an officer, "must have made an impression on the men; it was designed with that view." Wayne prided himself on his energy in crushing out attempted mutiny, though his official reports vary somewhat from the accounts given by other witnesses:

"A few leading mutineers on the right of each regiment called out to pay them in real, not Ideal, money; they were no longer to be trifled with. Upon this, they were ordered to their tents, which being peremptorily refused, the principals were Immediately either knocked down or Confined by the Officers who were previously prepared for this event. A Court Martial was ordered on the spot, the Commission of the Crime, trial and execution were all included in the Course of a few hours, in front of the Line paraded under Arms.

"The Determined countenance of the Officers produced a Conviction to the Soldiery that the sentence of the Court Martial would be carried into execution at every risk and Consequence. Whether by design or accident the particular friends and messmates of the Culprits were their executioners and while the tears rolled down their Cheeks in showers, they silently and faithfully obeyed their Orders without a moment's hesitation."

Wayne's account was not written until three weeks after the affair, when lapse of time may have softened his recollection of the exact course of events. In any case, he was certain that he had scotched rebellion, for in half a dozen letters, to Washington, Reed, Fishbourn, Polly, and others, he proudly wrote: "Thus was the hideous monster crushed in its birth, however to myself and officers a most painful scene. Harmony and the most perfect discipline again pervade the whole."

From the tone of his letters it appears that Wayne was more touched by the loss of his table linen and napkins through the carelessness of his caitiff servant Philip than by the bloody death of three soldiers. He snatched a moment while awaiting the sound of "the ear-splitting fife and the first stirring drum" to ask Sharp Delany to forward a fresh supply. Wayne used literary license in thus relating how "all the pomp and Glorious Circumstance of war" called him to horse, for he had no intention of departing for at least another day. He had letters to write, among them one to Mary Vining, telling her, "You will ever live in my fond memory," which, incidentally, is more than he ever wrote to Polly. He wished, too, to hear the latest news of Virginia, just come to camp by special courier.

That news was alarming. Lafayette and the British had been

dancing back and forth along the James seeking strategic advantage. Late in April, Cornwallis, at last recovered from his Guilford Pyrrhic victory, started north again, with 3,400 veterans, and these, added to 1,100 British in Virginia, could easily crush the poor force of 1,000 regulars and a few militia that Lafayette commanded. Lafayette, in fact, dared not fight, lest he be cut to pieces and his militia scattered. He played a waiting game, skirmishing a bit in order to keep up Virginia's confidence, but not risking a major battle. "I am not strong enough," Lafayette confessed, "even to get beaten."

His chief difficulty was that he had almost no scouts. Britain's redoubtable Tarleton, daredevil dragoon, had confiscated practically every fast horse in the state, leaving to Lafayette only plow horses and worn-out animals. Had it not been for a small body of Virginia volunteer cavalry and for the few men of the Baltimore troop of Light Dragoons, less than a few score in all, Lafayette's army would have been blind. These circumstances lent point to Lafayette's frenzied appeals to Wayne to hurry south. Steuben had only a few men in Virginia. Greene was much too distant to lend effective aid. Wayne was the only leader available to help the Marquis.

Wayne, however, was not yet completely ready to depart. Four of his officers, following the executions, offered their resignations. Wayne knew that they were shocked at the brutality of the drumhead court-martial and the subsequent shootings, but he chose to interpret their desire to quit the service as cowardice in the face of danger. He could not, under Continental custom, decline to accept the withdrawals, but before he forwarded the papers to Washington he blistered the four officers with violent tongue-lashings intended not so much to change their minds as to deter others from leaving. His purpose was achieved; no other officer asked permission to resign. With these preliminaries off his mind, Wayne at last gave the signal to start for Virginia. Just at what point he would meet Lafayette, Wayne did not know; the Marquis, he was confident, would hurry north to meet the Pennsylvanians and the two forces would join somewhere in northern Virginia. Wayne sent a special courier to tell Lafayette that the Pennsylvanians would proceed by way of

Frederick and Georgetown, though he reserved the right to change his course in the event that some other road seemed more desirable.

2

At daybreak on Saturday, May 26, 1781, drummers beat a reveille, and after a hearty breakfast the troops started south. The skies, following four days of rain, were leaden; the atmosphere was wet. Ruts in rough roads held muddy pools; gusts of wind shook water from the boughs overhanging the line of march. Gloom darkened the army; men made no open protests, but, still smoldering over Wayne's ruthless treatment of mutineers, they glowered at their officers and muttered sullenly out of the corners of their mouths. Wayne congratulated himself on his foresight in stripping his soldiers of their ammunition; with his troops in such a mood, it was better to carry all the cartridges and powder locked in closely guarded munition carts. Only after several days' marching, when men had worked off their grievances by steady muscular effort, would it be safe to trust them with loaded guns. Luckily, no enemy was near except for a few disarmed prisoners of war held under parole in Maryland.

Wayne's force disappointed him. Three months had elapsed since Washington had given him the assignment to lead Pennsylvanians south, yet, despite every effort in recruiting, Wayne had only 800 soldiers, many of them half-trained recruits, instead of the 1,500 shining veterans whom he had promised Lafayette. He could not drive them hard over the soggy road; rookies stepped gingerly over puddles, watching carefully each step they took; veterans, of whom Wayne expected more, had softened during their weeks at York. Lafayette's couriers dashed in constantly, appealing to Wayne to move rapidly, but the men could not respond. Though Wayne advanced the reveille each day in order to make earlier departures, the men could not cover more than fifteen miles before making camp for the night.

Roads grew worse as Wayne's column passed from Pennsylvania into Maryland; creeks swollen by recent rains proved difficult to cross. Beyond Taneytown, the men waded Pipe Creek through water waist-deep; a few miles farther, near James Wilkinson's home on Monocacy Creek, a ford was flooded too deep for infantrymen. Wayne waited some hours for the water to subside, but when he sent his mounted men across, the water lapped their saddles. Anxious to make all speed possible to join Lafayette, he gambled that wagons could be pulled across; he loaded stores and men upon them and ordered them into the creek, but the crescent-shaped ford was difficult to follow and the huge, loose stones upon the bottom rolled under the horses' hoofs. Many wagons toppled over, spilling soldiers and equipment into the swollen Monocacy. His haste resulted in the loss of an entire day, for on the morning following the Monocacy crossing Wayne ordered a halt so that his men might dry and clean their guns and salvage such goods as had not been spoiled. In his first five days' marching he had covered only fifty miles. By late afternoon of May 30, when his troops were again in good condition, Wayne ordered a review; he was anxious that when the column marched next day through Frederick, where some of Burgoyne's captured officers were quartered, the Americans should appear impressive.

Frederick was "a fine, large town, with a noble appearance, where most of the houses were of brick and stone." As Wayne anticipated, Burgoyne's men lined the main street to see the army pass, but to his disgust they did not seem impressed by the smartness of his troops. Some sneered at the motley force of Scotch-Irishmen, Pennsylvania Germans, and a sprinkling of Negroes; they were more interested in the black cockades with white decorations that the soldiers wore in honor of the French alliance than in the soldierly bearing of Wayne's men.

Wayne drove ahead to make up the time lost at the Monocacy. He struck his tents before daylight, and pushed forward. He halted in midmorning by a small brook, but in order not to break his ranks he allowed only six or eight men from each company, and these only under close watch of a sergeant, to fetch water in canteens. At noon he ordered his men to take off their knapsacks and relax while eating cold food, their first meal of the day; within an hour he was again upon the road, driving south to reach the Potomac. In his haste, Wayne shifted his plan of crossing at Georgetown, where boats and supplies were awaiting them, and passed the stream, going into Virginia twenty miles west, at Nolan's Ferry.

Four boats only were available here, and these were small leaky scows; rain fell in torrents. Soldiers unfamiliar with Potomac currents poled the clumsy craft across, and the transport took till midnight instead of being finished in the two or three hours that would have sufficed at Georgetown. One scow sank, drowning a sergeant and three soldiers, besides dumping Wayne's six field pieces into the river and ruining the ammunition. The men had to fish the ordnance from the water and then spend more hours in again taking the guns apart and drying each separate piece. Thus Wayne again lost time by his attempts at haste; just as he had wasted a day at Monocacy, so now he was compelled to halt until late afternoon on June 1 until the guns were cleaned, oiled, and reassembled. When at four o'clock he ordered his men to march, a sudden thunderstorm broke, so that he could cover no more than five miles. Rain fell in sheets from sunset until dawn; he was held up for thirty-six hours more.

Food supplies ran low. At Georgetown, where Wayne had told Lafayette to expect him, ample stores awaited his arrival, but Wayne's attempted short cut threw the schedule out of joint; supply carts bogged down on muddy roads. Not until June 3 could Wayne take up his march with assurance that food and forage were available, but then, after one clear day during which the troops went through Leesburg, rain again delayed the advance. Wayne's farmer's eye looked scornfully at these Virginia lands. He thought the people shiftless for their careless habit of planting tobacco year after year until the soil became so thoroughly impoverished that the land had to lie idle, growing up in scrub trees and underbrush. He wondered at their interest in cotton at a time when there was little demand for that commodity; he thought it would be better if they planted carrots and turnips to feed their scrawny cattle.

Lafayette, meanwhile, still showered him with feverish messages begging him to hurry. The British, quickly repairing bridges torn down by Virginia militiamen, were driving through good tobacco lands and were in the rich plantation country, sweeping onward irresistibly. Lafayette needed reinforcement quickly. Wayne plunged into the pine woods south of Leesburg, braving unexpectedly cold weather that suddenly closed down upon Virginia and that, even now, was bringing snow a foot deep in the near-by mountains, while the Marquis, desperate lest Cornwallis drive a wedge between the two American armies, hurried north. When Cornwallis unexpectedly changed his route and swam streams to enter the well-cultivated regions about Hanover, between Wayne and Lafayette, the Marquis changed his course. By a wide sweep around the right end, he dashed suddenly west, undiscovered by British scouts, until, well beyond Cornwallis's flank, he turned due north to the Rappahannock, twenty miles west of Fredericksburg. He came to the shores of that stream on June 4, while Wayne was still in the rain-soaked wilderness.

The rain which slowed Wayne's progress also hindered Cornwallis. In brook-filled country, the British could not readily chase the end-running Marquis. Cornwallis stopped the chase and billeted his officers in the handsome Virginia country houses, allowing them to relax in the comfortable Hanover Inn, feasting in its large and tastefully decorated salon and lounging on its wide porticoes while he waited for the creeks and rivers to subside.

Swarthy Banastre Tarleton, "the hunting leopard" of the British Army, was not content to dawdle. With Cornwallis's consent, he took 250 men, mounted on the best horses Virginia could supply, for a quick raid on Charlottesville, the temporary capital. His route led him over seventy miles of Piedmont country. He had only one stream to cross, and that close to its source; Tarleton hoped by steady riding to cover the distance within twenty-four hours. If he were successful, not only would large stocks of supplies be captured, but Governor Thomas Jefferson and such notables as Richard Henry Lee, Patrick Henry, Benjamin Harrison, and other members of the Assembly would fall into British hands. Virginia, Tarleton was convinced, would thus be paralyzed.

Early in the morning of June 3, while Lafayette was on his wide end-sweep and Wayne was passing Leesburg, Tarleton galloped out of Hanover. His best road would have taken him at once across the little gorge of the South Anna, over a high hill and through woods and barren country, but Tarleton avoided well-traveled ways for fear that rebel scouts might report his presence. He kept to bypaths, riding fast, and covered nearly half his distance before any American knew of his advance. He pressed on, undiscovered, after dark until at midnight he passed Cuckoo Tavern, near Louisa. Here, by luck, tall, powerful Jack Jouett, master marksman and expert horseman, saw Tarleton's cavalry sweeping by. Jouett, suspecting at once a raid against Charlottesville, rode like Paul Revere breakneck across country to the capital. At Louisa Inn he roused fat Landlord Johnson, who lived by day and night in a huge armchair, and shouted that redcoats were upon him; at Boswell's, he stirred up the sixty-year-old Scotch host who once was a colonel of militia. Boswell and his tall wife, together with one or two of the small Boswell children, spread the alarm. Early in the morning, Jouett hammered on Dr. Thomas Walker's door and told his news; by sunrise, he climbed the hill at Monticello and wakened Jefferson, thus enabling the Governor to get away on horseback barely a quarter-hour before Tarleton's men arrived, while Mrs. Jefferson and three children hurried off in their carriage to a refuge in the hills. A little later, Jouett rode breathlessly into Charlottesville, where he found legislators breakfasting. Hastily that body convened, in order that it might legally recess to Staunton; then the members fled into the mountains.

Tarleton did not come at once. He had halted his quick dash at the Walker house, where he demanded breakfast. Mrs. Walker deliberately worked so slowly in getting him a meal of salt herring, salt beef, and johnnycake that Tarleton was delayed. When he came into Charlottesville, two hours after Jouett had spread the warning, only a small handful of Assemblymen remained. The British did find a thousand flintlocks,

four hundred barrels of powder, and much clothing and tobacco; they burned public records in their two days' stay. "Like
birds of prey, they seized on everything that they could find."

John Graves Simcoe, clever commandant of the Queen's
Rangers, led a second raiding expedition, this one against
American stores at the Point of Forks west of Richmond, where
the Rivanna joins the James. Here Baron von Steuben was on
guard, watching over fifteen hundred guns, large stocks of
powder and shot, ten big French cannon, two hogsheads of
coffee, a barrel of brown sugar, and forty hogsheads of rum
and whisky. Simcoe's 100 dragoons and 300 infantry moved
more slowly than Tarleton's raiders, but they were no less successful. Some inkling, evidently, had come to Steuben of their
approach, for when Simcoe arrived, Steuben had ferried the
stores to the far bank of the river and all boats had been carried
off from the north bank where the British stood. Simcoe drew
up his men in so threatening an array that Steuben thought
them Cornwallis's main force. The Baron retreated thirty miles
in hot haste, leaving his stores behind. A sergeant of the
Queen's Rangers swam the stream, found a large canoe, and
paddled it back to his comrades, who crossed twenty at a time
to take the stores.

Wayne, meanwhile, slogged heavily ahead through low-
lying wilderness country. Instead of picking up speed, his progress slowed. On June 5, he made twelve miles, on the next day
only nine, and that night a violent electric storm blew down
his tents and so drenched everything in camp that on the seventh, when Wayne had hoped to join Lafayette, the army remained completely stationary. When at last the sun reappeared
and Wayne's men, "refreshed and furbished," sought to cross
the north branch of the Rappahannock, they found the stream
unfordable. Another detour was necessary; Wayne's troops did
not join the Marquis until June 10, when the armies met a
dozen miles south of Raccoon Ford on the Rapidan. They had
taken fifteen days to march the hundred and twenty miles from
York.

With Wayne's troops as reinforcement, Lafayette took the
aggressive. On the same day that Wayne joined forces with the

Marquis, the Americans turned about and hurried south. The British, in the meantime, had again united all their troops at Elk Hill, near Point of Forks, where they were poised for a descent in force on Charlottesville. Wayne and Lafayette, consulting as to a future course, decided to put themselves between Cornwallis and the temporary capital. To do so by customary highways involved exposing an entire flank to sudden British attack, but Virginians pointed out an alternative route whereby the desired movement might be effected with more safety. An old abandoned woods road, thickly overgrown with brush, ran through the pinewoods from Boswell's toward Charlottesville. Of this way Cornwallis knew nothing; if Lafayette and Wayne would send a few pioneers to clear the road, the Americans could march secretly and quickly to save the town.

Soldiers worked all night, chopping a path; at dawn the army advanced through dark woods, bordered by close-grown thickets. The road was rough and narrow, and men sweated profusely dragging heavy guns through the woods, but by night the two leaders halted their men in "an impregnable position" thirteen miles east of Charlottesville, between Cornwallis and the capital. They camped here all day on June 13, but the outwitted British chose to retreat.

From this time onward, the tide of invasion ebbed. Cornwallis steadily narrowed his hold on Virginia, withdrawing first to Richmond, then down the valley of the James toward Williamsburg. Wayne pressed hard upon the enemy's rear guard, threatening attack; Lafayette sent out numerous patrols so that wherever Cornwallis might scout, his horsemen would meet numbers of the patriots. Cornwallis imagined the Continental forces much greater than they really were. Impressed and bewildered, he hurried his retreat.

Twice, at least, Cornwallis seemed ready to accept battle, once when Tarleton came out to meet the Pennsylvanians and again when a foraging detachment, isolated from the main British Army, lined up to meet Wayne's advance, but on each occasion the British broke ranks before fighting began. Wayne clamored for a night attack upon the enemy, but Lafayette thought it wiser to trail about twenty miles behind Cornwallis.

By June 26, Cornwallis was penned in the narrow peninsula between the James and York rivers.

Just why he went there was incomprehensible. With all his confidence, Wayne labored under no illusions that the British were in forced retreat; Cornwallis had been neither outnumbered nor outgeneraled; his men were well fed, admirably supplied, and in excellent spirits. Wayne suspected that the retirement was a trap, that Cornwallis was baiting the rebels to follow, so that a fleet of transports from New York might land men behind the American lines. Indeed, had Clinton been willing to co-operate with his subordinate Cornwallis, such a maneuver might well have been successful. Cornwallis suggested that Sir Henry leave New York and come down to Virginia, but Clinton did not approve; instead, he called for large detachments to be sent at once by sea to New York.

Thus Cornwallis was badly weakened at a time when his strategic position was extremely weak. A brief skirmish at Hot Water Plantation, near Williamsburg, at dawn on June 26, when Wayne sent four platoons of Butler's infantry and Major McPherson's independent command into action against Simcoe, proved that Cornwallis was vulnerable, for the small force of Americans chased the British six miles, killing 40 men, capturing a number of prisoners, and taking horses and cattle. The Battle of Hot Water, though unimportant as a military engagement, restored the spirits of Virginia. Cornwallis thereafter ceased to "sport through the country without opposition"; Virginians no longer "seemed scared to death" at the very name of a dragoon, and the despondency which Wayne saw in Virginia countenances gave way to confidence. Cornwallis's retirement to Williamsburg caused patriots to hope that the end of the war was at last in sight.

With Cornwallis safely penned, Wayne and Lafayette rebuilt their army. The old guns thrown into the water when Simcoe surprised Steuben were fished out, and were again put into working order; cannon dumped into the James when the British left Richmond were overhauled. Lafayette sent off for supplies, asking for spears in the event that swords and guns were not available, and requisitioned munitions, medicines, and hospital stores in anticipation of a battle.

Militiamen, in fact, brought to Americans their only serious worry. Constant alarms and false rumors of attack kept the men alert, and caused them much unnecessary marching and counter-marching in the heat, purely for the purpose, so the soldiers said, of seeing "Some body's old field," but these were only to be expected. When militiamen who had signed for six weeks drifted out of service to go home for their harvests, little could be done to keep them under arms. "You might as well try," said Lafayette, "to stop the flood tide as to stop militia whose times are out."

Incessant alarms broke Anthony's sleep and made his temper shorter than usual. In addition, the continued heat and wetness caused him to grow irascible. He was worried, too, because after the Battle of Hot Water his friend Richard Butler had come down with a violent fever. Wayne feared that he would lose his best friend in the army; he was relieved when after a week of critical illness Butler began to convalesce. Cornwallis also put Wayne into better humor by giving him action. Under orders from Clinton at New York, the British general began to cross to the south side of the James, thus evacuating the peninsula. He sent his heavy baggage to Portsmouth, under escort of Simcoe's Queen's Rangers, and he made ready to transport the rest of his army over the river. In this fashion he weakened his rear and laid himself open to attack.

Lafayette, too, was certain that Cornwallis was vulnerable. Deserters, who were in reality clever British spies, brought conflicting rumors of Cornwallis's movements, but seemed to agree that the main body of the British were either now, or soon would be, on the south side of the James. At Lafayette's command, Wayne hurried to harass the supposedly few British who remained on the north bank of the river. With Walter Stewart, McPherson, and the French Major Galvan, Wayne rushed 500 men, almost all of whom were infantry, to Green Springs farm, adjacent to the scene of the Hot Water battle. Lafayette promised that the rest of the regulars would follow as a reserve.

Early on the morning of July 6, Wayne encountered the

enemy rear. Green Springs, as it happened, was a badly chosen battlefield, for the land was low and marshy and only a narrow causeway led to the British embarkation point; moreover, between the farm and the river lay a thick woods. Wayne took few chances, even though he was convinced that he had only a small rear-guard covering party with which to deal. He skirmished with outposts and drove back British pickets, but though he moved across the causeway, gaining ground steadily, he did not charge. Warily he watched the woods, not because he knew that Cornwallis lay in ambush, but because as a trained soldier he was habitually cautious.

Cornwallis played his role with consummate skill, tempting the Americans forward, even at the cost of heavy British losses. When men were shot down, he sent replacements forward from their ambush; as officer after officer fell before rebel sharpshooters, he substituted new leaders in their place. Cleverly, he simulated a steady falling back, so that the Americans would press on to victory. With the adroitness of a good chess-player, he allowed one gun to stand, abandoned in the open, as a gambit to lure the rebels into danger. Excitable Major Galvan jumped at the opportunity. With the Wyllys regiment and one field piece, he double-quicked to take the bait. Wayne, riding at the head of Stewart's Pennsylvanians, followed after, his broad face glowing with pleasure. A stray shot clipped the plume from his hat, and Wayne laughed at the narrow escape, but his eyes were on the Galvan charge. When an aide fainted and fell from a horse, he called the youngster an Irish Beauty and ordered him carried off the field.

The diversion prevented Wayne from seeing what was happening to Galvan. Lafayette, standing on a point of land jutting into the river to the right of Green Springs, saw clearly that the entire British Army was drawn up on open ground behind the woods, ready to spring upon Galvan and Wayne. The Marquis rushed reinforcements, but the regiments came too late. Galvan, dashing to the gun, found the British battle line, with field pieces pointing directly at the small American force. A redcoat wave swept out of the woods in two columns, less than sixty yards away. Galvan fired a volley and stood to load again, but the British came too quickly. Galvan retreated "in an order which does honor to American discipline."

Wayne came to the rescue. In desperate position, because by every rule of warfare the British should have forced the death or surrender of every man, he could not retreat upon the crowded corduroy causeway. Lafayette's reinforcements, save for two regiments under Lieutenant-Colonel Josiah Harmar and Richard Humpton, were not yet at hand. Wayne resorted to a characteristically daring move. Instead of retreating, he called for an advance! An ambushed force, caught in a hopeless trap, charged a British army which outnumbered it nearly ten to one! Wayne spurred forward, his men yelling, their bayonets pointed straight at the enemy. Cornwallis, taken aback, halted, wondering if he had been mistaken and if the entire American force was upon him. He hesitated; his men, bewildered by the rebels who were "making a devil of a noise of firing and huzzaing," fumbled with their guns. Wayne, seeing the British uncertainty, wheeled about and got his men away to safety, Cornwallis following with extreme deliberation. Wayne withdrew even his ammunition wagons, although two cannon whose horses had been shot were abandoned to the British.

For sheer audacity, for quick thinking in emergency, and for bravery, Green Springs marks a high point in Wayne's military career. His Trois Rivières exploit proved his courage even when he was inexperienced in arms; Stony Point testified to his resourcefulness; but in neither place had he been so outnumbered nor in such sudden, unexpected peril. Wayne himself was justifiably proud of his achievement; in half a dozen letters sent to Washington, Pennsylvania state officials, and the War Office as well as to Delany, he boasted of his success: "Every Circumstance considered, our small reconnoitering party who had the hardihood to attack Lord Cornwallis at the head of his whole army, with the advantage of so powerful a Cavalry, on their own ground and in their own encampment are more to be envied than pitied, as it not only frustrated the British General in his premeditated manoeuver but precipitated his retreat the same night."

Wayne lost 28 men killed, 99 wounded, and 12 taken prisoner at Green Springs, while Cornwallis had 75 dead or seriously hurt. Wayne found it hard to believe that British losses were fewer than his own; his enthusiastic letters boasted that 500 redcoats had been killed and wounded. He grew angry when in visiting his ten wounded officers he learned that army doctors were lax and inefficient and that medical supplies were not on hand. He took it upon himself to buy medicine and food at his own expense and to see that comfortable carriages were provided to take the men to Philadelphia. His thoughtfulness won him the thanks of his suffering officers.

Wayne's superiors lavished praise upon him for his Green Springs exploit. Lafayette mentioned him in special orders, and repeated his enthusiasm in private letters to Greene and Washington. Washington and Robert Morris sent Wayne their congratulations. Greene, however, in writing to Wayne warned that Cornwallis was not yet crushed. "Be a little careful and tread softly," he said, "for depend upon it you have a modern Hannibal to deal with in the person of Lord Cornwallis."

3

The Virginia campaign slowed pace. Cornwallis remained at Portsmouth, but day after day he marked time; Lafayette, from high, healthful ground at Malvern Hill, east of Richmond, kept close guard over the British. The two armies remained motionless. Wayne enjoyed no rest. His Pennsylvania Continentals, reinforced by 300 Virginia militiamen, 500 of Morgan's Riflemen, and a few dragoons, watched Tarleton's movements. The restless hunting leopard, whose dragoons rode Virginia's choice race horses, burst forth on a raid of devastation that was to carry him as far as New London, halfway across the state; Wayne's infantry was supposed to catch the cavalry and to check the raid.

It was a superhuman feat, to be accomplished only if Wayne's men chanced to hold a post past which Tarleton rode, so Wayne waited at Chesterfield, south of Richmond, where there was good water and a fine, level terrain. His dragoons scoured the country for signs of the hunting leopard, but to no avail, and Wayne went on to Good's Bridge, on the Appomattox, where he stayed ten days, with no incident to mark the camp save that one afternoon the wooden bridge fell unaccountably into the creek while soldiers sat fishing in the shade. Fortunately none were hurt.

Tarleton by this time had returned from his marauding, avoiding Wayne, and was again with Cornwallis, and the entire British Army embarked. No Americans knew where they were going. Wayne simultaneously received three letters: Stewart wrote to say that Cornwallis was off for Philadelphia; Wyllys that he was en route for Baltimore; and Lafayette that he was heading for either Carolina or New York. All agreed that the British move, wherever bound, spelled danger for the Continentals.

Wayne, having missed Tarleton, was on his way south through fertile Amelia County to join Greene in South Carolina when, at midnight of August 2, an express rider brought orders from Lafayette to swing about. By swift marches, Wayne went back to the Richmond area, prepared to hurry toward Baltimore or Philadelphia, but when he reached the James, word came that Cornwallis had landed, not at any of the places predicted in the letters, but at Yorktown in the same peninsula that he had left only a few weeks before. Here, at a little village of seventy houses, once the great tobacco-exporting port of Virginia, the British were throwing up defenses, and expecting momentarily a naval reinforcement from New York.

Wayne now held the highway between Richmond and the North while Lafayette closed in upon Cornwallis by reoccupying the handsome town of Williamsburg, whose two hundred and thirty white-painted houses bordered a mile-long central avenue stretching between the State House and the college. Once the pen was again completed, Wayne would draw closer to the enemy, scouring the area between the Pamunkey and the James for any British sympathizers, and tightening the land net about Cornwallis. The tour took him into interesting territory. The Pamunkey flowed through a valley with woods on either side, but the hills above gave wide vistas of rich tobacco lands. At Hanover, Wayne saw George Phillips's extensive plantation, whose innumerable living-rooms, guest chambers, kitchens, slave quarters, barns, and storehouses, each in its separate one-story wooden boxlike building, made Wayne, who was accustomed to the solidity of Chester County mansions, think of a toy village built of cards.

He liked the carefree life of Virginia planters, with their love for horses, their fox-hunting, and their long evenings of good companionship. Anthony could not match their idleness, but he enjoyed their capacity for friendship; their talk at night, gay, superficial, and full of banter, reminded him of his prewar evenings at the City Tavern before bluestockings such as Elizabeth Graeme Ferguson made a cult of intellectuality. Some of his more philosophical comrades thought that the Southern climate made Virginians indolent and unenterprising, others argued that the prevalence of slavery destroyed initiative, but Wayne was no prober into causes; for him, it was sufficient that the Virginians were generous and friendly; that they were also choleric, thin-skinned, and improvident only endeared them to him the more, since these were characteristics that Anthony well understood.

Other features of the Southern scene could never be transplanted. At formal dinners given in his honor, Wayne was shocked to see young slaves, boys and girls as old as fifteen, waiting on the table stark naked, or at most wearing nothing but a loose shirt that fell no further than the middle of the thigh. He glanced quickly at the ladies, but saw no sign of embarrassment. He went to parties on the lawns, where girls in huge gauze bonnets decked out by ribbons danced jigs and more formal minuets with officers while half-clad soldiers stood about the borders of the lawn, but again the girls, even those most delicately reared, were unperturbed.

While he was visiting about, plots and treacheries continued to boil about him. The restless Fishbourn, still angling for promotion, continued his underhanded correspondence with St.

Clair, using the opportunity to slander his supposed friends and to fawn upon the more successful major-general.

"Be assured, my dear General," he wrote St. Clair, "I ever shall esteem your character and revear the Man who has Honesty and Honor enough to despair any little, low artifices that may occasion disputes and quarrels. You cannot conceive how much of this Game that has been played against you. That man whom I knew you have took by the hand and salute by the kind epithet of friend, has many times joined in a convention that traded against you. R. Butler I mean, a man of more policy than wit, a man who would sacrifice his Soul for popularity altho he has not the capacity of a Stewart to obtain it. Such a man and such a character I despise. What I mean by making himself more popular is that he thinks and revears a Wayne as a God.

"I can never forgive or forget," he went on to assure St. Clair, "the Chekenery that was used toward you by General Wayne. . . . Great God that men should be allowed to carry on such acts. Why is there not some hidden curse in the Stores of Heaven to blast them to perdition?"

Perhaps Fishbourn, in thus condemning Anthony Wayne, for whom he professed such deep affection at times when Wayne was present, may, like Stewart at the Morristown dinner, have been carried away by drink. He confesses that the note was written at an inopportune moment, since he was obliged to write at a table "where the Bottles and scandals flow pretty considerable," but he adds, as reassurance, that "an honest man is the noblest work of God." The subject for the tribute was, of course, Arthur St. Clair himself.

Ignorant of the betrayals that were taking place, Wayne devoted himself to military duties. Little by little, while Cornwallis awaited naval reinforcement, Wayne drew closer to the penned-in enemy. In the last week of August, he was on the James, having passed by the country home of a Virginia farmer whose four-year-old son, Henry Clay, watched wide-eyed as the army swung along, and having thrilled an eight-year-old boy, William Henry Harrison, with the soldiers' shining bayonets and rumbling guns. He camped at Westover, where Colonel William Byrd had built a magnificent mansion on the crest of a hill overlooking waterfalls and rocky, wooded islands. Here he found a Philadelphia friend, for Colonel Byrd's widow, one of the Willing girls whose sister was Margaretta Wayne's schoolmistress, lived here with her children, two of them attractive young ladies just emerging from their teens. Wayne enjoyed his short stay at this magnificent estate; when he reluctantly moved on, he gave Mrs. Byrd a special permit entitling her to pass American sentry lines whenever she or her daughters wished to do so. She thanked him in a letter of appreciation which indicates that she, in her turn, had liked Anthony: "I shall ever retain the highest sence of your politeness and humanity and take every opportunity of testifying my gratitude. Should my judgment point out that you might suffer the smallest inconvenience from your indulgence to me, no consideration of self interest shall tempt me to use the flag. I shall ever think myself honored by a visit from General Wayne and very happy in receiving one from him. May ever felicity attend you in this life is the sincere wishes of the inhabitants of Westover."

But all was not as peaceful as these gay days and evenings might suggest. Wayne waged constant verbal warfare with civil leaders. His Virginia militiamen, who believed themselves bound for the Carolinas, made violent objection, warning that since their state had sent no pay, they would not set foot beyond the border. "Their impudence," Wayne told Thomas Nelson, the new governor who replaced Jefferson, "gives ground to fear that the other part of the troops may possibly catch the infection, for we have not a single private in the Pennsylvania Line that there is less sum due to than thirty half-joes." A half-joe, or johannes, was a Portuguese gold coin worth 36 shillings, or approximately $8.62 in specie. "Add to this," Wayne went on, "that our men are barefoot and the same causes may produce the same effects as heretofore."

In appealing to Pennsylvania for money and clothing, Wayne was more explicit than in dealing with Virginians: "There is not a single article of clothing in all this country. Our people are barefoot and bare-legged rather *high up*. For god's sake, forward shoes and overalls for if the Salvation of the army and the fate of America depended upon obtaining one pair they could not be procured in the *Antient Dominion*."

Virginia turned deaf ears. Nelson passed the buck to William Davies of the state War Office, who, he said, had sole authority to issue clothing, and the latter, after reading Wayne a lecture on carelessness, promised to send some shoes and uniforms "in less than two months."

A showdown was averted when Wayne's southward march was countermanded, for the militia were not asked to cross the border, but the need for clothing grew worse. Wayne commandeered a hundred and seventy-three pairs of shoes, eleven pairs of boots, and twenty pieces of coarse linen Osnaburg cloth, all belonging to the State of Virginia. In telling Nelson of his action, Wayne added that his men stood in much need of food. Nelson protested at the seizures and demanded that the footgear and linen be returned immediately. Wayne shot word back that had he not commandeered the goods, Tarleton would have taken them. He declined to send them back, though he refrained from issuing them to his men. "Delicacy has induced me to march the Pennsylvanians barefoot over sharp pebbles and through burning sands," he wrote to Nelson. The latter, instead of being convinced, went over Wayne's head and complained to Lafayette, demanding that every article taken by Wayne be restored to Virginia's control. The Marquis, not knowing what to make of the situation, relayed the letters to Wayne, but eased the tension by sending two hundred pairs of shoes and a quantity of overalls to replace the goods which Wayne had commandeered.

These bickerings ended quickly when Lafayette sent secret news that De Grasse's huge French fleet of twenty-eight sail of the line and six frigates was expected momentarily in the Chesapeake, and that Washington and Rochambeau with 6,000 men, the combined American and French armies, were coming posthaste from the Hudson. If the news, which Lafayette dispatched on August 25, were confirmed, no doubt remained that the British were at the mercy of the allies. Such an armada meant plainly that for the first time in the war England had lost control of the American waters, so that Cornwallis could expect no help from Clinton. It was evident that with virtually every trained soldier in the United States closing in at once on Yorktown, Cornwallis would be Burgoyned.

The news was true. On August 30, 1781, De Grasse passed Cape Charles, and two days later, on September 1, Wayne hurried to reoccupy Green Springs, to prevent Cornwallis from crossing the river to Portsmouth and so escaping into Carolina. On the same day, in the absence of Lafayette, who was in bed with a slight touch of fever, Butler and Stewart interviewed De Grasse, to plan for the landing of 3,000 white-uniformed Frenchmen. "Every door is shut," said Wayne jubilantly, "by the hard hearted fellows against poor Cornwallis."

Wayne's joy faded quickly. In his anxiety to join Lafayette, he took horse and rode ten miles across country to the French headquarters. He arrived at ten o'clock at night and dashed at once across the sentry lines. A picket challenged, but Wayne did not hear; the sentry leveled his gun and shot the General in the left thigh. It was good discipline, as Wayne admitted, but a painful method of discovering how alert American sentries really were. The ball grazed the bone and lodged about an inch from the inside of the thigh. "What is very extraordinary," Wayne said, "is that although I never had a symptom of gout before, the shot brought it upon me, as quick as electricity, so much so that I thought I was wounded in the foot, which continued much more painful than my thigh."

Wayne, laid up in hospital, took no part in the ceremony of welcoming the French fleet and the troops which came with it; he used his time to complain to Dick Peters that American ammunition was inferior. "*Your* damned Commissary of Military *plays false*. He has put too little powder in the musket Cartridges." Had the cartridges been perfect, Wayne implied, the ball and the buckshot, which had also been rammed in for good measure, would have gone completely through his leg. Wayne kept his bed for ten days; on September 12, two days before Washington's arrival, he rode out in a carriage.

Kept idle by "this Caitiff disorder," Anthony felt blue because he bore so small a part in the investment of Cornwallis's position. Contrary to his usual custom, he was far from confident. The French troops, he admitted, were the finest and best that he had ever seen, and allied numbers were overwhelming, but as he wrote Robert Morris: "I don't know how it is, but I have not felt so sanguine on the Occasion, as the Naval and land force sent us by our good and great ally would justify. Probably it is Occationed by our former disappointments when matters bore a flattering appearance."

Incapacitated for active service, he was able to hobble about, though the ball in his thigh caused pain, and on the rainy day following the carriage trip he dined with Washington. He retired early in order that he might be better able to bear the strain of an all-day review, September 14, when Washington inspected troops. It was a gala celebration, ushered in by a reception. Wayne and Edward Hand flanked the commander, presenting each man whom Washington did not know personally. Standing by the door, the three men saluted each officer, shook hands, and spoke a word or two until the entire corps had passed by. Then, at three o'clock, French guns sounded a royal twenty-one-gun salute in Washington's honor, and the entire army turned out upon parade.

The soldiers made a gallant showing, for the Continentals, dressed uniformly in the now standard buff and blue, drilled smartly under Steuben's watchful eye, while French privates, as immaculately turned out as if each man were an officer, marched with a precision that delighted every spectator. Certainly the French were colorful. The Marquis de Laval's Régiment Bourbonnais lent a somber note in their red-trimmed black uniforms, but they were followed by the Royal Deuxponts in white broadcloth faced with green and by the artillery in blue and white. The Marquis de St. Maime's Soisonnais looked debonair in white tricked out with pink, with pink plumes drooping from their caps, and De Custine's Saintonges, like the Royal Deuxponts, were brave in green and white. Their drum majors caught every eye as they stalked by in sharp-peaked, tinsel-covered hats with heavy feather plumes, flourishing ponderous batons; alert messengers and aides, in short, tight-fitting coats, silver-fringed waistcoats, rose-colored shoes, caps embroidered with regimental coats of arms, and bearing heavy canes, dashed back and forth looking important enough to be generals.

Those pastel-shaded troops were stern warriors; at least a third of the white-and-pale-blue Gatennais fell in battle, while other regiments merited equal praise for gallantry in action. Wayne himself, who cherished little love for foreigners, gave them credit for saving the United States: "Believe me, it was not to the exertions of America that we owe the reduction of this modern Hannibal; nor shall we always have it in our power to Command the aid of thirty-seven sail-of-the-line and 8,000 auxiliary veterans. Our allies are not to learn that on this occasion, our regular troops were not more than equal to one-half their land force, and altho' our prowess was such as to establish our Character as Soldiers, our means and numbers were far inadequate to the Idea they had formed of American *resources.*"

On September 28, Washington led 16,000 well-trained troops to within two miles of the doomed town where Cornwallis and his 8,000 men lay entrenched behind earthworks and batteries. The allies jubilated when they saw that Cornwallis, for all his sixty-five guns, gave way without a shot and let the besiegers come within half a mile of the village. Soldiers laid bets that the place would fall within a week. They lost their bets, for Washington took ample time to bring up siege guns from the James, to make fascines (bundles of brushwood) to use in filling up enemy entrenchments, and to construct gabions, the wicker baskets full of earth which served the purpose of the more modern sandbags. Not until October 6 did he venture farther, when 1,500 men dug a line of trenches by night in the rain, parallel to the British forts and less than six hundred yards away. Soon after, Knox and Steuben placed batteries close up and began bombardment. By October 11, fifty-two guns played on the British positions, and Cornwallis privately confessed: "With such works, on disadvantageous ground, against so powerful an attack, we cannot hope to make a very long resistance."

Owing to his wound, Wayne's part was small in these arrangements, but his Pennsylvanians were active. On the night of Cornwallis's gloom, they dug a second line of trenches seven hundred and fifty yards long, three hundred yards from the British lines. Wayne hobbled about, encouraging his men, while British shells burst all about. When one shell whistled by, Steuben threw himself into the half-dug trench, and Wayne followed, stumbling after him. In the haste Anthony caught his foot and fell heavily upon the Baron. "Ah ha, Wayne," Steuben laughed when he caught his breath, "you cover your general's retreat!"

The last stage was at hand. On the night of October 14, while the British enjoyed the pipes of wine distributed by Cornwallis to keep up their spirits, the Gatennais and the Royal Deuxponts stormed one redoubt while Colonel Alexander Hamilton with 400 New Yorkers and New Englanders swarmed a second. Cornwallis gave up hope. He tried a sortie and failed; he strove to escape to Gloucester across the York River, braving the French fleet, but a sudden storm threw his boats into confusion. American batteries pounded the town remorselessly.

Cornwallis sent a redcoat drummer to his parapet to "beat a parley," but the guns boomed away so steadily that the drummer could not be heard. A British officer appeared, waving a white handkerchief, and Wayne yelled an order to cease firing. An American ran out into the open, met the Briton, and tied a handkerchief around his eyes, preparatory to bringing him to Washington's headquarters. It was ten o'clock in the morning of October 17. The redcoat drummer boy beat on. "It was," said Ebenezer Denny, a fellow townsman of Dick Butler, "the most delightful music ever heard."

Two days passed while capitulation terms were proposed, rejected, resubmitted, and at last accepted. On October 19, 1781, 8,000 British soldiers, dressed in bright new uniforms, gave up their stronghold. Dick Butler had the honor of planting the first Stars and Stripes upon the enemy parapet, but Butler, too short and heavy to climb easily, detailed Lieutenant Denny for the duty. Denny mounted the parapet and was about to plant the flagstaff in the earthworks when Steuben rode out from the lines and ordered Denny to let him raise the colors over the fort. Denny, yielding to the Baron's superior rank, obeyed, much against his personal desires, but Wayne and Butler indignantly protested. Butler was so angry at Steuben's interference that he sent the Baron a sharp letter of complaint. Had not Rochambeau and Washington intervened, the Butler message would in all likelihood have led to a duel.

The British troops marched out, but Cornwallis, who professed himself too sick to take part in the final ceremonies, yielded command to Brigadier-General Charles O'Hara, his only other officer above the rank of colonel. As the redcoats left Yorktown, their colors furled and cased, their drums beating "as if they did not care how," their bands blared away at an old march, "Derry Down." Some Americans who, like Wayne, had been reading the *Gentleman's Magazine,* remembered that recently the periodical had published a new song, "The World Turned Upside Down," set to the old tune. By amazing coincidence, the song told how Goody Bull, or England, quarreled with her daughter America, and how the quarrel ended by the efforts of a farmer, whom Americans identified with the French. As the British band played "Derry Down," the Americans sang out the words:

> She be damned, says the farmer, and to her he goes,
> First roars in her ears, then tweaks her old nose,
> Hallo, Goody, what ails you? Wake! woman, I say,
> I am come to make peace in this desperate fray.
> Alas! cries the woman and I must comply?
> But I'd rather submit than the hussy should die.
> Pooh, prithee, be quiet, be friends and agree,
> You must surely be right, if you're guided by me.
> No thanks to you, mother; the daughter replied,
> But thanks to my friend here, I've humbled your pride.

O'Hara turned over his sword to Major-General Benjamin Lincoln, who a year and a half earlier had been forced to give up Charleston to the British. Then the beaten troops dropped their arms and unbuckled their cartridge cases, preparatory to going into captivity in western Virginia and Maryland; their officers, put upon parole, were wined and dined by Wayne and other American leaders before their departure for New York.

CHAPTER XIII

The Georgia Desert

CHIMNEY-CORNER soldiers thought the war was at an end. Philadelphia and the North went wild with glee, illuminating the towns, firing rockets into the sky, and spouting patriotic speeches at innumerable victory dinners. But except for voting official thanks and directing that a monument be set up to commemorate the triumph, Congress felt it needless to take further action. The states were even more lethargic. Pennsylvania, for example, used up all her cash in paying off civil employees, making no provision for the army. The Assembly brawled away its days, investigating corrupt practices in elections and threatening to arrest Wayne's one-time friend John Lacey for intimidation of electors, but made no move to help the army. Now that Cornwallis had surrendered, politicians saw no need for wasting money. Wayne felt differently. To his mind, Cornwallis was of slight importance; other phases of the war had arisen to occupy all the time and enterprise that the army had to spare. "I have for some time," he said, "viewed him as a fiery meteor that displays a momentary lustre, then falls to rise no more."

Yorktown had been taken, but British troops still held the Deep South in Charleston and in Georgia, where Greene battled constantly. Wayne was, as usual, anxious for active service, and he liked Greene personally, but now he hoped for his customary winter furlough. Counting on a few weeks' vacation from army duty, he plunged into speculation, committing himself by purchasing sugar for future delivery. He learned, to his dismay, that Washington expected him to go South, with Butler, Stewart, Craig, and Brigadier-General Mordecai Gist's Marylanders, to Greene's assistance. For the first time in his life, Wayne dodged a call to take the field. He asked Washington for a leave of absence, but the Commander-in-Chief pointed out that Anthony had enjoyed more freedom than any other general and that it was the turn of others to take vacations. Then he asked permission to remain a few days to finish up his private business, promising to rejoin the army immediately "if the exigencies of the case require it and circumstances permit." Washington granted consent, particularly since Wayne's old enemy Arthur St. Clair was to command the column and since with Wayne away dissension would be lessened.

Despite the wound that still pained severely, Wayne scurried about Yorktown to straighten out his speculations. As a hedge against possible loss, he asked Jeremiah Wadsworth, former commissary for the American Army, to lend him a large amount of money, but when Wadsworth found that Wayne could not repay the loan within four months, he declined. Three days after St. Clair's troops had marched, Wayne made a deal with John Irvin, a Yorktown merchant, whereby Irvin assumed the contracts.

Wayne mounted and rode slowly, favoring his wound, along the James, stopping to call upon the Byrds, John Page of Rosedale, and others of his friends, halting at Galt's Ordinary— Anthony called it an "ornery"—where he played billiards and ate sumptuously of rockfish, and diverging from his straight course to visit Blandford, the fine home of his friend Colonel Theodoric Bland. The tall, grave physician, as he knew, would not be home, but Wayne wished to know just how his fine estate had weathered British attack. He was glad to see that while devastation was evident, the buildings remained intact.

Wayne and his staff rode on toward Petersburg, a large town of three hundred houses, bigger than Richmond. They crossed the ferry over the Appomattox to Spencer Inn, which had a cramped, indifferent appearance from the outside but which within proved comfortable and indeed luxurious. The Spencer daughter played to him on a magnificent harpsichord, and Anthony let his thoughts turn, as they invariably did in times of leisure, to dalliance with love. Another lady cut short his stay

at Spencer's. Mrs. Bolling, who owned half the town, invited
him to shift his quarters to her mansion on the riverbank. Anthony enjoyed his Bolling visit, not only because the lively lady
of fifty entertained him lavishly, gossiping gaily about Virginians whom he knew, but because as a farmer he liked to see
how prosperous estates were run. He inspected her tobacco warehouses, looked at the big gristmill worked by water canalled
from the river, and marveled at the ingenuity with which slaves
cleaned cotton. On this, as on other Virginia plantations, two
wooden cylinders, slowly revolving in opposite directions, carried wooden teeth that combed out seeds from the cotton that
was passed between. Mrs. Bolling called the machine a "gin,"
which Wayne thought must be a contraction of the word "en-
gine"; she said that it made cotton-planting profitable.

At the Bolling plantation, Wayne received a letter from his
old friend Rush, commenting on the trip to Carolina. Ben was
pleased with Anthony's successes; he predicted further glories:
"South Carolina has been well watered with the blood of heroes.
It requires only to be manured with a few more British car-
casses to produce spontaneous laurels. This business, we expect,
will be effectually done in a soil naturally fruitful by men who
forced laurels out of the rocks of Stony Point." Nevertheless the
excitable physician warned Wayne to be careful. He gave admirable advice; if Anthony had followed it, he would have been
spared suffering and probably his life would have been prolonged. "Beware, my friend, not of bullets, for they do you no
harm, but of a bilious fever. Avoid the evening air, drink wine
moderately, wear flannel next to your skin and take a dose of
bark every day. Death from a fever or a flux may be natural to
a citizen, but a soldier can only die naturally and professionally
of a ball or a bayonet."

Wayne looked at the swamps that surrounded Petersburg and
thought that when poisoned night vapors rose from their stagnant waters, fevers would be inevitable. He had heard that
Georgia land lay low and that each summer men fell sick with
chills and fevers, but he felt himself above such perils. In mid-
winter, certainly, and on the high ground of North Carolina,
he need not fear swamp fever; certainly he had no intention of

wearing rough flannels. Anthony stuck the letter in his files and forgot all about it.

Now only two days behind the army, he rode leisurely, drawing rein to watch how Virginians trapped wild turkeys by building log stockades topped by heavy planks into which they spread a trail of corn. He wondered at the thin blue haze that floated in the air until tavern-keepers told him that it was smoke from distant forest fires. Careless wagoners left fires which, spreading, burned through dead leaves, set many miles of woodland ablaze. Riding further, he saw in the distance a pinewoods where a sea of flame, fanned by fresh winds, roared through a forest of gigantic evergreens. The treetops, red with fire, fell crashing to the ground. Travel, as Wayne saw, held peril in these Southern forests, especially on windy days when ancient tree trunks toppled over without warning. Even well-traveled roads, blazed at frequent intervals by bark slashed from the sides of tree boles, were blocked by freshly fallen trunks. On one breezy afternoon he had to turn his horse into the woods six times within a mile to ride around the fallen timber.

So long as Wayne rode in plantation-filled Virginia, riding was comfortable, for taverns were well appointed, and though they offered little more than coffee, ham and eggs, with cloudy cider, rum, and sweet peach brandy, and though their beds were "stuffed with shavings on a frame that rocked like a cradle," he could make shift. More often, near-by planters, lonesome and anxious for good company, sent slaves to the tavern to inquire if travelers had come and if so, to invite the strangers to stay overnight at the farmhouse, a practice which innkeepers would have resented strongly had not planters given lavish presents to compensate for loss of trade. In North Carolina, where farms were poorer, these alleviations ended. Frontier inns were log huts, one-storied and with but two rooms, sometimes with only one. Wayne soon came to know the signs: an earthen jug suspended from a pole sticking out from the side of a house meant that he must stay in a combination family bedroom, guest room, and barroom. At such an inn the only fare was ham and eggs, badly cooked unless Anthony's own men fixed the meal. He stayed but seldom in such a primitive retreat.

He was in the red-clay district of the midlands, where roads hardened at night into a rough, broken surface but softened by day into a slimy mire into which the hoofs of horses sank. Riding behind the army, he suffered grievously, for cannon had left huge, deep ruts and the passage of many horses and foot soldiers had broken any smoothness that the highway ever had. His wound ached with the roughness of his journey, but even this was preferable to being with St. Clair.

At Guilford Court House, scene of Greene's engagement, marks yet remained, ten months after the battle, to testify to its intensity. Wayne saw broken musket butts upon the field and remnants of torn equipment. Here, too, he saw a Negro's head stuck on a sapling beside the road, and a black right hand pierced by a tree limb on the other side of the highway. The victim had been hanged and cut to pieces for an assault upon his master. He pressed ahead into South Carolina, among the lands of the Catawba Indians. At Christmas he came to Camden, where Le Conte, the richest planter of the neighborhood, invited him to a fine dinner. It was a warm, pleasant day, without the need of a fire, and Wayne enjoyed the party hugely. For the next few days, his journeys were less pleasant. He went through marshes so soft that often he had to lead his horse, and he was wet to his knees in mud and water. The scenery changed completely; instead of pines and red clay, he passed through cane and groves of sharp-leaved palmetto; flocks of green parakeets flew over him; frogs croaked in the marshes; here and there a snake slithered from beneath his horse. On New Year's Day, 1782, he started off at sunrise "through a wilderness," wading twenty creeks, to make camp on low ground almost entirely surrounded by water. Then at last, crossing the Edisto River on January 4, he joined Greene at a town curiously named Round O. Greene welcomed Wayne, Gist, St. Clair, and the other leading officers with a sumptuous entertainment.

To keep Wayne and St. Clair in close proximity was to invite fireworks, but Greene had ample work for both. Charleston and Savannah were in British hands, and though Charleston was accounted the more important port, Greene wished to pen the British in both cities. With St. Clair and the Pennsylvania Line,

he drew a ring about Charleston; Wayne, with a few dragoons, some artillery, and about 500 men, went toward Savannah to cut off from any communication with the interior 1,000 British regulars, 500 Tory militiamen, and an indeterminate number of Indians. Wayne once more had an independent command, the assignment which above all others he most enjoyed, but for the first time in his military career he had no Pennsylvanians under him. He pleaded with Greene for at least one battalion of the men whom he knew and liked, but Greene could not spare seasoned soldiers for Georgia duty.

The situation proved worse than anyone had imagined. Georgia granaries were so bare that the countryfolk were starving. Wayne was forced to import rice and beef from South Carolina for both his own men and the civilian population. Local government was so weak that murder committed openly in tue streets of the temporary capital at Augusta went unpunished; beyond gunshot of the governor's office, state laws were disregarded. Insult, pillage, and rioting raged unrestrained. Plundering banditti, masquerading as patriots or loyalists—whichever best suited their convenience—stole Negroes, livestock, furnishings, and all forms of wealth that were not nailed down. "The rage ran so high," said Brigadier-General William Moultrie, "that what was called 'a Georgia parole,' and to be shot down, were synonymous."

The treasury was empty, too, for the state could collect no taxes, nor had it credit, since a Georgia paper dollar was so cheap that sixteen hundred equaled only $1 in hard cash. The state frankly ceased to be democratic, but allowed a majority of its nine-man Executive Council to appoint all officers, conduct finances, control the militia, administer justice, and what is more, to name their own successors. Despite this enormous, unrestrained power, the oligarchy broke down; when Wayne arrived on January 19, 1782, the state was virtually in anarchy. Two hundred and sixty of the most important citizens had been attainted of high treason to the United States; the remaining Whigs were hopelessly at odds with one another. Colonel John Skey Eustace, Adjutant-General of the state, made the situation clear to Wayne when the latter crossed the Savannah River from

South Carolina. He advised that Wayne summon small numbers only of militia and that he take pains to transport the men by water, for, he warned, upcountry men would never walk a step under any conceivable circumstance.

With true Georgia hospitality everyone welcomed Wayne. A long-forgotten Cousin William, son of Uncle Gabriel, offered to put Wayne up and told Anthony of his small son named after the illustrious general. Governor John Martin assured him that Georgia was happy to have him there, but added that the militia could not exceed 500 men, and that there was neither food, forage, nor munitions in the state. Neither would money be available for about a year, when estates confiscated from the Tories could be legally sold at auction. Others shook his hand and wished him well, but shut up like clams when he asked help. "I find this country," said Wayne despairingly, "a perfect desert."

Well he might, for he had camped at Ebenezer, twenty-five miles from Savannah, among swamps from which, old settlers said, poisonous miasmas spread. The town itself was pleasant, laid out as it had been in a neat, gridiron pattern by about five hundred settlers of German descent. The founders, who had come from Berchtesgaden—not then as well known as now—had not shared Wayne's opinion of the site, for to them the soil seemed fit for growing rice and wine grapes, cotton and good pasture. Their leader wrote home to Europe: "The earth is so fertile that it will bring forth anything that can be sown or planted in it, whether fruits, herbs or trees." The Berchtesgaden settlers had been happy here until British raiders laid the region waste; by Wayne's time, Ebenezer lay in ruins.

From Wayne's first appearance at his Ebenezer camp, Georgia provided constant action. Five hundred British rode out from Savannah to reconnoiter Wayne's force; they camped at Mulberry Grove, once a rice, silk, and cotton plantation twelve miles from the city on the Savannah River. Thence they intended to dash upon Wayne's camp. Anthony, ever alert, took the initiative. By so deploying his few men that they seemed to number at least 1,000, he frightened the British horsemen into a retreat to the city.

Three days later, on January 28, Wayne achieved a more important victory. Twenty-six Creek Indians and six white traders, headed by Joseph Cornell, came from the Altamaha River in southern Georgia to get presents (a polite word for bribes) from Sir Alured Clarke, British commander at Savannah. They brought ninety-three pack animals to carry back the gifts. Wayne heard of their approach, and summoned Colonel William McCoy of the South Carolina State Dragoons. "Your men," he said, "are dressed in scarlet. Go out and meet these Indians. They will think you British and will not be alarmed. Tell them that you have come to escort them to Savannah. Lead them to a place where we can surround and capture them."

The plan worked perfectly. McCoy rode out and called to Cornell to have no fear, that the dragoons were friends. Cornell, trusting the red uniforms, beckoned his Indians to follow, but before they neared the place of ambush some Creeks grew suspicious and bolted into the swamps. Wayne's men hurriedly closed in, and without a battle captured every man and all the horses. In dealing with the prisoners, Wayne used a combination of bribery and kindness. The braves, whom he was careful to call "kings of the Creeks," were kept under guard in a heated room and were bountifully provisioned and supplied with rum, so that when they went back to their people on the Altamaha, they would praise the liberality of Americans. Cornell, their leader, was alternately cajoled and threatened until he agreed, after substantial money gifts, to join Wayne's cause. He told of the near approach of 300 Choctaws and of the presence in the neighborhood of a hundred pack horses taking guns and ammunition to the Indians.

Wayne called Major Joseph Habersham, plain-spoken, forthright, and quick-tempered patriot, and told him of Cornell's disclosures. He suggested that the same guile which took the Creeks would work successfully against the Choctaws. "Better to make them our friends," he said, "than to bring on an inevitable war by murdering those within our power." Habersham found difficulty in following out Wayne's policy. On January 31 and February 1, rain fell heavily; the 120 men who comprised the whole militia of the State of Georgia refused to stir from

camp, lest "such bad roads kill our horses." Habersham dared
not demand their help, for fear his men would desert; he could
not leave without the malcontents, lest they plunder the people.
When finally the rain-shy militia agreed to march, they nearly
mutinied at hearing Habersham's orders to treat Indians with
kindness. They met a peaceful Chickasaw, and since the Major's
orders applied only to Creeks and Choctaws, they bayoneted
him to satisfy their loathing of all Indians.

As Wayne suggested, Habersham pretended to be British.
On approaching Choctaw country, he sent forward a Creek captive, one of Wayne's twenty-six well-treated "kings," to say
that Habersham was really Lieutenant-Colonel Thomas Brown,
a loyalist friend of Indians. In local annals, highly colored in
accordance with the intolerant spirit of the times, Brown is set
down as a most unmitigated scoundrel. "Brown was notorious
for murder, arson, theft, brutality and crimes too foul for utter-
ance. Bravery was his only redeeming trait. . . . To his ears,
the dying groans of a republican were more enjoyable than
strains of purest melody." To pass himself off as Brown must
have tried Habersham's soul sorely, but the Choctaws believed
the lie. One by one they dribbled into camp, until an Indian
who knew Brown well discovered the deception. He warned his
friends, and without a word to Habersham, they squirmed
through the sentry lines at night and disappeared.

Habersham, knowing that the game was up, ordered a pursuit, but his militia mutinied once more. Indians had no valuables; fighting was not worth the waste of shot and powder. But
since it would be a disgrace to go home empty-handed, the
militiamen suggested that they raid near-by white settlements.
Habersham pleaded with them not to rob their friends, but the
militiamen rode away in a body, sneering at Habersham. Only
a few dragoons remained, but when the Major turned to them
to stop the mutineers, they too departed, leaving him with only
six officers and two militiamen. The mutineers halted their flight
only long enough to capture three Indians, tie them to trees,
and hack them to pieces with swords.

The Indians, fully warned that Habersham was an American
and not their friend Colonel Brown, kept safely out of danger.

Although Habersham professed himself as eager, even with his tiny force, to attack the Choctaws and the rich pack-horse train, he was compelled to return to Ebenezer unsuccessful. There he learned that his rebellious militiamen had carried out their threat to raid the settlements by plundering the village of St. Andrew's and killing eleven white residents. Wayne listened to Habersham's report with rising anger. In the anarchic condition of the Georgia government, he could do nothing to punish the deserters or to guarantee that future state soldiers would be any more reliable; he could deal with them by military law only if he were willing to risk civil war. Even at Ebenezer, where Wayne had everything under his watchful eye, militiamen broke orders. Colonel James Jackson's Georgia State Infantry, set to guard the Creeks still held in their comfortable room, grew tired of watching Indians drink rum and eat. They turned their backs, Wayne charged, "through neglect or a worse motive," and every Creek escaped.

With his army rapidly evaporating, Anthony, in desperation, sought a larger, and more reliable, force. He wrote proclamations offering 200 acres, a cow, and two hogs to any British or Hessian soldier who would come over to the American side, but though through spies he papered Savannah with his offers, less than a hundred changed sides. He appealed to Greene for reinforcements, suggesting that Dick Butler bring a troop of Pennsylvania Light Infantry to Georgia, but Greene could not spare the men. Wayne received five thousand bushels of rice and corn from Carolina and "a little money for secret service," but not a single soldier.

2

"It is now upward of five weeks since we entered this State, during which period not an Officer or Soldier with me have once undressed for the purpose of changing his Linnen." Wayne hated Georgia, with its unruly militia, its poverty, its anarchy, and its swamps. Especially its swamps; everywhere Wayne turned he saw swamps; the state he thought one vast morass.

When there was high land, the ground was poor red clay covered with tough, coarse grass, with slash pine, or with larger trees that dripped untidily with gray Spanish moss.

Salt cost $2 a bushel in the Georgia desert, and such inhabitants as cured meat at all did so with wood ashes and red pepper; they drank a filthy concoction made of sassafras, molasses, and pine tops and called it beer; having no money of any value, the state paid its officers in rum and confiscated slaves. Councilmen, who wielded all the power in the state, received two gallons of rum, ten pounds of sugar, and a couple of quarts of salt as pay; the governor was told to take ten slaves as his reward for service. Such was the country Wayne had come to save, but instead of waging gentlemanly war, he faced guerrillas, Indians, and freed Negroes who did not know the principles laid down by Marshal Saxe. Had it not been that his alternatives would have been to go back to Greene and the obnoxious St. Clair or to resign, Anthony would have turned his back upon the place. He poured out his woes in identical letters sent to Greene, Frank Johnston, and Irvine, who would spread the news among influential Philadelphia circles, and to Stewart, for distribution to the Pennsylvania regiments:

"I have completed the tour of the Thirteen United States and made war in each of them and now command in the Sands and Swamps of Georgia. The duty we have done in Georgia was more difficult than that imposed upon the children of Israel. They had only to make brick without Straw, but we have had our army to form without men, provisions, forage and almost every apparatus of war to provide without money; boats, bridges, etc, to build without materials except those taken from the *Stumps* and what is itself more difficult than all, to make Whigs out of Tories in opposition to every let and hindrance thrown in our way by an unprincipled lawless banditti, all of which we have effected and have wrested the country out of the hands of the enemy, except the town of Savannah."

The document was propaganda, but in the main it was true. Anthony had not really warred in all the states, although he had set foot in all but Rhode Island and Connecticut—he had touched Massachusetts only on his Nova Scotia voyages—and

he certainly had not wrested all of Georgia from the British.
Sir Alured Clarke's vastly superior forces stayed in Savannah
of their own free will and not by dint of any power Wayne
might wield. In the existing state of the war, with the King
making speeches that implied a willingness to talk peace, Sir
Alured saw no reason for battling Wayne for control of sands,
swamps, and perfect deserts. Wayne's real fear was that Clarke's
Indian allies might suddenly descend upon the few Continental
dragoons and the 120 militiamen who remained at Ebenezer.
To stop this possibility, he bought Cornell with Greene's secret-
service funds and sent him with a message to the Creeks.

"I am no Englishman," Wayne told the Creeks, "but a plain,
open warrior born upon the same great island as yourselves.
All I ask is that you remain quiet spectators until this war is
terminated between us and our common enemy. After we make
peace, our wise men and great warriors will be happy to assist
in opening the paths that lead to our council fires. We will
brighten then the chains of friendship. But if," he warned, "you
are deaf to the voice of reason and wish to shed the blood of
people who have never injured you, if you prefer the hatchet to
the olive branch, we possess undaunted hearts, strong arms and
keen cutting swords."

Creeks knew of hatchets but they had never heard of olive
branches; they distrusted the promises of white men. They sent
Wayne no answer, but they prepared for war. So too did Colonel Brown, who with his regiment of "yallow boys" joined with
the "high jawbone gentlemen" of the Creeks to harass both
Wayne and Georgia settlers. They captured a dragoon and
scalped him, then they took the bloody trophy to Savannah and
paraded the streets with it, boasting that it was from the head
of Colonel Habersham. "We have," Wayne angrily burst out,
"taken a Chickasaw chief and we hold him as a victim. He and
a few British officers will eventually be sacrificed to the *manes*
of that brave unfortunate dragoon."

Before he could, as he put it, "bully the enemy at the lines of
Savannah with Jackson's little Legion and some *Crackers*," he
suffered a severe blow on the Altamaha. White Fish, a Creek
chief, distrusting the offer of an olive branch and hating the

British for not sending presents, made war indiscriminately. He killed a small Tory detachment, and then, learning that other troops were in the Altamaha neighborhood, he searched for further victims. He found a small American detachment, all wearing red coats to pass as Englishmen, and in a sharp fight White Fish killed most of them. Wayne vowed vengeance, but failed to punish White Fish. To keep his record clear, however, with the Georgians, he told the governor that the deaths had been avenged, although he had no ground whatever for saying so truthfully.

For all his fine speeches, Anthony's Indian tactics brought few tangible advantages, but he could not confess failure. Governor Martin would not be long in learning that White Fish remained alive and that the vengeance had been incomplete, but to create a temporary good impression Wayne anticipated his hopes. Overstatement was always a formidable weapon in his propaganda vocabulary. Weeks after the event, while the *"manes"* remained unsatisfied, Wayne reported that his leniency toward Indians had worked well: "I gave a spirited talk to the twenty-six kings and principal chiefs. So great is their gratitude for their liberation that it is not only likely to circumvent the enemy but to place me in a fair way of being adopted by one of the kings, and, was I at all inclined, might form an alliance with the charming princess of the lower Creek nation."

All of which was pure imagination, for inwardly Wayne was convinced that the war against Britons and Indians would drag on, as he told Dick Peters, for at least five years. Moreover, he was in the unhappy predicament of shouldering responsibility without any authority except that which the distant Greene chose to allow. He brooded over the prospect of a dismal future. Sunk in the swamps of Ebenezer, he proposed to Greene that the besieging army move closer to Savannah, but Greene objected. Wayne then suggested that his small force, enlarged by Colonel Thomas Posey, formerly of the Light Infantry, and some regiments of the Virginia Line, assail Savannah "to dig the caitiffs out," but he was again overruled. He saw himself condemned to rot away in Georgia living on "poor beef, swamp seed and aligator water."

Under such circumstances he lost his temper easily. He resented other officers who claimed authority, suspecting that they sought prestige at his expense. On one occasion, he learned that Colonel Jackson had jailed a soldier for impertinence to an officer. Wayne ordered the man set free; when the jailer volunteered that Jackson would not like the action, Wayne snapped back: "Jackson's a damned liar. Let him do his worst. God damn him, I don't care a damn for him."

He raged about the camp, looking for things to criticize. He thought himself insulted when he found that his washerwoman took laundry from other officers and he threatened to have her beaten if she dared wash for any other person than himself; he complained because his colonels grumbled in the presence of their orderlies and so stirred private soldiers to mutiny, though he himself talked loud and freely about the shortcomings of his officers. He drank too much and he entertained sour suspicions that murder plots were in the air. Much of this is traceable to idleness; Wayne invariably deteriorated when he stood inactive. In times of stress, Anthony was at his best; his mind moved swiftly and with smoothness; when he was in peril of death he was completely happy, but when there was nothing to do but to wait the pleasure of an adversary, he turned waspish.

Had he been with Greene near Charleston, he might have had cause for his worries, for the crack Pennsylvania Line, already mutinous on two occasions, rose in new revolt. "I thought," said Wayne, "I had effectually cured that distemper by a liberal dose of nitre, etc. administered at York in Pennsylvania." Sergeant George Goznall, a ringleader of the January mutiny, stirred his fellows to protest again about tattered clothing and lack of pay. Their dissatisfaction started, mildly enough, when Pennsylvanians tacked up in camp a rudely lettered placard reading "Can soldiers do their duty if clad in rags and fed on rice?"

Greene lost his head and leaped to the conclusion that British gold had won over his soldiers. He asked Josiah Harmar, who came from Pennsylvania, to look about for evidence, and Harmar heard a camp woman declare that she had heard some soldiers say that British cavalry would come to camp that night to capture all the officers. The evidence was purely hearsay and thoroughly anonymous, but it sufficed for Greene. He arrested Goznall, chiefly because the Sergeant had a known record of past insubordination. He also jailed five other sergeants, together with Peters, his orderly, and gave them a swift court-martial. All but one of the men were acquitted, although they were "sent away into the back country"; Goznall was shot. Even with this disposal of the assumed ringleaders, Greene continued to worry. He feared that British spies would foment another mutiny. "I am in hopes," he wrote to Wayne, "that pay and clothing are coming forward, but there is something at the bottom of this Spirit of discontent besides sufferings and want to be purged out."

That something, Wayne suspected, was short rations. For his own part, he avoided difficulty by feeding his men more rice and beef than the rules required. Greene tried to get along by issuing a pound and a quarter of meat and an equal weight of rice a day, but Wayne, after he set up a regular supply service, allowed an extra half-pound of beef and twice as much rice as Greene distributed. His officers drew as much food as they desired, apparently without regard for rationing. Anthony justified the additional cost by pointing to the fact that his men had built twelve bridges, a large number of boats, and three redoubts, had boiled their own salt, shod horses, and repaired wagons with no expense to the Government, and that the extra food was trifling in comparison to all the other things his men had done.

A British raid wrenched him out of his depression. Clarke, anxious to make contact with his Creek and Choctaw allies, again sent out the hated Colonel Brown, with about 450 men. By some slip-up in the American picket service, the expedition escaped notice until, on May 24, Wayne heard that Brown was eight miles from Savannah. Wayne ordered out his dragoons, now under Colonel Anthony Walton White, and put Posey's Virginians under arms. Between Brown and the Americans lay "a tremendous swamp of near four miles extent with many deep and dangerous morasses," over which one narrow causeway ran. Wayne weighed the dangers of a night march in such terrain, especially when it involved putting his men between two sections of the British Army, but, convinced "that the success of a nocturnal attack depended more upon prowess than numbers," he moved across the causeway in the dark.

At midnight, near the end of the causeway he saw enemy dragoons. Knowing neither their numbers nor their strategic position, he nevertheless was about to signal a charge when, to his astonishment, the British leader rode forward. Once more the enemy mistook Wayne's men for their own. It was a costly error, for Wayne took 18 dragoons prisoner. Brown was himself upon the causeway at the time with the remainder of his men. Wayne charged upon him; the British, taken by surprise, recoiled in confusion. Some fell off the causeway into the swamp, others, running to the end of the hard road, plunged into thick woods. White and Posey hurried after, with sword and bayonet, but in the dark could not chase a scattered enemy. The British lost 5 men dead and many wounded; in addition, Wayne took thirty dragoon horses. The American loss of men was as heavy as that of the British, but only two horses were shot and three others hurt. Wayne went down to within sight of Savannah looking for fugitives, but when none were found and when Clarke declined to sortie, he went back to Ebenezer.

Garbled reports of the fight with Brown reached Philadelphia, causing Anthony's friends to worry. When correct versions came, telling of Wayne's victory, a friend whose enthusiasm was surely greater than his poetic ability wrote verses mocking the pro-British clique:

> The old Tory rout
> Had spread round about
> That our brave Wayne, with 500,
> Were taken, or slain,
> Upon Georgia's plain;
> But, Tories, you've cursedly blundered.
> The case was, one Brown
> Had marched out of town,

> Well armed, and prepar'd for a tramp;
> But Wayne was aware,
> Prepared for the snare,
> And drove that Brown into a swamp.

Eleazer Oswald, an artillery officer at Monmouth, was then the editor of the *Independent Gazeteer, or The Chronicle of Freedom,* and he was asked to print the doggerel. With a fine appreciation of his patriotic duty, if not of literary merit, Oswald published it. As an editorial note, he added the request that the editor print the verses, together with his own comment: "Had you any reason to suppose the printer would dare to do otherwise?"

By Greene's explicit orders, Anthony could not move his camp closer to Savannah, yet as June wore on and huge clouds of mosquitoes rose hungrily from the surrounding swamps, he looked for more healthful ground. He did not know that insects bore disease, but they were unbearable pests, and Anthony was well aware that, from some miasmic vapor, his men came down with fever. Dense forests near Savannah shielded that town from the "noxious exhalations" of rice swamps, even where ground was wet and low; by moving toward the city, he could keep his men alive.

To do him justice, Wayne did not break Greene's orders abruptly; loyally, he complied with Greene's command to stay at Ebenezer just as long as he could do so safely. He smoked huts with burning pitch and with small wood fires, even when June heat grew intolerable; he hauled loads of pine boughs to make feverproof beds; he used up all the Peruvian bark he had in store—but sickness did not cease. Finally, when smudge fires failed to counteract the noxious vapors, and when his medicine gave out, he moved to higher ground at Sharon, within five miles of Savannah. He felt justified in doing so because Sir Alured Clarke was on the point of leaving. Wayne turned down an armistice, having no authority to make terms with the enemy, but he did so with reluctance, for the state militia, though promised land, cows, swine, and slaves as bounty for enlisting, refused to come on duty. After a month of coaxing, only seven men had volunteered. If Sir Alured learned how low Wayne's force had dwindled, he might never go away; if, on the other hand, the Americans closed in on Savannah, it might hasten Clarke's departure.

Perhaps Anthony became too confident; no doubt his men, worn down by fever, relaxed their vigilance. Certainly, after the defeat of Brown a month before no danger was expected, and with Sir Alured on the point of evacuation, there was no likelihood of an attack upon the van. Wayne carelessly set too few guards in front, and put only a single sentinel to watch the rear. He failed to consider the cleverness of the Creeks. That Indian nation was small, possessing no more than 5,000 warriors, but it had as chief a great Scotch-Indian leader, Alexander McGillivray, who later came to be known as "the Talleyrand of Alabama." From his capital at Little Tallassie, near modern Birmingham, the sickly McGillivray ruled an empire of western Georgia and Alabama. He liked Spaniards and he tolerated Englishmen, but Americans, particularly Georgians who butchered Indians, were anathema to him. Neither Wayne's bribes nor Cornell's purchased oratory convinced him that he ought to make friends with the new American republic.

McGillivray sent out Guristersijo, his general, with 300 warriors, to catch Wayne by surprise. He ordered the war chief to move by night, slipping through woods and crossing swamps in order to avoid detection; if by chance any white men were encountered, Guristersijo was commanded to kill them so that they might not spread alarm. Wayne had heard of Guristersijo, but by another name. Ten years before, when he served as Assemblyman, he warned Pennsylvania legislators against an Anglo-Indian alliance; he suggested that Americans ally themselves with a young chief named Emisti-Siguo who led the Creeks against the Choctaws. Indians changed their names when passing through some important personal crisis; the Emisti-Siguo of 1772 was now called Guristersijo.

Now the Creeks drew close to Wayne; on the night of June 23, they crossed a swamp near Sharon. Spies, squirming silently through tall grass and timber, came back with news that Wayne had but one picket. Yelling madly, the Creeks slashed down the sentinel and rushed headlong into camp at three o'clock in the morning. The distance between the sentry and the first large detachment, Posey's Virginians, was wider than Guristersijo had foreseen, and these Light Infantrymen had time to wake and grab their guns before the Creeks burst upon them. The Virginians fired blindly into the shadows and ran, leaving behind them two field pieces parked near Posey's tent. The shouts and firing roused the camp. Wayne woke, snatched his sword and pistol, and hurried from his tent. Posey's men reloaded hurriedly and fired again. Captain Isaac Gunn, half-dressed but wide-awake, shouted for his dragoons. Soldiers tumbled out of quarters. Over the shrill shriek of war whoops and the sharp bark of rifles, Wayne bawled an order: "Charge them! Drive them back!"

His men responded. Posey's men, abandoning firing for the bayonet, drove boldly into the dark; Gunn's dragoons plunged forward, slashing with their swords. Wayne, mounting the first horse he saw, rounded up more troops and hurried them against the Creeks. The Indians had no time to reload; they drew their tomahawks and slashed at the soldiers, but bayonets were longer and the Creeks could not come within striking distance of the white men. Gunn threw them into disorder; Posey pushed them into the Pipe-makers' Swamp that stretched along the left flank of the camp.

Guristersijo went down beneath Wayne's horse, but even as he fell, he pulled his trigger and shot the stallion dead. Wayne half fell, but recovered sufficiently to catch the Indian with a sword thrust. Other Indians, scattered in the swamp, fled for safety, some escaping to Savannah, though 18 Creeks lay dead upon the field. A dozen Creeks and a hundred and seven horses were taken prisoner. Wayne lost 13 killed and wounded. By his coolness a nearly fatal attack had been turned into a triumph.

The surprise had failed, but Wayne dared not sleep again that night; he feared that Sir Alured, less than five miles away, would sortie to assist the Indians. Posey, anxious to wipe out the stigma of having been caught unawares, demanded the privilege of going up to the British lines so that if Clarke advanced, the Virginians would be the first to fight. Just at dawn, a sudden stir within the British camp brought a cry of warning from the sentry. The Virginians cocked their guns; Wayne's men prepared again for action. Fearful that the dozen Creek captives would try to help Clarke, the Americans bayoneted every prisoner. It proved a false alarm; the British did not come. British resistance, indeed, ceased completely. Clarke had letters from Sir Guy Carleton, Clinton's successor as Commander-in-Chief, ordering evacuation of Savannah. When transports came to take the troops away, the British were ready to leave. Tory merchants in the town asked Wayne on what terms they might stay, and Wayne assured them that a reasonable time would be allowed to dispose of their property and settle their pecuniary concerns. By "reasonable time," it turned out later, Wayne meant until the end of the year.

On evacuation day, July 12, James Jackson, with his Georgia militia, led the American advance, Wayne following slowly after. As he rode down the wide central street, with its small frame houses on either side, Anthony remarked the town's close resemblance to Philadelphia. Each city was laid out in rectangular blocks without diagonal avenues, and each was tree-shaded and pleasant in appearance. Savannah, like Philadelphia, had small open "squares," for beauty and fresh air, though one or two were being used as market places; like Philadelphia, the town fronted on a bluff above a river.

Marks of the war were everywhere apparent. Churches and public buildings evidently had been used as hospitals; reckless soldiers had looted private houses. Imposing Christ Church was unharmed, as was the huge filiature where before the war Savannah capitalists had set up a silk mill; the courthouse and the council house were still undamaged. Here and there cannon shot, fired at the time when the British took the city, had caused damage that remained unrepaired. Worse still, smallpox raged, and slaves abandoned by the British refused to work again. These were civilian problems which Wayne purposed to leave for Governor Martin and the state government. He and all his men except invalids and horsemen were under orders to hurry to join Greene at Charleston.

Those orders could not be carried out at once. Sir Alured's evacuation fleet dropped anchor twelve miles from the city, and

Wayne feared that if the Americans withdrew, Clarke would immediately return. Brown, too, who supposedly had headed for St. Augustine, threatened to come back, so Wayne lingered in Savannah. His men, as always during idleness, got out of hand; officers lost their discipline. Wayne even sent McCoy, hero of the capture of the twenty-six Creek kings, to prison for disorder. Anthony spent his time searching shops for clothing and food, replenishing his larder with nine thousand pounds of fresh beef, and finding hats and shoes for 500 men. He drew up a proclamation for the people of eastern Florida, promising them immunity if they joined the Thirteen States, but threatening "calamity and ruin" if they refused. Anthony prided himself on the wording of that document, but when he sent Greene a copy, his superior curtly answered that the paper was "highcolored."

At last, twelve days after the evacuation, Clarke weighed anchor and departed, but two hours before Wayne's men were to set off for Charleston, Brown came back "with his motley crew of Regulars, Indians and tories" to within nine miles of Savannah. Wayne went to meet him, whereupon Brown took ship to an island twenty miles away. When Wayne again gave orders to leave Georgia, the Georgia Assembly, in session after a long suspension, petitioned him to stay. Wayne waited another week and then at last, on August 6, the troops marched away. Anthony, on a short furlough, lingered for a few days in the captured city.

3

"Resolved that a high sense of the great merits and Services rendered by the Honorable Brigadier-General Anthony Wayne is entertained by this House and that the same be acknowledged. . . . Resolved that the sum of 4000 Guineas be granted . . . for the purchasing an estate for Brigadier-General Anthony Wayne." Georgia appreciated what Wayne had done; its Assembly thus showed its gratitude. On July 31, 1782, nineteen days after he took Savannah, the state presented him with a plantation of 847 acres—Richmond, twelve miles northwest of Savannah, overlooking the river. To this were added, at a later time, additional lands called Kew, and large cowpens and a plantation in southern Georgia.

While on furlough, Wayne rode out frequently to view Richmond and Kew. He found them run-down areas, for the former Tory owners had fled six years before, and since then nothing had been done to keep the estates in good repair. All the Negroes working there had been stolen by raiders during Georgia's anarchy, or had run away. Broken floodgates and ruined irrigation ditches turned once-rich rice paddies into swamps; brush and bramble covered the upland; long marsh grass grew where formerly the owners raised a thousand barrels of rice yearly. Much needed to be done, but the land was fertile, and when the place was cleared for cultivation, the estates would yield a handsome income.

Privately, Wayne grumbled that the Assembly, by paying only £3,900 for Richmond, deprived him of many extra shillings which he could use in buying slaves and seed. His fiery temper blazed when he learned that his superior, Nathanael Greene, who had done nothing of consequence in Georgia, would get historic Mulberry Grove, worth £7,000. He kept his anger to himself when he thought how pleasant it would be to have Nathanael, and especially lovely Cathy Greene, within easy riding distance. Richmond charmed him; he looked forward eagerly to quitting Waynesborough to become a Georgia rice planter. "I am satiate," he assured his intimates, "of this horrid trade of blood."

Now that active field campaigning ceased, his thoughts inevitably turned to feminine society. There was in Georgia, as there usually was in Wayne's rest periods, a pretty girl whom he was courting. Polly as usual knew nothing of her; he carefully refrained from telling anyone who might take news to Pennsylvania—or to Wilmington. Mary Maxwell, daughter of one of Georgia's best families, filled his thoughts. The girl hero-worshiped him; in fact, she first came to his notice by sending him a new black-and-white cockade to brighten up his uniform. It was the case of the Schuyler girls all over again, but this time

Anthony was less discreet. He wrote her a pleasant note of thanks, and Mary answered with a charming message of no particular importance, but the correspondence quickened. Colonel Eustace, now Wayne's devoted friend, rode back and forth between army headquarters and Mary's home at Strathy Hall, carrying little letters whose tone grew warmer. Anthony had never seen the girl, but from Eustace, from McCoy, now released from jail, and from Georgians who knew the Maxwells, he was certain that Mary Maxwell would prove as charming as her letters. He wrote her asking her to call on him:

"As fine Ladies often wish a variety of little articles, not as a real addition to their charms (for I am clearly of opinion with Lady Wortley *Montague* on that head) but from Custom, which probably had its origins by the robbing *Flora* to adorn *Venus*, permit me to point out an easy way to obtain them.

"Col. McCoy Informs me that it is but a few hours' ride from *Strathy Hall* to this place—step into your carriage after breakfast and dine in Savannah. I will candidly acknowledge that I feel myself Interested in this advice, because it will put it *early* in my power to convince you of the Affectionate Esteem of your most Obt. and very Hum[l] Serv[t]."

Mary came and conquered. Wayne forgot Molly Vining, at least for the moment, and he gave no thought whatever to his wife or to any of the other girls. He spent so much time with Mary Maxwell and flirted with such skill that exaggerated rumors spread back to Philadelphia. Mary Maxwell's interest was not wholly due to Anthony's personal charm. She asked Anthony, in return for her attention, to rescue her nineteen-year-old Tory brother from the list of those proscribed by Georgia's confiscation laws. Anthony, too much enamored of social joys to pay attention to other interests, even those which Mary strongly urged upon him, delayed in taking up the matter with Governor Martin and the Assembly.

Certainly he paid slight heed to Rush's warnings as to night air and wine. His personal commissary had found much Madeira, and in addition Savannah yielded ample stocks of stronger liquor. With a new-found friend, Roger Parker Saunders, Wayne caroused nightly when he was not spending time with

Mary Maxwell. His brother officers knew that Wayne was always ready for gay evenings; his Savannah stay, especially after his troops had left to rejoin Greene, was filled with dissipation. Anthony's intense devotion to Mary Maxwell and to Roger Saunders brewed jealousies among his friends of longer standing. Again, as in the case of Michael Ryan, a displaced favorite complained that Anthony had turned cold. Colonel Eustace taxed him with inconstancy:

"Having observed a change in your Deportment *of very recent* origin, I have employed my consideration in constant exercise to trace the source and without effect. . . . If the inducement to your conduct have source *in any other person,* I beg the knowledge of them as I am not without suspicion this may have been achieved by some rascally Hypocricy. Being unus'd to Duplicity and having very little fondness for Whispering or ferret communications, I may probably have been depreciated in your good opinion of friendship by some practiser of this art."

Even his servants protested. His valet Philip took unpardonable liberties by criticizing Anthony; Philip's wife went about the town complaining that Wayne did not appreciate what people did for him. "Philip and I have done a great deal for the general over a long period of time, but he has never once requited us. He never pays us. He has never given me even a shift, and Philip has only had one shirt, but he dresses his damned negroes well. If ever we get back to Pennsylvania, I'll take care that Philip leaves his service."

Captain Fishbourn, the ever loyal, grumbled too at being shoved aside. At Stony Point, Fishbourn had resented Wayne's choice of Archer, then a newcomer, as courier to take the news to Congress, but he had excused Wayne at the time. As weeks and months passed without Anthony's making any effort to push Fishbourn for promotion, the Captain wondered if Wayne was deliberately ignoring his friends. Now that the Maxwell girl and Saunders monopolized his chief, Fishbourn lost his patience. He had not the courage to storm into Wayne's presence for a showdown, but he sent a note that amounted to an ultimatum. Wayne, he said, must recommend him to Congress for appointment as a major. To these complaints Wayne paid slight attention. He did, indeed, assure Eustace that neither Mary nor Saunders had spoken ill of him, and he treated that colonel with more courtesy, but neither Philip nor the valet's wife received a cent of pay, much less shifts and shirts, and Wayne failed to push Fishbourn's claim. Thus he showed again that self-centeredness which his enemies declared was an integral trait of his character.

He did find time during his courtship of Mary Maxwell to write two letters to Polly, though neither contained a word of intimacy or endearment. Each was limited to a cold recital of army movements and to orders concerning the rearing of the children:

"I experience much anxiety about the education of my little Girl and boy. I can never admit of any excuse for the neglect of a matter so essential to their interest and consequence in life. . . . Tell my son that when he is master of his Latin Grammar I will make him a present equal to his Sister's when she is mistress of her *French*. . . . In one year more he will be old enough for college.

"I am told my Daughter promises fair to make an excellent woman. Does she improve in her french, musick, dancing, drawing etc? She must be indulged in every little necessary as well as with pocket money for the purpose of procuring many little articles which may not come under what are generally deemed necessaries, but yet essential to her comfort and something to please her little *vanity*.

"Nature has been bountiful in giving them agreeable and pleasing features. I shall be much displeased if they do not move in the first circles."

Throughout his whole life, Anthony invariably showed more thoughtfulness for the pleasure of Margaretta—Peggy—than for his son Isaac. Modern educators would frown upon his spoiling the child by his insistence that she enjoy all the luxuries she wished for, but they would equally object to the bleak and stilted style in which he wrote to her. His letters, headed "My dear Miss Wayne," admonish her, in words as formally objective as if he were her headmaster, to "study your lessons and to

keep your head up." He signed them, as it has been noted he
did all letters, "Ant^y. Wayne."

Finally, he could prolong his stay at Savannah no longer.
Without slaves to work Richmond, nothing could be done to
put the plantation into production, but Wayne's speculations
had not prospered, and his cash ran short. He was needed, too,
in South Carolina to help Greene force the British out of
Charleston. He made one attempt, a full month after Mary
Maxwell's request, to free her brother, but when Governor
Martin refused to strike the boy's name from the list of those
proscribed, Anthony did not push the matter. He told Mary
that he had exhausted every possible effort; then, mounting his
horse, he rode toward Greene. The journey was not pleasant.
August was unusually hot, and the land, after several years of
constant foraging by two armies, was stripped of resources.
Wayne rode for miles through dreary country that showed few
signs of life except for turkey buzzards circling overhead.

Greene was camped at Ashley Hill, above Charleston, where
his men had an abundance of fresh water; but food was short
and supplies were unobtainable. The troops were tattered,
"many with but the remains of some garment pinned about their
waists with the thorn of a locust tree." More than a thousand
were so naked that they could not come on duty; almost all the
rest bore scars where heavy muskets and cartridge cases bruised
their unprotected shoulders and hips. Fever and dysentery were
prevalent; the camp was so ill-kept that Wayne smelt its stench
when he was far away. On active service, ills might be borne
which idle men could never tolerate. The troops, muttering
over the shooting of Goznall, dared not mutiny, even though
their food, they said, was perfect carrion, but in knots of twos
and threes they grumbled constantly.

Greene's authority was being flouted on all sides. Pennsylvania officers violently protested when he assigned a South Carolina officer to the Pennsylvania Line. Michael Rudolph, one of
Wayne's officers in the New Jersey campaign, led a cabal against
the appointment of Henry Laurens; when his cabal failed,
Rudolph and his brother officers handed in their resignations.
"The truth of the affair is," Greene told Wayne, "that they

intend to cram the thing down my throat, flattering themselves
that their number and consequence will deter me." Wayne replied that Rudolph probably planned to build up a praetorian
guard, "difficult to govern and impatient of insubordination."
He advised Greene to accept the resignations, but when the
latter did so, the officers canceled their requests and went to
Congress with protests against Greene. Congress upheld Greene's
right to appoint commanding officers.

Other evils filled the camp. Cavalrymen, feeling themselves
above common soldiers, impressed for their personal use the
best horses found in the neighborhood. For these they demanded government forage, but they regarded the animals as
their private property. Captain Isaac Gunn traded off "a public
horse" for two other horses and a slave, and swore at Greene
when the General refused to approve the deal. Indignantly,
Gunn demanded a court of inquiry, which, to Greene's astonishment, justified the whole transaction. Greene then threw aside
the court's decision, which so angered Gunn that for years thereafter he hated the General.

Wayne and Greene drifted apart in these broils. With nine
riding horses and six wagon animals in his personal train, Anthony asked the commissary of forage to provide them with
feed. The commissary passed on the requisition to Greene, who
flatly refused to honor the request. Wayne thought that Greene
delighted in turning down every plan which he suggested.
When Anthony asked to lead a Light Infantry detachment to
head off British foragers, Greene vetoed the suggestion, on the
flimsy ground that Gist, a brigadier of lower status, would feel
insulted. Wayne then proposed that he take his Georgia soldiers
and reconnoiter, but Greene again declined.

Greene felt that Wayne used little judgment in issuing passes
allowing private citizens to trade with British-held Charleston.
During the time the army fed on carrion, large quantities of
fresh provisions passed down the river to the city. Some of it,
certainly, went under Wayne's orders, for Saunders sent at least
one boatload to Charleston with Wayne's permission, and Anthony himself bought wine, porter, and cheese there, though he

denied that he paid for them with army goods. Greene warned Wayne that no more passes must be given and that every food boat going down the river would be confiscated. How far the growing split between Wayne and Greene might have widened is difficult to estimate, because too many factors were involved. Personal as well as professional jealousy entered into the situation. Had matters remained normal, it is probable that Greene would have dispatched Wayne with a force of men into the far interior to fight the Indians, as a means of getting rid of a bothersome subordinate.

4

On September 2, however, Wayne came down with a raging fever. He had already suffered from a touch of sun in Savannah, but he had passed it off as unimportant, nor had he kept the rules of health that Rush laid down. Now, in consequence, he was forced to stay in bed for a whole month. Daily he took strong emetics, followed by an ounce of Peruvian bark, but his health was slow in mending. Neither he nor his doctors diagnosed his ailment accurately, for he had a complication of troubles. His breast, never thoroughly healed since his fall at Germantown, still pained him; Wayne suspected that he had tuberculosis. He was bilious, his thigh wound ached, gout gripped his joints, and intestinal disturbance made him worry over his digestion. "I have this consolation," he declared, "that neither idleness nor dissipation has injuriously affected my constitution, but that it has broken down and nearly exhausted by encountering almost every excess of fatigue, difficulty and danger in defence of the rights and liberties of America from her coldest to her hottest sun." Doctors reassured him about tuberculosis; they told him that breast pains were usual effects of continued high fever. They prescribed "surup of whore-hond" as a never-failing remedy for the worst coughs, and suggested a long sea voyage to recruit his strength. This, of course, was impossible while the British held Charleston; meanwhile they recommended strict diet and moderate exercise.

Charleston was on the point of surrender, so that Anthony had only a few weeks to wait before he would be free of active army duty. When at last negotiations for evacuation were complete, Greene, as a compliment to the man who had taken Savannah, and to ease the tension between them, invited Wayne, Gist being ill, to lead the Light Infantry into the city. At the firing of the morning gun on December 14, the enemy abandoned their advance positions before Charleston, slowly withdrawing toward the harbor, where transports waited. Wayne followed them, at two hundred yards' distance. His eager men moved so fast that the British called back over their shoulders: "Slow down. You're too quick for us."

Charleston loyalists crowded the wharves to board the transports. Eighteen hundred Tory men, nine hundred women, a thousand children, and five thousand slaves pressed in disorderly haste to get away to Jamaica, to eastern Florida, or to England. Their houses, boarded tight, presented "one mournful scene of the most complicated wretchedness." After the civilians trudged retreating troops, withdrawing so slowly that nearly four hours were required to cover the three miles from the outer trenches to the harbor.

Wayne halted his men while the enemy embarked. At eleven o'clock he signaled for advance, and at the head of the line he rode through the city gates. Houses emptied of their British occupants were gay with improvised decorations. From balconies, doors, and windows Whigs who for two years had been compelled to hold their tongues cried out joyfully: "God bless you! Welcome! Huzza for General Wayne!" At three o'clock in the afternoon, Greene escorted Governor John Mathews into his now restored capital. Through streets lined with cheering people, the army marched to the State House, where they huzzaed and fired salutes. "It was a grand and pleasing sight," said a South Carolinian, "to see the enemy's fleet, upward of three hundred sail, lying at anchor in a curved line waiting for the tide."

That night, at Cathy Greene's instigation, the American officers gave a ball. Tadeusz Andrzej Kosciuszko, Polish cavalryman and engineer, decorated the long assembly room with fes-

toons of magnolia leaves and paper flowers; the army bands
played minuets. Lame, asthmatic Nathanael Greene looked on
indulgently as Anthony Wayne danced with vivacious Cathy.
The exercise, Wayne said, was good for him; it would shake
the musket ball out of his thigh. In the morning, as soldiers
and civilians lined the water front, the British squadron weighed
anchor and disappeared beyond the horizon. Wayne, with fine
sensitivity, did not raise the American flag over Charleston until
the fleet was well beyond the harbor. His critics noted that
Wayne, who treated mutineers with harsh brutality and who
was selfish, thoughtless, and heartless toward discarded friends,
acted as a chivalric gentleman toward a conquered enemy.

British evacuation did not at once restore tranquillity and
peace. Indians still ravaged the frontiers, particularly in southern Georgia, where Wayne had his cowpens; bandit gangs,
masquerading as Tories, raided isolated settlements, spreading
terror among peaceful citizens. Law and order had yet to be
restored. Until efficient civil government could be installed, the
army acted as police. Wayne could not spare the time to take
a sea trip, nor even to rest on land. He kept active and thereby
retarded his recovery. His cough hung on. The old problems
of food and clothing worried him; especially as states which
had no British troops within their borders showed themselves
reluctant to feed troops who seemed to serve no useful purpose.
The Northern division, under Washington, had at last learned
not to depend upon the states to send supplies; it followed the
European custom of contracting with food merchants for regular deliveries at fixed prices. Greene, who as a former quartermaster-general should have known better, continued the old
practice of imposing quotas on the states, and with the usual
disastrous results.

Robert Morris, newly appointed Superintendent of Finance,
shared the responsibility for failure. As one means of increasing
confidence in the Government, he gave the impression that the
United States Treasury contained plenty of gold. Thus American securities held their value and paper money ceased to de-
preciate; but the army suffered. Virginia, now that Cornwallis
had been captured, claimed her share of the supposed national

wealth; North Carolina not only appropriated no money for Greene's men, but asked a refund; Georgia, destitute and exhausted, held out her hand for government relief. The burden of supporting the soldiers under Wayne and Greene fell upon South Carolina, whose treasury, after months of war, was empty. No further food or clothing could be supplied the troops.

In this emergency, Wayne advised following the example of the Northern Army. From his contacts with merchants, he assured Greene that a number of business houses would compete vigorously for military contracts; he believed that Whig speculators could make deals with Charleston firms for surplus British army goods. Greene advertised for bids, but to his surprise only one offer followed. John Banks, a Virginian, proposed to feed and clothe the men in return for a cash payment of 1,100 guineas and for drafts on Morris for balances as they fell due. As Wayne had guessed, Banks planned to draw on Charleston for his supplies. The terms were high, but Greene had no alternative other than to turn troops loose to forage for themselves. On February 18, 1783, he signed a contract with John Banks. It was to cause him much future anguish.

The contractor, untrained in calculating costs for supplying so many men, ran on financial rocks. His funds gave out; when he tried to borrow money, Carolina patriots, themselves unwilling to assume responsibility, refused to help. Banks went to Wayne and Greene, confessing failure. Wayne prided himself on his business acumen and advised Greene to help out the contractor. Greene went personally on Banks's bond for £30,000. "Thus," said Wayne, "was a Calamity avoided that appeared to us dreadful, and order, discipline and control restored."

Jealous Carolina merchants saw the deal in a somewhat different light; to them it seemed a secret sharing of contractor's profits. Banks, they alleged, corrupted army officers. Rivals revived rumors that when Greene was quartermaster-general, he had formed a private partnership with Colonel Jeremiah Wadsworth, chief army commissary, whereby both men had drawn commissions on government purchases which Greene made from his own firm at fat prices set by himself and Wadsworth. This

Banks deal, some Carolinians suspected, was a similar illegal speculation. Thomas Sumter, who hated Greene for taking away the horses of his militiamen, was thoroughly convinced that the whole affair was criminal. Banks himself sedulously encouraged such reports, believing that if Greene were supposed to be his secret partner, his own credit would be enhanced. Wayne, worried because Greene had followed his advice, laid traps to catch Banks, and succeeded in intercepting a letter in which the contractor boasted that Greene took part in the business. Wayne showed the note to Greene. "He's an infamous scoundrel!" Greene burst out. "Shall I put him to death? I'd like to do it."

Wayne calmed down the indignant General, assuring him that no one outside a small circle of jealous business rivals credited the rumors and that to punish Banks would merely advertise the false reports. He recommended that Greene pay no attention to gossip, but that he watch Banks closely. Army supply, he pointed out, was more essential than gratification of a private grudge. The advice, it later developed, was most unwise. When a few months later Banks died suddenly, leaving notes unpaid, Nathanael Greene, as surety, was called upon to pay more than £8,000.

Food supplies under the Banks contract proved far from perfect, but the army did not hunger. Men complained, as soldiers always do, that the food was monotonous and insufficient; they said that Banks's beef cattle were so thin that two soldiers had to hold an animal on its legs while the butcher knocked it down to slaughter it; they objected to rice as "good enough for the sick, but rather washy for duty men"; they craved a change from their daily beef and rice and corn.

Winter, however, was not uncomfortable. After a week of Charleston, Greene sent Wayne, with the bulk of the troops, to James Island, south of the city, where they made camp near a wide pine forest whose air, physicians promised, would be pure and healthful. Spring came early, and James Island, although flat and sandy, was "a little Paradise"; officers enjoyed their stay. Charleston was but half an hour's rowing time away, and Wayne went frequently into town to dine with Greene and

Cathy on fish, oysters, and fine stone crabs. Common soldiers liked James Island, too, for work was lightened. Wayne suggested that if treetops and brush were piled high about the camp, fewer sentries would be necessary and more men could be freed from duty. In peacetime guards placed at the few openings left in the abatis would suffice to keep good watch; the rest of the men, after their daily drills were over, could fish and hunt and amuse themselves. They would have enjoyed firing their muskets at soft cabbage-wood logs, just to see the shot disappear into the spongy wood and the logs close up behind the bullet, but ammunition could not be wasted.

News that peace had been signed arrived on April 16, but Wayne was not present to enjoy the great celebrations that ensued. A few weeks earlier, Greene had sent him back to Georgia to keep an eye on threatened British invasions from St. Augustine, and to sign, if possible, a treaty with the Creeks. The former danger did not materialize, and McGillivray refused to consider any agreement with Georgia that involved surrender of Creek hunting-grounds. Georgia would deal on no other terms, nor would the ungovernable Georgia militiamen restore a hundred horses stolen from Indian peace commissioners while negotiations were in progress. The angered Creeks walked home, determined never to trust a white man again.

With nothing important left to do, troops once more deteriorated. Soldiers, restless to get back to their farms to plant new crops, drifted off, even though desertion involved at least a loss of pay. But since the money would be depreciated paper, deserters did not mind their loss. Those who stayed protested that they had enlisted for the war and that now that war was finished, they were entitled to discharge. Their grievance was similar to that of the Pennsylvanians at the Morristown mutiny. So bold became discontent that Greene had to point loaded cannon at them to overawe the troops. A hundred Virginia cavalrymen took all the best horses of the dragoons and rode away in the night; they were not overtaken, and when home in Virginia, were pardoned by their state officials. In June all soldiers were at last freed from duty; they received a six months' furlough, which in December became an absolute discharge.

Wayne too was restless. His health was not yet fully recovered and he dreaded another summer in the South. Sharp Delany, as friend and as physician, pleaded with him to come home: "There is no air within two hundred miles of you, either by sea or land, equal to your native air, and believe me that, and nothing else, will effect a compleat cure." Delany suggested that Anthony go with him on a trout-fishing trip into the interior of Pennsylvania, coming home to Waynesborough by way of the Susquehanna and the Lancaster Road.

Political reasons, as well as health considerations, called Wayne home. With the abatement of war spirit, Pennsylvania's ultraradicals were losing control and the moderates were gaining power. Wayne hoped for election to some state office that would provide him with a steady income. A pleading letter from Benjamin Rush much encouraged him. "Pennsylvania loves you," Rush wrote. "You are one of her legitimate children; let nothing tempt you to abandon her. . . . There are honors in store for you here." John Dickinson, one of Wayne's former fox-hunting friends, and author of the *Farmer's Letters*, was governor and this too, Wayne thought, would work in his favor. Dickinson consulted Wayne on army matters; through him, Anthony had the Pennsylvanians sent home from Charleston by sea rather than by a wearisome land march.

Nor was there much to do in the South. War operations ended, the states went over to civilian control. Wayne wished, to be sure, that he could start rice-planting on his Richmond estate, but without Negroes nothing could be done, nor could he raise capital to buy them until he returned to Philadelphia. Late in July, 1783, Wayne, furloughed from service, sailed for home.

CHAPTER XIV

Tortured Debtor

PHILADELPHIA planned a gala welcome to the deliverer of Georgia, but when his ship docked on Wednesday afternoon, August 13, Wayne was much too sick to be lionized. Fishbourn, now a Georgia merchant and his companion on the journey, reported that the General had come down with bilious vomiting and a recurrence of summer fever shortly after leaving Charleston and that he had spent the entire voyage in his bunk. Sharp Delany, who took Wayne under care at once, confidently promised that the sick man would soon recover. "His native air," Delany told inquirers, "will at once restore him."

More effective for Anthony than even the air was society. Mary Vining came at once, and so did Catherine Greene, who had sailed a fortnight before Wayne; Margaretta, a grown girl with pretty manners and a piquant air, spent afternoons at the bedside of her "beloved papa," though Polly, herself ill at Waynesborough, could not come. Wayne's old associates dropped in: Stewart, now a general, Peters, Johnston, Dickinson, Hartley, Morris, and even Arthur St. Clair.

They told him news, some of the highest importance, such as their desire to have him run for the Council of Censors, that curious body which by Pennsylvania law met every seven years to consider, like a Supreme Court, the validity of acts of the Assembly. Town meetings were being held to protest against easing the wartime restrictions on the Tories. Radical Whigs, they said, clamored for strict rules to prevent loyalists who had left the state from ever coming back to Pennsylvania. They gave him eyewitness stories of the latest Pennsylvania mutiny in June, when troops returning from South Carolina marched

to Congress to demand their pay, and so terrified that body
that it ran to Princeton for safety. No violence had been committed, Wayne's callers said, but the city had been in terror for
a week. When Wayne asked the outcome of the mutiny, they
said that no definite promises had been made except that of
prompt settlement.

Their lighter news was very welcome. Philadelphia weather
had been hot, with heavy rains and much lightning; the town
talked of a deadly battle between a blacksnake and a rattlesnake
that lasted until both fell dead; notorious bandits north of
Philadelphia had been taken prisoner, and their friends were
sending anonymous warnings, signed "The Royal Refugees,"
threatening to kill politicians in the city, but no one took the
warnings seriously; everyone was reading Captain Cook's *Last
Voyages*. Washington had recently returned to Albany after a
visit to Crown Point and Ticonderoga and was expected shortly
in Philadelphia.

Wayne drank in all the news and asked for more. He
wanted to know if the Front Street merchants had laid in new
stocks of Souchong, Congo, and Hyson teas, and if they had
replenished their supplies of port and Madeira. He asked if
women still crowded on the Water Street sidewalks to see
Stephen Girard open bales of dry goods. He inquired about
the taverns and if their punch was as good as ever, if one host
continued to make his unrivaled buckwheat cakes and another
his green turtle soup. He kept up a steady stream of questions
until Delany drove away the callers lest they excite his patient
unduly, and when they had gone, Delany sat down to talk
about the fine new fishing tackle he had seen on Market Street
near the Court House. Whether due to Pennsylvania air, or to
good comradeship, or to excitement, Anthony recovered rapidly, although for seven weeks he dared not be as active as he
could have wished. He joked in heavy fashion about his ailments:

"A very troublesome fellow, commonly known by the name
of Death, took the Liberty to call frequently at my Quarters
to know if I was ready for *Payment*. My friends were of Opinion that the *bond* would not be due until some thirty-three or

forty years hence. . . . A certain Doctor Issued a Noli Prose-
qui and I have just obtained a Habeas Corpus for my Liberation from my Chamber. . . . I know of no Statute or Law
upon which I could bring an action of Damages, otherwise I
would not suffer that same Caitiff *death* to pass with Impunity."

He played now a double role. In Pennsylvania, he allowed
his friends to think that he had returned to stay indefinitely;
they elected him censor from Chester County; they promised
that when the censor's duty was finished, he would be sent to
the Assembly. At the same time he wrote to Jackson and
Habersham that he would soon return to Georgia to make his
home permanently at Richmond. "It won't be long," he assured Habersham, "before I shall be with you, having determined to settle my lands in your Country, if *Curly heads* can
be procured at any reasonable rate." Habersham investigated
for him and found that Negroes could be bought at £70 a head,
provided Wayne agreed to take an entire gang of seventy-two;
but he recommended that Wayne wait until the British evacu-
ated St. Augustine, when, Habersham believed, prices would
fall sharply.

Wayne was very glad to wait, partly to take advantage of
lower future prices, but more because, as censor, he must remain in Pennsylvania until spring. October, when he was again
strong enough to move about, was a happy month, for Congress voted him his long-delayed promotion to a major-
general's commission, albeit by brevet, which gave the rank
without an increase in pay. He gave a rush order for a new
uniform; at the same time he bought a crimson-velvet-collared
suit for Isaac and a livery with scarlet cuffs and collar for his
servant Caesar. His tailor's bill amounted to more than £40;
he did not trouble to pay it for thirteen years.

In the same month, the Pennsylvania Society of the Cincinnati chose him vice-president, with the ever obtrusive St. Clair
as his chief. Presumably this organization of officers, formed in
the preceding May at Northern Army headquarters on the
Hudson, was to maintain friendships, assist dependent widows
and orphans of members, and honor the French allies, but
democrats raised a violent hue and cry against it as a danger

to the state and the beginning of a hereditary patrician dynasty. Rhode Island disfranchised the members; Massachusetts declared it, chiefly because of the provisions that made membership descend in direct male line, "dangerous to the peace, liberty and safety of the Union." Wayne's old friend Aedanus Burke, irascible upcountry Carolina democrat, wrote a violent pamphlet denouncing the Cincinnati, which Wayne read with mounting anger. In Pennsylvania the anti-Cincinnati fever did not blaze high; Wayne thought that the agitation would die down soon in other commonwealths.

He was absorbed in incidental interests. A new dancing assembly was being formed, and though Anthony's gout precluded his taking part, he pulled wires to have Margaretta included. Stewart planned a European trip and Wayne gave him a farewell party at the City Tavern; he consulted a quack physician who had an American Balsam at 6s. a bottle which was guaranteed as "a most effectual and infallible medicine for coughs, colds, asthmas, rheumatism, gravel, consumption and cholic." In his spare time, he dipped into Delany's copy of the newly published four-volume *Portable Military Library*. It was a Tory book with chapters on Cornwallis's march, Tarleton's raids, Lexington, and Camden, and it gave excellent advice which Wayne did not need on how to reconnoiter; but it said nothing about Green Springs or Stony Point. He chatted with his friends about the coming sale of Charles Lee's plantation, 2,800 acres adjoining Mount Vernon, and about the fall of James Mease, who was being sold out by the sheriff. Remembering his experiences with Mease during the Valley Forge winter, Anthony rejoiced that the red-tape-worshiper was in distress.

As censor, he again ran afoul of his old enemy. Once more St. Clair won preferment when the Council of Censors chose him as president, but Wayne was named to the important committee to inquire and report "whether the Constitution has been preserved inviolate in every part." His preference, of course, would have been to abolish it completely. He voted with Hartley in a minority to throw open meetings to attendance by "those who behave decently." But he had scarcely begun his investigations when he came down with another severe attack of gout. "I am well convinced," he said ruefully, "that there is not a single joint from the heel to the toe but what has been dislocated and probed twenty to twenty thousand times."

The attack came most inconveniently. Despite his censorship work, Wayne had planned to take the fast "Running Machine" that allowed those who left at three in the morning to breakfast next day in New York "without danger from wind or weather." He wished to welcome Washington, to celebrate the peace treaty, whose terms were published in late November, and to ask Washington and Knox to help him win a real major-generalcy with the pay that properly belonged to that position. Instead, he had to send regrets, but he wrote Washington of his ambitions, and he pointed out that his illness was really a war casualty: "Long want of health occasioned by the extreme of fatigue and loss of blood in assisting to vindicate the rights and Liberties of America from her Coldest to her hottest Sun deprives me of the honor and pleasure of attending your Excellency."

The gout attack did not continue long, and Anthony resumed his work with the censors. On January 1, 1784, he and Hartley pushed to victory their motion to end secret meetings of the censors and to open the doors to public attendance, and on the following day they voted their abhorrence of the Pennsylvania constitution. Wayne's group declared that a one-house legislative system was defective in offering "no check to an unjust and tyrannical faction . . . leaving no remedy to the people except revolution." He also carried resolutions condemning the Pennsylvania policy of electing Supreme Court judges for a seven-year term and having them removable by the Assembly; he protested against rotation in office as destroying the hope of re-election and thus limiting the right of people to elect whom they pleased. He suggested that a Senate chosen from among property-owners make laws in conjunction with a House of Representatives "consisting of persons most noted for virtue and wisdom." It was a most undemocratic plan, but Wayne balanced it by asking that governors be elected annually and that judges be appointed by the chief executive to serve during good behavior.

Anxious to kill the constitution of 1776, which at Ticonderoga he had called not worth defending, Wayne also moved a resolution calling for a convention to draw up an entirely new plan of government. The resolution stirred excited comment. By the provisions of that constitution which Wayne wished to supersede, a two-thirds vote was necessary for amendments or for cancellation, but because his motion carried, twelve to ten, Wayne insisted that the state was bound to call a new convention. The minority disapproved. In calling upon the public to reject the new proposals, the radicals charged: "The majority would forbid publishing reasons for dissent and so keep you in the dark. They would abolish rotation in office, and so keep hold by bribery, or bullying. We call upon you to defend your dearly bought freedom." Their tactics succeeded. When the censors met again, enough men changed their minds to vote down the proposal to call a constitutional convention. The form of government adopted in 1776 remained Pennsylvania's basic law until 1790.

Wayne's concern as censor was less with theory of government than with party interest. Whatever favored conservatives pleased him; he always turned down measures sponsored by the radicals. Everyone in Philadelphia knew, for instance, that the vote whereby conservatives were chosen to represent the city had been fraudulent. More ballots were cast than Philadelphia had citizens eligible to vote. On election morning soldiers marched, fully armed and officered, to the State House, where they overawed officials. Secret balloting was then unknown; electors walked up to the voting-place and deposited their ballots openly. At this Philadelphia election, voters who handed in democratic tickets were beaten back; conservatives who carried blue-paper ballots bearing the names of moderate candidates were not only welcomed but were allowed to cast plural votes. Out of sixteen hundred ballots cast at the election, five hundred and seventy were proved fraudulent.

Since the conservative blues won, Wayne voted to accept the returns, insisting in the face of overwhelming evidence that no violence was offered, that no one was intimidated, and that the path to the polls was always open. He admitted "an excess of votes," but explained that the conservative majorities were so high that the extra ballots did not affect the outcome.

Although his work as censor demanded much time, Anthony's evenings were for the most part free. With little regard for his gout, he again led a gay social existence, particularly with Hartley's merry group. Mary Vining joined them often and Cathy Greene spent as much time with them as the young wife of a sober Quaker dared to pass in frivolous amusement. The Wayne-Hartley group filled a peculiar niche in local society, ranking below both the official circle which Washington led and the Assembly Set of Philadelphia bluebloods, yet definitely above the sporting crowd. Twentieth-century slang would place Wayne among café society. To Anthony's contemporaries, the spectacle of emancipated young ladies moving with freedom in male society suggested lax morals; dowagers looked askance at Mary Vining and the other girls, just as Polly had looked on actors, but there was no evidence that moral rules were broken.

Wayne certainly savored life. He wined well and set a notable table; his dinner guests included all those eminent in statesmanship and public affairs. Undoubtedly he spent more for entertainment than he could afford; unquestionably his gout could have been eased had he not insisted on self-indulgence. He did not, however, turn slave to wine and gluttony. Always he maintained keen, boyish interest in local happenings. On a biting-cold January night, he took Margaretta to see the fireworks with which Philadelphia belatedly celebrated peace, and he saw with her the fire that destroyed the painted transparencies just as the demonstration was to start. He and Peggy dodged rockets which exploded prematurely and sent their fiery balls into the crowd. The people ran in confusion, pushing and shoving each other in their terror. In pulling Peggy away to safety, Anthony lost his beaver hat and Peggy dropped her brand-new bonnet.

Wayne had never known so cold a winter as that of'1784. On one evening the mercury fell fifty-three degrees, freezing ships tight in the harbor and bringing death to many. Hastily formed charitable societies, in which Peggy and Mary Vining took part, strove to comfort sixteen hundred distressed families. For three full months both the Delaware and the Schuylkill were frozen fast from shore to shore, blocking all river traffic as completely as though the city were besieged.

Conversation at his Philadelphia table turned not only on the weather and on politics, but on a variety of miscellaneous topics. Rush arrived one evening with a report of an Austrian woman who had given birth to octuplet boys, "all baptized and all well, including their mother," and he and Delany learnedly discussed the strange phenomenon; neither doubted that the event had actually occurred. News from Paris told of M. Joseph Montgolfier's "acrostique machine" which carried him eighty feet into the air. Lewis Hallam, the actor-manager, promptly informed the table that he would buy the machine, fasten it to an auditorium, and raise the building thirteen hundred miles perpendicularly above the State House so that plays again could be given in Pennsylvania. When Wayne, laughing, questioned whether even this would make plays legal, Hallam replied: "Yes, sir. The height will subtilize and enlighten the ideas of the play and make them more sublime, more rarified, and inoffensive even to the most immaculate Puritans." Others told of a newly invented Chinese mirror which not only reflected an exact likeness of any object placed before it, but also so preserved the reflection that only by smashing the glass could the likeness ever be lost, even after the original object had been moved away. The company thought £50 cheap for such a miraculous looking-glass.

Much discussion started when John Vining, Mary's brother, reported a movement for carving ten new states out of the territory west of the Alleghenies. They were, said Vining, to be called Sylvania, Michigania, Chersonesus, Assenisipia, Metropotamia, Illinoia, Saratoga, Washington, Polypotamia, and Pelisipia. Wayne, mindful of his former zeal for starting colonies in backward regions, thought the project highly feasible, but most of his companions disagreed with him, pointing out that these regions watered by the Ohio and the Mississippi were overrun by Indians, and that the better portions were already taken by Spaniards from New Orleans. When Wayne predicted that Americans would some day settle west of Pittsburgh, they called him an idealistic dreamer.

Anthony took much delight in teasing Mary Vining about the styles of women's clothes. He carefully clipped items from the papers describing the latest fashions, and although he did not always understand the terms employed, he liked to read the clippings aloud to her. One Paris fashion note, appearing in the summer of 1784, was, he said, all Greek to him: "The zone is totally abolished and the Persian sash regains its former situation and embraces the waist. Stays are exploded and dimity boddices take their place. The petticoat shortens daily for the purpose of exhibiting the shoeknot and embroidered clock which runs half-way up the leg, approaching the knee, from which a silk garter dangles to the ankle with a silver or gold tassel. That things below may appear to the best advantage, the hoop is contrived to jerk up and down in continual motion and from the elasticity of its form promises wonders."

Mary retorted that the item was understandable, but that the news undoubtedly was written by a man. No woman, she said, would be so stupid as to write of clothes in such a fashion. Anthony, still dwelling on the promise of wonders from the elastic hoop, grumbled that none of the news made sense. "Where does the wonder lie?" he asked. "There is nothing new under the sun; there can be nothing new under the hoop. Take away all the vanity from the outside and her ladyship of 1784 has no more to boast of than good old Eve of the year One." Mary, the emancipated, was shocked. She liked him better when he gave what he called his "Serious Advice to Ladies," warning them against the time they wasted in "deforming" themselves. "Employ a maiden blush instead of vermillion; relieve the voice of distress as the truest harmony; use the breath of love as fragrance. Fair virtue and fair water are best for clearing the complexion and smoothing the skin. Lastly, consider what a labor it is to live if paints, pastes, grease, wool, washes, etc. are daily necessary to put on." Polly may have followed his

precepts, but certainly Mary Vining did not. Nor did Margaretta, who worshiped her father, think that he knew whereof
he spoke.

2

October brought new honors in 1784. On behalf of Congress,
Henry Laurens presented Anthony Wayne with the gold medal
voted long ago to commemorate the victory at Stony Point.
The trophy was elaborate. On its face a crowned Indian queen,
wearing a mantle and a short feather apron, presented a wreath
to General Wayne with her right hand. Her left hand held a
crown which she seemed to be about to offer. At her feet an
alligator lay, perhaps in symbol of Wayne's services in Georgia;
a shield, striped like an American flag, rested against her left
knee. Around the top of the medal ran a legend: "*Antonio
Wayne, Duci Exercitus Comitia Americana.*" The reverse was
more appropriate than the medal's face. Troops in single file
marched up a hill toward a two-turreted fort over which the
British flag was flying. Other columns were shown, one along
a river's edge, another on the right of the fort. A piece of artillery stood on the plain at the foot of the hill, with ammunition
scattered over the ground; six ships were visible in the river.
The legend on the reverse side read: "*Stoney Point Expugna-
tum,*" with the date "xv Jul. MDCCLXXIX." It was an elaborate
medal, even though the promontory's name was misspelled and
though the Latin left much to be desired; Wayne thrilled at
the recognition.

In October, also, Chester County sent Wayne to the Assembly as its representative, thus restoring him to the political office
he had held before the Revolution. The session dealt chiefly
with the vexed question of how to treat loyalist refugees. During the war, ardent patriots had confiscated property belonging
to Tories and had denied such men all civil rights. Wayne believed that, as the war was over, the time had come to restore
Tories to equality. He took this stand as a matter of common
honor, but many political opponents credited him only with the

desire to place conservative voters on the rolls. Wayne grew indignant at the injustice done to Tories who had repented and who were now loyal Americans. In a dozen different ways, he said, Pennsylvania's intolerance worked against the best interests of the Commonwealth:

"The law violates the bill of rights. It is impolitic because it lessens the financial credit of the state, thus hampering the circulation of our money and injuring our trade and agriculture. It debases our state, particularly since every other state in the Union has revised or repealed its restrictions. Our laws favor tyranny; our policy opens the door to other limitations, even of a religious nature. We are continuing the spirit of hostility and of persecution of those who act according to their consciences. We are depriving ourselves of the services of a large number of men, but, even more, contrary to the divine revelations inculcating forgiveness of injuries and universal benevolence, we are, by confining power to little more than half our citizens, creating an aristocracy."

His eloquence failed; the Assembly voted forty-seven to eleven to continue discriminations against former Tories. Wayne, in mixed anger and cynicism, offered a bill to exempt all such disfranchised persons from tax payments, on the ground that "no part of a man's property can be justly taken save by his own consent or that of his legal representatives." He had no notion that the proposal would be taken seriously. To his amazement, he won more votes for it than for the bill to restore full civil rights to Tories. The tax-exemption measure lost only by thirty-six to twenty-two.

Since Wayne, as a conservative, was a minority member, his legislative service was not highly important. He sat on committees to revise election laws, to curb unlawful imprisonment, to repair the State House, and to draw up a divorce code, but he took no active part, knowing that he was named merely to give legal recognition to the Opposition. As a member of the committee to prepare laws for publication, a purely clerical task, he had more work to do, but nothing which gave special scope for his talents.

Re-elected to the Assembly, in October, 1785, Wayne remained in a Federalist minority, but his inability to carry legislation through the House did not prevent his making a gallant effort to swing the lawmakers to a more liberal point of view on censorship. Believing that the time had at last arrived for permitting the theater again to operate, Wayne pleaded eloquently for repeal of the ban on plays. On November 21, 1785, he introduced a bill to permit his friend Hallam to produce such tragedies and comedies during the winter months as might win the approval of the president of Pennsylvania and his Supreme Executive Council. In return for this monopoly Hallam was to pay a license fee of $2,000 yearly, which, said Wayne, "would be a very lucrative and profitable source of revenue to supply the necessities of the State." He was not to charge more than 4 shillings for gallery seats nor more than 8 shillings fourpence for the boxes. The proceeds of two performances each season, the bill provided, must be given to charity—for poor relief and for the benefit of those debtors who were jailed for owing less than 40 shillings. The measure was deftly drawn to win the support of Puritans by the censorship condition, of humanitarians by the charity clause, and of economists by the revenue-raising provisions.

Opponents of the bill damned it as unpatriotic and immoral. "We need no censorship for American plays!" shouted William Findley. "For English drama, yes! but our words and manners are too chaste to give any reason for us to fear that any improper play will be written in this country for centuries to come." Robert Whitehill seemed to think that what was needed was not so much a licensing of plays as a bill for the suppression of vice and immorality. He argued well, but when he made the mistake of suggesting that it would be wiser to jail all those who frequented the theater, Wayne saw an opportunity. "Washington went to the theater to see *Cato* during the war, and so did other officers. Such tragedies have been a stimulus to heroic action. In the plays of Shakespeare are strikingly delineated the most memorable events of English history. I trust that the American War will be thus consigned to future times."

"Perhaps the gentleman from Chester County is correct," John Smilie retorted, "but everyone knows that if a people give

themselves over to amusement, their manners are relaxed and
then ruin follows. Amusements are the means that politicians
use to divert public attention from important matters of statesmanship. To pass this bill will be to lose our liberties. We will
do better to devote our genius to writing history rather than
to writing plays."

Wayne rose again to his feet. "The theater," he argued, "is
a mirror for education, a school of manners, a source of virtue
and an exemplar of civilization. In Paris on certain Saints' days
which are celebrated with fasting and prayer they permit plays
in the evening. Dr. Franklin tells us that on those evenings
there is less immorality than on other days. While people are
at the theater, they do not frequent gambling houses or other
resorts of vice and licentiousness. Young men need relaxation,
but it should be innocent. Opening the theater offers that opportunity. Besides, if we have plays in Philadelphia, it may
induce Congress to return to this city, for there are many young
fellows in that body who do not choose to be debarred from
innocent pleasure."

The reference to Congress was unfortunate. Philadelphians
scorned that body for its cowardice in running away from the
city to escape the mutinous Pennsylvanians who had besieged
it on their return from South Carolina. At Wayne's plea that
opening the theater would bring the statesmen back, the gal-
leries burst out in hoots and catcalls—so much so that no
one could hear the climax of Wayne's speech. Smilie jumped
to his feet, motioned wildly for order, and shouted back that if
the passage of Wayne's bill meant that Congress would return,
that in itself would justify the defeat of the suggestion. He
called for a vote. Upcountry members, solidly opposed to the
city's luxuriousness, joined with the puritanical Quakers to put
down Wayne's bill. By a vote of 36 to 29, the drama bill was
laid upon the table.

Deprived of this last opportunity to do constructive service
for his state, tired of butting his head against the stone wall of
ultraradical opposition, Wayne looked more and more long-
ingly toward resumption of his planter life. His thoughts turned
toward Georgia and the rich profits to be made in rice; he

dreamed again of making a fortune. This, to be sure, involved leaving Waynesborough and abandoning Polly, but, thoroughly cold toward his wife, he gave that phase of the matter no second thought. It would be far more of a wrench to leave Mary Vining, for Anthony had worked out no feasible solution of his relationship with that charming lady. But Mary Maxwell still lived in Georgia. He resigned his Assembly seat and went South to his plantation.

3

Major Fishbourn, bright and glittering in his new uniform, entertained the Cincinnati on July 4, 1785, the ninth anniversary of the Declaration of Independence. His Savannah home, stocked with foods and wines from his recently opened commission house, echoed with gay talk as Wayne and half a dozen other officers indulged, to quote the contemporary newspaper, in "every demonstration of joy befitting the sons of freedom." Certainly liquor flowed freely. The company had just come from reviewing the Chatham County militia, in company with the Governor and the Speaker of Assembly; they had all dined at a civic dinner in the courthouse, where thirteen toasts were drunk. One of them, which they took on trust since none of the celebrants was in the slightest degree literary, was "to the enlightened writers of the age who have torn asunder the veil of superstition and who have shown tyranny and despotism in their proper colors." Another, which must have choked Major Habersham as he downed it, was "to the virtuous militia of the state of Georgia." These thirteen toasts no doubt had their effect, but they were followed by unlimited others at the special after-dinner party in the Fishbourn house.

By midnight, when the celebrants drank their final glass, the men were in a mood for jollity. Across the street was a tavern where a company of strolling players lodged. Two actresses were there, with a hurdy-gurdy. Someone suggested that the Cincinnati take up a collection to have the girls come out and sing. Uncertainly, the diners wavered across the unpaved, dusty road. They huddled beneath the shuttered windows of the tavern and called loudly for the actresses to show themselves. Someone inside fumbled with the door lock and the Cincinnati crowded to the entrance, prepared to greet the girls, but at the same instant that the door swung open, an upstairs shutter also moved. Two muskets snapped from the window, without effect, and the door slammed shut.

Thoroughly sobered, the Cincinnati hurled themselves against the door and forced it open, but when the first man, Daniel Gosse, pushed into the hallway, a bayonet jabbed him in the chin. The Cincinnati fell back hastily. Two more guns, loaded with swan shot, were fired at them, but miraculously no one was hit. Gosse, with blood streaming from his chin, charged into the tavern, with Fishbourn on one side of him and gouty Anthony Wayne close behind. The actors and Bill Platt, the tavern-keeper, warned the Cincinnati to keep off, but the angry officers pounded against the barred door. Platt reloaded a gun and John Brice, a Charleston carpenter who was one of his patrons, snatched it away and ran to the open upstairs window. He took careful aim and fired; nine buckshot poured into the already-wounded Gosse and killed him.

Four hours later, at five o'clock in the morning, a coroner's jury charged Brice and Platt with murder. Platt went free on bail because of an alleged illness, and Brice, finding an iron bolt loose in the prison, knocked down a jailer and escaped over the prison fence. Two weeks later he was recaptured. At a long trial a few weeks later, ending at midnight, the prisoners were found guilty and were sentenced to be hanged.

Wayne's return to Georgia, thus tragically begun, continued unhappily. He found Savannah in turmoil. Smallpox raged, and a hastily built hospital, called in Anthony's honor Fort Wayne, was filled with patients. A hotheaded city constable, who also held the post of scavenger, fired guns recklessly in the streets, shooting stray hogs, until an outraged citizen slashed him on the forehead and hit him over the head. The scavenger lodged a complaint against the attacker, but the city commissioners dismissed the charge, rebuking the constable for getting into trouble. He did his work so badly thereafter that when a man dropped dead in the streets, he let the body lie until dogs ate the flesh.

The Greenes brought Anthony some respite from the black series of misfortunes that befell his newly adopted city. They had rebuilt Mulberry Grove, having sacrificed their South Carolina plantation to pay off the holders of Banks's bills, and now their plantation was a show place of the neighborhood. Surrounding the mansion, which was reached by a mile-long tree-shaded avenue, were lovely flower gardens which bloomed as early as February. Wayne's own estate was a few hundred yards beyond the Greenes'.

Catherine Greene, active, lively, and vivacious, craving entertainment and excitement, found Georgia life absorbing. Although Nathanael, her lame, grave Quaker husband, worked so incessantly about Mulberry Grove, superintending his 60 acres of corn, his 130 acres of rice, and his extensive fruit orchards that he had no time for relaxation, Catherine found compensation in the company of Wayne. She won Anthony completely away from Mary Maxwell, for the Georgia girl, lacking Catherine's sprightliness, could not hold him in competition with volatile Cathy. Since his own rice plantations at Richmond and Kew were not yet sufficiently repaired to be put to cultivation, he had much leisure on his hands; he rode frequently to neighboring Mulberry Grove to entertain the lively wife of his old friend Nathanael Greene.

Small communities are always honeycombed with gossip, and Savannah buzzed excitedly about the frequency of Anthony's calls. More imaginative rumormongers whispered that Nathanael should be jealous and that it would be well for him to have a straightforward talk with Anthony, warning him away. This must have been based solely upon imagination, for when the reports reached Greene and he inquired, Cathy answered truthfully that Wayne's interest was "balm to my wounded heart," and she described their relationship as that between old and honest friends. Anthony indignantly demanded, "Is no character, however perfect, out of reach of envy, malice or detraction?" Greene accepted their protestations; he dismissed the rumors as absurd.

If Wayne were a lifesaver for Cathy, she in turn provided him with escape from the deadly indolence of Georgia planter life. Many Georgia country gentlemen lived useless lives, and Wayne, with his intense fondness for society, might have fallen into a hopeless snare of wastefulness and vice. Without even a working plantation to occupy his time, he would have found refuge from himself only in drink and dissipation. Other planters rose at dawn to inspect their rice and indigo and to look about the slave quarters to see if any Negroes were shirking work or needed medicine. They breakfasted at eight, and then rode to the county seat or to the nearest tavern to talk politics, ask market prices, play cards, or chat. At four they came home, usually with friends, for dinner, and if the company was pleasant, they sat drinking and smoking until sunset, when they turned to cards again until bedtime. It was precisely the type of life that most appealed to a convivial soul like Anthony Wayne. Cathy, by offering diversion, kept his mind alert and active, and saved him from excessive self-indulgence.

But Cathy's good influence did not last. Eight months after his arrival at Mulberry Grove, Greene died. A sudden summons had called him to Savannah to discuss business matters relating to the Banks affair, and he and Cathy rode off, utterly forgetting that they had asked Wayne to come that night for dinner. Nathanael spent too much time in the hot June sun, and on the twelve-mile drive home after his business was completed, he complained of severe headache. Cathy put him to bed as soon as they reached Mulberry Grove, but Nathanael grew worse. His forehead looked inflamed. Although physicians blistered him and took a little blood, the swellings increased and Greene relapsed into a stupor. Wayne sat by his bedside when, on June 19, 1786, Greene died.

"He was great," Wayne told James Jackson, "as a soldier, greater as a citizen, immaculate as a friend. The greatest honors of war are due his remains. You as soldier will take the proper order on this melancholy affair. Pardon this scrawl; my feelings are too much affected because I have seen a great and a good man die."

Cathy left Mulberry Grove immediately to stay with relatives in New York. Wayne found much difficulty in trying to readjust his life with two such friends missing from his side. Delany, who knew Anthony better than any other person, sensed the peril that faced him. With hot weather drawing close, when Georgia, "a paradise in spring," becomes "hell in summer" and "a hospital in autumn," Delany hoped that Anthony would come back to Pennsylvania. "You are blessed with Strength of Mind and Good Estate, and want no other exertions but what are completely within yourself. Therefore, my Friend, never hide from your feelings, never seek company, the bottle, or any other diversion to take You from Yourself, nor plunge deeper into debt. . . . You had better come here for a month or two."

Wayne, angry because he construed Delany's words to imply that he habitually flew to pleasure to shun business, did not go back to Pennsylvania in the summer of 1786. He stayed in Georgia, pleading with the Assembly to grant him more money, on the double ground that he had been voted 4,000 guineas but had received the equivalent of only £3,900, and that his friend General Greene, who had done so much less for Georgia, had received a greater reward. Anthony's appeal to the Georgia Assembly, begging for a larger grant, does not put him in the most attractive light, but political morality was lower in the late eighteenth century than it is today, and he acted upon the assurance that he had only to petition in order to receive. His hopes were unfounded; Georgia failed to increase her gift.

4

Wayne needed money desperately. Richmond was of no use unless it could be put to rice, but rice, a most demanding crop, could not be grown without spending a huge amount for slaves. Anthony had no cash, but he had two possible resources upon which he might borrow. His farms at Waynesborough and in Georgia were both unencumbered, and might be mortgaged, but he preferred to raise money on land certificates given him by

Pennsylvania as a bonus for military service. These, to be sure, sold at a ruinous discount, but he hoped to use them as collateral. For a loan of approximately $9,000, the American equivalent of £2,000, he offered to pay back $12,000, but his old friend George Emlen, owner of the house in which Wayne had been court-martialed for the Paoli affair, thought the certificates insufficient security, and another lender, close kin to his old Ticonderoga friend Jonathan Potts, shied off when Wayne seemed too eager.

His only recourse, accordingly, was to mortgage one or more of his estates. Negotiations on this matter dragged over a long term of years, and threatened to pull Wayne into utter bankruptcy. At Robert Morris's suggestion, he had applied to Messrs. Willem and Jan Willinks, Amsterdam merchants who had bought large blocks of American securities. He asked a loan of £5,000 on the security of Waynesborough, pointing out that Richmond was a vast estate of over 800 acres and that each acre of rich swamp soil should yield a ton of rice. His estimates were liberal, but he did not exaggerate in saying that his plantation was extremely fertile and that net profits should approach £3,000 a year. The Willinks asked difficult terms. European bankers had already lost large sums on Southern mortgages; Georgia was a notoriously bad risk. Before the Willinks would advance more cash, they demanded absolute guarantees of repayment:

Two Georgia lawyers of the highest standing must swear, the Willinks said, that the mortgage would stand as a prior lien "even if the state, or widows, or orphans, or other preferrent debts, had demands upon the borrower." They asked assurances that the loan would never be subject to any proceedings in a Georgia court, and in addition to a binding mortgage, they required a full power of attorney entitling them to sell any of Wayne's property at any time during the life of the loan. Even after these documents had been forwarded and were in their possession, the Willinks warned, the loan might not be granted, but the papers were prerequisite to even a consideration of the matter. In fact, they said, they much preferred to make no loan whatever. Only the bankers' high regard for Robert Morris, they insisted, induced them to give any thought to accepting another Southern mortgage.

Morris thought the terms impossible, but he suggested that Wayne visit the Dutch Minister, Peter John Van Berkel, and ask advice. Anthony did so, but Van Berkel, busy with diplomacy, misunderstood the purpose of Wayne's call. Thinking that Wayne was sounding him for information concerning the Amsterdam merchants' credit, the diplomat assured him that the Willinks had high commercial standing. Only in the event that Holland went to war, he said, would there be any question of the Willinks' ability to meet their obligations, and he guaranteed that there would be no war. Wayne rephrased his questions to correct Van Berkel's misconception. The Minister then pointed out that European bankers hesitated to lend money upon Southern plantations because of the high risks involved, but when Wayne suggested that Waynesborough was also pledged as security, Van Berkel was confident that no further hitch would halt negotiations.

Anthony withdrew Waynesborough from the market, where he had tentatively offered it for sale, and mortgaged it in the Willinks' favor. He sent the other necessary papers to Amsterdam, and waited for acknowledgment that the Willinks had placed the £5,000 to his credit. Since ocean voyages took six or seven weeks under the most favorable conditions, Wayne did not expect an answer from his Dutch bankers for at least three or four months, but since the loan was as good as made, he pushed his plans for developing Richmond.

His first step was to purchase slaves. He sent a hasty letter to Roger Parker Saunders, his old crony, saying that he had £5,000 in his possession and wished him to act as agent. Saunders shopped around and found better bargains than Habersham had discovered. Through Edward Penman, a Charleston broker, he bought from Samuel Potts of Southampton plantation, Georgia, forty-seven Negroes. Fifteen men, eleven women, nine boys, and twelve girls comprised the group for which Saunders agreed to pay £3,307 10*s*. The price was reasonable and the terms were easy, for Anthony was to pay £1,000 cash, and the balance in five equal yearly payments of £461 10*s*. each.

Wayne rolled the roster of his new slaves under his tongue. The men bore good English names, for the most part, with Sam, two Charleses, George, Norman, Harry, Dick, Simon, and Adam among them, but one was called Brutus and another Pompey; there was a Rentey, a Jolliboy, a Boson, and a Hector; the boys, Peter, Ned, Will, Bob, Jack and Johnny, were conventionally named, though there was one called Bissy and two others were London and Lancaster. The women were more oddly described as Cinga, Barnaba, Ebo, Sur, and two called Dye. Wayne was glad that he had a Molly and a Mary, a Peggy and a Sally, and a Phebe, too, to remind him of his Howell's tavern experience, but he wondered how Negro girls came to bear names like Charlotte, Sylvia, Phillis, Elsie, and Susannah.

The required equipment next occupied his attention, for after the ravages of war Richmond had nothing but its soil and its houses. Wayne shipped carriage horses fom Waynesborough so that William Little, the new overseer, could travel comfortably about the estate. He asked Saunders to buy five hundred barrels of rough rice (equal to about thirty barrels cleaned) for seed. At the same time Saunders purchased a new periauger (piragua), a small two-masted, flat-bottomed river boat with flat, egg-shaped leeboards. These purchases, together with tools, cost Wayne £240; he sent money for them to Saunders, but through some misunderstanding the latter thought the cash was intended as his personal commission. Bills for the periauger and the seed piled in upon Wayne for several years thereafter.

Disappointments faced the new rice planter. His slaves were not first-class; some of the men were old; many of the boys and girls were too young to do a full day's work. Wayne, with his usual exaggeration, complained that less than one-third were efficient laborers. Other misfortunes befell him. Something happened to his seed rice. Half of it disappeared, and Wayne was certain that Little had stolen it; four horses, with all their chains and harness, vanished utterly; a cow and a calf strayed off and could not be found. Nor was Little a steady worker; for two full months in the plantation's busiest time he took a holiday, so that Richmond produced but ten barrels of rice when

Wayne expected many more. He discharged Little and sent to Philadelphia for an expert overseer, one skilled in ditching. Ditchers did not come. Sharp Delany, who rose from a sickbed to hunt for them in Philadelphia, reported that none would be available until autumn. He did send two boxes and a canvas bundle containing four dozen shovels. Wayne made out, as best he could, to have ditches dug under his own engineering supervision. The delay in finding workmen cost him a summer in Philadelphia, for his original intention had been to stay in Georgia only until the overseer could get well under way.

Money problems plagued him. The Willinks declared that they would make the £5,000 loan provided war clouds then threatening Europe cleared away; meanwhile, they would hold his mortgages. Their delay in sending money caused embarrassment, for Wayne was obligated to pay sums that he could obtain from no other source. He took the Willinks' letter to Penman and on the strength of the half-promise by the bankers, he asked for more slaves. Penman shook his head over the matter but he sold Wayne nine Negroes, six men, two women, and a boy. Penman did not accept responsibility for this; he had Wayne draw on the Willinks in favor of Philip Jacob Cohen, another broker. The new drafts totaled 5,500 florins, which Wayne estimated as equal to £500. Penman reminded Anthony that the £1,000 down payment had not yet been made, and Wayne promised to send drafts for the amount within a very few days. They did not arrive immediately, and Penman, who appears to have been remarkably patient, although perhaps under Georgia's debtor-favoring laws he had no other alternative than to wait, waited several weeks. Then he dunned Wayne again. At the time, Anthony was traveling in southern Georgia, inspecting land. Not until five months after it was due did he pay the £1,000 cash; he did so then by yet another draft (for 11,000 florins) on the Willinks.

Penman, in addition to patience, evidently possessed endless confidence, for notwithstanding Wayne's delay in making settlement, he sold more slaves to Wayne on deferred payments. The terms were cheap, 65 guineas a man instead of the 70 which Wayne had been paying. The bills drawn on the Wil-

links mounted high, but Penman and Cohen eagerly accepted
Wayne's promises to pay. As additional security, they asked a
mortgage on Wayne's Georgia lands. Anthony pointed out that
he could not give this while the Willinks held a power of attorney, but they insisted. When he pleaded that he could not
wait, they allowed him to sail for Philadelphia before the signed
mortgages were delivered. Their delay cost them dear, for
Wayne never completed the papers. Penman and Cohen held
as security for payment of the debts only the drafts on Amsterdam which Wayne had offered.

Those drafts, as it turned out, were worthless. Although no
war broke in Europe, the Willinks refused to honor Wayne's
paper. The notes went to protest. Penman dispatched a hasty
letter to Philadelphia begging Wayne to make good. Wayne
could not credit the news that the Willinks had refused the
loan. He was certain, from what Morris and Van Berkel had
said, and from the Willinks themselves, that someone had blundered. "I find that information is a little exaggerated," he replied to Penman. "I believe that the Bills were not sent back
protested, altho noted for non-acceptance, which must be owing
to some mistake, for the House of Messrs. Willem and Jan
Willink must have too much regard for their own Character
as honest men and Merchants to hold Securities of my property in their hands to the amount of more than *ten thousand
Guineas* which, you know, they say 'was to intire satisfaction,'
and at the same time solemnly protest my Bills."

More than two years had now passed since Wayne had bought
his first Negroes, but he had yet to pay a farthing of his debt
except by drafts on the Willinks. Penman, as is understandable,
prodded him for the sums long overdue, but he had only the
defaulted bills on which to bring suit. New difficulties arose
here, for the drafts were made in Georgia to be paid in Amsterdam to satisfy a South Carolina debt. With all the international
and interstate complications that thus entered into the story,
Penman's chance to file suit successfully was slim. He could
do little more than plead with Wayne to pay the bills. Wayne
professed himself willing to do so, but only if Penman would
furnish him with at least fifty more slaves on credit. Not even

the easy-going Penman could stomach Wayne's proposition. He refused to lend more money, though he admitted that by adding fifty slaves Wayne could work himself clear of debt.

Wayne's bill, including interest charges and penalties of 15 per cent on the protested drafts, in January, 1787, totaled about £1,800, with £461 interest falling due in May. He had no cash, and no prospect of obtaining any, for Waynesborough still remained in the Willinks' hands under the mortgage and the power of attorney, which they refused to surrender, despite their denial of a loan. Even had he desired to sell Richmond or Kew, he could not have done so, for Georgia plantations were a drug upon the market. Faced with mounting debts and with no prospect of escape, Wayne offered Penman a compromise. If Penman would accept Richmond at a valuation of £7,500, Wayne would pay his bills; the balance due, after his debts were canceled, could be paid by Penman in "prime slaves at fifty guineas a head." In this way Anthony would be clear of debt and would possess a labor force to work Kew and his subsidiary plantation in southern Georgia. "I do assure you," he wrote Penman in making the offer, "that no person on earth can be more anxious to discharge a just debt than I am; indeed, I never experienced the *torture* of a debtor, until the *unfortunate* contract with your house, which I have had abundant reason to wish had never been made." But at the very moment that he was telling Penman that he had never known the tortures of a debtor, a Savannah merchant was demanding that he pay grocery bills of £65 dating back eighteen months, and his former overseer, the lax William Little, was clamoring for £41 pay due for more than a year and a half.

Penman refused the offer of Richmond. In desperation, Wayne put Waynesborough again upon the market for £6,000, but, with both a mortgage and a power of attorney in the Willinks' hands, no purchaser would buy. Suffering with renewed attacks of gout, and hurt by an accident, Wayne thought of going back to Pennsylvania, but, uncharacteristically, he wavered in making decisions. In one letter to Polly he told her to lime the fields and to plant them with rye, promising to be in Waynesborough within three months; on the same day he wrote to Delany that money difficulty "fixes an impenetrable barrier to that pleasure and happiness which I had fondly anticipated of enjoying in the social society of my friends in Pennsylvania." A month later he warned Polly "not to expect me until you see me," but immediately thereafter he left for Philadelphia, arriving there in August, 1787.

5

Georgia, a plantation state whose citizens were borrowers, threw protecting arms about its debtors, shielding them from legal action on the part of creditors; Pennsylvania, more commercial and more responsive to the pleas of moneylenders, took a hard-boiled attitude toward those who failed to pay their bills. So long as Wayne remained in Georgia, Penman could do little but entreat; in Pennsylvania, Penman could appeal to law. Wayne stepped off the packet that had brought him north, and found the sheriff waiting. Penman had brought suit for breach of contract, and Potts had followed his example. Unless Wayne satisfied their bills, now totaling £2,260, he must answer to the Court of Common Pleas of Philadelphia County.

Anthony roared indignantly. "This, sir," he complained, "is a conduct so very extraordinary and so cruel that I want words to express my feelings. It is the first warrant that was ever issued against me"—evidently he forgot Phoebe Stewart—"indeed, it is the first debt I ever owed and one of the most extortionate that was ever made." In telling of the "insidious conduct" of the creditors whom he now viewed as harpies, cormorants, rogues, and extortioners, Wayne assured his friends that the court action was unjustifiable. He told how he had several times offered to turn over Richmond or Kew in payment of the debt, and that Penman held a mortgage on both land and slaves—although, accurately speaking, Penman had nothing but Wayne's unfulfilled promise of such a mortgage; he called Penman "a

Tory caitiff" for bringing suit in another state than that in which the debt had been contracted.

He found, however, one wide loophole in the Penman-Potts proceedings. Ignorant that Waynesborough was in Chester County, the two creditors applied to a Philadelphia County court, which had no jurisdiction in the matter. To make his safety doubly certain, Wayne found a friend to take an affirmation that he was not even a Pennsylvanian! "The defendant," Rumford Dawes solemnly told the court, "hath not been a resident in this State for the space of two years." Dawes was economical with truth. His affirmation taken in 1787, at the very time that Wayne was a delegate to the Pennsylvania convention to ratify the new Federal Constitution, overlooked not only the fact that Wayne had been an Assemblyman, but also that Robert Morris had proposed him as governor. None of his friends with whom he spent the winter of 1786 in Philadelphia guessed that Anthony changed his voting residence while still a Pennsylvania officeholder.

Once more, Wayne patiently repeated his offer to turn over his plantations to extinguish the debts, though he was well aware that Penman would not take unsalable Georgia land in exchange for specie long overdue. He offered to go farther and return the slaves if that would satisfy his cormorant creditors. "Indeed, there are many of the old, superannuated negroes dead," Wayne admitted, "but I will make up the *number* in young, healthy, seasoned, working slaves now upon the premises. I will go further; I will give you the amount of the whole of the net proceeds of last year's *Crop* . . . and also that of 1785, together with the use of my Land, and all my labor and time and personal expences thrown in to the bargain." He thought it an irresistible offer. "Should this proposition *also* be rejected, it must produce a conviction to every candid mind that your object is *Oppression*, and I trust that I shall be exonorated by the World for that Conduct, which I most *certainly* shall pursue."

Penman, lured by the prospect of getting two years' rice harvest as a payment on his bill, inquired how much had been grown, but Wayne refused to tell. Unwilling to take a pig in a poke, Penman declined the offer. He began a new lawsuit in Chester County, once Wayne's legal residence.

Just where Wayne actually lived was a matter of dispute. His wife and children, and his ancestral estate, were certainly at Waynesborough, but Anthony himself claimed residence in Georgia. In fact, at precisely this same time he wrote to James Jackson asking for election to the Georgia Assembly. Two months later he asked Sharp Delany to have the Pennsylvania Assembly send him to Congress. No motives of statecraft were involved; Anthony was wholly frank. By contemporary Pennsylvania law, convicted debtors could be jailed. Wayne, knowing that Congressmen enjoyed immunity, sought election as a personal convenience. "A seat in Congress will leave me at liberty to transact my private business in any quarter within the United States, during the sessions."

Court action moved slowly in a suit for debt. Wayne, now a close student of Blackstone and well versed in legal procedure, knew that immediate decision was impossible and that, even if Penman and Potts should prove successful, he would not be summoned for arrest until after judgment had been given in their favor and until the sheriff had reported that there was no property upon which to levy. He waited in Philadelphia to see the result of an election for clerk of the Assembly until, finding that a majority was anti-Federal, he gave up hope of being sent to Congress. Then he sailed for Georgia. On the ship he had an inspiration. Neither Penman nor Potts had yet attached Waynesborough, although the Willinks held a mortgage on the property. Wayne consulted with Aedanus Burke, the anti-Cincinnati Chief Justice of South Carolina, and learned that quick action might save the farm from the clutches of the cormorants. Little, if anything, had ever been paid to his mother on the annuity which Wayne had agreed in 1776 to pay. If, Burke said, his mother could be persuaded to bring action, Waynesborough might be attached in her interest; in that case, he could baffle the bloodsucking cormorants and the "assassins of character." Accordingly, on July 16, 1788, Anthony asked William Lewis of West Chester to start suit in his mother's interest.

"The date of this letter," he went on to say, "causes me to recollect with a heavy heart the total reverse of fortune which has taken place in what appears to me but a short period—this morning. Nine years ago, I was in an enviable Situation—surrounded by a faithful, Effectionate and Gallant corps, clasped in the arms of Victory and hailed by my General the hero of Stoney Point—and, as he approached to embrace me, the blood, proud of the Occasion, flowed fresh from my wound, and more than met him—often, very often, have I had cause to regret that it ever ceased to flow until the last drop was drained—but a truce to these gloomy Ideas, future may yet be propitious now to the purport of this letter, which the day almost caused me to forget."

The anniversary did not drive from his mind the thought that Isaac, now at Princeton, might need money. He asked Sharp Delany to buy the boy some clothing, to pay tuition fees, and to advance whatever spending money might be needed. "I have a very fine appearance of a Crop . . . and shall make you a remittance out of the first of it."

Financial prospects brightened. His rice crop flourished; he estimated a clear profit of £1,000, and he felt assured that the cormorants could not take Waynesborough away from him. Richmond too was safe, since he had carefully refrained from signing any mortgages on that plantation, despite his statement to Lewis that Penman held such security. Moreover, he believed that Georgia would elect him to some public office. Not to the state Assembly, for rivals had spread word that Anthony Wayne sympathized with Tories! At the siege of Savannah, they declared, he had offered to pardon any loyalists who joined the patriotic army. The charge was true, but not in the sense that politicians gave it, for Wayne had promised amnesty at Greene's command and then only to weaken Sir Alured Clarke's military force, not to show special favor to the Tories. The accusation, nevertheless, had its effect; Georgia defeated Wayne for election.

A wider opportunity presented itself immediately. Wayne announced his candidacy for the United States Senate; he asked the Assembly to elect him. In reply to "Tory objections" that he was a Pennsylvania citizen, Wayne replied: "It is not true. I pledge you my word that I am a citizen of Georgia, and have not the most distant idea of ever leaving it, except upon public service." Again Anthony was disappointed; the Georgia Assembly, meeting in joint session, elected an opposition candidate.

Meanwhile, long, tiresome negotiations continued over Wayne's protested drafts. Throughout the whole year 1788, Penman, "the insidious Caledonian," and Cohen, his "Jew broker," clamored for cash. Penman, in addition, vainly demanded the Richmond mortgage which Wayne had agreed to give. Neither entreaties nor threats moved Wayne an inch. Penman, finding Waynesborough mortgaged to the Willinks, appealed to Anthony's sense of justice. Monotonously, Anthony answered with his stereotyped reply; the only terms that he would consider were either for Penman to take back the slaves and cancel the debt, or to buy either Richmond or Kew. His real intention was to sell one plantation in order to buy slaves to farm the other. More than four years had now gone by since Wayne had bought the Negroes. Despairing of ever getting any return, Penman at last agreed to take back the slaves, together with three hundred barrels of rice, but then, with some prospect of settlement looming up, Wayne refused to answer letters. Four months after Penman accepted the rice-and-Negro deal, Wayne broke silence by complaining of his "excess of rancour and avidity."

The fact was that Wayne had sold the rice to pay his own expenses. Moreover, he had other plans; Indians had been ravaging the Carolina and Georgia frontiers, scalping settlers, robbing farms, and burning buildings. Tired of "being buried in a damned river swamp," he applied for command of an army column to fight the Creeks. He asked James Madison, Knox, and Burke to help him gain the appointment. All answered cagily, Madison replying that he would support the man whom Georgia and the Carolinas endorsed, Knox saying that the appointment was a congressional affair. Burke alone was enthusiastic, but when Burke applied to the South Carolina Senators in Wayne's behalf, they passed the buck to Washington. Then Burke changed his tune, and, after saying "Georgia and South Carolina have been considered for five years past as nests of roguish swindlers," recommended that Wayne go home to Pennsylvania. "There is nothing in that country in the way of publick promotion and Employment which you could not have." Robert Morris, Pennsylvania's Senator, agreed unequivocally to help, perhaps to compensate for the Willinks fiasco, which he had advised Anthony to undertake.

Wayne would have none of it. Again he was enthusiastic over his prospects. In the autumn of 1789, Richard Wayne, Anthony's broker cousin of Savannah, had heard of a Florida slaveowner who wished to lease twenty-five slaves. Anthony agreed to take the slaves on condition that the owner was "not to interfere either directly or indirectly with the management of the negroes." For this, after harvest Wayne would pay the owner £10 per man. He expected to produce five hundred barrels of rice with his augmented labor force. Nothing worked out as he anticipated. Congress postponed indefinitely the plan for sending Federal troops to put down the Creeks, so that Wayne lost any opportunity to take command of the Southern department. The Florida slaves showed themselves so inefficient that at least half the rice in each barrel was ruined by carelessness; to make matters worse, the price of rice tobogganed. His cash income was so small that he was obliged to ask Delany to defray the expense of Isaac's college bills.

Penman, emboldened by a new Pennsylvania debtor law, then attached Waynesborough for the Georgia debt. Wayne, suffering again from gout, and realizing that Georgia land had so depreciated that plantations worth £1,000 five years ago would not bring £100 at forced sale, faced real disaster. Lewis, Delany, and Wayne all were taken aback by Penman's sudden move. Happy in the success of their maneuver to get judgments against Anthony on behalf of his mother, the triumvirate had overlooked the need for completing their success by attaching Waynesborough. Delany sadly sent Wayne the bad news that Jonathan Dickinson Sergeant, Penman's lawyer and one of the leading Pennsylvania political attorneys, had taken full advantage of the opportunity thus laid open.

Wayne, almost at the end of his financial rope, appealed to his mother for further legal intervention. Pessimistic again, as on the eve of battle, he wrote sadly that the request was "perhaps the last that I can be permitted to make." He sent a short note, too, to Mrs. Molly Wayne—the diminutive was that which, heretofore, he had reserved for Mary Vining—bidding her "adieu, a long adieu." "I did intend to write you a long letter, but my head will not permit me at present to write with any degree of coherency. Persecution has almost drove me mad."

Referring again to the Pennsylvania land certificates, issued as bonus for military service, Wayne urged Delany to take steps to preserve them for the use of Isaac and Margaretta. "Let the plunder of my other properties satiate the *harpies*, but let them [the certificates] be preserved as a modicum that seven years' hard service has left me—for my own part I shall not want it, but they will. Would to god that it was a thousand times as much for their sake. An ungreatful country with the addition of Insidious friends and Insatiate Sharpers have deprived them of a genteel competency and left me with a shattered Constitution to contend with misfortune in an Inhospitable Climate, from which, perhaps, *there is no return.*"

Penman, Cohen, and Potts, whom Wayne now called nothing but harpies, cormorants, bloodsuckers, and insidious leeches, proved patient with their slow-pay debtor. With all the legal weapons in their hands to get satisfaction for a just debt, owed by a man who made no effort to repay a penny, they delayed still longer to give him every opportunity. Wayne did not show a scrap of appreciation for their consideration; he failed to forward a single cask of rice to pay his bills. He sank into mental lethargy. Cathy Greene, brokenhearted at his silence, wrote from New York, but even she received no answer. She wrote again, chiding him for his neglect, complaining that he had failed to ask mutual friends about her health:

"I have waited with impatient hope of an answer. . . . I have felt resentment and flattered myself that I should be, in future, entirely indifferent whether you wrote or not—yet I confess I cannot yet arrive at that degree of tranquillity. To suppose you wanting in gallantry is doing you injustice merely but to suppose you incapable of feeling the professions you make —and to return *indifference* which amounts to insult to the Solicitude of friendship would I believe be a crime . . . yet my conscience has always been your friend as cincerely as You *formerly were mine.* I have condemned myself, after all the goodness with which you have treated me, for admitting for one moment to a *doubt.* Yet, why does he not write me one line acknowledging my letter, and saying he is yet my friend? Surely that could be no sacrifice to General Wayne when he knows what joy it would give an unhappy friend. Indeed, my dear General, you know not the conflict your long silence has occasioned in my bosom."

He roused himself long enough to write a one-page letter, devoid of sentiment, asking Cathy to plead with the President to name him to command the Southern army; later, when Cathy appealed to Congress to recompense her for the money spent by Nathanael in the Banks affair, he sent a note allowing her to quote him as defending Greene. Thereafter, he wrote no more.

For the first time in his life, Anthony was unresponsive to his daughter. Margaretta fell in love, and both she and Delany wrote to Wayne telling him that she was engaged to young William Atlee, son of that colonel whose promotion Wayne had fought. Anthony made no response. He did not go North for the wedding; he showed no interest in the personality or the abilities of his son-in-law. He snapped at Isaac for having wasted six years at college without finishing his education; he suggested that the boy, now twenty, be bound out to a lawyer, but he gave Delany carte blanche in determining Isaac's career. Delany followed Anthony's suggestion; the father thereafter lost interest in his son. Nor had he interest in matters which in former years would have been absorbing. A small boom started for Wayne's good friend Henry Knox as vice-presidential candidate, but Anthony took no notice of it. A Georgia county, looking about for a Congressman, invited Wayne to run, and actually cast eight votes for him, but he paid no heed. The Cincinnati chose him president, an honor which a few years earlier would have filled him with pride, but Wayne took it as a matter of course. He let his taxes go unpaid; he failed to call at the post office for his letters; he slumped in body and in spirits.

CHAPTER XV

Planter Politician

H EAD winds held back the periauger. The sun dipped into the western sky, darting slanting golden beams upon the lonely marshes bordering St. Mary's River. Negroes, sweating from their labor even on this January afternoon in 1791, poled the heavy boat about the narrow river bends, helping the periauger beat its way against wind and current, but though eight white men strained their eyes at each shift of course, no farmhouse and no human being broke the wide monotony of Georgia swamp. Henry Osborne, the state's Chief Justice, growled impatiently that they would never reach James Gray's polling-place before sunset put an end to voting. John Scott, army surgeon, reached down for a demijohn of rum that stood beside his seat, pulled heavily upon it, and shook his head despairingly. Bob Seagrove, Indian trader who knew the river's tortuous meanderings, gave up hope of getting to the place before the middle of the night. Once again, for the tenth or twelfth time that afternoon, he pointed to his soiled, creased sketch map. "The only way to reach James Gray's by dark is to cut across that swamp," he said. "It's wet and soft, but there are no rivers on the way. You'll be muddy to the neck when you arrive, but if you start now, you may vote before the sun goes down."

Osborne looked at his watch and at the sun. Georgia's strict election laws, which he had framed, commanded that polls close at sundown. These white men in the periauger, all freemen of six months' residence who carried paid-up tax receipts in their pockets, were needed if Anthony Wayne was to carry Camden County safely against James Jackson, candidate for re-elec-

335

tion to the United States Congress. With only twenty-five voters in the county, and these almost equally divided between the two contestants, a few more Wayne votes would spell success. Obviously, the periauger would not bring these voters to the polls before the sun went down. The Chief Justice did not hesitate. Gray's house lay due west over the swamp. Osborne, taking a compass from the periauger, ordered the Negroes to push for the shore. The white men scrambled out, stepped on the marsh that gave beneath their boots, and set off across the soggy lowland.

Soaked to the skin, slimy with marsh mud, eight tired men came to Gray's. They were already late; the sun had set. No one sat at the polls to take their votes. Gray, doing his chores by torchlight in the barn, came out to greet the late arrivals. Osborne demanded the right to vote, but Gray said that no officials remained. The registrars had waited after every known Camden County voter had appeared, but promptly at sundown the clerk had signed the election returns and had carried them away. The Chief Justice, disappointed and short-tempered, commanded that Gray go at once to the clerk's house, two miles away across the swamp, and bring the man back to reopen the polling-place. Gray protested that this would be illegal, that marsh travel in the dark was dangerous, and that in any case the eight men who demanded the right to vote were not Camden County residents; but Osborne cut him short. Peremptorily, he threatened Gray with punishment for contempt of court.

The action was illegal, but Gray dared not disobey. Nor did the clerk of elections venture to refuse. Gray brought the poor man back to the polls, where Osborne, using his authority as Chief Justice, forced him to reopen the balloting. Osborne's eight voters then proceeded to cast sixty-four votes for Anthony Wayne. Gray and the registrar, shocked at the spectacle of unknown men stuffing the ballot box, refused, even under the renewed threat of contempt of court, to certify the new returns. Osborne tore up the original certificate that showed that Wayne had fifteen votes to Jackson's ten, and replaced it by a new one giving Jackson ten and Wayne seventy-nine. One of his companions, looking on admiringly, remarked: "Mr. Osborne, you are a very good patcher." Another volunteered to take the patched return to Governor Edward Telfair as the official vote of Camden County. Gray ventured to ask if all this were legal, but was silenced by Osborne's sharp retort: "Never mind about legality; that's my business." The volunteer was more communicative. "It makes no difference," he said. "General Wayne had a majority at the first election, and since everyone who voted now was also in his favor, the new votes make no odds."

Equally remarkable occurrences took place in the other counties of the Lower Georgia Congressional District. In Glynn County, the official returns were sent to Telfair by Wayne's personal servant; they were twenty-six days on the way, and when they arrived, they were so distorted that on examination the whole vote had to be thrown out as palpably wrong. In Effingham County, Wayne in person arranged with the commander of the German Company of Militia to vote the entire group against Jackson in return for all the rum that they could drink. By eleven o'clock in the morning, the militia was roaring drunk. There had been a time when Wayne detested militia, but on election day they hired horses at Wayne's expense and rode, rolling in their saddles, shouting at the top of their lungs, to the polling-place to vote for Wayne, the man who promised to beat the Indians. In Effingham County, Wayne polled ninety votes to Jackson's seventeen. The overwhelming victory here was not wholly due to the rum-soaked militia; Wayne's friend Thomas Gibbons, Savannah mayor and one of the best lawyers in the state, threw out the regularly chosen election board, although he was not even a resident of Effingham, and put in two men of his own choosing. The new officials challenged Jackson voters, but allowed anyone to cast a Wayne ballot who desired to do so. Any boy over sixteen, they said, was eligible to vote, provided he was on Wayne's side.

Even with these aids to election, Wayne barely managed to pull through a victor, with 278 votes in the district as a whole against 273 for Jackson, the incumbent. When all the returns were in, Osborne and Gibbons loudly denounced the whole proceedings as unfair; in Chatham County, Wayne's home, Jackson's unprincipled partisans had counted twenty more votes

than were legally cast! They were indignant that a Congressman stooped to crookedness. Jackson had not been personally
involved, for he was at the national capital arguing valiantly
against an excise tax on spirits and protesting against the sale
of public lands to speculators instead of using them to reduce
the national debt. He had no suspicion that his re-election was
being contested, least of all by his close friend and client Anthony Wayne. Anxious to get the matter settled before news
reached Philadelphia, Wayne urged Telfair to issue a certificate
of election at once. He claimed to have been a Georgia resident for the required three years, although he had lived in
Philadelphia during the first half of 1788, and to have paid
his taxes, despite the fact that he had been advertised for nonpayment on 1,000 acres of Camden County land in 1789. But
then, so had James Jackson, while the Chief Justice was in ar-
rears on 27,607 acres and Seagrove on 48,105. Perhaps, as all
four men contended, they had actually paid their bills but
the collector had run off with the money.

In the midst of the election controversy, to Wayne's thunder-
struck amazement, he received a letter from Gibbons, his political manager in Effingham, demanding payment on the Potts
and Penman claims. The cormorants, at last taking the aggressive in Georgia, had retained Gibbons as their attorney. Wayne
repeated his customary offer that the cormorants take either
Richmond or Kew, together with the slaves, but he reduced
his price for the plantations from the £7,500 which he had
originally asked for each to £6,000 for them both. He went
on further to suggest that Gibbons also act as his attorney in
settling the long-protracted dispute. In return for a retaining
fee which Wayne, with nice delicacy, gave to Mrs. Gibbons
rather than to her husband, he asked that the lawyer act as
umpire, persuading his clients to accept the often repeated suggestion that they take land and slaves in lieu of cash.

His strategy succeeded. In March, 1791, six and a half years
after his purchase of the slaves, the cormorants, at Gibbons's
recommendation, agreed to take the two plantations and the
Negroes in full payment of the debt, which, with interest and
penalties included, amounted to £5,000. Wayne backed down

by accepting a much lower valuation of his estates; the harpies compromised by taking unsalable land and hard-worked slaves instead of the money which they really wanted. In consideration of a cash payment by Anthony of £100, all the cash he ever paid for his plantation venture, Potts and Penman gave him a general release of all claims and judgments against Waynesborough, so that by giving up all his Georgia lands except the cowpens Wayne regained control over his ancestral acres. With the eventual return by the Willinks of his deeds and mortgages, pledged for a loan that was never made, the business deal was finished.

In telling Polly of his arrangements, which he was obliged to do in order to obtain her relinquishment of dower rights, he appealed to her to persuade his mother to cancel the judgments which she held against him: "Having now cleared myself of all my oppressive debts, I wish to retire to my Sabine fields, but unless she relinquishes those Judgments it will be out of my power. If they are not relinquished, Waynesborough must be sold by the Sheriff." He repeated to Delany the same threat of sheriff's sale and gave instructions to advertise the property if his mother did not cancel her claims: "The small Modicum that may remain from the ruins of my Estate will be sufficient to begin the World anew in some obscure corner, far distant from my family, native air and early acquaintances until fortune is more propitious, but should she still continue Obdurate, I trust that my Conduct will be such as to Justify me in the eye of the World, and in the Opinion of all men of feeling, honor and Sentiment." His departure was not required. Elizabeth Iddings Wayne, widow of the long-deceased Isaac and mother of the General, showed much consideration by canceling her claims. Her son, who had promised in 1776 to pay her an annual annuity, failed to show appreciation, for after her relinquishment of claims he neglected, as in the past, to pay a single cent.

Negotiations with the cormorants were scarcely completed before Wayne, buoyant and jubilant over his release from debt, led a Southern celebration over the coming of George Washington. On May 2, the President arrived at Charleston for a tour of South Carolina and Georgia. From Charleston, Washington rode, escorted by light horse, to Purysburg on the Savannah River, where the Georgia delegation took him under their protection. Wayne, Washington, and three other notables of less prominence sat themselves in a barge rowed by twelve native-born American ship captains, who were dressed in jackets of light-blue silk, black satin breeches, white silk stockings, and round hats with black ribbons on which were printed in golden letters the words "Long Live the President." Ten miles from Savannah, a fleet of escort skiffs appeared, bearing a band which played gala airs while the leading citizens chanted "He comes, the hero comes." Again guns boomed, and the populace, standing on a high bluff above the river, cheered and sang. Mayor Thomas Gibbons, ballot-box stuffer and attorney on both sides in the Wayne-Penman lawsuit, gave him a formal welcome to the city.

Savannah's festivities had just begun. Late that afternoon, a formal civic dinner celebrated Washington's arrival. Sixteen toasts were drunk as cannon roared. By this time darkness had fallen, and Wayne escorted the President to the water front to see the magnificent lantern illumination of the harbor, with ships bright with colored lights forming a brilliant W. The next day, May 13, the President was the guest of the Cincinnati, with Wayne presiding. Sixteen more toasts, again to cannon accompaniment, were downed, after which Wayne led the President to a ballroom to be presented to ninety-six ladies, each "elegantly dressed in infinite taste." A concert closed the jubilee. Then the volunteer Light Horse, in silver-laced blue uniforms faced with crimson, reluctantly guided Washington from the city toward Augusta.

Wayne sailed for Philadelphia on July 3, 1791. The Cincinnati, meeting next day, the fifteenth anniversary of American independence, again chose him president of the society. He would far rather have had Arthur St. Clair's appointment to command the American Army, for St. Clair was expected to win glory crushing Indians who had recently defeated Wayne's old friend Josiah Harmar in what is now Ohio.

2

Congressman Anthony Wayne, representative of the First Georgia District, lounged comfortably at Philadelphia in his leather-bottomed armchair. Before him was his writing-desk, unlocked so that he might draw forth his writing-paper, scrawl a hasty letter with one of the numerous quill pens that lay ever ready to his hand, and blot it with the sand-shaker that stood upon the desk. Fellow members flanked him in a long semi-circle, three rows deep, facing Speaker Jonathan Trumbull.

Wayne was not, at the moment, looking at Trumbull, who sat enthroned upon his dais, one hand resting on the green-cloth table. The Congressman was admiring a full-length portrait of Marie Antoinette, the tall, blue-eyed Queen of France, which hung upon the wall above the wide fireplace. If he thought at all of statecraft while glancing at the picture of the handsome girl, he was certainly not dwelling on the long-winded debate about rules for codfisheries which the House was discussing, although he may have been congratulating himself on his success in winning a seat in Congress after previous disappointments in both Pennsylvania and Georgia. Perhaps he was musing, as he was wont to do, that he would have preferred being among the Senators, admiring the portrait of Louis XVI, for he dreaded going through the ordeal of election every two years when he might have been safe in office during six; but Congressmen enjoyed immunities and he was almost content.

Wayne took his seat November 1, 1791, a week after the Second Congress opened; seven days later, he made his maiden speech, asking a pension for the collateral heirs of a Revolutionary major. He was on the losing side; flaws in the major's record barred the heirs from profiting. As befits a freshman Congressman, Wayne sat silent during most of the session, though he voted regularly with the Federalist majority. He took no part in debates on apportionment, though the administration's bill gave Georgia only two seats instead of the three she had now; he had nothing to say upon the presidential-election law, nor upon the measure setting up a postal system. Together with his friend John Page of Rosedale he served on a select committee to discuss subsidizing an expedition to Baffin Bay. As a surveyor he approved, but he could see no reason why the United States should pay for experiments.

Catherine Greene's petition to be reimbursed for sums spent by Nathanael on the Banks accounts caused him again to break his silence. He fathered a resolution in her favor and he spoke in its behalf, but he found the opposition powerful. Thomas Sumter, "Gamecock of the Revolution" and anti-Federalist Congressman from South Carolina, lost his temper when the matter came before the House. Remembering how Greene had slandered Carolina militiamen as "locusts who did nothing but eat up food," Sumter violently attacked Greene's military record. He denied that South Carolina had been barren of supplies; he vehemently defended the state against Greene's accusation of lukewarm patriotism, and he insinuated that Greene was Banks's secret partner. Other Southern representatives aided Greene against the antiadministration bloc; Wayne spent busy days rounding up votes in behalf of his resolution. After two months of ceaseless lobbying, he jammed the resolution through by the slim margin of three votes.

Bills for frontier defense won Wayne's favor. By the Treaty of Paris, closing the Revolutionary War, Great Britain ceded to the United States all lands east of the Mississippi and north of the Ohio. Rich river bottoms, wide prairies where grass grew taller than a man, hardwood forests, and marvelous black soil thus came under American ownership. Indians protested that the land was not Britain's to transfer, since, they said, the tract had always been their hunting-ground. Miamī, Delaware, and Shawnee warriors took the warpath. During seven years, from 1783 to 1790, fifteen hundred white men died in seeking to settle this Ohio country; a thousand others fell prisoner to the Indians or were so badly mutilated as to be lifelong cripples. Each year the Americans offered peace, though never on terms favorable to Indian tribes, and yearly the Indians refused to yield. This was the struggle in which Harmar had been beaten. Some white men, even in the halls of Congress, charged that British officials were inspiring Indian resistance, and that the Englishmen in Canada supplied savages with guns and ammunition. Kentucky clamored for a bigger army to crush the tribes.

Wayne supported the bill to raise three additional infantry regiments, each of 912 men, for the duration of the Indian war. These were to be hurried to help Arthur St. Clair, newly named Commander-in-Chief of American Armies. That these regiments were necessary was evident. St. Clair's existing army, hastily recruited from the unemployed, was notoriously inefficient. Good men would not volunteer, and St. Clair had to accept "scourings and sweepings of the slums." Sickly and broken, racked by dissipation and debauchery, disorderly and wholly undisciplined, the little army was entirely unfit for active service in a wilderness. St. Clair was himself suffering from bilious colic, rheumatic asthma, gout, and a chronic cough.

To Wayne's astonishment, a storm of protest greeted the proposal to raise more troops of higher quality. He listened impatiently as two Virginians thundered against the danger of recruiting regulars. Such professionals, the Virginians charged, meant that the United States was growing militaristic; regulars, according to the Virginians, were heavy-footed men, terrified by war whoops. He snorted when the Virginians said that militia recruited from expert woodsmen were far better soldiers than trained professionals; he lost his temper when they said that whites provoked war by molesting Indians and by trespassing on ground that rightfully belonged to tribesmen. "Is this day set apart for oratorical flourishes?" he asked cuttingly.

News of the calamity that befell St. Clair's rabble turned the tide in Congress. On November 4, 1791, St. Clair suffered defeat at what is now the village of Fort Recovery, Ohio. Over two-thirds his entire force were killed or wounded; St. Clair himself had eight bullets pass through his clothes, one clipping his gray hair. Wayne's close friend Richard Butler, second in command, died in the battle, together with more than 600 men; the Indians lost only 150 killed and wounded. The news reached Congress in December. Almost immediately the bill to increase the military establishment passed, by twenty-nine votes to nineteen.

When Wayne was not on duty, he found good company among his colleagues. Tom Hartley, now his warmest friend and closest intimate except Sharp Delany, represented York and Lancaster; Page was here as a Virginia delegate; John Vining, Mary's brother, came from Delaware, and though he was an anti-Federalist, Anthony found "the pet of Delaware" so vivacious and attractive that their friendship ripened, to Mary's delight. Men whom Wayne had known in army service or in civil life mingled with Southern friends of newer standing; Pennsylvania's delegation had many of his old acquaintances. Anthony liked to stroll about the chamber, particularly when he could withdraw to the foyer beyond the rings of members' desks to that carpeted enclosure which Congressmen, remembering legal terms, called "without the bar." Interesting callers thronged there, some as lobbyists to push their pet measures through the House, others as casual visitors to pass the time of day. Wayne could stand and talk, or, in the rare moments when no people came, could gaze out one of the three large windows that gave a vista of the large, open square that stretched beyond the building. Always, before the House rose for the day, the Georgia Congressman arranged a dinner party where, as in his tavern days before the war, or as in his café-society period, he shared in bright, scintillating conversations.

Meanwhile, in Georgia political fevers burned high. Jackson had accepted defeat gracefully, and had taken a seat in the Georgia Assembly—until he discovered the methods that had been used against him. The deeper he probed, the more indignant the slender, ramrodlike warrior became. He demanded that Osborne be impeached. The Georgia House of Representatives heard testimony and, on Jackson's motion, voted to ask the state Senate for impeachment proceedings. Osborne indignantly declined to recognize the Senate's right to try him, on the ground that any offense committed in a congressional election was a Federal matter, but the Senate, accusing him of conduct unbecoming a Chief Justice, threw out his objections. Although Osborne stormed that Jackson was a "paper warrior," motivated by the "rankling murmur of small passions," the Senate proceeded to his trial. When evidence showed over-whelmingly that the Chief Justice was guilty, he took refuge in vituperation. He called Jackson contemptuously "Little Cayenne," and dared him to prove his case. "Come forth, thou brawling pygmy," Osborne shouted, "and say whether you have any cause to doubt my character!" Jackson came forth, and gave ample cause to doubt the honesty of the Chief Justice. The Senate found Osborne guilty, and not only fired him from the Chief Justiceship, but deprived him of the right to hold any other public office for thirty years. Further, it disbarred him as an attorney and fined him $600.

With Osborne out of the way, Jackson went after Mayor Gibbons, and challenged him to a duel. Three shots were fired on both sides, but neither man hit his adversary. Now that his honor had thus been satisfied, Jackson proceeded to unseat Wayne from the national House of Representatives. In vain Congressman Wayne tried to prevent a contest. Immediately upon Jackson's petition for investigation of the case, Wayne took the floor in self-defense. "This delay," he said, "is inexcusable. Mr. Jackson could have preferred his claim many months ago, but he waited. Why? Because he had no evidence, although nearly a year has gone by since the election. He now tries the same arts, the same practices, the same manoeuvers which he employed in the Georgia House of Representatives, bringing petitions signed by people who could neither read nor write, and who are under charge of perjury. I have not the most distant desire to postpone inquiry into the merits of my election, but I cannot refrain from mentioning that no other country in the world would permit such actions as Mr. Jackson has attempted."

Wayne's fellow members voted to defer consideration of the challenge while both parties to the suit sent letters to Georgia for documents to prove their case. Wayne especially sought certificates explaining the excess votes that had been cast and the right of Gibbons to name new election officers. In February, when the case came up again, Wayne asked for three weeks' postponement. On February 27 he sought further delay and

gained an additional two weeks' respite. He tried again, on
March 12, to postpone action, but after a two hours' debate
the motion was defeated.

Jackson opened the contest with a scathing denunciation of
Thomas Gibbons, "whose soul is faction and whose life has
been a scene of political corruption, who never could be easy
under any government." He then went on to produce affidavits
of fraud, bribery, and ballot-box stuffing, pointing out that in
some counties Wayne had more votes counted in his favor than
there were free males over the age of sixteen living in the district. Lewis vainly offered objections, and did succeed in preventing Jackson from telling the story of Osborne's impeachment, but he could not stem the tide. By unanimous vote,
Wayne of course not casting a ballot on the question, the United
States House of Representatives declared that Anthony Wayne
had not been duly elected to membership.

A further motion to give the seat to Jackson brought Anthony some satisfaction, for after hot discussion the House
voted not to do so. It was a close contest. When the roll call
ended, the count stood twenty-nine for seating Jackson to twenty-eight opposed. Then Speaker Trumbull, a Federalist, demanded that his name be called in order that he might vote
against the antiadministration Jackson. The count stood tied,
and by Congressional rules the motion failed, since it had not
gained a majority. The seat remained vacant until the close of
the session. Jackson was urged to run again, but he declined;
soon after, Georgia chose him as a Senator.

3

Even before the House voted to unseat him, Wayne anticipated its action; more than a month before the final vote, he
cast about for a Federal appointment. Richard Peters, worried
over Anthony's loss of fortune, suggested that he apply for
the post of Surveyor-General of the United States, and Anthony had some hopes that Washington might name him to

that office, but when the President appointed another man, Wayne thought again of army life and asked for the vacant job of Adjutant-General. This too failed to eventuate, but almost immediately a greater opportunity offered when Arthur St. Clair, triumphantly cleared by a Congressional investigation, resigned the leadership of the army to become Governor of the Northwest Territory. Wayne joined the scramble of those seeking to succeed St. Clair. From his wide acquaintance with leading politicians, particularly those of the dominant Federalist party, he enjoyed an inside track.

Trained in the tricks of politicians, Wayne electioneered with admirable skill. The President would make the appointment, but the recommendation of states would carry great weight. Anthony sought as much support as he could get. Pennsylvania strongly favored him. John Vining would rally Delaware to his support. To win Maryland, Wayne promised to name Henry de Butts, protégé of an influential Chestertown merchant, as chief aide-de-camp; his powerful friends in Charleston and Savannah would bring two more states into line. Other candidates made the remaining states less likely to support him at the outset, but no other aspirant would control as many votes, and if his ranks held firm, the favorite sons would slowly fade from the picture, leaving him as the outstanding choice. He set himself to talking of the exceptionally high qualifications that a commander-in-chief should possess, and of the essential need that proper army etiquette be employed in selecting a new leader.

The post required an honest man, of unquestioned sobriety, whose courage had been tried and whose experience was wide. Preferably, he should be an officer of resourcefulness and imagination, able to adjust himself to new and unusual conditions, a good disciplinarian and an expert in administration; he should be ambitious but not self-seeking, energetic but not rash, spirited without being foolhardy. In addition, the new commander should also be well known, in order to inspire confidence and to command co-operation. The specifications fitted Wayne, but the President summed him up in uncomplimentary terms. He was, Washington asserted, "more active and enterprising than judicious and cautious. No oeconomist, it is feared. Open to flattery, vain, easily imposed upon and liable to be drawn into scrapes. Too indulgent (the effect, perhaps, of some of the causes just mentioned) to his officers and men. Whether sober, or a little addicted to the bottle, I know not."

If Washington was really unaware of Wayne's heavy drinking, other officials could have resolved his doubts, for Wayne's tavern evenings were well known, and his propensity for self-indulgence was certainly no secret. Washington was no gossip-monger, but Wayne's conviviality could scarcely have escaped the President's attention. It is more likely that Washington, having set down unfavorable characteristics, was unwilling to damn Wayne's chances, and gave Anthony the benefit of a doubt. Having drawn up his specifications, the President then proceeded to canvass the eligible candidates. He drew up a list of twenty men.

The results were not encouraging. For one reason or another, most of the score of men considered were unsuited to the task. Benjamin Lincoln, first on the list, seemed at sixty "infirm and past the vigor of life"; for the same reason Lachlan McIntosh, Dan Morgan, and Maryland's Otho Howard Williams, all good men, had to be dropped from consideration. Steuben would have been an admirable selection, but native-born officers might protest. South Carolina's William Moultrie, sixty-three but still vigorous, stood high, but he was too little known; similar considerations barred Pennsylvania's Hand and Irvine, Connecticut's Jedediah Huntington, Massachusett's squint-eyed Rufus Putnam, and Carolina's Charles Cotesworth Pinckney, this last one of Washington's prime favorites. Virginia's George Weedon and Kentucky's Charles Scott were deemed inadequate and "no enemy to the bottle." Wilkinson had been too short a time in service, and Gist was "doubtful as to activity and attention to duty."

It was not a pleasant prospect, and Washington sought further. Personally, he hoped that Light Horse Harry Lee, Governor of Virginia, would be suitable, but when he sounded out his Cabinet, protest burst upon him. Lee was not upon the list of candidates; his highest active army rank, moreover, had been lieutenant-colonel. If he were named Commander-in-Chief over the heads of men who held higher rank, not a solitary general or colonel would remain in the service; every such officer, considering himself insulted by the promotion of an underling, would quit the army. Political considerations also made Lee ineligible. With the President, Secretary of State, and Attorney-General all from Virginia, the appointment of a Commander-in-Chief from the same state would lead to fears of Virginia domination, particularly as Pennsylvania had only slight voice in the administration. Knox and Hamilton, powerful in the Cabinet, urged that Pinckney be named to army leadership, even at the risk of angering Pennsylvania, and Washington hoped that Lincoln, for all his infirmity, might consent to serve, with Wayne as a brigadier, but neither Pinckney nor Lincoln won sufficient support.

As a last resort, early in April, 1792, Washington sent Wayne's name to the Senate, where, despite the furious opposition of United States Senator James Monroe, who still favored Lee, the appointment was confirmed. Lee protested vehemently. In a letter to George Washington, he told of "the extreme disgust" felt by Virginians at Wayne's nomination. Washington defended Wayne's appointment as the best that could have been made under the actual circumstances. "How far the appointment of G. W. [General Wayne] is a popular or an unpopular measure is not for me to decide. It was not the determination of a moment; nor was it the effect of partiality, or of influence; for no application (if that, in any instance, could have warped my judgment) was ever made in his behalf, from anyone who could have thrown the weight of a feather into his scale; but because, under a full view of *all* circumstances, he appeared most eligible. . . . G.W. has many good points as an officer, and it is to be hoped that time, reflection, good advice, and above all, a due sense of the importance of the trust which is committed to him, will correct his foibles, or cast a shade over them."

Wayne held no illusions concerning his popularity. Realizing that his appointment was due less to his own merits than to the fact that other candidates were unavailable, he knew that he could justify Washington's confidence only by buckling down to business. He spent long hours in consultation with army officers. He studied assiduously about the Shawnees, Delawares, and Miamis with whom he was to battle, and read the few books on them that were available. He talked with traders who knew the West and with missionaries such as John Gottlieb Heckewelder, who spoke Delaware Indian as fluently as he did English and was the War Department's expert on Indian affairs. Tall, sturdy Rufus Putnam had superintended a 1,500,000-acre settlement of veterans on the Ohio near Marietta, and he gave valuable hints to Wayne on Western affairs, while luckless Josiah Harmar stressed the need for discipline and for well-organized supply systems.

Most of the material proved of extraordinary value and led directly to future triumph, but Wayne found it necessary to check his data with exceeding care. Heckewelder, Putnam, and Harmar were authorities upon the Indians whose comments could be relied upon, but Philadelphia teemed with imaginative adventurers whose information was sheer fantasy. Such, for example, was Captain Isaac Stewart, who claimed to have lived among the Wyandots for twenty years and who reported that these natives of the Wabash Valley were red-haired blonds who spoke pure Welsh, and who darted as rapidly as a hundred miles a day to attack white settlements. Stewart talked, with typical frontier exaggeration, of Simon Girty, the Great Renegade, who, he said, yelled Indian songs as he crashed a huge war club against the skulls of white children and who cheered delightedly when Indians burned white women at the stake. He said that Girty was invariably drunk, that the renegade recognized no code of honor and held no oath sacred, but that he could outfight a score of soldiers. Later historical research holds that Stewart, like all frontiersmen, misrepresented Girty, but in Wayne's time the canards were generally believed.

Others reported curious animals living in the Ohio country, huge unknown beasts that stood so high above the ground that a full-grown man might walk erect beneath their bodies. Some spoke of a horrifying two-legged creature, goose-footed and covered with iridescent brown scales, which could leap eight feet high from a standing start and whose breath was fatal to a human being. Many believed, from the discovery of huge bones in the Ohio Valley, that elephants existed in the area. According to the news brought back by Wayne's informants, everything in the West was gigantic. Harmar said that catfish weighed a hundred pounds, that the air was black with birds, and that the prairies were alive with game; huge strawberries, far larger than anything seen in the East, surfeited the stranger; flowers more beautiful than those of coastal gardens lent unbelievable beauty to the Western scene.

Wayne's new duties kept him so busily engaged that he had no time to ride to Waynesborough to see ailing Polly; he was, he explained, far too absorbed in official business even to write her a line about his new appointment until nearly three weeks had elapsed. He was not wholly candid about the reasons for his silence; although all Philadelphia was well informed concerning army arrangements, and although social functions were being held to celebrate his promotion, Anthony told Polly that he could not write earlier because Washington had enjoined secrecy upon the matter, "nor," he added, "have I had an hour of leasure since my being appointed."

Entertainment filled his evenings. Mary Vining, whom Wayne called "my favorite fair," headed a gay group that included the political and diplomatic set where Wayne was invariably present, but in addition to the soirees of that charming hostess, Anthony mingled also with a rival group led by Mrs. Bab McLaine and by Mrs. Margaret Page, wife of John Page of Rosedale. The two circles did not meet, though Anthony professed himself anxious to bring them together. Mary's French mannerisms were too unconventional for acceptance in stricter social groups. "I believe," he assured Mrs. McLaine in telling her about Mary, "that you would have been pleased with each other, although it is not often the case with charming belles, but I know that you possess a good and feeling heart and that you have benevolence enough to draw a friendly veil over the little errors and imperfections even of a favorite." The forty-seven-year-old general, now gouty, heavy, and less agile than of yore, realized, probably for the first time, that he had grown middle-aged when at one of the McLaine parties he met a young girl, "the all-conquering" Miss Alexander, whom he admired, but who to his astonishment obviously cared more for the company of callow youths than for the society of the Commander-in-Chief.

While Wayne was completing his arrangements for campaigning, George Hammond, twenty-nine-year-old British Minister to the United States, shrewdly sized up his potentialities: "General Wayne is unquestionably the most active, vigilant and enterprising Officer in the American Service and will be tempted to use every exertion to justify the expectations of his countrymen and to efface the Stain, which the late defeat has cast upon the American Arms. His talents, however, are understood to be *purely* Military, and abstracted from that profession, not to be either brilliant or solid. In fact during the late War, his Services were rather those of an Active Partizan than of a General possessing abilities equal to the conduct of regular and extensive operations."

Hammond recognized that the United States was by no means satisfied with English policy. Frontier forts in American territory which were to have been surrendered to the Americans had not yet been delivered. British garrisons still held Detroit, Niagara, Oswego, and Michilimackinac. Americans were indignant at the failure of England to withdraw, and demanded that the administration take forceful steps to drive out British troops. "It would not be a matter of Great Surprise," Hammond continued, "should this Army be successful against its Indian Enemies, if a desire of gaining those Posts by force should be either artfully inspired into the Troops, or spontaneously conceived by them. In either of these cases, the discretion or rashness of the Commander-in-chief would finally decide the attempt and I must acknowledge that in the character of General Wayne the latter quality seems most likely to predominate."

The British viewed Wayne's appointment with considerable alarm, realizing that of all the generals proposed for the command Anthony Wayne was most dangerous from the point of view of England's interest.

CHAPTER XVI

Builder of Empire

S<small>T. CLAIR</small>'s defeat had wrecked American morale. Frontiersmen, remembering the atrocities that had followed Harmar's
disaster, fled hastily for safety into Pittsburgh, Wheeling, and
Louisville, or huddled at Marietta and Fort Washington, the
present site of Cincinnati. Indian tribesmen, jubilant at their
greatest victory over white soldiers, banded into a new confederation pledged to drive the Americans from lands north of the
Ohio. In this, they were led to believe, Great Britain would lend
effective aid with munitions and supplies.

Wayne's presence in the West was imperatively necessary.
The remnants of the American Army, undisciplined, undrilled,
and wholly disorganized, were melting away. Soldiers whose
terms had not yet expired had to be whipped back into shape;
recruits had to be secured; guns, uniforms, and ammunition
had to be replaced. Such work was Wayne's specialty, but even
in the darkest days at Valley Forge the need had never been
so pressing as in the spring of 1792. Wayne and his small escort,
a quickly gathered cavalry detachment, headed for Pittsburgh,
where Wayne planned to take active charge of the army, now
called the Legion of the United States—the American Legion—
four regiments of mixed veterans and raw recruits.

As far as York, Wayne rode through rich, rolling, limestone
country, green with growing grain. Thus far, he was familiar
with the scene, for he had ridden these narrow roads in Revolutionary days, when the rough trails were hammered smooth
by the hoofs of hundreds of horses. He had come this way to
plead with Congress for men, money, and supplies; he had followed the road at the beginning of his Virginia campaign; and

at York itself, Tom Hartley's town, he had shot down mutiny. The slow, stocky Germans, stolid and indifferent, who lived west of Waynesborough were well remembered. Beyond York both land and people changed. Wayne was riding into the wilderness; fields were smaller and less luxuriant, for the slaty soil was less fertile than Chester County farms; barns were smaller and less well kept; cabins were infrequent and of ruder style. As the road twisted around hills, small clearings cut from oak and hickory forests replaced the wide plantations that Wayne knew in the East.

Frequently he met enthusiastic welcome from the sandy-haired, freckle-faced Scotch-Irishmen who lived in these backwoods. These were men whom Wayne had known and liked when they were serving in the Pennsylvania Line. They had fought for him in Canada and at Brandywine, at Stony Point and Green Spring and in Georgia; they were the fighters whom Wayne boasted of as second to none as soldiers. But despite their welcome, Wayne caught an undercurrent of resentment, not against him as a leader, but against the cause he represented. These Scotch-Irishmen, who had fought so valiantly for freedom, feared new oppressions from the national Government set up by their valor. They hated Alexander Hamilton's centralizing tendencies; wishing for democracy, they detested the Federalistic trend which limited their liberty. Particularly, they showed anger against the national administration for its bungling of Indian affairs, for its creation of a salaried official class that smacked of aristocracy, for its failure to open the Mississippi to free navigation, and, most violently, for the excise tax of 7 cents a gallon on distilled spirits. This last grievance stirred vigorous resentment, since bad roads and consequent high transportation costs precluded hauling grain to market, and the only economical use that could be made of corn and rye was to convert them into whisky.

To Scotch-Irish frontiersmen, the whisky tax seemed unfair and unreasonable; they looked upon it as one more of the oppressions imposed by Eastern aristocrats upon the helpless West. Many Pennsylvanians living on small farms carved out of the woods resented the seaboard's refusal to tax land held for speculation in the West, which frontiersmen thought a fair means both of raising revenue and of forcing rich men to throw their huge realty holdings on the market; to Westerners, the whisky tax was nothing more than another selfish Eastern scheme to avoid tax burdens. Wherever Wayne passed, he saw tall Liberty Poles standing, bearing streamers lettered with defiance to the whisky tax. Some of these tall, stark flagpoles carried six-striped banners threatening secession of the six interior counties of the state if the detested tax should be continued. Scotch-Irishmen demanded to know Wayne's views upon the tax and upon the plan, which some tough Federalists proposed, of using the United States Army to put down opposition. It was no question for former privates to ask a Commander-in-Chief, but to their delight he angrily denied that citizen soldiers would be used against the populace. "The army," shouted Wayne, "protects the people; it does not oppress them."

The farther west Wayne rode, the more intense the opposition to the whisky tax. At Carlisle, a thriving munition-making settlement, the Liberty Pole stood in the central square in full sight of the newly enlarged stone jail. Even the fashionable set who picnicked at the famous sulphur springs two miles south of the town sympathized with the Whisky Boys who protested against the tax. Dickinson College, the newly established institution where Isaac Wayne had spent a year or two, joined the movement against the measure.

Wayne was now in comparatively unsettled country. The trail grew worse. Cut through the great woods, the thin track narrowed to a mere thread; stumps still stood in the middle of the path, necessitating frequent detours into the forest; big boughs, reaching from the trees on either hand, brushed the sides of the few clumsy wagons that tried to travel; horsemen leaped the loose boulders that blocked the way. Only recently this had been Indian country; even yet, at every mile or two a crude blockhouse marked the strategic points where Pennsylvania militiamen had stood on guard against surprise. Now flocks of wild turkeys, metallic-sheened, seemed the only tenants of the land. Wayne overtook them as they ran along the paths; he passed beneath large flocks roosting in the tree branches interlacing overhead. Few people disturbed their life, for on this yellow flint and black-slate soil settlers eked out but sorry livelihoods.

To Wayne's astonishment, he found a thriving tannery tucked away in the wilderness. An Englishman named Harris, working with Indian assistance, made leather that, to Wayne's practiced eye, was softer and more pliable than any he had ever manufactured in his own tannery. Harris explained that he used the bark of chestnut oaks to give a high, clear color, but that the secret of his leather lay in a special process called brain-tanning, carried on by rubbing a mixture of bear's brains and fat into the skins before they were smoked. "It is not a very cleanly process," Harris confessed, "but the leather is supple and is good for all manner of use and is durable."

Save for the Harris tannery and for a few sorry taverns, the road from Carlisle westward ran through monotonous forest. Chestnut and beech, Weymouth fir and the blue magnolia, which Pennsylvanians called the cucumber tree because of its long cones, mixed with the commoner oaks and hickories; rhododendrons and spicebush shaded the banks of creeks. Wayne noted the absence of wild life in these woods, for though people at the taverns talked much of bears and deer, copperheads and rattlesnakes, birds and small game, few living things except the turkeys were visible. Human beings were scarce, too. On his travels westward Wayne met a few expresses carrying army dispatches from Pittsburgh to Philadelphia, and on one occasion he overtook an emigrant plodding slowly to take up free land in the Ohio country, but otherwise the road was empty. Had it not been for the whisky tax, the tavern-keepers assured him, pack trains of spirits would be common, but the Federalists, they said, had killed that business.

Climbing the steep wall of the Alleghenies, Wayne saw before him the twelve-mile-wide valley of the Glades, a fertile, well-watered land lying as a corridor to the slope of Laurel Hill, the last mountain range upon the Pittsburgh road. This was the region where opposition to the excise was intense, since the imposition of that Federalist tax prevented sending either grain, flour, or even whisky to American markets. According to Glades farmers, Hamilton's policy would inevitably destroy all profitable communication between frontiersmen and the city folk; it could, they said, result only in driving the West into the more welcoming arms of Spain or perhaps into an alliance with the British up in Canada.

Hermon Husbands, once a violent North Carolina Whig, a rioter against the Crown as early as 1770, lived in the Glades and was active in his opposition to the excise tax. Barefoot and clad in dirty clothes, the seventy-year-old zealot rallied his neighbors against what he termed oppressive laws; he gathered them into meetings and harangued them upon the need for setting up a new nation, the New Jerusalem of the Prophet Ezekiel, which should rule the land between the Alleghenies and the Pacific from Hudson Bay to Mexico. Eventually, said Husbands, who now called himself Hutrim Hutrim, the Philosopher of the Alleghenies, the twelve tribes of the New Jerusalem would bring even the United States under their subjection. Wayne had no patience with the ravings of the wild philosopher. He ventured an objection, but Husbands' torrent of mystic oratory was too overpowering for purely verbal opposition. Wayne marked down the old man as a malcontent to be watched; then he rode on, over the desolate Laurel Hill where forest fires had ravaged the woods, to Pittsburgh, metropolis of the West.

Wayne saw the signs of Pittsburgh before he reached the little, tree-shaded settlement. Although the sky was clear, a cloud of smoke rose above the town, due, Wayne was told, to the burning of coal for fuel in almost all the houses. As he drew nearer to the town, he saw its hundred and fifty log houses, and its fifty more pretentious brick and frame mansions, standing on the triangular plain at the point where the Allegheny and the Monongahela unite to form the broad Ohio. Sycamores towering above gave a green appearance that reminded Wayne of a miniature of the capital city he had left. The dusty, unpaved streets where half-wild dogs and unguarded hogs roamed unchecked and where half-grown youths called Whisky Boys galloped at full speed, yelling loudly and firing rifles in the air, destroyed any illusion that the town was as sedate as Philadelphia. Across the Allegheny, too, upon the right, the dark shadow of woods that marked the beginning of the Indian country warned that Pittsburgh was not yet wholly safe.

Wayne, looking at Pittsburgh from a military standpoint, disapproved. The old French fort that once guarded the triangle was nothing but a ruin; Fort Fayette, standing a thousand yards from town on a low-lying marsh below a ridge of hills, was highly vulnerable. Its elevated blockhouses mounted heavy guns and its ten-foot palisades were strong, but the penlike structure was entirely wooden. If stealthy enemies came close with blazing faggots, the fort, with all its magazines and barracks, would go up in flames. Fort Fayette was also much too close to Pittsburgh, where temptations to carouse were numerous. Wayne was no Puritan, but the taverns and bawdyhouses of Pittsburgh repelled him by their sordidness; he thought of the diseases that they spread and of their devastating effect upon the welfare of his men.

He disliked also the town's political beliefs. Most of Pittsburgh, it seemed to Wayne, was touched by "demoncratic" principles. He felt isolated and friendless; he was homesick for the gaiety of the capital. He wrote to Bab McLaine regretting his loneliness and wishing for the presence of the "charming bells" who made up his circle of friends at Philadelphia: "I realy wish that you had possessed the power you mention, i.e. of 'Metamorphosing the troop of *fair* Ladies into a troop of well mounted Dragoons' on the condition that you would undergo a *temporary* change also, and march the troop to this place, when the power of Metamorphosing should cease in *you* and be vested in *me;* the first and instantaneous use I would make of that power would be to transform you into your Natural, and more pleasing form and *sex,* to cheer the heart and bless the arms of your Soldier." His desire for Bab did not lead him into an unfaithfulness to Mary Vining. In writing to Mrs. McLaine he took pains to remind her that his heart was still loyal to Mary, his "favorite fair."

2

West of the Alleghenies, everyone knew that war was certain. Indian attacks increased. Scouts reported that the wilderness was alive with war parties drawn from tribes as far north as Canada and from what are now Tennessee and Alabama to the south. A great Indian Council, to cement a firm confederacy, was gathering at the rapids of the Maumee River, the so-called Miami of the Lakes in northwestern Ohio.

Behind these warlike gestures, Wayne believed, the British pulled the strings. Lord Dorchester, the former Guy Carleton who had been Wayne's Ticonderoga adversary was now Governor of Lower Canada. With John Graves Simcoe, once leader of the green-uniformed Queen's Rangers, who, as Governor of Upper Canada, was in command at Detroit and Niagara, he incited the Indians to resist American advances. They insisted that the legal boundary of the United States was the Ohio River, and promised that the British would assist the tribes to fight the Kentuckians and Pennsylvanians who were crossing into Indian lands. "I am rather inclined to believe," said Wayne, "that we shall never have a permanent peace with the Indians so long as the British remain in possession of our posts on the margin of the Lakes and until the red people experience our superiority in the field, an event that I fondly flatter myself will take place at our next interview."

Simcoe spared no words in voicing his contempt for American leaders. He considered them despicable—corrupt and inefficient, and moved by avarice and vanity. "There is no person, perhaps," he assured Sir Alured Clarke, Wayne's one-time antagonist at Savannah, "who thinks less of the talents or integrity of Mr. Washington than I do." He was certain that the United States would sell out to the French, and he suggested that a Brunswick princeling be set upon the throne of America. If this could not be done, Simcoe urged that Wayne be bribed by a promise of support as Washington's successor. Wayne, he said, "breathed war" and could in no other way be brought to reason.

Wayne doubted that peace could be attained by skillful diplomacy; he preferred that Washington and the administration display force. French revolutionary wars put Britain in a serious predicament, and in this, in conjunction with rumored riots and rebellions within the British Isles themselves, the American Commander-in-Chief saw his nation's opportunity. In letters to friendly Senators, Wayne set forth his position clearly:

"Peace with the Indians is out of the question. The savages are stimulated by British emissaries to continue the war until the Ohio be made the boundary. That once granted, a chain of British forts would immediately be established from the source of that river to the Mississippi. . . . Shall peace be offered at so great a sacrifice of national honor, interest and safety, or shall government demand in the most pointed terms the surrender of the margin of the Lakes? The brilliant and rapid succession of the arms of France, the present complexion of affairs in Ireland and Scotland, all concur in pointing out as a very favorable crisis for making the demands of those posts which by rights ought to have been in our possession nine years since."

Knox would have none of it. Certain that the great mass of Americans, certainly in the East, opposed an Indian war, he held a tight rein on his commander. With an insight that was strangely modern for the late eighteenth century, he warned that white men must exercise great care not to commit acts that could be construed as aggression or as oppression of a weaker people: "If our modes of population and war destroy the tribes, the disinterested part of mankind and posterity will be apt to classify the effects of our conduct and that of the Spaniards in Mexico and Peru together."

Except with land speculators who looked for profits when new lands were opened to settlement, Indian war was not popular. Even in the House of Representatives Wayne had heard apologists explain that Americans had been the aggressors and that Kentuckians had deliberately broken treaties. Pennsylvania's anti-Federalist Senator William Maclay charged

OHIO CAMPAIGN
1792 ~ 1795

flatly that the only reason for war was to keep a large, unnecessary staff of officers employed. Even after the St. Clair disaster, when white resentment flamed high, Easterners calmly reminded warmongers that Indians had refrained from following up their victory. When told of the hysterical flight of settlers into frontier towns, these pacifists retorted that all news came from sources hostile to the Indians and that nothing had been heard of the Indian side of the story.

Washington yielded to the strong demand for peace. At his request, Secretary of War Henry Knox drew up a careful statement of disputes existing between the United States and the Indians living north of the Ohio. To make certain that no partisan element entered into this explanation, the Democratic Secretary of State Thomas Jefferson and the Federalist Secretary of War Alexander Hamilton checked over the paper before it was made public. As a further concession to the antiwar party, Washington dispatched Colonel John Hardin and Captain Alexander Trueman to invite Western Indian leaders to a conference at Philadelphia, ordering that all warlike actions cease until the suggested meeting should be held; he bade Knox write to Joseph Brant, a Mohawk chieftain, urging Brant to intercede for peace, and he hired Captain Hendrick (Aupumut), Stockbridge Indian leader, as an emissary to persuade the hostile Indians to listen to American suggestions. Captain John O'Beal, the Cornplanter, head of the Senecas, and Red Jacket, Seneca orator and statesman, were also approached with attractive invitations to come to Philadelphia.

Brant refused to intercede. "I was offered," he confessed, "a thousand guineas down and to have the half pay and pension I receive from Great Britain doubled, merely on condition that I would use my efforts to bring about a peace. But this I rejected. I considered that it might be detrimental to the British interests, as also to the advantage and credit of the Indian nations, until the Americans should make necessary concessions. Afterwards, I was offered the pre-emption rights to land in the amount of £20,000, currency of the United States, and £1500 per annum." Cynical statesmen were confident that the

British not only matched American offers but were even more generous.

While the negotiations were in progress, both at Philadelphia and later at the Indian Council, Wayne could take no active steps toward war, even though lawless tribesmen continued raids and massacres. While Knox impatiently awaited Brant, Pittsburgh shuddered at a tale of horror unfolded by twenty-two-year-old Massa Harbison, whose home was but a few miles northeast of the city. Mrs. Harbison, who as a child of eight had seen Wayne fight at Monmouth, reported that she and three small children had been captured, and that when one of the children, a three-year-old, had cried, the Indians took him by the feet and dashed his head against a wall. Her five-year-old son was tomahawked because he complained of being tired. Both children were then stabbed and scalped. Massa shrieked, but was struck unconscious by a heavy blow in her face. When she recovered consciousness, it was night and her captors were asleep. Massa grabbed a tomahawk and tried to kill one man, then, barefoot and half-clad, she ran through briers and over rocks, carrying her third child to safety. Hiding by day in hollow, fallen trees, traveling by night, with no food but a small bit of dried venison which she could not chew because of her swollen jaw, she found her way to Pittsburgh. Doctors took no less than a hundred and fifty thorns from her feet and legs, "some completely through her foot"; her body was lacerated in every part. Massa Harbison's recital stirred Pittsburgh to frenzy, but Wayne, bound fast by Washington's explicit orders, held back his infuriated army. Even when he learned that Trueman and Hardin had been killed, he could not launch a punitive expedition, lest he antagonize an Indian Council where Captain Hendrick was pleading for peace. The Legion had to remain calm, though two of its officers bearing a flag of truce had been brutally murdered.

Twenty-four Indian tribes, meeting in the largest Council ever held to discuss American-Indian relations, talked over the entire situation. Hendrick, as a known American agent, was hooted and laughed at as he spoke, so Red Jacket, whom the British called Cow-killer, and Farmer's Brother, both Senecas, took up the American argument. The Shawnee chief Painted Pole refused to listen. In picturesque Indian language, he accused Red Jacket of being in American employ. He threw down a gauge of contempt and defiance at Red Jacket's feet, daring that statesman to accept his challenge. Red Jacket, whom other Indians called cowardly, pleaded for time to consider what answer should be made. "You have talked to us a little too roughly," he said slowly. "You have thrown us on our backs." An hour later, Red Jacket and Farmer's Brother returned to the meeting, recommending peace. Other Indians, egged on by the Shawnees and by huge Buckongehelas, "Giver of Presents," chief of the Delawares, spurned a truce unless the Americans withdrew entirely from all land north of the Ohio and destroyed the frontier forts. If the United States agreed to these extreme terms, the Council decided, a final peace conference could be held when the leaves came out in the spring of 1793.

Brant, still faithful to the British, thoroughly approved. "It sets my heart right," he assured the Western Indians. He warned them that they must not be deceived by the seeming fair words of American leaders, not even those of the President. "General Washington," he said, "is very cunning; he will try to fool us if he can. He speaks very smooth and will tell you fair stories and at the same time, want to ruin us. Perhaps, in a few days, he will send out a flag of truce; that will be only to blindfold us. It will not do to turn about and listen."

Wayne's spies brought early word of the Indian decision. Convinced that only the surrender of territory beyond the Ohio would satisfy either the British or the tribesmen, he urged Knox to reject a patched-up, temporary truce with "savages who have become confident, haughty and insolent from reiterated success . . . and wanton and deliberate massacre." In a long, detailed dispatch to Knox, Wayne set forth a program of aggressive action, starting in the spring:

"I consider the Indian an enemy formadable only when he has a choice of time and ground. In the *fall* of the year he's strong, ferocious and full of spirits—corn is in plenty and venison and other game everywhere to be met with; in the *Spring* he is half-starved, weak and dispirited. Permit me to choose the season for operation. Give me time to manoeuver and discipline the army, so as to inspire them with a confidence in their own prowess . . . authorize me to direct ample and proper magazines of forage,, stores and provisions to be thrown into the advanced posts at the most favorable and convenient periods. . . . I would propose two strong, desultory parties of operation composed of mounted volunteers (and I am pleased to find among them an avidity for this kind of service) . . . these expeditions to take place as soon as the grass in the prairies would answer for pasture . . . should they have no other effect they would distract the Savage Councils and create a Jealousy for the safety of their Women and Children. . . .

"Give me authority to make these arrangements and I will pledge my reputation as an officer to establish myself at the Miami villages, or at any other place that may be thought more proper, in the face of all the savages of the wilderness."

Knox, without authority to approve such warlike moves, referred the suggestions to Washington. He, anxious to avoid war as long as possible, pigeonholed the letter. Wayne received only a formal acknowledgment of the receipt of his plan, with a promise that it would be considered. Not until eight months later did Knox reply, and then by throwing cold water on Wayne's scheme, but by that time it was too late to consider springtime operations.

Much, as it happened, had been gained for the Americans without the use of force. The Council failed to make peace with the United States, but dissension appeared among the federated Indian tribes. The Western Indians, particularly the Shawnees, Miamis, and Delawares, scorned the Six Nations of New York as dupes of the Americans, and refused to treat them longer as allies. Brigadier-General Rufus Putnam, conferring with the Potawatomis and other Wabash River Indians, made a temporary treaty which put them under American protection and so removed them from the ranks of hostiles; Colonel John Francis Hamtramck, Canadian-born officer in the American Revolutionary army, induced the Kickapoos of the Eel River in what is now Indiana to refrain from warlike action.

With Indians at odds with one another, and with the much-feared confederacy shattered, Washington hoped to avert war. Much would depend upon the outcome of the Council to be held when the leaves were all out in the spring. For this meeting the President sought to obtain particularly highly qualified envoys. Brant had expressed a special preference for Timothy Pickering, former member of the Board of War, and so Washington named him on the peace commission; as colleagues, the President asked Beverley Randolph and Major-General Benjamin Lincoln, former Secretary of War and special agent to the Creeks. Again, at Indian request, Washington invited a group of Quakers to accompany the commissioners, not in any official capacity but as "observors," as intermediaries between the envoys and the Indians.

Few at Philadelphia were confident that any lasting good would come of the conference; even Washington himself was skeptical. His Cabinet, frankly pessimistic, advised that "the treaty should proceed merely to satisfy public opinion" and persuaded Washington not to slacken Wayne's preparations for hostilities. Wayne's hope for a spring campaign had vanished; if he fought at all during 1793, he must fight in the fall when Indians were most effective. Indignant that his advice had been disregarded, certain that the crafty Indians had tricked the Government into giving them more time to get ready for a major war, he nevertheless drilled and disciplined his Legion.

3

Wayne thought Washington inconsistent. At Philadelphia, the President had stressed the need for having Wayne hurry to the army, but when Anthony reached Pittsburgh, he was ordered to delay for at least a year. Washington had been persuaded to let Wayne's preparations continue, but when Anthony drew plans, Washington vetoed the proposals. Wayne wanted to move the Legion westward before winter should set in; he wished to cut wide wagon roads through the woods from Fort Washington, the present site of Cincinnati, to the blockhouse forts already built by Harmar and St. Clair along the present Ohio-Indiana boundary, but Washington refused.

Everyone knew that the Indian Council would accomplish nothing except to delay an American advance until too late in 1793 for effective military operations; Washington himself admitted as much, yet, anxious to preserve not only the letter but also the spirit of the truce, the President forbade a general westward movement. Had he allowed Wayne to cut through the heart of the Indian country due north from Fort Washington to the Indian villages, the tribesmen would have been unable to unite effectively, but the President specifically forbade such operations. He did allow one portion of the Legion under Brigadier-General James Wilkinson to go to an advanced post at Fort Washington and another under Brigadier-General Rufus Putnam to winter at Marietta, but the main body of the Legion was required to stay in Pennsylvania.

Wayne swore angrily at Washington's decisions, but he improved his temper by seizing eagerly upon the President's permission to move the troops from Pittsburgh to a more secluded camp. He rode into the wilderness on a four days' trip searching for a suitable site northwest of the Allegheny River; finding none, he drifted down the Ohio on a barge inspecting localities suggested by his Pittsburgh friends. He liked the broad plateaus he saw, for on them could be built hut villages like those of Valley Forge and Morristown; high hills overhanging the riverbanks promised that the camp would be free from swamp fever, but, after all he had heard of Western fertility, he was disappointed to discover that much of the land was thin-soiled and poor in quality. Seven miles above the mouth of Big Beaver Creek, he found a place that caught his fancy. Twenty-two miles from Pittsburgh, it was sufficiently remote so that his men could not slip away to lose themselves in Pittsburgh's distractions, yet it was close enough for him to keep in contact with the city by barge or horse. Returning to Pittsburgh, he ordered a general removal of the army to the new site, which he christened Legionville.

Bad weather held up this movement. An especially dry season lowered the level of the river, never very deep, and pre-

vented transport of men and materials. Nearly a month elapsed
before sufficient rain fell to make navigation possible, but in
mid-November, 1792, the Ohio was deep enough to float big
barges, and on November 28 the Legion moved to its new
quarters. As the barges dropped down the river, a salute of
fifteen guns, one for each state in the Union, voiced the army's
gratitude for "the politeness and hospitality which the officers
of the Legion have experienced from Pittsburgh."

Wayne was now in Indian country. He was made aware of
this at once. While ground was being marked for huts, a raiding
party, dashing from the mouth of Big Beaver, carried off three
horses from the Legion, an insult which Wayne endeavored to
avenge by sending out a punitive detachment to track down the
thieves. The expedition failed, which superstitious soldiers construed as a bad omen, and to make matters worse, a lone Indian
approached within four hundred yards of the Big Beaver blockhouse and took deliberate aim at one of Wayne's captains. The
shot missed, but the Indian escaped.

Preparations for permanent winter quarters met a check. Snow
fell early in December, causing discomfort to the men and
worrying Wayne for fear the Legion must face a winter as
severe as that of Morristown; the river froze, so that supplies
did not arrive. Instead of having his troops in warm quarters
within two weeks, Wayne counted himself lucky to have them
under cover by Christmas; meanwhile the Commander-in-Chief
and his officers housed themselves in tents, as Washington had
done at Valley Forge.

He was more reconciled to his troubles when word came from
Knox praising him for what had been already accomplished.
The letter closed with the reassuring prediction: "Proceed, Sir,
in this line, and you will lay a foundation for your fame."
But Wayne, shivering in the cold, waiting for his new house
with its four big fireplaces to be finished, felt isolated. Despite
the Knox letter, he thought himself unappreciated; he was certain that his pay was much too small. He brooded over the
fact that his income was too meager to let him invite his officer
cronies to dinner as often as he desired; each time he paid
25 cents to post a letter he worried over the failure of Con-

gress to allow him the franking privilege. In confidential chats with his close friends he complained that as Commander-in-Chief of the Legion he actually received less pay than a major-general had received in the Revolutionary War. To relieve the strain upon his income, he sent mail back to Philadelphia by military couriers and he asked his friends in Congress to frank his private correspondence.

On New Year's Day, 1793, which he gave over to writing pathetic letters to his friends in lively Philadelphia, he voiced his homesickness in a message to Tom Hartley: "I am secluded not only from the gay world, but what I yet more esteem and regret, from the small but fascinating society in which we used to mix during the past winter. But whilst you, my friend, are basking in the sunshine of pleasure, I am destined to exist under a cold linnen cover in a howling wilderness with no other society than a Legion in arms perfecting themselves in the dreadful trade of Death."

Not everyone in Philadelphia credited him with loneliness. Strange stories drifted to the capital that Legion officers lived high, with Indian girls as sweethearts. The story of Ensign John Sullivan who ran a procurement service for supplying squaws to army men fitted perfectly with reminiscences that veteran Indian fighters told of Madame Grenadier, sister of the great Indian warrior Buckongehelas, who had been mistress first of a British general and later of an American Revolutionary War commander. There was a half-caste daughter, said Philadelphia gossip, who, while not as charming as the mother, had attractions that Wayne could not resist. She lived in an orchard house close by the fort, where Wayne was frequently a visitor. Almost certainly, the rumor was unfounded. Ever since his days at Golgotha, he had been averse to "black" mistresses. Moreover, at the time of his stay at Pittsburgh and at Legionville, he was too sick a man for love affairs.

Violent flux and bilious vomiting brought constant misery. Dr. John Carmichael, called in to cure the ill, failed dismally. Indeed, the physician's helplessness drove Anthony into a rage; Wayne ordered him away, insisting that he himself was a better doctor than anyone else in Legionville. Against the physician's horrified protests, Wayne, remembering the cure that had proved effective in Georgia, insisted on taking emetics, which, Carmichael insisted, were "both improper and dangerous to the last degree" but which gave Wayne relief. He dosed himself with bark, as he had in his Georgia days, whereby "the tone of my stomach altered for the better," yet it left him weak and thinner than he had been at any time since he returned, an invalid, from the Georgia campaign ten years before. He refused flatly to stay in bed; instead, he rode daily for an hour or two, inspecting redoubts and defenses, making them so strong "that all the Indians in the wilderness could not force them." Though "the monster" in his vitals gnawed him painfully, he continued doing two men's work each day.

Much of his relentless self-driving was designed to conceal his loneliness. That he yearned for comradeship was evident, for even in his formal correspondence his isolation crops out. Stiffly worded general orders, setting forth the parole and countersign for each day's use, are studded with names of people and places which he knew at home; perhaps he felt less remote from society when he heard soldiers call "Vining" to the sentries and when "Alexander" was the proper retort. Hardbitten soldiers from regions where the Welsh were strangers had a hard time pronouncing "Uwchlan" and "Tredyffrin," names of townships near to Waynesborough, but the Commander-in-Chief included these among his watchwords, just as he put in "Maxwell" and "Greene" and, recalling his distant days, "Robinson" and "Griffits" for the girls who no longer wrote to him.

He had by now lost all touch with Polly, who never sent a line. She was, to be sure, seriously ill, so much so that William Atlee, Margaretta's husband, despaired of her life, but she was quite capable of writing. In letters to her son Isaac, soft, plump law student with none of his father's driving energy, she poured forth her heart, condemning his "Earthly father" for carelessness and lack of morals, and praying earnestly that Isaac would turn out a better man than Anthony.

None of his family answered Wayne's repeated appeals for letters; for more than half a year after his departure for the

West, not a line of any sort reached him from Waynesborough. Then Isaac broke silence, asking for advice about continuing his law studies and mentioning his need for cash. Anthony replied to "Mr. Isaac Wayne—My dear friend," suggesting that he acquire a fluent speaking knowledge of both French and German and apply himself diligently to law. It is odd that Anthony failed to realize that he was attempting to shape the life of his son in precisely the same fashion that old Isaac had tried to rule his own. There was not a word of personal warmth in his letter to his son, nor did Wayne send messages by it to anyone except "your Mamma's Sister and friends." Thereafter the curtain of silence fell again, not to be lifted until April 28, 1793, when two letters came simultaneously, from Sharp Delany and from Atlee, telling him that Polly Penrose Wayne was dead. The letters were cold and formal, particularly that from Atlee:

"I am extremely sorry to be the messenger of bad news yet, notwithstanding the task is an unpleasant one, 'tis necessary it should be executed. Your poor Mrs. Wayne is no more; on Thursday evening last at 8 o'clock, she paid the Debt of Nature and bid a lasting adieu to the Cares of this world, after a close confinement of about ten days. Her sufferings were great but borne with a fortitude becoming a good Christian. Her departure was rather unexpected to us, not having discovered any material change for the last few days. Her Exit was, however, as easy as unexpected. She left us without a Groan." As a postscript, Atlee warned that Wayne's mother was also in critical condition. "The old Lady is following fast. She has been confined for upward of two weeks and is not expected to continue with us many days."

Wayne's response was more literary than heartfelt. Not for years had he been close in spirit to Polly; seldom had he bothered to write to her, and then only on cold business matters. In letters to Isaac, to Margaretta, or to such intimate friends as Sharp Delany, he failed to mention his dead wife. He acknowledged Atlee's message by replying, "I feel a sensation not in the power of language to express"; he went on to hope that Heaven would guard and protect his children, now grown up, and closed by bidding Atlee the usual "long and last adieu." Save for a hurried note to Knox declaring that his mind was in "a state of torture for the recent loss of my long loved and ever esteemed *Maria*"—the name that Mary Vining applied to herself—he never again wrote a line or spoke a word referring to his wife.

The Commander-in-Chief was preoccupied with worries about a threatened Indian attack. Joseph Collins, a ship captain turned spy, had come in from the Indian country with alarming news that both Shawnees and English were keen for war. As soon as the leaves were out, said Collins, the Indians, far from holding a peace conference with the Americans, would take the warpath. Nicholas Rosencrantz, another secret agent, learned from friendly Senecas that Collins's information was correct. Wayne rushed the reports by special military express to the capital, hoping that the administration would allow him to break camp at Legionville and move the Legion to Fort Washington in time to make a spring offensive. While waiting for Washington's reply, he redoubled his drills, ordering his dragoons to practice afoot as well as mounted, increasing target practice, and obliging his reluctant troops to dig yet more entrenchments. Waynesborough, farming, the tanning vats, and all the rural occupations of his Chester County life were no longer part of his career; Wayne was a soldier and nothing more.

4

Dandy Tony Wayne, surveying the Legion's clothing and accouterments, said that his soldiers looked like scarecrows. In words reminiscent of his Revolutionary War days, he reported to Knox that the men were almost destitute of clothing. He sent off a hurried call for proper uniforms. "For god's sake, send them forward," he pleaded, "that I may shut their clamorous mouths." The answer satisfied even his exacting wish. Clothing came quickly, heavy and of first-class material, well cut and elegant in style. The 1st Regiment—or Sub-Legion, as the regiments were customarily called—displayed white-trimmed costumes, topped off by a hat which had white feathers and a black panache of horsehair falling from its peak. Hamtramck, its commander, muttered that the white plumes made the soldiers look like "White Hats," the soldier nickname given to the British, but he consented to accept the uniforms when he examined their fine quality. Red-trimmed coats distinguished the 2d Sub-Legion; the 3d boasted yellow decorations and a black horsehair waterfall; the 4th was marked by green facings and black plumes. Each Sub-Legion had an eight-foot-high standard, in its legionary colors, surmounted by a life-sized silver bald eagle. "I promise you," Wayne wrote delightedly to Knox, "that the standards shall not be lost."

Other equipment left much to be desired. Wayne saw that his howitzers, few as they were, were poorly made, and that they were unfit for active use. Supplies stored for army use were hopelessly confused. Breaking open a box labeled "musket balls," he found it full of horseshoes; another supposedly containing infantrymen's uniforms turned out to hold rifle equipment. No reserve of biscuit had been created, although orders had required five tons. Worse still, smallpox ravaged the encampment, together with venereal disease. Carmichael was the only physician available, and there were no nurses. Wayne called for assistance, and pending the arrival of more medical men, he took the liberty to enroll two matrons, at $8 each per month, but these were overworked and without proper drugs.

He had hoped that men on the frontier, many of whom were expert Indian fighters, would at least know how to shoot, but when he tested them, he found that they were slow in firing and inaccurate in aim. They could at best shoot once a minute with their muzzle-loading flintlocks, and this only when they were at rest; in firing as they advanced, the fire was wider spaced. He undertook a scientific study of his muskets. By plugging up the regular touchholes and by drilling a new and larger opening, running obliquely instead of perpendicularly into the barrel, he made it possible for men to load more easily while on the run. "The Eye of the Soldier will therefore be perpetually upon his Enemy and he can load in a full trot without danger of losing any part of his powder, as he will have no other motion but biting off the top and introducing the cartridge into the piece and much quicker then he could load standing in the usual way."

The improvement doubled the speed of firing, but Wayne found that even his best marksmen were unreliable. He started daily competitions between the infantrymen and the crack-shot riflemen, offering a prize of a gill of whisky to the man who made the best record in each branch of the service, with a half-gill prize to the runner-up. He made a canny proviso: "Should the Infantry shot be better than those of the riflemen, then the riflemen will forfeit any claim to bounty for that day's practice." To the riflemen's dismay, the supposedly inferior infantry defeated the sharpshooters in about half the contests. "It's not infrequent for each corps to hit within one or two inches of the center and sometimes to drive it, off-arm, at fifty-five yards distance. The very men who four or five weeks ago scarcely knew how to load or draw a tricker," Wayne proudly wrote to Knox, "begin now to place a ball in a deadly direction."

Much more needed to be done before Wayne could take the field. His troops, enervated by long idleness, were soft in muscle and demoralized. Filled with the mistaken theory that freedom and equality gave each man license to ignore such orders as he disapproved, the men resented Wayne's demand that they do daily drills. They scoffed at his command that they practice firing with blank cartridges and with guns whose flints had been replaced by wooden snappers. They thought his field days silly, protesting vehemently when they were herded out of bawdyhouses and water-front taverns to go skulking through the woods on practice raids against nonexistent Indians. When, in addition, he forced them to dig breastworks and to fight sham battles whenever any civil dignitary or a friendly Indian chief came to visit the encampment, the army's anger flamed to fever point.

Low-type soldiers, recruited from the cities for service in a wilderness, could not stand the physical strain of Wayne's driving discipline. Many ran away, preferring to risk a guardhouse term, together with a stoppage of their small pay of $3 a month, to the unremitting labor ordered by their commander.

Desertions increased, forcing Wayne to offer a $10 cash prize to every citizen who caught a fugitive and an equal sum to any soldier who betrayed a companion's intention to escape. When this failed to halt the exodus, Wayne conceived a scheme for branding deserters on the forehead with the word "coward," but of this Knox would not approve. "Branding," said Knox cautiously, "is a punishment upon which some doubts may be entertained as to its legality. Uncommon punishments not sanctioned by law should be admitted with caution, although less severe than those authorized by the Articles of War." No law nor custom prevented Wayne from executing men who fled from camp, nor from giving them a hundred lashes, well laid on, nor from having them run the gauntlet naked while their comrades struck them with whips and clubs and stones.

His constant stress upon the imminence of Indian attack, intended to keep his men alert, made them jittery. The camp was frequently alarmed. Unexpected noises in the woods at night terrified sentries, who too often threw down their guns and ran to safety. Night after night Wayne was routed from bed by news that Indians were attacking; he formed his men in battle line and ordered a blind charge into the woods against an enemy who was not there. It was admirable practice for the troops, but after they had stumbled forward in the dark, or galloped madly by long detours to gain the supposed rear of the attackers, they grumbled openly that Wayne was a brutal martinet who cared nothing for the comfort of his soldiers.

Even his officers complained of Wayne's severity. Brought up in the lackadaisical tradition of Harmar and St. Clair, many majors, captains, and lieutenants were pleasure-seeking, if not drunken, leaders who looked on soldiering as an easy means for drawing government pay. Wayne thoroughly agreed with Brigadier-General James Wilkinson, his second in command, that "the old officers, with a few exceptions, had contracted ideas of speculation; some were rascals, some drunkards, almost all fools." In letters to Secretary of War Knox, Wayne heaped imprecations upon such men, winning the Secretary's approval of drastic action to weed the army of "drunken and unsuitable characters, whether commissioned, non-commissioned or privates."

The Commander-in-Chief did not delay in making use of his prerogative. He cashiered a number of officers, one for so slight an offense as talking out of the side of his mouth on parade, and accepted the resignation of such subalterns as seemed discontented with the new regime. "I had also an other motive," he wrote Knox in explaining why a good man had been dropped, "to produce a conviction to *some other officers* that if their resignations were offered, they would be accepted." He was intolerant toward those who asked leaves of absence, suspecting that many sought only to escape labor. Over and over again he snapped angrily at officers who sought furloughs, growling that they had "yet to learn the rudiments of war," assuring them that discipline would not be lessened but would be increased, and dismissing them with threats that unless they paid faithful attention to their duty, they would "find no difficulty in being dismissed the service." Evidently, he had entirely forgotten his own constant appeals for vacations during the Revolution.

Some few of the officers certainly merited Wayne's censure. Captain Ballard Smith of the 1st Sub-Legion proved particularly obnoxious. His running feud with his superior Major George Michael Bedinger, veteran of the Revolution, was well known, for Smith lost no opportunity for sneering at the Major as a former street singer masquerading as a gentleman. A noisy row broke out one evening in Smith's tent. Bedinger, summoned by the guard, hurried over, and was met by a bloody and disheveled noncommissioned officer who complained that a woman in Smith's quarters was slashing about her with the Captain's sword. Bedinger, knowing of Smith's contempt, chose not to irritate the Captain by personal interference, but sent a sergeant with a detail of men to take the woman into custody. The sergeant, breaking in, disarmed the girl, but before he could arrest her, she grabbed Smith's pistols and jumped into his bed, from which stronghold she defied the whole army to dislodge her. "I'm the little queen," she yelled, "who can whip you even if you are a sergeant." According to the story later told by the shocked sergeant, she let loose a string of "blackguard and abu-

sive expressions" which even he had never heard; she ended by
threatening to shoot off portions of his anatomy if he came closer
to the bed.

Smith, laughing drunkenly, ordered the sergeant to clear
out, and when the noncom answered respectfully that he was
acting under orders of Major Bedinger, demanded written
evidence that the sergeant told the truth. Unable to produce
the documents and not daring to ignore the orders of a captain,
the noncom withdrew, but came back almost immediately with
Major Bedinger. Bedinger ordered Smith under arrest. The
woman, it developed, was Polly Sprague, wife of one of Smith's
sergeants, who had deserted her husband for the Captain and
was living in Smith's quarters, "which conduct," the court-
martial proceedings quaintly declared, "produces discontent to
the sergeant." Smith's defense was that the girl had been so
cruelly treated that she had fled to him for protection. He further added that Polly had not been legally married to Sprague,
since he himself, "in a moment of gaiety," had read a service
over the sergeant and the girl, and that she was in reality the
wife of a common soldier of the 1st Sub-Legion. Smith needed
her, he said, as a nurse; he could not part with her.

The court-martial thought otherwise; Polly was ordered out
of the Smith tent, but with no other punishment, not even for
the slashing of the unlucky noncom who had tried to quiet her;
Ballard Smith received a sentence of six months' suspension
from the service. His successor was Lieutenant William H.
Harrison, eventually to be the hero of Tippecanoe and President of the United States. Wayne thought the punishment mild,
though he approved the finding. His failure to reverse the court-
martial's decision earned him Smith's intense hostility; in later
months Ballard Smith eagerly joined a cabal which was formed
against "the tyrannical, brutal and incompetent commander-in-
chief."

Yet Smith's punishment was mild in comparison to that
meted out to Sergeant Hopkins, found guilty of beating his mistress and of being abusive to Carmichael. Hopkins was jailed,
and in addition was reduced to the ranks. The difference, perhaps, is that Hopkins had talked back to an officer, and had thus

violated one of the most fundamental of Wayne's military
tenets. Stiffness of discipline was Wayne's chief concern. Any
sign of weakness earned his bitter hostility. When Ensign William T. Payne was caught weeping at the sight of a deserter's
being executed, the boy was charged with drunkenness and was
forced out of the army. When other officers differed among
themselves, he cursed them for taking their cases before court-
martials, and pointed out that dueling was the traditional means
for settling disputes. An officer who vainly offered a resignation
three times, only to have it curtly rejected even though Wayne
had let it be known that such requests were welcome, received
a warning letter that if the application was renewed, the man
would be arrested for mutiny.

No one could predict Wayne's course of action, nor his vacilla-
tions in mind. At one moment he would enjoin his officers to
Spartan living, but almost immediately thereafter he would
assure them that he neither wished nor intended "to deprive
them from participating in every rational amusement." He
pleaded for strict enforcement of all orders, but simultaneously
broke Washington's express orders so that he might squeeze his
old friend Butler's son into a vacant ensigncy, although the boy
was underage and one-eyed. Knox, as soon as he learned of the
act, canceled the appointment, declaring pointedly to Wayne,
"The lives of men are of too much importance to be confided
to the inexperience of raw youth." In Butler's stead, Knox
named Lieutenant Robert Mis Campbell, an energetic dragoon
officer.

Wayne talked economy too, as well he might, since the cost of
maintaining and drilling his new army was more than $42,000,
a huge sum for 1793, but he himself kept several dragoon horses
for his personal use. Here also Knox intervened, in a letter
that pointedly reminded Wayne that "cavalry horses must be
cherished and sacredly appropriated to the service for which
they are designed." When Wayne restored the dragoon horses
only to requisition others from the quartermaster, Knox sent a
second warning upon the subject.

Relations with civilian officers caused much concern. Once,
early in the Revolution, Wayne had insisted that the military

must in every matter except actual campaigning be subordinate to the civil government, but now he violated his own injunctions. He grew angry when Hagerstown, Maryland, authorities arrested messengers whom he had neglected to supply with military passes; and when his men were jailed and their horses requisitioned by Hagerstown people as race horses, Wayne sent peremptory commands that the prisoners were to be released at once. The puzzled Hagerstowners, who had merely carried out Wayne's earnest request to pick up every army man who could produce no proper credentials, wondered how they had offended, but they freed their prisoners and apologized for their actions.

Sarcastic Alexander Addison, Scotch-born Pittsburgh jurist, clashed with the Commander-in-Chief upon the point of whether the civil law or military rule should be supreme. When Addison freed a man from military service on the pretext that the recruiting officer, Captain William Faulkner, had enlisted the soldier unfairly, Wayne sharply ordered Addison to mind his own business. The Judge replied by charging that Faulkner had forged the enlistment paper. Wayne ignored the evidence, and ordered that civilians cease to interfere with army men. He demanded, in effect, the right of extraterritoriality for soldiers in the Pittsburgh area. This Addison, not unnaturally, refused, but he offered to refer the case to the Pennsylvania Supreme Court, which was scheduled to convene in Pittsburgh two months later. Wayne rejected the suggestion, but sent Faulkner, with a detachment of armed men, to take the recruit to camp by force. Addison, warned that Faulkner would shoot any man who resisted, gave up the soldier to the army. The whole West was in virtual rebellion against the excise tax. Captain Faulkner, fighting angry because thirty masked Whisky Boys had threatened to tar, feather, and castrate him unless he stayed neutral in the excise troubles, waited only for a good excuse to shoot up the town. Addison played safe by surrendering the soldier.

Quiet, diffident George Clymer, Philadelphia merchant whom Wayne had known at Ticonderoga, almost dragged Wayne into the excise quarrels. Appointed supervisor-general of excise, Clymer came West. Some strange quirk led him to think that he would be safer in disguise, and so he passed himself off as

Secretary Knox until, alarmed lest a Federalist Cabinet member might be roughly handled, the frightened excise supervisor came to Pittsburgh in the guise of a servant to a Legion paymaster. Clymer entered the Indian Queen Inn at Pittsburgh treading timorously, wearing a battered slouch hat, and pretending to have no interest in political affairs. No one recognized the signer of the Declaration of Independence, but he heard enough to convince him that Pittsburgh was balancing on the brink of rebellion. Next morning he hurried out to Legionville to take shelter with the army, but Wayne persuaded him to go back to the inn. Clymer returned to Pittsburgh with Wayne and a dragoon escort in his proper role of chief excise officer of Pennsylvania. Word spread quickly of their coming. Officers of the Legion, at the Indian Queen in violation of their leaves, ran hastily to cover. Chairs were overturned; noise was tremendous; general hurly-burly ensued. Clymer, hearing the confusion, thought that bandits were upon him. He fled in terror, watched by the guffawing Wayne, until he disappeared in the darkness on the road to Legionville. As long as he remained in Pittsburgh's danger zone, Clymer changed his lodgings nightly until, after a long, worried week, he departed with a heavy dragoon detachment for the East.

The Clymer episode was Wayne's only connection with the Whisky Rebellion, except for the inconvenience caused by the stoppage of mails between Philadelphia and the Legion. He waited impatiently for rain to swell the river so that his barges might float downstream toward Fort Washington. Repeatedly he practiced embarkation maneuvers so that when the Ohio proved deep enough, his Legion would lose no time in moving off; he had the barges calked and painted; he ordered heavy baggage packed for ready shipment. When at last, in April, 1793, Knox sent permission for the Legion to depart as soon as the river filled, he sounded depths impatiently. After a year in the vicinity of Pittsburgh, each additional day of waiting seemed interminable.

CHAPTER XVII

Down the Ohio

B ANDS played and banners fluttered in the warm spring wind as the Legion moved away from winter quarters. Huge fleets of barges, headed by boats bearing the right-wing rifle corps, dropped down the Ohio, each precisely in its leader's wake. Wayne, resting in the shade of an awning on his barge *The Federal*, watched approvingly. During the latter weeks at Legionville, his restlessness had grown, for the two months set by Secretary Knox as the probable duration of the winter quarters had lengthened into five; Wayne had begun to wonder if his troops would ever be allowed to go forward. But now on the last day of April, 1793, he was again upon his way.

The scenery was as charming as that which he had seen upon the Hudson when he was traveling toward Ticonderoga. The river, curiously white upon one side where Monongahela water flowed and deep green on the other from the less turbulent Allegheny, passed between high, timbered banks. The trees seemed veritably alive with turkeys, great ashy-gray birds with copper-colored necks; the woods were filled with deer which stood nervously watchful on the shore as the flotilla passed. Wayne forbade the men's taking potshots at the game. Roving Indians, peering from hilltops overlooking the river, might think such shots the prelude to attack and fire down into the barges. Under strict orders from Washington and Knox not to provoke hostilities, Wayne was overcautious.

Soon after leaving Legionville, the fleet moved past Fort McIntosh, the first army post on the right bank of the' Ohio, where in 1785 a treaty with the Indians had won for the United States the right to settle in the Northwest Territory.

This was the treaty which Indians now repudiated on the
ground that white men, by making unimportant Indians drunk,
had laid claim to land the signers never owned. Wayne paid
slight attention to past history; he was more concerned with
watching how the oarsmen steered the barges through the narrow gorge that marked the most northerly point of the Ohio,
where two chains of mountains hemmed in the stream and where
small islands so narrowed the channel that boats leaped forward
in the swift current. Rocks in the river required careful watching, but the army passed safely through, and, favored by a
strong current of perhaps three miles an hour, the barges passed
downstream over the Pennsylvania line into new territories.
Virginia's red soil stretched now upon the left; the right was
the vast Northwest Territory from which the Indians excluded
all settlers.

Wheeling, beautifully perched upon a high bank, was the first
important settlement along *La Belle Rivière*. The rough frontiersmen who lived in its dozen log houses insisted that their
town, only a few weeks old, was destined to become the Western metropolis. Already, though they had but two small stores
scantily furnished with trade goods, they enthusiastically
planned wide, smooth-paved highways to the East. Wayne
spent no time at Wheeling; its reputation as a wild, riotous,
outlaw settlement had been so sedulously spread by Pittsburgh
rivals that he feared to expose his Legion. He was anxious to
press on to Marietta, where Rufus Putnam waited with a Sub-
Legion and where ample stores of provisions and supplies
would be available.

From Wheeling to Marietta, few men were visible. The
barges passed through wild, unsettled regions where Wayne
saw lovely vistas of flower-covered hills. From the river he
glimpsed forest glades where magnolias bloomed and where,
in this early spring, honeysuckle spread sweetness on the air;
here and there, where forests thinned and there were open
prairies, he saw the meadows green with waist-high grass. Huge
flocks of birds, particularly pigeons and wild turkeys, became
visible; the river, scouts declared, was full of fish, not only
those hundred-pound catfish of which Wayne had heard but

also white perch, whose noise, frontiersmen solemnly averred, prognosticated rain. Great rock masses on the shore stood out in bold relief against the brilliant green of tulip trees. Wayne's barge carried him to Marietta, at the mouth of the Muskingum, where three hundred settlers hovered about the three log blockhouses to welcome the Commander-in-Chief. As the awninged barge with its twelve brightly painted oars, each lettered with the boat's name, touched the riverbank, fifteen cannon shot welcomed the Legion. Fort Harmar's garrison, brightly dressed in gala uniform, cheered Wayne as he landed; the New Englanders who had taken up land in the vicinity offered a feast in his honor.

The welcome cheered the General, but there were undertones of sorrow in his mind as he remembered that this site was one picked out by his old friend Richard Butler before that unfortunate soldier had been killed. He could not think of Marietta as a place of joy, nor was he happy there. He thought of the town primarily as a military center, and asked searching questions about its strength and concerning its strategic value. He seemed pleased to hear that the Muskingum was navigable for small boats to a point within a few miles of where the headwaters of the Cuyahoga started, so that by only short portages water traffic could be carried on between the river and Lake Erie. He beamed approvingly upon Marietta's Campus Martius, with its broad parade ground, its fine deep brick-lined well, its capacious storehouses and barracks. But when the proud New Englanders showed him their thousands of fruit trees, many of them in blossom, their mulberries and their vineyards, their vegetable patches and their mills, he grew restless to move on. No doubt there was a touch of homesickness in his emotions. The rich land reminded him of his Sabine farm, a memory he was resolved to erase entirely from his thoughts now that he was again a soldier.

Wayne signaled for the Legion to continue down the river. He passed the Little Kanawha, on the Virginia shore, caring little that it could be ascended fifty miles by barges like *The Federal*, for Virginia was white man's territory and needed no conquest, but he listened with interest to a hunter's story of a spring close by which burned whenever it came in contact with fire. It was his first knowledge of what would later be called petroleum, but Wayne paid only the attention that one gives to romantic travel yarns.

Gallipolis, now three years old, proved more entertaining. Its hundred and fifty residents, most of them French emigrants brought over to America by lavish promises of fortunes to be quickly won, made merry. Their square log houses, perched on a plateau above a morass of standing water, were wretched and uncomfortable, their little city lacked the trim cleanliness of Marietta, but the people were sociable and friendly. Old Frenchmen in their large crimson caps danced after dinner with wives who still wore the costumes of Bourbon times; younger settlers gave pleasant, vivacious entertainment to Wayne's officers. The General would have gladly stayed to chat with gay folk like these Gallipolis people, and especially to admire the work of their goldsmiths, watchmakers, sculptors, and glass-makers; he liked their gardens, laid out in the European style; he enjoyed their conviviality. But he could not linger; he was anxious to reach Fort Washington and set up his new head-quarters.

Thirty-six hours after leaving Gallipolis, the Legion reached the Great Scioto, a smooth, slow-flowing river navigable for two hundred miles. Fine, well-watered meadows stretched on either side; an island in the river was already lush with young grain; flowering trees gave excellent shade to the thirty cabins clustered where the rivers met. Yet for all its charm and beauty this Scioto region was a place of death. Before Wayne's coming, no less than a hundred and fifty white men had been massacred by Indian raids; the site was accounted one of the most dangerous on the frontier. Other Americans had been slow to settle, but a band of Swiss, attracted by the white mulberry trees, had moved in through Kentucky, to start silk-raising as an industry.

Wayne pressed on; he came to Limestone (now Maysville), a small but sprawling settlement at the foot of a steep hill where flatboats customarily unloaded to avoid the waterfalls that lay below. The town, already decaying because of the idleness of the residents, marked the river terminus of a land road through Kentucky.

Cincinnati was not far distant now. Twenty hours after pushing off from frowsy Limestone, *The Federal,* passing for hours through flat country where the Ohio for once flowed straight, came to Columbia, at the junction of the Little Miami. Columbia was a thriving town. Major Benjamin Stites, an old New Jersey officer whom Wayne had known at Monmouth and Morristown, lived here, governing a 20,000-acre land-development project, and there were other men whom Wayne knew well. He lingered gossiping with Stites while the flotilla passed onward toward Cincinnati; then, urging his oarsmen to greater effort, he swept triumphantly to Cincinnati to accept the greetings of the populace. Eleven hundred people crowded the high hills to watch the army barges come to town. Fort Washington, at the east end of the settlement, gleamed with fresh red paint; the square of long, low buildings where army mechanics labored and where food was stored was bright with flags and bunting. Wilkinson's Sub-Legion, lining the shores, set up a hearty cheer as Wayne approached; they fired a feu de joie; cannon boomed a fifteen-gun salute. Wayne's bandsmen answered with clash of brass and music from the fifes and drums.

Cincinnati, red-painted like Fort Washington, made much of Wayne. Arthur St. Clair, Governor of the Northwest Territory, stood waiting on the shore with Federal Judge John Cleves Symmes, whom Wayne had known in New Jersey. Mrs. Symmes, the former Susannah Livingstone, gay, saucy belle of Morristown days, smiled cordially at her old acquaintance. Leading merchants of the town, forgetting their vendetta against the army for the Legion's refusal to be ruled by civil law, entertained Wayne and his officers at an elaborate banquet. In the gay Cincinnati entertainments Wayne and St. Clair, each now supreme in his separate field, ended their long-drawn-out quarrel. Cincinnati was less inhibited than Pittsburgh. Heckewelder had told Wayne that it teemed with idlers and that its only counterpart was Sodom; it was a widely accepted comparison. Wayne's Legionnaires were not easily shocked, but the Cincinnati license was too broad even for them to bear with equanimity. "A man possessed of the least tincture of morality," said a sergeant, "must wish his stay here as short as possible."

Certainly Wayne felt that Cincinnati was no place to barrack the Legion. After a day or two of Cincinnati life, he hastily marched his men to safer ground. He knew that his new camp was much too close to the village, "filled with ardent poison and caitiff wretches to dispose of it," but he found no other suitable site between the two Miamis in the vicinity of the Ohio "except near some dirty village." He called his new cantonment Hobson's Choice, because, he said, he had no alternative. Arriving at Hobson's Choice on May 4, 1793, he remained there until October 7, waiting, as usual, for instructions from Knox and Washington.

2

Discord still ran rife. Wayne's ironclad discipline and his ruthless use of whip and jail silenced, if it did not utterly prevent, laxness in the rank and file, but there were subtler, and indeed more dangerous, dissatisfactions among the officers. Men of different rank and varied terms of service jealously guarded their special privileges; just as Revolutionary officers had watched for fancied insults, so the bored Legionnaires became suspicious of each other. Young men who knew little of army etiquette took their cue from those of higher status; they quarreled bitterly over who should take the van in practice marches or who should lead the right wing (the preferred position) on maneuvers. Envy, enmity, and hatred burned hot.

Factions speedily sprang up, centering about the personalities of the high-ranking generals. The soil was fertile, for Wayne, who had come with high hopes of pleasant association with his old friend Brigadier-General James Wilkinson, soon came to question the loyalty of his second in command. The two men, each aggressive, vocal, and intolerant, each an eager, quick-thinking fighter who could not stand boredom, swung from friendliness to angry hostility. Though each cloaked his feelings under a surface coating of formality, the Legion sensed their hatred. In mess hall and in tavern subalterns gossiped eagerly. In public the underofficers took sides, some applauding Wilkinson when the latter politely told Secretary of War Knox that Wayne knew next to nothing about Indians, others cheering Wayne when, as major-general, he forced Wilkinson, the brigadier, to cease correspondence with the Secretary. The Brigadier's partisans were delighted when Wilkinson rebuked his commander for making public certain secret-service documents; they laughed loudly when he cleverly disclaimed all thought of arrogance or impropriety in his remarks.

Generally speaking, officers of longer service sided with James Wilkinson, particularly since they disliked Wayne's bossiness; junior officers, dependent upon Wayne's favor for promotion, more often favored the Commander-in-Chief. The division was not ironclad, for the Legion was rent also by political divisions, the Federalists supporting Wayne and the "demoncrats" backing Wilkinson. Some leaders, too, who might normally have opposed the Commander-in-Chief doubted Wilkinson's integrity, suspecting him of dickering with Spain for questionable purposes.

Men disciplined by either general, whether justly or otherwise, joined the clique of his rival. Ballard Smith, for instance, when restored to service following his six months' suspension, became one of Wilkinson's most enthusiastic supporters, winning praise from that general both for sobriety and for character. Wilkinson's special enemies became Wayne's fast friends. Chief among this group was Captain John Armstrong—no relative of the hero of Kittanning—a veteran Pennsylvania officer who had joined the army after the Monmouth campaign. He had led a secret expedition up the Missouri River into Spanish territory and had explored the Indian country along the Wabash. His escape from an ambush where all of his command but seven men were killed was a frontier legend. In careless conversation, Captain Armstrong let slip remarks which Wilkinson chose to misinterpret as slanderous, and though the Captain vainly tried to explain his true meaning, Wilkinson put him under arrest. Ugly rumors that Armstrong had stolen army horses by burning off the military brand and substituting his

own, and that he had terrorized civilians, were then raked up
by Wilkinson and used to threaten Armstrong with court-
martial. The Captain asked time to call defense witnesses, but
the Brigadier would not consent. He hurried Armstrong before
a packed court on charges of speculation, theft, fraud, usurpation
of power, and insubordination.

Wilkinson's frightening list of charges awed the Captain, for
Armstrong, even after court-martial proceedings had begun,
was allowed to escape trial on condition that he quit army service. The Captain did so, but later he regretted his haste and
appealed to Wayne for reinstatement. The Commander-in-
Chief promptly appointed him to command a special corps of
mounted volunteers. Later, when Armstrong became sheriff of
Cincinnati, the grateful Captain arrested several of Wilkinson's
clique on trumped-up charges.

As an underling Wilkinson had less opportunity to show his
favor, for a brigadier cannot overrule the actions of a major-
general. Wilkinson's partisans sniped at Wayne's special favorites, either by bringing trivial accusations that would cause annoyance, if not conviction, or by an attitude of sneering contempt
that brought the victim into ridicule. Captain Isaac Guion, a
Wilkinson man, charged Captain Edward Butler, a Wayne
protégé of Light Infantry days who was now acting deputy
adjutant-general and inspector-general, with partial, unjust, and
unmilitary discharge of his duty, but when Wayne angrily demanded specific proof, Guion begged leave to postpone the
matter. Wayne pretended to be satisfied; in reality, he waited
only for a more convenient time to punish Guion for presumption.

John Sullivan the pander, another Wilkinsonian, took Henry
De Butts as his victim. Relying on Wayne's oversight in not
having definitely named De Butts as an aide-de-camp, Sullivan
pointedly ignored De Butts, and when the latter ordered Sullivan under arrest for insubordination, the Lieutenant professed
official ignorance of De Butts's rank. Technically, Sullivan was
in the right, but there was no doubt that he deliberately insulted
the aide. Wayne, furious because the court-martial with most
painful courtesy suggested that he make a formal announcement

of De Butts's appointment, did so, but he reprimanded Sullivan.

In less dramatic ways, Wilkinson's crowd showed contempt for their Commander-in-Chief. Although Wayne was only forty-eight, they referred to him in private as Old Tony; they joked about Tony Lumpkin; they jeered at him as "Mars" or the "Old Horse"; when they spoke of the "General" they invariably meant Wilkinson. Everyone knew what was going on, but no one could devise a means for softening the hatreds. Knox thoughtfully kept Wilkinson and Wayne as far apart as possible, flattering each by encouraging words; Federalist legislators buttered Wayne while the Opposition soothed Wilkinson; letters of friendly interest, often beginning "I am your true friend" but going on to insinuate that everyone else was an evil-minded enemy, poured in by every post. New men came to camp, carefully chosen from those whom Knox knew would be gentlemanly if not nonpartisan. Tom Posey, Wayne's friend at Stony Point and in the Georgia campaign, arrived as a new brigadier, assisting Wilkinson and Wayne, and so did Dr. Scott, Wayne's electioneering officer in the campaign for Congress. These were buffers, lessening the bitterness of conflict, but they could not end the backbiting and wirepulling.

Lieutenant Daniel of St. Thomas Jenifer, a Marylander with a curious middle name, proved singularly disturbing. Brusque, quick-tempered, and heedless of the feelings of others, he swaggered in mess rooms, to the annoyance of his fellows. He celebrated Christmas Day by telling Lieutenant Nathaniel Huston that the latter was no gentleman, and followed that insult by another quarrel in which he killed an ensign. The circumstances were so unpardonable that the matter came to Knox's attention and Wayne was obliged to make an official investigation. No sooner was Jenifer cleared on this charge than he was reprimanded for drunkenness, but when this was done, he celebrated by another drunken bout in which he characterized his fellow officers as cowards and damned rascals. This time in Wayne's view he went too far, since he spoke disrespectfully of De Butts, and so Jenifer was dismissed from the service. For some inscrutable reason, Jenifer's associates signed a round robin asking to have him pardoned.

Another Maryland boy, Ensign Campbell Smith, increased Wayne's worries. Arriving with a letter from his father, a prominent Baltimore attorney, in which the latter bade the Commander-in-Chief keep a parental eye on the lad, Smith claimed appointment as judge-advocate of the Legion. Wayne, as it happened, had another candidate, Ensign Charles Hyde, a Vermonter. Vermont's delegates to Congress firmly supported Hyde, and Wayne, weighing the political influence, promised him the place. A few months later, when Hyde's capacity was seriously questioned, Wayne regretted that he had not named Campbell Smith.

Still another of the virulent anti-Wayne coterie could have been won to Wayne had the Commander-in-Chief been more generous in making appointments. Captain Thomas H. Cushing, whose service started before Brandywine, was one of those unfortunates whose chances for promotion had been lost because he was a captive in a British military jail. Returning to duty after the Revolution, Cushing served as captain, but he considered himself entitled to a majority as soon as a vacancy occurred. But when an opportunity came, Wayne pushed two others over Cushing's head, to the anger of the injured Captain. Cushing hurried a protest to Wayne, but to no avail; he then lost his head and threatened to appeal to Wayne's superiors at Philadelphia. Wayne disregarded the threat, but Wilkinson promised to pull wires in Cushing's interest. Cushing became his right-hand man.

The Ballard Smith-Tom Cushing-Campbell Smith contingent did everything in its power to sabotage Wayne's plans. By letters home they undermined confidence in what the Commander-in-Chief was doing; adroitly they hampered Wayne's efficiency in the field. During the entire campaign against the Indians, the Legion faced the task of reducing not only open Indian opposition and covert British hostility, but also the hidden machinations of disgruntled officers.

3

Wayne's situation was perplexing. By Washington's express command, he could not push an army forward lest the truce be broken, yet everyone expected that war would certainly break out. He felt, then, that he must make adequate preparation, not only by drilling and maneuvering his highly trained Legion but also by putting his advanced defenses into good condition. Chief among these was the chain of three forts leading north into the Indian country. Twenty-five miles above Cincinnati, on the east bank of the Great Miami, stood Fort Hamilton, built by St. Clair. Two hundred soldiers garrisoned here manned the four big bastions and kept watch from the cannon platform while men cut hay upon the extensive plain that lay about the fort.

Fort St. Clair, set up by Wilkinson near a massive oak that dated back to the time of Christopher Columbus, was the second link in the fortified line of communications. This, like Fort Hamilton, was chiefly a storage stockade, and was particularly well planned because of its numerous clear, cool springs and the small brook that flowed near by. The present town of Eaton is close to the site.

Third, and most advanced, of the posts was Fort Jefferson, forty-four miles to the north, where St. Clair had made his headquarters. This was in flat country, but a near-by range of low hills caused Wayne to fear for its safety. If Indians or British planted cannon on the hilltops, Fort Jefferson would surely fall.

Wayne opened sixty-foot-wide roads, passable for army convoys, to all these posts. He ordered huge amounts of stores to be laid up at Fort Jefferson, the nearest stronghold to the Miami and Delaware villages on the Maumee River; he grazed large herds of cattle on the prairies north of Jefferson; and he reinforced his garrisons. These actions clashed with a promise made by Wayne to Cornplanter that "he would not advance nor establish any new posts in front of those we now possess."

Although Wayne made no fortifications and did not strengthen his defenses, Cornplanter complained that he was acting contrary to the spirit of his promise. Wayne admitted, in confidential notes to Knox, that his arrangements were preparatory to a forward move, and added that the steps already taken were not so great as those he had in contemplation.

Knox went half-heartedly through the motions of restraint. He issued a formal order forbidding any movement of troops "other than shall serve as escorts for the *ordinary* quantity of provisions for the advanced garrisons," leaving to Wayne the determination of what that amount should be and of how many men the advanced garrisons should consist. But at the same time that he thus went on record as observing the truce, Knox advertised in Philadelphia papers for bids for supplying rations to the Legion not only at Fort Jefferson but also at the Maumee Rapids in the Indian country. Undoubtedly he too anticipated a successful war.

Wayne, as always, preferred aggressive action. Once more, in warning Knox that war parties of Creeks and Cherokees were on their way to join the hostile Indians, he pleaded for permission to attack the Maumee villages. A frontal movement from Fort Jefferson, combined with a swift raid against the Indian flank, he assured Knox, would win an easy victory. This time Knox not only refused to countenance such a breach of the truce, but he ordered Wayne to bring back some of the soldiers already sent to Jefferson. Reluctantly, Wayne withdrew 184 men from the advanced posts, leaving 566 to guard the stores.

Knox was leaning over backward in his desire to avoid aggression. The leaves were all out and the time had come for the long-awaited Council of 1793 between Americans and the Indian confederation. Pickering, Randolph, and Lincoln, who had spent the winter poring over records of past treaties, studying old maps, and memorizing speeches delivered long ago by white men and Indian delegates, were ready to go forward to discuss peace. The Cabinet held long sessions to discuss what terms should be proposed; Washington prepared elaborate instructions for the guidance of his envoys.

Wayne was positive that no good would result from these

discussions. While the three envoys were preparing to attend the Council, he arranged a spy service to get advance information on Indian designs. Chief among his agents was William Wells, a Kentuckian who had been captured by the Indians when a boy of twelve. He had been adopted by the Miami tribe under the name of Blacksnake, but had now enrolled among Wayne's scouts. His record was already a lengthy one of war against the whites, since he had fought against both Harmar and St. Clair. As son-in-law of Little Turtle, war chief of the Miamis, he was a particularly effective secret agent. Wayne, knowing that no important action could be taken until the Council ended, sent Wells off on his mission and waited for the outcome of the talks.

In April, 1793, Pickering, Randolph, and Lincoln, accompanied by Captain Hendrick, Knox's Indian spy, set out to attend the conference. They carried with them instructions to state that the United States was willing to pay more money for lands already ceded, but that the Ohio River could not be the final boundary. No one at the capital seriously believed that the conference would be successful. American terms were too much at variance with Indian desires, and too little time was afforded for deliberations. The meetings were to be held chiefly to satisfy public opinion; while they were progressing, Washington told Secretary Knox, Wayne might push preparations for active war, provided the Legion did not advance.

The British were not lulled into security. Pennsylvania's action in making fortifications at Presqu' Isle, the present site of Erie, warned them that even should peace be signed with the Indians, the Americans, by garrisoning a fort on the Great Lakes and by the probable creation of a fleet on those waters, would challenge British rule. Rumors in Detroit that Wayne planned to march to attack that post, while devoid of truth, led the English to increase their garrisons; further and true reports that Wayne was widening roads into the Indian country spread alarm among the Indians. The British laid odds that the formal Council would never be held.

Lincoln, Pickering, and Randolph, arriving at Simcoe's quarters at Niagara, foolishly boasted that the United States, having

no real hope of peace, planned only to split the Indian confederacy by forming an alliance with the Six Nations of New
York against the Western Indians and the British. It was a
careless confession to make in such a place, because it held the
Indians firm to their allegiance to Great Britain. Even the Cornplanter, usually one of the strongest pro-Americans, turned
against his friends. He refused to call upon the commissioners,
although they had escorted his son from Philadelphia to Niagara. Simcoe jubilated at the ineptness of the three Americans:
"These gentlemen have much of that low Craft which distin-
guishes and is held for wisdom by people who, like the subjects
of the United States, naturally self-opinionated, have a trifling
share of Education—and indeed, by what I hear, their whole
behaviour has been of this Cast." Simcoe kept the commissioners
at Niagara until the Indians should be ready to receive them;
meanwhile he sent agents to the tribes encouraging them to
stand firm in their demands. For six weeks, while the British
and the Indians perfected their agreements, the three envoys
waited helplessly.

Brant came to ask Lincoln, Pickering, and Randolph why
Wayne's warlike measures were progressing. Pickering, whom
Simcoe termed a "violent, low, philosophic, cunning New Eng-
lander," replied by assuring Brant that since Washington had
expressly forbidden all aggression, the Indians must be mistaken. He volunteered to send a letter to Secretary Knox re-
questing him to stop Wayne from any advance. Brant also used
the opportunity to sound out the envoys concerning their willingness to agree upon the Ohio River as a boundary, and
learned that they were under orders not to agree to any such
proposal.

Even so the federated tribesmen might have been willing to
compromise had not the hothead Shawnees and Delawares
turned intransigeant. Believing that the Americans would be
helpless against an Anglo-Indian alliance, and angered by news
that Georgians had launched another unprovoked attack upon
the Creeks, the Delawares and Shawnees demanded war.

On August 11, 1793, nearly two weeks after the deadline
originally set for the completion of the treaty, the commission-

ers came to the reluctant conclusion that no conference would
be held. They sent messages to Washington, Knox, and Wayne,
informing them of the failure. News that the Council was not
to be held flooded in upon Wayne from several quarters simultaneously. A dispatch hurried to Pittsburgh from Niagara met
another relayed through Knox at Washington. Both messages
were put upon a fast light bateau and hurried downriver to
Hobson's Choice. On September 11, Wells, Rosencrantz, and
the Seneca chief Big Tree rushed in with news that the Indians
would go to war within two weeks.

The Commander-in-Chief had anticipated the news. Anxious
to be ready, impatient to advance, Wayne had already requested
Isaac Shelby, the Kentucky governor, to send him 1,500
mounted militia. He was not enthusiastic about using volunteers,
believing that militia were undisciplined and unreliable, but
Congress had insisted upon it. Wayne calculated that it was
actually more expensive to employ 1,500 highly paid Kentucky
volunteers for only four months than to hire an equal number
of regulars at $3 monthly for a three-year enlistment. In an
ironical note to Shelby, he expressed the hope "that the virtuous citizens of Kentucky are actuated by principles paramount
to pecuniary reward." Kentucky leaped at the chance to make
war at high pay. Shelby reported that he could get 2,000
volunteers, and that, if well officered, they could march into
any part of the enemy's country and lay it waste. To make sure
that they would be properly led, Shelby nominated his own
choice of generals and laid down a plan of campaign for Wayne
to follow.

Luckily the chief whom Shelby named, Charles Scott, was
highly acceptable to Wayne. A veteran of Monmouth and of
Stony Point, of the Virginia campaign and of two unfortunate
campaigns against the Indians, the sociable fifty-four-year-old
general was one of Wayne's most cherished friends. But not
even from Charles Scott would Wayne accept dictation as to
how a campaign should be run. "To detach mounted volunteers
by route of Limestone, as you propose," he wrote to Shelby, "to
move them fifty to a hundred miles wide of the army in order

to burn a few wigwams and to kill or capture a few women and children . . . would be an object unworthy of gallant mounted volunteers." He reminded Shelby that he was the general in command and that he would employ the Kentuckians as he pleased.

The volunteers had been called too early. Wayne had the mounted volunteers under arms as early as May, but when war was delayed, the Kentucky soldiers lost interest. By August, Scott reported sadly that the men were "giting a little flattend" and that enemies of both himself and Wayne who "dar not appere publicly" were "etarnally throwing cold water on the volunteer business." Wayne replied by counseling patience, which helped Scott not at all, and a whole month went by, during which Scott was "kept in one continuous train of perplexity and trouble to keep up the fever." When at last, on September 11, the Commander-in-Chief received official news that the Indian treaty had failed, and he demanded that Scott bring his 1,500 mounted volunteers, only 360 Kentuckians appeared for service.

4

The Indians lost no time in opening their attack. A war party of 40 Indians raided Major John Adair's camp and ran off with a number of his pack horses. Wayne sent a detachment to recover the horses, but although the pursuers captured some jerked beef, a few blankets, some scalping knives, and a little tobacco, the marauders escaped. Anthony swore that he would go out and burn the Indian towns. Wilkinson held the same idea. The pudgy, broad-mouthed Brigadier outlined a scheme to send troops to Grand Glaize, the Indian village at the junction of the Au Glaize and Maumee rivers, to "destroy their corn, captivate their wives and children and break up the settlements." Thus, he promised, the Legion could terminate the war at a single stroke. But as soon as Wilkinson agreed, Wayne changed his mind. He viewed the war, he said, as a more extensive rising than did Wilkinson. While he approved the general plan, his caution warned him that one short expedition would probably be insufficient to restore peace.

"This is not a common, or little, predatory war made by a few tribes," he assured his colleagues. "It is a confederated war forming a chain of circumvalation round the frontiers of America from Canada to East Florida, and unless the fire kindled at the Miami of the Lakes is extinguished by the blood of the *Hydry,* a little way in our front"—he referred to the supposed Anglo-Indian alliance—"it will inevitably spread along the borders of Pennsylvania, Virginia, Kentucky, the Territory Southwest of the Ohio, South Carolina and Georgia."

He was, it later developed, too conservative, since one campaign proved enough to crush the hydra, but he could not have anticipated such success. He held back from making a mad rush into danger zones. Temptation, to be sure, was great, for Indians swaggered boldly toward isolated farmhouses and even within gunshot of the forts, daring the Legion to attack. On one occasion a marauding party held up a provision convoy, putting the escort to flight and driving off with twenty wagons filled with corn. At another time, 50 Indians attacked an isolated station near Fort Hamilton, killing a civilian and two children; on yet another day, hostiles threw a party of dragoons into such panic that the soldiers fled in fright, leaving two sergeants and a subaltern to fight alone. The three dragoons fought so valiantly that the Indians withdrew. Wayne ordered every dragoon who had run away to be court-martialed before a tribunal ordered to convict the caitiffs.

Wayne could not set out immediately upon a punitive expedition. His army was again ill, this time with ague and influenza; his troops were admirably disciplined, but their sanitary service was execrable. Upcountry forts were insufficiently supplied with hay and forage, and the meat stored at Fort Jefferson was too bad to eat. Remembering the catastrophes that had befallen Harmar and St. Clair, he had no desire to campaign in autumn, when Indians fought best, unless his men were fully fit and unless every button was shined bright. Not until October 7, 1793, almost a month after receipt of news that the tribes had refused peace, was he prepared to take the field. Then, after his scouts had gone wide into the wilderness looking for ambush, he set out for the North. It was much too late for an autumn campaign; in fact it was at about the same season of the year that St. Clair had gone forth to defeat. Wayne hoped for a quick, decisive victory, but his real purpose was to be ready for a spring offensive in 1794.

His wide roads facilitated travel. Harmar and St. Clair had groped their way through underbrush and forest; Wayne enjoyed a wide wagon road over which artillery and supply trains could pass with ease and rapidity. His predecessors had gone forward without real knowledge of what was happening upon their flanks; Wayne, remembering the Guristersijo surprise, threw out parties to patrol the woods on either side. Harmar and St. Clair had bivouacked at night wherever darkness came upon them, their men huddled about brightly burning campfires set in open glades; on nights when they were not staying at a blockhouse Wayne required every camp to be well guarded by log barricades and by an abatis of timbers. His men worked hard; they grumbled at the labor—but the Legion moved in safety. Indian scouts, peering from thickets, saw a camp on active watch; they reported to their leaders that Wayne was a chief who never slept.

Six days after leaving Hobson's Choice, Wayne drove the Legion of the United States fifty miles into the wilderness. Each day he had hoped to meet the enemy, knowing that if only he could have a pitched battle with the Indians, much of the power of the hydra would be broken. To his disappointment, he saw no trace of the enemy; he came not only to Fort Jefferson but to the end of the good road six miles beyond that furthest outpost. By this time it was mid-October, and signs of winter were becoming visible. All Wayne's plans for early action had been ruined. Had he been allowed to wage war as he wished, there would have been huge deposits of supplies waiting for him at the head of the road, but the weak policy of politicians at the capital had prevented this. Washington and Knox against all reason had trusted that the Indians would sue for peace, and they had countermanded Wayne's arrangements. Although Anthony considered for two weeks the possibility of a quick thrust against Grand Glaize, he dared not venture deep into hostile territory without a well-established base.

The Legion halted, its irresistible advance stalled not by the enemy but by the Government's caitiff timidity. On November 6, a month after leaving Hobson's Choice, the fuming General, boiling with rage at the spoiling of his schemes, reluctantly ordered the Legion to build huts like those of Valley Forge. The cantonment was a pleasant site. Set on a beautiful peninsula on the banks of a winding creek, surrounded by rich prairie country, it had sufficient forage to feed a thousand cattle. The soldiers' huts were guarded by a deep trench and a strong stockade; in addition, a banquette (raised fire step inside the trenches) guaranteed powerful defense against attack. He called the camp Greeneville, in memory of his friend Nathanael Greene, though some intimates averred it was more probably named in honor of the lively and vivacious Catherine. In later years, the spelling would be officially changed to Greenville.

When Greeneville was completed, Wayne turned his attention to the improvement of the commissariat. Congress, much to his disgust, fed the army by private contract; for 1793 and 1794, it awarded the business to Robert Elliott and Eli Williams, small Western merchants with no previous experience in army work. The men were obligated to supply daily rations of a pound of bread or flour, and a pound of beef or three-quarters of a pound of pork, to each man. In addition, for each hundred men they must issue weekly a quart of salt, two quarts of vinegar, two pounds of soap, and a pound of candles. Wayne had required that 271,000 complete rations be collected before the close of 1793. It was his plan to relay the food into the Indian land as new territory was taken over. But the contractors saw no sense in piling up such huge stocks of meat and flour. They made no purchases other than those necessary to supply the daily needs of the expedition. At the back of their minds, no doubt, was the thought that by delaying their buying prices might be less and their profits much enhanced. To their dismay, Wayne ordered the supplies to be delivered immediately, before winter set in. The contractors were caught short. Having neither sufficient stores to meet Wayne's requisitions nor sufficient pack horses or wagons to transport such stocks as were available, Elliott and Williams could not meet the call.

They made the mistake of arguing with the Commander-in-Chief, pointing out that Greeneville warehouses contained 70,-000 rations, more than enough to feed the army for three weeks, and that additional supplies could be brought up within a very short time. Wayne, impatient with what seemed to him evasion and equivocation, demanded immediate compliance, and when the contractors confessed that their transport service was too small to bring up all the food at once, he ordered his quartermaster-general to buy two hundred and fifty horses and sixty oxen, at the contractors' expense, to hurry up the transport. Elliott and Williams protested at the cost, but Wayne warned of yet more drastic action. Unless the contractors complied at once with his demands, he threatened, he would buy fourteen hundred pack horses at their expense and use the quartermaster's corps to convoy food to Jefferson. Such action, if carried out, would bankrupt Elliott and Williams. Pack horses were not only expensive to buy, but they were uneconomical for transport. Each animal could be loaded with no more than three bushels of corn, and on the long trip from Cincinnati the horse would consume two-thirds of its load, delivering only a bushel or so each trip. Elliott and Williams would thus lose heavily, especially if in addition Wayne charged their account with the cost of the quartermaster's corps and of the army equipment used in the convoy.

Almost immediately the contractors gained an unexpected ally. Wilkinson's supporters told them that Wayne would not command the Legion long and that James Wilkinson would succeed him. It would be wise, said the malcontents, to disregard Wayne's threats. Moreover "the General" would look with leniency upon the contractors if Elliott and Williams would take orders from Wilkinson rather than from Wayne. As Wilkinson agents prophesied, Wayne failed to carry out his threats. Instead of buying the fourteen hundred additional horses, Wayne contented himself, somewhat inexplicably, with writing letters to the contractors upbraiding them for being dilatory. Wilkinson advised that the letters be disregarded and that the contractors send only a small dribble of supplies to camp. During one whole month the total stock of material sent to Greeneville consisted of thirteen hundred and sixty gallons of whisky, eighty bushels of salt, and one hundred and ninety-three bullocks so poor and so small, Wayne said, that "they had to be slaughtered to save their lives."

Wayne was too ill to supervise the contractors as closely as he wished. From October until the middle of December he was sick with a succession of ailments. His head ached miserably and the gout which now was chronic kept him in constant pain. He was obliged, in consequence, to rely implicitly upon reports from Wilkinson concerning the progress of Elliott and Williams in laying up supplies. Wilkinson slowed down the flow of food. Desiring to discredit Wayne at the War Department, the marplot sabotaged Wayne's plan to launch a spring attack in 1794. Knowing that the Commander-in-Chief would not advance unless at least a three months' stock of provision was laid by, Wilkinson secretly urged the contractors to delay while at the same time he assured Wayne that the dilatory contractors could not move faster because road transport was more difficult than usual.

By the year's end, Wayne had in store at Greeneville only 42,800 rations of flour, instead of the 271,000 he had demanded. Beef was rather more plentiful, though the 250,000 rations available were below the minimum he sought; other essentials were sadly lacking. No vinegar and no whisky could be found in camp; only five hundred rations of soap were available and only a thousand candles, while salt, so necessary for preserving slaughtered meat, was reduced to less than sixty bushels.

Wilkinson persuaded Wayne not to punish the contractors, assuring his chief that the flow of goods would steadily increase. On this assurance, Wayne amended his requirements, arranging with Robert Williams, Eli's brother, to have only 50,000 complete rations delivered "to a point 60 or 70 miles advanced of Greeneville." Since most of these supplies were already in storage at Fort St. Clair, transport would be the only problem to be solved. Two months later, however, the contractors had deposited even less than half the required amount of flour, and this at Greeneville instead of at the advanced post, and the meat supply was 10,000 rations less than it had been when the agreement was made. Wayne, worrying for fear a spring offensive would again be made impossible, demanded peremptorily that Elliott and Williams provide 250,000 complete rations within a month, but he obtained less than one-fifth that amount. By May 1, long after the time originally set for an advance, Elliott and Williams had on hand at Greeneville meat for only eight days and flour for nineteen, when Wayne had expected that food for three months would be available.

By this time Wilkinson, believing that the Wayne plans had been sufficiently sabotaged, loosed the curb which he had held upon the contractors. In a private letter to "Robin" Williams, he ordered that the flow of goods proceed at full speed. Then, writing to Wayne, he said: "The conduct of the Contractors is to me inexplicable." His delay had served its purpose. After two years' preparation, Wayne's desire to launch a campaign in the spring of 1794 was not to be fulfilled; if he advanced into Indian country, he must move in summer when the Indians were better able to resist. For his own selfish ends, Wilkinson thus subjected Wayne and the Legion to the imminent peril of a disaster as complete as that which had crushed Harmar and St. Clair.

5

"We stand on very ticklish ground; there is no calculating on anything but insult and oppression. I am sick of everything and almost every body around me." So wrote Major Tom Cushing to a more fortunate friend on furlough in Connecticut, in commenting on the morale of the Legion. He was not alone in his disgust; the Wilkinsonians showered letters upon their Eastern friends telling of the "abject servitude" to which Old Tony had subjected them. Even Dr. Scott, Wayne's Georgia friend, turned against the Commander-in-Chief, in a note congratulating an officer who left the army on his freedom "from the shackles of despotical restriction where the subordinate officer is subject to all the caprice, ill nature, to say nothing of the ignorance, of his weak superiors."

That Wayne, embittered by secret plots, suspicious even of his aides-de-camp, had turned sour is beyond all question. Restlessness, uncertainty, and inability to embark upon aggressive action, together with the constant ache of gout, made him captious, supersensitive, and unpredictable. He summoned courts-martial only to dismiss the courts before the trials were complete; he ordered men into arrest, keeping them prisoner for weeks without bringing them to trial or, in some instances, telling them of what crimes they were accused; suspecting Wilkinson of treachery, he insinuated much to officers in his confidence, but gave but little proof; he played favorites continually.

Again, as at Legionville and Hobson's Choice, clash of leaders induced restlessness among subordinates. Wayne's special favorite, Captain Edward Butler, Dick's youngest brother, puffed up with importance as deputy adjutant-general. He refused testily to perform his duties unless he felt in the mood; he interfered arrogantly with arrangements made by officers of higher rank. Major Cushing, never a man to suffer slights, went straight to Wayne with charges that Butler was an inefficient adjutant. Wayne paid no attention to the charges, retorting that Butler was a valuable officer. He warned Cushing to mind his own business and threatened to arrest the Major if the charges were repeated. Cushing shot back impudently that Wayne would do well to read the Articles of War. Wayne promptly ordered Cushing's arrest. "Your present situation," he told the fuming Major, "is the effect of your own choice. You have insulted, provoked and solicited it both verbally and in writing and that at a crisis when the utmost exertions of every officer was much wanted."

Guion took up the campaign against Butler, demanding that the adjutant be reduced in rank, but Wayne, hauling out of his pigeonholes an old charge against Guion for unmilitary behavior and disobedience of orders, silenced that complaint.

Colonel Hamtramck also joined the anti-Butler movement, alleging that the adjutant had twice usurped command of Hamtramck's troops and that Butler had been insubordinate. These were more serious charges, not only because of Hamtramck's rank, but also because he had been hitherto a strong Wayne man. If Hamtramck joined the Wilkinson cabal, Wayne would lose an influential ally. Wayne could not well ignore these accusations. He asked that Butler voluntarily relinquish the adjutant-generalcy for the time being, promising that if Butler thus co-operated, special favor would be extended at a later time. Butler would not make concessions to his enemies. Explaining to Wayne that all his accusers were drunken wastrels, he clung to his post. Wayne, loyal always to his pets, insisted that Hamtramck was completely in the wrong and that Butler was correct. Hamtramck, said Wayne, had disobeyed a general order which Butler carefully observed. The Commander-in-Chief accordingly rebuked Hamtramck for seeking to punish an officer whose only crime was following out Wayne's instructions. Hamtramck swallowed the reprimand, but thereafter relations between Wayne and himself were never as cordial as before. In private conversations with his cronies, Hamtramck said: "There is no doubt about it; the old man is really mad."

Once more, Wayne tried to restore harmony and discipline by stringent punishment. Ballard Smith, for all Wilkinson's certificates of sobriety, was again arrested for intoxication. William Diven, a Wilkinson lieutenant, received a formal reprimand in the presence of his troops for having called a Wayne man a liar and a coward. A captain facing punishment at Wayne's hands cut his own throat. Others, fearful that they might be denounced as enemies of the Commander-in-Chief, handed in their resignations. "I am to contend," wrote Wayne to Sharp Delany, "with a choice of difficulties: a savage enemy in front, famine in the rear, and a baneful leaven in the center of the Legion." He complained that envenomed arrows were pointed at him from a masked battery within the circle of his friends.

Those shafts were sharp as well as venomed. Wilkinson, while professing to be a friend of Wayne, knifed his commander in the back. While he and Wayne politely continued to invite one another to dinner, where they exchanged toasts to each other's good fortune, Wilkinson drew up formal charges to be

submitted to the Senate, alleging that Wayne was guilty of
fraud, speculation, and theft of army funds. In addition, Wilkinson audaciously intimated that Wayne knew far more about
a Kentucky plot to annex that region to Spain than the commander was willing to admit. The bold marplot insinuated that
delays in paying Kentucky mounted volunteers for their service
in the short 1793 campaign were due to Wayne's embezzlement
of funds. Scott's men, smarting over their inaction and their
subsequent dismissal, had looked impatiently for their money,
but months had passed without their receiving cash. Wilkinson,
as well as Wayne, knew well that a violent yellow-fever epidemic, which took the lives of three thousand Philadelphians,
had shut down every government department, and that no communications of any sort had been received from the capital, but
Wilkinson inspired the belief that delays were due to Wayne's
pocketing the funds. By the time the money was received, January, 1794, the mounted volunteers were convinced that Wayne
was a thief and that the cash distributed to them was but resti-
tution from his pockets.

Newspapers, meanwhile, flamed with accusations against
Wayne for his rigid discipline and for his alleged brutality and
cruelty. Acrostics were published using the initials of his name
to prove that A.W. stood for "Army Wretched." A letter, published first in the *Virginia Gazette* but widely copied, came from
"a gentleman in General Wayne's camp, who may be depended
upon," accusing the Commander-in-Chief of a whole sheaf of
faults:

Our informant states as matter of fact that the discontent, the
drinking, gambling, quarrelling, fighting and licentiousness in almost all ranks, exceeded all example. He adds, that these melancholy truths have been produced in a great measure by the conduct
and example of the General, whose manners are despotic, whose
judgment is feeble, infirm and full of prejudice; whose temper is
irascible and violent; whose language is indecent and abusive, and
whose conduct to his officers is capricious and irregular, being at one
time childishly familiar, and at another tyrannical and over-bearing.

That instead of restraining excesses by his authority; instead of
reprehending the dissolute and cultivating the meritorious officer, he

makes no distinctions but in favor of his tools, spies and toad-eaters.

That acting above all laws divine and human, he assigns the Sabbath for extraordinary fatigues, and overturns, without reason, or suppresses in violation of law, the proceedings of a general court martial.

That to the shame and disgrace of his cloth, he has confounded all ideas of infamy and honour, by permitting an officer who had been regularly cashiered by a general court martial for "fraud and forgery" to resign a commission, which he had in fact forfeited, dismissed him with honour.

That substituting domination for law, and private resentment for justice, he has arrested men of rank and worth on vexatious pretences, and has kept them in confinement, and denied a trial for months, whilst at the same time he has screened his pimps and parasites from justice, and has refused them to the law.

That such things should exist is lamentable, but that they do exist is too true to be denied, & it requires no spirit of prophecy to foretell what will be the end of a military corps, thus constructed and thus conducted.

Let those whom it concerns most, look to the consequences.

Wayne's friends were certain that Major Cushing was the author of this "Stubborn Facts" communication. Armstrong, now in office at Cincinnati, threw the Major into prison on what seems to have been little more ground than suspicion and general principles. Wayne himself preferred to disregard the "Stubborn Facts" communication. When his supporters prepared a reply, entitled "A Friend to Truth," he thanked them for their interest, but added that the answer was unnecessary.

"I am," he said, "much obliged to my friends for their kind interference upon this occasion but the libel signed 'Stubborn Facts' was so notoriously devoid of truth and so opposite to facts that I deemed it beneath my notice, conscious of my own rectitude of conduct and fully convinced that time would soon disabuse the public ear and shew those vile calumniators in their true colors, i.e. mutinous cowards and dirty tools of faction.

"I am not at a loss for the names of those assassins but I only consider them as catspaws of a Democratic, or rather Demoncratic, party both in and out of Congress who must shortly fall to rise no more. They have been very cautious to prevent detection by the secret manner in which they have transmitted the piece to the press.

"Those caitiffs are now in possession of the Sheriff of Cincinnati, one at the suit of Captain Armstrong for debt and scandal, the other by a demand from the civil authority for rescuing by force and arms his whore who was in custody of the Sheriff's officers. The first is a major, the second a captain in the Legion who perhaps provoked the civil durance in order to escape the dangers of the campaign or the sentence of a court martial. There is yet a third behind the curtain."

The third was in all probability Wilkinson himself, for by this time Wayne was certain that Wilkinson was an enemy. The two others were Major Cushing and Captain Guion, the latter of whom was in prison for taking his mistress down the Ohio with him while on active campaign. The offense was certainly not serious when viewed in the light of contemporary army morals, but in lieu of other grounds, it was sufficient to give Wayne and Armstrong a reason for holding Guion in jail.

At all events, murmurs, publications, and whispered insinuations had slight effect upon Wayne's superiors at the capital. Knox went out of his way to assure the Commander-in-Chief in a private, confidential letter that neither the President nor the Secretary of War were in the least influenced by "the disorganizers": "I have had no distinct view of the subject of the reports. In fact, they died of their own imbecility. I believe the main part consisted in your bearing authority with a rigid hand. You may rest assured that while I have any agency in the public affairs I shall sincerely endeavour to guard you from all misrepresentation."

The only fly in this ointment, so far as Wayne was concerned, was that persistent rumors reported that Knox would soon resign his post. Wayne, not certain who would succeed his friend, wondered whether it might not be possible to be appointed to the post himself. Once there, he could mete out punishment where he might think it most deserved.

6

Internal dissension failed to halt Wayne's preparations. Certain that the Indians were hopelessly divided in their councils and that neither the Six Nations on the east nor the Potawatomi and Wabash tribes upon the west would fight against Americans, the Commander-in-Chief planned for the inevitable war against Delawares, Shawnees, and Miamis. He hoped that Britain would not interfere, but in the light of a prediction by Lord Dorchester that Americans and British would be at war within a year, he feared that the Legion must fight both Indians and British. In that case, Wayne believed that a well-drilled Legion could defeat any force that Indians and British might raise against it. Ignoring local raids and minor skirmishes, whether they went in his favor or against it, he pushed plans steadily for a forward movement as soon as spring should bring good weather.

Just before Christmas he rose from a sickbed to lead a small force to occupy ground where two years before St. Clair had met disastrous defeat. No Indians opposed his progress as he marched twenty miles northward over heavy-timbered level country and took possession of the site. For purely propaganda purposes he gave the place the name of Fort Recovery. Placing a small guard to keep watch against surprise, Wayne set men to searching out, collecting, and "piously interring" the bones of St. Clair's men which still lay exposed upon the ground. Other soldiers looked for the cannon which had been lost, and when they had fished two six-pounders from the creek and dug up three three-pounders buried by the side of an old fallen tree, he had the ordnance cleaned and reconditioned. When all the work was done, he fired a last salute of nine volleys "from the same artillery that were lost but now recovered."

Fort Recovery was more than a mere propaganda gesture. Wayne ordered four blockhouses, each equipped with musket-proof doors and shutters and each fitted with embrasures for

small howitzers. This wilderness outpost was further strength-
ened by a strong fifteen-foot stockade, sunk deep into the
ground and firmly fastened at top and bottom. In front of this
a trench was dug; in addition, the land was cleared of trees for
a thousand feet about the fort, the timber being used as abatis.
Fort Recovery, the farthest American position in the Indian
country, was then deemed safe against attack. Wayne opened a
wide road to it from Greeneville, stationed eight companies with
artillery at the post, and waited for Indian reactions. So long as
no attacks were made, Captain Alexander Gibson, commandant
of the new fort, was to spend his time in scouting the sixty-mile
stretch of woods between Fort Recovery and Grand Glaize.
Other parties would fan out in all directions, mapping the country and reporting on Indian movements.

The Indians responded promptly. George White Eyes, a
Delaware, came under a flag of truce to Greeneville. Wayne
received him with elaborate ceremony, firing a salute in his
honor, giving a great banquet, and assuring him that the United
States had no thought of hostile moves against the Indians.
"The eyes and heart of the President of the United States are
ever open to the voice of peace," said Wayne. "He has instructed me, his chief warrior, to listen to that welcome voice
from whatever quarter it may come." He warned the Indians
not to listen to the advice of Englishmen, "those bad white
men who have neither the inclination nor the opportunity to
help the Indians." He demanded that the tribes call off their
raiding parties and that every white man in Indian possession
be delivered to Gibson at Fort Recovery within a month.

His words took the envoy somewhat aback. He had come, he
said, bringing "love to you all in hopes you will except it," but
he had also come to complain of Gibson's kidnapping activities.
Three young women, he said, had been spirited away; the Delaware ambassador demanded that the girls be given back unharmed. Wayne promised justice, but before he let White Eyes
leave, he took him on a tour of the Greeneville fort, impressing
him so firmly with its strength that the ambassador reported
to the British that Greeneville was guarded by 4,000 men, that
its circumference was two full miles, and that the cantonment

was heavily guarded. The next day, Wayne sent back the women with a message that if the tribes wished peace, they should send their military leader, Little Turtle, to confer with him before twenty days had passed.

Little Turtle, tall, sour-dispositioned, crafty war chief of the Miamis, was inclined to heed Wayne's invitation. The forty-year-old warrior, veteran of both the Harmar and St. Clair campaigns, called his fellow chiefs into conference. Standing straight before them, his foot-long silver earrings jingling as he tossed his head, his three huge nose jewels glittering in the firelight, he told Buckongehelas, leader of the Delawares, and Blue Jacket, Shawnee war chief, that Indian luck had been too good to last: "We have beaten them twice under separate commanders. We cannot expect the same good fortune always to attend us. The Americans are now led by a chief who never sleeps; night and day are alike to him. Notwithstanding the watchfulness of our young men, we have never been able to surprise him. Think well of this. There is something whispers to me, it would be prudent to listen to his offers of peace."

Stalwart Buckongehelas agreed with Little Turtle, but Blue Jacket bore them down. In searing, violent words, he accused the older men of cowardice, asked them if they were turncoats, and stormed angrily at the suggestion that the tribes restore the captives. He pointed out that William Wells, chief American scout, was the son-in-law of Little Turtle, and insinuated that "Wayne's money had bought Little Turtle's heart." Blue Jacket's sneers proved more effective than the caution of Buckongehelas and Little Turtle; the Indians resolved on war.

Wayne was not sorry that his offer was refused. Already convinced that the Indians were playing for time to remove their stores and "to withdraw women and children from pending destruction," he was anxious to take the field before the enlistment time of his men expired. Had Elliott and Williams been more efficient, he would by this time have occupied Girty's Town on the St. Mary's, halfway between Greeneville and Grand Glaize, but that had been impossible. Wayne had to rest content with sending out scouting parties and with cutting a wide road from Greeneville toward Grand Glaize.

As usual, Wayne talked too freely. He declared that he would push on to Girty's Town whether the Indians accepted his terms or not. From Girty's Town, he implied, he would go forward to the shore of Lake Erie, or perhaps to Detroit itself. Word of Wayne's rash boasts leaked quickly to the British. Simcoe and Dorchester were alarmed by Wayne's approach. They saw to it that the Six Nations, once friendly to the Americans, learned of the advance, and by cleverly tying up Wayne's loose talk with Pennsylvania's fort at Presqu' Isle, persuaded them that the "Fifteen Fires" were playing false with their pledged word.

Those once friendly Indians became convinced of Wayne's perfidy when Big Tree, a Seneca chief whom Americans sometimes nicknamed Stiff Knee, died suddenly at Greeneville. He had been urging the Delawares to accept Wayne's terms "if they wished to see their children grow up to be men and women." The Delawares declined, and Big Tree vowed to kill three of them "to avenge the death of Richard Butler." Then he turned despondent, and although Wayne gave him the brightly braided uniform of a captain in the Legion, his melancholy increased, and he committed suicide. To Wayne, the opportunity seemed ripe for propaganda. He concocted an explanation of Big Tree's death that convinced no one whatever but which instead roused much suspicion: "Captain Big Tree had some angry talk with the Delawares. Whether he ate and drank with them afterwards, or whether they gave him something which put him out of his reason, I cannot tell, but certain it is that, from that time to the moment of his Death, he was melancholy and deranged until the last moment of his death when stabbing himself with his own knife. . . . Brothers: I was informed by Captain Big Tree that many of your people had died last summer in consequence of something you had eat, when at the Council with the hostile Indians. . . . This mode of making war is cowardly and base."

None of the Six Nations credited the account; instead, cleverly encouraged by British agents, they brooded over the steady advances made by the United States into territory formerly Indian. Bear's Oil, head of the tiny group of Conneauts, expressed himself picturesquely in commenting on American aggression: "Our women and children are very uneasy. They say they cannot go out of doors to ease themselves for fear of spoiling General Washington's lands." Simcoe took full advantage of the anti-American emotions thus stirred up. Far down the Maumee River, at the rapids close to the present city of Toledo, the British held a stronghold which was called Fort Miamis, where Alexander McKee, their Indian agent, held yearly meetings to distribute presents to the Indians. For three years before Wayne's advance, Fort Miamis had been in disrepair, since the Indians had removed to Grand Glaize, but now that the Americans seemed bent on moving closer to the lake, Simcoe put the works back into good condition.

The reconstructed stronghold combined a heavy land battery with a powerful earthworks. Attackers must first cross a wide abatis, then leap a ditch and climb an elevated parapet before coming to the thick walls of the fort itself. Meanwhile, troops shielded behind safe protection could mow down an enemy either by musket fire or by cannon placed upon the bastion platforms. Simcoe believed that Fort Miamis could effectively prevent Americans from going down the Maumee to the lake and from ascending the stream by ship. The fort safeguarded Detroit against attack, since Wayne would surely hesitate about advancing to that post so long as Fort Miamis lay in his rear, threatening his long communication lines.

The British actions, like the American, became grossly exaggerated by popular report. A Potawatomi prisoner reported that Simcoe was about to loose the whole force of Britain's might against the Americans: "All the speeches sent by Simcoe are as red as blood; all the wampum and feathers are red; the war hatchets are bright red; even the tobacco is painted in that color." Further reports brought in by spies declared that the Indian confederates had mustered some 2,000 Chippewas, Wyandots, Shawnees, Delawares, Iowas, and Miamis. British regulars and Canadian militia numbered, it was said, almost as many, and there were false rumors that Simcoe planned to attack Greeneville before the end of June.

Wayne congratulated himself on his foresight in having

opened his new road from Greeneville to Girty's Town, since the wide highway gave him quick access to both Fort Miamis and Grand Glaize; he was pleased also when Captain Jemmy Underwood, a Chickasaw Indian friendly to the United States, came up from the south bringing with him a force of warriors, for these Indians, intent on "taking hair" from the Miamis and Shawnees, made first-rate scouts. Now that he had at last ironed out his difficulties with the contractors, Wayne was ready for swift action if the British made any move against him. His happiness was complete when in the last days of June, 1794, he received welcome news from Knox:

"If, in the course of your operations against the Indian enemy, it should become necessary to dislodge the party at the rapids of the Maumee, you are hereby authorized in the name of the President of the United States to do it. But no attempt ought to be made unless it shall promise complete success; an unsuccessful attempt would be attended with pernicious consequences."

CHAPTER XVIII

Western Triumph

SHARP war whoops barked as 2,000 Indians, pouring out from the forest, swept down upon the frightened pack train. Sixty quartermaster's men, unarmed and unguarded, caught wholly unprepared in the clearing near Fort Recovery, ran irresolutely here and there, some seeking to slash the straps that held the train together, others looking bewilderedly for safety. The convoy of three hundred and sixty horses was completely lost; eight men alone escaped the slaughter.

Gibson had been caught off guard. When the train was on its way with flour, he had kept careful watch until the stores had come to Fort Recovery; his garrison, together with the escort of 90 riflemen and 50 dragoons, had helped unload the packs. Happy that the flour was safely in the storehouse, Gibson had paid no heed to warnings that Jemmy Underwood had brought of Indians in the vicinity. He entertained the escort's officers, kept the men and horses overnight, and on the morning of July 30 opened the stockade gates. Incautiously, he sent the empty pack train out before the escorting troops were ready to leave; the long line of horses was well upon the road before any soldiers took off on their homeward trip to Greeneville.

Had the Indians been content to capture horses, their victory would have been complete, but the tribesmen lost their heads. Saginaws from Michigan, Mackinacs from the upper reaches of Huron, Potawatomis from the West, all eager for battle, all anxious to repeat the blow that had been dealt to St. Clair on this very spot, swung from their easy victory over unarmed hostlers to fall upon the fort. Vainly Blue Jacket and Little Turtle called them back; Canadian militiamen, whose faces had been heavily blackened as a disguise, shouted to the reckless Indians to come back to the forest; two or three scarlet-coated officers, whom Wayne called British, waved their arms for the excited tribesmen to return. Gibson too was impetuous. In the face of overwhelming numbers, he sent out 90 dragoons to charge 2,000 Indians. Many cavalrymen fell at the first fire; the rest, many running afoot, some crawling on the ground, turned back to the stockade. Gibson, reckless in his excitement, ordered out the riflemen, but they too met devastating fire as soon as they came into the open, and had to run for safety.

Within a few moments, Indians were all about the fort, firing upon the defenders from every quarter. Fort Recovery fired back steadily, until the Indians, unable to get through the high stockade, took cover behind the stumps of trees that had been cut to make an abatis. When no more savages were visible, Gibson's men continued shooting at the stumps. All day long the fight continued, Indians aiming at any man so reckless as to show himself, Gibson looping shells and six-pound shot into the woods. At nightfall, the attackers grew more bold; they came up to the stockade in the foggy dark, shouting and shooting, endeavoring to set fire to the timbers. Some, more distant than the rest, carried torches to search out their dead and to carry them away for burial. The defenses held, and at dawn the Indians ceased their attack.

Later in the morning, the enemy again fired at the fort, but when Gibson answered by shells, the Indians took refuge in the woods. For several hours there was silence, though here and there an Indian was seen, presumably hunting for dead and wounded comrades, and Gibson, hoping that this meant that the enemy was retreating, sent out Underwood to scout the woods. When the Chickasaw returned with news that hundreds of men were moving off across the creek, Gibson sallied out, yelling and waving his hands for the Indians to come back and fight, but although the tribesmen shouted in reply, they kept on with their retreat. Gibson's report to Wayne, telling of the attack, concludes with a polite postscript that indicates that no matter what the circumstances, Gibson never forgot his manners. "N.B.," his letter says, "excuse my haste."

Probably Blue Jacket, Little Turtle, and Simcoe were more annoyed than Wayne by this attack. The Indians were under orders not to fight, but only to watch for convoys. The Saginaw and Mackinac hotheadedness, by bringing on a skirmish, led those troops to believe that this one battle constituted a campaign; after a huge feast on roasted horse meat, these Indians from the Great Lakes considered their stint accomplished and announced that they were going home. The waste of ammunition had so diminished the supplies in Indian possession that it was doubtful whether the confederacy had enough left to fight another battle. "Such a disappointment," said a British agent with the Indians, "never was met with."

Wayne, knowing nothing of the breakup of the enemy army, was no more pleased than his opponents. Fort Recovery, to be sure, had been safe against attack; its design had been good. But he had lost 21 dead and 29 wounded, including several highly valued officers, against 38 Indians.

Like Blue Jacket and Little Turtle, Wayne also had difficulties with his Indian allies. Jemmy Underwood, unbeknown to Gibson, slipped out of Fort Recovery during the morning period of calm and scalped such enemies as he could find. Then, equipped with prizes to take home to show his prowess, he and his Chickasaw friends, like the Saginaws in the enemy camp, believed their work accomplished. Wayne argued with him, but to slight avail until, by a flash of inspiration, the General invented a special decoration to be awarded brave Indians who continued in the war. Any Chickasaw who remained, Wayne promised, would be entitled to a hat "with feathers in it, to show how he was respected by the whites." Jemmy and his friends stayed in service.

Coming at a time when Wayne was nearly ready to advance upon Grand Glaize, the attack on Fort Recovery caused the Commander-in-Chief to worry even more than usual over the thought that he might not return alive. He spent hours brooding in his quarters, seldom moving out of doors. Toward the end of the Greeneville stay, he wrote a final letter to his friend Delany:

"We are only awaiting the arrival of the Mounted Volunteers from Kentucky in order to have an interview with the hardy sons of the wilderness in their own towns, where we will probably meet with Mr. Simcoe at the head of the British troops and Militia of Detroit, between whom and the other Savages it may be difficult to discriminate in the hour of Action which from present appearances will be severe and bloody.

"Under those impressions and the uncertain events of War I have devised in the best manner I can all my Estate, both real and personal, to my Son and Daughter, and appointed you, my Son, and Mr. Lewis my Executors.

"As this may possibly be the last letter that fate will permit me to trouble you with, I have to request as the last favor that you will continue to be the friend and Guardian of my Orphan Children."

Waynesborough, by the will, was to go to Isaac, who in addition was to have a plot of land in Harrisburg, now the capital of Pennsylvania, and the Georgia cowpens; he was also to have 1,500 acres of land "granted by the Congress of the United States as some retribution for the loss of blood I sustained in defence of the Liberties of America in many a well-fought field from the frozen lakes of Canada to the burning sands of Florida." Margaretta's share comprised a house and lot in Philadelphia, on the east side of Second Street, 1,500 acres of land granted by the Pennsylvania Legislature in compensation for the depreciated paper money in which troops had been paid, and "my large landed estate in the province of Nova Scotia." The last-named bequest had no legal standing, since Wayne's rights to Nova Scotia land had long since lapsed.

He completed his preliminaries by appointing the troublesome Campbell Smith as judge advocate-general in place of Hyde—had he done so earlier he would have gained an influential friend instead of having a cunning enemy. Then he named Hamtramck as commander of the left wing, with Wilkinson at the post of honor on the right. Finally he drew up an order of march for the 2,169 soldiers of his Legion. The troops were to advance in double column, with dragoons in front, on the rear, and on either flank. Scouts ranged far into the woods in order to prevent surprise; within supporting distance in the rear 1,500 Kentucky mounted volunteers guarded the communication lines. As an additional precaution against his men's becoming scattered while en route, Wayne warned against unnecessary halts. If for any reason an accident required a wagon or a detachment to drop out of line, the Commander-in-Chief required the following groups to close the gap, so that the column would not be interrupted.

The same care that Wayne exercised on his march from Hobson's Choice to Greeneville was repeated during the advance from Greeneville to Grand Glaize. Each night a square camp ground of 75 acres was marked off and surrounded by breastworks of logs and an abatis of tangled branches. Four good redoubts were also built, three hundred yards distant from the line of trenches. While the troops were busy digging these defenses, dragoons and pack-horse men cut grass for their horses so that the animals could stand inside the breastworks, protected against raiding enemies. In the event of attack, Wayne provided, soldiers might use their artillery—always parked in the center of the camp—as a temporary breastworks, but as soon as possible he wished the rifle corps, infantry, and dragoons to charge yelling upon the enemy. These maneuvers, and camp-building too, had been practiced by the Legion daily for almost a year; Wayne had also held frequent field exercises to test the soldiers' prowess. Certain that his men were letter-perfect, he gave orders for the Legion to advance. The march, he assured Knox, "will be as rapid and as secret as the nature of the case will admit and before the enemy can be informed."

Early in the morning of July 28, 1794, Wayne gave the signal to march; his men, trudging forward in the heat, covered twelve miles on the good road to Fort Recovery. Passing this outpost at noon on the twenty-ninth, to the accompaniment of a salute from the St. Clair guns mounted on the blockhouses, the Legion pressed ahead, halting only long enough to let the baggage catch up with the main body of the army. Once they were in the wilderness, beyond the point to which wide roads had been built, the soldiers met greater difficulties. They proceeded to the banks of Beaver Creek "through thickets almost impervious, through morasses, defiles and beds of nettles more than waist high and miles in length," crossing numbers of winding creeks, bothered by mosquitoes larger than those which many of the soldiers had ever seen before. Then they had perforce to halt while the engineers built bridges. The task of bridging the seventy-yard-wide stream proved much more difficult than had been estimated; a job for which two hours had been allotted required a full day's work. Before sunrise on August 1 the Legion was again upon the road, "beating the Trail of the Pioneers" twelve miles to the St. Mary's River. Tramping over low, flat ground, through thick woods tangled with much underbrush, Wayne's army suddenly emerged upon an extensive open plain. The troops camped here, though many worried lest Indians might lurk near by in the woods, and since the day was hot, the soldiers went swimming in the St. Mary's.

Wayne himself now seemed uncertain; he sent out Wells and other scouts to look for hostile Indians; meanwhile the waiting troops fished. Then, rather than have men idle, Wayne changed his mind and ordered that the men erect a blockhouse, to be called Fort Randolph, for whose construction he allotted one day's time. The new fort, as everyone but Wayne anticipated, took much longer to complete. Wells came back with a report that no Indians were near by and that it was safe to move ahead, but Wayne, fretting because "the work of the garrison goes on with wondrous slowness," stayed on. Every available man was pressed into service, but a second day passed before Fort Randolph was in readiness.

To hurry up the work, the gouty Commander-in-Chief bustled about the camp, urging men to faster effort. On his rounds, he came to axmen chopping down a big beech tree whose trunk was to be used to make logs for the walls. Wayne, suddenly startled by loud shouts from his men, looked up in time to see the huge tree falling. Lame as he was, he leaped to safety, dropping beside a cut stump. The big beech fell heavily at the very place where Wayne had been standing. He did not escape unharmed; though the bole did not strike him, heavy boughs, their force of falling checked somewhat by the stump, hit him hard, inflicting serious cuts.

The accident still further weakened Wayne's failing health. "I find," he said, "that I have been injured inwardly, from the frequent discharges of blood and by an almost total loss of appetite; however, for a few days past, from a free use of bark and a partial state of rest, I feel much relieved, but still weak, and languid, nor can I expect to be restored to health until I experience a relaxation from anxiety and fatigue." Such relaxation was nowhere in sight. Without waiting for Fort Randolph to be finished, he set off again, early on August 4, toward Grand Glaize, leaving an invalid officer and 40 sick men to complete the work. The Wilkinson contingent professed themselves to be shocked at Wayne's callousness in so abandoning invalid soldiers to the mercy of the Indians; they did not consider that the entire Legion stood between the sick men and the enemy.

Wayne's route baffled his white opponents as well as the Indians. According to precedent, he should have descended the St. Mary's to the head of the Maumee as Harmar had done in 1790 and as St. Clair had intended to do in 1791. After reaching the Maumee his next step, according to customary strategy, would have been to proceed down that stream to Grand Glaize. But this, Wayne correctly thought, would bring on immediate conflict with the lurking enemy, on ground chosen by the Indians; it was, moreover, the route by which both Indians and British expected an advance, and on which they would be ready to receive him. An alternative route led straight to Fort Miamis, but this seemed dangerous to Wayne. The Delawares guarded the route jealously, and Wyandots and Shawnees living in the neighborhood would be alert to check the American advance.

Wayne's plan was more adroit. Well aware that each tribe was most concerned in protecting its own territory, he gave out conflicting rumors that he planned to march directly against the Miami village on the left and against Fort Miamis on the right. Thus, he correctly reasoned, each tribe would guard its own homes, lest their women and their children fall victims to the Americans. He himself meanwhile rushed the Legion directly through the undefended center of the Indian country, between the Miamis and the Delawares to Grand Glaize. He was in the very heart of enemy territory before the Indians knew of his whereabouts. The scheme, admirably devised, worked perfectly. The Indians, completely taken by surprise, learned only through an American deserter that Wayne had outmaneuvered them. By that time it was too late to organize effective resistance.

On August 8, eleven days after leaving Greeneville, Wayne's triumphant Legion strode into the deserted and undefended village of Grand Glaize. It had covered seventy-seven miles of marching through the wilderness and had taken the town without firing a single shot. Had a deserter not given warning of the Legion's coming, Wayne would have captured huge stocks of booty. As it was, he now stood astride the Maumee, between the army at the headwaters and that at Fort Miamis, ready to strike with equal efficiency against either objective. His strategy in thus dividing the enemy forces explains his subsequent triumphs.

Again Wayne halted while his men built a fort, with blockhouses, trenches, and stockades, and while they leveled a good road along the river. He stayed here for a week, completing the defenses; then, after calling the new stronghold Fort Defiance, and renaming Fort Randolph for Vice-President Adams, he hastened forty miles downriver to meet the Indian army, which he under-estimated as 700, at Fort Miamis. Eight or nine miles from the fort he halted, built yet another stockade, which he christened Fort Deposit, left his heavy baggage there, and made ready for a final battle.

He did not think the Indians would fight. In fact, he bet Wilkinson 10 guineas and a quarter-cask of wine that further peace negotiations would result. Within twenty-four hours of the wager, Wayne was called upon to pay.

2

Showers in the early morning of August 20, 1794, delayed Wayne's progress; not until eight o'clock did the Legion begin to thread its way from Fort Deposit along the narrow path between the thick woods on the left and the steep ravine and riverbank upon the right. Then slowly, because the ground was like an abatis, crisscrossed with decaying fallen timbers, the men moved downstream toward the British Fort Miamis. No one knew what the next few hours would bring. That Indians were in the neighborhood was certain, yet the scouts could find no traces of an army; whether the Shawnees, Miamis, Delawares, Wyandots, and others of the great confederacy had gone home, leaving the land to the Americans, or whether they were lurking in the forest, no one could learn. That the British troops would fight was taken for granted, yet the commander at the fort held his peace. Before noon, it would be finally decided whether the United States must fight the Indians; by that time, too, it would be settled whether the war would be between Americans and red men or be another war for freedom against the English.

Wayne suffered excruciating pain. His gout, following his exertions on the long ride from Greeneville, was worse than ever; to relieve the agony, he had his arms and legs so swathed in flannel bandages that he found it almost impossible to move. Three men labored to raise his heavy body into his saddle. The operation was sheer torture; tears started from the General's eyes. Hoisted at last into his saddle, he soon forgot his pain. Usually when setting out in early morning he walked his horse slowly until the stiffness disappeared from his bruised body and his racked joints worked more smoothly; but this morning was different. After he had ridden only a short distance, sharp rifle fire burst suddenly from clumps of tall grass. A small advanced corps of Kentucky volunteers riding down the river staggered before the volley. Surprised, although they had been warned to keep alert, the survivors swung about, spurred their horses, and galloped back for safety. Their quick dash threw the front ranks of regulars into confusion; they too broke and ran. The whole van of the Legion gave way simultaneously. Wayne jabbed his spurs into his stallion's flanks and hurried forward, forgetful of his pain.

Wilkinson, upon the right, hesitated to advance, for fear of ambush in the deep ravines ahead. Wayne, swearing at the Brigadier's caution, yelled to Robert Mis Campbell, dragoon leader, to clear the enemy from the tall grass. Wilkinson's ranks parted to let the horsemen through, then, closing gaps, the Brigadier moved to back up Campbell's cavalry. As Campbell's men galloped, their broad swords swinging in the sun, their horses jumping over fallen timber, ramming their way pell-mell into the ambush, Little Turtle's sharpshooters let burst with a second volley. Campbell fell dead; his men wavered. The Indians, thinking that their work was done, jumped from their hiding-places and ran to the woods on the left. Thus far, the Battle of Fallen Timbers was wholly in the enemy's favor; the Legion had scarcely fired a gun.

Wayne, hampered by his flannel bandages, tore them from his arms, regardless of his cuts and his gout; he galloped over to Hamtramck's position shouting for a charge; he yelled to the center to use the bayonet; he cursed at Wilkinson for not driving ahead. Discovering that Little Turtle and Blue Jacket stood in force in three columns in the woods, he bawled to Scott to go around by the rear and fall upon their flank. But the mass of fallen timber was too heavy; the Kentuckians could not penetrate the tangled wilderness. Meanwhile the close-packed Legion pounced upon the main force of the Indians with the bayonet, yelling triumphantly as the enemy gave ground for more than a mile. Wayne, said the Indians, fought like a tornado, sweeping everything before him.

Wayne's unending martinet drills now brought results. Blue Jacket, fighting as Indians always did in a long, extended line, had too thin a force to hold back the bayonet advance; moreover, by endeavoring to stretch his troops still farther, so as to catch the Legion on its flank, the Indian weakened his position. So complete was Tornado Wayne's success that the enemy had no time to stop and load; Wayne's men, taught to load as they advanced, did not hesitate an instant. Only scattering shots answered the American challenge; when these failed to halt Wayne's irresistible Legion, the tribesmen fled.

The main portion of the Battle of Fallen Timbers lasted only forty minutes, so short a time that the great bulk of Wayne's men took no part in the action. Kentucky's mounted volunteers fired hardly a shot, for they were trying to find paths through the woods for a flank assault upon the enemy; the rear guard could not get upon the field of battle in time to face the Indians. Only 900 soldiers of the Legion actually fought; the rest, available for reserve, came up when the conflict was complete. Fallen Timbers was an overwhelming victory. Wayne lost 28 men dead and 100 wounded; 40 Indians were left upon the field, but Wayne believed that many more were carried off by the retreating enemy.

Politically speaking, the aftermath of Fallen Timbers was quite as important as the battle itself. Terror-stricken Indians, fleeing from the Tornado's yelling victors, threw down their guns and ran to Fort Miamis, seeking shelter. To their astonishment and dismay, Major William Campbell, commanding the post, kept his gates locked tight. Blue Jacket, Little Turtle, and Tecumseh, the young war chief of the Shawnees, shouted for sanctuary, but Major Campbell paid no heed. The Indians knew now that their cause was hopeless, since their Father, the King of England, would not keep his promises. Wayne's task of making a peace treaty with the defeated tribes was thus assured.

Indeed, to demonstrate his utter mastery of the situation Wayne drew up his triumphant Legion in plain sight of the fort. Again heedless of his cuts and his gout, he and his aide, William Henry Harrison, rode within pistol shot of the works, openly reconnoitering its defenses. Dismounting and turning his back upon the walls, Wayne stooped to drink from a spring that bubbled amid the abatis. He waved to soldiers to come up, and they, with guns in their hands, stared contemptuously at the defenders. The gestures maddened the garrison. A captain of marines, angered by the careless freedom of Wayne and Harrison, seized a portfire to set off a gun, but Major Campbell ran toward him with a sword, threatening to cut him down if he persisted.

Campbell sent out a flag of truce with a message to Wayne inquiring "in what light I am to view your making such approaches to this garrison," adding that he knew of no war between Great Britain and America. Wayne retorted truculently that "were you entitled to an answer, the most full and satisfactory one was announced to you from the muzzles of my small arms." He showed his contempt for Fort Miamis by declaring: "Neither the fort nor its guns could much impede the progress of the Victorious Army under my command." Campbell swallowed the insult, but he warned Wayne not to repeat the offense. "Should you," he wrote, "continue to approach my post in the threatening manner you are at this moment doing, my indispensable duty to my King and country and the honour of my profession will oblige me to have recourse to those measures which thousands of either nation may hereafter have cause to regret, and which, I solemnly appeal to God, I have used my utmost endeavours to avert." Wayne answered, promptly and peremptorily, with a demand that Campbell clear out of Fort Miamis, since the post, according to Wayne, had been erected in defiance of the treaty signed between the United States and Great Britain at the close of the Revolutionary War. "I certainly will not abandon this Post," retorted Campbell.

The issue, thus sharply drawn, brought both nations to the brink of war, but neither Wayne nor Campbell dared start the conflict. Wayne went so far as to set fire to all the cornfields and prairies within sight of the fort, "even under the muzzles of the guns," hoping that Campbell would sally out to fight, but the British Major, with many sick men in his garrison, paid no attention. Wayne camped his men just out of rifle range, waiting a week for Campbell to do something, but when the Major held his peace, on August 26 Wayne led the Legion back to Grand Glaize, now called Fort Defiance. Here he stayed until September 14, leveling the ground before the blockhouses in such a way that every inch would be commanded by his guns,

digging trenches twelve feet wide and eight feet deep to safeguard the fort against a sudden raid, bombproofing the works,
and setting up stockades. It was hard work, and his men fell
sick with fever and ague; provisions, moreover, in spite of the
vast quantities of corn, beans, and pumpkins found in the Indian
gardens, ran low. The troops went on half-rations, regretting
now that they had burned the crops.

As always when the Legion was in idleness, internecine feuds
were renewed. Wilkinson, robbed of the chance to lead the
Legion, raged at Wayne's good luck; in every manner possible he undermined his leader's reputation. Angrily, he charged
that Wayne had been heartless after victory, and that wounded
soldiers had lain untended on the field of battle all day long
while Wayne swaggered in full view of Fort Miamis, and that
the bodies of the dead had "been left to ferment . . . the prey
of vultures" for two days after fighting ceased. "For a single
man sacrificed by such cruel negligence, a general deserves to
be hanged; damned, he certainly will be."

Wilkinson, talking to anyone who would listen, wondered
insinuatingly why provisions had fallen so low, and why
Wayne had left his heavy artillery behind instead of hauling
it through swamp and thick forest; he complained that the
Commander-in-Chief had marched upon the British fort without knowing its size, construction, or defenses. He made fun
of Wayne's "ridiculous gasconade," and mocked him for his
pride. "The General," Wilkinson scoffed, "is every moment
more inflated with his imaginary prowess and the importance
of his puny victory."

Antoine Lacelle, a French trader and Blue Jacket's brother-
in-law, was caught skulking about the battlefield in Indian paint
and costume. Wayne ordered him to headquarters to get information, but when Lacelle reported that the entire Indian
strength had been but 900, of whom less than half were actually
in battle, Wayne called him a liar. He loaded Lacelle with
chains and threw him into the guardhouse to improve the
Frenchman's memory; when the trader later reported that Little Turtle's army numbered 2,000, all of whom had fought
and that 400 had been slain, Wayne became more friendly.

Lacelle also testified that large numbers of Canadian militia, including Simon Girty, had also taken part in the fight at Fallen Timbers. Lacelle's information proved so pleasing that Wayne licensed him as one of the very few merchants permitted to trade with Indians of the Northwest Territory.

Wilkinson, impatient of subordination, could no longer restrain himself from taking his case directly before the highest authorities. In the summer of 1794, he twice dispatched trusted friends to Philadelphia with formal accusations against his Commander-in-Chief. The documents bristled with sharp charges. According to Wilkinson, Wayne's military conduct was habitually partial, oppressive, ungentlemanlike, and directly contrary to law. The commander, Wilkinson alleged, had wasted public money, and had violated every principle of justice, humanity, and common honesty. The statements were vague and without corroborative evidence, and Wayne's friends found slight difficulty in disproving them, but the innuendoes were poisonous.

A second set of charges revolved about Wayne's strict disciplinary methods. This was a rehash of "Stubborn Facts," which Tom Cushing had written with Wilkinson's aid. Credence had been lent the article by the commander's failure to refute the libels. His "silent contempt" had been construed as a confession of guilt; when Wayne told his friends that the charges were "as false as they are base and insidious" and that they were "the idle phantom of a disturbed imagination," Wilkinson retorted that Wayne had failed to touch the heart of the matter. In official letters to the President and the Secretary of War, the Brigadier presented the accusations anew, enlarged and in more critical form. Recklessly, moreover, Wilkinson attacked Wayne's whole plan of campaign as "improper and absurd"; the line of battle, he said, was "still worse." The boasted victory at Fallen Timbers, "about which there has been so much noise and gasconade," was said to be due rather to accident than to preconceived plan.

After Fallen Timbers, Wilkinson asserted in a fourth group of accusations, Wayne failed to follow up his victory. Had he pursued the Indians eight miles further, the Legion could have

captured a camp wherein 2,500 squaws and papooses were cowering in fear. On this score he was probably correct, but in view
of the overwhelming victory already won, the additional glory
of taking women and children prisoner would have added little to Wayne's laurels. Much more serious was Wilkinson's
direct assertion that the official reports on Fallen Timbers, particularly those describing Wayne's activity in giving orders,
were "replete with falsehood." Wilkinson insisted that Wayne
had virtually nothing to do with winning the battle. "I pledge
my honor that I did not receive an order from him during the
action, and Colonel Hamtramck, who commanded the left
wing, assures me that his case was exactly similar. Indeed, I do
not hear of a single order which he gave, except to poor Campbell who was sacrificed by a premature charge."

Wayne was not the only high-placed figure whom the Wilkinsonians assailed. Secretary of War Henry Knox, Wayne's
supporter and defender, came in for a share of acid criticism.
"If some very material alterations do not take place," Tom
Cushing threatened in discussing the Legion's leadership, "resignation is inevitable. There will not remain ten officers of in-
telligence, sobriety and honor in the army. The ministerial
arrangements may have been good, but they have always failed
in execution. A very general want of confidence (not to say
contempt for) the Secretary of War prevails. His manner of
introducing officers, their different and mixed characters, and
his treatment of them whilst in service, his open and glaring
falsehoods, his partiality and injustice, in a word all his actions,
as they respect the army, are so many proofs that it never can
be respectable while Henry Knox is Secretary of War."

The War Department promptly relayed the Wilkinson accusations back to Wayne, with the notation that he must of
course forward a reply for their records, but that no one in
Philadelphia took the charges seriously. Wayne wrote off at
white heat a sixteen-page letter calling Wilkinson "a vile assassin," an unprincipled scoundrel who was plotting against the
very independence of America, a villain in the pay of Spain,
and, in the words of verses quoted by the Commander-in-Chief
in his formal acknowledgment to the War Department,

To draw his portrait needs no pencil nice
For all his composition is vice on vice.

"Fortunately for America," Wayne added, "the wise and decisive conduct of her Guardian Angle the President of the United
States . . . with the success attendant upon the arms of the
Western Army over the numerous hordes of Savages etc. etc.
at the foot of the rapids of the Miami of the Lakes on the
20th of August I trust have broke the measures and frustrated
all the nefarious machinations, formed for the dismemberment
of the Union."

The Wilkinsonians, unaware that the Commander-in-Chief
knew of their plots, continued their disloyal practices. They
spread rumors among the Kentuckians that trouble with the
commissariat was all Wayne's fault, and that in order to line
the pockets of his special favorites he had starved the Legion.
"When the general's conduct is fully known and the secret
causes are developed," said Tom Cushing angrily, "it will un-
fold a scene of duplicity and injustice which no *policy* can justify! no *art* can palliate!" Cushing's spleen, like that of other
Wilkinsonians, poured out like a flood. He complained about the
"partial and unequal manner in which the officers are employed."
"Numbers have never seen the corps to which they belong, and
are rioting at home, in ease and pleasure, whilst those in the
field are exposed to the hardest duty, and the meanest fare—
some, who have served but a few months, have obtained furloughs and are gone home, whilst many of those longest in
service and who have seen the most duty, have been treated
with rudeness and affront for asking this indulgence. Applica-
tions to resign have lain for months unanswered. Discharges
have been peremptorily refused and to such length has the doc-
trine of passive obedience and non-resistance been carried out
that officers have been threatened with an arrest for mutiny
(and even the guard house) for avowing their right and their
determination to quit the service."

By this time, even the rank and file were complaining of the
morality of the Legion. An army sergeant writing to a Philadelphia newspaper protested that it was time that justice should

be done the men who had to suffer under the administration of "fops, coxcombs, pedants and debauchees" serving as commanders. "Good Heavens!" he burst forth, "what constitutes the man of honour? Is it ignorance, insolence, envy, malice, prejudice, duplicity, debauchery? If so, many of the officers of the Legion have an indubitable claim to that distinction." The sergeant threatened to write a book exposing the scandals of the Legion; when it was issued, two years later, it contained a scathing criticism of military men in general and of the Legion in particular:

In an army everything invites and leads to dissipation, debauchery and indeed an almost total extinction of virtuous principles and habits. Honour, a pitiful substitute for virtue, is the titular deity of soldiers. . . . The army is the best school in the world . . . but it is a lottery, in which the disproportion of the prizes to the blanks is immense and where a single youth has acquired a fund of useful knowledge and improved it to advantage by serving as a soldier, nine or ten, perhaps a much greater number, have been eternally ruined.

Military men consider themselves as a superior order of beings to those whose lot it is to cultivate the earth. They make use of nicknames, expressive of the most superlative contempt for the peaceful occupations and honest characters of farmers and mechanics. The idea of a chaste and permanent connubial connection is, to the immense majority of them, an object of ridicule. . . . In the vicinity of the residence of a military corps, adultery is always frequent. A soldier ever prides himself in seducing an innocent virgin or a simple wife. Hundreds of once innocent and happy females are to be seen in every army, who have become, from necessity or despair, the most abandoned beings in existence.

CHAPTER XIX

Double-Barreled Spy

ALTHOUGH his campaign had been brilliantly successful, Wayne continued to be puzzled. He could not yet understand how knowledge of his plans had so leaked to the Indians that Little Turtle had met him at so well-chosen an ambush as Fallen Timbers, nor why Major Campbell had closed his gates against the Indians. Following the battle, Wayne meditated over the problem, without reaching a solution; he talked with his intimates, whom enemies ridiculed as "the Cabinet"; he even sounded Wilkinson himself. All his probing failed to bring an explanation.

Then, unexpectedly, a guardhouse prisoner gave important information. Chaplain Davy Jones, Wayne's next-door neighbor and his army comrade since Ticonderoga days, had been visiting the jail and conversing with the prisoners. Among the men awaiting execution on desertion charges was one Robert Newman, former Kentucky schoolteacher, who said he was unjustly sentenced. He asked that Parson Jones take to Wayne a letter "written," Jones said, "in abstruse language." The gist of the message, Jones related, was that Newman knew of traitors in high places. Wayne promised that if Newman made a complete confesstion, clemency would be shown. He had the irons struck off the former schoolteacher, "so that he could change his shirt and get rid of the numerous inhabitants."

Newman, quartermaster of Kentucky volunteers, told how certain broadsides in which Wayne was maligned as an aristocrat, a despot, and an enemy of Kentucky freedom were widely scattered through that newly admitted state, together with handbills offering high rewards to any soldiers who deserted to the British cause. In consequence, said Newman, Kentuckians were afire with indignation against Wayne. Newman had been brought into the movement through the machinations of Wilkinson and James Hawkins, a well-known Kentucky land speculator and contractor. The youthful, idealistic schoolteacher, who yearned to be of service to his friends, had been enrolled as courier between the Legion and Alexander McKee, British agent for the Indians at Detroit. The mission seemed mysterious, but the suave Hawkins said assuringly that this was official business of the utmost importance, helpful both to the Americans and to the Canadians, that the service would be valuable to Hawkins personally, and that Newman would win renown. Newman carried out his orders. In his innocence, he assumed that Hawkins had some private agreement with the contractors serving the British Army whereby both sides would work together for a common profit. He had at the time, he told Wayne upon oath, not the slightest inkling that Wilkinson was involved; certainly he had no thought of treason.

On the evening before the Legion left Greeneville, Newman, who had arrived only a few hours earlier with the mounted volunteers, was walking down a company street in the vicinity of the quartermaster's office. A tall, good-looking officer whom he did not then know, but whom he later identified as Campbell Smith, darted from a hut and pushed a paper into his hands. Newman found that it was a sealed envelope addressed to Colonel McKee. He identified the writing as that of Wilkinson. At this point the Newman story strains the imagination, for the prisoner, though no woodsman and without a map, declared that he found his way speedily, and in advance of the Legion, to Fort Miamis. There he was gleefully received, and he gleaned more information about his mission. He picked up enough details to suspect that Wilkinson had predicted Wayne's imminent dismissal and that he was offering to make a deal with British leaders. Wilkinson, he understood, had either received a British bribe, or would soon be given one, to effect a new union of Kentucky, Canada, and the Northwest Territory, separate from both Britain and the United States! Major

Campbell was in the agreement; he had refused to admit the beaten Indians into the fort because he anticipated making a deal with Wilkinson and the American traitors.

No important Canadian outside Fort Miamis and Detroit appeared to be involved in the affair. Simcoe at Niagara evidently knew nothing of it, for Simcoe believed that Newman had been sent to Canada by Wayne "for some sinister purpose." He got rid of Newman by shipping him across the line into the United States. The bewildered former teacher went down to Philadelphia, where he passed himself off as Wayne's special envoy and where he asked for army transportation to rejoin the mounted volunteers. The War Department, accepting the story in good faith, gave him stagecoach passage to the Ohio country, adding $20 for traveling expenses. But no sooner had the stage rolled off along the newly built Lancaster Pike than Secretary Knox received a letter from Wayne reporting Newman as a deserter. A fast express sent after the impostor caught up with him at Pittsburgh; from that point to Wayne's headquarters, he was a prisoner in heavy irons.

His course thereafter was more simple; by throwing all the blame on Wilkinson and Campbell Smith, he won Wayne's favor. The Commander-in-Chief used Newman's information to discredit "that vile assassin Wilkinson"; in a private letter to Henry Knox, Wayne made the definite accusation: "I have strong grounds to believe that this man is a principal agent set up by the British and *Demoncrats* of Kentucky to dismember the Union. . . . Was peace once established with the Indians, no consideration would induce me to remain a single hour longer in the service should that worst of all bad men belong to it."

Newman, having proved the truth of his belief that if his frank confession "does no good, it can do no harm," now felt himself protected against Wayne's vengeance; it was necessary also to make himself safe against revenge by Wilkinson and Hawkins. He concocted a cock-and-bull story to the effect that Thomas Lewis, one of Wayne's aides, had intercepted Wilkinson's letter and that the note had been read by Wayne himself. Any betrayal of the Wilkinson plans, said Newman, should be laid to Wayne's foreknowledge of the plot. Even Newman's brother doubted the authenticity of this statement, believing that in return for disclosing the scheme to the General, Robert Newman had been promised cash from Wayne's secret-service funds. That payments were to have been made to Newman seems indisputable from assertions made by Thomas Lewis, but that vivacious aide while carrying the cash enjoyed himself so hugely at taverns and other places of resort that he spent not only all his own money but also the sums entrusted to him for Newman.

No matter what the truth behind the complex Newman matter may have been, the fact remains that the seriousness of its accusations against Wilkinson caused the Brigadier's charges against Wayne to fade into obscurity. The one answer to all Wilkinson's complaints was that Wayne's strategy had succeeded. The victory over Little Turtle and the smashing of the Indian confederacy, the bearding of the British, and the subsequent shattering of the Anglo-Indian alliance were too overwhelming victories to be forgotten. So thoroughly were the Wilkinson accusations disregarded that no official record of them now exists.

On the contrary, Wayne was warmly praised. Congress by a unanimous vote extended its thanks to him "for the good conduct and bravery displayed by him, the army, Major-General Scott and the mounted volunteers of Kentucky." Knox added his congratulations, while Washington authorized the sending of a special message reading: "The President has formed the most favourable judgment of your incessant industry in disciplining the troops, for your judicious managements and vigilance, and for your care in obtaining the necessary supplies." As further proof of the confidence imposed in Wayne by all branches of the administration at Philadelphia, he was appointed sole commissioner to negotiate a lasting peace between the United States and the hostile Indians of the West.

Armed with this authority, Wayne sent messages to the Delawares, Shawnees, Chippewas, Wyandots, Potawatomis, Miamis, "and all other tribes whom it may concern" that he was ready to make peace with them, provided they returned their prisoners at once. While he waited for an answer, he left Fort Defiance and struck southwest up the Maumee, to the Miami village at the confluence of the St. Joseph and St. Mary's rivers. This was an important strategic gateway, commanding the trails from Detroit and the Great Miami, from the Wabash, and from the East. To hold it firmly, Wayne built a log fort capable of resisting twenty-four-pounder guns. Colonel Hamtramck insisted that this post receive the name of Fort Wayne. Here, and at Fort Defiance, Wayne planned to create magazines sufficient to maintain the Legion in the event of a further forward movement. He cut a wide wagon road forty-eight miles long connecting the two posts.

Once the forts were built, the usual problems rose to plague the commander. Hundreds of Kentucky mounted volunteers, restless for want of useful occupation, milled about, drinking, gambling, rioting, and all too often talking over the plan to join Canada and Kentucky in a vast new inland empire. Wayne dared not discipline the volunteers too harshly, lest they desert him and go back to "demoncratic" Kentucky, where they would be not only forgiven but pampered.

Elliott and Williams came unwittingly to his assistance. Despite his wagon road and the facilities afforded them for transportation, they were defaulting in their duties; there seemed slight hope that they could fill the magazines before the coming of cold weather. Wayne resorted to the step that he had often threatened. He ordered Scott to turn the mounted volunteers into pack-horsemen to convoy flour over the new road to Fort Wayne. The Kentuckians resented their degradation; they almost mutinied at being demoted to the quartermaster's corps.

2

Greeneville's guns boomed out a twenty-four-round salute as the victorious Legion marched smartly back to its base on the evening of November 2. The heavy wall of forest, dull red with the late autumn tints of maples, glowing brown and yellow with oak and hickory, with here and there faint purplish hues of walnuts that had long since shed their leaves, echoed with the thunder of the cannon; great sycamores and graceful beeches threw long, slender shadow patterns over the clearing that lay about the fort.

Wayne's men prepared to take their ease again. For fifteen weeks they had been marching through the forest, fearing ambush yet plodding onward, passing through tangled underbrush and over swampy lowland, fording creeks and bridging rivers, fighting Indians at Fallen Timbers, cutting corn at Grand Glaize, building forts at every stopping-place, hauling stores and going through their never-ending drills. The men were tired of labor; they looked forward to a frolic. As the salute roared from Greeneville's cannon, the Legion quickened pace. Heads erect and chests thrown out as if they were upon parade, the army marched through an avenue of cheering garrison troops into the welcoming citadel.

The post had been improved since their departure. The Legion, setting forth upon its long campaign, had last seen Greeneville in the early summer, when the verdant meadow south of the fort was gay with flowers, and when to north and east the groves which had blossomed in the spring with magnolia, hawthorn, crab apple, pawpaw, and honey locust were crimson with fruit of plum and cherry. Now, in November, these were gone, but the soldiers did not miss the color. The returning men, happy to be once more at their base, looked with approval at the buildings that had gone up in their absence. For Greeneville seemed to these men from the Indian wilderness to have become a city. Within its mile-long palisade and its chain of circular redoubts were solid blocks of huts where men would be warm in winter. The blockhouse and bastions were reinforced by heavier defenses, capable, as Wayne boasted, recalling his Legionville phrase, of being held "against all the savages of the wilderness." Storehouses, mess rooms, headquarters offices, shops for artificers, and all the necessary buildings for a permanent cantonment had been erected. A giant Council House in which Wayne might talk to Indian ambassadors was in process of construction. For weeks the thud of hammers and the sound of axes had testified to the assiduous labor of the men whom Wayne had left behind.

The cheering and the artillery salute were but the start of a home-coming celebration. As soon as the soldiers were within the palisades, each man received a gill of rum. The officers, waiting only long enough to wash away their travel stains, enjoyed a feast where Wayne and Wilkinson, with all their staffs, dined sumptuously. The fare included all the food obtainable in the wilderness. Roast venison and beef, boiled and roast mutton, boiled and roast veal, boiled and roast turkey, duck, and chicken, raccoon and possum, boar meat and chicken pie, loaded down the tables. To follow these were mince and apple pies, preserves and jellies, plum pudding and plum cake, floating island, and, to cap the jubilation, dishes of ice cream, a dainty which army men had not seen since they had left the East. The officers, ignoring for the moment their rivalries and jealousies, dined merrily; in the evening they enjoyed a ball, although the men far outnumbered the few girls; at midnight, they broke up in high good humor. Two days later, Wilkinson received a furlough; with him went several of his chief supporters. Wayne, thus free of intrigue within his ranks, issued orders requiring that the customary two-hour drills and the maneuvers be continued.

Preparations now began for a final treaty with the Indians. Cleverly, Wayne again split the confederacy. By bribing Isaac Williams, a half-breed Wyandot from the Sandusky settlement, he spread dissension among that tribe, persuading Tarhe, the only Wyandot war chief left alive, that "the little finger of the Legion" could crush all the might that the Wyandots could raise. The Delawares and Miamis also became convinced that Wayne was irresistible; the Shawnees meditated moving west across the Mississippi. Simcoe and McKee pleaded with the tribesmen to make another stand, promising that in the spring the British would send aid, but Wayne and Isaac Williams pointed to the failure of the English to defend the beaten Indians after Fallen Timbers. The red men would not credit Simcoe's promises, since at their great crisis the British had not only refused to help but had barred their gates.

One by one, the tribes sent delegates to treat with Wayne. On New Year's Day, 1795, messengers arrived from Chippewas, Ottawas, Sacs, Potawatomis, and Miamis, petitioning for peace. Wayne assembled them in his newly completed Council House; he passed a pipe of peace, and gave them brandy to drink to the health of the Great Spirit. Then he stated his preliminary terms. If they would recognize the old treaties, ceding the Northwest Territory, and would surrender all prisoners, a final peace conference could be held in the early summer.

The Indians agreed. In a long speech, couched in symbolic language, Bad Bird, chief of the Chippewas, declared that their eyes were now open to recognize Americans as their true friends, and that their ears were sharpened to hear the voice of peace. Wayne, turning to his aide De Butts, who sat next to him, whispered drily: "The Legion are excellent oculists and aurists, and its bayonets are very proper instruments for removing film from the eyes and wax from the ears of savages. Possibly Congress may give us a three years' patent for our valuable discovery." He liked the quip so much that he embodied it in an official report to Knox.

The only point of disagreement was the place at which the final treaty should be arranged. The Indians asked that the conference be held at Kekionga (Fort Wayne); the Americans insisted that the tribesmen return to Greeneville for the ceremony. Resorting to the Indian use of symbolism, Wayne insisted that Kekionga would be unsuitable. "It was there," he pointed out, "that the hatchet was first raised; to bury a bloody hatchet there would disturb the spirits of the unburied dead. But if we bury it here, the hatchet will never again be found, because no bloody traces will mark the grave in which it rests."

His private reasons were less symbolic, but more practical. At Greeneville, the Legion would have more troops to overawe the delegates and the Greeneville citadel would be a powerful defense "against all the Indians in the wilderness." Besides, Wayne pointed out to Knox, the cost of holding a conference at Greeneville would be but half that of a meeting to be held scores of miles distant. He carried his point. On January 21, 1795, an armistice was signed binding both parties to cease from war until June 15; Bad Bird presented Wayne with a handsome string of blue wampum, "sent from the ladies of my village to the ladies of your villages," testifying to the cessation of warfare. Wayne, in return, supplied the delegates with rum sufficient for a drunken celebration.

Two weeks later, Blue Jacket, White Eyes, and Buckongehelas, representing Shawnees and Delawares, came into Greeneville to make a similar agreement. Blue Jacket held first a private conference with the Commander-in-Chief, in which he reported that the British had refused even to give the chiefs the presents that were usually distributed. Wayne took the hint and bribed Blue Jacket by a $300 yearly subsidy. Dressed in a bright scarlet coat with two glittering gold epaulets, given him by the Americans, Blue Jacket persuaded his colleagues to sign an armistice. The two Delawares, White Eyes and Buckongehelas, each uniformed in dress costumes, but with one epaulet instead of the two which Blue Jacket displayed, came over also to Wayne's point of view. As a proof of friendship, Blue Jacket left an unmarried sister in Wayne's care. In return, Wayne agreed to get for the Shawnee chief an American military commission, not because he wished to make Blue Jacket an officer in the army, but because the Indian admired the red seals and attractive engravings with which the documents were decorated. The administration, though loath to issue such papers, experimented with the creation of some specially ornate official documents that would strike the fancy of the chiefs.

During the period of the armistice, couriers dashed back and forth between Greeneville and Philadelphia, bearing messages relative to the terms to be demanded from the Indians. Washington declared that all that the United States required was that the Indians confirm treaties already signed, and that the nation would pay $25,000 in trade goods and give a yearly subsidy of $10,000 more in return for peace. If, in addition, Wayne could secure lands connecting the Ohio and Maumee rivers, together with control of the latter river from Fort Wayne to Lake Erie and from the head of the Wabash to the Ohio, the administration would be highly pleased. "Do not, however, insist upon this," wrote the Secretary of War, "for *peace* and not *increase of territory* has been the object of this expensive war."

Since the British had promised to relinquish Detroit, as well as other posts within the disputed territory, Washington desired Wayne to negotiate for a strip of land six miles wide along the west shore of Lake Erie and along the Detroit River from the Raisin River to Lake St. Clair. This, in the War Department's view, "would be a convenient appendage to Detroit and would give room for settlement." By a further communication, the Secretary of War suggested that concessions at the foot of Lake Michigan and along the Illinois River would be desirable to secure, but "it is probably not expedient to ask for them." Wayne was not to use duress and was to be absolutely accurate and truthful in dealing with Indians. He was cautioned to explain in clear detail exactly what ownership in fee simple meant to white men, so that Indians would not again be misled into thinking that they retained any rights whatever to the territory to be ceded. He was to be sure that every important chief was present at the Council, lest Indians claim that their delegates were not truly representative, but he must not make the mistake of allowing too many Indians to congregate, for, as the War Department warned, Pontiac had almost taken Detroit in 1763 by such a ruse.

Wayne's heart almost broke when he read the signature to this War Department letter. It was not signed by his old comrade Henry Knox, but by a new name, Timothy Pickering, the very man who had failed so dismally as Indian commissioner. Knox had warned that he was considering resignation, to take care of private business, and Wayne had hoped to be named Secretary in his stead. He had delayed too long in lining up political support; Pickering had entered the Cabinet before Wayne's supporters had been organized. Nor did Wayne like the general plan of treaty which the administration was suggesting. He wished a special clause forbidding white men and Indians to be neighbors. "I would beg leave to hazard an opinion," Wayne wrote, "that a kind of consecrated ground ought to be put between the savages and the white inhabitants; which Congress should make a point of holding in mortmain, and neither sell or suffer to be settled upon any pretext whatever."

This was rejected. Pickering flatly refused to consider the idea. "I do not know," he said, "what is so likely to be a fruitful source of disputes as an *undefined boundary* in which neither party can say, 'Here is the certain boundary which marks the end of my claims.' " Like Washington, Pickering also opposed the idea of broad territorial cessions, lest land-jobbers or marauders enter to cause trouble. It was a wise attitude to take, for Wayne was already finding that unprincipled white men, violating the truce, were goading the Indians to fresh revenge.

With all Wayne's care to avoid a breach of the truce, a reckless frontier party threatened to upset all arrangements. Wayne, immersed in manifold duties, had overlooked sending official word of the armistice to Arthur St. Clair, Governor of the Northwest Territory, so that the agreements not to venture into new areas were not officially known. A party led by Parson Findlay crossed the border and committed depredations. Wayne, incensed at the breaking of his truce, wrote a stinging protest to Governor St. Clair: "This Mr. Findlay cannot be a disciple of the meek Jesus, otherwise he would not thus wantonly bring war and desolation upon the innocent by the sinful aggressions of his guilty hordes of plunderers. . . . Unless some effectual measures are adopted to prevent predatory parties from Kentucky crossing the Ohio, the inhabitants of the Territory, over which you preside, will hold their lives and property by a very precarious tenure."

St. Clair, never patient with Wayne, threw the blame upon the Commander-in-Chief: "As I have never, Sir, had any information on the subject of the armistice that took place between you and the savages, nor any knowledge of it at all but from a newspaper, it is very difficult for me to know how to proceed in case of infractions, or to tell what is an infraction; and there may be doubt how far an agreement entered into by a military officer for a cessation of hostilities, however binding on him, is binding on the people. As yet, Sir, they have no notice of it, that I know of, in this territory that will bind them at all." Nevertheless, he did issue a proclamation calling upon civilians to abide by Wayne's agreement; he sent a message to

Governor Shelby appealing to that official to restrain Kentuckians from crossing into Indian territory. Wayne's purpose was achieved; the armistice was not again disturbed.

In the spring Indians began to gather for the Council. Many came by way of Fort Wayne, so crowding that post that Hamtramck's garrison had to go on half-rations to feed the delegates. Even this did not suffice; the stores kept there for emergencies became depleted, while liquor and tobacco were so exhausted that Hamtramck bought additional supplies from Antoine Lacelle, Blue Jacket's brother-in-law, at his own expense.

From Fort Wayne, the hordes of Indian delegates moved on to Greeneville, where Wayne quartered them in guardhouses beyond the advanced redoubts, under the guns of his bastions. All day long, parties of Delawares, Ottawas, Potawatomis, Shawnees, and Miamis wandered about the fort. They galloped their horses in the open meadows, trampling down jonquils and primroses, daisies, violets, and hyacinths growing luxuriantly about the cantonment; they danced and shouted all night long. Wayne dared not command them to keep the peace, lest they quit the conference. The chief leaders still held back. Blue Jacket, Buckongehelas, Little Turtle, and the rest lingered at Detroit, entertained by Canadian land-jobbers who kept them drunk. Wayne fumed at this duplicity, but he could do nothing to hurry the arrangements.

June 15, the day set for the opening of the Council, came with many of the principal Indian statesmen absent. Left to himself, Wayne would have proceeded with the treaty, but he was under orders to do nothing until the actual leaders were on hand. He convened such delegates as were present, in order to carry out the letter of the armistice, but he was well aware that the formal opening was but an empty gesture.

"I have cleared the ground of all brush and rubbish," he said, after the peace pipe had been passed, "and opened roads to the east, to the west, to the north and to the south, that all nations may come in safety and ease to meet me. The ground on which this Council House stands is unstained with blood, and is as pure as the heart of General Washington, the Great Chief of America, and of his Great Council; it is as pure as my heart which wishes for nothing so much as peace and brotherly love. I have this day kindled the Council fire of the United States; we will now cover it up, and keep it alive until the remainder of the different tribes assemble, and form a full meeting. . . . The heavens are high; the woods are open; we will rest in peace. In the meantime, we will have a little refreshment to wash the dust from our throats. We will, on this happy occasion, be merry, but without passing the bounds of temperence and sobriety."

Next day, a Potawatomi chief arrived; soon after, Buckongahelas appeared with a party of the Delawares; eight days after the scheduled opening, Little Turtle brought in seventy-three Miamis. All these received pork and whisky, but they complained that they were still hungry. Wayne told them that as soon as the Council began its work Washington would send food and liquor in abundance.

On July 4, nineteenth anniversary of American independence, Wayne gave an entertainment. The day opened with the boom of cannon, which Wayne described as "harbingers of peace and gladness," and continued with an elaborate field day in which the Legion, firing with blank cartridges, raised a fearful din. Flag-raisings followed; Sub-Legionary bands played martial music; and then the Legion was drawn up in parade formation to sing. Surgeon Joseph Strong led the soldiers in a seven-stanza hymn whose first lines read:

> In leagues of love we now unite
> Around the bank of peaceful light
> And hail the joy-clad day.
> No more shall ruthless foes pervade
> The vast domain of Western shade
> Or war-like music play.

The observance ended with a sermon on the theme of peace, justice, and, surprisingly enough, freedom from slavery. The next day being Sunday, Wayne led his officers to church to hear a second sermon on "The Altar of Peace."

By July 15, exactly a month after the day scheduled for opening the Council, all the great chiefs of the Indians at last assembled. The Council fire, "covered up" on June 15, was "stirred up and replenished," and round it gathered Wayne and his three chief aides, William Henry Harrison, Thomas Lewis, and Henry de Butts, together with James O'Hara and Parson David Jones. Nine French Canadian interpreters, together with the famous frontier scouts William Wells and Christopher Miller, and the half-breed Isaac Williams, acted as intermediaries between the Americans and such Indian chiefs as Little Turtle, Blue Jacket, Buckongehelas, the Bad Bird, and Tarhe, the great keeper of the Wyandot calumet. More than eleven hundred less important men represented the twelve tribes taking part in the arrangements.

Wayne opened the deliberations by reiterating that former treaties must be recognized. He then held up a huge carved copy of the coat of arms of the United States, and pointing to the eagle, indicated that the Indians could take their choice of either the sheaf of arrows held in one talon as a sign of war or the olive branch in the other which stood for peace. Little Turtle vainly pleaded that former treaties were not fairly obtained and that in any case too much land had been exacted from the tribes; he sought postponement, but to no avail. Wayne insisted on prompt action. During so much unnecessary delay, the Commander-in-Chief pointed out, the Indians must have considered their answer.

Wayne's demands called for greater cessions than Little Turtle had anticipated. At worst, he had expected that the victorious Americans would ask only for the Great Miami River as a western boundary, but Wayne, in line with his fixed policy of holding every inch of ground ever trod by his Legion, insisted that the Great Miami was unsuitable, since it would omit both Greeneville and Fort Recovery from the territory to be granted to the United States. He suggested a frontier drawn in a straight line running almost due south from Fort Recovery to a point opposite the junction of the Ohio and Kentucky rivers. Little Turtle, realizing that the additional cession would deprive his people of rich hunting-ground in the Whitewater River valley, just west of the present Ohio-Indiana line, protested vigorously, but to no avail. Wayne, who may or may not have known of the fertility of that area, insisted on its inclusion. The Indians, realizing that their only alternative was renewal of the war, reluctantly consented.

Another Wayne requirement, made and approved in all innocence, caused international complications. In order to prevent further British interference with American relations with the tribesmen, Wayne suggested that every white man residing among or trading with the Indians should secure a license from the United States authorities, and that unlicensed white men should be turned over by the Indians to Americans for punishment. The British promptly protested, pointing out that by the third clause of the Jay Treaty, British and American citizens enjoyed free rights of residence and passage in each other's territory. Whether Wayne knew of the Jay Treaty terms prior to the conclusion of the Greeneville agreement is open to doubt. He had been unofficially informed of the Jay Treaty fully four months before the Greeneville negotiations ended, but the United States Senate had failed to ratify it until late in June, 1795. In all probability, Wayne knew that his demand was in conflict with the Anglo-American agreement, but there is a possibility that, as a violent opponent of the Jay terms, he had hoped that the Senate would reject the arrangement. As soon as Great Britain heard of the Greeneville terms, Phineas Bond, the new Minister to the United States, received instructions to protest against them. By special stipulation made between Bond and Secretary of War Timothy Pickering, the United States recognized that licenses for residence and trade must be as freely granted to British subjects as to American citizens.

To prevent misinterpretations, Wayne explained the terms three times. He announced his desire to open up a series of broad avenues connecting the ceded areas, and he reiterated his idea of a "consecrated ground" between the area thus transferred to the United States and the lands retained by the Indians. Certainly, as he pointed out, the Indians were pleased. They had not liked the previous treaties and had, in fact, refused to look upon them as valid, but, Wayne said, they "cheerfully and unanimously" accepted the Treaty of Greeneville. Since the United States Senate had never ratified St. Clair's

Treaty of Muskingum of 1789, Wayne declared that he had won for the nation a land addition greater than any ever previously acquired.

By the final provisions, agreed upon on August 3, 1795, the Indians ceded land east and south of a line running from the mouth of the Cuyahoga, at what is now Cleveland, upstream to the portage site at Fort Laurens, in the neighborhood of Dover. Thence the line struck roughly westward through Loramie's Stores to Fort Recovery, from which it went southerly to the junction of the Kentucky and Ohio rivers. In addition, the tribes signed away their rights to lands at Chicago, Peoria, the mouth of the Illinois, Vincennes and Ouiatenon on the Wabash, Forts Wayne and Defiance, Sandusky, Fort Miamis, and the west shore of Lake Erie and the Detroit River. Wayne, in other words, gained everything that Washington and Pickering had termed either essential or desirable.

As a souvenir, Wayne presented to each important Indian chief an oval silver medal showing a bareheaded Washington presenting a peace pipe to an Indian; on the reverse the arms of the United States appear beneath a cloudy sky through which the sun of victory is breaking. The Indians, to testify to their appreciation of Wayne's fairness, gave him a yard-long peace pipe, elaborately carved and ornamented with much skill. The pipe was immediately charged with tobacco and passed about among the signers.

The Greeneville Treaty colors all later American relations with the Indians. For the first time in history the title of Indian nations to land lying within the boundaries of the United States was officially recognized, for while American ownership of territory lying south and east of the treaty line was confirmed, the United States by solemn covenant definitely admitted Indian ownership of all land lying north and west of the frontiers, even though such territory had supposedly been ceded to the United States following the Revolutionary War. By strict interpretation of the Treaty of Greeneville, no American citizen had any right to trespass upon Indian land without the license of the United States and, more important, the consent of the tribes to whom the land belonged. Violation of that pledge in later years when Americans swarmed over the frontier into Indian portions of Illinois, Indiana, and northwestern Ohio wrecked Indian faith in the honesty of American pledges.

Probably the Greeneville Treaty dictated the future course of American expansion. Ownership of scattered bits of land, set aside as military reservations, almost inevitably led to efforts to link the areas together by those "broad avenues" of which Wayne had warned. Consolidation of possession meant the taking over of great areas of Indiana and Illinois. This, in turn, increased American desire for the Mississippi and for a free outlet to the sea via the Gulf of Mexico. Had Wayne not won the Northwest Territory, it is probable that England would have overrun the region north and west of the Ohio, with the consequent shutting off of the United States from western expansion; with Britain pushed beyond the Great Lakes and no strong nation west of the Alleghenies, it was only natural for the United States, once it had reached the Mississippi, to look beyond the prairies to the Rockies and thereafter to the Pacific itself. Wayne's annexation of the Northwest Territory led to the purchase of Louisiana, to the Lewis and Clark expedition (officered by men trained in his Legion), and thus to the acquisition of Oregon and California. Anthony Wayne's military successes and his diplomatic triumphs were the beginnings of empire.

The work for which Wayne had been appointed Commander-in-Chief was now finished. He had succeeded triumphantly where Harmar and St. Clair had failed; by daring greatly he had broken the power of the Indians and by his defiance had destroyed the threat of an Anglo-Indian alliance. His long days of drill and discipline, his endless watchfulness, his careful preparation, had borne their fruit. Anthony Wayne, conqueror of the Northwest Territory, victor in what is now Ohio, southeastern Indiana, much of Illinois, and parts of Michigan, closed his active military career in a bright blaze of glory.

CHAPTER XX

With His Boots On

Bells chimed from every steeple in the capital as Major-General Anthony Wayne, conqueror of the Indian Confederacy, rode with the gaily uniformed Philadelphia City Troop into the center of the city. Again and again, all day long on Saturday, February 6, 1796, guns boomed their fifteen-round salute in honor of the hero.

Wayne was home again, for the first time in almost four years, savoring the warm welcome of his nation. His thousand-mile ride over the Wilderness Road had been a torture, for his gout ached painfully and he dared not ride too rapidly lest his flannel-swathed legs fail to grip his horse's flanks; for the first few hundred miles, through thinly settled Kentucky and the backwoods portions of Virginia, he had suffered agonies for want of comfortable beds at night. But now at last he was at home, where luxuries abounded. Hearing the sweet tones of Christ Church bells, striking their rapid octaves and their harmonies in tercet and in quint, ascending and descending fifteen times for the fifteen states, he felt a new delight. He knew that the machinations of his enemies had been in vain and that his campaigns against Indians and British were appreciated as the triumphs that they really were. He was at last receiving praise for himself alone. He was the sole hero.

The tidy, well-paved capital was scrubbed clean; its streets, geometrically laid out at right angles to each other, were gay with flags and bunting. Spanning High Street, in mid-city, a triumphal arch twenty-six feet high stood like a temple of peace, with four great columns and a highly ornamented cornice. Above it was a huge globe on which a great carved dove sat with an olive branch in its beak. As Wayne passed, artillery boomed again, marking his official arrival in the city. Crowds lined the sidewalks, many wearing the French tricolor, for this was also the eighteenth anniversary of the signing of the French alliance, and as they waited for the cavalcade to come, fathers wearing proudly the remnants of their Revolutionary uniforms told their sons of Trois Rivières and Ticonderoga, of Brandywine and Germantown, of Stony Point and Green Springs and Paoli. Some, remembering the great Guristersijo in Georgia, told of the General's exploits in the South; all who had ever been in the service snapped sharply to attention as Wayne's procession passed.

He paid, of course, his first respects to Washington and to the Cabinet, noting there, in some surprise, that Pickering was gone. Again he was hurt at being passed over, for Dr. James McHenry, a friend since early Revolutionary days, was the new Secretary of War. McHenry, he discovered, had also just arrived in town; the Wayne reception was his first official function. Then, after a brief visit with Sharp Delany, wan and pale after a long illness, and with his son Isaac, law student in William Lewis's office, he was taken over to the City Tavern.

In some respects the inn was a disappointment. Even in the four years while Wayne had been campaigning in the West, the City Tavern had lost much of its prestige. He found it faded and decayed, rather a businessman's hotel than a center for fashionable wits; but the company who waited for him brought back the brilliance of pre-Revolutionary parties. Effervescent Judge Peters, bubbling with bad puns, stood close to Francis Johnston, heavier and more sedate than he had been before he turned politician; Representative Tom Hartley moved about amid a score of Senators and Congressmen. No ladies attended, for this levee was purely masculine, but several men came over to whisper that they had messages from Mary Vining, still unmarried and expecting Wayne to come to see her when he was at liberty. He waited until he had greeted all the guests, and until De Butts and Thomas Lewis, the aides who had preceded him by about two weeks, had told him about political manipulations. They had, they said, discovered that the war portfolio was open, and they had endeavored to obtain the post for him, but Washington had thought Wayne too essential as an active soldier in the field.

After the reception, finding that the theater was legal again, Wayne would have liked to go with Mary Vining to see the new pantomime in the huge, conically roofed Art Pantheon which gave its address as "T'Other Side of the Gutter," but the time was not politically propitious. The Democrats had usurped the evening that they might demonstrate, by superb fireworks and by a special party at the Pantheon, their admiration for the radical French Republic. He stayed within doors lest by his presence he countenance the revels.

On the Wednesday following his arrival, the New Theatre, a magnificent affair copied after the Royal Theatre of Bath, staged a gala performance in Wayne's honor. Philadelphia society, packed into the double horseshoe tier of boxes, joined with two thousand other spectators to give him tumultuous applause when he and Mary came in to see *Warrior's Welcome Home*, a new ballet dedicated to the conqueror. It was preceded by a comedy, *The Provoked Husband*, which put everyone in high good humor, and was followed by a two-act musical drama, *The Children in the Wood*. The characters, said Wayne, were not at all like Indians. So successful was the party that five days later the same theater invited Wayne as guest of honor at a second play, *Everyone Has His Fault*, to be followed by the *Warrior's Welcome Home*, and by Wayne's favorite, *The Poor Soldier*.

The New Theatre had thus won two rounds from its opponent on "T'Other Side of the Gutter," but the Art Pantheon was not to be defeated. Its manager, Ricketts, a master showman, announced that Wayne would be the guest of honor at an evening when the Green Dragoons, assisted by several Indian warriors, would show entertainment never matched in previous theatrical history. Ricketts himself opened the main performance by dashing in on his horse Cornplanter, named in honor of Wayne's Indian friend, and then leaping a five-barred gate. Two other riders, a clown and a girl acrobat, cantered about the ring while Cornplanter leaped over their horses; then Ricketts jumped over seven members of the Green Dragoons as they stood huddled in the center of the ring. He made his audience gasp by leaping over the heads of twenty men, while simultaneously turning a somersault on Cornplanter's back. Ground and lofty tumbling by a company of six followed, and the evening closed with a pantomime, *The Triumph of Virtue, or Harlequin in Philadelphia.*

Wayne's time in the capital was not all holiday. Ten days after his arrival, the Treaty of Greeneville came up in the Senate for approval and the Commander-in-Chief was busy explaining its provisions. Soon after this a determined effort was begun to cut the army establishment in half. As during the time of his own service in the House, Wayne fought desperately for a professional army as opposed to hastily raised militia; he related his own experiences both during the Revolutionary War and with Kentucky's mounted volunteers. Not until the end of May was he successful in protecting the army against those who would reduce it to a flimsy skeleton.

Meanwhile, he was with Mary Vining constantly. Gossips reported that the two were deeply in love and some said positively that they were engaged. Mrs. Williamina Cadwalader, widow of Wayne's brother general John Cadwalader, seemed shocked to hear the news. "Such a weather-beaten, vulgar, affected old soldier, I should have thought," wrote Mrs. Cadwalader to her friend Ann Ridgely, "would not have suited her refinement. I at first heard it from Mrs. Ferguson"—Wayne's one-time flame Elizabeth Graeme Ferguson—"who had a person that had lived a year with Miss Vining; since then I have had a confirmation."

Neither Wayne nor Mary Vining publicly admitted their engagement. They sat together in the drawing-room of John Vining's Philadelphia home, or rode in Mary's daintily painted carriage through the streets; on one occasion, they went shopping so that Anthony could buy for her a set of Lowestoft porcelain, cream-white with deep-pink decorations. Evidently, they arranged that when Wayne should finish up his duties in the West, to which he must return in June, he would return to marry her, for in later years Mary Vining was to mourn him as the man who might have been her husband. During 1796 all that Philadelphia society knew was that gossip reputed them to be engaged.

Certainly Margaretta Atlee, Wayne's daughter Peggy, never mentioned Mary Vining as a future stepmother. Perhaps, however, Peggy was hurt because during her father's courtship two weeks had passed without her seeing him. "I was drawing unfavorable conclusions," she declared, "I thought that I was forgotten by a father whom I tenderly and affectionately love and respect." Neither in the correspondence of Isaac Wayne nor in the letters of any other intimate of Anthony is there reference to an acknowledged engagement of the Commander-in-Chief with the belle of Wilmington. Mrs. Williamina Cadwalader alone is contemporary evidence. "This is a strange affair of Miss Vining's," the Cadwalader letter admitted, "though 'none but the brave deserve the fair' and that he was brave is undoubted."

That Wayne intended to remain in the West is clear. He and former Secretary of War Knox discussed a scheme to start a company for developing the copper beds of the Lake Superior region; they sent a metallurgist to that area to make investigations and report on possibilities. Wayne thought much also of a new tanning process of which he had heard in Kentucky, whereby through the use of sulphuric acid skins lost their hair and softened quickly. A calfskin, Wayne learned, would tan in two days, and the strongest oxhide would be completely tanned in two weeks' time. If, thought Wayne, he set up a tannery in the forests, eliminating the need to transport bark long distances, the process would be even cheaper.

Politics attracted him; upcountry Pennsylvanians had backed the short-lived De Butts campaign to make Wayne Secretary of War; some voters in the interior urged him to run for the governorship. Wayne dallied with the idea, but the more he sounded out his friends, the less sure he was that Pennsylvania would vote Federalist; if he should run, he might not be elected.

Hopefully, though not with deep expectation of success, he purchased lottery tickets, for his own advantage and in the names of his children, thinking that if he won the capital prize, he might live for the remainder of his life upon the interest of his winnings; but his numbers were not drawn. Certain that something would turn up to free him from routine life in garrison duty, Wayne, now aging considerably, though his years had just passed fifty-one, took horse for the frontier. His immediate task was to supervise the delivery of the British posts to the United States.

His return was not pleasant. For the first few hundred miles, he rode easily, with no more than the customary pain that his gout always caused; but after he was well into the interior, he felt much worse. A slow fever seized him; he felt tired and weak, as though he had a touch of influenza, but when he took red Peruvian bark to reduce the fever, the medicine had no effect. He wondered if he should be bled, and he sent a letter to Dr. Rush asking his advice, but then the weather turned more favorable and he felt so much better that he forgot about his need for medicine.

At Greeneville, instead of facing only routine problems, he found the fort agog with rumors that the Spanish were invading American territories. According to report, Manuel Gayoso de Lemos, Spanish governor of Upper Louisiana, was not only erecting a fort at Chickasaw Bluffs (close to Memphis), where the Wolf River flows into the Mississippi, but was also beginning a second, and even greater, stronghold at the confluence of the Mississippi and the Ohio. Wayne did not hesitate. He sent a special envoy, in a twelve-oared racing barge, to demand by what right, and under whose orders, these defenses were being erected. He complained, too, that the Spanish were negotiating with the Chickasaws.

These forts were but part of the picture. Major Zebulon Pike —father of the famous explorer of the Arkansas—reported that the Spanish had exchanged "ambassadors" with the State of Kentucky, and that certain leading Kentucky Democrats were plotting to set up an independent republic under Spain's protection. The information recalled a chain of events that had taken place the year before, but which had been temporarily set aside while supposedly more important matters were being settled. In 1794, Henry Owens, a messenger trusted both by Kentuckians and by the Spaniards, embarked at New Orleans with a consignment of $6,000, said to be in payment for tobacco sold by Wilkinson to the Spanish Government. On his way up the Ohio, Owens was murdered, and the money was stolen by his oarsmen. Eventually, the murderers arrived at Fort Washington, where Wilkinson arrested them. After much correspondence with Spanish officials, Wilkinson placed the prisoners on board a boat and ordered Campbell Smith to take them to New Madrid, in what is now Missouri, to be tried for murder by the Spanish courts.

Wayne's friends got wind of the affair and suspected that the $6,000 payment to Wilkinson was the Brigadier's price for treason rather than a payment to be made for his tobacco. Wayne ordered his patrols along the Ohio to look out for the boat and to seize it at the first opportunity, alleging that since the murder had been committed on American waters, the trial must obviously be held in a United States court. He desired, also, to cross-examine the murderers to see if he could extort information from them implicating Wilkinson. Foolishly, Campbell Smith attempted to run past the American garrisons at night. He was detected and was stopped, and although he produced Wilkinson's written orders, he was forbidden to continue on his voyage. Although the murderers were said to have confessed in Spanish, American judges set the men free for want of evidence.

Sharp watch continued upon all river traffic. It resulted in Pike's discovery that a load of bacon being sent down the Ohio from Kentucky received a polite salute from Spanish guns. "It was," said Pike, with much restraint, "a very unusual compliment." On looking into the matter of the bacon that merited such attention, Pike discovered Judge Benjamin Sebastian, a Kentuckian long suspected of pro-Spanish leanings, among the passengers. With him was Dr. Thomas Power, whom Wilkinson had long befriended, and who was known to be a confidential agent of the Spaniards. Nothing could be proved concerning their intentions, but circumstances seemed suspicious.

By the time Wayne arrived at Greeneville, the entire anti-Wilkinson faction was convinced that Power, who spoke English, French, and Spanish as fluently as though each was his native tongue, was certainly a Spanish spy acting as go-between for Wilkinson and the Spaniards. Wayne ordered his arrest on sight, and when a young lieutenant caught the agent coming up the Ohio with a flatboat full of barrels of coffee, sugar, and tobacco, Wayne demanded that the boat be searched for money and for incriminating documents. Power kept calm while soldiers went over his boat from stem to stern. When they found nothing that could be used to prove his guilt, he swore that he would have the law on them for daring to interrupt an innocent trading voyage. He appealed to the Spanish consul at Louisville, the official whom Pike called an ambassador, and demanded satisfaction. But after the Americans had apologized for disturbing him, the gleeful Power showed the Wilkinson clique how he had hidden in the center of each barrel a sack of money for delivery to the Brigadier. Through a secret Kentucky spy Wayne learned how he had been outwitted. He dashed off an abusive letter to the lieutenant who had made the search, upbraiding him for not noticing that sending tobacco from New Orleans to Kentucky was "sending coals to New Castle." He was certain that Wilkinson was in Spanish pay as well as in the employ of the British, but he could not prove it.

The time was growing near when the British had agreed, in consideration for American ratification of the Jay Treaty, to abandon their long-disputed posts on the margins of the Great Lakes. Wayne, making a long tour of places where he thought forts might be desirable, turned his attention away from Spanish intrigues toward Detroit, Niagara, Oswego, Michilimackinac, and other frontier posts. Sending Captain Moses Porter as advance agent to take over possession of Detroit—a ceremony which he completed at noon on July 11, 1796—the Commander-in-Chief followed more slowly. On August 13, Wayne himself approached the city. His welcome was extraordinary. Before he came within sight of the town, a band of Indians swarmed about him, firing their rifles in the air, shouting what Wayne called "ear-splitting yells," and pawing him by frequent handclasps. Twelve hundred Indians accompanied him to the settlement.

He found a city unexpectedly well developed. "Here in the center of the wilderness," Wayne noted with much surprise, "you see ships or large vessels of war and merchant men laying at the wharf or sailing up and down a pleasant river about one mile wide as if passing and repassing to and from the ocean. The town itself is a crowded mass of wooden or frame buildings generally from one to two stories high, many of them well finished and furnished and inhabited by people of almost all nations. Among them there are a number of wealthy and well-informed merchants and gentlemen and elegant, fashionable and well-bred women. The streets are so narrow as scarcely to permit their carriages to pass each other."

Wayne passed the pickets that surrounded the town and entered the one main street, which ran parallel to the river. Approvingly, he noted that the gates at either end of the road were well defended by stanch blockhouses and that the gun platforms were sturdy. Old army custom required that the gates be shut at sunset, not to be opened until sunrise. No Indian was permitted to remain within the walls after nightfall. The citadel, too, won his approval. Four half-bastions with twenty-four gun embrasures, together with a bombproof barracks and storehouses, all surrounded by a deep ditch and further protected by a strong stockade, with an abatis strewn about the enclosure, made the place impregnable. Wayne issued orders for artillery to be brought up to the town. Then, with nothing more to worry him except the fear that the wooden city might become the prey of a vast conflagration, he drew up plans for permanent occupation.

Comfortably housed in Alexander McKee's residence, Wayne received many groups of Indians, with whom he talked over future relationships, now that he would take the place of Simcoe and McKee. He appraised them shrewdly, recognizing Blue Jacket as a man who with a little coddling from the Americans in the form of outward deference would be loyal to his new employers; he looked on Little Turtle, Blue Jacket's rival, as more dangerous, viewing him as a litigious personality who would argue and complain. It would be well, Wayne believed, to put them both under close American control by building for each man a special mansion under the guns of Fort Wayne. He recommended that high rewards be paid such scouts as William Wells, to keep them loyal, and to Isaac Williams to assure the United States of a willing spy within the Indian ranks.

He looked forward to closer and more personal relations with his officers. Wilkinson's intrigues had made him realize that his men looked on him with dread rather than with love, and that the higher ranks were jealous of his close friendships with young ensigns and lieutenants. Wayne resolved to be more conciliatory and less vacillating in his friendships, to give his troops more rest, and not to work them quite so hard upon the Sabbath.

Perhaps, Wayne mused, it would be better to remove headquarters from Detroit to some point closer to the capital. As soon as he should have completed his arrangements for supplying all the posts, he would move down to Pittsburgh, where he could be in closer touch with Philadelphia, and from which he could dispatch runners either to Fort Washington or to Detroit with equal speed. He would cut roads straight through the wilderness. From Pittsburgh, moreover, he could reach the Spanish settlements on the east shore of the Mississippi when it should be necessary to make war on those intruders.

2

The sloop *Detroit*, sixty-five-tonner operating in regular service on the smooth waters of Lake Erie, sailed briskly toward Presqu' Isle, carrying Major-General Anthony Wayne and Henry de Butts, his aide-de-camp, on a tour of inspection. Mid-November brought a pleasant Indian summer, with weather that was cool and nipping in the breeze, but with warm sunshine that made sitting in sheltered places an enjoyable relaxation. The General, tired by his frequent councils with long-winded Indians who talked in elliptical and always oblique phrases, bored by the paper work of a garrison, drank punch and chatted with his friend De Butts.

Never a historian, yet keenly interested in past military exploits, Wayne looked forward to visiting the old French military base from which army columns had set forth to penetrate the interior of Pennsylvania; he was anxious to inspect the British blockhouse. Former possessors of Presqu' Isle had used it as a point of departure for a conquest of a province; Wayne thought of it as a terminus for a new, and better, overland road to Pittsburgh. If, he mused, Captain Russell Bissell, now in command of the log blockhouse, had kept the place in good repair, if Pennsylvania, in laying out a new town, had been foresighted, and if the road to Pittsburgh would be feasible for army use, there was a glowing future for the harbor.

Wayne's thoughts on this five-day trip that started from Detroit on November 13, 1796, were not entirely centered on his army problems. For the first time since leaving Philadelphia, he had time to think about his own affairs. He knew that Waynesborough was in good hands, for Margaret Penrose, sister of Polly, was keeping house for Isaac and for some of Isaac's cousins; her hospitality, by all reports, was as lavish as Anthony could have desired. The farm ran smoothly now that it had been let for three years to a clever and resourceful man who paid a proper rental. Nor had Anthony much concern on money matters, since his monthly salary of $240, with his allowances for clothing and rations, was more than adequate. Indeed, the General was laying up a surplus fund. Sharp Delany, long his Philadelphia agent, had a balance of about £3,000 in Wayne's account, with more money steadily pouring in. Prospects brightened that Pennsylvania bounty lands which Wayne had once thought worthless would prove profitable now that the Indian menace was removed.

He had been, he confessed, bitterly disappointed at the failure of his mother to be more generous in her bequests. The "Old Lady," with an estate of more than £1,000 to distribute, had cut Anthony off with a bare £5, which, she decreed, was to be paid out of the money he still owed her on the annuity arranged in 1776. To make matters worse, she had left Isaac and Margaretta each £165, also to be paid by Anthony out of his delinquent dues. The remainder of her estate had then gone to the children of Ann Hayman, Wayne's sister; the Haymans were to be executors. Wayne was taken aback at the disclosure of his mother's preference for Ann. Certain that her memory was impaired by age and that she had drawn up a will in terms she never meant to be observed, he wrote a note to Isaac bidding him search desks and table drawers more carefully to see if some later and more favorable will might be discovered. "Examine secretly into this business," he told Isaac, "but keep it quiet; perhaps matters may be amicably accommodated should I live to return. In the meantime," he cautioned his son, "I must request you to keep on good terms with Captain Hayman and all your relations as far as possible and treat them with polite civility; at least, it costs nothing; add to this, it is prudent."

The unexpected shift of his mother into what Anthony called a "cold complexion" was inexplicable to him. Barely a few days before her death, he had heard, in a gossipy letter from Margaretta, that his mother was gay and cheerful: "The Old Lady says she never lived so perfectly to her mind as she does at present." He was certain that some hidden explanation could be discovered for his mother's callousness in what he persisted in referring to as "the paper said to be her last will and testament."

Isaac, now grown to manhood, was his chief reliance. As a boy, his slowness in acquiring polish, even after six years at Princeton and Dickinson, had cost him a grand tour to Europe— for Anthony did not think the lad capable of profiting by travel. Later he had developed into a plodding law student. At one time, when the boy was seventeen, there had been an indiscretion, which had caused his allowance to be cut to $10 monthly, but the lad had emerged safely from his scrape and thereafter he had led a calm and undistinguished life. At twenty-four Isaac was a routine lawyer, solidly grounded in such matters as wills and mortgages, land laws, and the rudiments of business methods —the departments of law wherein he could be of most use to his father. He was, Wayne thought, perhaps a bit too interested in land speculation; in this last year or two, Isaac had talked of buying land in lower Ohio and about Detroit, but Wayne had held the family purse-strings tight.

Peggy, high-strung, sentimental, emotional, and impulsive, brought more worries than her brother. The girl loved her family devotedly; she showered her affection upon her mother, her grandmother, her brother, and her father, and since her marriage upon her husband and an infant son, whom she proudly christened Anthony Wayne Atlee. As long as these were happy, Peggy was extraordinarily content. But then within a year death cut a wide swath in her circle, carrying away her mother, her grandmother, and her son. Peggy's world collapsed. The once gay girl brooded constantly; her spirits broke; she drooped in body and in mind. For more than a year, the stricken girl was brokenhearted.

Wayne, absent on the frontier, could be of no assistance. Never a man to express on paper his inmost thoughts, never able to pour out his sympathies fluently and convincingly, he wrote stiff, formal, impersonal letters that were worse than nothing. Peggy, sick with grief, construed his curt, short notes as proof that now her father also was lost to her. She dreamed that he was dead; so real was her hallucination that she spread a rumor that he had died in camp, drawing from the Secretary of War a formal note to ask whether there was any truth in the report. Anthony first heard of her collapse through a letter from her husband, William Richardson Atlee, who pleaded with him to send her just a line of loving reassurance: "My poor little Girl's sufferings have been great, nor has time blunted the edge of her sorrows. The death of a mother and grandmother was enough in the space of a few months for spirits like hers to contend with, but to be deprived of the only pledge of our tenderness and mutual affection and care was an additional burthen too great for support. She is wont to be cheerful, but in vain."

Nor was Atlee much support. The young lawyer, appointed through Wayne's influence clerk of the county court, found himself enmeshed in unhappy circumstances. A Grand Jury investigation conducted by his political enemies found a true bill against him on fourteen charges of extortion. He was acquitted, but he moved away from Chester, selling his newly built country house, which Margaretta liked so much, to take up residence in a new county. This too proved unfortunate; Wayne foresaw an imminent necessity of maintaining an invalid daughter and an unlucky son-in-law out of his major-general's salary. To make matters worse, Atlee showed signs of radicalism, advocating that the United States fight for the French revolutionaries against their British, Austrian, and German enemies. To Wayne, always a stanch Federalist, Atlee's advocacy of "demoncratic" principles was unforgivable.

Even the long-forgotten Willinks had risen from obscurity to plague poor Wayne. Out of a clear sky had come a message from the Willinks agent in South Carolina protesting that Wayne had been unjust: "Little did we expect to have heard our conduct blamed and called in question respecting the loan of money proposed to be negotiated on your Waynesborough estate in the year 1785, but to our great astonishment we are lately informed that this had been done at Charleston where it was said that after giving you permission to draw upon us, we had suffered your signature to be disgraced." The Willinks reminded Wayne that they had never given him permission to sign drafts; they charged him with inattention to their letters and with rashness and haste in his business relationships; they asked him for a public retraction and an apology.

With problems such as these to worry him, Wayne's thoughts detracted greatly from the pleasure of his voyage. He turned pessimistic; he brooded in melancholy vein. Gloomy and despairing, he thought of death. He wrote careful statements concerning his finances, and sent them on to Isaac; he made up lists of things that must be done when he was dead; above all, he issued careful instructions concerning the great mass of papers that had accumulated during his active career. There were trunks full of letters at Waynesborough, at his former lodgings in Philadelphia, at Fort Washington, and at Greeneville. He ordered Isaac to collect the documents and to sort them carefully: "Upon the examination of my letters and correspondence with a great variety of persons upon different subjects, which are very voluminous and rather promiscuously tyed together in bundles, you will find many miscellaneous, idle and juvenile letters that I fully intended to destroy, together with all such as are no longer useful or necessary; this duty, I must solemnly enjoyn you to perform immediately after my decease." In later years Isaac carried out the assignment to the letter. Few of Wayne's private letters escaped destruction. The son carefully kept every scrap of writing that had any possible bearing upon public affairs or upon military activities; these constitute the great bulk of the fifteen thousand Wayne manuscripts that still survive.

Arriving at Presqu' Isle on November 18, Wayne turned again to military duties. He inspected minutely the strength of Bissell's blockhouse, and he paraded the small garrison to check its readiness for instant action; he pored over arrangements for the new town that was being created, which in later years would be called Erie; he surveyed plans for the road cut through the woods toward Pittsburgh.

A week or two after Wayne's arrival at Presqu' Isle, his old complaint, the gout, returned in critical form, but the General, accustomed by long experience to its attack, took little care of it other than to swathe his arms and legs in flannel and to rest in a big armchair in the general's quarters in the upper story of the fort. By December 1, a new complication set in. Violent stomach pains, together with intestinal disorder, brought intense agony. No physician was on duty at Presqu' Isle, but at Pittsburgh Dr. John Culbertson Wallace, a former student of Dr. Rush's, was available. A fast express was sent over the newly cut military road to bring Dr. Wallace to attend the General. At the same time another messenger rushed East to ask advice of Dr. Rush himself. Young Dr. Wallace, flattered to be, at twenty-five, the physician chosen to attend the Commander-in-Chief of the American Armies, hurried at full speed to Presqu' Isle. In the meanwhile, Dr. George Balfour, a surgeon attached to the Western army, had also been summoned. Balfour arrived at the blockhouse early in the morning of December 15, just in time to see the General die; Wallace raced in on horseback a few hours later.

Two days later, Anthony Wayne lying in a plain coffin, clad in his major-general's uniform, was buried at the foot of the flagstaff of the blockhouse. On the top of the coffin, in round-headed brass tacks driven into the wood, was the marking:

A. W.
15 Dec. 1796

The news that Anthony Wayne was dead reached Philadel-phia on the last day of the year. Had he lived until New Year's, the Commander-in-Chief would have celebrated his fifty-second birthday.

Immediately upon Wayne's death, leadership of the army devolved, by right of seniority, upon the one man whom he most detested. James Wilkinson, succeeding to the command, at last gained the eminence for which he had plotted.

Twelve years later, Peggy Atlee, sick with the illness that was to cause her death, begged her brother Isaac to go out to Erie to bring back their father's remains for interment in the family burial plot in the churchyard of St. David's at Radnor. Isaac accordingly rode in a sulky across the state and, arriving at Erie, arranged with Dr. Wallace to disinter the body and pack it for shipment. When Dr. Wallace had done his work, Isaac drove back with his father's bones, and had them buried in St. David's churchyard in accordance with Peggy's wish. On an intensely hot Fourth of July, 1809, the Society of the Cin-cinnati, heading a procession of soldiers and citizenry more than a mile in length, conducted the funeral rites, with Chaplain David Jones preaching the sermon. Among the thousands at-tending the funeral was Mary Vining, who emerged for the first time in years from the seclusion of the Wilmington home in which she had voluntarily immured herself on hearing of Anthony Wayne's death.

Two years later, the Society of the Cincinnati, together with companies of militia from Philadelphia, Chester, and Delaware counties (the last of which was an offshoot of Wayne's own Chester County), erected a stone monument whose inscription reads, in part:

HIS MILITARY ACHIEVEMENTS

ARE CONSECRATED

IN THE HISTORY OF HIS COUNTRY

AND IN

THE HEARTS OF HIS COUNTRYMEN

Notes

This volume derives principally from manuscript sources. Anthony Wayne, always methodical and cautious, carefully preserved not only all letters sent to him but also fair copies of his own writings as well as, in many cases, rough drafts of documents considered by him but rejected in favor of some later version.

At the Historical Society of Pennsylvania—hereafter referred to as HSP—fifty folio manuscript volumes, each containing more than one hundred and twenty-five pieces, offer by far the best source of information on Wayne's public career. These, mainly military and official papers, were culled by Isaac Wayne from his father's writings for the use of Joseph J. Lewis, whom Isaac picked to be Wayne's biographer. Since the work was not completed at the time of Isaac's death in 1852, Isaac's will provided that Lewis should retain possession of the letters until the biography was finished. Thereafter, the will provided, the papers should become the property of Abraham R. Perkins, who was in turn to transfer the writings to the HSP.

A certain amount of confusion resulted. Lewis, busy with a crowded law practice, could not find time to write more than a hasty memoir of the General's career. He therefore called in the aid of Henry Barton Dawson, editor of the *Historical Magazine,* and arranged for collaboration. Dawson, receiving the letters in a huge trunk, stored the papers in a closet at the head of his bed and proceeded laboriously to copy out the writings. Some originals he turned over to George Bancroft, who copied about five hundred of the earlier letters in the six folio volumes now in the New York Public Library. These originals were returned; a dozen others, lent to a less scrupulous scholar at Lewis's peremptory request, disappeared when the borrower vanished, "a defaulter and a fugitive."

Later Lewis, freed from routine legal practice, revived his plan of writing a biography of Wayne, and canceled the collaboration agreement with Dawson. He called for a return of the papers, but he died before Dawson surrendered possession. Immediately upon Lewis's death, the Perkins heirs authorized the HSP to request the documents in order that they might be published, and after considerable delay they were given into the society's possession in January, 1890.

Charles Janeway Stillé, provost of the University of Pennsylvania and president of the HSP, then used the papers as the basis for his *Major-*

General Anthony Wayne and the Pennsylvania Line in the Continental Army, published in 1893, but he made but slight use of the manuscripts beyond Volume 9 of the folios. Hampton L. Carson, a later HSP president, planned to use the letters as the basis for a more extensive biography than that of Stillé, and for that purpose requested that the papers be sealed against indiscriminate use. Carson died before he had made an exhaustive search of the records, but the prohibition imposed upon general reading of the manuscripts continued until in 1937, by a gracious action of the Council of the HSP, the Wayne Papers, increased in 1917 and 1919 by the gift of Mrs. Charles T. Murphy from the Lewis estate, were opened for the use of the present writer.

Ever since the death of Anthony Wayne the private correspondence, separated by the action of his son Isaac from the public papers, had remained virtually untouched at Waynesborough. Approximately five thousand letters to and from the General have been preserved at the ancestral seat, now in the possession of William Wayne, his great-great-grandson. These comprise messages between members of the family, the General's business communications concerning Waynesborough and the Georgia estate, letters from intimate friends, and other matters of personal interest which Isaac Wayne believed should not concern the public. Because these letters have not been drawn upon for material before, scholars have generally believed that the papers were destroyed at Isaac's instigation. Through Mr. Wayne's courteous co-operation, these papers also have become available for the present work. This William Wayne Collection has been, it need not be said, of supreme importance for the study of the General's life.

Various historical societies possess miscellaneous Wayne manuscripts. The Cadwalader, Conarroe, Dreer, Etting, Gratz, Irvine, McKean, William Moore, Society, Stillé, Watson, and Provincial Delegates collections of the HSP contain numerous letters and documents either written by Wayne or concerning him. Several of these have been published in the files of the *Pennsylvania Magazine of History and Biography*—the *PMHB*, organ of the Society—but most of them remain in manuscript. At West Chester, the Chester County Historical Society has a number of Wayne documents, most of which have been printed in George Morris Philips's privately published *Historic Letters*. The same society also possesses a large number of autographs, evidently cut by Isaac Wayne from letters now in the ownership of the HSP.

In New York, the William Finnie, Charles Gates, John Lacey, Joseph Reed, Baron von Steuben, Walter Stewart, and Benjamin Van Cleve papers in the New York Historical Society are of value, as are the scattered Wayne papers of that institution. The William L. Clements Library at the University of Michigan not only has the invaluable series of Clinton Papers, but also a manuscript diary of Josiah Harmar, the Nathanael Greene Collection (especially important for Wayne's Southern campaign), and a series of letters between Wayne and other generals. In the John Pratt and the Governor Jonathan Trumbull collections at Hartford, the Connecticut State Library possesses material invaluable for understanding the jealousies in Wayne's army on the Western campaign.

In the Lyman Copeland Draper Collection at the University of Wisconsin, Madison, Captain Thomas Underwood's "Journal of an Army Officer," General Robert Todd's "Orderly Book, 1793-1794," and Nathaniel Hart's "Memoranda of Occurrences in the Expedition under General Anthony Wayne, 1794," all manuscripts dealing with the Ohio campaign, have proved fruitful. The University of Chicago owns the manuscript affidavit of Obadiah Newman describing the activities of his brother, the mysterious Robert Newman. Duke University has five letters from Wayne to Governor Martin, Greene, and James Jackson, together with one from Greene to Wayne. At the Delaware Archives, in Dover, the wills and inventories of estates of Mary Vining and Phoebe Vining are important, as are the wills and records of the Waynes at the courthouse in West Chester.

Still other important material, chiefly in the form of letters written by Wayne's associates to their friends in commenting on the General's character and tactics, may be found in the Georgia Historical Society, Savannah; the Torrens Collection of the Historical and Philosophical Society of Ohio; the collections of the Ohio Archeological and Historical Society; the Montgomery County Historical Society, Norristown, Pennsylvania; the Filson Club of Louisville; the Louisiana Historical Society, New Orleans; the Erie Museum, Erie, Pennsylvania; and the Crozier Theological Seminary, Chester, Pennsylvania. The last-named is particularly important for its letters exchanged between Wayne and David Jones, copies of which appear in the William Wayne Collection.

The writer is indebted also to Mrs. J. William Stair of York, Pennsylvania, for a manuscript copy of her speech on "The York Revolt of 1781," delivered to the York Historical Society in 1906, and to Clark University for the typescript of Fred Waldo Shipman's "The Indian Council of 1793," a master's thesis.

The invaluable *Pennsylvania Archives* (particularly the first three series, published at Harrisburg, 1853, 1879, and 1894), of New Jersey (Trenton, 1901, 1903, 1906, 1914, and 1917), of Delaware, and of Maryland contain corroborative material of great importance. E. A. Cruikshank's edition of *The Correspondence of Lieutenant-Governor John Graves Simcoe* (Toronto, 1923, 1924, 1925, 1926, 1931) puts into very convenient form the Simcoe manuscripts of the 1789-96 period.

In addition to the *PMHB*, the files of certain other historical society publications have been freely drawn upon. Chief among these are the *Mississippi Valley Historical Review*—shortened to *Miss. V. Hist. Rev.*—the *Quarterly* of the Ohio Archeological and Historical Society, the *Proceedings* of the New Jersey Historical Society, *Collections* of the Massachusetts Historical Society, the *Quarterly* of the Somerset County Historical Society (condensed for convenience as Somerset), the *Bulletin* of the Fort Ticonderoga Historical Museum, and the various publications of the historical societies of Georgia, Louisiana, Kentucky, Tennessee, South Carolina, Virginia, Delaware, Maryland, New York, Indiana, ·Illinois, and Michigan.

Newspaper files at the HSP, the Chester County Historical Society, the Savannah Public Library, and the Library of Congress have also been thoroughly ransacked. Full details of the books and periodical articles referred to in the following Sources will be found in the Bibliography, which follows Sources.

SOURCES

NOTE. *The references without name are to the Wayne Mss. (HSP), the first being the volume number, and those after, the number of the letter or letters.*

Chapter 1

Documentation covering Anthony Wayne's early life is scanty. By express injunction, given in a letter from Greeneville dated July 14, 1794, and now in the Family Papers at Waynesborough, he instructed Isaac to destroy all manuscripts dealing with personal, juvenile, or trivial matters. Isaac carried out the request, but he read the papers carefully enough to write a biographical memoir in the *Casket* (May, 1829, to January, 1830) from which something of his father's youth may be recovered (including the sham battle at the fort and the charge of Wayne's school sluggishness), and this has been the basis for subsequent writings. The family ancestry was well worked out by Edwin Jaquette Sellers. University of Pennsylvania records, admittedly incomplete, suggest but do not certify to Anthony's attendance at the Philadelphia Academy, although university historians, including Edward Potts Cheyney, definitely state that he was a student there. Deeds to the Waynesborough property recorded at West Chester, Pennsylvania, in Deed Book D 2, p. 1 *et seq.*, show the chain of title, and tax lists filed there, reprinted in *Pennsylvania Archives*, Ser. 3, Vol. 11, testify to the financial status of the Waynesborough property.

Chapter 2

Details of the Nova Scotia venture are contained in the Nova Scotia Papers at Waynesborough. The story of the Nova Scotia venture is further clarified by reference to the John Hughes Collection at the HSP. These papers contain a letter from Reuben Haines to Hughes, dated September 25, 1764, and one from Hugh Hughes, James Parker, and Benjamin Blagge to Hughes, written May 20, 1764, describing the colonizing methods used by McNutt. Wayne's agreement with John Hughes, dated March 14, 1765, is followed by an interchange of correspondence. Wayne wrote to Hughes on April 10, 1765, following Anthony's arrival in Nova Scotia, and after receiving additional instructions from Hughes, dated June 1, 1765, Wayne wrote three more letters, on July 9, August 5, and October 7, telling of his negotiation. These letters, once in the possession of William H. Holstein of Bridgeport, Pennsylvania, were presented to the HSP by William John Potts in 1893 and were intended for inclusion in Stillé's biography, but they arrived too late for Stillé's use and have remained unused until the present time, since no other biographer knew of their existence. Wilmot's grant, dated October 31, 1767, is entered in the Book of Records at Halifax, Liber 7, pp. 94-98. The fox hunt is from Hiltzheimer.

Chapter 3

From this point onward, letters at the HSP are plentiful, covering as they do the military details of Wayne's life. Social events in Philadelphia are based on Goodman, Parsons, Graydon, Allen, Wright, and Mackraby; the theatrical history derives from Pollock, with many valuable suggestions by Thomas Ridgway, Esq., who is not only a Wayne kinsman but is also an authority on colonial and early Federal drama. Phoebe Stewart's story is in William Moore's manuscript "Chester County Docket, 1719-1772" at the HSP. Lacey's "Memoirs" tell the story of that unhappy captain's experiences at Marcus Hook. The *Pennsylvania Packet* for May 23, 1774, was the issue which stirred Wayne's emotions so deeply that he took an active part in organizing Chester County; the issues of July 18, August 29, September 15, and October 10, 1774, describe his legislative services. The caucus call, issued August 13, 1774, is in 1:8, and the speech to citizens is in 1:18. Francis Johnston's troubles at Marcus Hook appear in letters to Wayne dated February 26, 1776 (1:28-30, 42). Thomas Hartley is introduced by a note from M. A. Lukens to Wayne, December 27, 1775 (1:15). Wayne's protest against Lacey's "Rot-Gut" is in a letter to Johnston dated Albany, May 4, 1776 (1:62).

Chapter 4

This chapter is based largely upon letters from the participants. Thomas Hartley writes to Jasper Yeates, dated Sorel, and published in *Pennsylvania Archives*, Ser. 2, Vol. 10; William Irvine's "Journal" and Wayne's "Orderly Book" for the period appear in the same volume. Wayne's own version of the affair is shown in a letter to Abraham Robinson, May 26, 1776, telling of the northward march (1:66), and in long accounts written to Benjamin Franklin (dated Sorel, June 13, and Ticonderoga, July 31, and now at the American Philosophical Society). Lacey, C. H.

Jones, Jeduthan Baldwin, and Wilkinson's *Memoirs* give additional testimony concerning the Canada campaign.

Chapter 5

The Ticonderoga episodes stem directly from Wayne's letters, either in Vols. 1-3 of the Wayne Mss. or in the William Wayne Collection. Additional material comes from the St. Clair Papers at the Ohio State Library, Lacey, Jeduthan Baldwin, Thacher, Hastings, and the *Bulletins* of the Fort Ticonderoga Museum. "Cannon Fever" appears in Wayne's letter to Polly, November 5, 1776, now at Waynesborough, and in a letter of the same date to Sharp Delany (1:96). The hospitalized volunteers are mentioned in letters to Richard Peters, Sharp Delany, and Benjamin Rush, dated November 5, 1776 (1:66). Wayne's complaints against diminishing the size of his garrison extend throughout the winter, beginning in a letter to Franklin dated Nov. 15, 1776 (1:122). He protests against the Albany Dutch "babies" to Schuyler on January 22, 1777 (2:70), and follows it up with other protests on February 12 (2:86). His phrase "I would rather risk my life" is found in a note to Delany, February 20, 1777 (2:108), and the "consolation in Hell" letter was sent on March 2 to Joseph Wood (2:120). He had previously complimented his men as "finest and best" in writing to Polly, August 12, 1776 (1:81). That Ty was well fed appears in Wayne's letter to Penrose, August 23, 1776 (1:82), but Lacey protested about the flour, and the "Orderly Book of the Northern Army" for November 29, 1776, describes the poor condition of the beef. That the deficiencies were only temporary is shown by Wayne's letter to Schuyler of December 15 (2:31) and by his own ration accounts, submitted April 26, 1777 (3:73, 83). Cold was more of a problem. On December 15, Wayne froze "by Shrewsbury Clock" in letters to Delany (2:30) and to Robinson (1:84). He thought of the place as Golgotha in writing to Peters on September 1, 1776 (see the Bancroft Collection, New York Public Library, Vol. 1, p. 88), and to George Clymer on December 15. Complaints that Schuyler stole mail are found in Kennedy's letter to his wife, August 5, 1776, published in *PMHB*, Vol. 8, p. 114, in Hartley's letter to Wayne, September 6, 1776 (1:97), and in Wayne's own writings to Franklin on July 29, 1776, to Abraham Robinson on December 15, to Sally Robinson on August 10, and to Richard Peters on December 1 (Wayne Mss., Vols. 1-2). The British Major Acland, in a memorandum to Sir William Howe dated January 6, 1778, and now at the William L. Clements Library, suggests that Schuyler was looked upon by the English as a possible convert. The Whitcomb riot, best told by Thacher, is touched upon by Wayne in a letter to Wood, April 2, 1777 (3:43), and in one to Craig, February 23 (2:112). Craig replied on March 10 (3:7). The Whiting case begins with a letter from Whiting to Schuyler of January 3, 1777 (2:73), and is continued by

Wayne's note to Schuyler of January 26 (2:74). Discussion over inoculation in correspondence from Wayne to Schuyler is found in 2:17-57. "Fortune is fickle" was written to Polly and to Sally on August 10, 1776 (*cf.* for the former 1:81 and for the latter 1:79). "I cannot submit . . ." was sent to Rush on November 5 (1:105), to Johnston on November 24 (2:14), and to Gates on December 1 (2:18). On November 12, 1776, Wayne asked Peters to promote Wayne's friends (*cf.* 1:121). Shee's case was discussed by Peters on October 10, 1776 (1:113), and by Johnston on November 17 (1:125 and 2:3). Wayne's views on discipline appear in his note to Captain North, December 11, 1776 (2:28), and as to the girls, to Captain Robinson, December 20, 1776 (2:37). The riflemen's mutiny is in Wayne's letter to Schuyler, February 12, 1777 (2:36); the Hay affair, February 9 (2:88), and the Coe-Holiday case in February, 1777 (2:92-107). Wayne's loneliness for Wood is shown in his letter of February 16, 1777 (2:96); his letters from Polly are in the Family Papers at Waynesborough under dates of June 23, July 6, August 23, and October 6, 1776. Wayne's letter to Sally of August 10, 1776 (1:79), and her reply of September 20 (Bancroft Collection, Vol. 1, p. 80), are reprinted in *PMHB*, Vol. 23, pp. 406 ff. He wrote to Sally and Hetty on February 16, 1777, in a letter now at Waynesborough. Hetty had already written him on October 30, 1776 (1:120). His two poems, undated, may be found in 2:44. The Udney Hay story is in Jeduthan Baldwin, and in Wayne to Colonel Lewis, March 3, 1777 (2:123). St. Clair's disappointment at the condition of Ticonderoga is in a letter to James Wilson dated June 8, 1777, in the St. Clair Papers at the Ohio State Library.

Chapter 6

This chapter is almost entirely drawn from manuscript accounts at the HSP or at Waynesborough. The ration dispute is in 3:83. Wayne's clothing troubles are related in a message to the Board of War, June 3, 1777 (3:89), and his own uniforms are discussed both in Graydon and in Abraham Robinson's letter of June 13 (3:98). The phrase concerning a musty paper brain appears in Francis Johnston's letter of May 31 (see 3:88). Polly wrote to her husband on May 31, and Anthony replied June 7 (3:93) and August 6. (The first and third of these are in the Family Papers.) Abraham Robinson wrote on August 23, 1776, about Peggy's schooling (1:83), and on October 14, 1776, Wayne gave Polly instructions for education (1:112). Sally sent oysters and tea on July 26, 1777 (*cf.* 3:116). The agreement for an annuity to Elizabeth Wayne, signed April 6, 1776, is at Waynesborough, together with three letters, June 30, 1776, August 24, 1776, and July 13, 1777, sent by Elizabeth Wayne to her son, concerning Priscilla's madness. Hetty wrote on July 13, 1777 (3:112). Attacks sent to Wayne on the Pennsylvania constitution are to be found in Rush to Wayne, September 24, 1776 (1:101), May 19, 1777 (3:84), and June 5, 1777 (3:91). Wayne replied, calling it a "sickly constitution," on June 2, 1777 (3:85), and thereby quoting from Francis Johnston's letter of November 17, 1776 (1:125). Peters criticized the document on October 16, 1776 (1:113), and May 27, 1777 (3:87), and Hartley opposed it on March 28, 1777 (3:34). Wayne again spoke of risking his life and reputation in letters to Peters on June 17, 1777 (3:102), and to Washington on July 8, 1779, for which see Ford's edition of Washington. The Ryan quarrel is in Ryan to Wayne, June 12, 1777 (3:110), and in Wayne's immediate reply of the same date (3:111). The City Tavern talk is from Adams, and the account of the Grant skirmish in Wayne to Rush, June 2, 1777 (3:85). The Morristown and Middle Brook descriptions are based on Sherman's "Washington's Army in Lowantica Valley," Johnson, Davis, Quincy, and Berger. Incidents there are reported in the *New Jersey Archives*, Vols. 1-5.

Chapter 7

Wayne invited Polly by letter on August 26, 1777 (3:120); he asks for a shirt on September 23 (4:12), says that his "sword points the way" on September 30 (4:26), and that "dawn is big" on October 3 (4:28). The clothes correspondence is Harper to Wayne, September 27 (4:15) and Frazer to Wayne, October 19 (4:34). He orders Washington to "push on" on September 19 (in Ford's edition), repeating what was said to Mifflin on September 15 (4:6). His war plan to Washington is dated September 2 (4:2). The Battle of Brandywine is described from contemporary sources in Vol. 1 of the *Bulletin* of the Historical Society of Pennsylvania by Joseph Townsend, by the British officer John Montrésor in *PMHB*, Vol. 5, by George Trevelyan in his *The American Revolution* (Longmans, Green & Company, 1907), by Thomas Sullivan in *PMHB*, Vol. 34, by the Hessians Stephen Popp (Vol. 26) and F. E. von Munchausen (Vol. 16). The best American versions are by F. D. Stone, *The Battle of Brandywine* (privately printed, Phila., 1895), F. C. Hooton, *Battle of Brandywine* (privately printed, West Chester, Penn., 1900), and Smith Burnham in the *Second Report* of Pennsylvania Historical Commission. Canby and the writer's *Valley Forge* and *The Delaware* contain full accounts. The Paoli story is best told by Wayne's defense at his courtmartial (4:23) and by the findings of the court-martial, October 13-15 (4:19). Samuel Hay, writing September 29, 1777, to William Irvine (*Pennsylvania Archives*, Ser. 2, Vol. 10, p. 599) gives a full account. See also J. S. Futhey in *PMHB*, Vol. 1, and the soldier accounts cited above. The box-bush legend is from Abraham Robinson's letter of September 22 to Wayne (4:13). Wayne describes the Battle of Germantown in a letter to Polly of October 6 (4:31) and, much later, in a letter to Peters of December 30, 1777 (4:61), telling of his wound. Trevelyan, Von Munchausen, and Montrésor discuss the fighting, and there are other soldier versions in *PMHB*, Vols. 11, 17, 23, 40. A. C. Lambdin gives a full account in *PMHB*, Vol. 1. Carter gives the Anna Lane incident, and Eager tells of Maryland fighters. See also the writer's *The Delaware* and *Valley Forge.*

Chapter 8

Wayne doubts Washington in a letter of October 27, 1777, to Washington himself (4:37), and more explicitly in letters to Gates, November 21, and to Mifflin, November 10, both in the Gates Papers at the New York Historical Society. The Rush strictures (*PMHB*, Vol. 27, p. 147) are answered by Robert Morris in a letter to Peters, January 25, 1778 (4:68), but Peters himself had criticized Washington in a message to Wayne of October 11, 1777 (4:32). Wayne's views on councils of war were expressed to Peters on November 18, 1777 (4:39). The whole question of advancing on Philadelphia is well discussed by W. C. Ford in a series of articles, "The Defences of Philadelphia," in *PMHB*, Vols. 19-21. Wayne saw "a pleasing dawn" in writing to Polly on November 1, 1777, but was not so optimistic when he wrote again on November 22 (both letters in the Family Papers). He became a "grandfather" by Peters to Wayne, December 6 (4:52). His plea of sickness was expressed to Peters on December 19, 1777 (4:55), and the furlough correspondence with Washington was on December 26 (*cf.* 4:58 and Washington's reply, 4:59, also Wayne's appeal to Peters, December 30, 4:61). The clothing quarrel is reported in *Pennsylvania Archives*, Ser. 1, Vol. 6, and some, but not all, the letters there printed may be found also in the Wayne Mss., Vol. 4. The foraging expedition, told by Stewart, is based on Wayne to Wharton, February 10, 1778 (4:82), and Wayne to Washington, February 25 (4:91) and March 14 (4:104). The Lacey quarrel is in the writer's *Valley Forge.* The Chew incident rests on the authority of a letter from Wayne to Governor Livingstone, February 26 (4:94); the Pulaski correspondence, on February 27 and 28, is in 4:95-97. Wayne's opinion of the Canadian expedition comes from his letter to Gates on January 26, 1778 (Gates Papers), and his love for Washington is expressed in a letter written to an unknown recipient from York on January 29, 1778 (4:72). His dislike for Brodhead was expressed to Peters on February 8 (4:78). The Priscilla Stephens matter is mentioned in a note to Polly dated February 7 (4:77), and the Prissy Walker letter to Wayne, dated June 21, 1778, is at Waynesborough.

Chapter 9

Wayne's war plans are described in letters to Washington dated April 21, 1778 (5:17), June 18 (5:53), and October 18 (5:115). His account of Monmouth is in a letter to Peters of July 12 (5:58), and in two to Polly, July 1 (5:57) and July 14 (5:59). Stryker has a very full account of this battle. The Fredericksburg camp is discussed in Patrick, and the Hay affair comes from two letters from Hay to Wayne dated October 6, 1778, and October 30 (5:107, 123). In letters to Johnston on August 10, 1778 (5:74), to Morris on September 8 (5:89), and to Joseph Reed on December 28 (6:42) Wayne threatens to resign. He complains of inadequate clothing for his troops in a series of letters during July and August, 1778, to Peters, Morris, Johnston, and Reed (5:58-74). He twice asks Washington.for a furlough, January 10, 1779 (6:70), and February 28 (6:76), and appeals to Morris on January 24 (6:62). His own clothing situation is described to Polly on August 13 and September 7, 1778 (Family Papers). Camp intrigues are discussed in Wayne's letter to Delany of July 20, 1778 (5:61), and in Robinson to Peters, October 1 (5:90). His troubles with St. Clair are aired in a letter to an unknown recipient dated October 14, 1778 (5:111), and are reflected in a letter from Udney Hay, August 7, 1778, to St. Clair and in one from St. Clair to Richard Butler, August 12, 1780 (both in the St. Clair Papers). The Lee correspondence begins with Wayne's criticisms of Lee's actions to Polly, July 1 (5:57), and to Irvine on July 14, charging that Lee's action "flows from insanity or worse" (5:60). Lee protested in a note of January 7, 1779, and an interchange of letters ensued that same day (6:53-55). Lee made a handsome offer later to drop the matter, August 11, 1779, in a letter now at the Chester County Historical Society and published in Philips. A curious letter, reporting Brodhead as calling Wayne a "bashaw with two tails," came from Cousin Michael Wayne on August 15, 1778 (5:77). Wayne flits "like the bee" in a letter to Stewart, February 28, 1779 (6:73), after he had followed Stewart's advice about the Easy Behavior set in Stewart's letter of November 29, 1778 (6:31). His family affairs are evidenced by letters to Polly on October 21 and November 12, 1778 (5:117 and 6:9), in Hannah Van Leer's letters of July 13 and August 13, 1778, both at Waynesborough, in Elizabeth Wayne's messages to her son of August 29, 1778, and February 14, 1779 (Family Papers), and in Robinson to Wayne on December 30, 1778 (6:44). As a lobbyist Wayne's efforts are described in letters from Mifflin to Wayne, November, 1778 (6:22), and Wayne's reply, November 23 (6:23), also in his "wide sea" letter to Jonathan Potts, January 10, 1779 (6:56), and in Wayne to Craig February 24, 1779 (6:69). The Mentges matter rests on two letters from Mentges to Wayne on March 9 and April 9, 1779 (6:81, 98), and the Mentges scandal is in Graydon. The troubles in camp over rank are shown by Craig's letters to Wayne of March 3 and March 6, 1779 (6:82, 83), and by St. Clair's letters to Reed of February 21 and March 5, 1779 (St. Clair Papers). The McPherson affair is told in Wayne to Peters, December 28, 1778 (6:41), and in St. Clair to Butler, August 12, 1780 (St. Clair Papers). The affair of the sword is told in a letter from an unknown sender at Wilmington, May 20, 1778 (5:40). Matters concerning the formation of the Light Infantry are revealed in correspondence from Wayne to Harmar, February 24, 1778 (6:74), and from Harmar to Wayne, March 8 (6:84). The Ryan application is in Ryan to Wayne, February 22 and April 9, 1779 (6:72, 96). St. Clair's championship of Ryan is revealed in St. Clair to Washington, May 31, 1779, and Washington to St. Clair,

June 1, 1779 (St. Clair Papers). Washington's orders to Wayne to report are dated June 21, 1779 (6:125); Wayne wrote to Polly on June 24 (6:126).

Chapter 10

Wayne's Light Infantry is described in Kapp and Wright. Wayne asked a special uniform in writing to Washington on July 4, 1779 (7:11), but was refused on the same day (7:13). The Butler case begins with a letter from Wayne to Washington, July 9, and continues with letters from Wayne to St. Clair, July 10, and from St. Clair to Wayne, July 11 (7:21, 26, 29). The Atlee controversy starts with a letter from Irvine to Wayne, March 1 (6:78), and one from Johnston to Wayne, July 10, closing with a letter from Wayne to Reed, August 6, 1779 (7:24, 84). The Arrowsmith case is in Wayne to Washington, March 23, 1779 (6:89). Wayne, bored on the Hudson (see Wayne to Henry Lee, August 24, 1779, 7:108), and to Delany on the same date (7:109), receives tea (Farmer to Wayne, August 28, 1779; 7:114), and porter (Johnston to Wayne, October 10; 8:39). Peters on July 11 (7:31) sends a ballad, which Wayne on August 30 has sung by his musical colonels (7:118). The Rooney case is in a letter from Rooney to Wayne, October 28, 1779 (8:116), and the McCormick complaint in Washington to Wayne, September 21 and 24, 1779 (8:23, 27), McCormick to Wayne, October 2 (8:41), and Wayne to Washington, September 23, 1779 (8:24).

The plan of the battle of Stony Point is in Washington to Wayne, July 1, 1779 (7:2), and Wayne to Washington, July 3, (7:9). Wayne's farewell to Delany on July 15 is in 7:43, and his report of the battle, July 17, is in the Chester County Historical Society. Johnstone compiled all available accounts of the battle, as did Dawson. Washington's official report to Congress appears in the *New Jersey Gazette*, August 4, 1779, as well as in Ford's edition of Washington. Wayne sent a supplementary report to John Jay, president of Congress, which was printed in the *Pennsylvania Packet*, August 26, 1779. Compliments on the taking of Stony Point came from Washington in General Orders of July 16 (7:45), from John Jay on behalf of Congress on July 27 (7:70), from Joseph Reed for Pennsylvania on July 20 (7:56), and from Schuyler on July 31 (Chester County Historical Society). Alexander Spottswood on August 9 (7:87), Adam Stephen on August 10 (7:89), Armstrong on September 15 (8:17), St. Clair on July 17 (7:49), and Charles Lee on August 11 (Chester County Historical Society) were other military men who sent congratulations. Sharp Delany on July 27 (7:69), Benjamin Rush on August 6 (7:83), and Polly on July 25 (Family Papers), praised the capture too, as did Congressman Thomas Burke on July 19 (7:52). An inventory of the stores taken appears in 7:46, 48, and the order for the distribution of prize money, signed by Washington on August 15, is in 7:91. Not so flattering are letters from Return Jonathan Meigs, August 22, and Isaac Sherman and Thomas Posey on the same day (7:95, 96,

101), complaining that they had not been given proper credit. Wayne replied to Meigs on August 23 (7:97), but received another complaint from Sherman on August 24 (7:98) and one from William Hull on August 25 (7:99). Wayne noticed these by a long letter to Posey on August 28. Wayne three times offered to repeat the exploit in letters to Washington, July 31, September 28, and October 9 (7:77 and 8:32, 54), but the Commander-in-Chief refused.

Chapter 11

"Blue devils" is in Wayne to Stewart, December 20, 1779 (9:96). The Wallace call, December 1, 1779, is in 9:84, and arrangements for Vining clothes are in Wayne to Magaw, March 12, 1780 (9:124), and Magaw to Wayne, February 8 (9:123). For the bridle see Wayne to Charles Lumm, December 23, 1779 (9:100). He asks more liberality toward Englishmen in a letter to Archer on December 1, 1779 (9:56). The Reed-Washington correspondence complaining of high prices and of the empty Pennsylvania magazines is in the Reed Papers, in the period November 15, 1779, to July 4, 1780. Stewart complains of White Wigs in a letter to Wayne on December 19, 1779 (9:94), and Wayne agrees in writing to Irvine on March 10, 1780 (Irvine Papers). Abraham Robinson, October 17, 1779, says that Wayne neglects his family (8:73), and on May 11, 1780, Wayne reports to Washington (10:15) that he has gone to Delaware. In the same letter he urges Washington to attack New York. He repeats the advice September 13, 1780 (10:73). Correspondence between Wayne and Lee and Burke on the Henry Lee quarrel appears during the period June 6-15, 1780 (10:23-30). The question of Wayne's accounts for spirits and for his confiscated cows begins February 13, 1780 (9:125 and 10:4), and continues until May 27 (10:18). His hasty note to Polly, June 9, 1780, is in 10:29. For additional data on army difficulties see Charlton, Marshall, De Chastellux, Elkanah Watson, Brissot, Schöpf, and Barbé-Marbois.

The attack on the blockhouse is in Wayne's report to Washington, July 21, 1780 (Casket, September, 1829, pp. 395 ff.), and in the Reed Papers at the New York Historical Society (Vol. 6, p. 60). The British version is in the Royal Gazette, July 22, 1780, and the New York Gazette, July 24, 1780. The "Orderly Book" of the First Pennsylvania (Pennsylvania Archives, Ser. 2, Vol. 11) gives additional data. Wayne's orders to Moylan on July 21 are included in the Casket. Pennsylvania Archives, Ser. 1, Vol. 8, prints much of the material. The text of the "Cow Chase" is in the Royal Gazette for August 16 and 30 and September 30, 1780. The dissatisfaction of Pennsylvania officers is well expressed in a letter sent by Wayne and Irvine to Washington on August 10, 1780 (10:55), and the subsequent correspondence of August 11 and 12 is in 10:56-58. McPherson's refusal to resign is dated August 12 (10:58). Wayne wrote to Reed about St. Clair's gossip on September 3, 1780

(10:65). Wayne's rush to protect West Point is related in his report to Washington of September 27, 1780 (10:77). On October 2 he wrote identical letters to H. A. Shiel, Johnston, Morris, and Reed expressing his disgust at Arnold. The revolt of the Pennsylvania Line, foreshadowed by Wayne's letter of October 3, 1780, to Grayson and Peters (10:94), and by his worry over the Ides of January (Wayne to Johnston, December 16, 1780, 11:50), is fully recounted, with all documents, in the *Pennsylvania Archives*, Ser. 2, Vol. 11, pp. 631-74. Wayne's special part is disclosed in his report to Washington, January 2, 1781 (11:101 ff.). The Craig case is in three letters, Craig to Wayne on February 9 and April 10, 1780, and Wayne's reply on May 11 (12:51, 52, 82). The Dunn affair, involving St. Clair, starts with Wayne's note to St. Clair of March 7 and St. Clair's reply the same day (12:63, 64). Wayne again wrote St. Clair on the same day (12:65) and Dunn closed the case on March 9 (12:68). Philadelphia social conditions are described in De Chastellux, Barnes, Brissot, Barbé-Marbois, and Hiltzheimer. Authority for the nickname "Mad Anthony" is vague; it seems to have arisen in the Isaac Wayne articles in the *Casket* about Jemmy the Rover.

Chapter 12

Stair (mss.), Denny, and Marshall are the best authorities for conditions in York, Pennsylvania, Tower and Louis Gottschalk's *Lafayette Comes to America* (University of Chicago Press, 1935) and *Lafayette Joins the American Army* (University of Chicago Press, 1937) for affairs in Virginia. Wayne's account of the York mutiny, extremely incomplete, is in letters to Fishbourn and Polly, both on May 25, 1781 (12:124, 126), and to St. Clair on May 26 (13:5). Butler had already warned, on April 28, 1781 (12:86), that the men were restless. The Southern campaign is described in Davis, in correspondence printed in *Pennsylvania Archives*, Ser. 1, Vol. 9 and Ser. 2, Vol. 11, and in Robert Kirkwood's *Journal and Orderly Book, 1780-1782* (Historical Society of Delaware, Vol. LVI, 1910). Lafayette's letters to Wayne begin with one dated March 7, 1781 (12:66), and grow increasingly frequent during April and May. Many of them are in *Pennsylvania Archives*, Ser. 1, Vol. 9. The Jouett ride is taken from Birch. Wayne's account of Green Springs is in almost identical letters sent on July 8, 1781, to Delany, Grayson, Washington, Reed, Irvine, and the War Office (13:70). At the same time, Galvan wrote to Peters on July 8 a version somewhat different (13:72). Johnston well discusses the Yorktown campaign. The perennial dispute over clothing begins again with letters from Wayne to Nelson on July 23, 1781 (13:97), and to Irvine on July 29 (13:112). Correspondence with Reed is in *Pennsylvania Archives*, Ser. 1, Vol. 9, and the Davies to Wayne letter of August 1 is in 14:2. The quarrel over the confiscated Virginia shoes is touched off by Nelson to Lafayette, August 3 (14:15), and continues with Wayne to Lafayette, August 9 (14:27), Lafayette to

Wayne, August 18 (14:37), Wayne to Nelson, August 19 (14:38), and Wayne to Lafayette on August 23 (14:41). The shooting of Wayne is reported in his letter to Polly on September 12, 1781 (14:64), and in one to Thomas McKean on September 13, 1781 (McKean Papers at the HSP). He tells Peters of it on the same day (14:66) and Morris on September 14 (14:68). A second letter to Morris on October 26 (14:85) refers to Cornwallis as "the modern Hannibal." The text of the song "The World Turned Upside Down" is by courtesy of the magazine *Life*.

Chapter 13

"Chimney soldiers" is in a letter from Stewart to Wayne, December 24, 1781, and repeated in David Jones to Wayne, December 28 (14:104). The "fiery meteor" was written to Reed on October 3 (*Pennsylvania Archives*, Ser. 1, Vol. 9, p. 430). Wayne asks for leave in a letter to Washington on November 4 (14:90), but, failing to get it, applies to Wadsworth on November 6 (14:94) for a loan, finally making a deal with Irvine on November 7 (14:95). Rush's advice is in a letter to Wayne dated October 30 (14:88). Eustace welcomes Wayne to Georgia on January 13, 1782 (14:112), followed by William Wayne on January 18 (15:2) and Governor Martin on January 19 (15:6). The Wayne-Greene correspondence, which runs intermittently through Vol. 15 of the Wayne Mss., is also to be found at the William L. Clements Library. On Indian affairs, the Cornell deposition of February 1 is in 15:27, and the reference to "kings of the Creeks" is in a letter to Lieutenant Clarke on January 29 (15:22). Wayne's order to Habersham, January 30, is in 15:24, and Habersham's report, February 8, in 15:39. Jackson's neglect is charged in Wayne to Greene, February 11, 1782 (15:41). Wayne issued proclamations (16:8) and appealed to Greene for secret-service funds. Getting them, he bribed Cornell (Wayne to Cornell, February 25, 15:62, and Wayne to Greene, February 28, 15:61). The Georgia hardships are discussed in virtually identical letters to Johnston and Irvine on February 24 (15:58) and to Stewart on February 25 (15:60). Brown's exploit was reported by Wayne to Greene on March 15 (15:119) and to Martin on March 26 (15:121). The White Fish war is referred to in Wayne to Martin, March 31 (16:6), Wayne to Greene, April 1 (16:11), P. Carr to Wayne, April 12 (16:45), Lyons to Wayne, April 13 (16:49), and Wayne to Martin, April 17 (16:60). The "spirited talk" is mentioned in Wayne to Thomas Moore, May 10 (16:125). Wayne wanted to attack Savannah (Wayne to Greene, May 27, 17:25). The "poor beef and alligator water" was used twice, once to Rush on April 10 (16:124) and again to Henry Laurens on June 15 (17:72). The quarrel with Jackson is found in two letters: Jackson to Wayne, May 10 (17:8), and Wayne to Jackson, May 19 (17:9). The laundress episode is in Eustace to Wayne, May 29 (17:32), and the grumbling colonels are in Wayne to Greene, April 28 (16:95). His fear of murder appears in an interchange of letters, Jackson to Wayne, April 29, and Wayne to Jackson, May 1 (16:96, 103). He warned Greene of mutinies on April 9 (16:36). The Goznall mutiny (described in *Pennsylvania Archives*, Ser. 2, Vol. 11) broke out soon thereafter (Greene to Wayne, April 21 and April 29, 16:72, 100). The ration problem was the topic for exchanges of letters between Greene and Wayne in the first week of June, 1782 (17:45, 52, 53), and in John Meals to Greene, June 2, 1782 (William L. Clements Library). Wayne reports to Greene on the Brown fight on May 24 (17:18), and the poem describing the victory is from the *Georgia State Gazette*, March 6, 1783. Correspondence relative to an armistice at Savannah appears in May, 1782, and is reported in Vol. 17 and in the Wayne-Greene Papers at the William L. Clements Library. The actual evacuation, in July, is reported in Vols. 17-18 of the Wayne Mss. Georgia's gift, issued May 1, 1782, is in 16:118 and for July 31, in 18:52. That he was "satiate of blood" appears in his letter to Polly of March 2, 1782 (15:66). Mary Maxwell's arrival is in a letter of April 25 (16:84), and the Eustace courier service began soon after (*cf.* Eustace to Wayne, May 29, 17:33). Wayne invited her to call, July 13 (18:13), and at that time she asked for help for her brother (*cf.* 17:101). Eustace worried over the affair (*cf.* 16:41), as did Fishbourn (16:53), and Mrs. Philip lost her head (*cf.* 17:32). During the interlude, on March 2 and May 30 Wayne wrote to Polly (the former, 15:66, and the latter, Family Papers). Wayne wrote Martin on August 9 asking for clemency (see 18:60), but the same day Martin refused (18:61). The Wayne-Greene difficulties were in late August, 1782, and are reflected in 18:66, 67, 69. Again in November Greene protested that Wayne issued too many passes (18:92, 93, 94). Wayne's fever is mentioned in letters to Morris, September 2 and 9, 1782 (18:75), and to Rush, December 24 (18:123). Fishbourn prescribed "whorehound" December 28 (18:124) and Delany, December 17, a sea voyage (18:120). Delany, February 12, 1783 (19:5), pleads with him to come home for better air. That Wayne approved the Banks deal is shown by a much later note to Catherine Greene, February 22, 1790 (19:104), reporting his conversation with her husband. Rush's offer of honors is expressed September 16, 1782 (18:79); the Dickinson letters are dated January 1, 1783 (19:2), and May 17, 1783 (19:19). Further material on the Georgia-South Carolina campaign is to be found in Greene, C. C. Jones, Gamble, Charlton, Barnwell, Hatch, and Denny.

Chapter 14

Wayne discusses his illness in two letters written October 1, 1783, one to Habersham (19:26) and the other to Jackson (19:27). On the same day Penman opens a long business correspondence by a letter to Wayne offering slaves. The Penman letters are all at Waynesborough. Tatem's bill for clothes, dated October 28, is also at Waynesborough. Elections to the Cincinnati appear in the *Pennsylvania Packet*, October 7, 1783, and to the censorship on November 13, 1783. Wayne's gout is mentioned in his letters to Irvine, December 9 (19:33), and to Washington, December 14 (19:35). His service in the censorship is in the *Pennsylvania Packet*, January 2 and 24 and August 12, 1784. Details of Philadelphia activities are from the *Pennsylvania Packet* for January-March, 1784. The "zone" is in the issue of July 27 and the "maiden blush" in that of November 13, 1784. Wayne's election to the Assembly is in the *Pennsylvania Packet* for October 16, 1784, and his service is mentioned in the issues for November 15 and December 6 and 9. His speech against intolerance is reported in the same paper for December 30, and his bill to exempt the disfranchised is in the issue of January 19, 1785. His great work for removal of the censorship, while not reported in the Pennsylvania papers, is found in the *New York Packet* of December 5, 1785, and February 6 and 9 and April 6 and 10, 1786. The Fishbourn riot is reported in the *Georgia Gazette* for July 7, 1785, and the Platt-Brice trial is in the issues from July 28 to December 22, 1785. Long after the slanders about Wayne and Cathy Greene, she described their relationship in a letter to Wayne, December 30, 1789 (19:102), to which he replied by a note of February 4, 1790 (19:103). Wayne appealed to Georgia for a larger gift on August 10, 1786 (19:54), after he had failed to secure a loan from Emlen, February 20, 1786 (19:50). Delany also failed, October 9 and November 1, 1786 (Delany Papers at Waynesborough). The Willinks Papers at Waynesborough contain the only data available on the Dutch loan, although there is a hint of the matter in Wayne to Van Berkel, October 22, 1784 (19:46), and in Morris to Wayne, June 4, 1785 (19:47). All other business correspondence mentioned in this chapter is preserved at Waynesborough. Wayne wrote to Polly on May 28, 1786, not to expect him (19:58). On November 15, 1788, he said prospects were brighter (*cf.* 19:71). His candidacy for the Georgia Senate is in a letter to Asa Emanuel, December 15, 1788 (19:72), and his denial of Pennsylvania citizenship is in a letter to the Georgia Assembly, November 1, 1788 (19:69). He applied for an army command to Burke, June 4, 1789 (19:81), and to others (*cf.* Madison to Wayne, July 31, 1789, 19:84; Knox to Wayne, August 9, 1789, 19:85; Butler and Izard to Wayne, October 1, 1789, 19:90; Morris to Wayne, October 23, 1789, 19:92). The Florida slaves are offered in a letter Richard Wayne to Anthony Wayne, September 30, 1789 (19:88), and accepted by Anthony on October 10 (19:91). He bids "a long adieu" to Polly on July 5, 1790 (19:107). Catherine Greene's letters are dated November 15, 1789, and December 30, 1789 (19:95, 102). He replies to her on February 4 and 22, 1790 (19:103, 104). Other personal letters to Delany and Polly are at Waynesborough. Georgia asked him to be Congressman (*Georgia State Gazette*, March 17, 1789), and the Cincinnati chose him president (*Augusta Chronicle*, July 18, 1790). His unpaid taxes are advertised in the *Georgia Gazette* of July 9, 1789, as are his uncalled-for letters. Dolores Boisfeuillet Floyd's monograph on "Richmond-Oakgrove Plantation," a manuscript at the Georgia Historical Society, partly printed in the *Georgia Historical Quarterly*, Vol. 24, Nos. 1-2 (March and June, 1940), is indispensable for its research into title deeds, mortgage records, and liens on Wayne's business deals in the South.

Chapter 15

Osborn's activities are described in affidavits published in the *Augusta Chronicle* of September 17 and October 8, 1791; militia voting in affidavits published in the *Georgia Gazette* for August 11, 1791; ballot-box stuffing in the *Augusta Chronicle* for September 17 and November 5, 1791. John M. Scott's deposition, made January 17, 1792, is in 19:113 and Daniel Millar's affidavit made the same day is in 19:114. In a letter to Gibbons, November 29, 1791, Wayne recounts the charges of illegal voting (19:124). Osborn's impeachment is described in the *Augusta Chronicle* for November 5 and December 3, 1791, and in the *Georgia Gazette* for December 8 and 29, 1791. The Jackson-Gibbons duel is from Gamble. Wayne's nonpayment of taxes is advertised in the *Georgia Gazette* of July 9, 1789, and the Washington reception is to be found in the *Augusta Chronicle* of May 5, 1791. Gibbons's demand for settlement is seen in a letter written to Wayne on January 13, 1791, and answered by Wayne on February 6, 1791; both letters are at Waynesborough. The settlements made with Penman and Potts appear in agreements made March 1, 1791, and supplemented by letters to Penman, April 10, and to Delany, May 19, all of which are at Waynesborough, and by a letter to Polly, April 13, 1791 (19:118). The description of Congress is founded on a letter from Theophilus Bradbury to Harriet Hooper, dated December 26, 1795, and published in *PMHB*, Vol. 8, p. 226; Wayne's unseating is described by Clarke and Hall, and by Gales, also, from the Jackson point of view, by Charlton. Congressional debates are drawn from United States Congress, *Debates and Proceedings, 1789-1793*. St. Clair's description of his men as "scourings" is in Denny, and is referred to by Cruikshank in his edition of Chew's(?) "Diary of an Officer in the Indian Country in 1794." Suggestion that Wayne was to be named surveyor-general is found in Hunt, and his application for the adjutant-generalship is in the *Georgia Gazette* for February 9, 1792. The De Butts appointment was sought in a letter from Murray to Wayne, April 9, 1792 (20:12). Washington's appraisal of candidates for the command, made March 9, 1792, is in Ford's edition. Lee wrote in protest on June 15, 1792, and was answered by Washington on June 30, 1792; both letters are in Ford's edition and in Lee. Monroe's letter to Lee, April 7, 1792, is in Lee, and his letter to Jefferson, June 17, 1792, appears in Vol. 1 of *The Writings of James Monroe*, ed. by S. L. Hamilton (7 vols., G. P. Putnam's Sons, 1898-1903). The British views are drawn from Simcoe, Vol. 1. Wayne's realization of the difficulties of his task was expressed in a letter to Knox, April 13, 1792 (20:16). His Philadelphia gaieties are described in letters written to Polly, April 24, 1792 (20:18), and to Bab McLaine, June 29, 1792 (20:45), and by notes from J. B. Cutting, April 17, 1792 (20:19), and Hartley (describing the "all-conquering" Alexander), December 21, 1792 (23:113). Stewart's account of Welsh Indians is in the *Georgia Gazette* of June 23, 1785, and the monster story is in both the *Philadelphia General Advertiser*, August 26, 1794, and the *Centinel of the Northwestern Territory*, October 11, 1794. Harmar's information was contained in a letter to Mifflin, November 9, 1789, in Denny. Corroborative material on the Western journal is in Baldwin, Schöpf, Elliott, Bernard, and Michaux, and also in a letter from Mead to Wayne, December 1, 1792 (23:63).

Chapter 16

Indian attacks are noted in Wayne to Irvine, July 20, 1792 (20:85), Putnam to Wayne, July 5 (20:55), and Daniel Strong to Wilkinson, June 25 (20:60). "No permanent peace" was used by Wayne several times, notably in letters to Irvine, July 20, 1792 (20:85), Knox, September 14, 1792 (21:95), John Berrien, January 1, 1793 (24:23), and James Gunn, February 8, 1793 (25:14). Knox cautioned Wayne about this on September 21, 1792 (21:112), and January 5, 1793 (24:38). Wayne reported that the "savages were haughty" in a letter to Knox, August 24, 1792 (21:38), and sent a plan of action which was rejected by Washington, as is seen in Knox to Wayne, September 1, 1792 (21:56), and April 27, 1793 (26:49). The anti-Washington ideas of Simcoe are in the Simcoe Papers under date of August 20, 1792, April 5, 1793 (for the "Brunswick princeling"), and June 2, 1793 (for Wayne "breathing war"). Brant's mission is based on a letter from Knox to Wayne, June 22, 1792 (20:33), and his bribe is recounted by Brant himself in a letter to Count de Puisy, quoted by Stone. In a letter to Henry Dundas, June 21, 1792, Simcoe predicted that Wayne would be Washington's successor. The O'Beal material comes from Smith and Stone; Massa Harbison's story is from Sipe; accounts of various Indian councils may be found in both the Simcoe Papers and in Shipman (mss.), which is largely based upon those papers. Wayne reported to Knox in letters written August 31 (21:52), October 26 (22:82), November 23 (23:42), and November 29, 1792 (23:59), and was praised by Knox on November 24, 1792 (23:44). Wayne felt that he was unappreciated, as is shown by his letters to Hartley on January 1 (24:24) and February 1, 1793 (24:107), and by his request for the franking privilege, Wayne to Gunn, February 13, 1793 (25:32). The Indian "sweetheart" rumors are in Lewis Bond to Wayne, January 1, 1793 (24:26), and the Madame Grenadier story is in Schöpf. Wayne describes his illness in a letter to William Hayman, December 28, 1792 (24:5). Other family matters are contained in a letter from Polly to her son Isaac, dated, without month or day, 1792, in the Family Papers. Polly's illness and death are detailed in letters from Delany to Wayne, April 19, 1792 (26:29), and Atlee to Wayne, April 20 (26:30). Wayne's emotion at the death of his wife is recounted in Wayne to Atlee, April 28, in the Gratz Collection at the HSP, and Wayne to Knox, April 29 (26:59). The Collins deposition is dated February 16, 1793 (25:40). Regulations concerning uniforms are in General Orders of September 11, 12, and 23 following Wayne's appeal to Knox on July 13, 1792 (20:74). Moses Porter reports on bad howitzers on October 4, 1792 (22:34), and Henly on the horseshoes, writing to Wilkinson, also on October 4 (22:34). Camp diseases are described by Wayne to Ashton, July 3, 1792 (20:53), and Wayne to Knox, August 3 (20:113), and in General Orders of August 19. New methods of loading rifles are outlined in letters to Knox, July 7, 1792 (20:61), and July 13 (20:74). Regulations for marksmanship practice are set forth in General Orders of July 21, August 8 and 25, and September 30, 1792, and the results are told to Knox on September 7 (21:70). Daily drills are required in General Orders of July 21 and August 8 and 30, and Knox is told of these in letters of August 17 (21:20), September 7 (21:70), and September 14 (21:95). The desertion problem is touched upon in General Orders of August 9, 1792, and on August 19, Wayne asks permission to brand deserters (21:8), but Knox refuses on September 14 (21:92). Further orders of August 31 and November 11 indicate that the problem was not solved. Wayne, writing to Knox on August 8, 1792 (21:3), complained that his men were nervous. He agreed with Wilkinson that the officers were "rascals, drunkards and fools," for which see Wilkinson to Wayne, November 1, 1792 (22:99), and Wayne to Knox, December 6, 1792 (23:69). Reasin Beall's application for leave of absence, December 24, 1792 (23:119), was refused, and nearly led to a court-martial, according to De Butts to Beall, June 13, 1793 (27:33). Ballard Smith's case is recounted in court-martial proceedings of September 29 and October 6 and 8, 1792 (49:35, 38; 22:40), and in Wayne to Knox, November 14, 1792 (49:47). The Hopkins court-martial, November 11, 1792, and the Payne court-martial are simultaneous (49:47, 51). Wayne reports to Knox on the frequency of court-martials on September 21, 1792 (21:115). The Butler appointment, asked by Wayne to Knox, September 21, 1792 (21:115), was refused on September 28 (22:23). In commenting on the Jenifer court-martial, June 6, 1793, Wayne recommends dueling (50:11). Army costs are detailed in a letter from Joseph Howell (Vol. 1 of Large Manuscripts of the HSP Wayne Collection, p. 52). Knox's criticism about Wayne's horses appears in letters of July 13, 1792 (20:72), and September 7, 1792 (21:69). Facts of the Hagerstown incident are in Abraham Jones to Wayne, October 1, 1792 (22:23), William Lewis to Wayne, October 1 (22:25) and October 22 (22:56), and De Butts to Lewis, October 12 (22:56). Addison's affair is in Addison to Wayne, December 6, 1792 (23:70), and February 6, 1793 (25:42), and Wayne to Addison, March 1, 1793 (25:60). The Clymer affair is in Wayne to William Taylor, October 5, 1792 (22:35), and in the *Georgia Gazette* of November 22, 1792.

Chapter 17

Wayne's opinion of Cincinnati was expressed to Knox on May 9, 1793 (26:77); the sergeant's testimony is from Elliott. For other opinions about the Ohio River country see Ashe, Heckewelder, Collot, Michaux, and McDermott. Wayne's account of the chain of frontier forts is in a letter to Knox, May 27, 1793 (26:119); they are also described by Young, Elliott, and Green, and by speakers at the dedication of monuments at Fort Recovery and Fort Jefferson. Army quarrels over command of the right wing were reported by Beall to Wayne, September 9, 1792 (21:75), and by Elliott. The Wilkinson relationship, beginning with friendliness in Wayne's letter of June 16, 1792 (20:27), passed through the stages of Wilkinson's rebuke on November 13 (23:19) and his complaint about secret service on November 28, 1792 (23:53), to active opposition. Wilkinson defended Ballard Smith on February 11, 1793 (25:20), and, according to Wayne's friends, persecuted Armstrong. See for this Armstrong to Wilkinson, October 21, 1792 (22:79), Wilkinson to Wayne, November 1 (22:95), Wayne to Armstrong, December 10 (23:80), Armstrong to Wayne, March 18, 1793 (25:88), and the Armstrong court-martial, February 13-March 3, 1793 (49:80). John Smith's case, beginning with Wilkinson's charges, March 27, 1793 (25:107), culminates in his court-martial, March 7-27, 1794 (49:94), after which Wayne protects the convicted man, Wayne to Smith, September 21, 1793 (29:65), and October 8 (29:112). Edward Butler's difficulties center about Guion, for which see Guion to Wayne, July 6 and 11, 1793 (27:97, 108), and Wayne to Guion, July 7 (27:98). Sullivan's court-martial, June 19, 1793, is in Vol. 50, pp. 15, 17. Jenifer's troubles began at Christmas, Huston to Wayne, December 26, 1792 (23:124), and continued with Gassaway's appeal to Knox, April 12, 1793 (26:13), and to Wayne, April 19 (26:27), before they ended with Wayne's report to Knox, April 29 (26:59), and with the court-martials of June 6 (50:11) and September 7, 1793 (50:39). Campbell Smith arrived with a letter from William Smith to Wayne on May 8, 1793 (26:75). Wayne appointed him aide on June 26 (27:60), but Smith was more ambitious, Smith to Wayne, September 13, 1793 (29:36). Charles Hyde appears in Hyde to Wayne, September 13, 1793 (29:37), and John Morgan to Knox, November 20, 1793 (Large Manuscripts of the HSP Wayne Collection, Vol. 2, p. 18). Cushing first enters on May 15, 1793 (26:95), and June 11 (27:26). The promise to Cornplanter is mentioned in Knox to Wayne, June 7, 1793, and Wayne to Knox, July 2, 1793 (27:87). Wayne asked for aggressive action in letters to Knox on July 10 and August 7, 1793 (27:105; 28:54), but was refused on July 20 (28:9). William Wells was introduced by Hamtramck on May 25, 1793 (26:109), and July 16, 1793 (27:125). Details of the Indian councils may be found in Simcoe and Shipman (mss.), together with the British fears of Wayne's advance. Wayne reported the failure of the treaty to Knox on September 17, 1793 (29:54), and to Scott on

September 18 (29:58). He had received information from Wells, September 16 (29:46), and from Wilkinson, September 14 and 18 (29:39, 56). Having called for Kentucky volunteers, Wayne to Shelby, May 18, 1793 (26:97, 98), June 14 (27:35), and July 1 (27:84), and having received replies from Shelby, written May 27 (26:120), June 24 (27:63), and June 27 (27:61), he now corresponded frequently with both Shelby and Scott during September, October, and November (see Vols. 26-29 *passim*). Wilkinson's plan to "captivate wives" is drawn from Wilkinson to Wayne, September 14, 1793 (29:39). The long correspondence with Elliott and Williams over rations is in Vols. 30-31 *passim*, and Wilkinson's letter to "Robin" is dated April 15, 1794 (34:113). Wayne's illness is mentioned in letters to Wilkinson of September 30, 1793 (29:87), and December 22 (31:102). Various orders for the march through the wilderness are found in General Orders after November 6. The founding of Greeneville—which has since dropped the third "e" to become officially Greenville—is in General Orders of November 6; the name was formally applied by General Orders of November 21, 1793. The march through the Indian country is admirably told by Wayne in a letter to Delany, July 10, 1794, in the William Wayne Collection. Contemporary accounts are in Wilkinson's highly prejudiced "Narrative," William Clarke, Boyer, Todd, Hart, and Underwood (the last three in the Draper Mss., University of Wisconsin). More recent accounts are in Priddy and Robb. For the British side, see Cruikshank's edition of Simcoe; the Indian version is in Young and Oskison. Correspondents in the *Centinel of the Northwestern Territory*, April 12, May 17, June 7, and June 14, 1794, give camp gossip concerning Wayne's alleged inefficiency.

Chapter 18

The attack on Fort Recovery is best described by Gibson's official reports, made June 30 and July 1, 2, 5, 10, and 18, 1794 (36:52, 55, 61, 72, 82, 92). Wayne's orders to Gibson were dated June 26 (36:46). Wayne reported to Knox on July 7 (36:76). The British version, made by McKee to Colonel England and to John Chew, July 7, are in Simcoe. The "Diary of an Officer in the Indian Country, 1794," edited by Cruikshank, is probably that of Chew, and is published in Simcoe also. Wayne's will, dated July 14, 1794 (36:86), is recorded at West Chester, Pennsylvania. General orders for the advance, certifying to Wayne's caution while on the march, are dated July 16, 21, 26, and 27; he told Knox about them on July 27 (36:107). The felling of the tree is told by Wayne in a letter to Isaac, September 10, 1794 (37:39). His bandaged legs were described in a letter from J. Porter to Thomas R. Peters, November 6, 1817 (48:10). The best description of Fallen Timbers is in Wayne's official report to Knox, August 28, 1794 (37:15), but Wilkinson's "Narrative," Boyer, Young, Robb, and others add details which Wayne omits. The Campbell-Wayne correspondence, officially released for publication by nearly every contemporary newspaper, is in Vol. 37, pp. 16-20. The information concerning Lacelle's testimony is from the *Virginia Gazette* of October 15, 1794. Wilkinson's objections to Wayne's strategy, culminating in an official charge lodged with the Secretary of War, are mirrored in Cushing's letters to his Connecticut friends in the Jonathan Trumbull Papers and the John Pratt Collection at the Connecticut State Library, together with a letter from Wilkinson to Pratt, May 16, 1795. A memorandum in Wayne's handwriting on "Expressions used by Major Cushing" (47:114) indicates Wayne's knowledge of intrigues against him. William R. Blue, writing to Wayne, January 8, 1795 (39:21), adds additional criticisms which had been heard on Kentucky. Wayne was attacked by a correspondent in the *Philadelphia Aurora* of May 19, 1796, and was defended in the same paper by James Elliot, August 21, 1796. Wayne's private reply to Knox on Wilkinson's charges, dated January 25, 1795, is at Waynesborough.

Chapter 19

The Newman case opened with a letter from Daniel Cooper to Wayne, August 15, 1794 (37:9), and was taken up by Parson David Jones (see Jones to Wayne, October 5, 1796, at Crozier Theological Seminary). Newman wrote to Wayne on December 1, 1794 (38:79), following his return to camp. Newman's experiences in Canada are described in the Simcoe Papers; John Stagg, October 4, 1794 (37:65), had also received him at Washington and Newman had been arrested at Pittsburgh (see Isaac Craig to James O'Hara, October 17, 1794; 37:106). Wayne wrote to De Butts about Newman on January 29, 1795 (39:37), and to Knox on January 29 and February 13, 1795 (39:38, 61). Robert Newman's own account is in the *Berkeley* (Virginia) *Intelligencer* of June 18, 1808, and an affidavit by his brother Obadiah, made July 13, 1796, is at the Chicago Historical Society. Knox's letter conveying Washington's praise to Wayne, December 5, 1794 (38:91), and the official thanks of the House of Representatives, also dated December 5 (38:92), testify to the high reputation earned by Wayne at Fallen Timbers. He was appointed peace commissioner April 15, 1795 (40:52), but he had already sent out a speech on September 12, 1794, to the hostile Indians inviting them to discuss a treaty (37:45).

Preliminaries for the treaty began in November, 1794, when Wayne sent out a letter of invitation to the Wyandots (38:20). The next day, November 5, he hired Isaac Williams as interpreter and intermediary (38:19), and a week later, November 12, told Knox of his plans (38:44). More details were given Knox on December 23 (38:44), and Williams was sent out January 4 (39:18). Wayne had already invited Tarhe to participate, January 1, 1795 (39:112). At the January conference Wayne spoke to the Indians on January 19, 1795 (39:28), to which the Indians replied on January 22 (39:31). This was when Wayne said he was an "excellent aurist and oculist," Wayne to Sargent, February 22, 1795 (39:74), and to Knox,

February 12 (39:60). An armistice was proclaimed on February 22, 1795 (39:56, 74), at which time the blue wampum was presented as reported by Buell. Blue Jacket's speech, made February 8 (39:56), had been followed by a bribe, Isaac Williams to Wayne, May 25, 1795 (41:21), and by Wayne's suggestion of a commission, Wayne to Pickering, March 8 (39:76), which was denied, Pickering to Wayne, May 7 (40:96). Pickering offered suggestions as to final treaty terms on April 8 and 15 and May 7, 1795 (40:35, 49, 96), and Wayne countered with a suggestion for a "consecrated ground" on May 15, 1795 (40:114), but Pickering rejected it on June 29, 1795 (41:115). The Findlay raid, Wayne to St. Clair, June 5, 1795 (41:49), led to two letters, St. Clair to Wayne on June 11 and to Shelby on June 20, both of which are in the St. Clair Papers. Wayne described the scene of the treaty to Pickering on June 17, 1795 (41:82), but fuller details are given by Buell, Young, and Elliot. The terms of the treaty are reported by Wayne to Pickering on August 9, 1795 (42:85), and are thoroughly discussed by Kent.

Chapter 20

The story of the Philadelphia stay is based chiefly upon the *Philadelphi Aurora* for February and May 23, 1796. The engagement has for its sole authority a letter from Willamina Cadwalader, dated February 20, 1796, in the Cadwalader Collection at the HSP. Wayne's other personal affairs—the "unfavorable conclusions" drawn by Margaretta in a letter of February 20, the lottery venture, mentioned in Wayne's letter to Isaac of November 10, 1795—are at Waynesborough. The "torture ride" was mentioned in a letter to Peters, November 18, 1895 (43:48), and the idea of the war portfolio was given in a letter from Truxton to Wayne, February 23, 1796 (43:104), as well as in the *Aurora*. There is no authentic documentary proof nor any family legend in either the Vining or the Wayne families of the more imaginary stories about Wayne's relations with Mary Vining 'as described in a recent fictionalized biography of Wayne. The complete story, so far as it may be documented after an exhaustive search of all existing records and legends, appears in the writer's *The Delaware*.

The Spanish matter was fully described by Wayne in reports to Pickering, June 17, September 3, and November 25, 1795 (41:81; 42:88; 43:44). Zebulon Pike's part in the venture is given in Pike to Wayne, February 24, 1796 (43:131), and Wayne to McHenry, July 8, 1796 (44:103). Power's newspaper article "Piracy on the Ohio," published September 13, 1796, is in Vol. 3 of Large Manuscripts of the Wayne Collection at the HSP. Wayne's arrival at Detroit is well told in his letter to Isaac of September 10, 1796 (46:47), and by his reports to McHenry on September 29, October 3, and November 7, 1796 (46:86, 105; 47:80).

The best accounts of Wayne's death are based on Isaac Craig's collection of letters, written by De Butts, Captain Bissell, and Dr. George Balfour in November and December, 1796. They appear in *PMHB*, Vol. 19, pp. 112-15. The story of the exhumation and subsequent reinterment is to be found in Sanford and Nelson, and in the letter of William H. Holstein, February 12, 1880, in the *Erie* (Pennsylvania) *Observer*.

The story of the preparation of Wayne's remains for the trip back to Pennsylvania is a curious one. Dr. Wallace found the corpse in almost perfect preservation. The body was of the consistency of soft chalk, but with the exception of a decayed foot and leg it was unimpaired by time. Faced by Isaac's order to pack the bones in boxes so that the remains could be strapped to the back of the sulky, Dr. Wallace, following a custom common to Indians of the neighborhood—dismembered the body and then dropped the limbs one by one into a large iron kettle full of boiling water. As each member was boiled, the flesh dropped from the bones. Wallace scraped the bones clean and packed them into Isaac's boxes. The flesh, together with the instruments used in the dissection and the cleaning, was reburied near the blockhouse. In 1878 it was once more moved, this time to be reinterred in a stone-lined grave within the blockhouse. Thus Anthony Wayne has two graves.

Bibliography

NOTE: *Publishers are given only for books published after 1880*

Allen, Paul, *A History of the American Revolution*, 2 vols., Baltimore, 1819

Allen, W. B., *A History of Kentucky*, Louisville, 1872

Anbury, Thomas, *Travels through the Interior Parts of America*, 2 vols., London, 1789

Armstrong, John, *Anthony Wayne*, Boston, 1839

Ashe, Thomas, *Travels in America, 1806*, London, 1808

Baker, William S., ed., *Itinerary of General Washington, 1775-1783*, The J. B. Lippincott Company, 1892

Balch, Thomas, *Papers Relating Chiefly to the Maryland Line during the Revolution*, Philadelphia, 1857

Baldwin, Leland D., *The Whiskey Rebels*, University of Pittsburgh, 1939

Barbé-Marbois, François, marquis de, *Our Revolutionary Forefathers*, Duffield & Green, 1929

Barclay, Sidney (Lydia Minturn Post), *Personal Recollections of the American Revolution*, New York, 1869

Barton, Thomas, *The Conduct of the Paxton Men, Impartially Represented*, Philadelphia, 1764

Bernard, John, *Retrospections of America, 1797-1811*, Harper & Bros., 1887

Bolles, A. S., *Pennsylvania, Province and State*, 2 vols., Wanamaker, 1899

Bolton, Charles Knowles, *The Private Soldier under Washington*, Charles Scribner's Sons, 1902

Boyd, Thomas, *Mad Anthony Wayne*, Charles Scribner's Sons, 1929

Boyer, John, *A Journal of Wayne's Campaign (1795)*, Cincinnati, 1866

Brissot de Warville, J. P., *New Travels in the United States of America Performed in 1788*, London, 1792

Burnaby, Thomas, *Travels through the Middle Settlements of America, 1759-1760*, London, 1798

Canby, Henry Seidel, *The Brandywine*, Farrar and Rinehart, 1941

Caughey, John Walton, *McGillivray of the Creeks*, University of Oklahoma Press, 1938

Charlton, T. U. P., *The Life of Major-General James Jackson*, Augusta, Ga., 1809

Chastellux, F. J., marquis de, *Travels in North-America in the years 1780, 1781, and 1782*, 2 vols., Dublin, 1787

Cheyney, Edward P., *History of the University of Pennsylvania, 1740-1940*, University of Pennsylvania Press, 1940

Clark, Daniel, *Proofs of the Corruption of Gen. James Wilkinson*, Philadelphia, 1809

Clarke, M. St. C., and Hall, David A., eds., *Cases of Contested Elections in Congress from the year 1789 to 1834, inclusive*, Washington, 1834

Cleaves, Freeman, *Old Tippecanoe*, Charles Scribner's Sons, 1939

Collot, G. H. Victor, *A Journey in North America*, 3 vols., Paris, 1826

Cooper, Thomas, *Some Information Respecting America*, 2d ed., London, 1794

Cutler, Manasseh, *Life, Journals, and Correspondence*, 2 vols., Cincinnati, 1888

Dawson, Henry B., *The Assault at Stony Point in the State of New York*, The author, Morrisania, N. Y., 1891

Day, Sherman, *Historical Collections of the State of Pennsylvania*, Philadelphia, 1842

Downes, Randolph C., *Council Fires on the Upper Ohio*, University of Pittsburgh, 1940

Drake, Francis S., *Life and Correspondence of Henry Knox*, Boston, 1873

Dunaway, Wayland Fuller, *A History of Pennsylvania*, Prentice-Hall, 1935

Egle, W. H., *An Illustrated History of the Commonwealth of Pennsylvania*, Harrisburg, 1877

Ellet, Elizabeth F., *Court Circles of the Republic*, Hartford, Conn., 1869

——*The Women of the American Revolution*, 2 vols., New York, 1848-50

Elliot, James, *Poetical and Miscellaneous Works*, Greenfield, Mass., 1798

Fersen, Hans Axel, graf von, *Diary and Correspondence*, Hardy, Pratt & Company, 1902

Fisher, Sydney George, *The Making of Pennsylvania*, The J. B. Lippincott Company, 1896

——*The Struggle for American Independence*, 2 vols., The J. B. Lippcott Company, 1908

Forbes, Archibald, *The Black Watch*, Charles Scribner's Sons, 1896

Futhey, John Smith, and Cope, Gilbert, *History of Chester County*, W. H. Everts, Phila., 1881

Gamble, Thomas, *Savannah Duels and Duellists, 1733-1777*, Review Publishing and Printing Company, Savannah, 1923

Goodman, Nathan, *Benjamin Rush*, University of Pennsylvania Press, 1934

Gordon, Alexander, *Anecdotes of the Revolutionary War in America*, Charleston, S. C., 1822

Gordon, T. F., *The History of Pennsylvania from Its Discovery to* . . . *1776*, Philadelphia, 1829

Graeff, Arthur D., *Relations between the Pennsylvania Germans and the British Authorities (1750-1776)*, Temple University, 1939

Graydon, Alexander, *Memoirs of a Life, Chiefly Passed in Pennsylvania*, Harrisburg, 1811

Graves, Robert, *Sergeant Lamb's America*, Random House, 1940

Great Britain, Courts, *The Trial of Lieut.-Col. Frederick Thomas on a Charge Exhibited by Lieut.-Col. Cosmo Gordon*, London, 1781

Greene, George Washington, *The Life of Nathanael Greene*, 3 vols., The Houghton Mifflin Company, 1884

Guild, Benjamin, *History of the American Revolution*, Boston, 1832

Harland, Marian (Mary Virginia Terhune), *More Colonial Homesteads and Their Stories*, G. P. Putnam's Sons, 1899

Hatch, Louis Clinton, *Administration of the American Revolutionary Army*, Longmans, Green & Company, 1904

Hay, Ian (J. H. Beith), *The King's Service*, London, 1938

Hay, Thomas Robson, and Werner, M. R., *The Admirable Trumpeter*, Doubleday, Doran and Company, 1941

Heckewelder, John, *History, Manners, and Customs of the Indian Nations Who Once Inhabited Pennsylvania*, Philadelphia, 1819

Hiltzheimer, Jacob, *Extracts from the Diary of* . . . *Hiltzheimer, 1765-1798*, ed. by J. C. Parsons. Wm. Fell & Company, Phila., 1893

Jacobs, James R., *Tarnished Warrior: Major-General James Wilkinson*, The Macmillan Company, 1938

Janson, Charles William, *The Stranger in America (1793-1806)*, London, 1807

Jefferson, Thomas, *Memoir, Correspondence, and Miscellanies*, ed. by T. J. Randolph, 4 vols., Charlottesville, Va., 1829

Jenkins, Howard, ed., *Pennsylvania, Colonial and Federal: A History*, 3 vols., Pennsylvania Historical Publishing Association, Phila., 1903

Johnston, Alexander, American Political History, 1763-1876, ed. and supplemented by J. A. Woodburn, 2 vols., G. P. Putnam's Sons, 1905

Johnston, Henry P., *The Storming of Stony Point*, James T. White, 1900

—— *The Yorktown Campaign and the Surrender of Cornwallis*, Harper Bros., 1881

Jones, Charles C., *The Dead Towns of Georgia*, Savannah, 1878

—— *The History of Georgia*, 2 vols., The Houghton Mifflin Company, 1883

Jones, Charles H., *History of the Campaign for the Conquest of Canada in 1776*, Porter & Coates, 1882

Jordan, John W., *Colonial and Revolutionary Families of Pennsylvania*, 8 vols., Lewis Publishing Company, N. Y., 1911-39, Vols. 1-3

Kapp, Friedrich, *The Life of Frederick William von Steuben*, New York, 1859

Knight, Lucian Lamar, *Georgia's Landmarks, Memorials and Legends*, 2 vols., privately printed, Atlanta, 1913-14

Knollenberg, Bernhard, *Washington and the Revolution*, The Macmillan Company, 1940

Leach, Josiah Granville, *History of the Penrose Family of Philadelphia*, privately printed, Philadelphia, 1903

Lee, Henry, *The Campaign of 1781 in the Carolinas*, Philadelphia, 1824

McCrady, Edward, *The History of South Carolina in the Revolution, 1775-1783*, 2 vols., The Macmillan Company, 1902

Maclay, William, *Journal . . . 1789-1791*, ed. by Charles A. Beard, Albert Boni, 1927

Marshall, Christopher, *Extracts from the Diary of . . . Marshall*, ed. by William Duane, Albany, 1877

Mellick, Andrew D., Jr., *The Story of an Old Farm*, Unionist Gazette, Somerville, N. J., 1889

Michaux, André, "Journal," in Vol. 3 of *Early Western Travels*, ed. by Reuben Gold Thwaites, Arthur H. Clark Company, Cleveland, 1904

Mills, W. J., *Historic Houses of New Jersey*, The J. B. Lippincott Company, 1902

Montgomery, Elizabeth, *Reminiscences of Wilmington*, Philadelphia, 1851

Moore, H. N., *Life and Services of Gen. Anthony Wayne*, Philadelphia, 1845

Nelson, S. B., *Biographical Dictionary and Historical Reference Book of Pennsylvania*, Erie, Penn., 1906

Nolan, J. Bennett, *George Washington and the Town of Reading in Pennsylvania*, Chamber of Commerce, Reading, 1931

Oskison, John M., *Tecumseh and His Times*, G. P. Putnam's Sons, 1938

Osler, Edward, *The Life of Admiral Viscount Exmouth*, London, 1835

Parkinson, Richard, *A Tour in America in 1798, '99, and 1800*, 2 vols., London, 1805

Patrick, Lewis S., *Washington's Headquarters and the Revolutionary Army at Fredericksburg in the State of New York*, Quaker Hill Conference Association, Quaker Hill, N. Y., 1907

Pennypacker, Samuel Whitaker, *Pennsylvania in American History*, William J. Campbell, Phila., 1910

Philips, George Morris, ed., *Historic Letters from the Collection of the West Chester State Normal School*, The J. B. Lippincott Company, 1898

Pleasants, Henry, *Anthony Wayne*, H. F. Temple, West Chester, Penn., 1936

Pollock, Thomas C., *The Philadelphia Theatre in the Eighteenth Century*, University of Pennsylvania Press, 1932

Pontgibaud, C. A. de M., chevalier de, *A French Volunteer in the War for Independence*, D. Appleton & Company, 1898

Preston, John Hyde, *A Gentleman Rebel: The Exploits of Anthony Wayne*, Farrar and Rinehart, 1930

Ramsay, David, *The History of the American Revolution*, 2 vols., Dublin, 1793

Reed, William B., *Life and Correspondence of Joseph Reed*, 2 vols., Philadelphia, 1847

Richardson, William H., *Washington and "the Enterprise against Powles Hook,"* New Jersey Title and Guarantee Trust Company, Jersey City, 1938

Robin, Claude C., *New Travels through North-America 1781*, Philadelphia, 1783

Robins, Edward, *Romances of Early America*, G. W. Jacobs & Company, 1902

Roosevelt, Theodore, *The Winning of the West*, 3 vols., G. P. Putnam's Sons, 1894-96

St. Clair, Arthur, *The St. Clair Papers*, ed. by W. H. Smith, 2 vols., Clarke, Robert & Co., Cincinnati, 1882

Sanford, Laura G., *History of Erie County*, The J. B. Lippincott Company, 1862

Scharf, J. Thomas, and Thompson, Westcott, *History of Philadelphia, 1609-1884*, 3 vols., L. H. Everts & Company, Phila., 1884

Schöpf, Johann David, *Travels in the Confederation (1783-1784)*, tr. and ed. by A. J. Morrison, 2 vols., William J. Campbell, Phila., 1911

Schouler, James, *Americans of 1776*, Dodd, Mead and Company, 1906

Ségur, Louis Philippe, comte de, *The Memoirs and Recollections*, 2 vols., London, 1825

Sellers, Edwin Jaquette, *English Ancestry of the Wayne Family of Pennsylvania*, The author, Philadelphia, 1927

Selsam, J. Paul, *The Pennsylvania Constitution of 1776*, University of Pennsylvania Press, 1936

Sherman, Andrew M., *Historic Morristown*, Howard Publishing Company, Morristown, N. J., 1905

Sipe, C. Hale, *Indian Chiefs of Pennsylvania*, The author, Butler, Penn., 1927

—— *Indian Wars of Pennsylvania*, The author, Butler, Penn., 1929

Smythies, R. H. Raymond, *Historical Records of the 40th . . . Regiment*, Devonport, Eng., 1894

Spears, John R., *Anthony Wayne, Sometimes Called "Mad Anthony,"* D. Appleton & Company, 1903

Stedman, Charles, *History of the Origin, Progress and Termination of the American War*, 2 vols., Dublin, 1794

Stewart, Frank H., *Foraging for Valley Forge by General Anthony Wayne*, Gloucester County Historical Society, Woodbury, N. J., 1929

Stillé, Charles J., *Major-General Anthony Wayne and the Pennsylvania Line in the Continental Army*, The J. B. Lippincott Company, 1893

Stone, William L., *Life of Joseph Brant-Thayandanagea*, 2 vols., New York, 1838

Stryker, William S., *The Battle of Monmouth*, ed. by W. S. Myers, Princeton University Press, 1927

Thacher, James, *Military Journal of the American Revolution*, Hartford, Conn., 1862

Tower, Charlemagne, *The Marquis de La Fayette in the American Revolution*, 2 vols., The J. B. Lippincott Company, 1895

Twining, Thomas, *Travels in America 100 Years Ago*, Harper Bros., 1894

United States, Presidents, *A Compilation of the Messages and Papers of the Presidents, 1789-1897*, ed. by James D. Richardson, 10 vols., Government Printing Office, Wash., 1896-99

—— Congress, *Debates and Proceedings, 1789-1793*, Philadelphia, 1843

—— *Debates and Proceedings . . . 1789 . . . 1791*, ed. by Joseph Gales, 2 vols., Washington, 1834

Wansey, Henry, *The Journal of an Excursion to the United States of North America in . . . 1789 . . . 1791 . . . 1794*, Salisbury, Eng., 1796

Washington, George, *Writings*, ed. by Worthington Ford, 14 vols., G. P. Putnam's Sons, 1889-92, Vols. 12-13

Watson, Elkanah, *Men and Times of the Revolution*, New York, 1856

Watson, John Fanning, *Annals of Philadelphia*, 2 vols., Philadelphia, 1856-57

Wharton, Anne Hollingsworth, *Salons Colonial and Republican*, The J. B. Lippincott Company, 1900

Wildes, Harry Emerson, *The Delaware*, Farrar and Rinehart, 1940

—— *Valley Forge*, The Macmillan Company, 1938

Wilkinson, Eliza, *Letters during the Invasion and Possession of Charleston, S. C., by the British in the Revolutionary War*, New York, 1839

Wilkinson, James, *Memoirs of My Own Times*, 3 vols., Philadelphia, 1816

Winterbotham, William, *Historical, Geographical, Commercial and Philosophical View of the American United States*, 4 vols., New York, 1796

Young, Calvin M., *Little Turtle*, The author, Greenville, Ohio, 1917

ORDERLY BOOKS

February-June, 1776, Marcus Hook, *PMHB*, Vol. 29, No. 4 (1905), pp. 470-78

October 17, 1776-January 8, 1777, Northern Army, Albany, 1859

December 1-16, 1776, Fort Ticonderoga, *Bulletin*, Fort Ticonderoga Museum, Vol. 3, No. 5 (January, 1935), pp. 218-25

February, 1778, Valley Forge, mss. at HSP

1792-1796, Ohio campaign, mss. at West Point Military Academy
See also Kirkwood and Wayne, Anthony, in the list following.

PERIODICALS

"Advice to American Farmers," *Packet and County Journal*, Norwich, Conn., April 17, 1789

Allen, James, "Diary 1770-1778," *PMHB*, Vol. 9 (1885)

Anderson, George P., "Pascal Paoli," *Publications*, Colonial Society of Massachusetts, Vol. 26 (February, 1925), pp. 180-210

Arnold, James Oliver, "Fort Greenville Traditions," *Quarterly*, Ohio Archeological and Historical Society, Vol. 17 (1908), pp. 60-63

Baldwin, Jeduthan, "Journal, 1775-1776," *Journal*, Military Service Institute, Vol. 39, No. 143 (September, 1906), pp. 257-73

—— "Diary, July 6, 1776-July 5, 1777," *Bulletin*, Fort Ticonderoga Museum, Vol. 4, No. 6 (January, 1938), pp. 10-40

Bangs, Isaac, "Journal of Massachusetts Militia," *Proceedings*, New Jersey Historical Society, Ser. 1, Vol. 8

Banning, Mrs. Henry G., "Miss Mary Vining of Delaware," *Every Evening*, Wilmington, Del., Aug. 18, 1928

—— "Miss Vining, a Revolutionary Belle," *American Historical Register*, July, 1895, pp. 1190-1205

Barnwell, Joseph W., "The Evacuation of Charleston," *South Carolina Historical Magazine,* Vol. 11 (January, 1910), pp. 1-26

Bell, Andrew, "Journal during the March of the British through the Jersies," *Proceedings*, New Jersey Historical Society, Ser. 1, Vol. 6

Berger, James J., "Phil's Hill: Home of Colonel Van Horn," Somerset, Vol. 1, No. 2 (April, 1912), pp. 81-85

Bicknell, Thomas Williams, "Major-General Anthony Wayne," *Journal*, American-Irish Historical Society, Vol. 10 (1910), pp. 277-300

Birch, John J., "The Ride of Jack Jouett, Hero of Virginia," *Americana*, Vol. 23 (October, 1929), pp. 454-57

Bland, Mrs. Martha Daingerfield, Letter dated Morristown, May 12, 1777, to Frances Bland Randolph, *Proceedings*, New Jersey Historical Society, Vol. 51, No. 3 (July, 1933), pp. 150-52

Bolander, L. H., "Arnold's Retreat from Valcour Island," *Proceedings*, United States Naval Institute, Vol. 55, Part 2 (December, 1929), pp. 1060-62

Bradbury, Theophilus, Letter dated Philadelphia, December 26, 1795, to Mrs. Harriet Hooper, *PMHB*, Vol. 8 (1884), p. 226

Buell, John Hutchinson, "Diary," *Journal*, Military Service Institute, Vol. 40 (1907), pp. 102 ff.

Burnham, Smith, "The Battle of Brandywine," *Second Report*, Pennsylvania Historical Commission (1918), pp. 33-43

Burkholder, Albert N., "Treason in Reading," *Historical Review of Berks County*, Vol. 3, No. 5 (April, 1938)

Carter, John Archer, "A Virginia Heroine," *D.A.R. Magazine*, Vol. 62 (May, 1928), pp. 289-92

Carter, Mary Hartwell, "The Staats House and Baron Steuben," Somerset, Vol. 2, No. 2 (April, 1913), pp. 81-87

Chapman, Thomas, "Journal of a Journey through the United States, 1796," *Dawson's Historical Magazine*, June, 1869

Chew, John (?), "Diary of an Officer in the Indian Country in 1794," ed. by Ernest Cruikshank, *American Historical Magazine*, Vol. 3 (1908), pp. 639-43; Vol. 4 (1909), pp. 69-71

Clarke, William, "Journal of General Wayne's Campaign against the Shawane Indians in Ohio, 1794-1795," ed. by R. C. McGrane, *Miss. V. Hist. Rev.*, Vol. 1 (December, 1914), pp. 418-44

Colver, William L., "Consider the Revolutionary Bullet," *Quarterly Bulletin*, New York Historical Society, Vol. 11, No. 4 (January, 1928), pp. 120-27

Cone, Stephen Decatur, "The Indian Attack on Fort Dunlap," *Quarterly*, Ohio Archeological and Historical Society, Vol. 17 (1908), pp. 64-72

Coulter, E. Merton, "Efforts of the Democratic Societies of the West to Open the Navigation of the Mississippi," *Miss. V. Hist. Rev.*, Vol. 11 (December, 1924), pp. 376-89

Davis, T. E., "Washington's Encampment at Middlebrook," Somerset, Vol. 1 (1912), pp. 5-14

Davis, William, "Journal of the Southern Campaign," *PMHB*, Vol. 5 (1881), pp. 290-311

Denny, Ebenezer, "Military Journal, 1791-1795," *Memoirs*, HSP, Vol. 7 (1860)

De Peyster, J. W., "Anthony Wayne," *Magazine of American History*, Vol. 15 (1886), pp. 127-43

Downes, Randolph C., "Indian Affairs in the Southwest Territory, 1790-1796," *Tennessee Historical Magazine*, Ser. 2, Vol. 3, No. 4 (January, 1937), pp. 240-68

Dupré, Huntley, "The Kentucky Gazette Reports the French Revolution," *Miss. V. Hist. Rev.*, Vol. 26, No. 2 (September, 1939)

Eager, John Howard, "The Battle of Germantown," *Maryland Historical Magazine*, Vol. 4 (1909), pp. 362-72

Eavenson, Howard M., "The Early History of the Pittsburgh Coal Bed," *Western Pennsylvania Historical Magazine*, Vol. 22, No. 3 (September, 1939)

Elliott, Charles Winslow, "Mutiny or a Bounty," *Coast Artillery Journal*, Vol. 82, No. 4 (July, 1939), pp. 330-38

Eve, Sarah, "Extracts from Journal, 1772-1773," *PMHB*, Vol. 5 (1881)

Fisher, Samuel Rowland, "Journal, 1779," *PMHB*, Vol. 41 (1917), pp. 145-97

Folsom, Joseph Fulford, "More Light on Chaplain J. Caldwell's Death," *Proceedings*, New Jersey Historical Society, Vol. 1, New Ser., No. 1 (January, 1916), pp. 1-12

—— "The Preakness Valley and Reminiscences of Washington's Headquarters in the Dey Mansion," *Proceedings*, New Jersey Historical Society, Vol. 6, New Ser. (1921), pp. 217 ff.

Frelinghuysen, Joseph S., "Washington at Morristown," *Proceedings*, New Jersey Historical Society, Vol. 15, No. 1 (January, 1930), pp. 72-84

Futhey, J. Smith, "Speech at Dedication of Paoli Monument," *Proceedings of Dedication*, West Chester (Penn.), 1877

"General Collot's Reconnoitering Trip down the Mississippi, 1796," *Louisiana Historical Quarterly*, Vol. 1, No. 4 (April, 1918), pp. 303-26

Good, James W. (Secretary of War), "Farmer, Soldier, Patriot," *National Republican*, Vol. 17 (November, 1929), pp. 18-20

Green, James A., "A Visit in 1929 to the Sites of Forts in Western Ohio Built by Generals Arthur St. Clair, Anthony Wayne and William Henry Harrison," *Quarterly*, Ohio Archeological and Historical Society, Vol. 38, No. 4 (October, 1929), pp. 601-12

Hastings, Hugh, "Ticonderoga under Three Flags," *Journal*, Military Service Institute, Vol. 50 (1912), pp. 88 ff.

Heckewelder, John, "Narrative of a Journey to the Wabash, 1792," ed. by J. W. Jordan, *PMHB*, Vol. 12 (1888)

Henderson, Archibald, "Isaac Shelby and the Genet Mission," *Miss. V. Hist. Rev.*, Vol. 6, No. 4 (March, 1920), pp. 45-69

Hunt, Gaillard, "Office-Seeking during Washington's Administration," *American Historical Review*, Vol. 1, No. 2 (January, 1896), pp. 238-50

Irvine, William, "Extracts from Papers," *PMHB*, Vol. 5 (1881), pp. 259-75

Johnson, Willis Fletcher, "The Meaning of Middlebrook," *Proceedings*, New Jersey Historical Society, Vol. 12, New Ser., No. 3 (July, 1927), pp. 289-308

Johnston, Alexander, "Some Account of the Society of the Cincinnati," *Memoirs*, HSP, Vol. 6 (1858)

Jordan, John W., "Colonel Thomas Hartley," *PMHB*, Vol. 25 (1901), pp. 303 ff.

Kennedy, Samuel, Letter dated Ticonderoga, August 5, 1776, to Mrs. Sarah Kennedy, *PMHB*, Vol. 8 (1884), p. 114

Kent, Charles A., "The Treaty of Greenville," *Journal*, Illinois State Historical Society, Vol. 10, No. 1 (January, 1918), pp. 568-84

Kimball, LeRoy Elwood, "Military Events at Stony Point and King's Ferry," *Scenic and Historic America*, Vol. 3, No. 4 (July, 1934)

Kinnaird, Lawrence, "The Ascendency of Alexander McGillivray, 1783-1789," *Florida Historical Quarterly*, Vol. 10, No. 2 (October, 1931), pp. 59-85

Kirkwood, Robert, "Journal and Orderly Book, 1777, 1780-1782," *Papers*, Historical Society of Delaware, Vol. LVI, 1910

Lacey, John, "Memoirs," *PMHB*, Vol. 25 (1901)

"Legislation of the Northwest Territory," *Quarterly*, Ohio Archeological and Historical Society, Vol. 30, No. 1 (January, 1921)

Levermore, Charles H., "The Whigs of Colonial New York," *American Historical Review*, Vol. 1, No. 2 (January, 1896), pp. 238-50

Lewis, Joseph J., "History of Chester County," serialized in *Village Record*, West Chester, Penn., during 1824

Lisle, Clifton, "Waynesborough," *Ladies' Home Journal*, Vol. 39 (May, 1922), pp. 16 ff.

Livingood, Louis J., "A Pioneer Doctor," *Historical Review of Berks County*, April, 1936

McDermott, John Francis, "Gallipolis As Travellers Saw It, 1792-1811," *Quarterly*, Ohio Archeological and Historical Society, Vol. 48, No. 4 (October, 1939), pp. 283-303

Mackraby, Alexander, "Philadelphia Society before the Revolution," *PMHB*, Vol. 11 (1887)

McPherson, William, Letter on resignation, dated November 24, 1780, *PMHB*, Vol. 11; p. 503

Maryland Officers, "Grievances of the Maryland Line," *Maryland Historical Magazine*, Vol. 4 (1909), pp. 362-72

Merlin, John R., "Critique of the Army Ration," *Military Surgeon*, Vol. 50 (January-February, 1922)

Millis, Walter, "Rugged Patriot," *Michigan Historical Magazine*, Vol. 20 (April, 1936), pp. 127-51

Moore, Captain Samuel, "Extracts from Orderly Book, June-July 1776," *PMHB*, Vol. 18 (1894), pp. 253 ff.

Murray, Nicholas, "Memoirs of the Rev. James Caldwell," *Proceedings*, New Jersey Historical Society, Vol. 3 (1848-1849), pp. 79 ff.

Nickell, M. F., "The Historic Home of Anthony Wayne," *Mentor*, Vol. 17 (March, 1929), pp. 23-26

Parish, John Carl, "The Intrigues of Doctor James O'Fallon," *Miss. V. Hist. Rev.*, Vol. 17 (September, 1930), pp. 230-63

Pennypacker, Samuel W., "The Capture of Stony Point," *PMHB*, Vol. 26 (1902), pp. 360-69

Priddy, O. W., "Wayne's Strategic Advance from Fort Greenville to Grand Glaize," *Quarterly*, Ohio Archeological and Historical Society, Vol. 39, No. 1 (January, 1930), pp. 42-76

Proceedings: At Dedication of Monument at Paoli, West Chester, Pennsylvania, 1877

    Relative to Calling the Conventions of 1776 and 1790 and the Council of Censors, Harrisburg, 1825

    Unveiling of Fort Jefferson Monument, *Quarterly*, Ohio Archeological and Historical Society, Vol. 17 (1908), pp. 112-31

Unveiling of Fort Recovery Monument, *Quarterly*, Ohio Archeological and Historical Society, Vol. 22 (1913), pp. 419-54

Unveiling of Monument at Cooch's Bridge, Wilmington, *Papers*, Historical Society of Delaware, 1902

Quincy, Eliza Susan, "Basking Ridge in Revolutionary Days," Somerset, Vol. 1 (1912), pp. 34-43

Reeve, Enos, "Letter Books, 1780-1782," *PMHB*, Vols. 20-21 (1896-97)

Richardson, William H., "The Enterprise against New York, November 1780," *Proceedings*, New Jersey Historical Society, Vol. 15, New Ser., No. 3 (July, 1930), pp. 388-91

Robb, H. L., "Mad Anthony Wayne's Campaign against the Indians in Ohio," *Military Engineer*, Vol. 13, No. 72 (November-December, 1921)

Robins, Edward, "Portrait of a Wilmington Belle in Colonial Days," *Evening Bulletin*, Philadelphia, January 22, 1940

Rodney, Thomas, "Letter to Maia," *Every Evening*, Wilmington, Del., February 11, 1933

Rowan, Archibald Hamilton, "Delawareana," *Every Evening*, Wilmington, Del., January 23, 1937

Scamp, Henry A., "The Girty Legends and Romances," *Magazine of History*, Vol. 12, No. 5 (November, 1910), pp. 243-52; Vol. 13, No. 5 (May, 1911), pp. 219-29

Sherman, Andrew M., "Mutiny of the Pennsylvania Troops in Morris County," *Journal*, American-Irish Historical Society, Vol. 17, pp. 93-98

—— "Revolutionary Camping Grounds of Connecticut Brigades in Morris County, 1779-1780," *Journal of American History*, Vol. 10 (April, 1916), pp. 321-30

—— "Washington's Army in Lowantica Valley, 1776-1777," *American Historical Magazine*, Vol. 3 (November, 1908), pp. 581-96. (The same article appears in *Journal*, American-Irish Historical Society, Vol. 10 (1909), pp. 300-22.)

—— "Wick House and Its Historical Environment," *Americana*, Vol. 4 (1909), pp. 251-60

Sherman, Walter J., "Fort Industry—a Historical Mystery," *Quarterly*, Ohio Archeological and Historical Society, Vol. 38, No. 2 (April, 1929), pp. 231-59

Shira, Donald D., "Pioneer Physicians of Ohio," *Quarterly*, Ohio Archeological and Historical Society, Vol. 48, No. 3 (July, 1939)

Steel, John, "Morristown," *Dawson's Historical Magazine*, Vol. 9, p. 137

Stillwell, Adeline W. Voorhees, "Washington's March through Somerset County, N. J.," *American Monthly Magazine*, Vol. 40, No. 1 (January, 1912), pp. 7-8

Stoddard, R. H., "Anthony Wayne," *National Magazine*, Vol. 12 (1858), pp. 213-20

Stone, Frederick, "Philadelphia Society a Hundred Years Ago," *PMHB*, Vol. 3 (1879)

Stough, Mulford, "The Yellow Fever in Philadelphia, 1793," *Pennsylvania History*, Vol. 6, No. 1 (January, 1939)

Thornton, Edward, Letter to Sir Thomas Bland Burges, dated Philadelphia, June 11, 1792, *PMHB*, Vol. 9 (1885), pp. 214-16

Tuttle, J. F., "Hibernia Furnace and Surrounding Country in the Revolutionary War," *Proceedings*, New Jersey Historical Society, Ser. 2, Vol. 6 (1879-81), pp. 148-73

Von Kraft, John Charles Phil, "Journal," *Collections*, New York Historical Society, 1882

Wall, Alexander J., "The Flag with the Eagle in the Canton," *Quarterly Bulletin*, New York Historical Society, Vol. 17, No. 3 (October, 1933), pp. 51-67

Ward, Townsend, "The Insurrection of 1794 in the Western Counties of Pennsylvania," *Memoirs*, HSP, Vol. 6 (1858)

Wayne, Anthony, Letters to William Irvine, *Historical Magazine*, Vol. 6 (1862), pp. 322-23, 336-42

—— Letter to George Washington dated Richmond, Georgia, April 6, 1789, *PMHB*, Vol. 27 (1903), pp. 109-10

—— "Orderly Book of the Northern Army, December 1-16, 1776," *Bulletin*, Fort Ticonderoga Museum, Vol. 3, No. 5 (January, 1935), pp. 218-25

—— "Orderly Book, Fourth Pennsylvania Battalion, 1776," *PMHB*, Vol. 29, No. 4 (1905), pp. 470-78

Wayne, Isaac, Newspaper account of his father's death, *American Republican and Chester County Democrat*, West Chester, Penn., November 2, 1852

—— "Biographical Memoir of Major-General Anthony Wayne," *Casket*, Vol. 1, May, 1829-January, 1830

Werner, Raymond C., "War Scare and Politics in New York, 1794," *Quarterly Journal*, New York State Historical Society, Vol. 11, No. 4 (October, 1930), pp. 324-34

Whitaker, Arthur Preston, ed., "Two Letters of Harry Inness, 1794-1795, on the Spanish Intrigue," *Miss. V. Hist. Rev.*, Vol. 15 (September, 1928), pp. 236-48

Wiley, Richard T., "Ship and Brig Building on the Ohio," *Journal*, Ohio Archeological and Historical Society, Vol. 22 (1913), pp. 60-61

Wilkinson, James, "Letters to Hugh Shiells, 1784-1791," *Register*, Kentucky State Historical Society, Vol. 24, No. 72 (September, 1926), pp. 259-67

—— "Narrative of the Fallen Timbers Campaign," ed. by M. M. Quaife, *Miss V. Hist. Rev.*, Vol. 16 (June, 1929), pp. 81-90

—— "General James Wilkinson," *Louisiana Historical Quarterly*, Vol. 1, No. 2 (September, 1917), pp. 79-116

Woodbury, Margaret, "Public Opinion in Philadelphia, 1789-1801," *Smith College Studies in History*, Vol. V, No. 1-2 (October, 1919)

Wright, John W., "The Corps of Light Infantry in the Continental Army," *American Historical Review*, Vol. 31 (April, 1926), pp. 454-61

Index

510

INDEX

(A. W.'s mother-in-law), 25; Joseph (A. W.'s brother-in-law), 45; Margaret (A. W.'s sister-in-law), 458; Mary ("Polly"), see Wayne, Mary Penrose; Thomas (A. W.'s brother-in-law), 24, 42

Peters, Rev. Richard, 25, 42, 114

Peters, Richard, 42, 48, 72, 82 f., 90, 93 f., 101, 144 f., 147 ff., 151, 166, 170, 179, 185 f., 233, 263, 281, 303, 346, 370, 449

Peters, Sally Robinson, 43, 46, 53, 55, 77, 83, 90-94, 101, 108, 111, 116, 145, 159, 166, 179

Petersburg, Va., 269 f.

Philadelphia, 3, 10, 40, 51 f., 84, 89, 102 f., 106 ff., 113 f., 118, 122 ff., 127, 136, 140, 143, 150, 153 f., 158 f., 172, 177 f., 188, 202-08, 217, 228 f., 239, 256 ff., 288, 324 f., 338, 394, 405, 417, 428, 448-52, 457 f., 461, 463; descriptions of, (1758) 8 f.; (1759) 9 f.; (1766) 26 f., 34; (1769) 35; (1776) 78; (1777) 108 f.; (1778) 115; (1779) 172 f.; (1781) 230-34; (1784) 309-12

Philip (A. W.'s servant), 244, 292 f.

Pickering, Timothy, 366, 392 ff., 440 f., 445 f., 449

Pike, Maj. Zebulon, 453 ff.

Pinckney, Charles Cotesworth, 348 f.

Pipe-makers' Swamp, Battle of, 286 f., 354

"Pitcher," Molly, 165 f.

Pittsburgh, Penna., 158, 311, 353, 356 ff., 363, 366-69, 379 f., 382, 385 f., 395, 433, 457 f., 462

Plots against: Greene, 294 f., 299 f.; Wayne, 259 f., 377, 386-90, 400-07, 427 ff., 437, 457; Washington, 144 f.

Porter, Capt. Moses, 455

Portsmouth, Va., 254, 257, 263

Posey, Maj. Thomas, 180, 196, 281, 283, 287, 389

Postage, 94, 368. See also Franking.

Potawatomi Indians. See Indians.

Potts, Dr. Jonathan, 81, 321

Potts, Samuel, 322, 327 ff., 333, 338 f.

Power, Dr. Thomas, 454 f.

Presqu' Isle (Erie), Penna., 393, 411, 457-63

Princeton, N. J., 52, 78, 91, 105 f., 123, 229, 304, 330

Prohibition, 30, 232

Promotion, 82 f., 348 f., 390

Pulaski, Casimir, count, 122, 155 f.

Punishment, 50, 242 ff., 375

Putnam, Col. Rufus, 180, 190-91, 348, 350, 365, 367, 382

Quakers, 3 ff., 8 f., 31 f., 43, 120 ff., 172, 314 f., 366

Quebec, Canada, 46 f., 52, 61

Queen's Rangers, 251, 254, 359

Race Street tavern, 11, 21, 24

Rachel (servant), 141

Racing, 10-11, 30-31

Radeaux, 58, 68

Radicals, 82 f., 101 f., 150, 171, 175 ff., 204, 302, 308

Radnor, Penna. See St. David's Church.

Raisin River, 440

Ramapo River, 97, 208

Randolph, Beverley, 366, 392 ff.

Rank, army, 44, 82 f., 175-78, 215, 221 ff., 225, 348 f., 386

Rapidan River, 249, 251

Raritan River, 103, 106

Rations, 48 f., 53, 60, 69, 74 f., 96 f., 126, 282 f., 300, 392, 397, 399-402, 429

Reading, Penna., 123, 158

Red Jacket ("Cow-Killer"), 362 ff.

Reed, Joseph, president of Penna., 178, 198, 203 ff., 216, 218-21, 227, 229 f., 244, 314

Rhode Island, 279, 306

Rice, 275, 283, 285, 290, 302, 315, 320 f., 328-32   [269

Richmond, Va., 238, 251-52, 257 f.

Richmond Plantation, Ga., 289 f., 294, 302, 305, 316, 318, 320-27, 330, 338

Robinson, Abraham, 23 f., 77, 111, 134 f., 141, 174, 206